Fundamental Principles
of Restaurant Cost Control
Second Edition

D1249344

Fundamental Principles of Restaurant Cost Control
Second Edition

David V. Pavesic, Ph.D., CHE, FMP
Professor, School of Hospitality Administration
Robinson College of Business
Georgia State University, Atlanta, GA

Paul F. Magnant, MBA, CFBE, FMP,
CCE, CEC, CHE, CHM, CCI

PEARSON
Prentice
Hall

Upper Saddle River, New Jersey 07458

Library of Congress Cataloging-in-Publication Data

Pavesic, David V.
  Fundamental principles of restaurant cost control   /   David V. Pavesic, Paul F. Magnant.—2nd ed.
    p. cm.
  Includes bibliographical references and index.
  ISBN 0-13-114532-0
  1.   Restaurants--Cost control.   I. Magnant, Paul F.   II. Title.
  TX911.3.C65P38 2005
  647.95'068'1—dc22
      2004014806

Executive Editor: Vernon R. Anthony
Associate Editor: Marion Gottlieb**Editorial Assistant:** Beth Dyke
Production Editor: Patty Donovan, Pine Tree Composition, Inc.
Production Liaison: Janice Stangel
Director of Manufacturing and Production: Bruce Johnson
Managing Editor: Mary Carnis
Manufacturing Manager: Ilene Sanford
Manufacturing Buyer: Cathleen Petersen
Creative Director: Cheryl Asherman
Senior Marketing Manager: Ryan DeGrote
Senior Marketing Coordinator: Elizabeth Farrell
Marketing Assistant: Les Roberts
Formatting and Interior Design: Pine Tree Composition, Inc.
Printing and Binding: Phoenix Book Technology
Cover Design Coordinator: Miguel Ortiz
Cover Designer: Miguel Ortiz

Pearson Education LTD
Pearson Education Singapore, Pte. Ltd.
Pearson Education, Canada, Ltd
Pearson Education—Japan
Pearson Education Australia PTY, Limited
Pearson Educaçion de Mexico, S.A. de C.V.
Pearson Education Malaysia. Pte. Ltd.

10 9 8 7 6 5 4 3 2 1
ISBN 0-13-114532-0

To my wife and partner Tana. Your love and support has made this possible.

David V. Pavesic

To the infinite patience of those who care about me; my wife Addie, my daughter Michiko, my mother, and my co-author.

Paul F. Magnant

Contents

7   Purchasing   253

8   Inventory and Storeroom Management; Receiving; and Accounts Payable   289

Preface

The second edition of the *Fundamental Principles of Restaurant Cost Control* has been "kicked up a notch" with the addition of Paul F. Magnant as co-author. Paul was one of my many students in the hospitality management program at Florida State University back in the 1980's. He served as the department head and assistant professor of hospitality management at Johnson and Wales University, Norfolk. We ran into one another at the annual hospitality educator's conference in the summer of 2002. We had not seen or talked in over 15 years.

He had come to this conference with the intention of getting me to autograph the bound course packet of articles I put together as a supplemental text for my class on cost controls at FSU. He had kept them for over twenty years and told me he referred to them often when he was in the industry and now as an instructor. He then said the words that when uttered to a college professor will absolutely leave them speechless. Paul said something that went like this. "I just want you to know how much I appreciate what you taught me in your classes. I did not fully appreciate it at the time I was a student, but as a manager and restaurant owner, I finally grasped the practicality of what you said in your lectures and these notes when I put them to use on the job. They restored a financially troubled restaurant to profitability and this success did not go unnoticed by my employer. It helped me earn a significant promotion and several pay raises." He further went on to tell me that he had used these materials to train countless managers and chefs under his guidance throughout the years. Many of them have gone on to very successful careers as restaurant general managers.

Hearing comments like this from a former student gives an instructor, whether he or she is teaching management or culinary, a feeling that is best described by words like validation, fulfillment, absolution, and justification. As a restaurateur who turned to teaching, I have been able to walk the talk with my students, colleagues, and consulting clients. It is a myth that "those who can't do, teach." When a graduate of a hospitality or culinary program has a successful industry career, their former teachers take pride in knowing they provided some of the knowledge used for an objective and critical review of operations. Fortunately, we get to take some of the credit for that success and find great satisfaction in the possibility that we might have made a difference. When a former student validates that thought in their own words, it is the most sincere form of flattery to an instructor. Thus was the case with me when Paul expressed those thoughts.

Over a cup of coffee, we talked and caught up on what had transpired in the fifteen years since we last spoke. The conversation turned to my cost control book and that I needed to write a second edition. I also mentioned that I wanted to write it primarily for culinary schools and asked for his input because Paul has taught hundreds of students in the area of cost controls. The more we talked, the more I felt that Paul would be an excellent co-author for the second edition. Paul brings his experience as a foodservice manager and entrepreneur into his classes. That, along with having earned his ACF certifications, has added an additional credential and point of view that helps make this version better than the first.

Thus we both set out to make the second edition of this text even more practical and helpful to both the student and the instructor. The text contains twelve chapters ranging from general cost controls to financial analysis. We introduce cost control from a "systems perspective." It covers all the important aspects of restaurant cost control stressing food, labor, and beverage cost controls. We have expanded the chapter on Menu Sales Mix Analysis and have included a CD program of Cost/Margin Analysis, developed by Pavesic. It is a most practical and easy to use tool for analyzing both your food and beverage sales mix. With this software, you will find it easy to use spreadsheets that analyze almost any menu. This will position you to manage your menu to maximize your profit potential. End of chapter problems that can be solved by using Excel spreadsheets are indicated in the text with the spreadsheet accessible on the enclosed disk. Excel supplemental products (ISBN: 013-119368-6) are available at a discounted price when packaged with this textbook. Please consult your local Pearson Prentice Hall sales respresentative for details.

We have expanded the financial analysis chapter to include balance sheet and the statement of cash flows. We now cover the three most important financial statements that an owner or manager uses and explain them in a simple, easy to understand format. We cover break even and closing point, two of the most useful financial tools for an operator.

The appendices of the book include the most comprehensive glossary of culinary, financial and cost control terms heretofore assembled. In addition, the terms in the glossary are *italicized* in the body of the text so students can quickly look up the meaning of a new term. The appendix also contains material on the economic importance of customer service and a summary of the current wage and hour laws that pertain to restaurant and food service operations.

The support materials have been expanded to include a student study guide as well as an instructor's manual. Paul has done research on the instructional value of graphic organizers and we have included them in both the student and instructors' materials. Organizers such as these have been proven to increase student retention and improve the level of understanding of material. We have included some case studies and the use of Excel spreadsheets so the computer is integrated into teaching and learning. (Student Study Guide; ISBN: 013-119368-6)

The instructor's manual contains PowerPoint slides and lecture notes for each chapter, key terms, goals, and objectives, homework problems, and review quiz questions. A midterm and final exam are also included. The Instructor's Manual can be found online through our online catalog at www.prenhall.com. Once you are at the catalog page for the book, choose the link to Instructor Resources from the menu on the left.

We have written this text much like one would write an article for a trade journal like *Restaurant Business* or *Restaurant Hospitality.* It does not read like a textbook. Both Paul and Dave are available should you have a question or comment. You can reach Dave at hrtdvp@gsu.edu and Paul at paddiebk6@aol.com.

 ## Acknowledgments: David V. Pavesic

To my editor, Vern Anthony, for his encouragement and assistance in bringing this second edition to print; to Marion Gottlieb for her patience and help in preparing the manuscript elements for production; to Georgia State University and the School of Hospitality for giving me the platform to develop the content for this book over the past 17 years; and to my co-author and former student, Paul F. Magnant for validating that what I have been teaching for over 25 years is relevant and practical.

 ## Acknowledgments: Paul F. Magnant

It is appropriate for me to say thank you to my mentor and co-author who even twenty years later is still providing me with valuable lessons for my career and in life—Dr. David V. Pavesic. He has shown me, through his actions, how to be professional while delivering tough lessons in a kind manner.

There is one other person from my academic training that I should acknowledge for her mentorship. That person is Dr. Stacy B. Plichta from Old Dominion University. Her tough training in the area of research methods and quantitative analysis has prepared me to continue to conduct meaningful research that will contribute to my field of interest—hospitality.

From my early years, I can remember working for Rose Marquardt who at the time was the Food and Beverage Director of the Sheraton City Squire. She taught me how to develop a daily flash report and to take corrective actions for problem areas. My most significant operations development came from my general manager at Sara Hotels, Mr. Orr Rivero, who taught me perseverance and many techniques on how to become a better manager through motivational styles that I still use today.

During the time that my wife and I had our restaurant, I became aquatinted with a family physician and entrepreneur by the name of Steven Selznick, MD. It was under his tutelage that I learned how to use the knowledge that I already possess to become financially independent and free of debt. For this lesson I am very grateful. He and his wife Karen, along with Joe and Patty Alverez, have been role models for us in parenting as well as how to help others achieve their dreams in life. We are grateful for their unselfish contributions to our professional development.

I could not close this section without a tribute to my parents. Lt. Col. Paul Alfred Magnant and Charlotte Faye Magnant (Higgins). Through their love and caring they instilled in me a belief that I should follow my dreams and a true and sincere appreciation for the diverse culture in which we live. My father used to comment "don't look at the package look at the contents," that is what is important about a person. My father became my best friend and confidant in his later years. I was always amazed at how nothing ever intimidated him. He simply had no fear. This was truly inspirational to a young man in his developmental years. My mother was a very successful elementary school teacher. Her creative nature and development of learning methods for students with learning handicaps still influences me today. It was my mother who helped me become a better husband and father through her early teachings on how marriage is a partnership. We are best friends today.

Lastly, and certainly not the least, is my wife, Addie Marie Magnant (Ishii). I met Addie in 1984 while at my first placement right out of college. She only wanted to be friends then, but I persisted and sure enough, seven years later got my first date. After seven family interviews I was given the family's blessing and we were married. Addie is my number one cheerleader. We have been married for over 12 years now and have been recently blessed with our first child Michiko Addie Magnant. If it were not for her encouragement and support, we would not enjoy the wonderful life we have today as a family. She is my best friend and I love her dearly.

About the Author

David V. Pavesic Dr. David V. Pavesic is a second-generation restaurateur. His family owned and operated two Italian restaurants in Chicago from the mid 1940's until 1974. He earned his bachelor of science in business administration from Florida State University and majored in hotel and restaurant management. He received an MBA from Michigan State University, majoring in hotel, restaurant, and institutional management. He received his Ph.D. from Florida State University in higher education administration.

Upon graduation from Michigan State, he served as chairman of the hotel and restaurant program at Metropolitan Junior College in Kansas City, MO. After three years he went to work for Regan's Restaurants, a family-owned chain of six restaurants in the metropolitan Kansas City area as general manager of operations. He later accepted a position as the director of food service at Rollins College in Winter Park, FL. He then founded Angelo's Italian Restaurants, Inc. in Casselberry, FL where he opened two casual dining restaurants. He sold his controlling interest in the restaurant to return to academia as an instructor in the Department of Restaurant Management at Florida State University and earned his doctorate while on the faculty.

He joined Georgia State in 1986 as an associate professor in the Department of Hotel, Restaurant, and Travel Administration. In 1988 he was named program director of the Cecil B. Day School of Hospitality Administration and served until 1996. He is director emeritus, senior professor, and graduate program director.

Dr. Pavesic has served on the industry boards of the Missouri, Kansas, and Georgia Restaurant Associations, the Board of Directors of the Atlanta Convention and Visitors Bureau, American Hotel and Motel Association, and the Council on Hotel, Restaurant and Institutional Education.

He has consulted for independent restaurants, private clubs, and contract food service accounts in the areas of kitchen layout, menu analysis, cost controls, menu design and operational analysis. He has delivered presentations to professional associations like the National Restaurant Association, National Association of Catering Executives, American Hotel and Motel Association, and Club Managers Association of America.

He is one of the most prolific authors in hospitality journals. He ranked 9th out of 108 "most influential hospitality management scholars" from 1989–1999, 10th in the top 37 most cited hospitality faculty from 1997–1999 and 17th out of the top 100 authors in terms of publication in the premier hospitality journals. He has written eight books including *Menu Pricing and Strategy* with the late Jack Miller, this text and the six Restaurant Manager Handbooks on topics ranging from cost control to menu design.

He has had over 30 articles published in refereed journals, eight chapters in books of other hospitality educators, and given numerous speeches, workshops, and seminars at academic and industry association conferences. He received the Southeast CHRIE research award in 1993. He has developed his Cost/Margin Menu Analysis software for menu sales mix analysis which is in use in both academia and industry. His current research is about to explore restaurant failure rates, hoping to dispel the misconception that restaurants have the highest failure rate of all retail service entities.

He is an avid collector of old restaurant and hotel books and magazines and is developing a historical database of materials. He has been married to his college sweetheart for 37 years and has a daughter and son who have blessed him with four beautiful grandchildren. He currently resides in Woodstock, GA and can be reached at 404-651-3678 or hrtdvp@gsu.edu.

Paul F. Magnant   Paul F. Magnant is a native of Central Florida and was the Department Chair and Assistant Professor of the Hospitality Department of Johnson & Wales University–Norfolk, Virginia Campus. He has taught at Valencia Community College, Stetson University, and Daytona Beach Community College. He is a Certified Executive Chef and Culinary Educator (C.E.C., C.C.E.), a Certified Food and Beverage Executive and Foodservice Management Professional (C.F.B.E., F.M.P), a Certified Hospitality Educator and HACCP Auditor/Manger (C.H.E., C.H.M.), and Certified Culinary Instructor (CCI). Magnant has nearly two decades of operational experience in the food service sector, including five years as chef–owner/operator of a full service restaurant and four years in sales and distribution with Pepperidge Farm Inc. (a division of Campbell's Soup Co.) where he was awarded the Super Merit Award and Merit Award for being in the top 1 percent of the national sales force. In addition, he has served as the Food and Beverage Director of Sara Hotels Inc. (Gothenburg, Sweden) and held management positions with Sheraton Corporate Hotels (Seattle, WA and New York City), Red Lion Hotels (Costa Mesa, CA) and The Palace Hotel (Walt Disney World, FL).

Currently in the final stages of pursuing his Ph.D. in Urban Services with a concentration on "Food Safety Training and Management" at Old Dominion University, Magnant has already earned his MBA from Nova Southeastern University and a bachelor of science degree in Hospitality Administration and Psychology from Florida State University and is currently working toward obtaining two additional culinary certifications.

He resides in Norfolk, Virginia with his wife of over 12 years, Addie M. Magnant (Ishii), and their daughter Michiko. Magnant has conducted valuable research in the areas of instructional skills for culinary and hospitality students. He is active in the local chapter of the American Culinary Federation as the Educational Committee Director and has conducted consulting and training work for several nationally known foodservice and hospitality organizations. Chef/Professor Magnant along with his wife Addie (who is also a chef), have both distinguished themselves in the classroom by finding methods and techniques for bringing out the best in students.

MENU SALES MIX ANALYSIS
David V. Pavesic
Cecil B. Day School of Hospitality Administration
Georgia State University

The purpose of this software program is to provide instructors and students of cost controls a practical tool for demonstrating how the menu sales mix can impact overall food cost, gross profit and revenue. Point of Sale (POS) technology has allowed operations to track the sales of every item on their menu to determine their respective popularity, cost, revenue and profit contribution. Typically, the data is displayed in a spreadsheet format, which is difficult to interpret and use as a decision-making tool. While the information provided in the spreadsheet format is useful, the graphing of the spreadsheet data can provide even more detailed insight to the dynamics of the menu sales mix.

This program allows the user to categorize sales not only by meal periods, but by up to five separate menu categories; e.g., appetizers, side orders, entrees, desserts, and miscellaneous. A separate program is also included for the sales mix of alcoholic beverages, which are categorized by spirits, beer, wine, liqueurs, and miscellaneous categories. The menu categories are viewed separately and then combined in a summary spreadsheet providing cost information that can be compared to figures reported on the monthly income statements.

The unique aspect of this program is the graphing feature which allows the instructor to show the differences between the three most frequently used methods of menu sales mix analysis, Menu Engineering, (Smith and Kasavana) Cost/Margin Analysis (Pavesic) and the Miller Matrix (Miller).

The program is written in Excel 97 and enhanced with Visual Basic for Applications. The program is "menu driven" with protected macros for all the calculations and graphing functions. After entering only the menu item name, its food cost, menu price and number sold, with the click of the mouse, the data is automatically converted into a 23 column spreadsheet which is then converted to graphs in any of the three menu analysis methods.

INSTRUCTIONS FOR LOADING MENU ANALYSIS 3.5L

It is important to note that you will need to save the program on our hard drive to add new data. It should be saved in your "My Documents" folder and can be opened when you are in Excel 97 or later versions. The program will ask you if you want to *"enable macros"* and **you must answer "yes"** to load the program. It will not work with Lotus 123.

INTRODUCTION

Upon opening the program, click on the *README tab.* We suggest that you print out a hard copy as a ready reference. Read it over to get an overview of the program components and operation. The following examples are offered to familiarize you with the program. There are five different menu categories and eleven different TABS (Sheets) in this program. They are: Appetizers, Side Orders, Entrees, Desserts, Miscellaneous, Summary, Averages & Totals, Cost/Margin Graph, Miller Matrix Graph, Menu Engineering Graph, and the README tab.

Select the "Appetizer" category by clicking on the tab at the bottom of the screen. You will not that at the TOP menu bar the word "Appetizer" now appears. You will find it located between <u>W</u>indow and <u>H</u>elp. Move the cursor to "Appetizer" and click. A drop down menu will appear with options labeled "Calculate" and "Clear." Click "Calculate" and a spreadsheet with sample data will appear with all the 23 columns filled and extended. (The "Clear" function will erase all sample data and allow you to enter your own figures. But for this orientation do not clear the data until you are ready to enter your own data). Look over the spreadsheet to familiarize yourself with the column headings. Note that each menu item is named and numbered starting with the number "one." This is extremely important as it represents the identification of individual menu items on the graphs. The numbers on the graphs correspond to the specific menu items on the spreadsheet. Space does not permit the description of all 23 columns and their calculations. This information can be seen on the README file. You may wish to go through and view each of the five different menu categories. All utilize the same spreadsheet format. Not that the midpoints are different on each spreadsheet. This is because each menu category has different food costs and popularity.

Click on the "Summary" TAB and then the "Calculate" button. A spreadsheet will appear with all the menu items summarized on a single spreadsheet. Note that there are a total of 78 different items on this spreadsheet. (The last item is Mahi Mahi). Scroll up and you will find entries from each of the five spreadsheets "summarized" in this single sheet. You will also not that the midpoints have been recalculated and are based on the entire menu sales mix. This is the number that would be compared to you actual food cost on your monthly income statement. *You do not have to use all five menu categories when entering your data as the "summary" function totals only those categories with data. (Be sure to clear sample data from unneeded categories before hitting the "calculate" summary button.*

Click on the "Cost/Margin" TAB and you will see the words "Cost Margin" in the top menu bar. Click on it and a drop down menu will appear. This same drop down menu will appear for all three of the menu analysis methodologies. The drop down menu selections will be for the five menu categories. When you click on any one of them, another menu appears to the right with two options. They are: *"Individual"* or *"Summary."* Each one will produce a graph for the specific menu category you select. In this example, click "Appetizers." You will see the name of the graph and the menu items it represents. You will also see a *vertical black line and a horizontal purple line.* These lines are drawn automatically through a calculated mid-point designated by the number zero.

After you have viewed each of the five menu categories and clicked the "Calculate" button for each one, you can now click on the *Summary* TAB to produce the Summary Spreadsheet. You can now display the entire menu sales mix, all five categories, on a signal graph. Select any one of the graphing methodologies and click on "Summary." You will see why we have added the "Individual" category graphing option with the "Summary" midpoints. With more than 70 items on a single graph, it becomes extremely crowded and difficult to analyze individual menu items. To correct this, we added the option that allows you to view any of the individual menu categories plotted on a graph with the *Summary* midpoints of the entire menu sales mix. It is the graphing of the spreadsheet data that provides the most valuable information to the student as they can see how each menu category contributes to the overall menu sales mix.

Therefore, to eliminate the crowding on the *Summary* graphs, the program allows you to plot individual menu categories on a graph with the *Summary* midpoints. To activate this feature, go back up to the menu bar and click on the menu category you want to view. Instead of clicking on "Individual," click on "Summary" for Cost/Margin, Miller Matrix or Menu Engineering analysis for Appetizers or any of the menu categories you have been using. What you will get is a single menu category sales mix plotted against the *Summary* midpoints. We believe that this feature is beneficial in seeing how each menu category lines up against the entire menu sales mix.

The *Averages and Totals* TAB brings you to a very useful table that summaries the midpoints for each menu category as well as the midpoints for the summary sales mix. Note that the weighted food cost percentage is 36.8% and the different average food costs for each of the menu categories. You can see that *Appetizers* help lower the overall food cost percentage because they average 31.14% while *Desserts* and *Miscellaneous* items have a food cost of 46.48% and 43.66% respectively.

The midpoint for food cost on the Summary sheet is unrealistically low because it is calculated based on the cost shown in standardized recipes for standard portions. It does not take into account allowances for food consumed but not sold, as would be the case with employee meals, quality control waste, complimentary meals, discounts, and give-away food items used in the bar for happy hours. Subsequently, before you can compare this percentage to the one on the monthly income statement, allowances for food consumed but not sold must be added. This can amount to an additional 1.5-3.5 percent. When this allowance is added to what is basically the *Potential Food Cost* it becomes your *Standard Food Cost Percentage* which can then be compared to your *Actual Food Cost Percentage* shown on your income statement. (*The computing of the Actual Food Cost on your income statement must follow the Uniform System of Accounts for Restaurants methodology, which requires that a month end inventory of all food be taken. Without an inventory, you cannot have an accurate cost of food sold*).

In Column C are the average number sold or cut off points for popular and not popular items. Further note that the cut-off points for *Desserts* and *Miscellaneous* items are far below the 176 cut off for the entire sales mix. This points out the importance of individually assessing the popularity of items within their respective menu category as well as against the entire sales mix.

Columns F, G, H, & I reveal important management information that should be pointed out to your students. In terms of items sold, 44 out of every 100 items are *Side Orders (Snacks)*. *Desserts* and *Miscellaneous* items account for only 7 out of every 100 items sold. Almost 42c out of every dollar spent on food cost goes to items in the *Side Order* category. The point that needs to be made to students is that this kind of analysis tells them where management needs to concentrate its controls because that is where it stands to lose the most. The same *Side Orders* account for over 44c of every dollar of contribution margin and over 43c of each dollar of food revenue. This same kind of analysis can be done for alcoholic beverages. A separate program for alcoholic beverages is also available by email request.

INTERPRETING THE DATA

Teaching students to intuitively analyze financial data is certainly one of the more challenging aspects of the teaching-learning process. The spreadsheet and graphs assemble the data and organize it into reports that still required management to interpret. The data will reveal how the menu design, pricing, internal merchandising and up-selling strategies are impacting your menu sales mix and ultimately the food cost percentage, gross profit dollars, and total sales revenue. The graphs allow students to see which menu items are the ones that need to be adjusted to improve the financial results and which items are contributing the most to their profit goals and cost standards. They can quantitatively determine whether their decisions are improving their overall financial results. If the food cost percentage declines and the average individual and weighted gross profit increases, it indicates that the changes instituted had a positive outcome on the menu sales mix.

Remember that the food cost calculated by this program is really the *potential food cost* and is based on the assumptions that there is zero waste and perfect portioning, which is rarely the case. In addition, it assumes that the food cost is based on current prices paid to purveyors. Therefore, it can be unrealistically understated because there will be food that is consumed but not sold. The cost of these items must be added to the food cost. The amount of variable will depend on adherence to standards of purchasing, preparation and portioning. In restaurant with full menus and items made from scratch, allowances for waste and quality control will be greater than in operations with limited menus and where convenience ingredients are used.

Once the sales analysis program has classified all the menu items into one of the five categories for Cost/Margin, Miller Matrix and Menu Engineering, a strategy for improving or optimizing their overall impact on the menu sales mix can be put into action. The characteristics of the menu items will point you in the direction of what specific strategy would be best.

ABOUT THE AUTHORS

David V. Pavesic, Ph.D., CHE, FMP is a professor and graduate program director in the Cecil B. Day School of Hospitality Administration in the Robinson College of Business at Georgia State University. Nicholas Yu and Pinaki Mitra were graduate research assistants who helped put my program into its present format. I also acknowledge my late colleague, Jack Miller, the creator of the Miller Matrix and Don Smith and Michael Kasavana, the creators of the Menu Engineering methodologies. If you have any difficulties with the program whatsoever, please feel free to contact me with your comments and questions. I can be reached at school at 404-651-3678 or at by Email at mailto:hrtdvp@gsu.edu.

Fundamental Principles
of Restaurant Cost Control
Second Edition

1

The Value and Importance of Cost Controls

■   ■   ■   ■   ■   ■   ■   ■   ■   □   □

1. Cost controls are not enough to insure the financial success of your restaurant. It is just one important component of your overall business plan.

2. Costs eventually reach a point where they cannot be further reduced without compromising food quality, customer service, and price-value.

3. Sales volume can hide a multitude of cost control sins. Therefore, a marketing strategy to build customer awareness and traffic is essential once costs are contained.

4. You eventually have to spend money to save money. Investment must be made in people, equipment, systems, and programs to control costs. You will get what you pay for when it comes to employees and equipment.

5. It takes time and talent to assemble, organize and analyze financial and operational data. Whether you will achieve success or suffer failure will depend on two things: 1. How well you are able to collect relevant cost and sales data, and 2. How well you will be able to interpret that data and use it to determine if your decisions have been the right ones.

6. Cost controls need to be *preventive, not corrective.* If cost controls are only implemented *after* a problem has been discovered, you are addressing only the *symptom* and not the *cause.*

7. Cost controls need to be *proactive* more often than *reactive.* Cost controls are most effective when they are designed to *prevent* losses in the first place rather than to *correct* them after they have been discovered.

8. Cost standards are needed to provide management and ownership with information about the effectiveness of day-to-day operations.

9. Your cost control program is only as strong as your weakest area. Controls must be addressed from the back door to the front, covering all activities in between.

10. Your physical presence, while valuable, is not sufficient for cost control purposes. Written records are your eyes when you are not present.

E very Decision You Make Is a Financial One

We have been teaching **cost control** and menu planning for some time now and it is amazing how often we all underestimate the effects of our daily decisions on our financial future. This could be prevalent in both our foodservice careers as well as our personal lives. A **cost control strategy** is an essential element of any foodservice operation's planning. This includes the long-range strategic plan that involves the vision of the operation's success, annual and monthly financial goals, as well as the daily evaluation of productivity. It is not the *only* element but one of several important elements necessary for the operation to be able to effectively compete in the marketplace. It has been reported that pretax income in commercial restaurants is down about 4 percent and that operating expenses have increased by 6 percent. Coupled with the rising costs of food and labor, restaurant profitability has been cut significantly.

The difference between financial success and failure in the restaurant business is basically 3 percent of sales. After expenses and taxes are paid, the restaurants showing profits have bottom lines ranging from 0.5 to 3 percent of sales. That small percentage is the difference between going out of business and being a solvent entity.

The decisions we make every day have a significant impact on the likelihood that a restaurant will remain viable. This is the reason we must have a system of cost control procedures as part of our overall business plan. When business is good, even the marginally efficient operations can show a positive cash flow. But when there is heavy competition and demand slows down, these marginal operators are the first to feel the negative effects on their cash flow. During such economic periods, only the strong will survive. But the "will to survive" is simply not enough. We can assume that entrepreneurs do not "plan to fail" when they decide to risk their capital and go into business; however, many of those who are not successful simply "fail to plan."

This is why taking a **systems approach** to cost control and menu planning is essential to the success of a foodservice operation. By systems approach we mean that there is a documented plan with procedures for how each operational element is going to be handled, from the initial steps of ordering and receiving food and beverages through the collection of payment from the guest to the depositing of funds and reconciling of our month-end financial statements. Often in the foodservice industry, no such planning exists or if it does, it is very unofficial. Typically we will rely on the common sense of a manager or owner. The problem here is that the system is only as good as the person who is directing it. Now in sole proprietorships, this can be effective. But when they are absent from the restaurant what happens to the process? Typically, as long as the owner or manager is present the plan is in effect. However, their presence becomes so critical that they are unable to free themselves from the restaurant for fear that things will not function properly. By creating a system and then delegating responsibility and authority to other key employees who have been trained, the presence of the owner or manager is no longer critical to the continuity of the system and achieving the desired results.

An additional benefit to creating a system is that it allows for more time to be spent on other activities. For the manager, it may mean staff training or local marketing efforts. For the owner/operator it may mean that they can concentrate on activities more strategic in nature. Both manager and owner need to have a life away from the restaurant. Without a break, job and career burnout are likely to occur. In your first few years in management, you need to give 100 percent to your job to become established. However, most individuals are not willing to trade a career for a family—they want both. In any case the argument is very strong for creating a system that can be understood and used by employees when the manager is absent.

There is no way around it: Cost control is a *numbers game.* At first glance, paying attention to numbers is viewed as a job for the accountant, controller, or consultant. It involves accounting and that is work that will at first seem tedious and dull. However, if you want to make money, a detailed assessment of what is going on in your restaurant is necessary and you need numbers to do that. Just as you evaluate food quality and service in the dining room you need qualitative and quantitative standards. The quantitative numbers you collect must be organized, interpreted, and compared to the organization's goals. These numbers may represent what happened during a particular meal period, day, week, month, or even year.

The interpretation of the numbers is something you cannot delegate. You must understand what these numbers mean in terms of productivity of your prime resources (food, beverage, labor) so you can lead by managing the activities of others in the operation in a proactive manner. Not to do so is a formula for failure. You have to know what is going on in your own operation and cannot rely on being told that you have a problem. The numbers are your keys to your success. You review them over and over to measure how close you came to your planned results until their meaning is clear and you have answers to any deviation from the original plan. Comprehension of numbers comes from an understanding of the relationship each outcome has with the input(s) that produced it. This is just like cooking, we know if something is over cooked (outcome) to lower the temperature or reduce the cooking time (inputs). With a constant review, a resulting familiarity with numbers will be developed just from knowing the activities that caused the results and comparing it to your standards.

Eventually you will find yourself looking forward to preparing and reviewing the numbers and calculating the ratios and percentages that reveal the information you need. "The truth is that the drudgery of the numbers will make you free" (Geneen, Harold "A Case for Managing by the Numbers," *Fortune,* Vol. 10, No. 7 pp. 78–81 Oct. 1, 1984). The very fact that you go over the progression of those numbers week after week, month after month, means that you have strengthened your memory and familiarity with them so that you retain a vivid and complete picture of what is going on in your operation. Knowing what happened in the past can provide insight into what is likely to happen in the future.

Understanding the numbers puts you in a position to influence the financial outcome of the foodservice operation; in other words, you are in control. You become aware of significant variances from your standards. This information will help you determine what needs to be done either to sustain the financial gains or to keep costs within prescribed standards. When you have mastered the numbers, you are no longer reading numbers any more than you are reading words when reading a book—you will be reading meanings. Your eyes will be seeing numbers but your mind will be reading the story behind the numbers, such as labor productivity, portion control, purchase prices, marketing promotions, new menu items, and competitive strategy.

Controls are Proactive and Preventative

The stepfather of one of the authors was a self-made restaurateur, and was the role model that made him decide on majoring in restaurant management in college. He was the classic trial-and-error entrepreneur. He was not formally educated in business let alone restaurant management. When his restaurant closed in 1974 he had been in business for 27 years at the same location. When the author sought his advice prior to opening his first restaurant back in 1973 his stepfather told him that if he were starting off today with the same knowledge about the business he had 27 years ago he would not have lasted a year in business given the level of competition from the chains and the overall economy. (The U.S. economy was in a recession in 1973.) His reluctance to give him his opinion was both surprising and disappointing to the author at the time.

The author had to reach his own conclusions and it was not until after his stepfather had passed away that his mother told him the reason why his stepfather was not comfortable giving him restaurant advice. She said he was worried that if he followed his advice and it was wrong, he would feel terrible. He had also told her that he did not know the "why" behind "what" he did. In addition, what worked for him at the time would not likely work in the present economy and markets.

Knowing "why" you do or do not do something is what distinguishes *professional restaurateurs* from *amateurs.* You will be taught the "why" behind what you do in your culinary courses. (There is a reason why you add the acidic lemon juice to the alkaline cream based sauce instead of the the other way around.) Once you understand "why" cost controls are important you will understand "what" you need to do and "why" it must be done a certain way.

C ontrols are Part of the Entire Management Process

The management process of *Planning, Organizing, Leading, and Controlling* (POLC) is a "system" that provides you with a way of achieving your profit goals. *Planning* is conducted when you design your menu and establish your food and labor cost standards. Planning gives you a clear picture of what it is you want to accomplish. *Organizing* is the system used to establish the procedures for accomplishing your objectives. *Leading* is using the information you collect within the process we call "cost controls" to guide the activities and efforts of the human resources of the organization. *Controlling* is the measurement of the actual results and comparing them to the plan. See Figure 1–1. Having said this, one of the authors remembers the experience of opening his own restaurant. During the initial stages of writing the business plan for the operation he had to complete several planning projects. These included developing the menu, purchasing specifications, standardizing the recipes and costing them out, as well as determining the minimum required culinary skill level of kitchen staff. The organizing stage occurred when he applied for funding, chose a management team of qualified individuals, and assembled

Management Process	Cost Control Application	Examples
Planning	Creating a vision of what it is you want to accomplish and establishing what tools you will need to get there.	Standard Recipe Cards Menu Layout and Design Break Even Analysis Scheduling Budgeting
Organizing	Creating a systems approach to how measurements will be calculated, what is to be measured, when, and by whom?	Establishing Policies (procurment, receiving, storing, issuing, inventory, etc.) Security of Assets (inventory)
Leading	Establishing the relationships to influence the employee's behavior toward achieving established goals within the system.	Relationships to hold employees accountable Creating a climate and culture of genuine concern for maintaining the established cost control standards
Controlling	Measuring the actual performance in the language of numbers, ratios and percentages. Then comparing them to the plan to form an analysis of the results.	Food Cost Beverage Cost Labor Cost Menu Mix Horizontal & Vertical Analysis

FIGURE 1–1
The Systems Approach to Cost Control

the necessary facilities and equipment for the operation. The leading function occurred when he presented the philosophy of the operation and shared his vision with the management team so that they could influence the future staff. This would ensure continuity of the "service attitude" in the restaurant at all times. Lastly, the controlling function occurred when the management team measured their results and compared them to the budget and weekly forecast.

The story of Christopher Columbus serves to explain the preventive aspect of cost control. When he set out for the New World, Columbus had no plan on how to get there, how long it would take, and what to expect along the way. He had to battle rough seas, going aground on sandbars, and coral reefs. When he finally got to where he was going, he didn't know where he was. But like many entrepreneurs attempting to open their own business, Columbus was willing to take the risk. According to government figures, a restaurant investor is given a 1 in 20 chance of getting their money back in five years.

However, today we cannot just set sail in the business world without charts and maps. The competition is too great, and we will perish before we reach our destination. If we were in Columbus' shoes, we would stay out of dangerous waters and sail around storms that threaten to wreck us. If we cannot avoid certain adverse conditions, we batten down the hatches to minimize loss or dock at a friendly port until danger passes. Such "dangers" include economic recessions, inflation, unemployment, interest rates, and tax laws that all foodservice businesses must endure. Only those who are prepared with a plan will survive the storms. Cost controls are our survival kit. You cannot enter the restaurant business without having a comprehensive plan. Richard Melman, a very successful and innovative restaurateur and president of Lettuce Entertain You, Inc., told an auditorium full of people in the foodservice industry that 80 percent of the success of any restaurant idea is determined before the doors are opened. The restaurant business is no longer for novices to learn as they go or to proceed on a trial-and-error basis.

One must remove as much of the risk of failure as possible before the ship ever leaves port. With the proper maps, reports, and instruments, you can avoid running aground on a coral reef, you will know where to stop along the way to get supplies and rest, and in bad weather, make necessary preparations to minimize damage. While planning is critical, it does not imply that cost control is a one-time program or a pre-opening exercise; it is ongoing and present throughout the life of the business.

If we look at opening and owning a restaurant like the voyage of Columbus, we would find ourselves competing against other entrepreneurs who have the latest charts, equipment, and expertise to help their businesses succeed the first time. When things are going right, cash flow is positive, and business is good, cost controls may appear unnecessary. High sales volumes can hide a multitude of cost inefficiencies that become evident during low sales periods. It is much harder to make a profit when sales revenues are low because every dollar of expense takes away from the bottom line.

Marginal operations that show a profit during peak volume periods do not know how much additional profit they could have made had they been more cost-conscious. Too many become "converts" to cost controls after suffering losses and they are seeking a way to "heal their wounds." Keep in mind that the *primary purpose* of cost controls is to *maximize profits, not minimize losses.*

Cost control is not a project instituted in response to hard times but a culture ingrained in the everyday practices of a business, just as components of the chef's uniform are designed for a specific function and not just appearance. As a philosophy, it places a premium on getting the greatest value for the least cost in every aspect of the restaurant's operations. After all, we apply this philosophy to our personal hard-earned income. We shop for ways to optimize our purchases and get the most for our money. We are careful with what we have on hand so as to avoid having to throw it away and we want to earn the most we can and become successful in our careers.

A large part of what it takes to remain in business today encompasses the ability to keep waste to a minimum and to utilize resources as efficiently as possible. This pertains not only to food and beverage, but also to labor, energy, and other operating expenses. When you keep costs under control, you can sell your products and services at a lower price and provide greater price-value to your customers. Even if you charge the going rate in the market, you will make more money than your competitors charging the same price.

Why don't all operators have cost control programs? The answer may be that they are not aware of the waste that is going on around them and therefore do not see a need for it. The truth is that you cannot "see" a lot of the waste with *just* the naked eye. It takes a system utilizing records and reports to see the magnitude of the waste or inefficiency that is very likely taking place.

The first step in correcting any problem is to realize that you, in fact, have one. It is often assumed that there is no problem until something is discovered to be missing or profit margins begin to shrink. By that time, the damage has already been done. Without controls in place to detect variances and shortages, owners and managers remain open to losses. When a loss is discovered, you must take the appropriate action to limit adverse effects on the financial well being of the operation. Again, foodservice operational success does not happen by chance, but as the result of some very careful advance planning, organizing, leading and controlling.

D efinition of Cost Control

The word *control* is not a particularly friendly and welcome word as it implies "restrictions" and "limits." Its dictionary definition says it is a "process or function" that is used to "regulate, verify, or check" that which is accomplished through some "method, device, or system." Control means to exercise authority over and to restrain.

Every foodservice operation, regardless of its size or method of service, should have a cost control system in place. Owners and managers need to regularly assemble and review information about the expenses being incurred and the revenues being received. They need to compare the actual results to established standards and budget guidelines for purposes of analysis.

What do we need to place under control in the restaurant business? The answer is, all items of income and expense. The major areas are food, beverage, and labor costs which are often referred to as *prime costs*. Did you know that, over the life of a restaurant, more dollars will be spent on food, beverage and labor than on the capital costs of building, land, and equipment combined? We are talking about millions of dollars, and that is why we devote such detailed attention to these three expenses.

Purpose of Cost Controls

Regardless of the type of hospitality enterprise you end up working in or operating, cost controls will be a major part of your responsibilities. You may not be purchasing food and beverage, but you will have labor and overhead expenses that must be monitored. Cost controls encompass all areas from the back door to the front door, from purchasing and checking deliveries to making the bank deposits and paying the bills. This cycle of activities is shown in Figure 1–3. All activities must be monitored to some degree. These examples can be generically transferred and applied to all segments of the hospitality industry, and they apply to multi-unit operations as well as single location operations.

Cost control is more than just computing percentages and ratios; it involves making decisions after the information has been compiled and interpreted. Operations such as *cost accounting* and *bookkeeping* provide the tools used in cost control for gathering the information needed for control to take place. Therefore, a more complete definition of cost control can be explained by citing its purposes, which are:

1. To provide management with the information necessary to make day-to-day operational decisions

2. To monitor the efficiency of individuals and departments

3. To inform management of what expenses are being incurred, what incomes are being received, and whether they are within standards or budgets

4. To prevent fraud and theft by employees, guests, and purveyors

5. To be the basis for *knowing where the business is going*, not for discovering where it has been

6. To emphasize *prevention* and not correction

7. To *maximize profit* not minimize losses

A key aspect of cost control is *prevention* not correction. Prevention is brought about through *planning.* Correction is the activity that takes place after the historical data is compared to the plan. If you wait for losses to occur before you develop a plan, the damage has already been done and you are still one step behind. If you have taken a course or read a book on the *principles of management,* you may recall the term *putting out fires.* "Fires" are major and minor incidents that management must deal with on a daily basis. If a large portion of a your time is spent dealing with the same problems that occur repetitively, all you are doing is "correcting after the fact." If a problem can be prevented from reoccurring, your time can be devoted to more important matters such as developing ways to increase sales through marketing efforts and dealing with customer service. It is the cost control process that helps you focus on diagnosing the root cause of a problem after identifying the symptoms. Without correcting the root cause of a cost control problem, you will find yourself having to deal with the same problems over and over.

I s Your Physical Presence Sufficient for Control?

Some owners or managers assume that, because they are on the premises working during all the hours that the establishment serves food and beverage, no detailed records or system of control needs to be in place. This is not entirely true since theft is only one of many reasons for establishing a system of cost controls in a foodservice operation.

Many independent, family-owned businesses do not see cost controls as necessary. They view them as a device for theft prevention that would be interpreted as a sign that they are distrustful of family members working for them. They fail to see the main purpose of cost control is that of providing information to management and owners on the results of the day-to-day operations. This information is not a "nice" to know item, it is a "need" to know area that will be required for making business decisions in the future. Its ancillary purpose is to detect fraud and theft.

Many operators become converts to cost control only when it is too late. Losses are excessive and they are like a terminally ill patient: All you can do is make life as comfortable as possible until the inevitable happens. Cost control is the basis for knowing where you're going and why, not for just discovering what you have done and where you've been. That is the difference between prevention and correction.

ost Control Versus Cost Reduction

Cost control is more than the accumulation and interpretation of information, filling out department reports, taking inventories, costing out recipes, and computing percentages and ratios. It involves interpreting those figures and taking the necessary steps to maintain profitability.

There is a difference between the terms cost *control* and cost *reduction*. Cost *control* is accomplished through the compiling, assembly, and interpretation of data and ratios on revenues and expenses. This control is a system of measuring what is actually happening in the operation. Armed with the cost control information, we can determine what happened and why. **Cost** *reduction* is the actual changing of the factors that will influence food, beverage, and labor cost in some manner, which results in the lowering of the ratio. Cost reduction is the "action" taken to bring costs within accepted standards. An example of this might be to choose an alternative ingredient in a recipe that is similar in taste and presentation to the original item but is less expensive to use. This would result in a lower percentage of the price being used for the menu item.

Cost controls provide owners and managers with the information necessary to determine the efficiency of their operation and the basis for making operational decisions. Cost controls become the "eyes" of the owner, franchisor, or manager when they are not physically present. Keep in mind that many cost inefficiencies are not detectable or preventable simply by one's physical presence in the restaurant. It does not matter how intelligent you are, or how many hours you put in each day at the restaurant. No one can possibly see everything that can cause costs to be out of line. Even if it were possible to observe all business activities and transactions, you still could not ascertain their immediate effect on the financial results of the foodservice operation.

A national pizza chain utilizes an inventory system that is tied into its menu sales mix. It allows management to detect over-portioning and waste based on standardized quantities for each ingredient used on its pizzas. For example, the system revealed that the use level of mozzarella cheese exceeded standard by approximately 25 pounds over a 30-day period. While initially this seemed to be a significant quantity, it averaged less than 2 grams of cheese per pizza; based on the number of pizzas sold. That kind of variance cannot be detected by simply watching; it takes written cost records of what was purchased and what was sold. Remember, the difference between success and failure in most hospitality enterprises is 3 cents on the dollar!

The further removed the owner or manager is from the actual operation of a restaurant, either in terms of distance or frequency of visitation, the greater the need for proper cost control records. Through required written reports, franchisors of McDonald's, Taco Bell, and Wendy's keep their corporate eye on the thousands of franchisee units across the country from their district and regional offices.

Systems Approach to Managing Your Costs

A systems approach to cost control is very closely related to the *process* of management by objectives (MBO's). In this instance, a manager will create goals, most likely expressed in profits, that will be the result of an entire team's efforts of cost containment and sales efforts. Once the goals have been established, the team creates a set of objectives that include many separate action steps to be completed throughout the entire process of the daily operation of the foodservice establishment. By establishing a system for the execution of these objectives, each person on the team is assigned specific areas of responsibility and can then be held accountable for their performance. An additional benefit of a systems approach is that the success of the system is contingent upon the interpersonal interaction of separate functional areas of the operations. These include purchasing, production, service and record keeping. All of these must communicate effectively and in an efficient manner to be successful.

An adaptation of a systems model developed by Spears and Gregoire (2003) is shown as a cost control system in Figure 1–2. The systems approach organizes the cost control functions into a step-by-step procedure to show how they are integrated to accomplish the desired result.

As stated earlier, the beginning of the creation of a system is to establish *goals* for the organization. Every goal should contain three elements: first, the result should be specific in terms of exactly what is to be accomplished; second, it must be measurable by some means, either in a quantitative (dollars or percentages) or qualitative measurement (satisfaction scales of 1-5) and third, the result should be "time sensitive." In other words, there is a deadline for the accomplishment of the goal. Keep in mind that there are several goals for an organization at any one time. We are going to focus on the ones related to cost control.

> Example: During the month of February we will achieve sales of $84,000 with a sales ratio of 80-20 (80% Food Sales & 20% Beverage Sales) while maintaining a combined cost of food and beverage of 29%, resulting in a profit of $12,600 or 15%.

Once the goals have been determined, resources have to be gathered to begin implementing your strategy to achieve your goals and objectives. This step will include **input** areas directly related to the resources of the organization. One example of input is the purchasing of food and beverage products in the raw state as required by the purchasing specifications. Others include the establishment of a theme/plan for the final serving of these menu items, acquiring the culinary skill required to prepare such items, getting the level of investment capital required to start and run the operation as well as determining what menu is required to attain the goal and meet your objectives.

> Example: The menu can only be as successful as the skill of the individuals preparing the food purchased, and the right equipment, and the equipment they have to work with. In other words, if you have a highly skilled chef and can afford to pay the wages required by a complementary supporting staff, they can create menu items from scratch. If you do not, you may have to purchase foods that are partially prepared, such as stuffed flounder ready to bake.

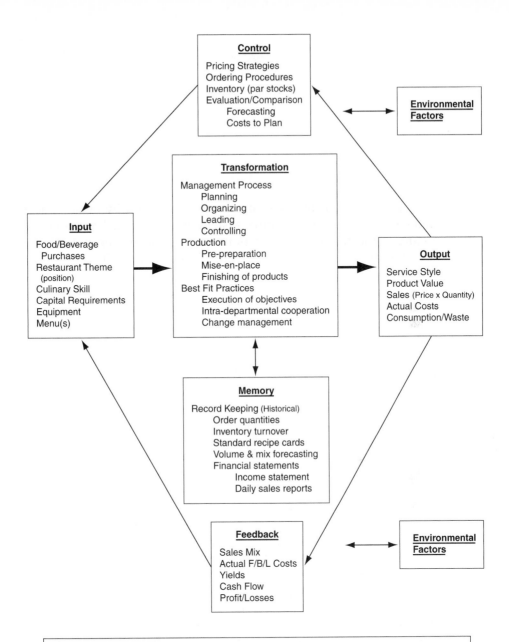

Environmental factors may include:
Weather, Seasonality of foods, Business Cycles, Availible labor pool, Market pricing, Political climate, Economic conditions (macro/micro), as well as Competition.

FIGURE 1–2
A Cost Control Systems Model
Source: Adapted from *A Foodservice Systems Model* by M.C. Spears & Mary B. Gregoire, 2003. Taken from Foodservice Organizations, a managerial and systems Approach 5th ed. Prentice Hall, Upper Saddle River, 2003. p. 7 (ISBN# 0-13-048689-2)

The *transformation* stage is the point in time when management decisions are made (planning, organizing, leading and controlling), production is executed, and what we call best-fit practices are communicated. These best-fit practices are valuable to the success of an organization in terms of arranging interpersonal relationships that promote cooperation and allow the organization to be flexible enough to deal with changes on a daily basis. The transformation stage is the part of the system that manipulates all input and turns it into the desired output. The ability to rely on our experience here is directly linked to the successful transforming of goods into a final product for guests to consume. We call this the memory part of the system. In this area, we create forms for record keeping and begin the historical process of archiving certain pieces of information about our plan for later use in comparing the actual results to the initial goals. Examples of these records are: quantities ordered during specific time periods, pricing structures, inventory turnover ratios, specifications and standard recipe cards, forecasts, as well as financial statements of income and daily sales. All of these, combined with an experienced management team, can assist in achieving the desired cost control goals.

> Example: You have just been informed that a bus load of 55 senior citizens are arriving in 40 minutes for your early bird special. You have to conduct your planning quickly to set aside a section for service, alert the kitchen that a large party will be arriving soon and will be using the early bird menu, organize your front-of-the-house staff to meet the needs of the large party without interfering with other guests, reinforce the check control policy (many of them have requested separate checks) as well as many other issues. You can see that communication is very important in this example. By alerting the kitchen to the arriving group, you've given them the time to begin production of extra quantities of items such as baked potatoes, rolls, and house salads (all of which are included in the early bird dinner). The dining room is ready to serve 55 people simultaneously. The bar may even be prepared to mix drinks that are popular with this age group.

The *output* is the tangible result of the effort put forth in the transformational stage. Here we can see the final product. This may be food quality, quantity (portions), actual costs, waste, perceived value, and guest satisfaction in accordance with the established service style. This is where the rubber meets the road in terms of meeting your objectives. The sales will reflect the quantity (covers) and price (average check) that will determine whether or not there is a profitable relationship between input and output. This leads us in two directions for the follow up to our performance.

> Example: Let's revisit the parameters of our original goal. Let us assume that during the month of February we had sales of $85,000 with a ratio of 85/15, a food and beverage cost (combined) of 31% and a profit of $13,000. This lists the output of sales, cost, and sales ratio.

The first is the *feedback* from the actual performance. This is represented in many forms in information that the system collects for us (after we set it up initially). This information is the foundation of the decision process used in shaping the restaurant's outcomes in order to achieve a profitable pattern of operations. Examples of the types of information collected are; menu sale mix, actual yields, actual costs of food, beverage and labor as well as cash flow information and determination of profits/losses. The second is the *control* function of the system. This is the area where we evaluate the measurements (**feedback**) of actual costs (food/beverage/labor), pricing strategies, inventory levels, out of stock situations (resulting in a lost sale) as well as the performance of our menu (variety, position on the page, pricing, portion size, etc). This is where the management of any variance from the actual performance to the planned performance is useful to achieve success.

> Example: We need to measure the output in order to be able to compare the results to our original goal. These measurements of sales mix (what percentage of entrees were lobster, steak, chicken, pasta), average check, yields, and food/beverage/labor costs, allow us to begin the process of evaluating our efforts relative to the goal. Next, we will determine what options we have for making the appropriate changes so that we may expect an improved outcome during the next business cycle.

So far we have only discussed the events that are controlled by the organization internally. These internal components of the system are very important but should not be the only focus of the management team. There also exist several external components, which we will call *environmental* **factors**. These include events or situations that may have an impact on the operation and, while not under the direct control or influence of the management, need to be recognized for the potential impact they have on the output of an organization. These include weather, availability of food items, the up and down periods of the business cycle, labor pool availability and skill levels, the political climate (local and national), economic conditions, and competition. These are prevalent in the control and feedback portions of the system.

Example: Management's Role

Effective cost control systems must start at the top of the organization. No control program can function well unless management establishes, supports, and enforces its standards and procedures. Employees are quick to notice when standards are not followed and when management fails to act to bring variances from standards into line. Employees seem to deviate from set standards only as much as management allows.

Regardless of the type of restaurant, cost controls will be a major part of management's total responsibility. Cost controls encompass all areas from the back door to the front, from purchasing to checking deliveries, making bank deposits, paying the bills, and all the activities in between. Central to every food or beverage operation are 12 primary function areas (see Figure 1–3). Central to the 12 primary functions are the menu, sales analysis, and inventory records. The menu drives the control process and will be covered in Chapter 5. The menu determines what the customer will buy (the menu sales mix), the specifications for the items purchased, and the quantities held in inventory. These are critical elements of the cost control records.

The systems approach we have just described is basically a way of thinking about your restaurant's operations. It is a way of organizing the functions of selling food to the public and it is also a device for helping you solve management problems. Before we describe the various functions of cost control, there are two very important points we need you to understand. First, a system is only as strong as its weakest component; and second, you will find that you will be stronger at certain functions than others. The systems approach requires that the various functions work to accomplish the same objectives. This means that all the elements of the operation need to come together to accomplish the objectives of restaurant. You cannot tolerate rifts between the kitchen and the dining room staff, lunch staff and dinner staff, day managers and night managers, or bussers and servers. If everyone sees their job only as it directly affects them, the system will fail.

Think of your restaurant system as a grouping of separate components that work together toward the ultimate goal. Your job as manager or executive chef will be to direct all the interdependent, interacting components through the intervening variables into an organized, cohesive team to ultimately satisfy the customer.

The steps in the **cost control cycle**, in sequential order and surrounding the menu, inventory, and menu sales mix records, are:

1. Purchasing
2. Receiving
3. Storage
4. Issuing
5. Pre-preparation (i.e., rough prep)
6. Portioning
7. Preparation (for service)
8. Order taking/guest check
9. Transfer of food from kitchen to dining room

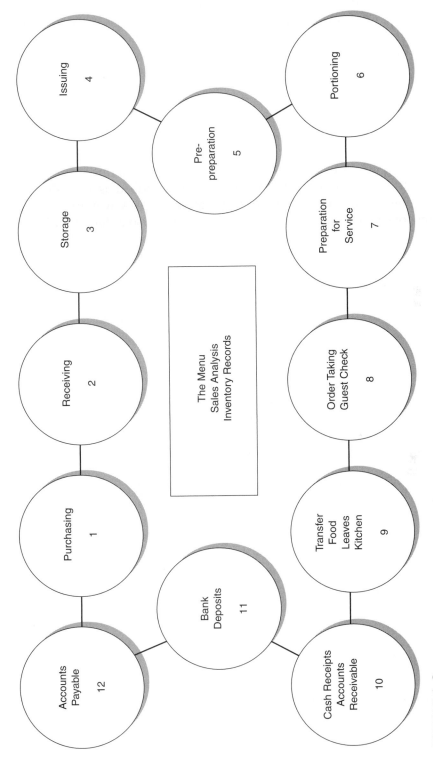

FIGURE 1–3
Cost control cycle.

10. Cash receipts/Accounts receivable
11. Bank deposits
12. Accounts payable

Many of these functions overlap and are performed at the same time. Because all of these steps are interrelated they must be monitored, or you will never uncover the real cause of any variance between actual and standard food cost. Controls for each function area must be operative as soon as the personnel are assigned or have access to the function area. Another way to approach the 12 function areas is using the analogy of a chain with each function area being a single "link" in the chain. That chain can only be as strong as its weakest link.

Some owners and managers are very good at controlling costs in one or more function areas while others are ignored. That can leave many opportunities for losses to occur and go undetected until they become excessive and are noticeable in the monthly financial report card of the owner/manager— the income statement. The function areas can be separated into two categories, front-of-the-house and back-of-the-house. Basically, this separates the functions of the kitchen (back-of-the-house) from the dining room and bar (front-of-the-house).

If all the effort is placed on controlling expenses in the kitchen and the dining room is neglected, financial goals may still not be attained and unwarranted pressure may be placed on those who are not at fault. Closely monitoring recipes, waste, and portioning is for naught when customers are not charged for food served or when sales are underreported. While the emphasis here has been on food cost–related concerns, cost controls are also concerned with beverage and labor cost inefficiencies as well as other overhead expenses such as linens, supplies, utilities, and other controllable expenses.

Each of the function areas will be covered more thoroughly later in this text, but a brief summary and description of each function here provides an overview of the importance of each area. The starting point of the cost control process actually begins when the menu is planned and designed. The menu will have the greatest influence on the complexity of your cost control procedures. It will impact your labor cost, inventory, equipment needs, and space requirements. Standardized recipes will be prepared for all menu items detailing the steps, ingredients, yields, and portion costs. This information becomes the basis for the detailed cost control and cost reduction methods that will be systematically followed.

Forecasting the sales mix (the number of times a menu item is sold within a time period) of menu items is the basis for determining purchasing and preparation quantities. Detailed sales records by meal period, day, and week will make forecasting more accurate. A properly designed menu will make the menu sales mix more predictable and allow management to predict sales levels for scheduling staff, determining purchasing quantities, and inventory levels.

Many individuals in the functional areas of both the front-of-the-house and back-of-the-house use the information gathered for cost control purposes. For example, sales analysis data such as customer counts and the mix of menu items sold helps the dining room manager in scheduling servers and bus help. During meal periods when there will be possible waiting times for guests, the bar manager may need to increase staff and overall preparation in order to keep patrons on property until their table is ready. This information tells the person doing the purchasing what and how much to keep in stock, and the kitchen manager how much to prepare each day. In addition, management interprets the information to plan a schedule of advertising promotions to optimize every opportunity to grow sales as well as to be able to compare food consumed numbers to the actual food sold in order to determine whether a variance exists. And if a variance does exist, management can move on to determine the cause and take steps to keep it from reoccurring.

Purchasing

The inventory system is a critical component of the purchasing function. Before placing an order with a supplier, you must know what is already on hand, how much will be used, and allow for a small cushion of inventory (also known as safety stock) so the items will not run out before the next scheduled delivery. This safety stock is necessary in case of purveyor vehicle breakdowns, occasional incomplete orders, or just plain communication errors in ordering. Once the owners have established the standardized purchase specifications, the manager then *orders* the quantities needed from the approved suppliers. Records are kept that indicate all the necessary information to conduct the purchasing function; for example, purveyors, prices, unit of purchase, product specifications, and the like. This information should not be kept only in the mind of the person doing the purchasing but needs to be put down on paper for future reference. This can be done using a purveyor order guide that is also used to verify the order upon delivery. You never know when a person may become ill, be transferred to another location, or quit. This is yet another reason for the development of a system that can be followed even if member of the team is absent. In order to accomplish the function of purchasing, information must be obtained on *what* and *how much* to purchase. This information is obtained from the menu sales mix analysis, which tells you how much of each menu item you plan to sell from day to day. With an estimate of the customer counts expected, order quantities can be accurately estimated.

Receiving

The function of the receiving process is to ensure and verify that all merchandise ordered has been received. Inspection is conducted to check for correctness of brands, grades, varieties, quantities, weight, count and that prices charged are those that management has approved. Substitution of brands or grades, damaged products, incorrect prices, weights, counts or goods that do not meet quality standards need to be noted, returned, or credit taken. Products purchased by weight must be checked for correctness using a properly calibrated scale.

The establishment is constantly purchasing merchandise of great monetary value and adequate security measures should be instituted at the receiving area. Remember that inventory is just as valuable as money in a bank account. Unfortunately, this point of view is often not adopted, and this important task is left to employees who are not trained in the system and therefore do not know what to look for. The result is that the operation is left to the mercy of delivery personnel and purveyor. Fortunately, most purveyors are ethical and professional and few will intentionally defraud a client. But honest mistakes occur and, if undetected, could cost the operation.

Storage

Every food ingredient and supply item must be placed in storage until it is time to use it. The orderly placement of items in storage is essential so that they can be easily found and counted for inventory. The items must be stored properly—for example, proper temperature, ventilation, and free of contamination by chemicals or vermin—so they remain in optimum condition and will not deteriorate. Storage must be secure so expensive items are safe from theft. A method of product rotation and labeling is necessary to avoid waste as a result of spoilage or out-of-date products. Likewise it will create order and add a sense of organization to the storage areas making it more efficient for personnel to find what they are looking for during preparation times. Proper equipment, such as a #10 can rack or using Lexan containers along with a proper labeling procedure, are aids to good storage methods.

Issuing

The term *issue* is generally used for taking items out of storage for use. While most restaurants do not have full-time storeroom personnel, procedures for the removal of inventory from storage must be part of the cost control process. Simply installing locks on dry goods storage areas, reach-in and walk-in coolers, and freezers, that limit access will be a major deterrent to theft and unauthorized entry. In cases where the chef or cook is preparing food items, he or she will "take" the necessary ingredients from storage themselves. The head bartender will restock the bar with inventory from the liquor storage area. These individuals have the authority to remove items from storage for specific use, and they assume responsibility for the products from that point until they are consumed or sold.

Although there is no physical act performed on the merchandise except to transport it to the appropriate area where it will be processed, consumed, or sold, the function is an extremely important one in all food-service establishments. Without adequate issuing controls, no determination of true costs can be made. The three elements necessary to assess food and beverage cost are (1) beginning inventory, (2) number sold, and (3) ending inventory. You must know how much you had to begin with so you can compare sales figures to what you have left over.

Proper cost allocation to the respective department using the ingredients or supplies must also be noted. For example, foods transferred to the bar (e.g., lemons, limes, fruit juice, olives, celery, cherries, and nonalcoholic mixes) are all inventoried as food items. The product used by the bar should be noted and charged against liquor sales and not food cost. Unless issues to the bar are recorded, proper cost allocation will not be possible. This is another reason for having secure storage areas and placing accountability on employees removing items from these areas; it affects the final food cost at the end of the accounting period.

Prepreparation

The function of pre-preparation is the preliminary processing which many food items undergo before they are ready for the final cooking process prior to serving to the customer. This is referred to as "rough" or "pre-prep" preparation by some culinarians. Examples are vegetable cleaning and cutting, meat cutting, and processing of ingredients for recipes. The procedures followed by the production staff should minimize waste and utilize as many of the byproducts as possible. Excessive trim on vegetables and meats will increase the edible portion cost of the final product. Each recipe card will take into account the standard yield of each food item. If the yield is too low or high it will result in an inconsistent product and this will affect the cost as well as quality of the final product. That is why standardized recipes must be followed and preparation quantities adjusted according to projected customer counts and the menu sales mix history. Restaurants with fixed or static menus must eliminate leftovers, as they have no way to incorporate them into the menu. This will result in increased costs and a loss to the operation. This can be avoided with proper production planning and organization.

P reparation

This refers to the final preparation or "cooking to order" done when the server places the order with the kitchen. Chefs often refer to this as "firing the order". The preprepared ingredients are combined or finished off prior to plating for service to the guest. This step is a critical control point in both food cost and quality control. The best ingredients and standardized recipes can be ruined by poor and sloppy final preparation and presentation.

P ortioning and Transfer (Food Leaves Kitchen for Dining Room)

Food cost can be lost with over-portioning of ingredients and accompaniments. Management should regularly monitor final preparation to be sure that quality and portioning standards are being followed. Many restaurants consider this such a critical function that managers are assigned to expedite orders from the kitchen. They will monitor order times, portions, presentation, and food quality with military-like precision.

Excessive leftovers indicate either improper preparation procedures or inaccuracies in the forecasting of the menu sales mix. Over-portioning can impact recipe yields, sales revenue, and eventually profits. Food that the guest leaves on the plate can result from poor preparation, sloppy presentation, or standard portions that are excessive. In every operation the size of the portions must be determined based on the target customer, meal period, and price point. Food cost is not the only basis for determining menu price. What the customer in a given market is willing to pay must be taken into account. The price of a lobstertail dinner will undoubtedly be more expensive if the location is downtown Manhattan than the end of Duval Street on Key West. The question then becomes whether the restaurant can sell the food item at the price the customer is willing to pay and still make an adequate profit. For example, practically every moderate-priced food service operation serves a hamburger of some type. How to prepare it, what size portion to use, and what specific accompaniments are included are variables under the control of the owner and manager when the menu is written. The price to charge will be determined by what the competition charges, the specific check average desired, the competing items on the menu, and many other "indirect" cost factors. This is discussed in greater detail in the chapter devoted to menu pricing.

Order Taking/Guest Check

In order for the cost control process to work, every item sold, or issued from the kitchen, needs to be recorded accurately. That recording can be a simple paper guest check or a point-of-sale computer. Once it is entered into the system, it can be tracked and monitored. Safeguards must be established that make it impossible to get food out of the kitchen or drinks from the bar without having the transaction entered into the system. In the case of a written guest check, a portion of the check is submitted to the kitchen and only items written on the check are prepared. No verbal orders should be accepted for food or beverages from anybody, including management and owners.

Guest checks are typically serially numbered and signed out to specific waiters. Unused checks are turned in at the end of the shift and kitchen copies are paired up with the guest copies. Missing checks are noted, as are discrepancies between food checks and guest checks, and errors in price extensions and additions. Electronic Point of Sale (POS) systems, such as Micros, Squirrel, Posi-Touch and Aloha, eliminate the need for printed checks and separate all server sales.

Cash Receipts

Whether your operation utilizes a cashier or has the servers carry their own banks, monitoring sales is critically important to cost controls. The amount of food and beverages served by the kitchen and bar will determine the amount of sales receipts that need to be turned in at the end of the shift by servers and bartenders. It can be a mystery to many chefs why they follow all of the steps under their control only to have the food cost overstated (too high) because all of the revenue is not being collected for various possible reasons. Not ringing menu items up correctly on guest checks, overcharging customers, providing items to a guest and not charging at all, falsification of credit card tips, and lost checks must be monitored at the end of each shift. Management must compile all the sales information for each meal period so a historical financial record can be established. It is this historical record that helps management forecast the future as well as determine the possible causes of lost revenue.

B ank Deposits and Accounts Payable

The revenues must be deposited in a bank account in a timely fashion and charge slips sent to the credit card company for payment. Funds are transferred from these accounts or drawn upon to pay for food, beverage, and labor costs. Proper auditing of these accounts must also be conducted to reduce fraud and theft. It is a common technique to have two different individuals perform the deposits and bank reconciliation to the daily sales report. This eliminates the temptation to commit a fraudulent act.

A n Ongoing Process

As mentioned earlier, cost control is not a response that is undertaken after a loss has been uncovered or when revenues and profits have already begun to shrink. Cost control is an ongoing process that must be so ingrained in the minds of all employees that it becomes institutionalized and becomes a permanent part of the culture and philosophy of the company. The control philosophy becomes institutionalized when all employees innately place a premium on getting the greatest value for the least cost in every aspect of the company's operations without sacrificing quality or customer service. This is where the leadership of the management is so important in influencing the attitudes and thinking processes of all employees towards awareness of cost control problems and the need to follow procedures.

Ongoing appraisal is an important part of the control process. A foodservice enterprise must establish goals and have a strategic plan to achieve those goals within the time frame and the budget it has to work with, while also maintaining the qualitative standards of performance. Thus, proper control implies the exchange of information for planning, organizing, leading, and control (measurement) of goals and objectives.

Five elements of a cost control strategy must be present for it to be effective in controlling costs. They are:

1. Advance planning
2. Devices or procedures to aid in the control process

3. Implementation of the program

4. Employee compliance

5. Management appraisal and enforcement

A cost control program cannot be successful unless you have the complete cooperation and participation of all employees and managers. In addition, a cost control program must be assessed against the following questions:

1. Do the cost controls provide *relevant* information?

2. Is the information reported in a *timely* manner?

3. Is the information easily *assembled* and *organized*?

4. Is the information easily *interpreted*?

5. Are the *benefits/savings* greater than the cost of implementing the controls?

When the cost of the controls exceeds the savings gained, the control may be doing more harm than good. Purchasing a $25,000 point-of-sale system that is not going to be fully utilized is a waste of money. Leasing of automated dispensing equipment that counts draft wine and beer at a cost of $300 a month to save $75 worth of beverage is not cost-effective.

Although the scope of this book is cost control, control is only one part of the total operational program of a successful business. You may have adequate cost controls and still go out of business because having costs under control will not assure financial success. Think about why a Burger King or Church's Fried Chicken shuts down or sells out. The likely reason they closed was not due to poor cost control practices but rather due to *inadequate sales revenue to retire debt and return a minimum profit.* A business must have adequate sales revenue, which implies a marketing perspective be used along with a cost control program! This component must also be in your overall business plan.

Low costs will not make much of a difference without adequate sales volume. There is an old saying in business: "Volume hides a multitude of sins." This basically means that if you have the sales volume, it can make up for cost inefficiencies. However, the time to maximize profit is when business is good, not when it is near the break-even point.

If you were a manager in charge of a business currently returning an average of $1000 profit per week with sales of $10,000 and your boss said that wasn't good enough and expected $1500 profit per week, which strategy would you pursue to increase profit—increase sales or reduce costs? Which do you think is the fastest and easiest way to increase the bottom line? If you said increase sales, you would have to increase sales by $5000 to realize an additional $500 profit while operating the same as you have been in the past.

(Currently, a 10 percent bottom line is being earned, $1000/$10,000.) Assuming that profit will continue at the 10 percent-of-sales ratio, $500 is 10 percent of $5000. Now think of how you would go about increasing sales. You would probably need to advertise and advertising costs money. If you spend $500 on newspaper or radio ads, you will now need to increase business by an additional $5000. What do you think your chances are of doubling sales volume if your business is flat?

Using your personal monthly budget as an example, what would be the fastest way to increase your disposable income—increase your income or cut back on expenses? The answer is cut back on unnecessary expenses. Clearly, expense reduction remains the fastest way to increase bottom line in business. However, you reach a point where cost/expenses cannot go any lower or you will suffer grave consequences regarding the quality of your food, beverage, and service (or personal lifestyle). In the long run, customers will start going to competitors as they find your prices too high, portions too small, service too slow, and the like. You must never forget that you will incur expenses and need to spend money to make money. No business can grow the top line (sales) by *just* reducing costs. Failure to spend enough on remodeling, training, advertising, and quality ingredients may move money to the bottom line faster, but eventually overall business will suffer.

Some operators become too "bottom line oriented" and forget about the qualitative aspects of the business. The brown-edged lettuce that you keep on the salad bar instead of throwing it out, the purchase of lower-quality ingredients to keep food costs low, or failure to *not* charge a guest after a complaint are the little things that can hurt you in the long run. These are pennies; don't be "penny-wise and dollar-foolish" when it comes to controlling cost. The marketing perspective keeps you in touch with the competitive world as a reminder that you cannot forget the importance of food quality and customer service. In the best-selling book, *In Search of Excellence,* the authors reported that in companies that really paid attention to customer service and the quality of their products, their bottom lines had a way of meeting their financial expectations.

The Importance of Standards

Setting standards is an integral part of any cost control program. What is your definition of a standard? The dictionary says it is simply a measure that establishes a value. **Standards** establish a minimum acceptable level of performance or results. Think of it as a benchmark, rule, or policy that requires consistency and limits the number of unknown variables you need to control for in your operation to attain the goal at hand. These standards become the yardsticks with which management sets qualitative and quantitative levels of performance for the operation. Actual results are compared to the standards to see if they exceed or fall below acceptable levels.

When establishing standards, one defines the desired result as a point of comparison against which the actual results achieved and the resources consumed in the process of creating revenue will be measured. The difference between resources planned and the actual amounts used is referred to as the **variance.** Management must reduce or eliminate the negative discrepancies between the predetermined standards and the actual results. A positive variance occurs when performance exceeds that standard. When this occurs, management will praise or reward those responsible. Although standards can show where individuals or departments have not met expectations and corrective action must be taken, they are more important as preventative measures that reduce or eliminate how often corrective action must be taken.

Recalling the principles management, what is the distinction between a *formal* standard and an *informal* one? Typically, a formal standard is put in writing while the informal standard is not. However, one could argue that the formal aspect has nothing to do with whether or not it is written but with what is the common everyday practice. The formal standard is the one that management follows on a day-to-day basis.

Managers employed by corporate chains are not asked to establish standards; they are more often held responsible for making sure they are followed. Remember, employees will deviate from prescribed standards only as far as management allows. We use terms like *tight ship* and *by the book* to express that things must be done a certain way. Management sets the acceptance level for standards.

Standards become part of the philosophy and culture of a business. Employees should conduct themselves as if they are owners or investors. If this takes place all employees will uphold the standards. Both cost and quality standards must be ingrained in employees so they become second nature. This occurs only when employees are thoroughly committed to the values of the company. Setting standards is an important part of cost control. You cannot let employees set standards nor can you openly adopt the standards of another operation and expect to achieve the same results.

Each operation must establish its own standards relative to its financial idiosyncrasies and position in the marketplace. This is necessary because all of the variables that will influence cost standards differ from operation to operation; even within a chain of fast-food outlets. Rent, property taxes, interest rates, amount of debt financing to equity, depreciation schedules, and the like, all affect the acceptable cost standards.

When it comes to standards, McDonald's Corporation probably is the quintessential authority. Yet if you randomly select any two McDonald locations, you will find that they are not running the same month-end food cost percentage nor do they return the same profit-per-dollar of sales. Why would two identical McDonald's not necessarily have the same food cost percentages or profit percentages? Ruling out fixed and overhead expenses, differing wage rates, menu prices, purchase prices, waste, and theft, what could be the cause? Consider that one McDonald's does around 23 percent of its total sales volume at breakfast while the other does only 15 percent. The reason they are not the same is because their menu sales mixes are different. Different menu items will have different food costs and gross profits. Breakfast typically runs a lower food cost percentage and lower check average than lunch and dinner sales mixes.

After cost standards are set, one can examine the income statement relative to these standards and break down figures by day, meal period, and department. Cost standards must, however, be determined from observations and calculations occurring under actual operating conditions, not by unrealistic and highly controlled laboratory-like conditions. The danger with such highly controlled conditions is that costs will be understated because factors like recipe yields will be overstated and waste understated. Always understate your yields on items requiring portioning unless they are pre-weighed, counted, or pre-portioned. A very few items will, however, result in 100 percent yield; for example, precut steaks should not show any variance between sales and number removed from inventory.

The following five steps are important to the establishing of standards as an integral component of any cost control program.

1. Establish standards of performance and results for *all* individuals and departments.
2. Charge all individuals to follow established standards to prevent waste and inefficiency.
3. Monitor adherence to standards as a preventive control measure.
4. Compare actual performance and results against established standards.
5. Take timely and appropriate action when deviations from standards are detected. (Dittmer & Griffin, 1994, p. 47.)

The whole aspect of cost control and standards is an area that must be mastered by chefs and managers alike because a restaurant is essentially a production operation. It processes raw materials and combines them into end products purchased by the customer. This is further complicated by the fact that we must deal with a perishable product that can be stored or stockpiled for only limited durations. If we overproduce and do not sell out within a given time period, it turns to waste.

Products must be produced on demand. The customer determines demand. We must manufacture a variety of products simultaneously on the same production line. In addition, the items produced may change three times during a 24-hour period. Controlling quality is a particularly difficult problem because what is produced is also purchased and consumed in the same place at the same time. Therefore, quality control responsibility falls upon the employee closest to the customer.

In a factory, one can inspect what is being produced on the line and reject bad lots or take hours and days to test for quality. In food service, the employee must make judgments on the spot. A supervisor cannot inspect every product produced. Therefore, the employee is responsible for the final qualitative check prior to serving food to the customer.

Your job as manager will be to see that your staff is adhering to your standards. If, for example, portioning standards were not being followed, you might implement some of the following cost *reduction* techniques: require the use of measured scoops and ladles; specific sized bowls, cups, and glasses; as well as weighing portions individually; portioning by count; and pre-portioning items in advance.

Cost control is a very basic and fundamental management activity. Pretend you are an owner and you have a situation where you have to downsize your management team. You have two managers who are equally efficient in their jobs. One may be slightly more effective with scheduling staff and the other is more adept at cost control techniques, always has an answer for you even before you know the question yourself. Which one do you keep? This is not an easy decision because the elements of a restaurant's success are not exclusively cost related. What we must never forget is that the goal of any business is to survive and prosper. You have to be able to monitor your costs and recognize when and where costs deviate from standards. It could mean the difference between being employed and even being promoted. Do not lose track of the qualitative and revenue-enhancing aspects when implementing a cost control program. Remember that cost controls are not an end in themselves. Once costs have been contained, the only way to increase bottom line is to increase sales revenue.

The cost control concepts and principles given in this chapter are not by any means limited to commercial restaurant applications. They apply equally to institutional foodservice and not-for-profit businesses. Although there may be differences in terminology, the principles are fundamentally the same.

ey Concepts

- Cost controls in and of themselves are not enough to ensure the financial success of a restaurant.
- Seeking the lowest possible cost for food, beverage and labor is NOT a sound or valid business strategy.

- Cost control is proactive and preventative, not corrective after the fact.
- Cost *control* and cost *reduction* are two different functions.
- You physical presence in the restaurant is not sufficient for cost control purposes.
- Your cost control program is only as strong as its weakest functional area.
- Standards are an important component of any cost control program.
- Your decisions ultimately have a financial result somewhere in the organization.
- You must have a system for cost control in order to have continuity and efficiency when you are not present.
- Cost control awareness must be created at all levels of employment in a foodservice operation.
- A system is a combination of functions and policies that work together as a device for problem solving and cost containment.
- Environmental factors are variables that a manager/chef needs to consider on a daily basis for whatever cost impact they may pose to the operation.

Key Terms

Cost Control	Systems Approach	Planning
Cost Reduction	Input	Organizing
Cost Control Cycle	Output	Leading
Cost Control Strategy	Feedback	Controlling
Standards	Environmental Factors	

Discussion Questions

1. What is the purpose of cost control?
2. Why are cost controls not enough to ensure financial success and profitability?
3. What needs to occur for any hospitality enterprise to remain in business?
4. What is wrong with the following statement? "Achieving the lowest overall cost is the primary goal of cost control."

5. Every decision you make is a financial one! What is meant by this statement?
6. How does a systems approach help set you up for success in terms of controlling your costs?
7. What is meant by the following statement? "Cost control is a numbers game!"
8. How can cost control be related to the management process?
9. In a systems approach, what are the three components of creating a "goal"? How do goals become successful outcomes?
10. Illustrate the example of "the systems model" in the chapter and explain each component in the process.
11. How does a systematic approach differ from the common charismatic approach to controlling costs?

Problems

1. In the chapter text, the authors provide the following example of how a small variance in portion control can affect profitability. A national pizza chain utilizes an inventory control system that is tied into its menu sales mix. It allows management to monitor use level of key ingredients to detect over-portioning, waste and theft. It compares standardized portion usage for each ingredient used to the actual use levels at the end of the month after inventory has been taken. In the example given in the chapter, the standard portion size was exceeded by only 2 grams per pizza but the overall impact amounted to a 25 pound variance over a month. What would this kind of over-portioning do to food cost and potential profits before taxes if this went on for 150 of their locations for 3 months? *Assume the cost of the mozzarella cheese was averaging $2.25 per pound.* What would happen if over-portioning of sausage toppings on pizzas went undetected for the same time period? *Assume that the cost of the sausage was $3.10 per pound and that the standard portion amount was exceeded by 10 pounds per month at all 150 of their locations.*

2. Using the Excel template provided, determine the actual usage, inventory variance, standard cost, actual cost, and cost variance for the items shown below. Assume that tomatoes are 5 × 6 size and yield six slices per tomato; apple pie yields 7 slices per pie; hamburger buns are priced per dozen; all other items are priced per pound. Assume food sales for the period are $6442. Is the cost variance within acceptable limits for a week of sales activity?

Ingredient	Standard Portion	Number Sold	Standard Usage	Beginning Inventory	Purchases
Sausage (oz)	7	234	102.38	80	50
Mozzarella (oz)	6	535	200.63	140	100
Tomatoes (slice)	2	430	143.33	80	80
French Fries (oz)	6	670	251.25	150	180
Shrimp (oz)	8	149	74.50	58	50
HB Buns (ea)	1	875	72.92	24	60
Apple Pie (slice)	1	210	30.00	5	30
Hot Dogs (oz)	4	120	30.00	15	25
Chicken Tenders (oz)	6	345	129.38	85	80
Food Sales					
Standard Food Cost %					
Actual Food Cost %					
Cost Variance %					

3. The importance of cost control cannot be overstated. Assume that the restaurant you are managing is producing a profit of $1,000 (10%) per week on sales of $10,000 and that the owner does not feel that this is acceptable. The owner feels that a figure of $1,500 profit is attainable for a week's business.

■ How much do your sales have to increase if profit remains at 10% of sales to bring in an additional $500 profit?

Ending Inventory	Actual Usage	Inventory Variance	Purchase Price	Standard Cost	Actual Cost	Cost Variance
24			$ 1.79			
35			$ 2.79			
12			$ 1.29			
68			$ 0.98			
33			$ 4.50			
10			$ 1.79			
4			$ 3.50			
9.5			$ 2.39			
30			$ 2.39			

- How can you increase sales? What additional costs will you likely incur in attempting to increase sales? If you spent an additional $500 to increase sales, how much would your sales have to increase to achieve the additional $500 in profit?

- What short-run strategy would you suggest to increase the bottom line profit besides trying to increase sales? Why is this not a good long-term strategy?

2

Cost Ratios

1. Cost control requires more than the mathematical calculation of ratios and percentages.

2. The interpretation of numbers cannot be delegated.

3. Review the numbers over and over until their meaning is clear and you have answers to your questions.

4. Comprehension of numbers comes only from regular review.

5. Understanding the numbers puts you in control.

6. When you understand the numbers, you will be reading the story behind the numbers and will have a composite picture of what is going on in your operation.

7. Success or failure often depends not only on how well you collect data, but also on how well you are able to convert it into knowledge that will help you better manage your restaurant.

8. Inventory, sales figures, customer counts, and average checks are merely accounting data. They do not tell you much until you put them into a format that allows you to compare actual to projected figures.

9. A restaurant operator without ratios and numbers is at a significant disadvantage in today's economy.

10. Numbers allow you to back up your opinions with facts.

The preceding principles must be considered when you are preparing your financial reports. Restaurant cost controls require both owner and manager to be on the same page in terms of the meaning and calculation of the numerous ratios that are used to analyze food, beverage, and labor costs. This is absolutely necessary because the terms can have different interpretations depending on the segment of the foodservice industry (e.g., fast food, commercial, or institutional foodservice) and the source of the terminology (e.g., industry trade journal, academic textbook, accountant or financial lender). In addition, several cost control software packages are now on the market with built-in formulas for calculating ratios and percentages. It is important to review the documentation provided to understand how the ratios are being calculated before you jump to conclusions when a percentage or ratio does not meet your standard. The variance may be due to the way it was calculated and not be a true indication of the cost or profit activity in your restaurant.

The Board of Directors of the National Restaurant Association publishes its *Uniform System of Accounts for Restaurants* (USAR). The USAR establishes a "common language" for the industry that makes it possible to compare ratios and percentages across industry lines and to report industry-wide sales and cost figures to its membership in annual studies and reports. The new seventh edition of the USAR is an essential guide for the restaurant operator on the subject of restaurant accounting.

The emphasis of this chapter will be on operating ratios and the statement of income and retained earnings. The goal is to produce financial statements that are in fact "management tools" and not simply reports for the Internal Revenue Service.

Keep in mind that the mere calculation of the ratios and percentages is not "cost control." The numbers must be interpreted by owners and managers, who then take appropriate action. When ratios and percentages are not within standards, management will immediately begin their investigation to determine the cause of the variance. Knowledge of food, beverage, and labor cost components is absolutely necessary to reveal the story behind the numbers.

F ood Cost Ratio/Percentage

This basic ratio is perhaps the most misinterpreted of all the ratios because it can be calculated so many ways. In its simplest calculation it is *food cost* divided by *food sales*. How one arrives at *food cost* is very important. One must ascertain whether the food cost figure is food *sold* or *consumed* as there is a big difference in the **food cost percentage** between the two.

In addition, for the food cost percentage to be accurate, it is absolutely necessary that a month-end inventory be taken. Without an inventory figure, the food cost percentage shown on an income statement is inaccurate and relatively useless to owners and managers.

We continue to be amazed at the number of restaurant operators who do not take a monthly inventory. Those who do not, very likely do not have their accountant prepare a monthly income statement. If they do, the food cost figure on the statement can only be an estimate of the food cost. It is naive to think that monthly purchases and inventory will even out over the year. The amount of food inventory will vary from month to month even if business volume were the same every month (which it isn't) because the amount on hand on the last day of the month will vary depending on which day of the week the month ends. Think about the inventory on hand on a Friday compared to a Monday or Tuesday.

It is equally important to distinguish the difference between food *consumed* and food *sold*. Remember, all food consumed is not sold. Total food purchases for the month, as indicated from delivery invoices and adjusted for returns and credits, is added to the *beginning inventory* to get *total food available for sale*. Subtracting the month-end food inventory gives you the **cost of food consumed**. Remember, food consumed is all food used, sold, wasted, stolen, or given away to customers (complimentary meals) and employees. **Cost of food sold** is found by deducting known waste, employee meals, complimentary meals, discounts, food transfers to the bar, and any other known food usage for which full price was not received from the total food consumed.

This figure is divided by *food sales.* Most accounting software programs will automatically divide food cost by *total sales* unless you adjust them to do otherwise. If beverage sales are included in the sales figure, it will lower and understate the food cost percentage. Remember the accounting principle that says to match costs with the revenues they produce. Only food sales should be used when calculating food cost ratios.

Example

(Calculated from figures shown in Four Faces of Food Cost)

Cost of Food Consumed = $9000/$25,000 = 36%

Cost of Food Sold = $8650/$25,000 = 34.6%

THE FOUR FACES OF FOOD COST

I Maximum allowable food cost This is the highest food cost can be and still allow the operation to realize its profit goal. If the month-end food cost percentage exceeds this, profit expectations will not be achieved. The percentage will be different for every operation, including chain operations, because of the financial idiosyncracies of each location. The calculation is as follows for a restaurant selling only food and non-alcoholic beverages:

1. Express labor costs, controllable and noncontrollable overhead expenses, excluding food cost, in dollar amounts. Refer to past accounting periods and year-to-date averages to get accurate and realistic cost estimates.

2. Add the monthly profit goal as either a dollar amount or a percentage of sales.

3. Convert dollar values of expenses to percentages by dividing by food sales for the period used for expenses. We *suggest that you use monthly figures that are neither under nor overstated. Do not use the highest sales or the lowest sales figures for calculating your operating percentages.* Subtract the total of the percentages from 100 percent. The remainder is your **Maximum Allowable Food Cost (MFC) Percentage.**

Example

Assume the following are weighted averages calculated from past accounting periods and represent "conservative" sales revenues and "liberal" expenses. *Resist overstating your sales revenues and understating your expenses. Be conservative with sales projections and liberal with expense estimates.*

Food Sales[1]	$25,000
Overhead[2]	$6,900
Payroll[3]	$6,000
Minimum Profit[4]	$2,000 or 8 percent of sales
Beginning Inventory	$5,300
Ending Inventory	$4,900
Purchases	$8,600
Employee Meals	$350
Potential Food Sales[5]	$25,500
Potential Food Cost[6]	$8,000
Allowance for Waste[7]	1.5%

Convert to percentages by dividing costs by total sales. *Note:* If alcoholic beverages were served, expenses would be divided by *total* sales to calculate percentages. Also, carry out calculations to two decimal places and do not round off.

Labor Cost Percentage: $6000/$25,000 = 24.0%
Overhead Percentage: $6900/$25,000 = 27.6%
Profit Percentage: $2000/$25,000 = 8%
Total: 59.6% (24.0% + 27.6% + 8%)
Maximum Allowable Food Cost = 40.4% (100% − 59.6%)

[1]This restaurant does not serve alcoholic beverages of any kind.
[2]Includes fixed, variable, and controllable expenses; does not include food cost
[3]Includes hourly employees, payroll taxes, and benefits
[4]Profit can be expressed as a dollar value or percent of sales
[5]Based on menu sales mix and listed menu prices
[6]Based on menu sales mix and standardized recipe costs
[7]Management builds in quality control costs and complimentary meals given to customers

Note: Although not shown in this example, if you track the amount of food transferred to the bar, discounted or promotional meals that are comp'ed, known waste, and include a management allowance for quality control waste, these amounts would also be deducted from Cost of Food Consumed to arrive at Cost of Food Sold and the Actual Food Cost Percentage.

Employee meals are the actual cost of the food eaten by employees and credited to food cost. The amount is arrived at by tallying the food checks of employees or totaling the cost of ingredients used for employee meals. Known waste is the amount recorded on waste sheets for food that was discarded because of improper cooking, spoiled, or spilled food. Quality control waste would be food discarded by management because it did not meet quality standards of appearance, e.g., brown lettuce, improper cuts. (The food is edible but not of a quality that can be served to a paying guest, so it is discarded.)

II Actual food cost percentage (AFC) This is the food cost percentage that the restaurant is *actually* running and is found on the monthly income statement. It is calculated by dividing cost of food sold by food sales. Here is a way to tell whether you are calculating cost of food *consumed* or food *sold* percent. If there is a line item on the income statement deducting for *employee meals,* you are calculating cost of food *sold.* If there is no allowance for employee meals, as is the case in most operations, the food cost being expressed is food *consumed.* Cost of food consumed will always be a higher figure than cost of food sold. If inventory is not being taken, the food cost shown on the income statement is basically just an estimate based on purchases and is not accurate.

How can you tell, when looking at the financial statements, if an operation is taking monthly inventory? One way is to look at the current assets section of the balance sheet. If the operation is not preparing a monthly balance sheet, it is probably not taking monthly inventory, and the food cost shown on the income statement is really an estimate or a total of the invoices for the month. In the current assets section of the balance sheet there should be entries for food inventory, beverage inventory, and supplies inventory. They should be shown separately if the restaurant is following the *Uniform System of Accounts.*

Beginning Inventory	$5,300
Add Purchases	$8,600
Total Food Available for Sale	$13,900
Less Ending Inventory	$4,900
Cost of Food Consumed	$9,000
Less: Employee Meals	$350
Discounts and Promotions	0
Food Transfers to Bar	0
Food Transfers to Other Units	0
Known Waste	0
Quality Control Waste	0
Plus: Bar Transfers to Kitchen	0
Cost of Food Sold	$8,650

Actual Food Cost Percentage = 34.6% ($8650/$25,000)

Note: Although values are not shown in the example, if you track the amount of food transferred to the bar, e.g., drink garnish and snacks; food transfers to other units, discounted or comp'ed meals, recorded or known food waste, and include an allowance for quality control waste. Each of these amounts would be deducted from Cost of Food Consumed to arrive at the Cost of Food Sold and the Actual Food Cost percentage. Alcoholic beverages used by the kitchen are credited to the bar and charged to food cost.

Employee meals are the actual cost of the food eaten by employees and credited to food cost. You calculate employee meals by tallying the food checks of empolyees or totaling the cost of ingredients used in employee meals if a special meal is prepared. "Known waste" is the amount recorded on waste records for food that was discarded due to improper cooking, spoiled food, spilled or spilled food. "Quality control waste" would be food discarded by management because it did not meet quality standards of appearance or freshness. The food is still edible, but not of a quality that can be served to a paying customer. Food transferred to other units is common in a chain or multiple unit operation. If one unit runs short of something, they will "borrow" from a sister location.

III Potential food cost percentage (PFC) Potential food cost is also referred to as *theoretical food cost*. This is the lowest your food cost can be because it assumes that all food consumed is sold and that there is zero waste, over-portioning, and no theft. It is calculated based on the weighted menu sales mix of the number sold of each menu item multiplied by the ideal recipe cost. The weighted cost is divided by the weighted sales (number sold × menu price) of all items on the menu. A complete explanation of the menu sales mix is provided in Chapter 5.

IV Standard food cost Because PFC is unrealistically low, it must be tempered with allowances for unavoidable waste, employee meals, and quality control losses to make it a realistic goal for management. This is the food cost percentage that is compared to the AFC and is the standard that management must meet.

Standard Food Cost Percentage is derived by taking the Potential Food Cost Percentage of 31.372 percent and adding allowances for employee meals (1.4%) and the management allowance for unavoidable waste (1.5%). In these four examples, food cost ranged from a high of 40.4 percent (MFC) to a low of 31.372 percent (PFC). The difference between cost of food consumed and food sold was 1.4 percent.

You can see why it is important to clarify how your figures will be calculated if you are seeking to make comparisons to other operations. A more detailed analysis of the four faces of food cost is covered in the following chapter.

Food cost calculations. The calculation of the food cost percentage for an individual menu item is found by dividing the edible portion cost of the entree with all accompaniments by its respective menu price. If the cost of a steak dinner is $5.57 and the menu price is $12.95, the food cost percentage is **43 percent ($5.57/$12.95).**

If you are pricing a menu item to achieve a targeted food cost percentage, you simply divide the edible portion cost of the entree and accompaniments by the desired food cost percent expressed as a decimal or **$5.57/.43 = $12.95.**

Food sales. The National Restaurant Association includes revenues derived from the sale of food in the restaurant, including the sale of coffee, tea, milk, and fruit juices, which are usually served as part of the meal. If there is no alcoholic beverage service, the soft drink sales would also be included in this category.

PRIME FOOD COST

Prime food cost was developed first by restaurateur Harry Pope, who realized that marking up food cost only on items made from scratch sometimes understated the total cost of producing the item. He decided to include the cost of *direct labor* with the food cost. Direct labor is labor incurred because an item is made from scratch on the premises, such as steak cutting and baking pies and breads. The restaurant is incurring additional labor to cut steaks and operate a bake shop. The labor costs associated with the items produced are allocated directly to the items that caused the labor to be incurred. In addition to the raw food cost of the steaks and baked goods, an additional cost for the labor incurred is added to each steak, pie, and loaf of bread. When food cost and direct labor are added together, it is referred to as prime cost. **Prime cost**, as defined by the National Restaurant Association for purposes of interpreting the figures in the Annual Industry Operations Reports, is the total of the cost of food sold, cost of beverage sold, and the associated payroll costs and employee benefits. Prime cost is applied to every item on the menu that requires extensive direct labor before it is served to the customer.

Indirect labor is that labor that cannot be charged to any particular menu item and is therefore allocated to each menu item in the form of overhead. Examples are labor for dishwashing, line cooks, bartenders, and servers.

TRADITIONAL LABOR COST RATIO

This is the traditional ratio of payroll to *total sales* reported on the income statement. Payroll may include both hourly and management wages, but it is recommended to separate management salaries from the hourly employees. Management salaries and benefits should be carried as administrative expenses and separated from direct controllable expenses. This important distinction needs to be noted when analyzing labor cost percentages. If management salaries are included, the payroll percentage will run 8 to 14 percent higher than the hourly payroll percentage.

Note: The National Restaurant Association includes the *entire* restaurant payroll, including management salaries, hourly wages, extra wages, overtime, vacation pay, and commissions or bonuses paid to employees, when it reports salaries and wages. Employee benefits are reported separately and include federal retirement taxes (Social Security), federal and state unemployment taxes, and state health insurance taxes. Other items considered benefits are workers' compensation insurance premiums; welfare plan payments; pension plan payments; accident, health, and life insurance premiums; education benefits; and any other fringe benefits employees receive.

Because the **traditional labor cost ratio** is subject to distortion due to wage and sales fluctuations, is historical in that it reports what happened in the past, and is nonspecific as to job category, day, and meal period, other ratios must be used to interpret the productivity of employees. The following examples explain those ratios.

Example

The following data are used in the calculation of the labor cost ratios.

	Unit I	Unit II
Sales	$12,680	$14,000
Payroll	$2,220	$2,450
Covers	2,400	2,500
Labor Hours	1,065	1,155

Traditional Labor Cost Ratio

Unit I $2220/$12,680 = 17.5%

Unit II $2450/$14,000 = 17.5%

Both units have the same labor cost percentage. *Which unit is using labor more productively?* The answer requires that the traditional labor cost percentage be supplemented by other ratios.

Sales per labor hour Some operations determine the number of employees to schedule based on the sales per labor hour. It is calculated by dividing total sales by the number of hours worked or scheduled. If, for example, you were to use sales of $25 per labor hour as a standard, in a time period in which $100 in sales was brought in, up to four employees could be scheduled. If only $75 were forecasted, only three workers would be scheduled.

This calculation is useful only for "variable cost" employees or those employees who are added to the schedule over the "fixed cost" employees as business volume warrants. Fixed cost employees are those who must be scheduled to staff the restaurant during the slowest hours of business, often called the "skeleton crew." Additional employees (variable cost employees) are added to the schedule when business volume exceeds what the fixed cost employees can handle on a qualitative and quantitative basis.

Using sales per labor hour to schedule employees does not work when one figure is used for all meal periods. This methodology was initially used in fast-food operations. However, when breakfast was introduced and the drive-through windows installed, scheduling on the basis of sales per labor hour resulted in severely understaffed operations. Managers soon realized that scheduling had to take into account the number of transactions required to achieve the sales per labor hour they used as a standard. Breakfast had a much lower average check (fast-food operations use the term "average transaction") than lunch or dinner. When a drive-through window was added it increased the number of transactions per minute and required more employees. Employees are scheduled not by sales, but by customer counts. For that reason, the value of sales per labor hour for scheduling has its shortcomings.

Example

Unit I $12,680/1065 = $11.91 sales per labor hour

Unit II $14,000/1155 = $12.12 sales per labor hour

Unit II appears to have an edge on Unit I. However, would your interpretation be influenced by the knowledge that Unit II has a high number of tourists frequenting it and Unit I has strictly a residential clientele? The spending patterns of tourists are much more liberal than local residents eating out on week nights. Thus the check average could be higher in Unit II.

Covers per labor hour Because sales per labor hour did not always work the way it was intended, a more efficient way to schedule and analyze labor cost needed to be developed. It is not dollars in sales that drives scheduling as much as the number of customers that need to be served. Covers per labor hour is calculated by dividing the number of customers served by the total number of labor hours worked or scheduled. The number of covers per labor hour will be different for each job category.

Example

Unit I 2400/1065 = 2.25 covers per labor hour

Unit II 2500/1155 = 2.16 covers per labor hour

While the difference is only decimals, it is significant in terms of productivity. Unit I is better than Unit II in this ratio.

Labor cost per labor hour This ratio is best compared to past periods. It is calculated by dividing the total hourly payroll (management excluded) by the number of labor hours worked or scheduled. This figure cannot be evaluated based exclusively on a higher or lower number. If higher wages means more experienced and productive employees have been scheduled, overall payroll may still be low because fewer employees need to be scheduled to handle the business. Conversely, lower labor cost per hour may mean less productive employees and payment of minimum wage as a starting rate of pay.

Example

Unit I $2220/1065 = $2.08
Unit II $2450/1155 = $2.12

Unit I has a lower cost, which reflects a better operating position than Unit II, if it is assumed that the staffs are comparable in experience and tenure.

Labor cost per cover Another comparative ratio is calculated by dividing the total hourly payroll by the number of customers served. A lower figure is preferred because it means that the operation is using labor more productively than an operation with a higher labor cost per cover.

Example

Unit I $2220/2400 = $.925
Unit II $2450/2500 = $.98

Unit I has a lower labor cost per cover served, indicating that it is again more productive than Unit II. When all the ratios are reviewed and compared, it is clear that Unit I is more productive than Unit II because it has a lower labor cost per labor hour, a higher covers served per labor hour, and a lower labor cost per cover. These interpretations cannot be made from the traditional **labor cost percentage**.

B everage Cost Ratio

The **beverage cost ratio** is calculated when alcoholic beverages are sold. It is found by dividing beverage cost by beverage sales (calculated the same way the cost of food consumed is sold, with all the same assumptions regarding the taking of a fiscal inventory). A single beverage cost ratio cannot be given as a standard because the percentage will vary depending on the sales mix of spirits, beer, and wine sold. Restaurants will run a higher beverage cost than lounges with entertainment because more beer and wine will be sold with food. Beer and wine typically will only have a mark up yielding a cost range from 25 to 50 percent.

Mixed drinks have a much higher markup and therefore correspondingly lower beverage costs, sometimes in single digits. Thus the more mixed drinks that are sold, the lower the beverage cost percentage. It is recommended that beverage sales be separated into three categories: beer, wine, and spirits and liqueurs. Inventory should be tallied separately as well to determine the separate beverage cost for each beverage category.

When calculating beverage cost, you consider only beverage sales. However, in a restaurant with both food and beverage sales, a ratio of food and beverage cost to total sales may also be shown on the income statement.

B everage Sales

The National Restaurant Association includes on the financial statements revenue for the sale of wine, spirits, liqueurs, beer, and ale. Beverage sales *does not include* coffee, tea, milk, or fruit juices, which normally are served with the meals and therefore considered food. Apparently, some operations that serve alcoholic beverages also include the sale of soft drinks in beverage sales. Since the consumption and sale of soft drinks can be significant, the allocation of soft drinks to food or beverage sales will, in most instances, lower the cost of food or beverage sold since the ratio of product cost to selling price of soft drinks is in the single digits.

A verage Check

This calculation is more than simply dividing the total food and beverage sales by the total number of covers (customers) served. You can arrive at an **average check** this way, but it is more important to recognize how this figure compares to the average check you need to achieve your daily sales goals. If you need to get a $10.00 average check and the average is only $8.00, you will have to examine your menu prices. In addition, the check average should be calculated for each separate meal period, especially when different menus are used so it can be of comparative value to the operator. Rules must be established as to how small children and adults who order beverages only are counted or customer counts can distort check averages. Once a policy is made about how customers are counted for purposes of house counts and check averages, it should not be changed or historical comparisons will not be possible. In an inflationary economy occurs or when menu prices are increased, customer counts are the best indication of business growth or decline.

Seat Turnover

Restaurateurs monitor business by another ratio called **seat turnover**. This is the number of times they can fill an empty chair or booth during a meal period with a different paying customer. Restaurants with low check averages must turn tables frequently in order to achieve the sales volume they need to stay in business. Fast-food restaurants are the prime example of low check averages and high seat turnover. They rely heavily on carryout and drive-through business to increase the number of transactions. Did you ever notice that the seating in fast-food outlets is not designed for your comfort and that the lighting is very bright? This is done purposely to speed up seat turnover. The calculation for seat turnover is the number of customers (covers) served divided by the number of seats (chairs) in the dining room. The seat turnover is impacted by the type of food served, the type of service, and the meal period. Breakfast and lunch are characteristically quicker turnover meal periods than dinner. The rate of seat turnover and the average check are inversely related. The higher the average check, the slower the seat turnover.

Seat turnover is also impacted by the size of the parties and the allocation of tables for two, four, and six or more. All the tables can be filled, but if less than 85 percent of the chairs are filled, the restaurant is not optimizing the use of the dining room. The efficiency of the seating of guests is impacted by three factors: the person doing the seating, the size of the parties entering the restaurant, and the allocation of table sizes. An analysis of party size and tables should be examined if long lines and empty chairs are evident. The person doing the seating needs to match parties to tables to get the most people seated as quickly as possible.

Inventory Turnover

This ratio is used to evaluate the amount of food and beverage inventory relative to monthly consumption levels. The amount of inventory kept on hand varies inversely with the frequency of deliveries and the amount of storage space. Restaurants with limited dry and refrigerated storage have higher **inventory turnover** ratios than operations with ample storage space. However, the square footage of storage space should never be the determining factor for inventory levels.

Food inventory needs to turn over more frequently than beverage inventory. The biggest reason for this is perishability. However, tying up capital in perishable food inventory or excessive beverage inventory is not putting your cash to its best use. It is much easier to control cash in a bank account than to control perishable food and costly beverage inventory in a restaurant.

Inventory turnover is calculated by dividing the cost of food (or beverage) consumed by the average inventory. Average inventory is simply beginning inventory plus ending inventory divided by two. This average is then divided into the cost of food (or beverage) consumed. Using the figures from "The Four Faces of Food Cost" covered earlier, the calculation for food inventory turnover is shown.

Example

Average Inventory = ($5300 + $4900)/2 = $10,200/2 = $5100

Food Inventory Turnover = $9000/$5100 = 1.76 times

The number 1.76 tells us that the inventory turns over in dollar value 1.76 times per month. When this figure is divided into 30 days, it provides another way to examine the dollar value kept in inventory in terms of the number of days of business it should support. In this case, 30/1.76 = 17 days. In a city like Atlanta, where deliveries are at least once a week, this turnover rate appears to be much too low. Given the fact deliveries could come weekly, no more than a 7 to 10 day supply is needed. This would leave the operation in a more liquid cash position. The industry rule of thumb for food inventory is three times a month or a 10-day supply.

With alcoholic beverages the inventory turnover is much lower and is examined from an annual rather than monthly turnover rate. This is necessary because of higher spirit and wine inventories. Some restaurants with extensive wine cellars will have over $100,000 in wine inventory alone. If a restaurant served primarily beer with some wine, the turnover would be higher than where spirits and wine were the primary sellers. Beer is perishable and has a limited shelf life. Wine improves with age, and liquor maintains its quality if unopened and stored at proper temperatures.

RATIO OF FOOD SALES TO BEVERAGE SALES

Food sales are also expressed as a percentage of total sales in operations that serve alcoholic beverages. If total sales were $100,000 per month, food sales were $75,000, and beverage sales were $25,000, the ratio of food to beverage sales would be 75–25, or 75 cents out of every dollar taken in would be for food and 25 cents from beverages.

The industry "rule of thumb" for this ratio has been 75–25. In some operations the ratio is almost 50–50. The greater the percentage of beverage sales, the greater the profit as there is a greater contribution margin (menu price minus beverage cost) from a dollar of beverage sales than from the same amount of food sales.

Impact of the Sales Mix

While this is not a ratio, it is an important concept that needs to be understood before any critical cost analysis can be conducted. The **menu sales mix** is the number sold of each item on the menu. Each item will account for a certain percentage of total items sold and impact the sales and food cost differently. As stated in Chapter 1, two McDonald's in the same city will not have the same standard food cost because their menu sales mixes are not the same. Even if we assume that all waste and portioning are equal and that portion cost prices charged are equal, if the sales mix is different, the cost of food consumed and/or sold will be different.

If the sales mix from one McDonald's shows a higher percentage of its total sales at breakfast, where food costs are typically lower than the food costs on hamburgers and other lunch sandwiches, it will impact the actual food cost percentage. Subsequently, when a variance in food cost percentage occurs between two restaurants with identical menus and prices or even when there is a unexpected variance in food cost at a single unit, one of the first things to look for are shifts in menu item popularity and the change in overall menu sales mix before you jump to the conclusion that waste and theft are the reason. This concept will be thoroughly explained in Chapter 5.

B reak-Even Point (BEP)

Break-even (and closing-point) calculations provide owners and managers with another tool to use in financial analysis and forecasting the necessary sales volume to produce desired levels of profit, or the impact on required sales of increases and decreases in fixed and variable expenses. In its most basic definition, the **break-even point** (BEP) is when sales equal expenses and neither a profit nor a loss is incurred. The equation for Break-Even Sales Point is Cost of Sales (Food and Beverage) + Labor Costs + Overhead Cost (Fixed and Variable).

A business may continue to operate indefinitely at break-even if the owner and manager are drawing salaries from the business but when there are investors who expect a return on their money, a profit must be realized. The BEP equation can be modified to include a minimum profit as well as the expenses. The equation for the point in sales to achieve minimum point/sales profit = Cost of Sales + Labor Costs + Overhead Cost + Desired Profit.

Break-even can be expressed in either accounting terms or cash flow terms. Sometimes we can show an "accounting" loss on the income statement, though it is just on paper and not a cash flow loss. A cash flow loss is where the operation must actually reduce its retained earnings to cover expenses in excess of sales.

While break-even analysis is a useful management tool, it must be remembered that the break-even point is "theoretical"—an approximation rather than an absolute figure. The reason for this is that in order for the break-even point to be accurate, the following conditions must exist:

1. Costs/expenses must be expressed as either fixed or variable costs. Fixed costs are expressed in dollar values and variable costs expressed as a percentage of sales. In reality, many costs/expenses are not purely fixed or variable and possess some of each at different sales levels. This alone can affect the break-even calculation significantly.

2. Variable costs remain the same percentage of sales at all levels of sales. The only true variable costs on the income statement are food costs and beverage costs. These two costs are always expressed as a percentage of sales. This can occur only if the menu sales mix remains constant from period to period.

3. Fixed costs must remain fixed. While there are more examples of purely fixed costs, several are semi-fixed costs. Utilities, for example, are fixed at the minimum bill, but when the outside temperature reaches 95 degrees and the operation is running at capacity in terms

of customer counts, the bill will exceed the minimum due to the volume of activity and the time of year and be a variable cost.

For these reasons, the actual break-even point is really not a specific sales point but rather a range of sales that may run $200 to $300 higher or lower. It is more realistically and accurately calculated for the short term; for example, meal periods, day, or week, than for a month or year. The variance from actual break-even will depend on how realistically the costs are expressed as dollars and percentages of sales. Costs that are semi-variable (both variable and fixed properties) and semi-fixed (both fixed and variable properties) need to be correctly estimated for break-even to be precise.

Break-even can be used to determine not only the point where sales and expenses are equal but also the following:

1. The amount of sales needed to realize a predetermined profit
2. The impact on break-even if fixed or variable expenses are increased
3. The impact on break-even if fixed or variable expenses are decreased
4. The point where it would be better for the operator to close the door for a slow meal period or day because the costs of opening the door are not being covered. It can also be used to explore the feasibility of expanding operating hours and days.
5. The number of customers that need to be served at a specific check average to achieve a particular sales level
6. The sales level needed to pay for equipment or remodeling
7. To determine the purchase or asking price for a business
8. The impact on break-even if menu prices are increased or decreased (discounted)
9. The number of additional customers that need to be served at discounted prices to break even
10. The break-even point for a meal period, day of the week, week, month, and year

Breakeven and closing point are covered in Chapter 12.

Contribution Margin

Contribution margin is also referred to as "gross profit." It has a different interpretation when used in the context of break-even, vis-à-vis menu sales analysis and menu pricing. In the break-even context, contribution margin is what remains after all variable expenses, expressed as a percentage of sales, have been totaled and subtracted from 100 percent. For example, if variable costs of food, beverage, and direct operating expenses totaled 64 percent, the contribution margin would be 100% − 64% = 36%, or .36, when expressed as a decimal.

Another way of describing contribution margin is that it is the excess of revenue (sales) over the variable costs incurred in generating the sales. What remains is the contribution margin, which is used to pay fixed expenses. If there is money left over after fixed expenses, a profit is realized.

The contribution margin is a critical element of the break-even calculation. The break-even point can be calculated mathematically by dividing fixed costs (expressed as dollars) by the decimal equivalent of the contribution margin.

$$BEP = \frac{\text{Fixed Costs Expressed as Dollars}}{100\% - \text{Variable Cost}\%}$$

Contribution margin in the context of menu sales analysis and menu pricing is the difference between the menu price and the raw food cost. For example, if a steak dinner with accompaniments sells for $12.95 and has a raw food cost of $5.57, the contribution margin to cover labor, overhead, and profit is $12.95 − $5.57 = $7.38. Contribution margin in this application is not expressed as a percentage of sales but as a dollar value. Different methods of menu sales analysis look at the individual contribution margin as shown above or as the weighted or total contribution margin. If the operation sold 35 steaks per day, the weighted contribution margin from the steak would be $7.38 × 35 = $258.30. Each menu item would be tallied and summed, giving the total weighted contribution margin for the entire menu sales mix.

Break-even is also discussed in some texts as the "cost/volume/profit equation." It is a set of analytical tools that examines the relationships between costs, sales volume, and profit and how these elements impact the break-even point of the operation. It is important to understand the relationship of these elements. For example, the lowering of the contribution margin will increase the sales necessary to break even. The sales must be converted to customer counts with a desired check average to ascertain whether the increase is realistic given the seating capacity of the dining room, the seat turnover, and the competition for business.

On the other hand, an increased contribution margin brought about by increased menu prices or lowered product costs through smaller portions or reduced accompaniments may lower the BEP but result in a drop in customer counts. Also, the amount of fixed costs will make a huge difference in break-even and what contribution margin is necessary. Each operation must calculate its own break-even point and not attempt to use some rule of thumb or industry average.

C losing Point

Closing point as a very useful variation of break-even analysis is another management financial tool. Closing point was first introduced by Peter Dukas in his book, *Planning for Profits in the Food and Lodging Industry*, Cahners Publishing Co. 1976 pp. 20–22., 1976. Dukas defines **closing point** as where the sales do not cover the costs incurred in opening the restaurant. Understand that fixed costs continue to be paid regardless of whether the restaurant is open for business or closed.

If a restaurant is opened for a particular meal period as opposed to remaining closed, it will incur expenditures for labor, food, supplies, maintenance, and the variable portion of overhead expenses (e.g., increased utilities). Rent and debt service continue even if the restaurant does not open for business. Subsequently, if the cost of "opening the doors" is $300 and only $250 in sales is realized, the operator will have an additional $50 in expense that would not have been incurred had the restaurant remained closed.

Closing point is calculated by dividing the cost of opening the restaurant that is best expressed in dollar values (e.g., labor cost) by the contribution margin percentage.

H ow to Interpret National Restaurant Association Industry Averages

These are aggregate figures that may differ significantly when compared to your restaurant's income statement. Do not focus on food, beverage and labor cost percentages individually. Rather, look at the Prime Cost Percentage and compare that to your restaurant's Prime Cost. What you want to achieve is a Prime Cost in the mid sixties. It doesn't matter that your food cost percentage is a few percentage points higher than the median shown for your restaurant category. The same holds true for your beverage or labor cost. These costs will be different depending on your menu prices, menu sales mix and factors unique to your concept or location. When you add them all together and arrive at Prime Cost, you can see how you stack up to industry averages. Note that the lower the Prime Cost Percentage the greater the pre-tax-income. If Prime Cost exceeds 65%, pre-tax-profit is reduced. Therefore, concentrate on your Prime Cost Percentage because it includes the three major expenses your restaurant has, food, beverage, and labor. Over the life of your business, more money will be spent on those three expenses than any capital investment related to your business.

In Table 2.1, showing the Restaurant Industry Dollar, note that there are significant differences in costs between full service and limited service restaurants. In addition, percentages will vary depending on which quartile a restaurant is in (e.g., lower or upper). Notice how the median and average differ. Keep in mind that these percentages are compiled from both limited and full service restaurants with and without alcohol.

Tables 2.2–2.5 show the breakdown of cost per dollar sales by type, food only versus food and beverage, location, whether the operation is profitable or showing a loss, type of menu, single-unit, franchise or company-owned, form of ownership, and sales volume. All amounts shown are medians. The statistical definition of a median is the value that represents the middle value where approximately half of the data falls above and half below the median (middle) value. This differs significantly from the statistical average or mean.

RANGES OF FOOD, BEVERAGE, AND LABOR COST RATIOS

The figures quoted here are those reported in the Restaurant Industry Operations Report, 2002, prepared for the National Restaurant Association by Deloitte & Touche LLP. Assumptions are that the figures reported follow the *Uniform System of Accounts for Restaurants,* seventh edition. Keep in mind that figures shown in Table 2.6 are medians and are averages that include all types of operations ranging from fast food to continental table-service operations, single-unit independents, multi-unit company owned, and multi-unit franchise operated and have varied menus (e.g., French, Mexican, Steak/Seafood, Italian, and American). Subsequently, comparison of any of these figures to any specific restaurant will not necessarily be an indication that your restaurant is above or below the industry average.

 ## K ey Concepts

- Ratios are essentially just a mathematical relationship between two numbers.
- The relationship between the two numbers must be directly related to result in a useful ratio, e.g., food expense to food sales, whereas, food expense to telephone expense is not remotely connected or useful to management.
- Cost ratios are valuable analysis tools for the owner and manager.
- Calculating cost ratios does NOT constitute cost control.

Table 2.1   The Restaurant Industry Dollar

	Full Service Restaurants	Limited Service Restaurants
Where It Came From		
Food Sales	75%*	95%*
Beverage Sales (alcohol)	25%*	5%*
Where It Went		
Cost of Food & Beverage Sold	34%	35%
Salaries and Wages	31%	29%
Employee Benefits	4%	2%
Prime Cost	69%	66%
Occupancy Costs	6%	6%
Other**	19%	23%
Income Before Income Taxes	6%	5%

The following percentages are averages computed from per-seat sales and cost figures of the lower, median, and upper quartiles of those restaurants reporting.

	Lower	Median	Upper	Average
Food Cost	36.95%	36.00%	37.30%	36.75%
Beverage Cost	25.04%	28.04%	26.04%	26.37%
Total Cost	34.14%	36.11%	33.85%	34.70%
Labor and Benefits	NA	NA	NA	33.00%
Prime Cost	NA	NA	NA	64.70%

The average cost percentages above are based on using sales and costs-per-seat figures. Both limited and full service restaurants with and without alcoholic beverages are included in the average. Therefore, these figures are not representative of any specific restaurant segment/category and should be interpreted with those limitations in mind.

Author's Note: The above percentages are to *Total Sales* and this understates food and beverage cost percentages. This is not the industry practice for computing food and beverage cost. These percentages should be computed by dividing cost of food sold by *Food Sales* and cost of beverage sold by *Beverage Sales*. A beverage cost of 7% does not correctly reflect the cost to sales ratio. Therefore, the only way to make sense of these percentages is to add food and beverage cost to Salaries and Wages and Employee Benefits. This number is referred to as Prime Cost and is a more relevant and useful ratio.

Source: *2001 and 2002 Restaurant Industry Operations Report, National Restaurant Association and Deloitte & Touche LLP.

All other figures are 2002 by the National Restaurant Association and Deloitte & Touche

**Includes the following: Direct Operating Expense, Music and Entertainment, Marketing, Utilities, Repairs and Maintenance, Depreciation, Other Operating Expense (Income), General and Administrative, Corporate Overhead, Interest, and Other.

Table 2.2   Full Service Restaurants (Average Check Per Person Under $15) Cost per Dollar of Sales*

	Total Cost of Sales (in cents)	Total Payroll and Benefits (in cents)	Prime Cost (in cents)
All Restaurants	32.1¢	34.0¢	67.2¢
Type of Establishment			
Food Only	33.0¢	35.4¢	69.1¢
Food and Beverage	32.1	33.7	67.1
Restaurant Location			
Hotel	**	**	**
Shopping Center or Mall	31.2¢	33.7¢	66.9¢
Sole Occupant	32.6	33.5	66.8
Other	31.5	36.8	69.6
Profit versus Loss			
Profit	31.7¢	33.0¢	65.9¢
Loss	34.8	38.0	71.7
Menu Theme			
Hamburger	**	**	**
Steak/Seafood	**	**	**
Pizza	**	**	**
Sandwiches/Subs/Deli	**	**	**
American (varied)	32.8¢	34.5¢	68.7¢
Mexican	28.6	34.4	62.5
Italian	**	**	**
Other	31.9	37.4	66.9
Affiliation			
Single Unit - Independent	32.5¢	34.9¢	68.8¢
Multi-Unit - Company Operated	31.8	33.3	65.9
Multi-Unit - Franchise Operated	**	**	**
Ownership			
Sole Proprietorship	31.7¢	33.8¢	68.0¢
Partnership	31.5	34.5	65.5
Public Corporation	**	**	**
Private Corporation	32.5	33.6	67.2

(continued)

Table 2.2 Continued

	Total Cost of Sales (in cents)	Total Payroll and Benefits (in cents)	Prime Cost (in cents)
Sales Volume			
Under $500,000	34.4¢	32.8¢	67.7¢
$500,000 to $999,999	32.6	36.9	69.3
$1,000,000 to $1,999,999	32.8	33.8	67.3
$2,000,000 and Over	28.8	33.3	65.3

*All amounts are medians.

**Insufficient data.

Table 2.3 Full Service Restaurants (Average Check Per Person $15 to $24.99) Cost per Dollar of Sales*

	Total Cost of Sales (in cents)	Total Payroll and Benefits (in cents)	Prime Cost (in cents)
All Restaurants	33.5¢	34.3¢	67.4¢
Type of Establishment			
Food Only	**	**	**
Food and Beverage	33.3¢	34.3¢	67.4¢
Restaurant Location			
Hotel	31.6¢	40.0¢	71.4¢
Shopping Center or Mall	32.8	34.0	66.3
Sole Occupant	34.3	31.5	67.4
Other	30.7	36.1	67.8
Profit versus Loss			
Profit	33.2¢	32.1¢	66.4¢
Loss	35.3	38.9	74.1
Menu Theme			
Steak/Seafood	36.4¢	29.4¢	67.2¢
Pizza	**	**	**
Sandwiches/Subs/Deli	**	**	**
American (varied)	33.5	35.0	68.2
Mexican	**	**	**
Italian	**	**	**
Other	**	**	**

(*continued*)

Table 2.3 *(Continued)*

	Total Cost of Sales (in cents)	Total Payroll and Benefits (in cents)	Prime Cost (in cents)
Affiliation			
Single Unit - Independent	33.3¢	34.3¢	67.1¢
Multi-Unit - Company Operated	34.7	33.9	67.6
Multi-Unit - Franchise Operated	**	**	**
Ownership			
Sole Proprietorship	34.5¢	32.5¢	66.0¢
Partnership	30.2	34.9	66.3
Public Corporation	**	**	**
Private Corporation	33.3	34.4	67.5
Sales Volume			
Under $500,000	**	**	**
$500,000 to $999,999	32.8¢	37.2¢	68.7¢
$1,000,000 to $1,999,999	34.3	34.3	68.3
$2,000,000 and Over	32.1	31.1	63.7

*All amounts are medians.
**Insufficient data.

Table 2.4 Full Service Restaurants (Average Check Per Person $25 and Over) Cost per Dollar of Sales*

	Total Cost of Sales (in cents)	Total Payroll and Benefits (in cents)	Prime Cost (in cents)
All Restaurants	33.7¢	35.0¢	67.8¢
Type of Establishment			
Food Only	37.3¢	35.5¢	72.3¢
Food and Beverage	33.5	35.0	67.4
Restaurant Location			
Hotel	33.9¢	44.6¢	79.3¢
Shopping Center or Mall	31.6	31.0	63.6
Sole Occupant	33.6	34.5	65.7
Other	33.7	35.0	68.8

(continued)

Table 2.4 *Continued*

	Total Cost of Sales (in cents)	Total Payroll and Benefits (in cents)	Prime Cost (in cents)
Profit versus Loss			
Profit	33.8¢	34.1¢	65.4¢
Loss	32.8	38.9	72.8
Menu Theme			
Steak/Seafood	35.5¢	31.1¢	66.3¢
Pizza	**	**	**
American (varied)	32.8	37.7	70.2
Mexican	**	**	**
Italian	**	**	**
Other	33.3	35.8	68.7
Affiliation			
Single Unit - Independent	33.4¢	36.3¢	68.8¢
Multi-Unit - Company Operated	36.2	31.6	67.3
Multi-Unit - Franchise Operated	**	**	**
Ownership			
Sole Proprietorship	34.7¢	34.5¢	63.7¢
Partnership	33.7	34.8	66.9
Public Corporation	36.9	36.7	73.6
Private Corporation	33.6	35.8	68.9
Sales Volume			
Under $500,000	33.5¢	27.8¢	61.3¢
$500,000 to $999,999	35.4	37.1	69.4
$1,000,000 to $1,999,999	32.8	38.0	70.2
$2,000,000 and Over	34.1	34.1	66.2

*All amounts are medians.

**Insufficient data.

Table 2.5   Limited Service Restaurants Cost per Dollar of Sales*

	Total Cost of Sales (in cents)	Total Payroll and Benefits (in cents)	Cost Prime (in cents)
All Restaurants	31.8¢	29.9¢	61.6¢
Type of Establishment			
Food Only	30.8¢	29.9¢	61.0¢
Food and Beverage	**	**	**
Restaurant Location			
Hotel	**	**	**
Shopping Center or Mall	31.3¢	29.3¢	63.8¢
Sole Occupant	29.8	30.4	60.3
Other	38.0	29.2	68.5
Profit versus Loss			
Profit	31.2¢	29.5¢	59.8¢
Loss	32.0	35.0	68.5
Menu Theme			
Hamburger	**	**	**
Steak/Seafood	**	**	**
Pizza	**	**	**
Sandwiches/Subs/Deli	39.6¢	27.5¢	63.6¢
American (varied)	26.5	29.5	56.5
Mexican	**	**	**
Italian	**	**	**
Other	33.8	33.0	68.7
Affiliation			
Single Unit - Independent	35.2¢	30.4¢	68.6¢
Multi-Unit - Company Operated	26.8	29.9	57.1
Multi-Unit - Franchise Operated	**	**	**
Ownership			
Sole Proprietorship	**	**	**
Partnership	26.1¢	29.2¢	55.6¢
Public Corporation	**	**	**
Private Corporation	34.4	30.4	67.9
Sales Volume			
Under $500,000	38.0¢	28.9¢	68.6¢
$500,000 to $999,999	31.6	31.3	63.2
$1,000,000 and Over	28.5	29.2	57.6

*All amounts are medians.

**Insufficient data.

Table 2.6   Median Percentages of Sales for Statement of Income and Expense for Restaurants with Food & Beverage Sales

	Full Service <$15 (%)	Full Service $15–$24.99 (%)	Full Service > $25 (%)	Limited Service <$10 (%)
Food Sales	82.1	78.0	72.4	100.0
Beverage Sales	17.9	22.0	27.6	n/a
Food Cost	**33.6**	**34.4**	**33.6**	**31.7**
Beverage Cost	**28.1**	**29.9**	**31.8**	**n/a**
Total Cost of Goods	**32.1**	**33.3**	**33.5**	**31.7**
Gross Profit	**67.6**	**66.5**	**66.4**	**68.3**
Salaries and Wages	30.8	30.2	30.3	27.5
Employee Benefits	2.9	2.8	3.8	1.8
Total Labor Cost	**33.7**	**33.0**	**34.1**	**29.3**
Prime Cost	**65.8**	**66.3**	**67.6**	**61.0**
Direct Operating Expense	5.9	6.0	5.5	4.5
Music and Entertainment	0.2	0.6	0.3	0.0
Marketing	1.8	2.0	2.5	0.7
Utilities	3.3	2.9	2.4	30.0
Rent/Occupancy Costs	5.4	5.6	5.5	6.2
Repairs and Maintenance	1.5	1.8	1.4	1.2
Depreciation	1.7	1.8	1.5	1.7
Other Expense (Income)	0.0	0.1	−0.1	2.1
Administrative & General	4.0	4.6	4.2	3.1
Corporate Overhead	4.1	3.6	3.0	6.0
Total Operating Expenses	**60.9**	**60.5**	**62.4**	**60.7**
Interest Expense	1.1	0.8	0.8	0.5
Other Expenses	0.7	0.4	0.1	n/a
Pre-Tax Income	**5.7**	**4.0**	**2.4**	**12.2**

Source: 2002 Restaurant Industry Operations Report, National Restaurant Association & Deloitte & Touche Excerpts taken from Exhibits A-11, B-11, C-11 & D-11

- Management must compare ratios either to budgeted or historical ratios and interpret whether the difference is positive or negative.
- Knowledge of food, beverage, and labor cost components is absolutely necessary to be able to interpret the story the ratios reveal.

K ey Terms

Maximum Allowable Food Cost	Beverage Cost Ratio	Menu Sales Mix
Actual Food Cost	Cost of Food Con- sumed	Break-Even Point
Potential Food Cost	Cost of Food Sold	Contribution Margin
Standard Food Cost	Average Check	Closing Point
Traditional Labor Cost Ratio	Seat Turnover	
	Inventory Turnover	

D iscussion Questions

1. What is the benefit of following the *Uniform System of Accounts for Restaurants* in the preparation of your restaurant's financial records?
2. What is the caution you must exercise when comparing industry averages to your restaurant's cost ratios?
3. Why do restaurant owners and managers compute and analyze ratios?
4. Any two numbers can produce a ratio or percentage. What are the characteristics of a relevant and useful ratio?
5. What must you know and understand to be able to interpret your restaurant's numbers?
6. Why do we say, "The interpretation of numbers cannot be delegated?"

P roblems

Problem 1

Given:

Ending inventory May 31st	$6,200
Total of Delivery Invoices for April	$9,700
Ending Inventory April 30th	$5,100

	$	%
Employee Meals	$ 860	
Food Sales for April	$31,775	

Using the template provided, compute the following:

1. Total Food Available for Sale in April
2. Cost of Food Consumed in April
3. Cost of Food Sold in April
4. Cost of Food Consumed Percent
5. Cost of Food Sold Percent
6. Inventory Turnover for April

Problem 1

	$	%
For the Month of April		
*Ending Inventory March 31st		
Purchases		
Total Food Available for Sale		
Ending Inventory April 30th		
Cost of Food Consumed		
Employee Meals		
Cost of Food Sold		
Food Sales for April		
Cost of Food Consumed %		
Cost of Food Sold %		
Average Inventory		
Inventory Turnover		
Days of Inventory		

*Ending Inventory March 31st = Beginning Inventory April 1st.

Problem 2

Clay Aiken manages a sports bar in Savannah, Georgia and has been keeping track of his sales and customer counts since he opened the restaurant. The restaurant has 150 seats. Clay believes he needs to average at least $2500 per day to achieve his minimum monthly profit objectives. The following table contains the sales and customer counts for a typical week. Using the template provided, you are to calculate the average check and seat turnover for each day of the week. After you have completed the table, answer the following questions:

- Which days are the most productive in terms of seat turnover?
- Which days are the least productive in terms of seat turnover?
- How many customers per day are needed to achieve his sales objective of $2500 per day with an average check of $12.50?

Sales Period	Date	Sales	Guests Served	Average Sales Per Guest	Seat Turnover
Monday	1/5	$2,300	190		
Tuesday	1/6	$2,560	201		
Wednesday	1/7	$2,200	179		
Thursday	1/8	$2,700	225		
Friday	1/9	$5,230	365		
Saturday	1/10	$4,975	330		
Sunday	1/11	$3,975	280		
Total		$23,940	1,770		

Problem 3

Clay has maintained a sales history for January through June for the past two years. Using the template provided, you are to calculate the absolute (dollars) and relative (percentage) sales variances for the first six months of the years using the template provided.

Month	Sales This Year	Sales Last Year	Variance	Percentage Variance
January	$ 28,500	$ 25,000		
February	$ 23,500	$ 21,500		
March	$ 26,500	$ 23,800		
April	$ 25,600	$ 22,600		
May	$ 27,000	$ 29,000		
June	$ 27,500	$ 27,300		
Total	$158,600	$149,200		

Problem 4a

Clay (from Problem 3) wants to forecast his sales for the last six months of the year and will use the 6.3% predicted change in sales to estimate his sales increases for July-December. Complete the spreadsheet shown below using the template provided.

Month	Sales Last Year	Predicted Change	Projected Sales Increase	Revenue Forecast
July	$ 26,600.00	6.30%		
August	$ 27,000.00	6.30%		
September	$ 31,000.00	6.30%		
October	$ 28,000.00	6.30%		
November	$ 27,200.00	6.30%		
December	$ 27,300.00	6.30%		
6-Month Total	$167,100.00	0.00%		

Problem 4b

Clay wants to develop his sales forecast for the next 12 months. Using the template of the spreadsheet shown below, determine the weighted average check for last year.

Month	Sales Last Year	Guest Count Last Year	Check Average
January	$ 28,500	2,400	
February	$ 23,500	2,500	
March	$ 26,500	1,900	
April	$ 25,600	2,600	
May	$ 27,000	2,100	
June	$ 27,500	2,150	
July	$ 26,600	2,250	
August	$ 27,000	2,975	
September	$ 31,000	2,645	
October	$ 28,000	2,650	
November	$ 27,200	2,700	
December	$ 27,300	2,800	
Total	$325,700	29,670	

Problem 4c

Using the weighted average check calculated in part b, determine Clay's sales forecast assuming the customer forecast increases shown.

- Which months show lower sales than the previous year?
- Why did this occur even with increased customer counts?

- Comment on why the sales for these lower months may actually be understated.
- What is the total sales forecasted for next year?

Month	Guest Count Last Year	Guest Count Forecast	Weighted Check Average	Projected Sales
January	2,400	2,520		
February	2,500	2,625		
March	1,900	1,995		
April	2,600	2,730		
May	2,100	2,205		
June	2,150	2,258		
July	2,250	2,363		
August	2,975	3,124		
September	2,645	2,777		
October	2,650	2,783		
November	2,700	2,835		
December	2,800	2,940		
Total	29,670	31,154		

3

Food Cost Controls

PRINCIPLES OF FOOD COST CONTROL

1. Food cost has four dimensions, or faces, and you need to understand the relationship and relevance of each one.

2. Calculate your operation's food cost percentage. It is unique from any of your competitors' and from restaurant industry averages.

3. If you concentrate on selling only menu items with low food costs, your overall sales and revenue will not be optimized.

4. Low food cost and high gross profit are not mutually exclusive. Promote the menu items that are popular, low in food cost and return a high gross profit.

5. You must accurately forecast how much of each item you are going to sell and purchase and prepare appropriate quantities.

6. You must adhere to the four standards if you expect to achieve consistency in quality, costs and profits. They are: standards for purchase specifications, recipes, portions, and yields.

7. You must understand the difference between cost of food *consumed* and cost of food *sold.*

8. Having to deal with leftovers will raise your food cost and limit your flexibility in menu planning.

9. Be aware that menu sales mix will cause identical restaurants to have different month-end food costs even when menu prices, recipe costs, portioning, and waste are equal.

10. Keep track of the cost of food eaten by employees; it amounts to more than you think.

In order to effectively control food cost, you must be able to accomplish four things:

1. Accurately forecast what and how much you are going to sell
2. Purchase and prepare according to sales forecasts
3. Portion effectively to achieve standardized yields
4. Control waste and theft in both back and front of the house

Before you can correct a problem, you need to realize that you, in fact, have one. If we do not know we have a theft problem, we do not set up a system to stop it. Many of the reasons for high food cost cannot be detected by management unless detailed cost control records are kept. These records are not simply the accounting reports prepared by the company accountant but rather managerial accounting reports that are far more detailed. If you do not have a cost control program that allows you to determine if anything is missing or out of compliance with standards, you are operating in the dark.

When a problem does become evident, it may be too late, as serious damage to the financial well-being of the operation may have already occurred. In today's competitive economic environment, one must be able to detect and prevent such losses from occurring.

"Very few operators have a *cost control system,* but most have a *cost accounting* system. The former *controls* costs, the latter *records* costs" (Dukas, *Planning for Profits in the Food and Lodging Industry,* 1976, p. 56). It is important to distinguish between these two terms. Accounting records must be kept for tax purposes; cost controls must be kept for operational purposes. Cost control is the accumulation and interpretation of costs that allows management to highlight and pinpoint how, when, and where costs are incurred. Each cost is measured against a budget or standard, and the variance noted.

Food Cost Myths and Misconceptions

Food cost percentage is sometimes misused and its importance both over- and understated. Calculating a monthly food cost is relatively meaningless if one does not take a physical inventory at the end of every month. *A physical inventory is where you count every food item and extend its cost using the most recent AP price.* A daily, weekly, or monthly food cost percentage does not inform the operator whether the food cost percentage is good or bad if it is not compared to a realistically determined food cost standard that requires knowing not only what you purchased during the month, but what you have on hand in dry storage and refrigeration. Remember, food items on your shelves are not expenses until they are consumed. They are *current assets* while they remain in your inventory.

Proponents of the contribution margin approach, also known as gross profit return, to cost analysis, place little or no importance on the food cost percentage. They are concerned only with the dollar difference between the menu price and the menu item food cost. This approach is not the best strategy, especially when demand is low and competition for customers is intense. High contribution margin comes from the higher priced menu items and, during such economic times, higher prices can result in reduced demand. The gross profit approach does optimize profit in markets where demand is greater than supply and where demand is price inelastic, as sometimes is the case with private clubs and resorts, and celebrity restaurants.

Achieving a low food cost and a high contribution margin are *not* mutually exclusive attributes and, actually, your menu needs to have both kinds of items, and you need to look at both in your food cost analysis. You will rarely, if ever, rely on only one and ignore the other completely. Exclusive reliance on achieving a low food cost percentage can result in lower check averages and lower revenues because low food cost items are typically the lowest priced items on the menu. Ignoring food cost for contribution margin will cause the monthly food cost percentage to increase because high contribution margin items, while the highest priced items on the menu, are typically the highest in food cost as well. In highly competitive markets, the contribution margin approach may not be the correct strategy for building customer counts.

Basics of Food Cost Control

Foodservice professionals must have a complete understanding of food cost and contribution margin in order to answer questions such as the following: How does one determine a food cost standard for an operation? What factors influence the food cost percentage? And, how is it calculated? What is a good food cost percentage?

Food cost control begins with the establishment of standards. A standard is the generally accepted result that management uses to define a level of excellence and attainment. Standards serve as benchmarks for acceptable results. One compares actual results to the expected standard and assesses whether it meets, exceeds, or fails to meet the standard. Standards of cost control become the basis for comparison in measuring or judging capacity, quantity, content, value, and quality. The essence of operational analysis is *comparison*. Only after cost standards are set, can you examine managerial cost control reports and financial statements by comparing the results to the expectation standards. Standards are used to evaluate individuals, departments, units, and even divisions of a business.

Food cost controls require you to break down sales and costs by the day, meal period, and department. The cost standards must, however, be objectively determined from observations and calculations occurring under actual operating conditions and not from unrealistic results only obtainable under controlled conditions, as is the case in test kitchens where new menu items are created. Costs can sometimes be *understated* because recipe yields in controlled tests are optimized and waste is negligible. These high yields are not likely to occur in an understaffed kitchen that has just been inundated with orders. Therefore, it is more realistic to *understate* your yields on items requiring portioning unless they are pre-weighed, counted, or pre-portioned in advance. Certain items will demand 100 percent yields (e.g., precut steaks), but items like Prime rib will have yields that will vary daily.

The Importance of Standards

Four main standards that help develop quality, consistency, and low cost are:

1. Standardized purchase specifications
2. Standardized recipes
3. Standardized portions
4. Standardized yields

STANDARDIZED PURCHASE SPECIFICATIONS

Standardized purchase **specifications** describe in detail the ingredients used in the standardized recipes. Specifications will include, among other things, the brand, size, variety, and grade of recipe components. Purchase specifications serve not only as quality control measures but also as cost control measures. Both quality and price are agreed upon before the purchase is made, making recipe costing consistent from week to week and from unit to unit in multiple location operations.

Specifications also reduce misunderstandings between buyer and purveyor on what to ship and how much to charge. Specifications are an important element in the overall food cost control program. Chapter 7 covers the ordering process and purchase specifications in detail.

STANDARDIZED RECIPES

Every menu item produced should have a standardized recipe. The recipe becomes the basis for determining the cost of the menu item. In order to assure consistency in quality and cost, purchase specifications are established. In multi-unit operations with the same menu and prices, consistency in cost, quality, and plate presentation are critical. Standardized recipes allow different individuals at remote locations to produce identical products if they use standardized ingredients. If the proper ingredients are used (e.g., brands, varieties, grades, size, etc.) and the recipe followed, a predictable yield and consistent quality will be produced. If portioned properly, it will yield a standard number of orders that, when sold at the prescribed menu price, will return the desired cost percentage and profits.

A **standardized recipe** is one that has been customized to a specific restaurant or foodservice operation based on the actual ingredients, cooking time, temperature, methodology, and cooking equipment available. It is rare that a recipe can be copied right from another operation or cookbook without some adjustment to the ingredients, equipment, or method. For example, you may decide to use fresh ingredients when the recipe calls for canned, frozen, or dehydrated. Whenever alterations are made to a recipe, you need to check your end product to be sure it results in the quality and quantity you want. The recipe is then checked and rechecked for all factors.

The standardized recipe is the basic component of a food cost control program. If an operator does not know the cost of the ingredients of every item on the menu, objective assessment of the month-end food cost percentage is impossible. The standardized recipe contains the following information:

1. The name of the recipe
2. The yield in number of portions, weight, or volume
3. Ingredient form, quality, and quantity
4. Equipment, utensils, pots, and pans required in preparation
5. Preparation methods, cooking methods, time, temperature, holding procedures, and even how leftovers can be utilized
6. Plate presentation and garnish

There is the assumption that the persons preparing from the standardized recipes have general culinary knowledge and understand the meaning of the terms and instructions used in the written recipe. There is a significant difference between the terms *mix, beat*, and *whip*, for example.

The ingredients are typically listed in the order of use. The recipe will state the quantity in terms of measure or weight and not in general terms like, "one apple, peeled and cored." What variety of apple and how big of an apple needs to be specified. The correct wording would be more specific, like "one cup of peeled and cored Red Delicious apple, diced."

Accurate measurements are very important to obtaining cost and quality consistency in food production. In food preparation, recipe quantities are expressed in a combination of three ways: *weight, volume,* and *count. Weight* is expressed in grams, ounces, and pounds. *Volume* is expressed in terms of tablespoons, cups, quarts, fluid ounces, and gallons. *Count* refers to the number of individual items, for example, *6 medium whole eggs* or *3 5 × 6 ripe tomatoes.* Quantities need to be expressed in the *largest* full measure. For example, if an original recipe called for 2 tablespoons of peanut oil and the recipe were expanded to a quantity that required 16 tablespoons, convert tablespoons to a larger measure. Since 2 tablespoons are in an ounce, 16 tablespoons equal 8 ounces or 1 cup. That is the quantity used on the expanded recipe.

In the past, chefs found it necessary to guard recipes like the secret formula to Colonel Sanders' combination of 16 herbs and spices or the Coca Cola formula. They believed that this preserved their job security and the restaurant owners absolute dependence upon them to remain in business. However, we now accept the realization that the menu and kitchen do not exist to serve the chef; rather, the kitchen exists to serve the foods that the customers want to eat. Many owners and managers have been "held hostage" by chefs who would not allow their recipes to be written for fear that their services will be devalued. However, most American-trained chefs and corporate chefs rely heavily on standardized recipes that they have helped develop. These recipes become the property of the restaurant, not the chef.

Food cost control requires that standardized recipes be used as a tool for the chef and management. The written recipe assists with training cooks, educating service staff, and controlling food cost and product quality. Accurate recipe costing and menu pricing demand that standardized recipes be followed. Standardized recipes are useful in assuring that a menu offered by the restaurant is consistent from one cook to another and from one location to another. Recipes are also the basis for inventory purchase units. This control tool frees management from being dependent on any single individual in the kitchen. Imagine what it would be like to run a restaurant where the menu was completely dependent on existing knowledge at the time of hiring any given chef or cook. With standardized recipes in place, any knowledgeable food preparation worker can follow them and get fairly satisfactory results, and reduce leftovers from over-preparation.

The standardized recipe specifies the type and amount of each ingredient, the rough preparation and cooking procedures, the portion size, and yield. While standardized recipes cannot make chefs out of ordinary cooks, anyone with a basic knowledge of cooking terminology can combine ingredients to produce a consistent chili or spaghetti sauce. There is no "magical" touch that a chef has that turns onions, garlic, olive oil, tomatoes, and spices into a great marinara sauce; however, there is something that one of the author's grandmother was never able to show or tell him as to why her homemade biscuits always were twice as high as his. Baking differs somewhat from cooking because there seems to be some "special touch" in combining the ingredients listed on the recipe that is very critical to producing a fluffy biscuit or flakey pie crust.

When one of the authors opened his restaurant, Angelo's Italian Cuisine, in Casselberry, Florida, he hired a wonderful Italian woman to be the restaurant's chef. She guarded her recipes as if they were government secrets and she was the only one who made the signature Angelo's spaghetti sauce. Keep in mind that, as the owner, he did not know the recipe for the sauce that was served on 90 percent of the food leaving the kitchen. She would prepare a double batch every time she had a day off so others never had to make it. If we ran low, we would call her and she would come in to make another pot.

She did not get along very well with the author's partner and one day he had had enough and fired her. She thought that the author would never allow that to happen, but each partner respected the other's decisions and she was not taken back. Needless to say, it was very stressful as the preparation of the signature Angelo's sauce was pondered. It was not only the sauce, but most of the entrees on the menu, that she was relied on exclusively to prepare. The approximate ingredients that went into everything were known, so they were written down on 5 × 7 cards. What resulted was that both partners and three other employees all learned the recipe and could prepare the sauce and all the other items that had previously been made only by that chef. Liberation! Confidence and independence were renewed as control of the food production process was regained. Angelo's Italian Cuisine operated for eleven years and was voted the favorite Italian restaurant in Orlando for three years running without having a chef. The author still has all the recipe cards in his files. They are yellowed with age and stained with tomato sauce and olive oil but he keeps them because they are a symbol of his independence from his temperamental chef.

We do not recommend that you wait until your chef quits or is fired to develop your standardized recipe file. Start with whatever recipes you are now using and begin with the most popular menu items. Weigh and measure quantities that may be currently added by the "handful" or "pinch." Quantities prepared should be based on storage life and sales demand. However, it was noted when making homemade Italian sausage and meatballs that the steps of "get ready" and "clean up" took the same amount of time whether 25 or 50 pounds was made. Consequently, there are optimum batch sizes that should be prepared and the product kept frozen or in vacuum tight packaging until needed.

One thing we recommend be included on your recipes is a list of the pans and utensils needed to prepare the item. The old *mise en place*, "everything ready," is essential in quantity food production. But, the purpose of this book is not to detail the steps in standardizing a recipe. There are many wonderful books available and I will defer to culinary experts at Johnson and Wales University, the Culinary Institute of America, and the many other fine culinary programs on this subject.

Production Control and Leftovers

For production control, only enough food to meet the demand for the day is prepared, with the objective of eliminating leftovers completely. A **leftover** is defined as any prepared food that cannot be sold the next day in its original form at its original price. Most commercial restaurant menus are fixed, or static, in that they offer the same items every day, with the exception of two or three seasonal changes. Consequently, they do not have an outlet on their menu for "daily specials." Besides, what kind of customer acceptance would you expect for items that are put on the menu driven exclusively by foods that are left over? Even employees will balk at eating items that are made from leftovers.

Whenever leftovers are incorporated into the menu, food costs are likely to increase rather than decrease. This is true because additional ingredients must typically be added to create the "new" menu item and it will be priced considerably lower than what the primary leftover ingredient would have returned had it sold in its original form. Consider the leftover Prime rib that is made into beef stroganoff or beef burgundy. As a luncheon special, it will have to be priced under $7 when it would have originally been priced at twice that amount. Consider, too, the additional ingredients and labor required to offer the item will reduce the profit return.

When chefs are asked if they had their choice of not having to deal with leftovers versus having to work them into the menu, the majority would elect not to have to work with them. Incorporating leftovers into the menu can cause standardized recipes to be altered. Whether it is the homemade vegetable soup that suddenly incorporates an additional vegetable ingredient or changing the lineup of a menu to incorporate yesterday's roast chicken, compromises are made. In the case of the soup, the customer will notice that there is inconsistency in the ingredients, and the food cost will be higher because the additional cost is not reflected in the price.

Now there are some who, in reading this section are thinking, "How can he say that food cost would be increased by using leftovers?" If the alternative to using leftovers is throwing it away as waste then yes, using leftovers will lower food cost. However, the cost will still be higher than if the food were sold in its original form at the original menu price. There are exceptions that have been brought to my attention by chefs over the years. One is BBQ ribs of beef made from the leftover bones from a 107 Rib. Since the cost of the bone is figured in when the Prime rib is sold, the leftover ribs basically contain only the cost of the BBQ sauce and accompaniments. The other exception is leftover food from a buffet or banquet that has been paid for with the guarantee. If a restaurant put these items out for sale in the restaurant, they would have basically zero food cost. There may be several other "extended" dishes like stew, goulashes, and casseroles that are expanded with the use of rice or noodles that can return a low food cost. However, they will not bring in the gross profit that the original item would have, and very few contemporary restaurants have menus that will permit the addition of such daily specials.

Even in an institutional operation such as a school or hospital foodservice, having to incorporate leftovers into the menu disrupts the menu cycle that has been balanced in terms of taste, texture, preparation method, and variety. Most foodservice contractors must adhere to specific menu parameters requiring a certain number of entrees, salads, vegetables, and desserts. Further, the requirements may call for entrees that offer one beef, pork, poultry, and fish item. Trying to incorporate yesterday's leftover roast chicken may require that two extended dishes be offered instead of one, and now the production manager has to move the turkey that was purchased for that day to another menu. Consequently, a domino effect of changes on future menus occurs.

This is the reason why operators will design menus and preparation methods that will eliminate leftovers completely. The first step in eliminating leftovers is accurate forecasting of customer counts. If the same menu is placed before guests day after day, a predictable menu sales mix will result. From sales histories, management can make predictions on how much to purchase and prepare. Standardized recipes and portioning result in standardized yields so we can prepare the optimum amounts.

How do restaurants like Applebee's, Chili's, Houston's, and Outback Steak Houses keep leftovers to a minimum? Remember, a leftover is a prepared item that cannot be sold the next day at its original price. Uncooked steaks are not leftovers because they can be sold the next day. These are restaurants whose menus cannot incorporate leftovers in the form of daily specials. Some restaurants do not have the expertise in their kitchens to entrust that a cook will be able to prepare and cost out a dish made of leftovers.

The most effective way to eliminate leftovers is to *cook to order*. If an item is refrigerated until it is cooked for service, there are no leftovers. Many menu items do not lend themselves to being cooked to order; for example, Prime rib, BBQ ribs, and chicken. These items need to be partially cooked and finished off on the char broiler or in a convection oven. To reduce leftovers of these items (if the item is more than two days old it will not be served to a paying guest and is therefore a leftover), they are cooked in small batches in quantities based on the menu sales mix and forecasted customer counts.

If quantities required are large or the cooking times extended, cooking to order is not practical. In such cases, cooking small batches frequently will keep leftovers and waste to a minimum. Another way leftovers are reduced is through the use of technology in the cooking equipment. Equipment such as convection steamers allow individual orders of fresh vegetables to be cooked in a matter of minutes. The new combi-convection-steam ovens can cook half inch pork chops in 12 minutes. Quartz ovens and broilers, and clamshell broilers can take frozen items to table-ready in minutes. There is no reason to have leftover baked potatoes, french fries, and baked bread and biscuits if management watches production quantities based on customer forecasts. If there are some leftovers, they will be minimal and can be discarded as quality control waste.

Portioning Standards

When food cost percentages exceed standards, one must examine the elements that can cause the variance. You will want to refer to the list of "130 Reasons for High Food Cost" at the end of this chapter. However, management can observe many things on the job that will indicate that cost standards are out of line or compliance. For example, over- and under-portioning can be a cause of high food costs and low price-value perceptions of customers, even when standardized recipes are being followed. Some of the things that signal to management that portioning standards may need to be reevaluated follow:

1. Not using measuring tools to portion food (e.g., scoops, ladles, scales)

2. Lack of size standards for serving bowls, plates, cups, and glasses. It is impossible to put more than 10 ounces of juice in a 10-ounce glass

3. No portion markers used to cut pies and cakes. Management should notice miscut pieces being served or wasted. Remember, the profit comes from selling the last two pieces, not the first ones

4. Customer comments to servers and cashiers about portions being too small or large

5. Amount of plate waste or lack thereof. Check the bus tubs and soiled dish table. Are certain menu items seen coming back? It may

be due to taste as well as portion size. Are plates completely empty (portions too small)?

6. Return trips to salad bar to fill up
7. Sales of side orders and appetizers
8. Sales of desserts
9. Use of doggie bags
10. Production yields, number sold, and leftovers do not add up

The Four Faces of Food Cost

You may have *cost control* systems in place that will help you detect the preceding signals. The *cost reduction* response is the *action* taken to bring costs within standards. For example, strict compliance to serving food with measures, scoops, and ladles will be enforced. Specific employees will be responsible for marking and portioning cakes and pies. Numbers sold of certain menu items will be tallied and compared to production quantities and leftovers.

Food cost is not a one-dimensional concept or calculation. It cannot be accurately and completely analyzed from just a single percentage. In order to fully understand and appreciate the relevance that food cost percentage has in the financial results of any foodservice operation, one must approach food cost from not one, but four different perspectives. In its most basic and fundamental presentation, food cost is expressed as a percentage of total food sales.

Food cost is calculated by dividing the food expense by the food revenue. Typically you will see the formula:

$$\frac{\text{Total Food Cost}}{\text{Total Food Sales}} = \text{Food Cost \%}$$

This calculation is for the overall food cost percentage for all food sales, as shown on the monthly income statement. It can also be calculated for individual menu items by using the formula:

$$\frac{\text{Menu Item Food Cost}}{\text{Menu Item Price}} = \text{Menu Item Food Cost \%}$$

The food cost referred to in the formula is the "raw food cost" of preparing the menu item or items. The cost is worked up from the standardized recipe and is called the "standardized cost." The food cost of any given menu item is going to be influenced by three factors under management's control and responsibility. They are not the only factors that influence food cost percentage, as we will see, but we must start with these three.

1. The "as-purchased" price of the ingredients (quality)
2. The portion size (quantity)
3. The menu price charged

By altering any one of these three variables, you can change the food cost percentage. However, once the quality, quantity, and price have been established and the menus printed, these are not sufficient in themselves to guarantee that the food cost goals will be achieved. In order for that to occur, management must assure that the standards are adhered to in purchasing specifications, standardized recipes, and standardized portions. In addition, waste and theft must be controlled, guests charged, and revenue collected.

The food cost figure that appears on the income statement example (see Table 3.1) is shown as an "absolute" or dollar value and as a "relative" value or percentage of food sales. Where do we get the figures for the food cost on the income statement? It starts with the assumption that a complete and accurate inventory is taken at least monthly of all food cost related items.

The following tip is recommended by the National Restaurant Association in the seventh edition of the *Uniform System of Accounts for Restaurants*. The separation of food cost into the cost of food served to customers and that eaten by employees as part of their employment benefits is a critical step that should be taken. This separation indicates more clearly the direct relation of menu prices to food costs and distinguishes between **cost of food** *consumed* and **cost of food** *sold*. Please refer to Tables 3.2 and 3.3.

Where does the figure for purchases come from? It is the total of all invoices for food received during the month whether they have been paid or

Table 3.1   Income Statement Angelo's Restaurant, April 200X

	$	%
Food Sales	$ 36,700	72.39%
Beverage Sales	$ 14,000	27.61%
Total Sales	$ 50,700	100.00%
Cost of Sales		
Food Cost (Consumed)	$ 15,500	42.23%
Employee Meals	$ (1,200)	(3.27)
Food Transfers to Bar	$ (450)	(1.23)
Discounts and Comps	$ (270)	(.74)
Food Cost (Sold)	$ 13,580	37.00%
Beverage Cost	$ 2,940	21.00%
Total Cost of Goods	$ 16,520	32.58%

Table 3.2   Cost of Food Sold Worksheet w/o Numbers

	Beginning Inventory (Which is the ending inventory for the previous month)
+	Food Purchases for the Month
=	Total Food Available for Sale
−	Ending Food Inventory (Taken last day of the month)
=	Cost of Food *Consumed*
−	Employee Meals
−	Food Transfers to Bar
−	Discounts and Complimentary Meals
+	Beverage Transfers to Kitchen
=	Cost of Food Sold

not. Let's add some numbers to see how the numbers used in the example were derived.

Let's look closely at the important differences between the cost of food consumed and the cost of food sold percentages.

$$\text{Cost of Food Consumed } \frac{15{,}500}{36{,}700} = 42.23\%$$

$$\text{Cost of Food Sold } \frac{13{,}580}{36{,}700} = 37.00\%$$

The difference of 5.23% represents $1920 in food inventory that was consumed and not sold. The point is, you need to know which of these two food costs is being reflected on the income statement. How can you tell? The first thing to look for is employee meals. If an allowance for employee meals is

Table 3.3   Cost of Food Sold Worksheet

	Beginning Inventory Food	5,800
+	Food Purchases	15,000
=	Total Food Available for Sale	20,800
−	Ending Food Inventory	5,300
=	Cost of Food Consumed	15,500
−	Employee Meals	(1,200)
−	Food Transfers to Bar	(450)
−	Discounts and Complimetary Meals	(270)
=	Cost of Food Sold	13,580

shown somewhere on the statement, it is as close as you're going to get to cost of food sold. Inquire as to whether the accounting systems follow the *Uniform System of Accounts for Restaurants.* If they do, employee meals are deducted from cost of food consumed. However, unless the restaurant tracks employee meals, the figure it reports as employee meals may be just an estimate and not an actual cost. Many restaurants give their employees a "free" meal and do not calculate the actual cost of what employees eat.

Since 1967, when restaurants came under the jurisdiction of the Fair Labor Standards Act and were required to pay the federal minimum wage, the cost of employee meals took on a new aspect of importance. Under the Wage and Hour Law, an employer can take a credit against the minimum wage for the *cost* of meals given to employees without charge. If an operator takes a meal credit against the minimum wage, it must be able to show the *true and accurate costs* of the meals eaten by employees. The meal credits are then prorated on an hourly basis for the hours worked. Different meal credits will be determined based on the time of day and type of meal eaten. For example, the *reasonable cost* of a breakfast meal will be lower than that of a lunch or dinner meal. An example should clarify how the meal credit is used.

Assume the employee is paid $5.50 per hour and works an average of 8 hours per day. The total daily wage rate would therefore be $5.50 × 8 hours or $44.00. Assume further that the employee is given a free meal with a reasonable food cost of $2.00. A credit against the hourly wage can be claimed in the amount of $.25 per hour *($2/8 hr).* Therefore, the hourly wage would be reduced from $5.50 to $5.25. In addition, if the employee is given a 30-minute break to eat, the employee will be paid only for a total of 7.5 hours, and the payroll savings would total $4.62 per employee per day *($5.25 × 7.5 = $39.38 versus $5.50 × 8 = $44).* When you have a crew of 25 employees, the savings can be significant. In this simple example, over the year this would amount to a reduction in payroll of *$42,158! ($4.62 × 365 days × 25)*

How do you monitor food consumed but not sold, such as employee meals, discounts, and complimentary meals? You could have employees write checks for their food. In fact, if the policy is that a check must be presented for a customer's meal, employees should be required to follow the same procedure and not be allowed to order employee meals verbally. Once they are written, you can collect them and estimate what employee meals are costing you.

What about discounted and complimentary meals? Again, all complimentary meals should be separated and tallied at the end of the month. Most restaurants attach coupons to guest checks to determine how the promotion is proceeding and have actual records of the cost of the discounted food. "Known" waste can be recorded as well. At the end of the night, the kitchen prepares a list of food that is being discarded, and management checks it and signs off. Waste forms are part of the daily reports at McDonald's and Wendy's. With all known employee meals, discounts, complimentary meals, and waste recorded, food cost percentage shown on the income statement becomes a more accurate figure as to what is being controlled or not controlled by management and employees.

The calculation of a food cost percentage is a simple mathematical calculation. The determination of a food cost standard for any given foodservice operation is not quite so simple. What is a good food cost percentage? Can individual operators use industry averages or some universal rule of thumb to establish a food cost percentage for their particular operation? The answer is a resounding NO!

Operators *cannot* arbitrarily select another's food cost percentage to use as a standard for their operation. National restaurant chains are becoming more sophisticated in establishing standard costs because a single food cost standard cannot be assigned to all locations. Although standardization in menu offerings, purchasing, preparation, portioning, and pricing are assumed, identical food cost percentages are not likely to occur. They will not be identical even if waste, theft, and over-portioning were assumed to be equal. Even if two operations achieved identical food cost percentages, their bottom line profits may still differ significantly. The point is that there are too many operational and financial variables that make it impossible for one's food cost percentage to be exactly comparable to any other operation.

Among the influencing variables, aside from waste, theft, and inconsistencies in following recipes, specifications for ingredients, and portioning, the *menu* will have the greatest impact on food costs. The menu affects the purchase requirements, storage space and temperature, equipment and utensil needs, and the number and skill levels of employees. The menu must utilize employees productively and satisfy the customers. The reason for the variance in food cost percentages is twofold: (1) differences in the ratio of sales by meal periods, that is, breakfast, lunch, and dinner; and (2) the *sales mix* of individual menu items.

As is often the case in restaurant chains serving three meal periods (e.g., Denny's and Shoney's), the units with the greatest percentage of total sales being accounted for during breakfast hours will likely achieve a lower food cost percentage than those with lower breakfast volumes. Even chain restaurants with static daily menus or single meal periods will not sell individual menu items in the same proportion. (This is referred to as the *menu sales mix.*)

Each operation, whether chain or independent, must establish its own standard food cost. The menu sales mix cannot be absolutely controlled so variances in food costs will occur. Many managers and operators express food cost in a *single* percentage and do not know how to develop their own standard food cost. In order to completely comprehend food cost, it must be expressed and analyzed from the four perspectives listed in Table 3.4.

Table 3.4   The Four Faces of Food Cost

Food Cost	Origin
1. Maximum Allowable Food Cost (MFC)	calculated from operating budget
2. Actual Food Cost (AFC)	shown on income statement
3. Potential Food Cost (PFC)	determined by sales mix
4. Standard Food Cost (SFC)	PFC + allowances

MAXIMUM ALLOWABLE FOOD COST PERCENTAGE

The first and most important of the four faces of food cost is the **maximum allowable food cost** (MFC). It answers the question, "What food cost percentage does the operation need if it expects to achieve its minimum profit objectives?" Although the name may be new, the methodology as to how it is derived is not. It was first presented by the Texas Restaurant Association in the early 1960s. The MFC can be calculated from historical accounting records or from proforma figures if opening a new restaurant. Every restaurant will have a different and unique MFC due to different overhead expenses, depreciation schedules, interest rates, taxes, labor rates, and insurance expenses, all of which will impact the bottom line. These costs will, in turn, influence the actual maximum allowable food cost percentage needed to achieve the restaurant's minimum profit objectives.

The procedure for calculating the MFC is as follows:

If using historical financial statements, select a representative accounting period not biased by high or low extremes in revenues or expenses. In most cases, year-to-date or weighted average figures will prove to be more representative and reliable. Express all expenses first in dollar values that accurately reflect the expenses incurred. If using proforma figures, be liberal with estimating expenses and conservative with revenues.

Express payroll and related expenses separately from other fixed and variable expenses. *Exclude* any food cost in this calculation because we will calculate it *after* we have determined all other costs and added a minimum profit. Included here would be advertising, utilities, supplies, repairs and maintenance, depreciation, rent, interest, and so forth. After listing all overhead expenses, add in an amount for the *minimum* profit you are willing to accept for investing your time and money.

Convert each of the dollar figures to percentages by dividing by the total sales for the period of time reflected in your expense and profit figures. For example, if all expenses and profit were expressed as monthly, divide by a month's sales. After converting the dollars to percentages, sum the percentages and subtract from 100 percent. Note that there is no allowance for food cost and what you have calculated is total costs plus profit, but *without* food

Table 3.5 Maximum Allowable Food Cost

Sales	$50,700	
Labor	$12,675	25%
Overhead	$11,661	23%
Minimum Profit	$ 4,056	8%

25% + 23% + 8% = 56%

100% − 56% = 44% MFC

cost. Therefore, the difference between the sum of the percentages and 100 percent is the maximum allowable food cost.

The name comes from the value of the calculation. It tells you the *highest* your monthly food cost can go and still allow you to achieve your *minimum* profit expectations. It represents a "high water mark" for your food cost. You should establish menu prices to achieve food cost below this percentage. For the sake of example, assume that labor cost is $12,675, overhead (fixed and variable expenses) is $11,661, and minimum profit is $4,056 per month. If sales were $50,700, then labor would be 25 percent, overhead 23 percent, and profit 8 percent. See Table 3.5. The total percentage of expenses and profit *without food cost* is 56 percent. That means that the *maximum allowable food cost* is 44 percent.

ACTUAL FOOD COST PERCENTAGE

The second food cost, **actual food cost** (AFC) percentage, is frequently discussed between managers and operators and is reported on the monthly income statement. If the operation follows the *Uniform System of Accounts for Restaurants*, seventh edition, the percentage shown is considered to be the *cost of food sold* because it will typically *deduct only* the cost of employee meals. You will need to inquire as to whether food transfers, allowances for discounts and complimentary meals, and recorded waste have also been deducted. If the *Uniform System of Accounts for Restaurants* is not followed, the income statement will more likely reflect the *cost of food consumed*, which shows the difference between the total of food available for sale less ending inventory. Food consumed is all encompassing and includes food sold to customers, eaten by employees, stolen, wasted, given away, or simply discarded. *The cost of food consumed will always be a higher number and percentage than cost of food sold.* The AFC indicates what the food cost is currently running but is really of little value unless the operator knows what the food cost *should be* running. Again, for the sake of example, assume for comparison that the AFC for the month, shown as Food Cost (Sold) in Table 3.1, was 37 percent. This formula is Cost of Food *sold* divided by *food* sales.

While the AFC percentage is lower than the MFC by 7 percentage points (44% − 37%) and profit will increase from 8 to 15 percent (8% + 7%), you still cannot evaluate this as good or bad based on these two food cost percentages. MFC is a value arrived at from financial statements and sets the upper limits of food cost, and AFC tells us what we ran during the most recent accounting period. In order to make a judgment as to the food cost efficiency, one must establish a benchmark value or standard for comparison. Before one can arrive at the standard food cost, the menu sales mix must be examined and Potential Food Cost determined.

POTENTIAL FOOD COST

From the menu sales mix we can calculate the third food cost, referred to as *potential food cost* (PFC). Sometimes called "standard food cost" or "theoretical food cost" in the literature, it is influenced by the actual menu sales mix. This food cost percentage utilizes the menu sales analysis and the recipe cost of each item on the menu. The calculation of the PFC reflects the fact that the most popular items will have the greatest effect on the resulting food cost percentage. The number sold of each individual menu item is multiplied by its respective food cost and menu price. The total *weighted* food cost for the menu sales mix is divided by the total *weighted sales*. The PFC is calculated from only the *cost of food sold*. It indicates what the food cost would be in a perfectly run operation where all food consumed was sold, and where there was zero waste and perfect portioning given the existing menu sales mix. It is the lowest food cost can ever go and is not an achievable percentage in 99.99 percent of foodservice operations. This is why it is a "theoretical" percentage. In actual practice, revenue is not received for all food consumed, and this fact alone will cause AFC to always be higher than PFC. The example in Table 3.6 demonstrates this concept.

Note in the example menu sales mix that none of the five menu items actually have a food cost percentage equal to the PFC of 33.84 percent. Three items have a food cost percentage greater than the PFC. If the sales mix were to shift away from lower food cost percentage lamb shank, veal Marsala, and shrimp scampi to any of the higher food cost percentage broiled chicken, cobb salad, or grilled salmon, the PFC will increase. When we compare AFC to PFC a significant variance of 3.16% is revealed (37.00% − 33.84%). But remember, we have to make allowances for food *consumed* and not *sold* before we can make a qualitative judgment as to whether our AFC is above or below our standard. Adjustments must be made so we can properly evaluate this percentage and that is why we have a fourth food cost called Standard Food Cost Percentage.

You will notice that while the total weighted sales shown in Table 3-6 is essentially identical to the food sales shown in Table 3-1 ($36,697 and $36,700,

Table 3.6 Computing Potential Food Cost

Menu Item	Item Food Cost $	Menu Item Price	# Sold	Indv CM	Wgtd CM	Wgtd Cost	Wgtd Sales	Food Cost %
Lamb Shank	$ 5.55	$ 18.50	345	$ 12.95	$ 4,468	$ 1,915	$ 6,383	30.00%
Broiled Chicken	$ 3.36	$ 9.20	688	$ 5.84	$ 4,018	$ 2,312	$ 6,330	36.52%
Veal Marsala	$ 5.00	$ 17.20	390	$ 12.20	$ 4,758	$ 1,950	$ 6,708	29.07%
Shrimp Scampi	$ 5.50	$ 19.35	300	$ 13.85	$ 4,155	$ 1,650	$ 5,805	28.42%
Cobb Salad	$ 4.00	$ 11.15	462	$ 7.15	$ 3,303	$ 1,848	$ 5,151	35.87%
Grilled Salmon	$ 5.75	$ 13.25	477	$ 7.50	$ 3,578	$ 2,743	$ 6,320	43.40%
Totals			**2,662**		**$ 24,280**	**$ 12,418**	**$ 36,697**	**33.84%**

Formulas (PFC)

Indv CM = Menu Price *minus* Food Cost Indv CM = Individual Contribution Margin

Wgtd CM = #Sold × Indv CM Wgtd CM = Weighted Contribution Margin

Wgtd Cost = #Sold × Item Food Cost

Wgtd Sales = #Sold × Menu Price

Food Cost% = Item Food Cost *divided by* Menu Item Price

PFC = Total Wgtd Cost *divided by* Total Wgtd Sales **PFC% = $12,418/$36,697 = 33.839%**

a coincidence), the weighted food cost was $3,082 ($12,418 and $15,500) less than the *cost of food consumed* and $1,162 ($12,418 and $13,580) less than the *cost of food sold* in Table 3-1.

Although every operation will have its own specific *potential food cost,* one cannot assume that achieving the PFC will automatically achieve the budgetary profit objectives. In a situation where an existing restaurant's sales mix was examined, the PFC exceeded the MFC. This restaurant had a existing overhead and labor expenses that required food cost to be unrealistically low for the segment of the market it sought to attract. While nothing could be done in the short run to lower property taxes, interest, and insurance, labor cost and other controllable overhead were brought into line to bring the operation closer to break-even.

Since the potential food cost of 33.84% is an unobtainable benchmark for food cost, (because it assumes that all food consumed is sold and that there is zero waste or theft) it must be "adjusted" to reflect employee meals, unavoidable waste, quality control standards, and other "known" situations where food is *consumed* and not *sold.* If employees are given a free meal, this can amount to an additional 2–3 percent of food cost. A guest satisfaction guarantee policy could add an additional percent to food cost when meals are discounted or given as complimentary by management. In addition, restaurants like Houston's have very high quality control standards that may find management discarding up to $100 in raw food per day. Such quality control standards need to be reflected in adjusting the PFC upward to arrive at an obtainable food cost standard.

STANDARD FOOD COST PERCENTAGE

The *Uniform System of Accounts for Restaurants* calculates Cost of Food Consumed as Beginning Inventory + Purchases + Delivery Charges to get Total Food Available for Sale (TFAS). Ending Inventory is then deducted from TFAS to get Cost of Food Consumed. When no provision for employee meals is made, food costs are called gross cost of food consumed. In fact, this figure includes all food that is "consumed" from waste, theft, spoilage, employee meals, complimentary and discounted food, and food transfers to other departments, e.g., the bar.

Typically, only employee meals are broken out as a separate food costs. The cost of the food eaten by employees is deducted from gross cost of food consumed in computing the gross profit. A figure for the cost of employee meals can be arrived at in more than one way depending on how employee meals are recorded and tracked. Officers and managers frequently order from the menu and sign the check. These transactions are therefore recorded and can be audited to determine the sales value of the food eaten. The approximate total cost of their meals can be determined by assigning a standard portion cost for each item ordered. This can be quickly and easily done when a Point of Sale (POS) system is used and where food costs are also contained within the system's database. In operations where POS systems are not used or do not contain food cost data, one can arrive at employee meals food cost by multiplying the total sales value of the meals eaten by officers, managers, and employees by a food cost percentage representative of the entire menu sales mix. This gives you a general idea of the cost of food eaten by employees and it will be credited against food consumed to lower the number.

If hourly employees are given a free meal, the amount that can be deducted for employee meal expense would be the cost of the food, not the sales value of the food. (*Additionally, this amount can also be used as a credit against the hourly minimum wage*). Again, a POS system would tally all the food items eaten by employees (assuming that employee meal transactions were entered into the POS system). The total cost of the food consumed based on standardized portions can then be calculated. The amount of employee and officers meals is then shown as a payroll-related expense or fringe benefit expense. For example, if the total retail sales value (*based on actual menu prices*) of the food eaten by employees and managers in a month was $3,546 and the PFC was 33.84 percent, the amount deducted from gross

Cost of Food Consumed would be *$1,200* (*.3384* × *$3546*). This is one of the numbers that is subtracted from Cost of Food *Consumed* to determine the Cost of Food *Sold* in Table 3.1.

There are several other ways that food is "consumed" where partial or no sales dollars are received. One occurs when meals are discounted or offered as complimentary. Management often empowers servers to "comp" portions of the check when they deem it appropriate. The item may be deducted from the check and replaced with another item or food may be served free as with a "buy-one-get-one-free" promotion. In both cases, food is consumed and no money is taken in, thereby causing the food cost percentage to increase.

The discounted and complimentary meals need to be tallied, either manually or within a POS system. The food cost of the meals comped or discounted is tallied the same why it is with officer and employee meals, either based on total sales times the Potential Food Cost of the menu sales mix or but extending the cost of each item individually. This amount is deducted from Cost of Food Consumed and then debited to public relations or advertising expense.

One can begin to see that if cost of food consumed is not adjusted for these uses of food that the food cost percentage will seem out of line with standards. The objective is to account for the food that is consumed but not sold. When this is accomplished, the variance between Actual Food Cost and Standard Food Cost represents *avoidable waste and shrinkage*. Since many of the causes for the higher costs are due to management policy, adjustments must be made to be fair to the kitchen manager and staff, especially if a bonus is tied to the food cost percentage.

Another way that food is consumed that will affect the overall food cost percentage comes from food transfers to other departments or sister units within a chain. For example, if the restaurant has a full bar, a sizable amount of food items are consumed there. Consider the lemons, limes, celery, olives, fruit juices, fresh fruits, cherries, and other non-alcoholic ingredients used in the making of drinks. There are also food items ranging from peanuts and popcorn to cheese, chicken wings, nachos, and even carved roast beef served to bar patrons at no charge during happy hours. The cost of these food items should be charged to the bar, not the kitchen. Similarly, the kitchen should be debited with the cost of the wine, beer, and liqueurs used in the preparation of food items.

Perhaps the biggest reason that these types of adjustments to food cost are not made is the difficulty encountered in compiling the necessary data. However, with more and more operations installing computers and POS systems, access to this information has become as easy as taking a sales reading.

The definition, calculation, and application of the Standard Food Cost percentage (SFC) is an important concept in the analysis of food cost. The SFC percentage is the food cost target or goal set by management. This is what the food cost "should be" at the end of the accounting period. The manner in which the food cost is calculated for income statement purposes is germane to proper interpretation by management.

As previously explained, the food cost shown on the income statement in an operation following the *Uniform System of Accounts for Restaurants* is the "Net Cost of Food" which deducts officer and employee meals. However, it does not deduct any of the other uses of food such as discounts, complimentary meals, and transfers to the bar.

The SFC is used as a benchmark for management and is typically compared to the resulting food cost percentage shown on the income statement. While the calculation of the cost of food consumed is largely "objective," the calculation of the SFC is at least partially "subjective." The subjectivity comes from "management allowances" for unavoidable waste and quality control which are intuitively determined.

Stated simply, SFC is the Potential Food Cost plus allowances for all *known* food that has been consumed in any way whatsoever. This includes employee meals, complimentary meals, recorded waste, discounts, food transfers to bar, and management allowances for unavoidable and quality control waste.

Using the figures from Table 3.6 to calculate the Standard Food Cost Percentage, we start with the Potential Food Cost Percentage, which is 33.84 percent. We then add the equivalent percentage allowances for all known food consumed but not sold. Table 3.3 shows the following food allowances: Employee Meals to $1,200; Transfers to the Bar, $450; and Discounts and Comps, $270. This totals to $1,920. We can convert this to a percentage by dividing it by the Food Sales ($36,700) shown in Table 3.1 to arrive at 5.23 percent.

The allowance percentage of 5.23 percent is added to the PFC of 33.84 percent to get the Standard Food Cost of 39.07 percent. If we compare the SFC to the Cost of Food Consumed Percentage, we see that the SFC is *approximately* 2 percent higher than the 37.00 percent AFC (Food Cost Sold) shown in Table 3.1. This 2 percent amounts to an approximate savings of $760 ($36,700 × .0207) and would be the amount of the bonus earned by the chef and kitchen crew for that particular month. This tells management that food costs were contained, but one should be aware that if this low cost was achieved by serving lower quality food or skimping on portions, it could have a negative affect on business in future months. Also, when AFC is lower than SFC, check the extension of the month end inventory. If it is overstated or includes non-food items like paper supplies and dishwasher chemicals, it will result in understating the cost of food consumed and lower the overall food cost. Typically, an acceptable variance between SFC and AFC in a QSR restaurant should be plus or minus one quarter of one percent (.25 percent). This kind of variance occurs due to over-portioning, excessive leftovers, unrecorded employee meals, customer walk-outs, and outright theft which are unknown and unrecorded.

Exactly which food items, if any, that caused this discrepancy needs to be determined. However, the problem could be in the dining room and not the kitchen. Consider that if food can be obtained from the kitchen without entering an order into the POS system or by turning in a handwritten check, there will be no record that the transaction ever occurred. Therefore, a server or cashier can collect the money and never turn it over to the house. Such a scam would require at least two people to perpetrate, but it could happen.

Cost control systems that do not allow food to leave the kitchen without a written or printed check forces the transaction to be entered into the POS system where it can be tracked. This includes food requested by managers as well as employees. Another cause could be that the food never got to the restaurant. If the deliveries were not checked, the order could be shorted and the restaurant still billed for merchandise it did not receive. This is, perhaps, the easiest to detect from order quantities, inventory counts, and sales analysis. Such an investigation would never be conducted until food cost indicated a problem. That is why written records are so critical for cost controls. You cannot visually see or detect such discrepancies.

If all of the recorded allowances are tallied and deducted from gross cost of food consumed, one would not add those same allowances to the potential food cost in arriving at a SFC. Management would also add a percentage for unavoidable waste and quality control to the PFC and compare that percentage to the Cost of Food "Sold." (CFS in this instance would be gross cost of food consumed less all recorded and known uses of food not sold, e.g., employee meals, discounts, etc.) In foodservice operations with very limited menus such as pizza delivery units, the avoidable waste allowance may be as little as one quarter of one percent. This is possible given the type of ingredients used and that little or no scratch preparation is done in the unit. Most pizza components are pre-cut and even pre-measured. Subsequently, if the PFC were, for example, 33.30 percent, the actual food cost would need to be less than 33.55 percent to be within the food cost standard. If it were higher than 33.55 percent, management would be required to provide a written explanation, e.g., oven failure that resulted in improperly cooked pizzas that were discarded or delivery problems resulting in late delivery times and discounted or free pizzas. Details on the toppings and size of the pizza would be included in such a report. In full service restaurants the variance would be much greater, e.g., 1–142%.

Table 3.7 shows an example of the four faces of food cost. Maximum Allowable Food Cost is the highest your food cost can be and still allow you to achieve your minimum profit objectives and it is determined from historical or proforma costs and profits objectives. Actual Food Cost is the one that should be on your monthly income statement. It is a cost of food *sold*—not

Table 3.7   The Four Faces of Food Cost

Maximum Allowable Food Cost	44.00%
Actual Food Cost	37.00%
Potential Food Cost	33.84%
Standard Food Cost	39.07%

cost of food *consumed.* It deducts all known food that is not sold and requires that a physical inventory be taken beforehand. Potential Food Cost is based on your menu sales mix and assumes that all food is sold and portioned perfectly. It is unrealistically low and needs to be adjusted for "allowances." **Standard Food Cost** is the benchmark that is compared to AFC. It is derived by adding allowances for employee meals, etc. to the PFC.

The concept of food cost must be examined from multiple perspectives in order to understand the total impact it has on operating profit. The four faces of food cost must be individually calculated for each operation because no two operations will be identical in all contributing variables. Maximum allowable food cost determines whether the potential food cost for the menu sales mix will allow profit objectives to be realized. The PFC must be adjusted with allowances to arrive at the standard food cost, which is the "realistic" food cost objective. The actual food cost taken from the income statement should not exceed the SFC. When it does, losses being incurred are exceeding allowances set by management.

The most important aspect of operational analysis is being able to interpret the figures on departmental cost reports. You need to know what the numbers are telling you. Once a variance from standard cost has occurred, examination of the probable causes must be undertaken. The simple calculation of a food cost ratio or percentage is only the beginning of the investigation process. Knowing how to interpret a ratio requires knowing all the possible reasons for the cost control variance. Only then can a remedy be prescribed.

In order to control food costs effectively, one must be familiar with the numerous causes of high food cost. One needs to start the process by examining the largest or most frequently occurring costs first. A small cost variance that occurs frequently can add up to a sizable cost variance if left unchecked. Keep in mind that cost control covers more than just the back-of-the-house. The cause of the higher than standard cost could result from activity taking place outside the kitchen. The following list of 130 reasons is by no means exhaustive and complete, but it will provide you with areas where you can begin your investigation.

Remember, a restaurant exists to sell food to customers. Any control measure that reduces sales volume or costs more than the resulting savings is counterproductive. Also, controls put in place for the convenience of the operation that are not "customer-friendly" are also counterproductive.

One Hundred and Thirty Reasons for High Food Costs

Menu

Poor forecasting of business volume

Menu offerings that do not appeal to clientele

Poor menu design for cost control

Too many items on the menu

Monotonous menu choices

No balance between high and low food cost menu items

Poor promotion of low cost items

Improper pricing of menu items

Failure to adjust prices when food costs increase

Purchasing

Excessive inventory of perishable items

No competitive purchasing policy

No detailed specifications

Poor relationships with suppliers

Use of fixed versus flexible standing orders

Not monitoring markets for supply and price

Graft between buyer and purveyors

No regular and organized inventory procedures

No formal written inventory records

Overbuying

Par stock levels too high—slow inventory turnover

Fictitious company invoices being sent for payment

Reprocessing of paid invoices for payment

Failure to take discounts for early payment

Failure to obtain quantity discounts

Failure to lock in prices with suppliers

Not counting on-hand quantities before placing orders

Frequent run-outs requiring retail purchases

Receiving

Theft by delivery person

Failure to check invoices for correct prices, quantity, quality

No system to assure proper credit for returned merchandise

Not weighing items purchased by weight

Failure to adhere to purchase specifications

Signing invoices without checking deliveries

No backup record of purchases to compare to delivery invoice

Acceptance of less than complete shipments with "full" billing and failing to receive back-ordered items

Lack of security at delivery entrance

Storage

Improper storage temperature of perishable items

Failure to rotate inventory (FIFO)

Failure to properly cover supplies

Poor sanitation of storage areas

No periodic report of dead stock or inventory turnover

Spoilage due to vermin

No daily inspection of perishable foods

No locks on storage areas

Unorganized storage areas

No limited access to storage areas

No written record of issues

No "forced issues" of dead stock

Uncovered containers of prepared mixes and food items

Cooler doors not sealed properly or correctly closed

Leftovers not properly saved at the end of the day

Paper Controls

No serially numbered guest checks

No audit of cash register readings

No control of voids and payouts

No reconciling of kitchen checks with guest checks

No reconciliation of statements to invoices

No record of reported waste and spoilage

Poor order book maintenance and system for recording invoices and purchases

Preparation/Processing

Excessive trim waste on meats and vegetables

Inability to incorporate trim/by-products into production items

Overproduction

Failure to follow standardized recipes

Failure to follow standardized cooking techniques

Not cooking in small batches

Inadequate or improper processing equipment and utensils

Preparing too much food in advance

Failure to check portioning standards

Over-reliance on value-added (convenience) products

Overcooking foods with resulting low yields

No production/menu mix history to guide production amounts

Oversized portions

Using more costly varieties/grades than needed for intended use

Excessive use of high cost convenience foods

Failure to update recipe costs

Failure to utilize ingredients in multiple menu items

Failure to rotate stock so oldest is used first (FIFO)

Refrigerator temperatures above 40 degrees

Improper storage of potentially hazardous foods

Lack of filtering for deep fryer oil

Thawing too much product for volume of business

Inadequate preparation quantities and run-outs during meal periods

Oven and fryer thermostats off calibration causing foods to burn

Service Transfer Functions

No standardized dishes, bowls, cups, and so on for plating

Failure to use measured portioning tools, e.g., scoops, scales, ladles

Food issued from kitchen without written checks

No recording of waste and returned items

Carelessness, spillage, waste

Failure to adhere to portioning standards

Standard portions too large

Inadequate customer counts for food bars/buffets

Servers over-garnishing plates

Servers over-portioning of condiments and salad dressings

Sales

Server theft

Cashier theft

Customer walkouts

Improper recording of items on guest check

Inaccurate price extensions on guest checks

Errors in addition on guest checks

Intentional or accidental omission of items from check

Poor menu design to promote low-cost high-profit items

Lack of internal selling by servers

No calculators provided for servers to total checks

No records of past sales for use in forecasting business

No monitoring of complimentary meals and discount coupons

No monitoring of voids and overrings

Failure to charge for add-on items, e.g., coffee, tea, blue cheese

High incidence of bad checks and invalid credit cards being accepted

Missing guest checks

Failure to reconcile kitchen requisitions with guest checks

No record of mistakes and returned food orders

Ability of servers to get food from kitchen without recording sale

Resetting cash register readings

Under-ringing of guest checks

Guest checks not serially numbered and assigned to servers

Failure to use creative pricing strategies to build volume

Failure to promote low cost menu items

Failure to adjust menu prices when ingredient costs increase

Excessive complimentary meals due to customer send-backs

Discounts improperly taken on guest checks by servers/managers

Not charging customers for coffee, tea and soda

NSF checks and invalid credit card charges

Other

No allowance taken for employee meals

No monitoring of employee meals

Failure to adhere to control rules and policies

Collusion between receiving and purchasing agents

Theft by delivery person

Errors made by accounts payable bookkeeper

Failure to deduct food transfers to bar

Failure to credit food cost for food items used in bar area, e.g., hors doeuvres, fruit juices, etc.

No reconciliation of food "sold" to food "consumed"

The Fallacy of Gross Profit: The Impact on the Bottom Line

Ever since the introduction of Menu Engineering sales analysis (Smith and Kasavana, Hospitality Pub. Inc., Okemos, MI, 1982), the consideration of food cost percentage has been de-emphasized and overlooked. Advocates of the gross profit approach (also called contribution margin) treat food cost and gross profit as mutually exclusive, often citing that "You bank *dollars* not percentages."

Treating food cost percentage and gross profit in this way can sometimes lead to a false sense of "profitability" that does not translate to the bottom line unless a number of other variables fall into place. The truth is that, in most cases, the examples provided to show the benefits of high gross profits over low food cost percentage will reveal some very startling evidence that indicates the gross profit scenarios sometimes return less gross profit per dollar of food cost and require more sales to achieve the "dollars" they put in the bank.

While gross profit is important, completely ignoring food cost can lead to reduced profits and is not always practical. The same is true for food cost; a goal of achieving *the lowest overall food cost percentage* can sacrifice revenue and profit. Typically, items with low food cost are the lowest priced items on the menu. A menu sales mix made up of primarily low food cost items will result in a lower check average, and unless customer count increases, overall revenue will be lower as well.

A balanced menu sales mix will contain both items with low food costs and items with high gross profits. **The Cost/Margin Analysis,** *International* (Pavesic, *Journal of Hospitality Management,* Nov., pp 127–134, 1983) seeks to identify items on the menu that are both low in food cost and high in contribution margin. On the other hand, reliance on selling only items with high individual gross profit (menu price less raw food costs) will result in a higher overall food cost because the high gross profit items on the menu have higher food costs (e.g., steaks, seafood, prime rib) and are often the highest priced items on the menu.

The gross profit method of pricing works best in operations like country clubs and destination restaurants with long waiting lines. However, in competitive markets, reliance on gross profit pricing may result in declining customer counts. In other words, if price inelasticity exists, gross profit pricing seems to work best. However, most operations are in markets where price elasticity exists and higher prices can mean reduced demand. Therefore, those relying on gross profit pricing will not see an increase in the bottom line return unless customer counts hold steady and fixed cost percentage declines more than food cost percentage increases due to higher sales levels.

The figures that follow will demonstrate this theory using the sales mix data previously offered to show that the gross profit approach is superior to the food cost approach. The results show that the *financial efficiency* is lower with gross profit pricing examples and the increases in cost are far greater than the additional dollars returned from the effort.

A *middle ground* position is recommended and the *Cost/Margin Analysis* provides an alternative that combines food cost and gross profit. Cost/margin *optimizes* both food cost and contribution margin and is not subject to the biases of a reliance on a single measure.

We start with the premise that sales increases must occur for gross profit to offset the increased food cost percentages. While fixed costs (e.g., rent, loan payments, insurance, overhead) remain stable from month to month, the percentage of overall sales they account for will vary inversely with sales. Consequently, higher sales will result in lower fixed cost percentages and reduced sales will cause fixed cost percentages to increase.

Menu sales mix "A" in Table 3.8 shows the overall results when a "low food cost" is achieved while sales mix "B" shown in Table 3.9 is offered to show the results that occur from a sales shift to higher gross profit items with higher food costs. Sales mix B was presented at a past NRA seminar as an example of an "improved" financial performance over sales mix A.

Table 3.8   Menu Sales Mix "A"

Menu Item	Number Sold	Menu Price	Food Cost	Food Cost Percent	Item Gross Profit	Weighted Gross Profit
Lobster	42	$28.50	$14.90	52.3%	$13.60	$ 571.20
NY Strip	74	$16.50	$ 7.40	44.8%	$ 9.10	$ 673.40
Prime Rib	143	$17.25	$ 7.25	42.0%	$10.00	$1430.00
Chop Steak	88	$ 8.95	$ 2.75	30.7%	$ 6.20	$ 545.60
Pasta	72	$ 7.50	$ 1.80	24.0%	$ 5.70	$ 410.40
Grilled Fish	_96_	$ 7.95	$ 2.40	30.2%	$ 5.55	$ 532.80
Totals	515					$4,163.40

Total Weekly Sales: $6,975.55; Total Weekly Food Cost: $2,812.15; Food Cost %: 40.3%

Sales mix B shows 10.9 percent more in sales revenue, or $758.95, over sales mix A. However, in realizing that sales increase, it consumed $564.55 in additional food cost. This is 20 percent more than in sales mix A. Sales mix B realized a 4.7 percent increase in overall gross profit, or $194.40 over what was achieved in sales mix A.

When you analyze these changes some rather startling percentages jump out. Consider that the additional sales of $758.95 used an additional $564.55 in food inventory. The food cost to sales ratio is 74.38 percent! How comfortable are you offering items for sale on your menu that would result in a 74 percent food cost? This occurred because the sales increase was 10.9 percent while the increase in food cost was 20 percent, resulting in an increase in overall gross profit of only 4.7 percent.

Table 3.9   Menu Sales Mix "B"

Menu Item	Number Sold	Menu Price	Food Cost	Food Cost Percent	Item Gross Profit	Weighted Gross Profit
Lobster	62	$27.00	$14.90	55.2%	$12.10	$ 750.20
NY Strip	101	$15.50	$ 7.40	47.7%	$ 8.10	$ 818.10
Prime Rib	180	$16.25	$ 7.25	44.6%	$ 9.00	$1620.00
Chop Steak	54	$ 9.95	$ 2.75	27.6%	$ 7.20	$ 388.80
Pasta	52	$ 8.50	$ 1.80	21.2%	$ 6.70	$ 348.40
Grilled Fish	_66_	$ 8.95	$ 2.40	26.8%	$ 6.55	$ 432.30
Total	515					$4,357.80

Total Weekly Sales: $7,734.50; Total Weekly Food Cost: $3,376.70; Food Cost % 43.7%
Example used at NRA Seminar on "Your Menu Is Like a Supermarket," Educational Foundation, National Restaurant Association, 1996.

Proponents of the gross profit approach would focus on the additional $194.40 in gross profit and not call your attention to the fact that the actual food cost percentage increased from 40.3 to 43.7 percent! We do not have the complete income statement to be able to determine what happened to the overall bottom line profit dollars and percentages. It is unlikely that a sales increase of 11 percent lowered fixed cost percentages to offset the 3.4 percent increase in food cost.

In the examples provided to show the advantages of gross profit over food cost percentage, the customer counts remain the same in both scenarios, an unrealistic assumption that will not hold true in highly competitive markets. Also, the sales mix cannot be "manipulated" perfectly. Techniques of menu design can increase the likelihood that certain items will be read and improve the chance that they will be selected by the patron. However, other forces in the marketplace influence the customer traffic on any given day or meal period. Menu pricing is only one aspect of the total operating picture that impacts the overall menu sales mix.

If this does not have you questioning the soundness of ignoring food cost for gross profit pricing, consider the following financial results. Sales mix A returned $1.48 in gross profit for every dollar of food cost expended ($4,163.40/$2,812.15) while sales mix B returned only $1.31 ($4,357.80/ $3,316.70). Sales mix B had to generate $1.77 in sales to return $1 of gross profit ($7,734.50/$4,357.80) while sales mix A needed only $1.67 to return $1 of gross profit ($6,975.55/$4,163.40).

The purpose of this explanation is to tell restaurateurs not to completely abandon their low food cost philosophy for the gross profit approach. It is not for everyone. In fact, most operators in competitive markets where demand and price elasticity are at work need to keep food cost percentages within standards of acceptance and not forsake it for gross profit. We recommend considering a middle-of-the-road approach, similar to that of the Cost/Margin analysis (Pavesic, *International Journal of Hospitality Management,* Nov., pp. 127–134, 1983). Cost/margin is covered in complete detail in Chapter 5.

 ## Key Concepts

- Food Cost is not a one-dimensional concept or calculation. You need to understand the relationship between the four Faces of Food Cost.
- Your restaurant's food cost percentage is unique from any of your competitors.

- You must understand the significant difference between food *consumed* and food *sold.*
- The menu sales mix will cause the food cost percentage of two identical restaurants to differ, even with the same menu items, menu prices, recipes, portions, and purveyor costs.
- You must take a month-end physical inventory to know your true monthly food cost.
- Food cost control begins with the establishment of standards.
- Don't be food cost-wise and gross profit-foolish.

ey Terms

Specifications	standardized portion	Maximum Allowable
Standardized Recipe	The Four Faces of	Food Cost
mix	Food Cost	Actual Food Cost
beat	Cost of Food Con-	Potential Food Cost
whip	sumed	Standard Food Cost
misen place	Cost of Food Sold	Cost/Margin Analysis
Leftover		

iscussion Questions

1. Discuss the importance of taking a monthly physical inventory as it relates to calculating month-end food cost percentage?
2. Why is it important to distinguish between cost of food *consumed* and cost of food *sold?*
3. Explain the relevance and importance of standards in food cost control.
4. Regarding leftovers and waste, discuss the signs that can be observed that would alert an owner or manager that their standardized portion sizes are not being followed or are in need of revision. *Students can answer this question from the perspective of an employee, e.g., server, busser, dishwasher, or cook; and from the perspective of a regular customer to a restaurant. You can substitute "standardized recipe" or "standardized purchase specifications" in place of "standardized portions" and elicit an entirely different set of observations.*

P roblems

Problem 1

As foodservice professionals, you must thoroughly understand the complexities of food cost and be able to review it from four different perspectives. This is necessary because it cannot be approached from a single dimension or calculation, e.g., food cost divided by food sales on your income statement. In the following exercise, you will compute the four dimensions (faces) of food cost and gain a clearer understanding of the food cost components. Using the Excel template provided on the accompanying diskette, compute the answers to the following, showing all of your calculations and labeling the numbers used in your calculations. *Set your percentages to two (2) decimal places. Do not round up or down.*

1. Maximum Allowable Food Cost Percentage
2. Actual Food Cost Percentage
3. Potential Food Cost Percentage
4. Standard Food Cost Percentage
5. Inventory Turnover in both times per month and number of days

Problem 1
Four Faces of Food Cost

Food Sales	$ 25,000
Overhead	$ 6,900
Payroll	$ 6,000
Profit	$ 2,000
Beginning Inventory	$ 5,300
Ending Inventory	$ 4,900
Purchases	$ 8,600
Employee Meals	$ 350
Potential Food Sales	$ 25,500
Potential Food Cost	$ 7268
Recorded Waste	$ 125
Food Transfers to Bar	$ 250
Discounts and Comps	$ 225

Calculate the following:

Maximum Allowable Food Cost %

Actual Food Cost %

Potential Food Cost %

Standard Food Cost %

Average Inventory

Inventory Turnover

Inventory Days

Problem 2

2. There are a number of factors used by management when evaluating the mix of menu items to determine which items to emphasize. Food cost has traditionally been the most important factor, but since the introduction of Menu Engineering (Smith and Kasavana, 1982), attention has turned away from food cost to individual contribution margin or gross profit. The relevance and importance of food cost has been deemphasized and overlooked. This problem parallels the example given in the book on *The Fallacy of Gross Profit.*

Using the data and template on the accompanying diskette, you are to complete the spreadsheets and analyze them to determine which of the two sales mixes produces the optimum financial results. Don't be fooled by totals. You will need to follow the analysis used in the text to arrive at the correct answer. Remember, you must back up your opinions with financial support.

Problem 2

Sales Mix A Menu Item	No. Sold	Menu Price $	Food Cost $	Food Cost Percentage	Item Gross Profit	Wgtd. Gross Profit	Wgtd. Food Cost	Wgtd. Sales
Chicken Tenders	57	$ 5.95	$ 2.98					
Buffalo Wings	89	$ 4.95	$ 2.23					
Sirloin Burger	120	$ 5.50	$ 2.31					
Fish Sandwich	42	$ 4.95	$ 1.52					
Veggie Wrap	127	$ 4.50	$ 1.00					
Slice Pizza	80	$ 3.95	$ 0.95					
Totals	515							
Total Sales A								
Total Gross Profit A								
Wgtd. Food Cost % A								

Sales Mix B	No. Sold	Menu Price $	Food Cost $	Food Cost Percentage	Item Gross Profit	Wgtd. Gross Profit	Wgtd. Food Cost	Wgtd. Sales
Chicken Tenders	69	$ 5.95	$ 2.98					
Buffalo Wings	44	$ 4.95	$ 2.23					
Sirloin Burger	143	$ 5.50	$ 2.31					
Fish Sandwich	127	$ 4.95	$ 1.52					
Veggie Wrap	75	$ 4.50	$ 1.00					
Slice Pizza	57	$ 3.95	$ 0.95					
Totals 515								
Total Sales B								
Total Gross Profit B								
Wgtd. Food Cost % B								

	Sales	Food Cost	Gross Profit	Food Cost %	Sales/ GP	GP/FC
Sales Mix A						
Sales Mix B						
Difference B-A						
Sales Increase Percentage						
% Increase in Food Cost						
Sales Inc. to Food Cost Inc. %						
% Increase in Gross Profit						

4

Yield Cost Analysis

FUNDAMENTAL PRINCIPLES OF FOOD COST CONTROL

1. You need to consider direct labor as a cost along with raw food cost when costing menu items made from scratch.

2. Convenience products do not need to be marked up as much as items made from scratch because you do not have to recover direct labor costs.

3. If you can eliminate a job by purchasing pre-cut foods, you can reduce your payroll.

4. The Cost per Servable Pound will always be more than the As Purchased price per pound when there is trim and cooking loss.

5. Yield factors are a useful tool to chefs in costing out menu items.

6. Consistency in quality, taste, yield, are requirements for controlling recipe cost.

7. Your costs and yields are only as good as your standards of purchase specifications and standardized recipes.

8. Realistic productivity standards must be established for each preparation task.

9. Productivity must address qualitative as well as quantitative factors.

10. Prime Cost Control is the key to profitability.

In Chapter 3, a restaurant was compared to a factory where raw materials are transformed into the final product that is then consumed by the customer within minutes of completion. The production process is guided by the standardized recipe, which if followed will result in quality and quantity standards being achieved. In order to calculate the *plate cost* (also called *edible portion cost,* or *EP*), you must first determine the cost of your ingredients. The data required for this calculation are (1) the purchase price of the ingredients and (2) the edible yield.

 ## ield Terminology

There are several terms used in yield cost analysis with which you should be familiar.

As-purchased (AP) weight: The weight of the product as delivered to the restaurant by the purveyor, including bones, fat, and unusable trim.

Edible portion (EP) weight: The amount (weight or volume) that is available to be portioned after loss in carving or shrinkage in cooking. No further losses will occur due to trimming or shrinkage in cooking.

Waste: The amount of unusable product that is lost due to processing, cooking, and portioning or by-products for which there is no salable value.

Usable trim: By-products that result from processing or cooking that can be sold as other menu items to recover all or part of their cost. For example, trim resulting from cutting steaks in the restaurant that is used for ground beef, sirloin tips, or stew are usable trim. They are costed as *equivalent products* that can be purchased from suppliers; for example, the market price for ground beef, sirloin tips, and stew meat.

Yield: The yield is the net weight or volume of food after it has been processed and made ready to serve. This refers to the yield from a ham or turkey that has been weighed after cooking, but *before* portioning.

Standard yield: The yield that results from following the standardized recipe and processing procedures. It is the amount of usable product available for portioning after all processing and cooking have been completed. The yield percentage is calculated by dividing the as-purchased weight by the yield weight.

Standard portion: The size of the portion indicated on the standardized recipe and the basis for determining the plated portion cost of the menu item.

Yield Factors

The following discussion of yield cost factors offers an extremely practical procedure for costing out items that involve trim losses, cooking shrinkage, or usable trim. One very valuable tool accompanying these calculations is the *portion divider*, which makes determining order quantities of items with trim and shrinkage simple and accurate to estimate. Once the as-purchased price has been determined, portion costs can quickly be calculated whenever market prices fluctuate.

The calculations are relatively easy to do when you are dealing with any food item that only has to be portioned prior to plating. Such items are often referred to as *convenience foods*. A **convenience food**, however, is any food item purchased with some preprepararation labor already performed on it. Some or all of the production steps to bring the particular product to that level of readiness are performed *outside* the restaurant by the processor. A frozen Sarah Lee muffin and pre-mixed cookie dough are easy to cost out and are examples of "convenience foods."

Would you classify raw fresh chicken cut into eight pieces a convenience food? According to the definition given earlier, it is because it eliminates the need for the restaurant to cut up the chicken after it has been delivered. Yes, it will cost a few cents more per pound than you would pay if it were purchased whole, but consider the labor-intensive task of cutting hundreds of chickens if you were a KFC or Popeye's chicken franchisee. Think of the money these restaurants save on equipment and space by purchasing pre-cut chicken, not to mention the reduced number of workers' compensation claims for employees who would likely cut themselves performing this duty. Other examples of convenience foods are frozen french fries, pre-cut steaks, pre-pattied hamburgers, bottled salad dressing, and shredded cabbage.

Calculating Plate Cost

Calculating the **plate cost** for a convenience food is not difficult. In the case of pre-mixed cookie dough, if one 24-ounce package costs $2.50 per pound, the cost of 24 ounces would be $3.75. If the portion size is 0.75 ounce of dough for each cookie, you should get 32 cookies from each package (24/0.75 = 32). Therefore, the food cost per cookie is approximately $.12 ($3.75/32 = $.12). If you sell them for $.39 each, the food cost percentage is 30.7% ($.12/$.39 = 30.77 percent). This calculation is easy because there is no waste or loss in processing.

If you knew that the food cost for making the cookies from scratch was approximately 25 percent lower than the purchased dough, would you make them yourself? By using the pre-mixed dough, the restaurant eliminates having to purchase the preparation equipment, raw ingredients, and the labor cost of a baker to prepare the cookies. The price paid for these ready-made products or ingredients raises the food cost over what they would be if made from scratch on the premises, but the operation simplifies its purchasing, can hire less skilled employees at lower wages, and does not have to carry large inventories of ingredients that complicate the purchasing and storage functions.

C osting Convenience Foods

With most convenience foods, all you have to do to determine portion costs is to simply count, weigh, or measure the size of the portion to determine how many orders you can get. You divide the number of servable portions into the as-purchased price to get the portion cost. However, even with convenience foods, an allowance for normal waste due to portioning must be factored in the cost of each portion. This may be as little as one portion per case or as much as 2 percent of possible yield.

In the case of the cookies, what if you discovered that you were getting only 28 and not 32 cookies out of each 24-ounce package of dough? If you get only 28 cookies at $.39, your food cost per cookie increases from $.12 to approximately $.14 or 35.9 percent. The total revenue from a package of dough drops from $12.48 to $10.92 (28 × $.39 = $10.92). You did not just increase your cost per cookie by $.02; you reduced sales revenue by $1.56.

Some allowance for waste must be made even with raw cookie dough. It should be very minimal if the dough is weighed or portioned with a measured scoop. Most convenience foods would have minimal or no allowances for waste (e.g., pre-portioned steaks, pre-portioned desserts like pie and cheesecake). Portion cost calculations are not this simple when it comes to items *made from scratch* in the kitchen. When you cut your own steaks, bake your own pies, make your own gravies and soups, the costing out of the recipe and servable portions requires much more than dividing portions into as-purchase prices. Whenever you process, trim, cook, or otherwise perform any preparation step on a menu item, you will end up with less weight, count, or volume of product to serve than when you started. Therefore, the cost per pound, per ounce, or per piece will be greater than when you started.

Because of this loss, the cost per servable pound will be greater than the cost per pound as purchased. The greater the trim loss, cooking shrinkage, and portioning loss, the higher the cost per servable pound relative to the purchase price per pound.

A calculation of the actual portion cost for every menu item must be made. Although this may be done only a few times during the year, the fluctuating market costs of the ingredients requires that menu prices be updated and adjusted. With the system that is explained in this chapter, this process is reduced to a simple yet accurate bookkeeping adjustment. Efficient cost controls demand such data be part of the overall cost control program. Without such records, costs cannot be accurately determined.

The cost of the edible portion is rarely calculated from the invoice price, referred to as the *as-purchased price (AP) per pound or unit.* Determination of portion costs for items like frozen french fries that are packed 5 six-pound bags to a case at a cost of $15 a case is a simple calculation of the cost per pound divided by the portions per pound. If the portion's size is 5 ounces, the portion cost for the french fries is $.16 ($15/30 lb = $.50/lb; 16 oz/5 oz = 3.2 portions per pound; $.50/3.2 portions/lb = $.16. That food cost may actually be understated because it assumes you will get 3.2 portions per pound. If you get only 3 portions per pound (allowing for over-portioning and a waste factor), the true portion cost is $.50/3, or $.17. An additional cost of $.03 to $.05 per portion should be added for the frying oil and the catsup typically served with the fries.

Another example of a convenience product would be ready-made cheesecakes purchased from a specialty baker. All the operator has to do is cut the cake into portions and serve. The same applies to all ready-to-eat pies and cakes. If the cost of the cheesecake is $15.00 and 12 servings are cut, the cost per slice is $1.25. One important thing to keep in mind is that the profit is in the last three or four pieces that are sold! Some operators will pre-plate each piece and wrap it to insure proper portioning and yields. It is always a good idea to calculate portion costs on less than 100 percent yields, even with convenience foods. Doing so, you build in a cushion for error and quality control. There will always be a questionable item that should not be served. Do not allow food cost decisions to be counterproductive to quality control standards. When in doubt, throw it out. Build quality control losses into your food cost! This is applicable to both convenience and scratch-prepared foods.

Costing Items Made From Scratch

Most menu items contain ingredients that require trimming, processing, and preliminary cooking that will result in shrinkage of some kind. Consequently, whenever the weight or volume of cooked product is less than the AP weight or volume, the EP cost will be higher than the AP price. This requires that *yield cost analysis* be conducted on these menu items to determine their true cost per portion. The buyer for a foodservice operation uses yields to help determine quantities to be purchased and kept on hand to meet production needs. For example, if cutting yield tests for a whole salmon weighing 20 pounds produces 16 pounds of steaks or fillets, only 80 percent of the original as-purchased weight will be usable. This has significant implications on the plate cost of each portion and on order quantities.

Over time, the chef or owner will discover the optimum size to purchase that results in the highest yield and least amount of waste. Thus, purchase specifications are developed that indicate the minimum and maximum weight of a single fish and even the specific variety of salmon.

Certain cuts of meat will have both trim loss and shrinkage during cooking. Yields must be measured and portion cost determined after cooking. The amount of product that remains after processing, cooking, and portioning is called the *yield.* The ratio of the *edible portion* to the original weight is called *yield percentage.*

Yield tests do not have to be taken every time the product is prepared. If standardized purchase specifications, standardized recipes, and standardized portioning are followed, you can assume that the yields, and therefore portion costs, should remain consistent over time. The only variable that will change the portion cost is the price paid to the purveyor.

Yield tests should represent a weighted average of several tests, not just a single test. Operations where standardized recipes and purchase specifications are inconsistently applied will have a variance in food cost that will fluctuate from day to day and month to month. Close adherence to standards assures that variances will be minimal and that costs will be consistent over time.

In **cooking from scratch**, there are two primary steps in making an item ready for sale. They are (1) **pre-preparation** (that is, *rough preparation*), which includes such steps as butchering, vegetable cleaning, processing foods such as slicing meats, boning fish, cleaning shrimp, peeling and chopping vegetables, making salad dressings, and the like; and (2) preparation, which is taking the partially processed ingredients and completing the cooking or combining with other pre-prepped ingredients in advance of serving the item to the customer.

Owners, managers, and chefs need to have at their disposal the most accurate portion costs for all the major entrees and accompaniments on their menus. In addition, they need to monitor the purchase prices of key ingredients so they can adjust menu prices when necessary. The calculations and formulas that follow can simply, quickly, and accurately translate increases in *as-purchased prices* to update portion costs. In addition, once yields have been standardized, quantities to order for busy periods and special parties can also be determined quickly, easily, and accurately.

The accuracy of your costs and quantities is dependent upon diligent adherence to standardized purchase specifications, recipes, and portioning. If you have tight standards and follow them religiously, your costs will be consistent and accurate, and they will not have to be recalculated unless you change any of the three standards. Without consistent standards you cannot accurately determine purchase quantities and food costs.

R ecipe Costing

Ideally, every item on your menu should follow a recipe "standardized" for your operation. Consistency in quality, taste, yield, and cost are critical to controlling both the quality and the cost of each menu item. Just because you do not see a printed recipe being used does not mean the absence of recipes in the operation. Most chefs have memorized the recipe and even when they seem to be not measuring spices and seasonings, they know the precise amounts required for the recipe. However, recipes are very useful when it comes to costing the menu item.

A recipe for most food items (baked goods are the exception) has been compared to a road map showing how to get from one location to another. There are interstate and county roads, two lane and four lane highways, the business route or by-passes. Any of them will get you to your destination. Just as you can alter your travel route, so can you alter recipes to fit your tastes and those of your customers. However, once a recipe has been perfected, no alteration of the recipe is permitted unless changed by the chef or management. After all, once you have perfected your house dressing, special beef gravy for your Prime rib, or that special dessert, customers expect it to taste the same every time they order it. In addition, since the menu prices are based on actual food costs of ingredients and yields, it is important that the recipe be followed for food cost consistency as well.

You will recall from your food production classes that a standardized recipe is a set of instructions describing the way a particular establishment prepares a particular dish. It is customized based on the cooking equipment, pots, pans, and utensils used as well as the ingredients and preparation methods. In addition, when one conducts a recipe costing, the assumptions are:

- The recipe is followed
- The purchase specifications of the ingredients are followed
- The cooking and portioning standards are followed

Remember, a standardized recipe "standardizes" quality, quantity, and food cost. In the following exhibits, we have provided food cost sheets for five items and then totaled the cost of the entire meal. Yields of fresh ingredients and weight-volume of ingredients for quantities needed were determined from yield tests and standards published in tables and charts of volume-measure-to-weight-measure conversions. Bulk costs have been converted to recipe quantity costs for ease of calculation.

You will need to know your units of measure to determine recipe ingredient costs, e.g., ounces in a pound; ounces in a cup, quart, gallon; teaspoons and tablespoons per ounce; etc. We recommend adding 5 percent to your recipe cost for acceptable waste and quality control loss. This is a way to minimize the likelihood that borderline questionable quality items will not be served to customers by cooks and managers concerned about raising their food cost for the month. In addition, a server or manager can comp a meal when service or other circumstances warrant without adversely affecting food cost standards.

In Tables 4.1–4.5 you see samples of recipe costing forms showing a salad, with dressing, entrée, vegetable, and dessert. The costs shown would be different for your operation depending on the price you pay for the ingredients and the yield you actually obtain. You will note that we have added 5% for waste and quality control. This amount can vary between 1–5% of the recipe cost. When you divide the amount by the number of portions, the ad-

Table 4.1   Recipe Cost—Spinach Salad

Menu Item: Spinach Salad			Portion Size: 4 oz	
Number of Portions: 20			*Cost Per Portion: $1.15	
Ingredients	**Purchase Unit**	**Price/ Unit**	**Recipe Quantity**	**Recipe Cost**
Baby Spinach	Lb	$3.57/lb	3 lbs	$10.71
White Mushrooms	Lb	$2.50/lb	8 oz	$ 1.25
Red Onions	Lb	$ .70/lb	8 oz	$ 0.35
Strawberries	Pint	$3.49	1 pint	$ 3.49
Vinaigrette Dressing	See Table 4.2			$ 6.00
Cost of Recipe				$21.80
Add 5% for Waste/QC				$ 1.09
Total Cost of Recipe				$22.89

*Cost Per Portion: Divide Total Cost of Recipe by number of portions it produces.

Instructions: Purchase Unit and Price Per Unit will be given or found on delivery invoice. Recipe Quantity is amount called for in the recipe. You will cost out each ingredient in the recipe and total the amount. Add 5% of the total (for waste and quality control-QC) to get Total Recipe Cost. Divide this amount by the number of portions it is supposed to produce to calculate Portion Cost. Note: You will need to count the "actual" number of portions the recipe produces to determine the "actual" portion cost. If over portioning occurs, the total number of portions will be less than the recipe amount and your cost per portion will be higher.

Table 4.2   Recipe Cost—Vinaigrette

Menu Item: Raspberry Vinaigrette   **Quantity: 45 ounces**
Number of Portions: 20   **Cost Per Ounce: $.14**

Ingredients	Purchase Unit	Price/ Unit	Recipe Quantity	Recipe Cost
Red Wine Vinegar	Pint	$ .58	1 cup	$ .29
Rice Wine Vinegar	Pint	$1.20	1 cup	$ .60
*Lemon Juice	Lemon	$ .25	3 T	$ .25
Thyme	Tablespoon	$ .36	1 T	$ .36
Salt			TT	$ .05
Pepper			TT	$ .10
**Fresh Garlic	Lb	$1.20	1 T	$ .06
Honey	Pint	$3.50	4 oz	$ .88
Strawberry Preserves	½ Pint	$1.25	1 cup	$ .63
Olive Oil	Quart	$4.96	1½ cups	$1.86
Vegetable Oil	Quart	$1.25	2 cups	$ .63
Cost of Recipe				$5.71
Add 5% for Waste/QC				$ .29
Total Cost of Recipe				$6.00

*1 Lemon = 3 T juice

**20T = 1-lb

Table 4.3   Recipe Cost—Chicken Divan

Menu Item: Chicken Divan   **Portion Size: 1 Breast**
Number of Portions: 20   **Cost Per Portion: $2.90**

Ingredients	Purchase Unit	Price/ Unit	Recipe Quantity	Recipe Cost
Boneless Chicken Breast	Each	$1.50	20	$30.00
Chicken Stock	Gallon	$1.46	1 gallon	$ 1.46
Broccoli	Heads	$1.29	4 heads	$ 5.16
Cream of Chicken Soup	11 oz Can	$ .79	8 cans	$ 6.32
Mayonnaise	Quart	$1.60	2½ cups	$ 1.00
Lemons	Each	$ .25	4 each	$ 1.00
Curry Powder	Tablespoon	$ .17	1½ T	$ .26
Sharp Cheddar	Lb	$5.40	1½ lbs	$ 8.10
Bread Crumbs	Cup	$ .42	3 cups	$ 1.26
Butter	Lb	$2.42	¼ lb	$ .61
Cost of Recipe				$55.17
Add 5% for Waste/QC				$ 2.75
Total Cost of Recipe				$57.92

Table 4.4   Recipe Cost—Cauliflower

Menu Item: Cauliflower Bake *Portion Size: 1/5 head*
Number of Portions: 20 *Cost Per Portion: $1.33*

Ingredients	Purchase Unit	Price/ Unit	Recipe Quantity	Recipe Cost
Cauliflower	Head	$3.25	5 heads	$16.25
Mayonnaise	Quart	$1.60	1½ cups	$ .60
Chinese Mustard	½ pint	$1.28	6 oz	$ .96
Swiss Cheese	Lb	$3.36	1 lb	$ 3.36
Bread Crumbs	Cup	$ .42	1 cup	$ .42
Parsley	Tablespoon	$ .04	2 Tablespoons	$ .08
Cherry Tomatoes	Pint	$3.49	1 pint	$ 3.49
Vegetable Oil	Quart	$1.25	2 oz	$ .08
Salt				$ .05
Granulated Garlic	Tablespoon	$ .16	½ Tablespoon	$ .08
Cost of Recipe				$25.37
Add 5% for Waste/QC				$ 1.27
Total Cost of Recipe				$26.64

ditional cost amounts to pennies more per portion. For example, with the Chicken Divan, $2.75 divided by 20 portions equals $.14 per portion. Think of this amount as your insurance against wasted meals, re-made entrees, and unsold leftovers that will likely occur. If the kitchen minimizes these occurrences, the Actual Food Cost will be less than Standard Food Cost and they can earn a bonus. The extra also covers the costs of table condiments, e.g., mustard, catsup, mayonnaise, and steak sauce, that customers will put on their food. These are elements of food cost that the kitchen staff does not have under their direct control and that they cannot influence one way or another.

We suggest that you refer to Chapter 4 of *Applied Math for Food Service* by Sarah R. Labensky (Prentice Hall Publishers, Upper Saddle River, NJ, 2003) on yield tests where you can find common yield percentages for common produce items. Table 4.6 shows the cost of the entire meal. The table d'hôte meal cost in this example is $6.29 which would be marked up to a menu price range of somewhere between $15.75–$18.95 resulting in a range of food cost of 33–40 percent. You will learn that pricing is not a simple mark up of cost and there are many "indirect" costs and factors that ultimately influence the price charged on any menu item. Factors such as the type of restaurant (casual or white tablecloth), location (suburban or downtown), meal period (lunch or dinner), and several other factors covered in detail in Chapter 6 on menu pricing will be considered before arriving at the menu price.

Table 4.5

			Portion Size: 1/10 of pan	
Menu Item: Chocolate Pizza				
Number of Portions: 20			Cost Per Portion: $.90	

Ingredients	Purchase Unit	Price/ Unit	Recipe Quantity	Recipe Cost
White Chocolate	Lb	$2.59	½ lb	$ 1.30
Butter	LB	$2.42	½ lb	$ 1.21
Eggs	Dozen	$1.32	4 each	$ .44
Granulated Sugar	Cup	$ .26	2½ cups	$ .65
Cake Flour	Cup	$ .22	2 cups	$ .44
Pecans	Cup	$1.90	½ cup	$ .95
Vanilla Extract	Oz	$ .60	1 Tablespoon	$ .30
Raspberry Jam	Cup	$1.50	1 cup	$ 1.50
Kiwi	Each	$ .69	3 each	$ 2.07
Strawberries	Pint	$3.49	1 pint	$ 3.49
Bananas	Lb	$ .55	1 lb	$ .55
Blueberries	½ pint	$2.99	½ pint	$ 2.99
Apricot Jam	½ pint	$2.99	12 oz	$ 2.25
Cost of Recipe				$17.06
Add 5% for Waste/QC				$ .86
Total Cost of Recipe				$17.92

Table 4.6   Menu Costing Sheet

Use this sheet to summarize the portion cost of each menu item to arrive at the "total meal cost."

Menu Item	Cost Per Portion
Spinach Salad w/dressing	$ 1.15
Chicken Divan	$ 2.90
Cauliflower Bake	$ 1.33
Chocolate Pizza	$ .90
Total Meal Cost	$ 6.28
Menu Price © 40% Food Cost	$15.75*
Menu Price © 33% Food Cost	18.95*

*Prices rounded up or down to .25, .50, .75, or .95

C osting an Oven-Ready Prime Rib Without Usable Trim

In the example that follows, you need to focus on the *methods described* and not the actual numbers derived. The prices and yields are not necessarily representative of what you would achieve with a like product nor are they presented as industry standards. Further, assume that the final figures given are the result of a weighted average of dozens of yield tests, not a single one. As statisticians will tell you, if you want to get a valid and reliable conclusion from any test, your sample universe is critical. In addition, the larger your sample (of Prime rib yield tests you conduct) under all kinds of conditions and with different employees, the more representative your yield standard will be of actual yields in your restaurant.

Further, after testing different grades, weights, and brands of products, you discover that certain ones produce better yields. Thus you will establish a purchase specification for the ingredients, and will accept no substitutions at any price. In the following example, it is assumed that the quality and yield grade that give the best product, the best cooking method and temperature, and the best portioning procedures have been determined in this manner.

With such standards in place, cost and yield predictions on Prime rib becomes more accurate. As a result of this consistency, you will be able to calculate several numerical constants to quickly determine the cost per servable pound, cost per portion, and the amount to purchase. To demonstrate these factors, two yield tests will be conducted to explain how to determine these same factors for your own use. In the first yield test, we will be using a product that has only servable product and waste. Waste has no value and the more waste you have from cooking shrinkage or carving loss, the smaller will be your standard yield, the fewer salable portions you will get, and the greater will be your cost per servable pound.

All weights less than a pound are expressed as decimal fractions to eliminate the necessity to convert pounds to ounces in the math required. For example, 4 ounces is a quarter of a pound, or 0.25 pound, eight ounces is a half a pound, or 0.5 pound, and so on. To convert ounces into decimal equivalents, simply divide the number of ounces by 16, the number of ounces in a pound.

The first test will be on a 109 oven-ready Prime rib. It is a USDA Choice, yield grade 3. Yield grade is an indication of the ratio of lean to fat. A yield grade of one (1) will weigh under 17 pounds as purchased and have less fat and marbling. A yield grade 5 will have a 25 pounds as-purchased weight. This yield grade is an important addition to your purchase specifications when purchasing primal beef cuts. The purchase specifications require it to weigh between 19 and 22 pounds.

The Institutional Meat Purchasing Specifications (IMPS) number 109 is a standard of identity that translates into a very specific description of this cut of beef. IMPS describe products customarily purchased in the food service industry. Refer to *The Meat Buyers Guide* published by the North American Meat Processors Association, Reston, VA, 1997. The USDA specifications say that a 109 rib

> ... is prepared from a 7 rib primal rib (no. 103) by a straight cut across the ribs at a fixed point measured three inches from the extreme outer tip of the rib eye muscle at the 12th rib and continuing in a straight line through a fixed point 4 inches from the extreme outer tip of the rib eye muscle at the sixth rib. The chine bone is removed.

The original as-purchased weight is 20.25 pounds. See Table 4.7. Since the rib is *oven ready* there is no trimming before cooking. It goes right into the oven and is roasted at the prescribed temperature until the desired internal temperature is reached. Remember, cooking at high temperatures increases shrinkage. The new cook-and-hold low temperature roasting cabinets reduce shrinkage from 25 percent to less than 10 percent. That translates to an additional 15 percent yield. In the case of this rib, it would have meant an additional 3.0375 pounds of rib to sell. This yield test is not using such an oven. The cook-and-hold oven cooks at 250 degrees for about 6 to 8 hours, depending on the degree of doneness sought. An additional advantage of the cook-and-hold oven is that the meat is cooked to the same degree of doneness throughout instead of well done on the end cuts and rare in the middle.

The weight of the cooked rib is 16.375 lb or 16 lb 6 oz. That means we had cooking shrinkage of 3.875 lb or 3 lb 14 oz. This is 19.136 percent of the original as-purchased weight. After it sits for about 20 minutes, it is cut into portions. If the entire rib were portioned at one time, as might be the case if it were for à banquet, the yield will be higher than if it were portioned for à la carte dining room service.

Typically, prime rib is sold in two or three sized cuts, all cut from the same rib. This would increase the likelihood of over-portioning and waste from miss-cut portions that may not be served to customers. Thus this yield test would be more appropriate for a banquet situation than for à la carte portions.

When conducting yield tests in a controlled environment to esimate costs for a table-service restaurant, remember there are many distractions in an actual restaurant kitchen, and the fast pace does not allow the time and attention often given in a test kitchen. Under such controlled conditions, most yields will be greater than will occur in the actual operation. Therefore, if costs and prices are determined by unrealistically high yields, the food cost goals will not be achievable in the individual units serving the public.

Out of the original 20.25 lb purchased, the combined shrinkage and carving loss was 9.0625 lb, or 9 lb 1 oz. This is 44.75 percent of the original as-purchased weight. Keep in mind that the results are approximate yields on

Table 4.7 Standard Yield Calculations w/o Usable Trim

Item: Oven ready rib, IMPS 1110R (109)
Quality grade: Choice (upper half)
Yield Grade: 3
As-purchased price per lb.: $3.43
As-purchased weight: 20.25 lbs.
Total cost: $69.46
Summary of Yield Test Results (The figures represent the weighted average yield determined from several similar yield tests).

	Decimal Wgt.	Lbs & Ozs	% of Total Wgt.
Loss in Cooking	3.875 lbs	3 lbs 14 oz	19.136%
Loss in Carving	5.1875 lbs	5 lbs 3 oz	25.617%
Total Loss (Waste)	9.0625 lbs	9 lbs 1 oz	44.753%
Servable Weight	11.1875 lbs	11 lbs 3 oz	

1. Percentage of servable weight

   Formula: $\dfrac{\text{Servable Weight}}{\text{As-Purchased Wgt}}$ $\dfrac{11.1875}{20.25} = 55.25\%$

2. Cost per servable pound

   Formula: $\dfrac{\text{As-Purchased Price/lb}}{\text{\% Of Servable Weight}}$ $\dfrac{\$3.43}{.55246} = \$6.21$

3. Cost factor per servable pound

   Formula: $\dfrac{\text{Cost Per Servable Pound}}{\text{As-Purchased Price/lb}}$ $\dfrac{\$6.21}{\$3.43} = 1.810$

4. Cost per portion (Assume 8 oz portions or 2 per lb)

   Formula: $\dfrac{\text{Cost Per Servable Pound}}{\text{No. of Portions Per lb}}$ $\dfrac{\$6.21}{2} = \$3.11$

5. Portion cost multiplier

   Formula: $\dfrac{\text{Cost Factor Per Servable/lb}}{\text{Portions Per lb}}$ $\dfrac{1.810}{2} = .905$

6. Number of pounds to purchase (Assume 100-8 oz portions)

   Formula: $\dfrac{\text{Total Portion Weight}}{\text{Percent of Servable Weight}} = \dfrac{800 \text{ oz}}{.5525} = 1448 \text{ oz}$ Or **90.5 lbs**

Note: Since each rib will weigh between 19–21 lbs, 5 ribs are needed.

what you can expect on *all the ribs* when purchasing and cooking specifications remain the same. If a restaurant does not adhere to such standards, any given rib will vary to a greater extent from the average of the yield test figures.

The percentage of servable weight is 55.25 percent of the original as-purchased quantity. Since there is only salable product and waste, the cost per *servable pound* of the 11.1875 lb of servable Prime rib cannot be $3.43. Remember, the total cost of the rib as purchased was $69.46. We cannot assign any value to the cooking shrinkage or trim loss. Therefore, we have to recover the total cost of the rib from the amount we have to sell.

There are two ways to calculate the **cost per servable pound**. The first is to divide the total as-purchased price, $69.46, by the servable weight, 11.1875 pounds. The result is $6.21 per pound. However, there is a better method that incorporates the yield percentage. Simply divide the as-purchased price per pound by the percentage of servable yield, or $3.43/0.5525. You will get the cost per servable pound of $6.21. The second method is better because you can estimate your yield percentage easier than you can calculate the actual pounds and ounces of servable product. Servable yield is what determines your cost per servable pound. In this case, there is an increase of $2.78 per pound, or over $.17 per ounce from purchase to the plate.

This makes a significant difference when computing actual food costs. Remember, the figures here are really the weighted average of many such cooking and carving tests, and you can expect that any given rib you roast and carve will have the same yield if you uphold your purchase and preparation standards. For this reason, we can calculate a *constant value* that will allow you to quickly determine the cost per servable pound regardless of the as-purchased price per pound.

The cost factor for converting any as-purchased price per pound to the cost per servable pound is found by dividing the cost per servable pound, $6.21, by the as-purchased price per pound, $3.43 ($6.21/$3.43 = 1.81). The cost factor per servable pound, 1.81, has no value like dollars or pounds; it is just a mathematical constant. It will remain constant as long as all the variables remain constant; for example, purchase specifications, cooking methods, and carving procedures. With this factor, you can convert any as-purchased price per pound to your cost per servable pound by multiplying the cost factor, 1.81, times any as-purchased price per pound that you are quoted by your meat purveyor. As proof, you multiply $3.43 × 1.81 = $6.21. If the market price increases to $3.50, the new cost per servable pound would be $6.34 ($3.50 × 1.81). This is a valid factor based on the average yields.

Once the cost per servable pound is calculated, it is simple to determine your portion costs. Simply divide the cost per servable pound by the number of portions per pound. In this example, we are serving only 8-ounce portions, or two portions per pound. Therefore, $6.21/2 = $3.11 per portion. You would add the food cost of the salad, bread and butter, potato, vegetable, and condiments to get your total plate cost.

Since most restaurants offering Prime rib serve more than one size portion, you will find it useful to be able to convert any as-purchased price per pound directly to a portion cost. This is accomplished quickly and accurately with the use of what is called the **portion cost multiplier.** This constant is calculated by dividing the number of portions per pound into the cost factor per servable pound, or 1.81/2 = .905. With the portion cost multiplier, you convert the as-purchased price per pound to your portion cost by multiplying it by the as-purchased price per pound. In this example, $3.43 × .905 = $3.11. If the price increases to $3.50, your new portion cost for 8 ounces is $3.50 × .905 = $3.17.

For the sake of example, assume you are going to serve an 8-ounce Prime rib to 100 people. How many ribs do you need to purchase? The first thing you need to do is calculate the total edible portions you need. In this case it is 800 ounces (8 oz × 100 portions). Since we know that the percentage of servable weight for the prime rib is 55.25%, all you have to do is divide 800 ounces by .5525 and it reveals that you would need to buy 1448 ounces or 90.5 lbs (1448/16).

You cannot call up your meat purveyor and order 90.5 pounds of 109 ribs. Since the average weight of the ribs will be between 19 and 22 pounds, you will need to order a minimum of 5 ribs (90.5/20.5 lbs = 4.4 ribs). If this were a banquet, you would have a built-in allowance for additions, and if they are under guarantee, you will still charge for the full 5 ribs.

Proof

As-Purchased Weight	90.5 lb
Less Waste of 44.75%	(40.5) lb
Servable Weight	50 lb

50 lb × 16 oz = 800 oz

800 oz/ 8-oz portions = 100 portions

The application of utilizing the percent of servable yield to other products that do not have usable trim is extensive. Assume you have a delicatessen or sandwich shop that uses precooked meats for your sandwiches. In this example, we are testing the various forms of corned beef. You sell reubens and corned beef sandwiches and your portion size is 4 ounces. (The following example is adapted from C. Levinson, *Food and Beverage Operation*, Prentice Hall, Englewood Cliffs, NJ, pp. 188–189, 1989.)

The corned beef products we are testing are:

Waste or Shrinkage

Raw Corned Rounds	25%
Raw Corned Briskets	50%
Cooked Corned Rounds	5%
Cooked Corned Briskets	10%

This same test could be done with roast beef, turkey breast, and ham, as they are all similar in the ways they can be purchased. The percent of servable weight for each of the corned beef products would be 75 percent, 50 percent, 95 percent, and 90 percent, respectively. We will compute another factor called the **portion divider** by (*multiplying the percentage of servable weight by the number of portions per pound, in this case, four.*)

The portion dividers are:

Raw Rounds	$0.75 \times 4 = 3.0$
Raw Briskets	$0.50 \times 4 = 2.0$
Cooked Rounds	$0.95 \times 4 = 3.8$
Cooked Briskets	$0.90 \times 4 = 3.6$

Assume the following are as-purchased prices per pound:

Raw Rounds	$1.45
Raw Briskets	$1.05
Cooked Rounds	$1.95
Cooked Briskets	$2.25

The cost per servable pound can be computed by dividing the as-purchased price per pound by the percentage of servable weight.

Raw Rounds	$1.45/0.75 = $1.93 lb
Raw Briskets	$1.05/0.50 = $2.10 lb
Cooked Rounds	$1.95/0.95 = $2.05 lb
Cooked Briskets	$2.25/0.90 = $2.50 lb

Another method of calculating the portion cost is to divide the original as-purchased price per pound by each respective portion divider.

Raw Rounds	$1.45/3 = $.49
Raw Briskets	$1.05/2 = $.53
Cooked Rounds	$1.95/3.8 = $.52
Cooked Briskets	$2.25/3.6 = $.63

Raw rounds end up being the lowest cost per portion, but selecting them assumes that you have the equipment and personnel to properly cook them. There is labor cost that must be considered. Other considerations that may override cost are the taste preference of your clientele and your quality standards. It may be that only corned beef brisket will meet customer expectations. Therefore, your decision on which one to use cannot be based only on cost. Quality and customer preferences are sometimes more important than food costs in the selection process.

To determine how much to purchase for 700 sandwiches, divide the number of covers by the portion divider. Using cooked briskets, we would need at least 195 pounds (700/3.6 = 195). Proof: $195 \times .90 = 175.5 \times 16 = \dfrac{2808 \text{oz}}{4} = 702$ or 700.

Costing a Prime Rib with Usable Trim

In the previous examples, there were only two end products to deal with, servable portions and waste. This example considers *usable trim* as an additional end product of in-house butchering of meat. This example simulates a butchering and cooking test on a Primal rib, IMPS 103. To elect for this alternative, you would need to have the skilled labor to do the meat cutting, have a meat saw, and have a menu that allows you to sell the resulting usable by-products. If the restaurant has a fixed or static menu, it will not be able to

Table 4.8   Yield Test with Usable Trim

Item: 103 Primal Rib
Grade Choice, Yield 2
Total Cost: $90.75

As-Purchased Weight: 33 lbs
As-Purchased Price/lb: $2.75

	Weight	Market Value
Usable Trim		
Cap Meat	1.55 lb	$4.40
Short Ribs	3.25 lb	$9.07
Ground Beef	1.25 lb	$1.25
Total	6.05 lb	$14.72
Waste	3.3 lb	0
Total Trim	9.35 lb	
Weight of Oven-Ready Rib	23.65 lb	

Total: *As-Purchased Price* less the market value of the usable trim equals the cost that needs to be recovered from the oven-ready rib. $90.75 − $14.72 = $76.03 or $3.21/lb ($76.03/23.65 lb)

incorporate short ribs, stew meat, or ground beef into the menu. The breakdown of the rib is shown in Table 4.8.

The breakdown of the rib yields are: waste trim (fat, gristle, bone), cap meat, short ribs, and ground beef trimmings. Each of these by-products is collected in a separate pan for weighing prior to determining its market value. The industry standard for determining the value of usable trim is to assign a market value based on what it would cost to purchase these items from a supplier. You would simply ask your supplier to obtain prices on such trim or similar items. Fat and bone, although sold to rendering companies, is not given a value. Total value of all usable trim in this test comes to $14.72, and the breakdown is shown in Table 4.9.

The calculations follow simple word problems such as "If one pound costs $2.25, how much does 0.75 of a pound cost?" The value of the usable trim is *deducted* from the total as-purchased price of the rib ($90.75 − $15.02). The difference of $75.73 is the amount you need to recover from the sale of the

Table 4.9   Butchering Yield Test

Item: 103 Primal Rib Grade USDA Choice, Yield 2
Total Cost: $90.75
As-Purchased Weight: 33.0 lb   As-Purchased Price/lb: $2.75/lb

Description	Lb	Oz	Decimal	%	Value
103 Rib	33	0	33.0	100	$90.75
Waste/Trim	3	5	3.3125	10	0
Usable Raw Weight	29	11	29.6875	90	$90.75
Usable Trim					
Cap Meat	1	9	1.5625	4.73	$ 4.73[1]
Short Ribs	3	4	3.25	9.85	$ 9.07[2]
Hamburger	1	4	1.25	3.79	$ 1.25[3]
Total	6	1	6.0625	18.37%	$15.05
Oven-ready Rib	23	10	23.625	71.59%	$75.70[4]
Shrink/Carving Loss	9	10	9.625	29.17%	0
Servable Weight	14	0	14.0	42.42%	$75.70
Cost per Servable Pound					$ 5.41[5]

Market Value of Usable Trim

[1]Cap Meat $3.03/lb

[2]Short Ribs $2.79/lb

[3]HB Trim $1.00/lb

[4]$90.75 − $15.05 + $75.70 Cost per pound at oven-ready stage $75.70/23.625 or $3.20

[5]$75.70/14 lb = $5.41 lb

Prime rib. The cost of the usable trim will be recovered from the sale of the menu items in which they are used. Of course, the assumption is that you have an outlet for these items; that is, daily luncheon specials or a special of the day.

The butchering test has converted the 103 rib into a 109 rib like the one purchased oven ready in the first cooking and carving yield test. This one is a little larger as it weighs 23.625 pounds or 23 pounds, 10 ounces. This costs out to $3.21 per pound. This is compared to the $3.43 paid for the 109 oven-ready rib. However, we must consider that you have to pay a skilled meat cutter and invest in additional equipment that will add to labor and overhead costs (see Table 4.10).

The cooked rib is carved to determine the yield of edible portions. After cooking and portioning, there is 14 pounds of servable product. The total cost is still $75.73, so the cost per servable pound is $5.41, which is less than the $6.21 of the 109 rib in the previous example. This would be the way to go if you had the skilled labor, space, equipment, and ability to sell the usable trim. If you use the trim in employee meals, it would reduce only your cost of providing employee meals.

You can now calculate the constant cost factors. The first is the cost factor per servable pound, which is the cost per servable pound divided by the as-purchased price per pound ($5.41/$2.75 = 1.967). This factor converts the AP price per pound into the cost per servable pound by multiplying it by the market price per pound ($2.75 × 1.967 = $5.41). The portion cost is calculated by dividing the cost per servable pound by the number of portions per pound; in this case $5.41/2 (8 oz) = $2.71.

Table 4.10 Comparison of Yields

	109 Oven-Ready Rib	103 Primal Rib
AP Price/lb	$3.43	$2.75
Oven Ready		
Cost Per/lb	$3.43	$3.20
% Servable Weight	55.25%	42.42%
Cost/Servable lb	$6.21	$5.41
Equivalent Market		
Cost	$81.12*	$75.73**

Cost saving of 103 rib is $5.39 plus the $15.02 of usable trim.

*23.65 lb @ $3.43

**23.65 lb @ $3.21

Special Note: Whenever there is usable trim, you cannot calculate the cost per servable pound by dividing the percentage of servable weight into the as-purchased price per pound. The reason is that the resulting cost does not take usable trim into account; it assumes all trim is waste. All other constant factors still apply.

You calculate the portion cost multiplier by dividing the cost factor per servable pound by the number of portions per pound, (1.967/2 = 0.9835). The portion cost multiplier converts the AP price per pound into the portion cost ($2.75 × 0.9835 = $2.71).

You can still use the **percentage of servable weight** (after cooking and carving loss) of the prime rib to determine the quantity or order. We are once again seeking 100-8 ounce portions so we need a total of 800 ounces. You divide the total portions needed weight by 42.42% and you will get 1886 ounces or 117.87 pounds. You can prove your calculations with 117.87 lb × 0.4242 = 50 lb. With two portions per pound, you would get 100 portions.

S teak Cutting Yield Test

An example using steaks instead of Prime rib will review all the yield calculations. As in any yield test, the less waste one has, the greater the yield and the smaller the difference between the as-purchased price per pound and the cost per servable pound. The only way waste can be recovered is by charging it to the cost of the salable cuts. If waste and trim are excessive, cost will be high and will be reflected in the menu prices charged.

As in the previous examples, the first step is to weigh out the usable trim, assign a market value, and then subtract it from the total AP price. In this case, the value of the 19 eight-ounce steaks is $22.96. See Table 4.11.

Since the 19 steaks weighed 9.75 pounds, divide the weight of the steaks into $22.96 to get the cost per servable pound, or $2.36. With two steaks per pound, the portion cost is $1.18 ($2.36/2). However, that is an average cost knowing that steaks may be over or undercut in successive yield tests. Therefore, the assumption is that they will even out over the long run and $1.18 per steak is a representative cost. In this yield test, the 19 steaks weighed 156 ounces, not 152 ounces. Therefore, the cost per steak was actually $1.21. In another yield test, 19 steaks may weigh only 149 ounces and would carry an actual cost less than $1.18. The more consistent we are in our purchase specifications and cutting efficiency, the smaller such variances will be.

You can now calculate the constant cost factors. The cost factor per servable pound is $2.36/$2.05 = 1.151. To convert any AP price per pound, multiply it by the cost factor, $2.05 × 1.151 = $2.36. The portion cost multiplier, which allows you to convert the AP price per pound directly to your portion cost, is 1.151/2 = 0.5756. Proof: .5756 × $2.05 = $1.18.

Once again, determine the amount to purchase by simply dividing the percent of servable weight of the steaks into the total portion weight needed. If we need 100-8 ounce steaks, you simply divide 800 ounces by .8298 (9.75 lbs/11.75 lbs) and you will get 964 ounces or 60.25 pounds. You can order 5 Top Butts if you specify that they all weigh between 12.25 and 12.5 lbs each.

Table 4.11 Steak Yield Test

Primal Cut: Top Sirloin Butt IMPS No. 184
Quality Grade: USDA Choice (upper half)
Yield Grade: 3
AP Weight: 11.75 lbs
AP Price: $2.05 lb
Total Cost: $24.09

	Yield	Market Value
Waste Trim	1.125 lbs	0
Stew Meat @ $1.29 lb	.875 lbs	$1.13
Steaks 19 @ 8 oz ea.	9.75 lbs	$22.96
Totals	11.75 lbs	$24.09

COST PER SERVABLE LB $24.09 − $1.13 = $22.96/9.75 lbs = $2.36/lb

Cost Per Steak @ 2 steaks per lb = $2.36/2 = $1.18

Cost Per Steak for 19 steaks = $22.96/19 = $1.21*

Portion Cost Multiplier 1.151/2 = .5755

Proof: AP Price/lb $2.05 × PMC .5755 = Cost Per Portion $1.18

Amount To Purchase for 100 8 oz steaks (800 oz)

Total Portion Weight/% of Servable Wgt 82.98% (9.75 lb/11.75 lb) 800 oz/.8298 = 964 oz or 60.25 lbs

Proof: 60.25 lbs × .8298 = 50 lbs = 100 8 oz steaks

*Note: The cost per steak based on the actual weight of the 19 steaks is slightly higher than the cost per steak based on the cost per servable pound divided by 2 portions per pound.

Reason for difference: 19 × 8 oz (avg) = 152 ounces

19 @ 9.75 × 16 = 156 ounces

The steaks are not all exactly 8 oz each. An additional four ounces was used.

Since our tests are based on standardized purchase specifications, recipes, and cutting procedures, we can assume these yields will represent actual yields on all like items in the future. So, with a card file of cost factors and your calculator, you can quickly and accurately determine portion costs and purchase quantities. When your menu is being updated, a quick check of market prices will tell you which items may need to be increased when you reprint the menu.

Buyers have the option of purchasing cuts of meat in different forms. They may purchase a rib that is oven ready and merely has to be placed in the oven and cooked, or they may elect to purchase the item fully cooked and processed, or do the butchering on a primal cut. The purveyor charges different prices at each stage of the processing. Buyers, therefore, must be able to calculate their servable yields so they can compare prices at different stages of product preparation.

On items with usable trim, you will also be able to develop yield factors that will allow you to estimate just how much trim you will get from any given 103 rib or 184 Top Sirloin Butt. In fact, your meat purveyor has set the cost factors so that the sales representatives can tell you how much it will cost you to have them cut the steaks for you. The price they quote factors in both the cost of the labor to cut the steaks and the usable trim and waste that results.

Costing a Deluxe Hamburger Platter

Yields need to be known for all food items, not just the entrée. Consider the ingredients and accompaniments that go into the common hamburger platter. The menu description says "A quarter pound of grilled lean ground sirloin, served on sesame seed bun, with lettuce, tomato, onion, and pickle accompanied by a side of french fries and cole slaw."

Let's look at the list of items and their respective AP costs.

Ground sirloin at $2.24/lb

Sesame bun at $.98 per dozen

Lettuce at $13 for a case of 24 heads

Tomato at $7.50 for a lug of 5 × 6 size

Onion at $8.50 for 50 lbs

Pickle at $4.50 gallon

French fries at $.50 lb

Homemade cole slaw consisting of shredded cabbage at $.40 lb, shredded carrots at $.59 lb, and dressing at $4.50 gallon

Condiments of mayonnaise, mustard, catsup

Costs based on repeated yield tests and allowance for waste are as follows:

Ground sirloin: $2.24/4 = *$.56* for a quarter pound pattie

Bun: $.98/12 = *$.09* (round up to next penny)

Lettuce: (yield 20 portions per head) $13/24 = $.55 head/20 = *$.03*

Tomato: $7.50/30 = $.25 each/5 portions per tomato = *$.05*

Onion: 50 lb yields 45 lb edible product. Cost per servable pound = $8.50/45 = $.19 lb; portion 2 oz = *$.03*

Pickle: $4.50/75 portions = *$.06*

$.50 lb 3 portions/lb = $.1666 per portion or 17¢

French fries: *$.20* ($.17 + $.03 for frying oil)

Cole slaw: Recipe for 10 pounds of slaw; 8 lb shredded cabbage at $.40 = $3.20; 1 lb shredded carrots at $.59; 1.5 cups of cole slaw dressing (1.5 cups = 12 ounces; 128 oz (1 gallon)/12 = 10.7 portions/gallon; $4.50/10.7 = $.42.

Total cost of 10-lb batch = $3.20 + $.59 + $.42 = $4.21 or $.43 lb, or *$.08* for 3 ounces.

Condiments: Catsup at $17.00 for 24/14 oz bottles = $.71 bottle, or $.05 oz = *$.10;* Mustard at $8.00 for 24 8-oz jars = $.34 jar, or $.04 oz = *$.04;* Mayonnaise at $3.50 gallon, or $.03 oz = *$.03.*

The cost of the ground sirloin patty, bun, lettuce, tomato, onion, pickle, fries, and slaw comes to $1.10. You need to add something for the condiments that will be used on the burger and fries. In this case we have assigned a cost of $.11 which bring the total cost of the hamburger platter to $1.21. The yields would basically stay the same on all items, and the only adjustment in cost would come from price increases on the ingredients. Yields on each item would be recorded for reference each time items containing them are placed on the menu. If a 1 ounce slice of American cheese were added and the cost was $1.76 per pound and each slice weighed one ounce, this would add an additional $.11 to the cost of the platter. Your menu price would reflect your cost plus the competitive price point for this item in your market.

When you have multiple locations all serving the same menu, it is necessary to have written specifications on how each menu item is to be prepared and plated. Consider the example shown in Figure 4.1 describing the Deluxe Hamburger.

While such instructions may seen elementary to an experienced short-order cook or chef, written standards are of value in the event of inquiries regarding the care and safety used in the preparation of food. The absence of such written standards could be construed to imply lack of management direction in the event of a health department inquiry. Photographs of properly plated food would typically accompany a written specification.

Prime Cost and Pre-Cut Products

Prime Cost is the sum of food cost and labor cost. If the food cost is 32% and labor cost is 34%, Prime Cost would be 66 percent. If the food cost for 10 lbs. of bulk carrots to be cut by your employee into sticks for crudités is $2.80 and the labor cost to cut them is $6.75, the Prime Cost would be $9.55! The labor can be more than the cost of the raw ingredients. Whenever there is direct labor involved in the scratch preparation of a menu item, you need to consider the labor cost and include that in the total cost of that menu item.

Our history has always been to closely monitor food cost so that when a purveyor gives us a price on processed food items, the as-purchased price per

Ingredients: 1 4 oz ground beef patty; 1 large sesame hamburger bun; shredded lettuce, 1 slice tomato, 1 slice onion, pickle, 5 oz French fries, 3 oz cole slaw.

Plate: 9" Round

Method:

1. Hamburger must be cooked to minimum of 165 degrees F or medium well stage. The grill should be set at 375 degrees. The cooking time is four minutes, or two minutes per side.
2. Lightly brush inside of hamburger bun with Koala Gold and place on grill to toast, approximately one minute.
3. Place bun on 9" round plate open faced with cooked hamburger patty on bun bottom. Place the lettuce, tomato, onion, and pickle chips on the bun top.
4. Place 3 oz soufflé cup of cole slaw on the left side of the plate.
5. Place the French fries on the right side of the plate.

Variations: If cheeseburger is ordered, place one slice of cheese on hamburger patty after one side has been cooked. Place burger cheese-side up on bun bottom. If grilled onions are requested, place them on top of hamburger patty.

FIGURE 4–1
Deluxe Hamburger Platter

pound is much higher than the same product purchased in bulk form. Chefs who looked primarily at food cost percentage would balk at purchasing pre-cut and value-added products because they cost more per pound than the unprocessed potatoes, onions, or cabbage. In addition, because they had an employee scheduled to perform these processing duties, if they purchased value-added products, the employee would not have anything to do. Subsequently, many of us have not considered pre-cut items because they appear initially to negatively impact our food cost percentage. However, in these days and times, labor has become more expensive than food and if you can reduce or eliminate labor cost, in the long run you will save money. Therefore, we need to move from food cost control to Prime Cost control. When you minimize Prime Cost, you maximize profit.

Today, many progressive-minded chefs and managers are beginning to integrate Prime Cost into their costing and pricing decisions on items that are "scratch prepared" in the restaurant. Using the steak example, assume that the restaurant cut all its steaks in house. When you purchase a primal cut like a No. 184 Top Sirloin Butt instead of pre-cut steaks, the as-purchased cost per pound will be lower. However, in order to process the primal cut into steaks, you will have to pay for the labor to cut the steaks. In addition, you have to find a use for the trim that is leftover and recover the cost of any waste that results, e.g., excess fat and gristle.

The National Restaurant Association claims that, for many restaurants, labor cost now exceeds food cost. This is a trend that will continue in the future as hourly wages and salaries increase. Food cost, typically running in a range of 35%–45% will eventually have to be lowered to a range of 25%–35% to offset the proportional increases in labor cost percentages. It is not uncommon today for a full-service, casual dining restaurant to have a food cost less than 30 percent.

As labor becomes more expensive, the only real place that full-service restaurants can cut costs is in the back-of-the-house. One way many chefs and kitchen managers are dealing with having to reduce their kitchen staffs is to purchase more pre-cut produce and other value-added products. (These items used to be referred to as "convenience foods" which to chefs meant canned or dry mix sauces or frozen portion-cut items. Pre-cut items have greater acceptability today as chefs and kitchen managers see that quality is not compromised by purchasing peeled potatoes, onions and garlic, carrot and celery sticks, shredded cabbage, eighth-cut fryer-broilers, portion cut fish and beef. Additional benefits include more consistency in portions and quality, fewer cuts and trips to the emergency room, elimination of waste and bi-products (for which they really did not have a use), easier and more accurate portion control, simplifying of purchasing, and even freeing up space in walk-ins and storerooms.

Yes, **pre-cut produce** does cost more than bulk produce, but it eliminates the need for you to have even a minimum wage worker in the kitchen to do these menial tasks. It is a waste of labor to have your skilled kitchen workers peeling garlic, slicing potatoes, and peeling onions. They did not go to culinary school to do this menial work. They take the processed ingredients and combine them into delicious entrées attractively presented.

Subsequently, today's chefs and kitchen managers need to look at the prime cost of each menu item, not just its raw food cost or gross profit. To demonstrate this important point, the example that follows shows how you need to look at pre-cut and value-added products when comparing them to identical scratch-prepared items.

In this example, assume you have one salad prep employee who is scheduled 40 hours per week and you pay this employee $9 per hour. (While that is their hourly rate for the purposes of determining their weekly pay, the actual hourly cost is more like $13.50 per hour when you add the costs of social security, meals, uniforms, workmen's compensation insurance, unemployment insurance, and other benefits.) This amounts to $108 per day ($13.50 x 40 hrs = $\dfrac{\$540}{5\ \text{days}}$ = $108). Further assume that they perform the tasks shown in Table 4.12.

There are five steps you can follow to implement a Prime Cost Reduction Plan in your restaurant.

1. Choose a production job that is labor intensive
2. Allocate work hours to the task

Table 4.12   Employee Tasks and Times

Task	Time Allocation
Prep 2 cases of salad greens	1 hour
Shred 50# of cabbage for cole slaw	.5 hour
Prepare 20 lbs of carrot and celery sticks	1 hour
Peel and cut 100 lbs of potatoes	1.5 hours
Slice 1 case each zucchini and mushrooms	1 hour
Peel and cut 50 lbs onions	1 hour
Peel 2 lbs of garlic	.5 hour
Core and slice 40 lbs tomatoes	1 hour
Total Productive Hours	7.5 hours*

*Achieving a full eight hours of productive labor is not realistic. Generally, if you can average 75% you are doing better than average. Employees are not machines and cannot go full speed the entire day. Subsequently, this output is more than the average that could be produced in a day. Your labor cost would be for the full eight hours and that is what is used in this example.

3. Substitute processed or pre-cut products to eliminate the job or shift

4. Validate the proposed prime cost reduction

5. Use labor turnover as an opportunity for implementation

A PRACTICAL EXAMPLE

Table 4.12 shows the tasks performed by the employee during the eight hour day. As previously stated, this output may be more than a single employee can produce in a single shift.

The total of $169.99 shown in Table 4.13, represents the raw food cost of the ingredients purchased to yield the quantities listed. It does not include the cost of the labor needed to prepare these items. The prime cost of preparing these items from scratch in-house amounts to $277.99 ($169.99 + $108). When the labor factor is added to each item, the prime cost can be calculated for each respective produce item.

In Table 4.14 the costs are listed for the equivalent quantities of pre-cut produce adjusted to equal the yield produced from bulk product. You will note that the cost of the labor exceeds the raw food cost on the carrots, celery, and garlic and is over 40% of cost on potatoes and onions. These are items that should be targeted to be purchased in pre-cut form. Table 4.15 shows the cost to the operation when the equivalent quantities of product produced in Table 4.14 are purchased pre-cut from a supplier. The cost of the equivalent quantities produced in Table 4.13 would be $400.59. This represents an increase in food cost of $230.60 per day with the assumption that the quantities

Table 4.13   Cost and Yield of Bulk Produce Processed in House

Commodity	Yield %*	As-Purchased Price	Cost Per Servable lb	Total Food Cost
1 case iceberg lettuce	73%	$16.95/24 heads ($.71 ea) 30 lbs or $.57/lb	$.97 ea 21.9 lbs or $.77 lb	$16.95
½ case romaine	75%	$35.90/24 heads ($1.50 ea) 30 lbs or $1.20 lb	$2.00 ea 22.5 lbs or $1.60 lb	$17.95
¼ case curly endive	81%	$16.75/24 heads ($.70 ea) 30 lbs or $.56 lb	$.87 ea 24.3 lbs or $.69/lb	$4.19
50 lbs green cabbage	80%	$.25/lb	$.32 lb Yield 40 lbs	$12.50
10 lbs carrots	81%	$.28/lb	$.35 lb Yield 8 lbs	$2.80
10 lbs celery	69%	$16.75/36 $.42 lb 40 lbs	$.47 ea $.61 lb (6.9 lbs) Yield 27.6 lbs	$3.25
100 lbs potatoes	78%	$.25/lb	$.32 lb Yield 78 lbs	$25.00
1 case zucchini	94%	$14.50/20 lbs	$.78 lb Yield 18.8 lbs	$14.50
1 case mushrooms	94%	$14.50/10 lbs	$1.55 lb Yield 9.4 lbs	$14.50
50 lbs yellow onions	91%	$20.25	$.45 lb Yield 45.5 lbs	$20.25
2 lbs garlic	88%	$1.30/lb	$1.48 lb Yield 1.7 lbs	$2.60
40 lbs tomatoes	80%	$35.50/40 lbs	$1.11 lb Yield 32 lbs	$35.50
Total Raw Food Cost				$169.99

*Yields are taken from *The Book of Yields*, 4th Edition, 1998, Chef Desk Publishers, Sonora, CA.

Table 4.14 Cost of Pre-Cut Equivalent Items

Commodity	Food Cost	"Total" Labor Cost*	Prime Cost
Iceberg lettuce	$16.95 or $.77 lb	NA	NA
Romaine	$17.95 or $1.37 lb	NA	NA
Curly endive	$4.19 or $.74 lb	$13.50**	$52.59***
Green cabbage	$12.50 or $.32 lb	$6.75	$19.25
Carrots	$2.80 or $.35 lb	$6.75	$9.55
Celery	$3.25 or $.61 lb	$6.75	$10.00
Russet potatoes	$25 or $.32 lb	$20.25	$45.25
Zucchini	$14.50 or $.78 lb	$6.75	$21.25
Mushrooms	$14.50 or $1.55 lb	$6.75	$21.25
Yellow onions	$20.25 or $.45 lb	$13.50	$33.75
Garlic	$2.60 or $1.48	$6.75	$9.35
Tomatoes	$35.40 or $1.11 lb	$13.50	$48.90
Total prime cost	$169.99	$108****	$277.99

*Labor cost is calculated as the hourly rate equivalent of all costs of employing the scheduled worker, so the hourly rate would be computed at $13.50 ($540/40 hrs).

**Includes labor for all first three ingredients.

***Cost of salad mix consisting of three lettuces.

****Total of column will actually be less than figure shown because not a full eight hours was assigned to tasks.

Table 4.15 Daily Cost of Pre-Cut Produce

Item	AP Price/lb	Quantity (lbs)	Extension
Salad Green Mix	$ .94	68.7	$64.58
Shredded Cabbage	$ .78	40	$31.20
Carrot Sticks	$1.09	8	$8.72
Celery Sticks	$1.44	6.9	$9.94
Peeled Russet Potatoes	$1.01	78	$78.78
Zucchini Moons	$3.05	18.8	$57.34
Sliced Mushrooms	$1.50	9.4	$14.10
Peeled Yellow Onions	$1.16	45.5	$52.78
Peeled Garlic	$1.85	1.7	$3.15
Sliced Tomatoes	$2.50	32	$80.00
Total			$400.59

represent average daily requirements ($400.59 − $169.99). However, remember, if you purchase the pre-cut produce it allows you to eliminate one salad-prep worker per day and reduce you labor cost by $756 over the seven day week ($108 × 7 days).

This results in an increase in prime cost of $125 per day to use the pre-cut produce versus doing it in-house. Based on these calculations, the use of pre-cut produce does not result in lowering prime cost. However, pre-cut produce is still being test marketed and purveyors of pre-cut produce are lowering their markup and starting to use "price points" that demonstrate greater value to encourage chefs and kitchen managers to consider greater use of pre-cut products. In this example, costs used were representative of actual costs of both food items and labor.

The chef or kitchen manager will need to assess whether the convenience of having pre-cut is worth the extra cost. There are some apparent good values in pre-cut where the scratch labor represents a cost greater than 50 percent of the price to purchase the item pre-cut, for example, as it is with carrot and celery sticks, onions, garlic, and potatoes. These are items that should be purchased pre-cut because they will result in a savings over scratch preparation. Pre-cut foods are practical when large quantities must be processed in short periods of times where labor and space limitations exist. Other benefits of pre-cut foods that contribute to making them a value, in spite of their higher as purchase costs per pound are:

- Pre-cuts have no trim waste
- Pre-cut quality is more consistent than with scratch preparation
- Pre-cut costs are more consistent than costs for bulk ingredients
- Pre-cuts take up less storage space than bulk ingredients
- Pre-cuts allow for accurate portioning and recipe costing
- Pre-cut foods never call in sick
- Pre-cut foods never claim workmen's compensation benefits
- Pre-cut foods do not file for unemployment benefits
- Pre-cut foods do not require uniforms
- Pre-cut foods do not need benefits like insurance, paid vacation, or meals
- Pre-cut foods do not steal or break things
- Scheduling pre-cut foods is at management's complete discretion

In summary, as long as the cost of labor continues to increase restaurants will be looking for ways to reduce their dependence on labor. The kitchen remains the one area where management will continue to seek efficiencies in food preparation. Subsequently, the use of processed foods is likely to increase in the future. This will move management's attention away from separating food and labor costs and will result in focusing on both—the prime cost. They will seek to lower prime cost and pre-cut processed foods will be valuable toward that end.

 ## ey Concepts

- When there is trim loss or cooking loss in the processing of ingredients, the edible portion cost per unit will always be greater than the as-purchased (AP) cost per unit.
- Rarely will you get a 100% yield from scratch prepared items; therefore, final portion costs must include an allowance for unavoidable waste.
- The decision to use or not use convenience products like pre-cut produce should not be made entirely on the basis of food cost. You need to consider that you are able to save on labor when you use convenience foods.
- When you are comparing pre-cut produce costs to bulk produce costs, you need to add your cost of the labor to process the produce in-house.

 ## ey Terms

As-Purchased Weight	Yield Factors	Cost Per Servable
Edible Portion Weight	Convenience Food	Pound
Waste	Plate Cost	Portion Cost Multiplier
Usable Trim	Cooking from Scratch	Portion Divider
Yield	Yield Tests	Percentage of Serv-
Standard Yield	Pre-preparation	able Weight
Standard Portion	(rough preparation)	Pre-Cut Produce

 ## iscussion Questions

1. Discuss the pros and cons of using pre-cut produce versus scratch cut produce in a kitchen. What are the factors that a chef will use in his or her decision to purchase pre-cut produce or prepare it in-house.
2. What assumptions allow us to say that the yield factors we have calculated today on items like the Prime rib and steaks, are accurate and consistent over time?

3. Discuss the importance of costing out all menu items made from scratch.

4. How can you use product yields in your purchasing decisions?

Problem 1

Recipe Conversion

You are to first compute the conversion factor and expand or reduce the recipe as called for in the example. Use proper abbreviations for amounts used in recipe, e.g., cups = C, Tablespoon = T, Teaspoon = t, Pounds = lbs or #, etc.

1. Convert 50 8-oz portions to 150 8-oz portions of Curried Lamb. *You will need to convert expanded quantities to the largest whole measure, e.g., if you go from 1 Tablespoon to 8 Tablespoons, the correct amount should be ½ cup because 8 T = ½ cup.*

2. Conversion factor _____ (show calculations)

3. Compute the cost of the recipe and cost per portion

Ingredients	Amount for 50	Amount for 150	Cost Extension
Lamb Shoulder, boneless, 1" cubes	18 lbs		
Water	2½ gallons		
Unsalted Butter	2 lbs		
Curry Powder	1/3 cup		
Granny Smith Apples, diced	2 quarts		
Vidalia Onions, diced	2 lbs		
Ground Cloves	½ teaspoon		
Bay Leaves	2 each		
Marjoram	1 teaspoon		
All Purpose Flour	1½ lbs		
Sea Salt	1 Tablespoon		
Ground Black Pepper	½ Tablespoon		
Total Cost			
Cost Per Portion			

Problem 2

1. Convert 100 8-oz portions down to 60 7-oz portions of Hungarian Goulash. *Convert required quantities to largest unit of measure as explained in previous example.* **Note: In this example, the portion sizes are different. This will require an extra calculation to determine the conversion factor.**

2. Conversion factor _____ (show calculations)

3. Compute the cost of the recipe and the cost per portion.

Ingredients	Amount for 100 8-oz	Amount for 60 7-oz	Cost Extension
Beef Chuck, 1´ cubes	36 lbs		
Minced Garlic	1 ¼ ounces		
All Purpose Flour	1 lb 4 ounces		
Chili Powder	1 ½ Tablespoons		
Spanish Paprika	10 ounces		
Tomato Puree	1 quart		
Brown Stock	2 Gallons		
Bay Leaves	4 each		
Caraway Seeds	2 Teaspoons		
Spanish Onions, minced	3 lbs 8 ounces		
Kosher Salt	1 Tablespoon		
Black Peppercorn	1 Teaspoon		
Total Cost			
Cost Per Portion			

Table of approximate weights of dry items by volume units. To be used to cost out recipes conversion homework.

Food Product	Tbsp.	Cup	Pt.	Qt.	Price/Unit
Lamb Shoulder	N/A				$ 2.87/lb
Beef Chuck	N/A				$ 2.25/lb
Unsalted Butter	½ oz	8 oz			$ 1.99/lb
Curry Powder	¼ oz	4 oz			$11.83/lb
Apples, diced	N/A	6 oz	12 oz	24 oz	$ 2.12/lb
Onions, diced/minced	¼ oz	4 oz	8 oz	1 lb	$ .69/lb
Ground Cloves	¼ oz	4 oz			$18.72/lb
Bay Leaves	N/A				$14.05/10 oz 130 count
Marjoram	$\frac{1}{8}$ oz	2 oz			$ 8.49/12 oz
Flour	¼ oz	4 oz			$ .25/lb
Kosher Salt	$\frac{1}{3}$ oz	5.25 oz			$ .65/lb
Pepper, ground	¼ oz	4 oz			$11.15/lb
Pepper, whole	¼ oz	4 oz			$12.68/18 oz
Garlic, minced	¼ oz	4 oz			$ 2.23/lb
Chili Powder	¼ oz	4 oz			$ 9.83/18 oz
Paprika	¼ oz	4 oz			$ 5.71/lb

Food Product	Tbsp.	Cup	Pt.	Qt.	Price/Unit
Tomato Puree					$ 2.86/#10 can
Brown Stock					$ 1.46/gallon
Caraway Seeds	¼ oz	4 oz			$21.20/lb
Sea Salt	$\frac{1}{8}$ oz	2 oz			$ 3.59/lb
Mushrooms	NA	8 oz	1 lb	2 lbs	$ 1.99/lb
Beef Tenderloin	NA				$ 8.95/lb
Wine					$ 8.95/750 mL
Mustard					$ 2.40/gal
Espagnole Sauce					$ 3.00/gal
Cream					$ 4.56/$\frac{1}{2}$ gal

Problem 3
Costing a Deluxe Hamburger Platter

Ingredient	AP Price	Portion	Portion Cost
Ground Sirloin Patty	$ 2.50 lb	4 oz	_____
Hamburger Buns	$ 1.80 dz	1 each	_____
Lettuce	$ .60 hd	20 portions/hd	_____
Tomato	$10.50/30	5 portions/tomato	_____
Onion	$ 9.00/50 lbs	90% yield/2 oz portion	_____
Pickle	$ 5.00 gal	75 portions/gal	_____
French Fries	$ .60 lb	3 portions/lb	_____
Total			_____
Cole Slaw			
Cabbage	$ .50 lb	8 lbs	_____
Shredded Carrots	$ .69 lb	1 lb	_____
Slaw Dressing	$5.00 gal	12 oz	_____
Total		10 lbs	_____
Cost Per Portion of Slaw		3 oz	_____
Condiments			
Catsup	$18/24-14 oz	1 oz	_____
Mustard	$9/24-8 oz	1 oz	_____
Mayonnaise	$4.50 gal	1 oz	_____
Total			_____

Total Cost of Hamburger Platter _____

If American Cheese is $2.99 lb and a one ounce slice is the serving size, how much will need to be added to the above cost?

Problem 4: (without usable trim)

> Primal Cut: Oven Ready Rib IMPS 109
> Quality Grade: Choice (upper half of grade)
> Yield Grade: 3
> AP Weight: 23.375 lbs
> AP Price/lb: $3.24
> Cooking Shrinkage: 2.1875 lbs
> Carving Loss: 4.25 lbs
> Serving Portion Size: 14 ozs

Determine the following, showing all formulas and calculations:

1. Servable weight
2. Percentages for:
   Servable Weight %
   Cooking Loss %
   Carving Loss %
3. Cost per servable pound
4. Cost factor per servable pound
5. Portions per lb
6. Cost per portion
7. Portion cost multiplier for 14-oz cut
8. Quantity to order for 125 14-oz portions

Problem 5: (with usable trim)

> Primal Cut: Boneless Strip Loin, Short Cut #174
> Grade: USDA Select (upper half of grade)
> Yield Grade: 3
> AP Weight: 12.25 lbs
> AP Price/lb: $2.90
> Waste and Trim: 1 lb 5 oz or 1.3125 lbs
> Stew Meat 4 oz @ $1.38/lb
> Luncheon Steak: 5 oz @ $3.50/lb
> Strip Steaks: 18 @ 9 oz, total weight 10 lbs 2 oz

Determine the following showing all formulas and calculations:

1. Cost of the steaks
2. Cost per servable pound
3. Cost per steak based on 9 oz
4. Cost per steak based on actual cutting yield
5. Cost factor per servable pound
6. Percentage of servable yield
7. Portion cost multiplier for 9 oz steak
8. Quantity needed for 100 9 oz steaks

Problem 6

Recipe Costing

Using the templates provided, cost out the following recipes and then determine the cost of the entire meal by portions. Assume 20 portions per recipe. Purchase prices are given and you will need to determine the cost of the recipe quantity.

Menu Item: New England Clam Chowder   Portion Size: 6 oz

Ingredients	Purchase Unit	Price/Unit	Recipe Quantity	Recipe Cost
Chopped Clams	4 oz can	$1.20/can	32 oz	
Water	NA	NA	24 oz	
Smoked Bacon	Lb	$3.95 lb	5 oz	
Diced Onion	Lb	$.79 lb	½ lb	
Corn Starch	Cup	$.25	¼ cup	
Red Potatoes	Lb	$.79 lb	1 lb	
Whole Milk	Gal	$2.25 gal	40 oz	
Heavy Cream	Pint	$2.25 pint	4 oz	
Kosher Salt	Cup	$.50 cup	1 T	
White Pepper	Cup	$4.64 cup	1 t	

Menu Item: 4 Bean Salad   Portion Size: 3 oz

Ingredients	Purchase Unit	Price/Unit	Recipe Quantity	Recipe Cost
Cut Green Beans	8 oz can	$.89 can	2 cups	
Red Kidney Beans	8 oz can	$.79 can	2 cups	
Garbonza Beans	8 oz can	$.69 can	2 cups	
Yellow Wax Beans	8 oz can	$.59 can	2 cups	
Onion	Lb	$.79 lb	4 oz	
Green Pepper	Lb	$.89 lb	6 oz	
Vegetable Oil	Gal	$3.90	1 cup	
White Vinegar	Gal	$3.06	½ cup	
Wine Vinegar	Gal	$4.60	½ cup	
Sugar	Lb	$.60 lb	4 oz	
Kosher Salt	Lb	$.50 cup	1 T	
White Pepper	Cup	$4.64 cup	1 t	

Menu Item: Chicken Tenders   Portion Size: 6 oz

Ingredients	Purchase Unit	Price/Unit	Recipe Quantity	Recipe Cost
Chicken Tenders	Lbs	$5 lb	5 lbs	
Buttermilk	Quart	$1.45 qt	1 quart	
All Purpose Flour	Cup	$.07	3 cups	
Kosher Salt	Lbs	$.50 cup	1 t	
White Pepper	Cup	$4.64	½ t	
Granulated Onion	Cup	$2.50 cup	½ t	
Granulated Garlic	Cup	$2.50 cup	½ t	
Vegetable Shortening	Lbs	$.50 lb	5 lbs	
Mayonnaise	Gal	$6.10 gal	2 cups	
Yellow Mustard	Gal	$2.35 gal	½ cup	
Honey	Quart	$7.84 qt	½ cup	

Menu Item: Sugar Cookie Tart   Portion Size: ⅒ Cookie

Ingredients	Purchase Unit	Price/Unit	Recipe Quantity	Recipe Cost
Pillsbury Sugar Cookie Dough	12 oz Pkg	$2.25 pkg	2 pkgs	
Cream Cheese	3 oz Pkg	$.59 pkg	2 pkgs	
Sugar	Lb	$.60	2 oz	
Vanilla	Cup	$5.45 cup	2 t	
Kiwi	Each	$.79 ea	2 each	
Strawberries	1 Pint	$2.75 pint	1 pint	
Bananas	Each	$.35 ea	2 each	
Blueberries	Pint	$3.65 pint	1 pint	
Apricot Preserves	8 oz Jar	$1.25 jar	1 jar	

Weights and Measure U.S. Customary Units and Metric System Equivalents

1/8 teaspoon = dash

1 teaspoon = 1/3 Tablespoon or 60 drops

3 teaspoons = 1 Tablespoon or ½ fluid ounce

2 Tablespoons = 1 fluid ounce

4 Tablespoons = 2 fluid ounces or ¼ cup

16 Tablespoons = 1 cup or 8 fluid ounces

1 cup = 8 fluid ounces

1 pint = 2 cups or 16 fluid ounces

2 pints = 1 quart or 32 fluid ounces or four cups

2 quarts = 64 fluid ounces or 8 cups or 4 pints

1 gallon = 128 fluid ounces or 4 quarts or 8 pints or 16 cups

1 teaspoon = 4.93 milliliters

1 Tablespoon = 14.79 milliliters

1 cup = 326.59 milliliters

1 pint = 473.18 milliliters

1 quart = 946.36 milliliters

1 gram = 1/30 oz

1 liter =

1 quart = 95% of 1 litre or 30 ounces

1 ounce (weight) = 28.35 grams

8 ounces or ½ lb = 226.8 grams

1 pound = 453.6 grams

2 lbs 3 oz = 1 kilogram or 1000 grams

Conversion Formulas

# of ounces *times 28* = # of grams

# of grams *divided by 28* = # of ounces

Teaspoons *times 5* = milliliters

Tablespoons *times 15* = milliliters

Fluid ounces *times 30* = milliliters

Fluid ounces *times .03* = liters

Cups *times .25* = liters

Pints *times .47* = liters

Quarts *times .95* = liters

Ounces (weight) *times 28* = grams

Pounds *times .45* = kilograms

Milliliters *times .04* = teaspoons

Milliliters *times .07* = Tablespoons

Milliliters *times .03* = fluid ounces

Liters *times 30* = fluid ounces

Liters *times 4.2* = cups

Liters *times 2.1* = pints

Liters *times 1.06* = quarts

Liters *times .026* = gallons

Grams *times .035* = ounces

Kilograms *times 2.2* = pounds

To convert Celsius to Fahrenheit multiply by 1.8 and then add 32

Example: 176.5 degrees Celsius times 1.8 = 317.7 + 32 = 349.7 or 350 degrees F.

To convert Fahrenheit to Celsius subtract 32 then multiply by .555

Example: 350 degrees F minus 32 = 318 times .555 = 176.5 C

5

Menu Sales Mix Analysis

FUNDAMENTAL PRINCIPLES OF MENU DESIGN

1. The menu is the starting point for all restaurant planning and design.
2. The menu is more that just a list of items your kitchen prepares.
3. The menu is your most important internal marketing tool.
4. The menu communicates your restaurant's personality to the public.
5. Give your menu design and production the same time, effort, and budget you give to any major capital investment decision.
6. Cost/Margin analysis helps pinpoint menu designing, pricing, and packaging decisions.
7. The techniques of menu psychology can make things easier for the operator.
8. The menu format impacts the area of sales concentration.
9. The menu design impacts the average check and the gross profit return on each sale.
10. Key components of menu design are the texture, color, and weight of the paper; the type font; and the ink color.

The frequency of additions and deletions from restaurant menus is increasing rather than slowing down. Menu changes at casual theme restaurants and family restaurants are taking place at several times a year where in the past, the menu remained static all year long. If you have eaten at a Chili's or Applebee's, you have seen how they have introduced new menu items every 90 days. This is occurring because the public demands it. Menu revisions must occur to replace slow selling items that have fallen out of favor with the dining public with new trendy dishes being offered by competitors. They are finding that they cannot just offer the traditional steak, salad, and potato or the typical "coffee shop food" of country breakfasts and pancakes. While such items are perennial favorites and will continue to be offered, they have to introduce new items to attract repeat and new customers. In addition, many traditionally static menus are being augmented with ethnic, fusion and seasonal items.

Keep in mind that increasing menu offerings and making frequent changes in menu selections impacts both the customer and the operation. Introducing new menu items will impact everything from ordering and inventory to the equipment and skills of the kitchen staff. The preparation of ingredients prior to cooking for service may change significantly and thereby impact labor costs. This is all the more reason to have an effective and easy way to monitor your menu sales mix. **Menu sales mix** analysis is not done solely to determine the popularity of menu items. It also tracks food costs and gross profits. Foodservice operators in all segments of the market will discover that customers are scrutinizing their menus and if they cannot find at least four or five items they like, they may view the selections as too limited for their tastes.

Your menu is the first and foremost cost control and marketing tool in your operations' arsenal. The menu should come before you hire and train you employees, before your servers' suggestive selling efforts, and before your POS system captures sales analysis data. If you accept the premise that your menu is the number one component of your restaurant's strategic plan, you will plan and design it with the same care and attention given to a major capital expenditure.

We are continually astonished by the number of fine restaurants that have designed menus that do not do justice to the investment, talent, and professionalism of the owner, chef, and management. We are referring to the physical menu, e.g., its appearance, size, configuration, construction, layout, color and overall appearance. This is especially surprising where the owner has spared no expense in the dining room décor or kitchen design. Owners spend many weeks deciding on china patterns, linens, silverware, glassware, and tabletop accessories because they know the importance of table and plate presentation. The menu design should be given the same budget and attention as the table settings. Consider that your menu is your restaurant's calling card. (*Early menus were actually referred to as "menu cards."*) It is the most important internal marketing tool you have to influence which items are selected by your guests. The menu impacts everything from the average amount spent by each guest to the flow of product and personnel in the kitchen and dining room. The menu drives profit and cash flow by calling the guests' attention to certain sections of the menu and to specific menu items much in the same way department store counter displays entice shoppers to pause and inspect a particular garment or accessory. The theory is that if they stop to look, you have increased the odds that the item will be ordered. There is zero chance of purchase if they never noticed the item in the first place.

The menu design should be congruent with the image of the restaurant and the expectation of the guest of the overall dining experience. The menu design not only has to fit the experience, it has to be of a size that is comfortable for the guest to handle, and should fit the given size of the table, the place setting, and the table accessories. In other words, it cannot be too big or too small. The menu design should reflect the philosophy of the owner or chef. This can be portrayed with a menu that is printed on recycled paper, uses no artificial dyes, and is tied with a twig or raffia as opposed to being printed on synthetic paper or laminated and stapled.

A menu needs to be comprised of more than just paper and printed words. It needs illustrations and graphics to break up the monotony of the printed page. The layout and the content needs to be easy to read and interpret. This is where a graphic artist can turn your menu into a merchandising and communication tool that will make your menu more than a mere list of food offerings. Money spent on menu design is money well spent because it will pay you well to have a menu that is a consistent and effective marketing tool day in and day out.

Yet, the menu, often times, is the last thing management does prior to opening the restaurant to the pubic. We will concede that there are many successful restaurants with menus that fall short of what we would consider worthy of the professional staff that owns and manages them. A poorly designed menu in a upscale, full service restaurant is analogous to having the maître d'hotel in a tuxedo but wearing a pair of running shoes. If the restaurant is a success, the menu, no matter how it is designed and produced, will be assumed to be effective, albeit by default. This is the only reason we can think of as to why some highly acclaimed restaurants have menus that are poor calling cards for what the customer ultimately receives when they dine there.

Many menus are mere *lists* of what the restaurant has to sell. The way it is designed and printed fails miserably in enticing the guest to purchase items the restaurant prepares best and that return the highest profits. The only way to guide purchases is by designing the menu to have certain items jump out and get the attention of the guest. You need to realize that restaurant guests do not *read* menus like they read a book or newspaper. They do not necessarily start in the upper left corner and read until they come to the last page of the menu. Guests scan menus and therefore are more likely to notice (and stop to read) something that catches their eye. This may be a graphic box, a section with larger or bolder type, or an illustration or dot matrix color screen surrounding menu copy.

We use such techniques to feature items the restaurant does best and wants to sell more than others. The reasons may be that these items help improve the average check, have low food costs or high gross profits, or are easy to prepare and serve. Even with evidence that this strategy in menu design works, many operators will still use menus that are lacking in the elements of effective menu design.

The point we are making is this; the menu design *validates* the restaurant's expertise and professionalism. The entire process of menu design is not expensive. If all you have been doing is providing your printer with a list of your menu items and allowing the printer to lay it out and select the color, paper and size, your menu is not an effective cost control, marketing, and communication tool. Any menu, regardless of its design, will produce a predictable menu sales mix when used over an extended period of time. Consider how much there is to gain from a menu designed to feature the items your restaurant does best and wants to sell! As a manager, it is much easier to order food and determine preparation quantities when you can predict with accuracy the number of orders of each item you are going to sell that day.

The costs of designing and printing a menu must be separated into *fixed costs* and *variable costs*. *Fixed costs* include the paper, cover, typesetting, and the actual printing. If the menu is to be laminated, that would be another fixed cost. Fixed costs are inherent to any menu production regardless of whether it is printed in-house or by a printer or menu designer. Under *variable costs* in menu design are what are referred to as *creative aspects* that make your menu unique and special. Custom art and graphics are usually one time costs that, when amortized over several printings of the same menu, amount to only a few dollars per menu.

The Restaurant Concept, Location, and Menu

The menu is the starting point of all planning and design for a foodservice operation. If you have a specific operational or menu concept in mind, the location must be selected with care to be sure customer traffic will support the concept. Granted, destination restaurants will draw customers from more distant points than family and fast-food operations, but the fact remains that a major part of the success of the restaurant will rest upon its location. You may design a wonderful menu in terms of offerings, ingredients, and preparation methods and still not be financially successful if the restaurant is not in the right location.

On the other hand, if you have a specific location in mind to build a restaurant, you need to be very flexible on the restaurant concept and menu. If the location and customer traffic favor a family restaurant or cafeteria, a white tablecloth operation with a fresh seafood menu may not be successful. The rule therefore is, if you have a specific concept and menu in mind, you must be flexible on the location. If you have already picked out the location, you must be flexible on the concept and menu.

The Menu Determines Equipment Needs

Once the concept has been determined, the equipment selection and kitchen space requirements are specifically designed around the menu. The kitchen of a foodservice establishment is designed after the menu has been written and the recipes determined for all items. Once the kitchen is installed, the equipment becomes a limiting factor in future menu decisions. The kitchen equipment package and layout will impact what the operation can prepare. Certain kitchens are more flexible than others and can adapt quickly to menu changes. However, in the highly specialized fast-food industry with limited menus and equipment packages, the addition of new menu items is difficult. Space has been reduced to a minimum, and new pieces of equipment are difficult or impossible to add without major renovation.

There is no universal equipment package that can be suggested by foodservice consultants unless they see a menu complete with recipes and forecasted volumes of product that will need to be prepared within specified time periods. However, certain "essential" pieces of equipment are likely to be found in just about any foodservice operation, such as refrigerators, ice machines, work tables, dishwasher and dish tables, open top ranges, and deck ovens. However, the real challenge is to make the right decision concerning what size (capacity) and how many of each piece of equipment are needed.

The selection of specific pieces of equipment requires knowledge of the type of equipment best used for the job to be done. In selecting a piece of equipment to cook steak, for example, you have to choose among charbroilers, infrared broilers, quartz broilers, whether the heat source is above or below the cooking grates, and whether it is gas or electric. Once this decision is reached, the selection of a manufacturer and model must be made from an extensive list. There are approximately 24 different manufacturers that produce broilers and, to complicate the decision even further, they will probably show you several models with various options and features. In short, a broiler is not just a broiler, and you will find that to be the case with deep fryers, griddles, and even reach-in refrigerators.

Another consideration is the size or capacity of the equipment. Deep fryers, for example, are available from 7.5-pound fat capacity up to hundreds of pounds. The size and capacity of a fryer needed by a small neighborhood bar selling breaded mushrooms as snacks is considerably different from that of a high-volume seafood or chicken restaurant. Consider the "downtime" that all equipment eventually requires for maintenance and repair. You can still "limp" along with one of two ovens, but business may come to a standstill if your single piece breaks down in the middle of the dinner rush.

Since you will have a choice of several manufacturers for the equipment, the one you select will be determined by considerations other than price. Reliability, reputation, and service record are more important than just the lowest price when it comes to commercial cooking equipment. Shop for the lowest price only after you have determined the best equipment for your menu needs. If you are unable to conduct such a study on your own, seek out information from local equipment distributors. Many have kitchen design consultants who can help you write your equipment specifications.

Such decisions cannot be made without a detailed chart or spreadsheet that "tracks" each menu item from the delivery of ingredients to final warewashing and storage of flatware and kitchen utensils. The correct number and size of kitchen equipment, utensils, pots and pans, china, glassware, and silver cannot be accurately determined by simple rules of thumb. You will find that someone has tried to simplify the selection of such based on the number of seats, beds, meal periods, or even the total number of patrons to be fed. Rest assured that they will not be accurate for all applications.

In order to determine the optimum number and capacities for each piece of equipment, utensil, and storage area, such intervening variables as the state of the raw ingredients upon delivery, storage temperature required, delivery frequencies from distributors, product perishability, preparation methods, product service presentation, and even final warewashing must be examined. You must start with the detailed recipes and service specifications for each item on the menu. Therefore, the menu planning team needs to consist of food production and dining room service representatives.

What you must ultimately do is visualize the delivery, storage processing, preparation for service, presentation to the guest—tabletop arrangement included—and the warewashing of all pots, pans, utensils, and flatware. You cannot do this without being familiar with the preparation and service of the food items. This requires consultation with the food and beverage manager, chef, maître d', and equipment distributor. This is too important a task to be left for rules of thumb.

The menu preparation methods determine the type of equipment needed. The quantities prepared of each item determine the size or capacity of the equipment, and the peak production demands will influence the number of pieces and specific sizes needed. In addition, budget and space restraints will further limit your choices. Rarely does one have an unlimited budget and complete flexibility in selecting and arranging kitchen equipment. Plumbing, ventilation, and building codes will restrict placement in many situations, particularly when you are occupying a leased building or one that has already been wired, plumbed, and vented.

This equipment planning process can be better understood if you contemplate the following. Each of us has some food item we like to prepare. For those who have a tough time combining dry cereal and milk, seeking the counsel of your mother or grandmother will be required. However, for those who are "kitchen crusaders" and are at home with fresh ingredients and sharp knives, this will be a simple exercise. Remember, if you have never made the dish, you will not be able to "visualize" the preparation from start to finish.

Assume you are asked by friends who are planning a party to cook the main course at their apartment or home. You will be required to bring all the necessary pots, pans, and utensils. You want to be sure that the kitchen you are going to use is equipped with the essentials such as sinks, refrigeration, ovens, and range top so you will start by assuming that you have nothing with which to work. This is what it is like when you are planning a new kitchen from the ground up. Unless you specify it in your list of equipment, you will not have it available.

Whether your specialty is Texas-style chili with beans, lasagna, chicken Divan, or Chinese sweet and sour pork, you will need to be as specific as you can in stating quantities of ingredients and preparation methods. For example, one "scoop" of mashed potatoes is too vague. Instead, state no. 12 scoop, 4-ounce ladle with 9-inch handle, 4-1/2 inch flexible spatula, 5-quart saucepan.

In a foodservice operation, this exercise would be conducted for every appetizer, entree, side dish, vegetable, and dessert and repeated for each meal period. Once all the recipes have been written, the results are then converted to an equipment matrix or spreadsheet. See Figure 5–1.

You must go through this process mentally, and then on paper, to determine quantities and sizes of pots and pans, refrigeration, and freezer space as well as the number of burners on a range top or wells in a steam table. The planning process considers even auxiliary equipment such as scales, trash receptacles, can openers, cutting boards, dollies, and heat lamps. The more detail, the better the matrix.

From the matrix you begin to prepare the item specifications in advance of obtaining price quotations or bids from distributors or manufacturers. New projects seeking financing cannot afford to underestimate their capital requirements, and lending institutions want documentation that shows system and planning went into the design process. Visit distributor showrooms, equipment shows, and new installations, if possible. Talk to service people

Menu Item	Top Sirloin Steak	Shrimp Scampi	Fried Catfish	BBQ Ribs	Eggplant Parmesan
Primary Storage	Walk-in refrigerator	Walk-in freezer	Walk-in freezer	Walk-in refrigerator	Walk-in refrigerator
Primary Cooking and Processing	Slicer	Sink and range (gas)	Sink	Deck oven	Range (gas), slicer
Secondary Storage	Reach-in refrigerator (line)	Reach-in refrigerator (line)	Reach-in refrigerator (line)	Reach-in refrigerator (line)	Reach-in refrigerator (line)
Secondary Cooking and Processing	Charbroiler	Salamander broiler	Deep fryer	Charbroiler	Salamander broiler
Utensils	9-inch clam tongs; SS spatula; 14-inch slicer (knife); cutting board	14-inch colander	9-inch clam tongs	14-inch slicer; 9-inch cleaver; cutting board	9-inch clam tongs
Landing Areas	Cutting table	Countertop	Breading table	Cutting table	Breading table
Pots and Pans	SS full size 2.5-inch pan	18 × 24 sheet pans	SS full size 2.5-inch pan; SS full size 6-inch pan	SS full size 2.5-inch pan; 18 × 24 sheet pans	15-inch iron skillet; 2.5-inch fill perforated SS pan; SS full size 2.5-inch pan
China and Flatware	10-inch pewter plate	5.5 oz casserole; 9.5-inch round dinner plate	1.5-inch oval platter	10-inch pewter plate	5.5 oz round casserole; 9.5-inch round dinner plate
Silverware	Standard place setting plus steak knife	Standard place setting plus serving spoon	Standard place setting	Standard place setting	Standard place setting plus serving spoon
Glassware	Standard water glass	Standard water glass	Standard water glass	Standard water glass	Standard water glass
Sanitation	Standard dish and pot washing	Standard dish and pot washing	Standard dish and pot washing	Standard dish and pot washing	Filter cone holder
Auxiliary Equipment	Platform scale; dollie, portion scale	Platform scale	Platform scale	Platform scale; dollie	N/A
Quantities and Time Period	40 lb/day, 120 covers	15 lb/day, 25 covers	10 lb/day, 15 covers	30 lb/day, 15 covers	Half case/day, 40 covers

FIGURE 5–1
Equipment Matrix

about maintenance records of certain manufacturers, and ask chefs and managers for their opinions on equipment and manufacturers.

The Role of the Modern Menu*

The menu concept should evolve over time with serious thought given to each item served. The personality of a restaurant is a direct result of the menu offerings. The menu concept will entail decisions on the kind of food and beverage served, the preparation methods, the type of service, and the theme and decor package. You must expand your definition of a menu. It is an oversimplification to consider it a mere list of what the restaurant or food-service operation has to offer. Traditionally, menus have been considered simple bills of fare without any consideration for the way the menu can affect the revenue and operational efficiency of the establishment.

You must start with the assumption that the items have been selected with customer preferences in mind and possibly even after some rather detailed market studies have been undertaken. Menus that are driven by factors other than customer preferences and consider only the personal likes and dislikes of an owner, manager, and chef will not serve the operation well.

The menu should not attempt to be all things to all people. Although you may try, you cannot cater to everyone's tastes. There has never been a restaurant that successfully appealed to every customer and offered items from eggs and bacon and fast-food fare to gourmet French and continental cuisine on a single menu. If you try, you may become known for variety, but without any menu identity or house specialties, nothing is done particularly well. Therefore, menus must emphasize what your staff does well and what the majority of your clientele want to eat.

A menu will be impacted by the skill levels and availability of the food preparation staff. This is not meant to imply that the menu is employee driven. The fast-food segment of the food-service industry is noted for its limited and simple menu offerings. This has allowed such operations as McDonald's, Wendy's, and Burger King to employ unskilled employees. However, the expanding tastes of today's more sophisticated customer are requiring even fast-food operators to expand their menus and include more elaborate menu items. Arby's, for example, has broken the $4 price range for sandwiches. It has offered a roast chicken club that combines sliced chicken breast, crisp bacon, lettuce, tomato, and mayonnaise on a grilled poppy seed roll. Arby's new sandwich offerings are a sharp contrast to the simple sliced roast beef sandwich with which it started.

*Adapted with permission from "*Introduction to Hotel & Restaurant Management,*
5th Ed, 1988 Kendall-Hunt Publishing Co.

Imagine you are planning to dine out at a new restaurant for the first time. You have not been inside or even seen its exterior. You begin to formulate expectations about the restaurant and menu based on advertisements on television or in the newspaper and from word of mouth among friends and business associates. However, a copy of the menu is handed to you. When you pick up and look at a menu, images should begin to form in your subconscious in regard to the food, decor, prices, and ambiance of the foodservice operation. When you actually see the restaurant and step inside, you will compare your perceptions derived from the menu to the actual theme and decor. A well-designed menu will project an accurate identity and personality for the establishment without the customer ever having set foot in the establishment.

Heretofore, the independent restaurant operator knew many of his or her customers. The owner greeted, seated, and even personally prepared the food for customers. The menu design wasn't considered important in projecting the personality of the restaurant because the owner was present in the establishment. This type of personal attention exists today primarily in owner-operated establishments. In Los Angeles, the personalities of individuals like Wolfgang Puck and Michael McCarthy are now personified in the menu and decor, as they have opened multiple locations and their physical presence is not possible.

In Chicago, Richard Melman, president and co-founder of Lettuce Entertain You Enterprises Inc., spreads his genius and innovations in restaurant concepts. His popular concepts are Maggiano's Little Italy and The Corner Bakery, now under the direction of restaurant powerhouse Brinker International. As is the case with all corporate chain restaurants, the personality of the restaurant rests not so much with the unit manager but with the company's corporate image. The personality of the chain is represented in the menu and decor of the restaurant. Independently owned and operated restaurants have an added advantage when the owner or manager personally interacts with the customers.

The reality is, however, that as one expands to two, three, and more units, the personality of any one individual becomes diluted and ceases to be the main identity or personality of the restaurant. According to the National Restaurant Association, 80 percent of the 500,000 plus *commercial* restaurants in existence today are independently owned and operated and they account for approximately only 20 percent of the 2 billion annual commercial food sales each year. Corporate national and regional chain operations with absentee owners transact the remaining 80 percent. The top 100 chains account for close to 50 percent of the food and beverage sales annually.

In chain restaurants, the personality of a manager, maître d', or chef is not the primary vehicle for establishing and maintaining the personality or image of the restaurant concept. The menu plays the most significant role in establishing the public image and personality because managers, chefs, and maître d's are often transferred. The menu, through the image it communicates, remains the most permanent link between the operation and the dining public.

When a friend suggests that you try a new restaurant, don't you usually inquire about the kind of food served there? This does not mean that the personality of an owner, chef, manager, or maître d' has little to do with the success of a given restaurant, but, given the high turnover of personnel and normal promotions and transfers that take place, it would be somewhat impractical to try to sustain a restaurant's popularity on the strength of the personality and physical presence of any individual. Relying exclusively on that aspect holds the operation hostage. It is because of this that the menu needs to be well planned and designed from the outset. Chain restaurants have obviously used their menus to project their personalities to the public in an effective manner.

To demonstrate how the visual impact of a menu can paint certain images in your mind and form expectations, consider the following. Picture in your mind's eye a large black leatherette menu cover with a gold cord around the fold. Does it elicit feelings of formality, double-digit prices, white tablecloths, French or continental food, and waiters in tuxedos?

Country Pride Restaurants have a menu design that gives the distinct impression they are family restaurants with prices and menu items families would appreciate. The surprising incongruity of it is that you will not find these restaurants in shopping centers. Country Pride is owned by Truck Stops of America, and its restaurants are found on interstates with truckers as the major customer base. When a menu is designed properly, the image and expectations elicited by the size, color, shape and material used on the menu should communicate the personality of the restaurant accurately. It is beyond the scope of this chapter and text to go into the elements of proper menu design.

The menu is also an integral cost control tool. The menu determines the degree of sophistication and detail of your cost control system. Cost control does not just involve methods to control waste and theft. The ultimate purpose of cost control is to provide management with the information it needs to make decisions concerning day-to-day operations. The menu will influence which items sell and impact your overall food cost percentage, contribution margin (gross profit), the average check, and total food and beverage revenue. Achieving food cost percentage and gross profit objectives does not happen by accident. It is built into the menu design from the very beginning.

The menu may just be the most important internal advertising tool used to direct customers to make their selections when they order in the restaurant. Not only can it influence what customers will order but how much will ultimately be spent. The menu can determine not only the volume of business you will do, but strongly influence the ultimate success or failure of the restaurant. Using forecasted customer counts and average check targets, the menu design can directly influence sales revenue. Management is constantly forecasting business volume and relating this knowledge to decisions on how much to buy, store, and prepare as well as how many employees to schedule. The menu will have a bearing on every one of these decisions.

A properly designed menu can direct the attention of the diner to specific items and increase the likelihood that those items will be ordered more frequently than random chance predicts. Although the customer's selection cannot be "controlled," it can be "directed." The profit picture brightens, the food cost improves, and the check average increases when the customer chooses an item that contributes positively toward these ends.

The menu is the only piece of printed material used by a restaurant that the customer will positively pick up and read. Because it impacts in so many areas and has a significant influence on the success or failure of a restaurant, it deserves to be given the attention, planning, and financial consideration reserved for matters requiring major investment consideration. More money will be spent on real estate construction, equipment, and furnishings, but nothing is more important than the menu when it comes to the overall success or failure of a restaurant concept. To make a profit, you have to plan for a profit. There is no room for guesswork when it comes to the menu. A poorly planned and designed menu not only can increase you food costs but also add to your payroll, complicate your purchasing, upset the flow of work in the kitchen, destroy your service, drive away customers, and reduce your sales revenue.

The Evolving Menu

The competitive nature of the foodservice market for the dining public's business and the changing tastes of more adventuresome palates, dictate that menus change frequently to reflect the trendy preferences that will attract new clientele and keep the regulars coming back for more. With the high cost of commercial real estate, construction, and leases in prime locations, building space must be kept to a minimum without sacrificing production efficiency or customer service aspects. The fact that menus will "evolve" over time requires kitchen design and equipment packages to conserve space and be versatile to allow quick adaptation to achieve production flexibility without expensive renovation costs and premature replacement of under-depreciated equipment.

As a case in point, Burger King was very slow to enter the breakfast market pioneered by McDonald's and Hardee's. The major reason cited was the lack of a griddle to cook eggs and pancakes. Remember that Burger King uses a flame broiler, which does not lend itself to cooking scrambled eggs. However, because of its desire to serve breakfast items, Burger King enlisted the help of the AMF Wyott Company to design a griddle that would allow conversion of deep fryers into griddles during the breakfast hours. The fryers would be set at 375 degrees and fry oil was pumped through the griddles that were placed in the fryers. The oil heated the griddle surface to 350 degrees, and Burger King was able to cook eggs and other breakfast items requiring a griddle.

Such flexibility can be achieved if kitchens are well planned and equipped. Every square foot of kitchen space must be productive space and utilize equipment selected for its versatility, ease of operation, sanitation, maintenance, and energy efficiency. The more uses a piece of equipment has, the greater the ability to add new menu items in response to changing customer preferences. Some of the most versatile pieces of equipment are the tilting skillet, which can be used to fry, braise, grill, sauté, and stew items; the infrared hotel broiler, which is the workhorse of the classical hotel kitchens for steaks, chops, fish, and poultry; the steam-jacketed kettle; the griddle; the salamander broiler or its variation called a cheese melter; and, perhaps the most versatile, the open burner gas range. It is recommended that equipment be installed on casters for ease of movement within a bank of equipment and have the gas and electricity brought to the equipment on flexible quick-disconnect hoses and receptacles.

New menu items must be evaluated as to how they will impact the kitchen and service staff. You must determine how a new item will flow through the kitchen from the time it enters the back door through storage, issuing, preparation, cooking to order, service, and dishwashing. You must be conscious of overloading particular stations or individuals with items requiring complicated processing, which can reduce efficiency. However, one word of caution: If an item is desired by the customers but requires more than the average processing and preparation, you should examine ways in which the item could be turned out more quickly and efficiently. This usually requires some preprocessing, partial assembly, and workstation rearranging.

Because the tastes of the dining public have become more adventuresome, menu offerings are being expanded. This is taking place even in the fast-food segment previously noted for its limited menu offerings in terms of both ingredients and preparation methods. You might think that there is a greater need for efficient equipment selection and layout in operations with extensive menus, scratch preparation, and finesse in plate presentation than in operations with limited menus, particularly fast-food operations. However, just the opposite is true. The extensive menu foodservice operations like most hotel kitchens and fine dining restaurants, are a "craftsman's workshop" with all sorts of specialty tools and equipment. They have order and system to be sure, but the high check average and the lower seat turnover allow time for chefs to "personalize" each dish. Mass production is not the rule.

Contrast this to the "assembly line" fast-food or limited menu operations. Speed in preparation of menu items is critical in serving large numbers of customers in relatively short periods of time. The check average is low so the number of transactions must be high to achieve revenue objectives. Therefore, the high volume-low check average operations are hurt more by inefficient kitchen layouts than are the fine dining restaurants.

Goals of an Effective Menu

The goals of an effective menu can be summarized in five statements. An effective menu is one that:

1. Emphasizes what the clientele wants and what the restaurant prepares and serves best.
2. Is an effective communication, merchandising, and cost control tool.
3. Obtains the necessary check average for sales and profit considerations.
4. Utilizes staff and equipment in a productive and efficient manner.
5. Makes forecasting sales more consistent and accurate for purposes of purchasing, preparation, and scheduling.

A menu can be written on a continuum ranging from what can be described as "limited" to "extensive" in the number of selections. The aspect of limited versus extensive menus can be examined for two perspectives:

1. The actual number of items listed on the menu, referred to as "variety"
2. The number of ways a product is prepared or presented

The most simplified and limited menu in terms of both parameters is best exemplified by the menus of fast-food operations. There has been considerable broadening of the menu variety in some fast-food operations while others have held fast to doing only a few items. KFC, long noted for its "We Do Chicken Right" strategy, has expanded the number of ways it prepares chicken. It used to be that the Colonel's recipe was the only way it was sold, and now you can get extra crispy, spicy, chicken nuggets, hot wings, and roast chicken.

From the limited/limited menu, we progress to a limited/extensive menu; that is, limited in variety but prepared and presented in an extensive number of ways. Examples of such a menu would be in restaurants like Red Lobster. They offer fish, shrimp, and other seafood prepared by frying, broiling, baking, and steaming with a variety of accompaniments such as vegetables, rice, pasta, and potatoes. Also, restaurants like Chili's and Applebee's demonstrate how variety in preparation can broaden an otherwise limited selection of items.

The next progression in menu item development would be the menu that offers an extensive variety of items prepared or presented in a limited number of ways. The best examples are coffee shop and family restaurants like Denny's, Shoney's, and International House of Pancakes, as well as restaurants like Bennigan's and Ruby Tuesday.

The fourth and final menu category is the operation with a menu that is extensive in both variety and preparation methods. Usually, fine dining French and continental restaurants with certified chefs and large kitchens are in this category, as are many hotel restaurants and private clubs. However, after seeing menus like those used by the popular TGI Friday and Houlihan's restaurant chains, I would have to categorize menus like theirs as extensive in both the number of items and the preparation as well as presentation.

Menus expand to broaden the customer base and to appeal to more people. However, if operators had their druthers, they would probably want to limit their menus for some very logical reasons. **Limited menus** require less equipment and space than extensive menus. Preparation of items can be simplified and speeded up, which is clearly what fast-food operations consider most important. With simple menus, less skilled employees are needed, and with the labor crisis what it is, many operators believe that the answer lies in hiring "alternative labor sources" such as the handicapped, mentally retarded, elderly, and disadvantaged. Such labor sources are sure to move menus toward the limited end of the continuum. Inventory and storage space is minimized with limited menus, cost controls are less complicated, and quality control is easier. In addition, overall operating costs are lower than in full menu operations.

However, proponents of extensive menus believe that to be competitive and financially successful, a restaurant must offer variety. You cannot limit menu offerings for operational cost reasons and disregard the competitive repercussions of such reasoning. **Extensive menus** have their advantages as well. An extensive menu will appeal to a broader range (base) of customers. Extensive menus appeal to first-time customers more than limited menus. Some believe that patrons are more likely to try a new and unfamiliar restaurant if the menu offers a wide range of choices. In addition, regular customers will not become bored with the menu and are more likely to return more often.

Restaurants with extensive menu offerings are more responsive to customers' changing tastes as they can add new items easily because of their extensive inventories of ingredients. Therefore, new items will appear more often and more quickly than in operations with limited menus. This menu flexibility has a built-in competitive benefit that creates product differentiation and allows the operator to charge higher prices for unique items. Clearly, the advantages of the extensive menus are driven by marketing-oriented reasons rather than the cost-oriented perspective of the limited menu advocates.

The advantages of one are the disadvantages of the other. Most operators will try to strike a balance between the two extremes and emphasize the positive aspects of limited and extensive menus. Figure 5–2 shows, in matrix form, the four categories of extensive/limited menus by the number of menu items and the variety of preparation methods.

Extensive menus require more equipment and more kitchen and storage space for ingredients. Equipment needs will be more specialized, and skills of kitchen workers will need to be at a higher level. It is more difficult to maintain quality control and waste is greater. The inherent danger in the attempt to provide variety is that the identity of the operation is lost. You must have some signature menu items that will build the restaurant's identity and reputation. Remember, you cannot be all things to all people. Ingredients must be utilized in more than one dish, and "daily specials" need to be used to work off excessive inventories of perishable ingredients. Record keeping must be more sophisticated as well.

FIGURE 5–2
Limited and Extensive Menus

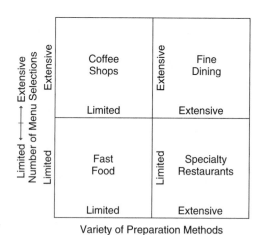

Extensive menus are certainly more costly to produce than limited menus and, therefore, will be priced accordingly. However, the truly adventuresome diners are willing to pay for their sophisticated tastes. This means operators catering to this market can charge a premium for increased variety and unique menu items.

Regardless of these factors, an optimum number can be given as to the extensiveness of entree selections. Twenty to 24 entrees is a number that can provide variety and be efficiently managed. Studies have shown that if you take a sales analysis and count the number of each entree sold for a period of 30 days or more, that approximately 60 to 75 percent of the items sold will be concentrated among the same 8–12 menu items. This means that of the total entrees sold, these 8 to 12 will make up the majority of items sold. This will be the case whether there are 60 entrees or 20 entrees. You can see that offering more than 24 entrees is of little value.

Types of Menu Formats and Item Listings

The frequency of menu changes and the format for listing entree accompaniments will vary among various foodservice operations. To begin with, there are three basic types of menu formats used in menu design. The one you use will depend on the type of foodservice operation and your target market. They are (1) static or nonchanging menu format; (2) cyclical menu format; and (3) static and cyclical, combination format. Some consider a fourth category, called market format.

Commercial foodservice establishments, particularly the larger chains, primarily use the static or fixed menu format. Essentially, the menu items stay the same from day to day, and changes are made only to delete slow sellers and add new or seasonal items. Their menu selections are therefore carefully selected and monitored for popularity with their customers. Much product research goes into testing and developing new and unique items that will provide product distinctiveness over their competition.

However, with the intense competition for the public's dining dollars, no operation, whether chain or independent, can expect to sustain a product or price advantage over the long run. The reason is that if someone develops a popular new item, others will follow to negate the advantage. Consider when the very popular fajitas were first introduced. Fajitas were likely copied from an independently operated Mexican restaurant and now are served in just about every type of operation from table service to fast food. The higher check restaurants have even upgraded the traditional ingredients by substituting chicken or beef with shrimp. This is why it is almost imperative to have new products being tested so you can introduce at least four or five a year in the hopes that you may discover a new food trend. Remember, for multi-unit operations the menu, not a manager or chef, is the key element in maintaining the image of the concept with the dining public.

There are some fairly obvious operational benefits of a limited or **static menu**, especially from a cost and quality control perspective. That is why they are so widely used. Fixed menus can be effectively used in establishments whose target market is large in numbers and diverse in customers or where frequency of visitations is no greater than three or four times per month.

Remember, a static menu is not necessarily a limited menu in both number of items and preparation methods. Fast-food operation menus are static and limited but almost all table service chains, from family restaurants like Bob Evan's, Shoney's, and Denny's to the "fern bars" (noted for their abundance of hanging plants) like Bennigan's, Houlihan's, and Ruby Tuesday are static yet extensive in the number of items or preparation methods.

Static menus have many of the advantages of limited menus and some further distinctions are worth mentioning. Leftovers are virtually eliminated because almost all the cooking is done to order. The forecasting of purchase and preparation quantities is easier and more accurate. Generally, the same percentage of items sold will prevail night after night. With static menus the kitchen personnel become specialists in preparation, and quality control is more easily accomplished. And, the cost of menu printing and production is reduced. Imagine the cost of changing menus for a chain such as Bennigan's or IHOP nationwide. The cost could easily reach five figures when you consider production costs, printing, and paper.

The life span of a static menu is growing shorter and shorter. Menu changes in casual, moderately-priced restaurants like Applebee's and Chili's and family restaurants like Denny's and IHOP are beginning to occur with much greater frequency than in the past. Some casual operations are introducing new menu items 3 or 4 times a year.

With the growing dining sophistication of the customer and the increased frequency of eating out, menu offerings need to change more often than in the past. Slow selling items must also be eliminated and replaced with new menu offerings. Of course the classic static menu example is seen in the fast food restaurants. But we are seeing more and more hamburger, chicken and pizza chains introducing new sandwiches, salads, desserts, and pizza crusts and toppings. Even hot wings have been added to Domino's and Papa John's menus.

The opposite of the static menu is the cyclical or changing menu. A **cycle menu** is an organized schedule for presenting different preplanned menus in a set pattern over a specified number of days. It is used primarily for food-service operations that often cater to a "captive clientele"; that is, students on a school meal plan, in hospitals, in industrial plants, or in large office complexes feeding employees who cannot leave the premises to eat.

Cycle menus are usually designed to provide nutritionally balanced offerings as well as variety in food groups, preparation methods, and plate presentations. Although primarily used in the institutional foodservice segment, they have been adapted and used in commercial foodservice operations. They offer variety to regular clientele who visit the restaurant two or more times in a week, usually at lunchtime. If a menu remains static, regular clientele could become tired and bored with the menu selections. To alleviate this, a cycle of daily specials is prepared to supplement the regular static menu. However, purely cyclical menus are not practical or necessary for most commercial operations.

Many menus will be **combination menus**; a combination of the static and cycle menus for certain meal periods and days of the week. These "specials" are advertised through menu clip-ons, blackboards, table tents, and back-lit menu signs. They were once referred to as "blue plate specials" and offered the clientele a form of table d'hôte menu at a very reasonable price. They also allowed the foodservice operator to serve the lunch clientele faster and more efficiently than cooking to order from the regular menu.

À la carte prices each course or menu item separately. Fast food restaurants traditionally have priced each sandwich, drink, and accompaniment separately allowing the customer to exercise control over how much they spend. However, more and more fast food operations are offering *value meals*. The price is reduced if one purchases the "bundled" menu items. The purpose is to increase the average check or transaction per person and is fundamentally a form of table d'hôte pricing.

Table d'hôte pricing, in the classical sense, includes all courses at one price. Because more items are included, the price charged will reflect that fact. Over the years, inflation pushed up prices making *table d'hôte* menus seem out of reach for most of the dining public. In addition, customers became more concerned with how many calories they were consuming and the nutritional values of foods. Table d'hôte menus were seen as expensive and offered more food than one really needed or wanted to consume.

Today's menus use a pricing format that is a combination of á la carte and modified table d'hôte. Luncheon and dinner specials are likely to be priced table d'hôte, while the regular luncheon and dinner entrees will be served with one side dish and bread and butter only. Most commercial restaurants include salad and bread with dinner and charge extra for potato or vegetable. One budget steakhouse includes the potato but not the salad in the price of the steak. Apparently the reasoning is that more people are likely to purchase an additional á la carte salad than potato and this strategy increases the likelihood of building their check average.

Psychology of Menu Design

Remember that a menu is more than just a list of what the restaurant has for sale, and the way a menu is designed is as important as the items it lists. A menu must be designed to allow an operation, whether it be a commercial table-service restaurant, private club, or fast-food operation, to achieve its sales goals, keep its costs in line, and return a desired profit. This does not happen by accident—it must be planned for ahead of time.

When certain practices are incorporated into the graphic design and layout of a menu, they can actually "influence" the menu selections of the guests. This is accomplished through techniques referred to as **menu psychology**. The influence is not subversive or subliminal in any way. The truth is that any given menu design or format will produce a predictable sales mix of menu items if used week after week without change.

The well-designed menu can help management sell certain items more often than if the items were "randomly" placed on a menu. If management were given their druthers of indicating which items they would prefer to sell more than others, their decisions would differ based on the criteria they deemed most important. Specific items might be singled out for emphasis for a number of reasons. When such items are emphasized, they will sell more of those items than if they had just randomly placed them on the menu. Menu psychology techniques cannot make unpopular items popular or make liver and onions outsell southern fried chicken or sirloin steak. However, they will allow an operator to sell more liver than would otherwise be sold if left to random chance.

A well-designed menu can make things a lot easier for the operator. Not only can it help keep costs in line, but it can even help distribute the workload in the kitchen. Think about the advantages of such a menu: You can influence the minimum amounts a customer will spend so you can realize the check average you need to achieve your daily sales projections based on seating, customer counts, and hours of operation. Being able to guide a customer's selection will improve the accuracy of sales forecasts, purchase and preparation quantities, and even labor scheduling.

The menu is also important in projecting the image or personality of a restaurant. Depending on the type of operation, the menu can be the main communication link between the customer and the restaurant. It is especially important in the moderate-priced table-service operations where management or chef personalities are not visible or well known to the restaurant patrons. The old saying, "You can't judge a book by its cover," should not apply to menu covers. The menu cover should project an accurate image of what to expect in terms of decor, degree of formality, price range, and, in some cases, type of food served. If a menu cover leaves one with vague or incorrect expectations, it is not doing its job. The most important aspect of menu psychology is to design the menu in such a way as to get the customers' attention and influence their decision to select certain items over others. Generally, you want to emphasize items that have low food cost, have high gross profit, help increase the average check, are easy to prepare, or are combinations of these criteria. You don't want to leave this to chance or have the printer or graphic artist pick the items for emphasis.

The concept of "menu psychology" was first introduced to the industry through menu seminars conducted by two educators and consultants. The late Jack Miller, author of several books including *Menu Pricing and Strategy*, 4th ed. (Van Nostrand Reinhold, NY, 1996), and long-time instructor in the hospitality program at St. Louis Community College, and his colleague, Joe Gregg, were the ones who popularized the concept of menu psychology. They were strongly influenced by the writings of the late Albin Seaberg, author of the book *Menu Design* (CBI, Van Nostrand Reinhold Pub., New York, 1983).

The techniques of menu psychology are most applicable to the printed menu; however, some of the theory works with verbal menus. The material presented herein is limited to printed menus since it is far and away the most universal method of displaying food and beverage offerings. We recommend that verbal menus be used to "supplement" printed menus and do not approve the use of complete verbal menus for a number of reasons.

Verbal menus take away time from customer service. The time spent on recitation and question-and-answer follow up may consume an extra 15 minutes of order-taking time, time that could be put to more direct customer service. The majority of servers do not do an adequate job when it comes to describing and explaining the menu. The presentation may range from monotone and indifference to speeding through the spiel to get on to more pressing matters. Customers don't pay absolute attention and are reluctant to ask for items to be repeated. A printed menu is paced for all customers to reread as often as necessary.

Verbal descriptions have a place and serve an important purpose in upselling guests. Verbal up-selling can reinforce the printed menu for even greater emphasis. Verbal menus are not an alternative to printed menus. A well-known west coast restaurant relegated its verbal recitations to the slag heap of gastronomic history. After going back to printed menus, it found that the sale of its daily specials increased, and the waiters were free to lavish an even greater level of service on their parties.

What are the specific menu psychology techniques employed in the design and production of a menu? Some involve such elements as the print style and size, the paper and ink color, the texture and finish of the paper, graphic design, artwork, and illustrations. Actually, anything used to direct the reader's attention to certain parts of the menu to increase the likelihood of certain items being selected more than just randomly is a technique of menu psychology.

The menu should "showcase" those items you want to sell the most for whatever reason. Once you get the customer's attention, you increase the chances of certain items being selected. Many menus are expensive pieces of artwork, graphic designs, paper, and even leather. Some are printed in full color, which is very costly. Yet some elaborate menus that win awards do very little to improve the operation's menu sales mix.

Menu psychology techniques are borrowed from the retailing industry, which has used window, counter, and mannequin displays to boost sales of specific items. The menu is to a restaurant what a merchandise display is to a major department store. You want the customer to see all the things you have for sale. When Houlihan's redesigned their original menu several years ago, the company felt that the design on the old menu, which lumped all types of items next to one another on the same foldout page, was contributing to customers ordering only appetizers and not dinner items. The new menu was designed to lead the customer from the high-margin specialty drinks on the cover, to the appetizers on the first page, to the complete dinners inside.

In a study of a menu sales mix from a popular casual theme restaurant (shown later in Tables 5.3, 5.4, 5.5, and 5.6) we found over three fourths of all menu items sold were either snacks or appetizers. It is of interest to note that both restaurants were using multiple-page menus where dinner entrees were listed on the back pages. Apparently customers didn't page through to the end, which may have contributed to the resulting sales mix. A recent Gallup survey studied the time customers spend reading a menu and found the average time to be 109 seconds. Customers become impatient if they have to read more than 6 pages.

Since menu psychology techniques are designed to get the patrons' attention, it is important to understand the way a customer typically looks at or "sights in" on the menu content. Studies have monitored the eye movement across a page. Through the use of laser beam technology, a device attached to the forehead of a subject allows the eye movement to be recorded. This has been referred to in a number of books and articles as "**gaze motion**" or "eye tracking." Figure 5–3 shows random eye movement across a plain, three-panel menu. Note that the eye first focuses on the center and passes over that point at least two more times. This finding has resulted in the center panel being the prime menu sales area.

It must be noted that eye movement is not static. This study did not test to see if graphics, photographs, color, or typefaces were used to "draw" the eye. Menu psychology can create "eye magnets" that will alter random eye movement and direct it to an area of emphasis. The areas of emphasis would be used to list the items that the operator wishes to promote the most. Since the first grade, when we were taught to read, we learned to begin reading at the upper left side of a page. This is the most natural reflex when one's eyes are not directed anywhere in particular. After a quick scan of the page, we begin serious reading at the upper left.

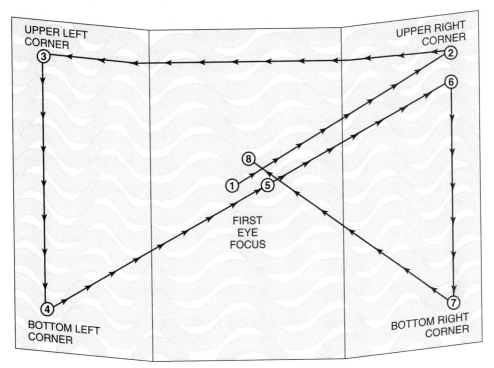

Eye movement across the three-fold menu.

FIGURE 5–3
Eye Movement Chart

Another important menu psychology technique that should be used to compliment gaze motion is called the principle of primacy and recency. This psychological phenomenon explains why people are more likely to remember or recall the first or last thing they see or hear. This is put to use in menu design along with gaze motion in the following way. If the menu is designed to draw the eye to a certain panel or section on a page, place the items you want to sell in that location, since it is the first place the eye focuses. The fact that it is the first or last thing customers read increases the chance of those items being ordered by more than random chance.

Menu psychology is not designed to make people buy items they do not want any more than counter and window displays do in department store windows. It does, however, make the customer give them a little extra thought, which will pay off with some when it comes to their purchase decision. I suggest that in operations where the menu is verbally presented, the order in which the items are given can impact the guest selection. Again, the first and last items mentioned should be the ones the management prefers to sell.

This is taken one step further when putting menu items in a list format on a printed menu, chalkboard, menu board, or drive-through menu. Try to remember the first item on the drive-through menu at McDonald's. It is not the regular hamburger. It will likely be their "feature" sandwich and one they are using in their national advertising. It will be followed by the Big Mac and Quarter Pounder. McDonald's wants to sell more of those items so they are the first ones the customer will read. Notice how some fast-food operations are listing their drink prices from large to small. They want to sell more large sizes.

If you have ten or more items you want to list in a particular section of the menu, the principle of primacy and recency suggests that you divide the items into two lists so you can better merchandise the items you want to sell. The items in the middle of the lists are somewhat lost, and this is where you can "hide" high-cost or labor-intensive items. You see, primacy and recency can work in reverse to de-emphasize selected items. Remember, all we are doing is trying to increase the odds that certain items will be ordered more often than random chance would permit. If an item is remembered, it may be selected more often.

In some cases, in an attempt to "catch the eye," menu design ends up fighting itself by confusing the customer. When you overuse graphics, artwork, or special lettering, a cluttered and disorganized menu results, forcing the reader to return to the upper left-hand corner. Very few commercial restaurant or club menus effectively use gaze motion and primacy and recency to full advantage.

Customers will react to the physical form of the menu, its shape, paper texture, size, cover material, and color. The customer begins to interpret the message the menu is trying to convey. This is where one can judge the effectiveness of the menu design. Does it clearly indicate which items the operation specializes in and does the menu project the correct image?

Since the menu plays such an essential role in determining whether a restaurant realizes its cost, revenue, and profit objectives, the resulting menu sales mix must be examined to see how it helps or hinders the restaurant from reaching its financial goals. The *menu sales mix* is the number sold of each menu item.

While the selection process can never be completely controlled through menu design, it can be greatly improved, even on menus offering multiple selections of appetizers, entrees, and desserts. When the same menu is used week after week, a predictable sales mix will result, allowing management to accurately forecast how much to order and prepare in advance.

VISUAL ELEMENTS OF MENU PSYCHOLOGY

There are techniques in menu layout and design that will increase the effectiveness of the menu as a marketing, communication, and cost control tool. There are four visual elements that will be described here.

FONT SIZE AND FONT STYLE

If everything is the same size and font, nothing stands out. Increase the size of the font to attract attention; decrease in size to avoid attention to a particular item. The use of bold type can also increase awareness and can actually direct the eye along a prescribed navigational path. It follows that selective use of font sizes and font styles for specific menu items is a technique that will draw the customers' eye and therefore their attention. It is this attention that increases the odds that the customer will give more consideration to ordering that item than if they had not noticed it at all. This technique is effective when the entire menu is limited to a maximum of three different font styles. When four or more font styles are used, the drawing power of the font is diluted and the eye never rests in any one specific area.

COLOR AND BRIGHTNESS

Increase the brightness or color (shading) of visual elements to attract attention and establish a menu grouping or category. In printing jargon, this is referred to as dot matrix screening. The brightness of a color can be lightened or darkened by reducing or increasing the number of dots. For example, a 80% screen of red would be very dark while a 20% screen would appear a pale pink color. Lighter screens are used as backgrounds for textboxes on menus and are effective eye magnets. The use of color ink for menu section headings can also be an effective way of getting the guests' attention.

SPACING AND GROUPINGS (SECTIONS)

Directing attention to a certain part or section of the printed menu can also be accomplished by placing the elements in a confined area or space on the menu. The use of borders to frame a menu item or group of menu items is one way to use this menu psychology design technique. An example would be an appetizer section of a menu set off by a box border or dot matrix screen. The grouping of all the appetizers within a designated area encourages reading them all as one unit. This has been described by Gestalt psychologists as the Law of Proximity.

SIMILAR ELEMENTS

The fourth and final visual element is referred to as the Law of Similarity. In much the same way that spacing and grouping of related menu items can contribute to the guest reading the entire section before moving on, the use of similar elements such as brightness, color, size, or shape encourages menu items to be viewed and read together. Thus, switching from regular to bold type, changing fonts, or introducing a different color signals to the reader that they are moving from one section to another, e.g., appetizers to salads.

SIMPLICITY, REGULARITY AND SYMMETRY

While all these visual elements can be used to guide the customers' eye around the menu to items that provide the best overall return, the entire menu must remain uncluttered and easy to read. Another Gestalt principle known as the Law of Pragnanz, states that figures with simplicity, regularity, and symmetry are more easily perceived and remembered than those that are unusual or irregularly shaped. If for example, several appetizers are contained in a rectangular border, do not use a circle or square around other appetizers and place it adjacent to the first. This is because a different shape suggests a different category, e.g., side dishes or salads.

For additional information about menu design, we suggest that you consult the following texts: *Menu Pricing and Strategy*, 4th Edition (Van Nostrand Reinhold, NY 1996), Miller and Pavesic, *Profitable Menu Planning*, 2nd Edition, (Prentice Hall, Upper Saddle River, NJ 1998 Drysdale).

C ost/Margin Menu Sales Mix Analysis

Operators have long sought a method for analyzing their sales mix to determine the impact each menu item has on resulting sales, costs, and profits. It is common practice to adjust menu prices and food costs when profit projections are not realized. The analysis will reveal specific menu items that should be aggressively promoted and positioned in prime sales locations on the menu. It is shortsighted to conclude that lost sales revenues and profit are due solely to poor purchasing, over-portioning, rising costs, and excessive waste. Much of your financial success is determined by the mix of menu items you sell on a regular basis in your restaurant.

Operators who have costs and waste under control must look to the menu sales mix as a possible cause of reduced profits. Certain items on the menu need to be aggressively promoted while others need to be de-emphasized or dropped from the menu. The categorization of each menu item will greatly affect the ultimate strategy used by management to improve the sales mix.

Heretofore, menu sales analysis has used *either* food cost percentage or item contribution margin (selling price minus food cost) to define an optimum sales mix. Both perspectives use the number sold (popularity) of each menu item to determine its respective impact on cost and gross profit.

Those utilizing the food cost perspective have reasoned that it is better to sell the popular low food cost menu items. Each menu item is classified according to its popularity and food cost percentage. An item is either popular and high cost, popular and low cost, not popular and high cost, or not popular and low cost.

The shortcoming of this perspective is that if you promote the menu items with the lowest food cost percentages, you will sacrifice revenue because the lowest food cost items are also the lowest priced items on the menu; e.g., chicken and pasta. Therefore, your average check will fall, and unless you increase your customer counts, overall revenue will not be optimized. Lower sales will cause fixed cost percentages to increase (fixed cost percentages react inversely to sales revenue increases or decreases) and cancel out any lowering of the food cost percentage.

Proponents of the contribution margin or gross profit perspective completely ignore food cost percentages and concentrate on the amount of dollars a menu item contributes to profitability. Here, menu items are classified into four categories according to their popularity and item contribution margin. Menu items are either popular and high in contribution margin, popular and low in contribution margin, not popular and high in contribution margin, or not popular and low in contribution margin.

Concentrating only on item contribution margins and ignoring food cost percentage results in a higher food cost percentage. This occurs because the items with the highest item contribution margins are the items with the highest food cost percentages on the menu, for example, steaks and seafood. While this works well in exclusive restaurants and country clubs where demand is price inelastic, it will be ineffective when used in competitive markets on menu items with market-driven prices.

When price elasticity exists, promoting the highest priced items on the menu will cause demand to drop even though the average check may increase. If customer counts are already flat or declining, this pricing philosophy will not be effective. (See Chapter 3 and the section titled, The Fallacy of Gross Profit: The Impact on the Bottom Line.)

Both the food cost perspective, referred to as the *Miller Matrix,* and the contribution margin approach, also known as *Menu Engineering*, are heavily biased to either low food cost or high individual contribution margin. These perspectives are treated as being mutually exclusive when, in fact, both low food cost and high contribution margin must be optimized in a menu sales mix.

A third approach combines the elements of both low food cost percentage and high total contribution margin and reduces the biases that are inherent in the Miller and menu engineering methods. The premise is that *the true optimum menu sales mix is one that simultaneously optimizes (not maximizes) total dollar contribution margin and total sales revenue while keeping the food cost percentage as low as possible.*

The methodology used to accomplish this is called *Cost/Margin Analysis*; the name reflects both food cost and contribution margin criteria in its analysis. Every item on the menu is examined from three, not just two, perspectives. Using the criteria of popularity (number sold), item food cost percentage, and the *weighted* **contribution margin** (total gross profit), menu items are grouped into one of eight categories instead of four.

The eight classifications of menu items afforded by the cost/margin analysis provide a greater in-depth perspective of the impact individual menu items have on the total sales mix. (See Table 5.1.) The items that need to be emphasized are those that have a high sales volume (popular), are low in food cost, and return a high *weighted* contribution margin.

Menu items with high individual contribution margins that are unpopular, will have less impact on the total gross profit than popular items with moderate to low individual contribution margins. High-volume items with moderate to low individual contribution margins will put more *dollars* into the cash register than low-volume items with high individual contribution margins. This is why the *weighted contribution margin* (individual contribution margin times the number sold) is a more relevant criterion on which to assess the sales mix potential of promoting certain menu items.

In Table 5.2 we have seven menu items in the sales mix. When items are ranked by *individual contribution margin*, the lobster tail is the top-ranked item and one that would be targeted for promotion. Because it is the highest priced item on the menu, it is more difficult to increase its sales. It is one of the two least popular items on the menu, and, in spite of the $10.45 individual contribution margin, contributes only $627 in weighted or total contribution margin. The chicken breast, the menu item with the lowest individual contribution margin of $5.90, is the top-selling item on the menu and brings in the

Table 5.1   Cost/Margin Menu Item Classifications

Sales Volume	Food Cost %	Weighted Contribution Margin
High (popular)	Low	Low
High	**Low**	**High**
High	High	High
High	High	Low
Low (not popular)	High	High
Low	High	Low
Low	Low	High
Low	Low	Low

Table 5.2 Rankings of Menu Items by Individual and Weighted Contribution Margins

Menu Item	No. Sold	Menu Price	Food Cost/$	Food Cost/%	Individual Contribution Margin	Individual CM Rank	Weighted Contribution Margin	Weighted CM Rank
Sirloin Steak	240	$9.95	$3.95	39.7	$6.00	6	$1,440.00	3
King Crab	50	$15.95	$6.00	37.6	$9.95	2	$497.50	7
Lobster Tail	60	$18.45	$8.00	43.4	$10.45	1	$627.00	5
Prime Rib	180	$14.50	$5.50	37.9	$9.00	3	$1,620.00	2
Whitefish	80	$8.75	$2.50	28.6	$6.25	5	$500.00	6
NY Strip	150	$12.45	$5.75	46.2	$6.70	4	$1,005.00	4
Chicken Breast	280	$8.50	$2.60	30.6	$5.90	7	$1,652.00	1

highest gross profit dollars of $1,652. This demonstrates that a popular, lower food cost menu item with a lower individual contribution margin can bring in more gross profit dollars than an unpopular high food, high individual contribution margin item.

The data needed to conduct Cost/Margin Analysis are the same data needed for the Miller and Menu Engineering analysis:

1. The number sold of each menu item

2. The food cost of each menu item

3. The menu price of each item

In the example that follows, sales data for a full month (the minimum period we recommend for this type of analysis) was used from a popular national fern bar restaurant chain, the menu items were classified into the following four categories:

1. Appetizers

2. Snacks

3. Entrees

4. Desserts

A total of 72 different menu items were examined. (See Tables 5.3 through 5.7.)

Excel software with the addition of Visual Basic was employed to generate the multi-column spreadsheets and graphs that are shown. *A diskette of this program has been included with your text for your own use.* These same spreadsheets and graphs can be viewed on your computer using the disk. Menu item sales are tallied and cut-off points for popularity, high and low food cost percentage, and high and low weighted contribution margin are calculated. We will first explain the formulas for each of the cut-off points and then calculate them for each of the four menu categories and for the entire menu sales mix.

Each menu item is first classified as *popular or unpopular (high or low volume)* according to an adaptation of the method first used by Kasavana and Smith (*Hospitality Publications,* Inc. Oke Mos, MI, 1982) in their *Menu Engineering* methodology. The formula for high and low sales volume (number sold) is:

1.00/number of menu items × 0.7 (constant) × sum of all items sold

APPETIZERS (TABLE 5.3)

$$1.00/17 \times .7 \times 6256 = 257.60 \text{ or } 258$$

Any appetizer that sells more that 258 is a high volume or popular menu item and any that sell in an amount equal to or less than 258 are low volume or not popular. How many appetizers are considered popular according to this standard?

SNACKS (TABLE 5.4)

$$1.00/34 \times .7 \times 8651 = 178.11 \text{ or } 178$$

Any snack that sells more that 178 is considered high volume or popular and any that sell in an amount equal to or less than 178 are low volume or not popular. How many snacks are considered popular according to this standard?

ENTREES (TABLE 5.5)

$$1.00/14 \times .7 \times 3397 = 169.85 \text{ or } 170$$

Any entree that sells more than 170 is considered high volume or popular and any that sell in an amount equal to or less than 170 are low volume or not popular. How many entrees are considered popular according to this standard?

DESSERTS (TABLE 5.6)

$$1.00/7 \times .7 \times 794 = 79.4 \text{ or } 79$$

Any dessert that sells more than 79 is considered high volume or popular and any that sell in an amount equal to or less than 79 are low volume or not popular. How many desserts are considered popular according to this standard?

THE TOTAL MENU SALES MIX (TABLE 5.7)

$$1.00/72 \times .7 \times 19,098 = 185.68 \text{ or } 186$$

When the entire menu sales mix is summarized in a single table, the cut-off point will change significantly. You will notice immediately that only appetizers would be considered popular menu items and that desserts will always rank dead last in popularity. This is why we added a word of caution about interpreting these mathematical cut-off points as final and absolute. You must continue to look at each menu category separately so you are comparing like items and can put their value to the sales mix in better perspective. If you did not do this, you would incorrectly assume that the desserts are such poor sellers that they should be eliminated from the menu. This points out the importance of comparing appetizers to appetizers and desserts to desserts in making menu decisions. While you can normally expect that there will be one entree sold to each customer, the ratio of appetizer and dessert sales to actual customer count is rarely more that 40%. How many menu items would be considered popular by this standard?

Table 5.3　Appetizer Cost/Margin Spread Sheet

Item No.	Item Name	No. Sold	Menu Price	Item Food Cost	Supp. Cost	Total Cost	Item Contribution Margin	Weighted Food Cost	Weighted Contribution Margin	Wgtd Sales	Item Food Cost %
0	Midpoint	257.60					$2.26		$832.55		31.14%
1	Onion Soup	507	$1.95	$0.42		$0.42	$1.53	$212.94	$775.71	$988.65	21.54%
2	Bowl Soup	290	$1.85	$0.10		$0.10	$1.75	$29.00	$507.60	$536.50	5.41%
3	Spin/Salad	349	$1.95	$0.30		$0.30	$1.65	$104.70	$575.85	$680.55	15.38%
4	Batter	256	$3.75	$1.09		$1.09	$2.66	$311.74	$760.76	$1,072.50	29.07%
5	Fr Cheese	1602	$2.95	$1.14		$1.14	$1.81	$1,826.28	$2,899.62	$4,725.90	38.64%
6	Fr Mush	257	$2.95	$0.87		$0.87	$2.08	$223.59	$534.56	$758.15	29.49%
7	Zucc	289	$2.95	$0.66		$0.66	$2.29	$190.74	$661.81	$852.55	22.37%
8	Guac	170	$2.95	$0.69		$0.69	$2.26	$117.30	$384.20	$501.50	23.39%
9	Fing App	383	$3.75	$1.32		$1.32	$2.43	$505.56	$930.69	$1,436.25	35.20%
10	Skins BC	551	$4.45	$1.90		$1.90	$2.55	$1,046.90	$1,405.05	$2,451.95	42.70%
11	Skins Combo	175	$4.45	$1.81		$1.81	$2.64	$316.75	$462.00	$778.75	40.67%
12	Skins Chill	29	$4.45	$1.86		$1.86	$2.59	$53.94	$75.11	$129.05	41.80%
13	Nacho1	585	$3.95	$1.02		$1.02	$2.93	$596.70	$1,714.05	$2,310.75	25.82%
14	Nacho2	129	$4.25	$1.34		$1.34	$2.91	$172.86	$375.39	$548.25	31.53%
15	Nacho3	385	$4.95	$1.19		$1.19	$3.76	$459.34	$1,451.36	$1,910.70	24.04%
16	Nacho4	130	$4.95	$1.60		$1.60	$3.35	$208.00	$435.50	$643.50	32.32%
17	Fr Fries	138	$1.65	$0.17		$0.17	$1.48	$23.46	$204.24	$227.70	10.30%
	Total	6256						$6,399.80	$14,153.40	$20,553.20	

Next, the cut-off for *high and low food cost percentage* is calculated by dividing the weighted food cost by the weighted sales for each menu category. You are essentially calculating the Potential Food Cost for each menu category. Any item that it greater than the PFC is a high food cost item and any menu item that is equal to or less than the PFC is considered a low food cost item. These mathematical calculations should be interpreted by management and should not be considered absolute and final. We use these mathematical formulas to be able to compare results from one period to the next and from one restaurant to another.

APPETIZERS (TABLE 5.3)

$$\$6400/\$20,553 = 31.14\%$$

Any appetizer with a food cost percentage greater than 31.14% is considered a high food cost item while those that are equal to or less than 31.14% are considered low in food cost. How many appetizers are low in food cost?

Total Sales %	Total Food Cost %	Items Sold %	Wgtd Cont Margin %	Popularity	Food Cost	Indv. Cont Margin	Wgted Cont Margin	Miller Matrix	Cost/ Margin	Menu Engineering
4.81%	3.33%	8.10%	5.48%	Popular	Low	Low	Low	Winner	Sleepers	Plowhorses
2.61%	0.45%	4.64%	3.59%	Popular	Low	Low	Low	Winner	Sleepers	Plowhorses
3.31%	1.64%	5.58%	4.07%	Popular	Low	Low	Low	Winner	Sleepers	Plowhorses
5.22%	4.87%	4.57%	5.38%	Popular	Low	High	Low	Winner	Sleepers	Stars
22.99%	28.54%	25.61%	20.49%	Popular	High	Low	High	HVHCMARG	Standards	Plowhorses
3.69%	3.49%	4.11%	3.78%	Not Popular	Low	Low	Low	LVLCMARG	Sleepers	Dogs
4.15%	2.98%	4.62%	4.68%	Popular	Low	High	Low	Winner	Sleepers	Stars
2.44%	1.83%	2.72%	2.71%	Not Popular	Low	Low	Low	LVLCMARG	Sleepers	Dogs
6.99%	7.90%	6.12%	6.58%	Popular	High	High	High	HVHCMARG	Standards	Stars
11.93%	16.36%	8.81%	9.93%	Popular	High	High	High	HVHCMARG	Standards	Stars
3.79%	4.95%	2.80%	3.26%	Not Popular	High	High	Low	Loser	Problems	Puzzles
0.63%	0.84%	0.46%	0.53%	Not Popular	High	High	Low	Loser	Problems	Puzzles
11.24%	9.32%	9.35%	12.11%	Popular	Low	High	High	Winner	Prime	Stars
2.67%	2.70%	2.06%	2.65%	Not Popular	High	High	Low	Loser	Problems	Puzzles
9.30%	7.18%	6.17%	10.25%	Popular	Low	High	High	Winner	Prime	Stars
3.13%	3.25%	2.08%	3.08%	Not Popular	High	High	Low	Loser	Problems	Puzzles
1.11%	0.37%	2.21%	1.44%	Not Popular	Low	Low	Low	LVLCMARG	Sleepers	Dogs
100.01%	100.00%	100.01%	100.01%							

SNACKS (TABLE 5.4)

$$\$13,714 / \$38,800 = 35.35\%$$

Any snack with a food cost percentage greater than 35.35% is considered a high food cost item while those that are equal to or less than 35.35% are considered low in food cost. How many snacks are low in food cost?

ENTREES (TABLE 5.5)

$$\$8,520 / \$20,405 = 41.76\%$$

Any entrée with a food cost percentage greater than 41.76% is considered a high food cost item while those that are equal to or less than 41.76% are considered low in food cost. How many entrées are low in food cost? Note how much higher the food cost is for entrées compared to appetizers and snacks.

Table 5.4   Snacks Cost/Margin Spreadsheet

Item No.	Item Name	No. Sold	Menu Price	Item Food Cost	Supp. Cost	Total Cost	Item Contribution Margin	Weighted Food Cost	Weighted Contribution Margin	Wgtd Sales	Item Food Cost %
0	Midpoint	178.11					$2.90		$737.81		35.35%
1	Snk Stik	165	$4.95	$1.30		$1.30	$3.65	$214.50	$602.25	$816.75	26.26%
2	Snk Clams	293	$4.95	$0.68		$0.68	$4.27	$199.24	$1,251.11	$1,450.35	13.74%
3	Snk Shrimps	129	$7.95	$3.04		$3.04	$4.91	$392.16	$633.39	$1,025.55	38.24%
4	Snk Chk	370	$4.95	$1.57		$1.57	$3.38	$580.90	$1,250.60	$1,831.50	31.72%
5	Snk Combo	307	$4.95	$1.43		$1.43	$3.52	$439.01	$1,080.64	$1,519.65	28.89%
6	Shrimp Salad	246	$5.95	$3.05		$3.05	$2.90	$750.30	$713.40	$1,436.70	51.26%
7	Chef	352	$4.45	$1.91		$1.91	$2.54	$672.32	$894.08	$1,566.40	42.92%
8	Spin	280	$4.45	$1.88		$1.88	$2.57	$526.40	$719.60	$1,246.00	42.25%
9	Chk Sal	551	$4.25	$1.94		$1.94	$2.31	$1,068.94	$1,272.81	$2,341.75	45.65%
10	Taco Chk	206	$4.25	$1.66		$1.66	$2.59	$341.96	$533.54	$875.50	39.06%
11	Taco Chili	98	$4.25	$1.64		$1.64	$2.61	$160.72	$255.78	$416.50	38.59%
12	Changa	275	$4.95	$1.82		$1.82	$3.13	$500.50	$860.75	$1,361.25	36.77%
13	Super	86	$4.25	$1.38		$1.38	$2.87	$118.68	$246.82	$365.50	32.47%
14	Beet-C	71	$5.45	$2.33		$2.33	$3.12	$165.43	$221.52	$386.95	42.75%
15	Turk-C	262	$4.95	$2.00		$2.00	$2.95	$524.00	$772.90	$1,296.90	40.40%
16	Ham-C	139	$4.85	$1.83		$1.83	$3.02	$254.37	$419.78	$674.15	37.73%
17	Chik-C	81	$4.45	$1.86		$1.86	$2.59	$150.66	$209.79	$360.45	41.80%
18	Philly	912	$4.75	$1.60		$1.60	$3.15	$1,459.20	$2,872.80	$4,332.00	33.68%
19	Club	264	$4.75	$1.50		$1.50	$3.25	$396.00	$858.00	$1,254.00	31.58%
20	Chk Sal Sand	147	$3.95	$1.46		$1.46	$2.49	$214.62	$366.03	$580.85	36.96%
21	Rueben	257	$4.95	$1.52		$1.52	$3.43	$390.64	$881.51	$1,272.15	30.71%
22	Dip	643	$4.85	$1.94		$1.94	$2.91	$1,247.42	$1,871.13	$3,118.55	40.00%
23	Chk Sand	321	$4.95	$1.56		$1.56	$3.39	$500.76	$1,088.19	$1,588.95	31.52%
24	Q-Day	309	$3.95	$1.12		$1.12	$2.83	$346.08	$874.47	$1,220.55	28.35%
25	Q-Ham	212	$3.95	$1.34		$1.34	$2.61	$284.08	$553.32	$837.40	33.92%
26	Q S/S	554	$4.75	$1.41		$1.41	$3.34	$781.14	$1,850.36	$2,631.50	29.68%
27	Q-Sea	196	$4.65	$1.68		$1.68	$2.97	$329.28	$582.12	$911.40	36.13%
28	Q-Sea S/S	238	$5.35	$1.86		$1.86	$3.49	$442.68	$830.62	$1,273.30	34.77%
29	Soup/Sal	231	$0.95	$0.22		$0.22	$0.73	$50.82	$168.63	$219.45	23.16%
30	Muffin	341	$0.85	$0.27		$0.27	$0.58	$92.07	$197.78	$289.85	31.76%
31	Kid Chk	52	$2.25	$0.98		$0.98	$1.27	$50.96	$66.04	$117.00	43.56%
32	Kid Stk	15	$2.45	$1.08		$1.08	$1.37	$16.20	$20.55	$36.75	44.08%
33	Kid Burger	40	$2.25	$1.01		$1.01	$1.24	$40.40	$49.60	$90.00	44.89%
34	Kid Shrimp	8	$3.45	$1.49		$1.49	$1.96	$11.92	$15.68	$27.60	43.19%
	Total	8651						$13,714.36	$25,085.59	$38,799.95	

Total Sales %	Total Food Cost %	Items Sold %	Wgtd Cont Margin %	Popularity	Food Cost	Indv. Cont Margin	Wgted Cont Margin	Miller Matrix	Cost/ Margin	Menu Engineering
2.11%	1.56%	1.91%	2.40%	Not Popular	Low	High	Low	LVLCHMARG	Sleepers	Puzzles
3.74%	1.45%	3.39%	4.99%	Popular	Low	High	High	Winner	Prime	Stars
2.64%	2.86%	1.49%	2.52%	Not Popular	High	High	Low	Loser	Problems	Puzzles
4.72%	4.24%	4.28%	4.99%	Popular	Low	High	High	Winner	Prime	Stars
3.92%	3.20%	3.55%	4.31%	Popular	Low	High	High	Winner	Prime	Stars
3.77%	5.47%	2.84%	2.84%	Popular	High	High	Low	HVHCMARG	Problems	Stars
4.04%	4.90%	4.07%	3.56%	Popular	High	Low	High	HVHCMARG	Standards	Plowhorses
3.21%	3.84%	3.24%	2.87%	Popular	High	Low	Low	HVHCMARG	Problems	Plowhorses
6.04%	7.79%	6.37%	5.07%	Popular	High	Low	High	HVHCMARG	Standards	Plowhorses
2.26%	2.49%	2.38%	2.13%	Popular	High	Low	Low	HVHCMARG	Problems	Plowhorses
1.07%	1.17%	1.13%	1.02%	Not Popular	High	Low	Low	Loser	Problems	Dogs
3.51%	3.65%	3.18%	3.43%	Popular	High	High	High	HVHCMARG	Standards	Stars
0.94%	0.87%	0.99%	0.98%	Not Popular	Low	Low	Low	LVLCMARG	Sleepers	Dogs
1.00%	1.21%	0.82%	0.88%	Not Popular	High	High	Low	Loser	Problems	Puzzles
3.34%	3.82%	3.03%	3.08%	Popular	High	High	High	HVHCMARG	Standards	Stars
1.74%	1.85%	1.61%	1.67%	Not Popular	High	High	Low	Loser	Problems	Puzzles
0.93%	1.10%	0.94%	0.84%	Not Popular	High	Low	Low	Loser	Problems	Dogs
11.16%	10.64%	10.54%	11.45%	Popular	Low	High	High	Winner	Prime	Stars
3.28%	2.85%	2.97%	3.51%	Popular	Low	High	High	Winner	Prime	Stars
1.50%	1.56%	1.70%	1.46%	Not Popular	High	Low	Low	Loser	Problems	Dogs
3.28%	2.85%	2.97%	3.51%	Popular	Low	High	High	Winner	Prime	Stars
8.04%	9.10%	7.43%	7.46%	Popular	High	High	High	HVCMARG	Standards	Stars
4.10%	3.65%	3.71%	4.34%	Popular	Low	High	High	Winner	Prime	Stars
3.15%	2.52%	3.57%	3.49%	Popular	Low	Low	High	Winner	Prime	Plowhorses
2.16%	2.07%	2.45%	2.21%	Popular	Low	Low	Low	Winner	Sleepers	Plowhorses
6.78%	5.70%	6.40%	7.38%	Popular	Low	High	High	Winner	Prime	Stars
2.35%	2.40%	2.27%	2.32%	Popular	High	High	Low	HVHCMARG	Problems	Stars
3.28%	3.23%	2.75%	3.31%	Popular	Low	High	High	Winner	Prime	Stars
0.57%	0.37%	2.67%	0.67%	Popular	Low	Low	Low	Winner	Sleepers	Plowhorses
0.75%	0.67%	3.94%	0.79%	Popular	Low	Low	Low	Winner	Sleepers	Plowhorses
0.30%	0.37%	0.60%	0.26%	Not Popular	High	Low	Low	Loser	Problems	Dogs
0.09%	0.12%	0.17%	0.08%	Not Popular	High	Low	Low	Loser	Problems	Dogs
0.23%	0.29%	0.46%	0.20%	Not Popular	High	Low	Low	Loser	Problems	Dogs
0.07%	0.09%	0.09%	0.06%	Not Popular	High	Low	Low	Loser	Problems	Dogs
100.02%	99.99%	99.99%	99.99%							

Table 5.5 Entrées Cost/Margin Spreadsheet

Item No.	Item Name	No. Sold	Menu Price	Item Food Cost	Supp. Cost	Total Cost	Item Contribution Margin	Weighted Food Cost	Weighted Contribution Margin	Wgtd Sales	Item Food Cost %
0	Midpoint	169.85					$3.50		$848.88		41.76%
1	Cordon	148	$6.45	$1.90		$1.90	$4.55	$281.20	$673.40	$964.60	29.46%
2	BBQ Shrimp	240	$7.45	$3.18		$3.18	$4.27	$763.20	$1,024.80	$1,788.00	42.68%
3	8 oz	215	$6.95	$2.89		$2.89	$4.06	$621.35	$872.90	$1,494.25	41.58%
4	10 oz	167	$8.95	$4.04		$4.04	$4.91	$674.68	$819.97	$1,494.65	45.14%
5	Smk Stk	338	$6.95	$2.97		$2.97	$3.98	$1,003.86	$1,345.24	$2,349.10	42.73%
6	Fr Shrimp	132	$7.95	$3.58		$3.58	$4.37	$472.56	$576.84	$1,049.40	45.03%
7	S $ S	161	$8.75	$2.81		$2.81	$5.94	$452.41	$956.34	$1,408.75	32.11%
8	BBQ Chick	83	$6.95	$2.31		$2.31	$4.64	$191.73	$385.12	$576.85	33.24%
9	Smo Chick	203	$6.75	$2.01		$2.01	$4.74	$408.03	$962.22	$1,370.25	29.78%
10	Fing Din	208	$5.95	$2.08		$2.08	$3.87	$432.64	$804.96	$1,237.60	34.96%
11	Burger	330	$3.95	$2.16		$2.16	$1.79	$712.80	$590.70	$1,303.50	54.68%
12	Burg Plat	729	$4.65	$2.28		$2.28	$2.37	$1,662.12	$1,727.73	$3,389.85	49.03%
13	Eggs Benedict	401	$4.25	$1.75		$1.75	$2.50	$701.75	$1,002.50	$1,704.25	41.18%
14	Stk & Eggs	42	$6.75	$3.38		$3.38	$3.37	$141.96	$141.54	$283.50	50.07%
	Total	3397						$8,520.29	$11,884.26	$20,404.55	

DESSERTS (TABLE 5.6)

$$\$887/\$1,909 = 46.47\%$$

Any dessert with a food cost percentage greater than 46.47% is considered a high food cost item while those that are equal to or less than 46.47% are considered low in food cost. How many desserts are low in food cost?

Table 5.6 Desserts Cost/Margin Spreadsheet

Item No.	Item Name	No. Sold	Menu Price	Item Food Cost	Supp. Cost	Total Cost	Item Contribution Margin	Weighted Food Cost	Weighted Contribution Margin	Wgtd Sales	Item Food Cost %
0	Midpoint	79.40					$1.29		$145.92		46.48%
1	Royal	96	$2.45	$1.02		$1.02	$1.43	$97.92	$137.28	$235.20	41.63%
2	Cake	41	$2.45	$0.95		$0.95	$1.50	$38.95	$61.50	$100.45	38.78%
3	Delight	62	$2.75	$0.97		$0.97	$1.78	$60.14	$110.36	$170.50	35.27%
4	Kid Sundae	64	$1.50	$0.45		$0.45	$1.05	$28.80	$67.20	$96.00	30.00%
5	Rocky	226	$2.45	$0.97		$0.97	$1.48	$219.22	$334.48	$553.70	39.59%
6	Apple	195	$2.45	$0.97		$0.97	$1.48	$189.15	$288.60	$477.75	39.59%
7	B'day Cake	110	$2.50	$2.30		$2.30	$0.20	$253.00	$22.00	$275.00	92.00%
	Total	784						$887.18	$1,021.42	$1,908.60	

Total Sales %	Total Food Cost %	Items Sold %	Wgtd Cont Margin %	Popularity	Food Cost	Indv. Cont Margin	Wgted Cont Margin	Miller Matrix	Cost/ Margin	Menu Engineering
4.68%	3.30%	4.36%	5.67%	Not Popular	Low	High	Low	LVLCMARG	Sleepers	Puzzles
8.76%	8.96%	7.07%	8.62%	Popular	High	High	High	HVHCMARG	Standards	Stars
7.32%	7.29%	6.33%	7.36%	Popular	Low	High	High	Winner	Prime	Stars
7.33%	7.92%	4.92%	6.90%	Not Popular	High	High	Low	Loser	Problems	Puzzles
11.51%	11.78%	9.95%	11.32%	Popular	High	High	High	HVHCMARG	Standards	Stars
5.14%	5.55%	3.89%	4.85%	Not Popular	High	High	Low	Loser	Problems	Puzzles
6.90%	5.31%	4.74%	8.05%	Not Popular	Low	High	High	LVLCMARG	Prime	Puzzles
2.83%	2.25%	2.44%	3.24%	Not Popular	Low	High	Low	LVLCMARG	Sleepers	Puzzles
6.72%	4.79%	5.98%	8.10%	Popular	Low	High	High	Winner	Prime	Stars
6.07%	5.08%	6.12%	6.77%	Popular	Low	High	Low	Winner	Sleepers	Stars
6.39%	8.37%	9.71%	4.97%	Popular	High	Low	Low	HVHCMARG	Problems	Plowhorses
16.61%	19.51%	21.46%	14.54%	Popular	High	Low	High	HVHCMARG	Standards	Plowhorses
8.35%	8.24%	11.80%	8.44%	Popular	Low	Low	High	Winner	Prime	Plowhorses
1.39%	1.67%	1.24%	1.19%	Not Popular	High	Low	Low	Loser	Problems	Dogs
100.00%	100.02%	100.01%	100.01%							

THE TOTAL MENU SALES MIX (TABLE 5.7)

$$\$29,522/\$81,666 = 36.15\%$$

When you average all the menu items together and calculate the Potential Food Cost Percentage for the entire sales mix, you can see how the average is weighted to the most popular items, appetizers and snacks. The menu had 36

Total Sales %	Total Food Cost %	Items Sold %	Wgtd Cont Margin %	Popularity	Food Cost	Indv. Cont Margin	Wgted Cont Margin	Miller Matrix	Cost/ Margin	Menu Engineering
12.32%	11.04%	12.09%	13.44%	Popular	Low	High	Low	Winner	Sleepers	Stars
5.26%	4.39%	5.16%	6.02%	Not Popular	Low	High	Low	LVLCMARG	Sleepers	Puzzles
8.93%	6.78%	7.81%	10.80%	Not Popular	Low	High	Low	LVLCMARG	Sleepers	Puzzles
5.03%	3.25%	8.06%	6.58%	Not Popular	Low	Low	Low	LVLCMARG	Sleepers	Dogs
29.01%	24.71%	28.46%	32.75%	Popular	Low	High	Low	Winner	Prime	Stars
25.03%	21.32%	24.56%	28.25%	Popular	Low	High	High	Winner	Prime	Stars
14.41%	28.52%	13.85%	2.15%	Popular	High	Low	Low	HVHCMARG	Problems	Plowhorses
100.01%	99.99%	99.99%								

Table 5.7 Cost/Margin Summary Spreadsheet

Item No.	Item Name	No. Sold	Menu Price	Item Food Cost	Supp. Cost	Total Cost	Item Contribution Margin	Weighted Food Cost	Weighted Contribution Margin	Wgtd Sales	Item Food Cost %
0	Midpoint	185.68					2.73		724.23		36.15%
1	Onion Soup	507	$1.95	$0.42		$0.42	$1.53	$212.94	$775.71	$988.65	21.54%
2	Bowl Soup	290	$1.85	$0.10		$0.10	$1.75	$29.00	$507.50	$536.50	5.41%
3	Spin/Salad	349	$1.95	$0.30		$0.30	$1.65	$104.70	$575.85	$680.55	15.38%
4	Batter	286	$3.75	$1.09		$1.09	$2.66	$311.74	$760.76	$1,072.50	29.07%
5	Fr Cheese	1602	$2.95	$1.14		$1.14	$1.81	$1,826.28	$2,899.62	$4,725.90	38.64%
6	Fr Mush	257	$2.95	$0.87		$0.87	$2.08	$223.59	$534.56	$758.15	29.49%
7	Zucc	289	$2.95	$0.66		$0.66	$2.29	$190.74	$661.81	$852.55	22.37%
8	Guac	170	$2.95	$0.69		$0.69	$2.26	$117.30	$384.20	$501.50	23.39%
9	Fing App	383	$3.75	$1.32		$1.32	$2.43	$505.56	$930.69	$1,436.25	35.20%
10	Skins BC	551	$4.45	$1.90		$1.90	$2.55	$1,046.90	$1,405.05	$2,451.95	42.70%
11	Skins Combo	175	$4.45	$1.81		$1.81	$2.64	$316.75	$462.00	$778.75	40.67%
12	Skins Chili	29	$4.45	$1.86		$1.86	$2.59	$53.94	$75.11	$129.05	41.80%
13	Nacho1	585	$3.95	$1.02		$1.02	$2.93	$596.70	$1,714.05	$2,310.75	25.82%
14	Nacho2	129	$4.25	$1.34		$1.34	$2.91	$172.86	$375.39	$548.25	31.53%
15	Nacho3	386	$4.95	$1.19		$1.19	$3.76	$459.34	$1,451.36	$1,910.70	24.04%
16	Nacho4	130	$4.95	$1.60		$1.60	$3.35	$208.00	$435.50	$643.50	32.32%
17	Fr Fries	138	$1.65	$0.17		$0.17	$1.48	$23.46	$204.24	$227.70	10.30%
18	Snk Stk	165	$4.95	$1.30		$1.30	$3.65	$214.50	$602.25	$816.75	26.26%
19	Snk Clams	293	$4.95	$0.68		$0.68	$4.27	$199.24	$1,251.11	$1,450.35	13.74%
20	Snk Shrimps	129	$7.95	$3.04		$3.04	$4.91	$392.16	$633.39	$1,025.55	38.24%
21	Snk Chk	370	$4.95	$1.57		$1.57	$3.38	$580.90	$1,250.60	$1,831.50	31.72%
22	Snk Combo	307	$4.95	$1.43		$1.43	$3.52	$439.01	$1,080.64	$1,519.65	28.89%
23	Shrimp Salad	246	$5.95	$3.05		$3.05	$2.90	$750.30	$713.40	$1,463.70	51.26%
24	Chef	352	$4.45	$1.91		$1.91	$2.54	$672.32	$894.08	$1,566.40	42.92%
25	Spin	280	$4.45	$1.88		$1.88	$2.57	$526.40	$719.60	$1,246.00	42.25%
26	Chk Sal	551	$4.25	$1.94		$1.94	$2.31	$1,068.94	$1,272.81	$2,341.75	45.65%
27	Taco Chk	206	$4.25	$1.66		$1.66	$2.59	$341.96	$533.54	$875.50	39.06%
28	Taco Chili	98	$4.25	$1.64		$1.64	$2.61	$160.72	$255.78	$416.50	38.59%
29	Changs	275	$4.95	$1.82		$1.82	$3.13	$500.50	$880.75	$1,361.25	35.71%
30	Super	86	$4.25	$1.38		$1.38	$2.87	$118.68	$246.82	$365.50	32.47%
31	Beef-C	71	$5.45	$2.33		$2.33	$3.12	$165.43	$221.52	$386.95	42.75%
32	Turk-C	262	$4.95	$2.00		$2.00	$2.95	$524.00	$772.90	$1,296.90	40.40%
33	Ham-C	139	$4.85	$1.83		$1.83	$3.02	$254.37	$419.78	$674.15	37.73%
34	Chk-C	81	$4.45	$1.86		$1.86	$2.59	$150.66	$209.79	$360.45	41.80%
35	Philly	912	$4.75	$1.60		$1.60	$3.15	$1,459.20	$2,872.80	$4,332.00	33.68%
36	Club	264	$4.75	$1.50		$1.50	$3.25	$396.00	$858.00	$1,254.00	31.58%
37	Chk Sal Sand	147	$3.95	$1.46		$1.46	$2.49	$214.62	$366.03	$580.65	36.96%
38	Rueben	257	$4.95	$1.52		$1.52	$3.43	$390.64	$881.51	$1,272.15	30.71%
39	Dip	643	$4.85	$1.94		$1.94	$2.91	$1,247.42	$1,871.13	$3,118.55	40.00%

Total Sales %	Total Food Cost %	Items Sold %	Wgtd Cont Margin %	Popularity	Food Cost	Indv. Cont Margin	Wgted Cont Margin	Miller Matrix	Cost/ Margin	Menu Engineering
1.21%	0.72%	2.65%	1.49%	Popular	Low	Low	High	Winner	Prime	Plowhorses
0.66%	0.10%	1.52%	0.97%	Popular	Low	Low	Low	Winner	Sleepers	Plowhorses
0.83%	0.35%	1.83%	1.10%	Popular	Low	Low	Low	Winner	Sleepers	Plowhorses
1.31%	1.06%	1.50%	1.46%	Popular	Low	Low	High	Winner	Prime	Plowhorses
5.79%	6.19%	8.39%	5.56%	Popular	High	Low	High	HVHCMARG	Standards	Plowhorses
0.93%	0.76%	1.35%	1.03%	Popular	Low	Low	Low	Winner	Sleepers	Plowhorses
1.04%	0.65%	1.51%	1.27%	Popular	Low	Low	Low	Winner	Sleepers	Plowhorses
0.61%	0.40%	0.89%	0.74%	Not Popular	Low	Low	Low	LVLCMARG	Sleepers	Dogs
1.76%	1.71%	2.01%	1.78%	Popular	Low	Low	High	Winner	Prime	Plowhorses
3.00%	3.55%	2.89%	2.69%	Popular	High	Low	High	HVHVMARG	Standards	Plowhorses
0.95%	1.07%	0.92%	0.89%	Not Popular	High	Low	Low	Loser	Problems	Dogs
0.16%	0.18%	0.15%	0.14%	Not Popular	High	Low	Low	Loser	Problems	Dogs
2.83%	2.02%	3.06%	3.29%	Popular	Low	High	High	Winner	Prime	Stars
0.67%	0.59%	0.68%	0.72%	Not Popular	Low	High	Low	LVLCMARG	Sleepers	Puzzles
2.34%	1.56%	2.02%	2.78%	Popular	Low	High	High	Winner	Prime	Stars
0.79%	0.70%	0.68%	0.84%	Not Popular	Low	High	Low	LVLCMARG	Sleepers	Puzzles
0.28%	0.08%	0.72%	0.39%	Not Popular	Low	Low	Low	LVLCMARG	Sleepers	Dogs
1.00%	0.73%	0.86%	1.15%	Not Popular	Low	High	Low	LVLCMARG	Sleepers	Puzzles
1.78%	0.67%	1.53%	2.40%	Popular	Low	High	High	Winner	Prime	Stars
1.26%	1.33%	0.68%	1.21%	Not Popular	High	High	Low	Loser	Problems	Puzzles
2.24%	1.97%	1.94%	2.40%	Popular	Low	High	High	Winner	Prime	Stars
1.86%	1.49%	1.61%	2.07%	Popular	Low	High	High	Winner	Prime	Stars
1.79%	2.54%	1.29%	1.37%	Popular	High	High	Low	HVHCMARG	Problems	Stars
1.92%	2.28%	1.84%	1.71%	Popular	High	Low	High	HVHCMARG	Standards	Plowhorses
1.53%	1.78%	1.47%	1.38%	Popular	High	Low	Low	HVHCMARG	Problems	Plowhorses
2.87%	3.62%	2.89%	2.44%	Popular	High	Low	High	HVHCMARG	Standards	Plowhorses
1.07%	1.16%	1.08%	1.02%	Popular	High	Low	Low	HVHCMARG	Problems	Plowhorses
0.51%	0.54%	0.51%	0.49%	Not Popular	High	Low	Low	Loser	Problems	Dogs
1.67%	1.70%	1.44%	1.65%	Popular	High	High	High	HCHCMARG	Standards	Stars
0.45%	0.40%	0.45%	0.47%	Not Popular	Low	High	Low	LVLCMARG	Sleepers	Puzzles
0.47%	0.56%	0.37%	0.42%	Not Popular	High	High	Low	Loser	Problems	Puzzles
1.59%	1.77%	1.37%	1.48%	Popular	High	High	High	HVHCMARG	Standards	Stars
0.83%	0.86%	0.73%	0.81%	Not Popular	High	High	Low	Loser	Problems	Puzzles
0.44%	0.51%	0.42%	0.40%	Not Popular	High	Low	Low	Loser	Problems	Dogs
5.30%	4.94%	4.78%	5.51%	Popular	Low	High	High	Winner	Prime	Stars
1.54%	1.34%	1.38%	1.65%	Popular	Low	High	High	Winner	Prime	Stars
0.71%	0.73%	0.77%	0.70%	Not Popular	High	Low	Low	Loser	Problems	Dogs
1.56%	1.32%	1.35%	1.69%	Popular	Low	High	High	Winner	Prime	Stars
3.82%	4.23%	3.37%	3.59%	Popular	High	High	High	HVHCMARG	Standards	Stars

Item No.	Item Name	No. Sold	Menu Price	Item Food Cost	Supp. Cost	Total Cost	Item Contribution Margin	Weighted Food Cost	Weighted Contribution Margin	Wgtd Sales	Item Food Cost %
40	Chk Sand	321	$4.95	$1.56		$1.56	$3.39	$500.76	$1,088.19	$1,588.95	31.52%
41	Q-Day	309	$3.95	$1.12		$1.12	$2.83	$346.08	$874.47	$1,220.55	28.35%
42	Q-Ham	212	$3.95	$1.34		$1.34	$2.61	$284.08	$553.32	$837.40	33.92%
43	Q S/S	554	$4.75	$1.41		$1.41	$3.34	$781.14	$1,850.36	$2,631.50	29.68%
44	Q-Sea	196	$4.65	$1.68		$1.68	$2.97	$329.28	$582.12	$911.40	36.13%
45	Q-Sea S/S	238	$5.35	$1.86		$1.86	$3.49	$442.68	$830.62	$1,273.30	34.77%
46	Soup/Sal	231	$0.95	$0.22		$0.22	$0.73	$50.82	$168.63	$219.45	23.16%
47	Muffin	341	$0.85	$0.27		$0.27	$0.58	$92.07	$197.78	$289.85	31.76%
48	Kid Chk	52	$2.25	$0.98		$0.98	$1.27	$50.96	$66.04	$117.00	43.56%
49	Kid Stk	15	$2.45	$1.08		$1.08	$1.37	$16.20	$20.55	$36.75	44.08%
50	Kid Burger	40	$2.25	$1.01		$1.01	$1.24	$40.40	$49.60	$90.00	44.89%
51	Kid Shrimp	8	$3.45	$1.49		$1.49	$1.96	$11.92	$15.68	$27.60	43.19%
52	Cordon	148	$6.45	$1.90		$1.90	$4.55	$281.20	$673.40	$954.60	29.46%
53	BBQ Shrimp	240	$7.45	$3.18		$3.18	$4.27	$763.20	$1,024.80	$1,788.00	42.68%
54	8 oz	215	$6.95	$2.89		$2.89	$4.06	$621.35	$872.90	$1,494.25	41.58%
55	10 oz	107	$8.95	$4.04		$4.04	$4.91	$674.68	$819.97	$1,494.65	45.14%
56	Smk Stk	338	$6.95	$2.97		$2.97	$3.98	$1,003.86	$1,345.24	$2,349.10	42.73%
57	Fr Shrimp	132	$7.95	$3.58		$3.58	$4.37	$472.56	$576.84	$1,049.40	$45.03%
58	S $ S	161	$8.75	$2.81		$2.81	$5.94	$452.41	$956.34	$1,408.75	32.11%
59	BBQ Chick	83	$6.95	$2.31		$2.31	$4.64	$191.73	$385.12	$576.85	33.24%
60	Smo Chick	203	$6.75	$2.01		$2.01	$4.74	$408.03	$962.22	$1,370.25	29.78%
61	Fing Din	208	$5.95	$2.08		$2.08	$3.87	$432.64	$804.96	$1,237.60	34.96%
62	Burger	330	$3.95	$2.16		$2.16	$1.79	$712.80	$590.70	$1,303.50	54.68%
63	Burg Plat	729	$4.65	$2.28		$2.28	$2.37	$1,662.12	$1,727.73	$3,389.85	49.03%
64	Eggs Benedic	401	$4.25	$1.75		$1.75	$2.50	$701.75	$1,002.50	$1,704.25	41.18%
65	Stk & Eggs	42	$6.75	$3.38		$3.38	$3.37	$141.96	$141.54	$283.50	50.07%
66	Royal	90	$2.45	$1.02		$1.02	$1.43	$97.92	$137.28	$235.20	41.63%
67	Cake	41	$2.45	$0.95		$0.95	$1.50	$38.95	$61.50	$100.45	38.78%
68	Delight	62	$2.75	$0.97		$0.97	$1.78	$60.14	$110.36	$170.50	35.27%
69	Kid Sundae	64	$1.50	$0.45		$0.45	$1.05	$28.80	$67.20	$96.00	30.00%
70	Rocky	226	$2.45	$0.97		$0.97	$1.48	$219.22	$334.48	$553.70	39.59%
71	Apple	195	$2.45	$0.97		$0.97	$1.48	$189.15	$288.60	$477.75	39.59%
72	B'day Cake	110	$2.50	$2.30		$2.30	$0.20	$253.00	$22.00	$275.00	92.00%
	Total	19098						$ 29,521.63	$52,144.67	$81,866.30	

of 72 tracked items at or below this percentage. Sixteen low-cost menu items were snacks, 13 were appetizers, 5 were entrées, and 2 were desserts. This is the same percentage you would use to arrive at your Standard Food Cost at the end of the month. You would add allowances for food consumed but not sold to arrive at the SFC to compare to your Actual Food Cost shown on your income statement.

Total Sales %	Total Food Cost %	Items Sold %	Wgtd Cont Margin %	Popularity	Food Cost	Indv. Cont Margin	Wgted Cont Margin	Miller Matrix	Cost/ Margin	Menu Engineering
1.95%	1.70%	1.68%	2.09%	Popular	Low	High	High	Winner	Prime	Stars
1.49%	1.17%	1.62%	1.68%	Popular	Low	High	High	Winner	Prime	Stars
1.03%	0.96%	1.11%	1.06%	Popular	Low	Low	Low	Winner	Sleepers	Plowhorses
3.22%	2.65%	2.90%	3.55%	Popular	Low	High	High	Winner	Prime	Stars
1.12%	1.12%	1.03%	1.12%	Popular	Low	High	Low	Winner	Sleepers	Stars
1.56%	1.50%	1.25%	1.59%	Popular	Low	High	High	Winner	Prime	Stars
0.27%	0.17%	1.21%	0.32%	Popular	Low	Low	Low	Winner	Sleepers	Plowhorses
0.35%	0.31%	1.79%	0.38%	Popular	Low	Low	Low	Winner	Sleepers	Plowhorses
0.14%	0.17%	0.27%	0.13%	Not Popular	High	Low	Low	Loser	Problems	Dogs
0.05%	0.05%	0.08%	0.04%	Not Popular	High	Low	Low	Loser	Problems	Dogs
0.11%	0.14%	0.21%	0.10%	Not Popular	High	Low	Low	Loser	Problems	Dogs
0.03%	0.04%	0.04%	0.03%	Not Popular	High	Low	Low	Loser	Problems	Dogs
1.17%	0.95%	0.77%	1.29%	Not Popular	Low	High	Low	LVLCMARG	Sleepers	Puzzles
2.19%	2.59%	1.26%	1.97%	Popular	High	High	High	HVHCMARG	Standards	Stars
1.83%	2.10%	1.13%	1.67%	Popular	High	High	High	HVHCMARG	Standards	Stars
1.83%	2.29%	0.87%	1.57%	Not Popular	High	High	High	Loser	Standards	Puzzles
2.88%	3.40%	1.77%	2.58%	Popular	High	High	High	HVHCMARG	Standards	Stars
1.28%	1.60%	0.69%	1.11%	Not Popular	High	High	Low	Loser	Problems	Puzzles
1.73%	1.53%	0.84%	1.83%	Not Popular	Low	High	High	LVLCMARG	Prime	Puzzles
0.71%	0.65%	0.43%	0.74%	Not Popular	Low	High	Low	LVLCMARG	Sleepers	Puzzles
1.68%	1.38%	1.06%	1.85%	Popular	Low	High	High	Winner	Prime	Stars
1.52%	1.47%	1.09%	1.54%	Popular	Low	High	High	Winner	Prime	Stars
1.60%	2.41%	1.73%	1.13%	Popular	High	Low	Low	HVHCMARG	Problems	Plowhorses
4.15%	5.63%	3.82%	3.31%	Popular	High	Low	High	HVHCMARG	Standards	Plowhorses
2.09%	2.38%	2.10%	1.92%	Popular	High	Low	High	HVHCMARG	Standards	Plowhorses
0.35%	0.48%	0.22%	0.27%	Not Popular	High	High	Low	Loser	Problems	Puzzles
0.29%	0.33%	0.50%	0.26%	Not Popular	High	Low	Low	Loser	Problems	Dogs
0.12%	0.13%	0.21%	0.12%	Not Popular	High	Low	Low	Loser	Problems	Dogs
0.21%	0.20%	0.32%	0.21%	Not Popular	Low	Low	Low	LVLCMARG	Sleepers	Dogs
0.12%	0.10%	0.34%	0.13%	Not Popular	Low	Low	Low	LVLCMARG	Sleepers	Dogs
0.68%	0.74%	1.18%	0.64%	Popular	High	Low	Low	HVHCMARG	Problems	Plowhorses
0.59%	0.64%	1.02%	0.55%	Popular	High	Low	Low	HVHCMARG	Problems	Plowhorses
0.34%	0.86%	0.58%	0.04%	Not Popular	High	Low	Low	Loser	Problems	Dogs

The cut-off for the *average weighted contribution margin* is calculated by dividing the total weighted contribution margin by the number of menu items in the menu category. Any items with a weighted contribution margin greater than the average are considered high contribution margin items and those equal to or less than the average are considered low contribution margin items.

APPETIZERS (TABLE 5.3)

$$\$14,153/17 = \$832.53$$

Any appetizer that returns a weighted contribution margin greater than $832.53 is considered a high contribution margin appetizer while those that return an amount equal to or less than $832.53 are considered low in contribution margin. Which appetizers return a high weighted contribution margin?

SNACKS (TABLE 5.4)

$$\$25,086/34 = \$737.82$$

Any snack that returns a weighted contribution margin greater than $737.82 is considered a high contribution margin snack while those that return an amount equal to or less than $737.82 are considered low in contribution margin. Which snacks return a high weighted contribution margin?

ENTREES (TABLE 5.5)

$$\$11,884/14 = \$848.86$$

Any entrée that returns a weighted contribution margin greater than $848.86 is considered a high contribution margin entrée while those that return an amount equal to or less than $848.86 are considered low in contribution margin. Which entrees return a high weighted contribution margin?

DESSERTS (TABLE 5.6)

$$\$1,021/7 = \$145.86$$

Again it is obvious that desserts do not contribute much at all to the overall weighted contribution margin. However, within the dessert category, any dessert that returns a weighted contribution margin greater than $145.86 is considered high in contribution margin.

THE ENTIRE MENU SALES MIX (TABLE 5.7)

$$\$52,145/72 = \$724.24$$

Again we want to point out that all desserts would be considered low in weighted contribution margin when compared to the weighted contribution margin of the popular appetizers and snacks. This points out that decisions cannot be based entirely on the mathematical values used to determine cutoff points and why you need to look at each menu category separately when making decisions on which items to promote or eliminate from your menu.

We have not calculated the cut-off points for all four menu categories and the entire menu sales mix. The cut-off points are summarized later in Table 5.8. Keep in mind that what we are ultimately seeking to find are those menu items that combine the benefits of low food cost and high contribution margins. These two attributes are *not* mutually exclusive. Through the *Cost/Margin Analysis* we will identify the menu items that are popular, low in food cost and return a high weighted contribution margin. These items are referred to as **Primes**. The other categories are *Problems* (not popular, high food cost, low contribution margin), *Standards* (popular, high food cost, high contribution margin), and *Sleepers* (not popular, low in food cost, low in contribution margin). Each will be explained in detail later in this chapter.

The most valuable aspect of the Cost/Margin methodology comes when the spreadsheet data are graphically displayed, plotting each menu item by category and its food cost percentage and weighted contribution margin. A basic *X-Y* graph is used to plot individual menu items. The *Y*, or vertical, axis displays the food cost percentage and the *X*, or horizontal, axis the weighted contribution margin. Graphs should be prepared for each menu category calculating cutoff points *separately* for each one. It is important to compare items within their respective categories as it reveals a different perspective for assessing menu items.

Note that each graph is divided into four quadrants by vertical and horizontal lines intersecting the plot of the potential food cost and average weighted contribution margin (AWCM). (See Figure 5–4.) Although the

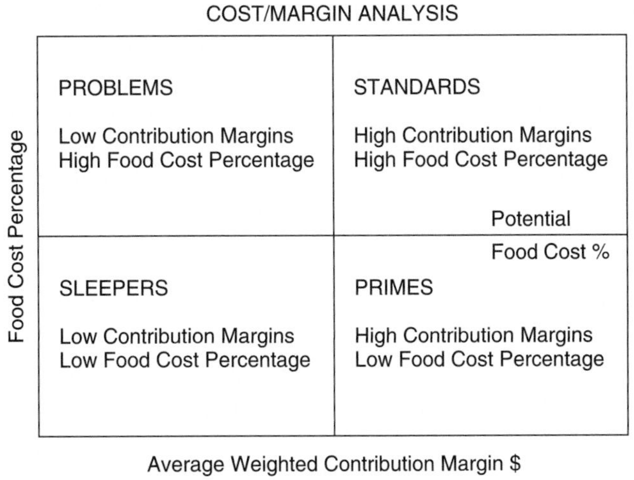

COST/MARGIN ANALYSIS

FIGURE 5–4
Graph quadrants.

graphs plot food cost percentage and weighted contribution margin, the figures really plot a third variable, popularity. Since cost/margin uses "weighted" contribution margin, popularity is reflected in the "weight" of the number sold of each menu item. Although not perfect, most of your popular menu items will be plotted to the right of the vertical AWCM line. The interpretation of the graph is based on the location of each plotted point relative to the intersecting lines.

Items that fall below the horizontal PFC line are those considered low in food cost while those plotted above are considered high food cost items. Items plotted to the left of the vertical AWCM line are considered low in contribution margin while those plotted to the right are considered high.

The items referred to as *Primes* that are both low in food cost and high in individual contribution margin satisfy both food cost and contribution margin standards and are found in the lower right quadrant. The more items in this quadrant, the better the sales mix results in terms of lowering food cost and increasing contribution margin. It is not realistic to have all items in the *Primes* quadrant and a menu will generally contain *Problems, Standards,* and *Sleepers.*

Items located in the upper-right quadrant are high in food cost and high in contribution margin and are referred to as *Standards*. They are the traditional items found on most table-service restaurant menus, (e.g., steaks, Prime rib, lobster, seafood). They are usually the highest priced items on the menu and have the highest food costs. All menus need to have *Standards* to "balance" the menu with items that help raise the average check.

The items in the lower left are called *Sleepers* because they are low in food cost and low in weighted contribution margin. The reason they are low in contribution margin is that they are not very popular menu items. They are often new dishes that are being tested. Every restaurant needs to test new menu items to keep its menu fresh, and often we seek to add low food cost items at low prices to create some demand. The inclusion of *Sleepers* in the sales mix helps "soften" the negative higher-than-average food costs of *Problems* and *Standards.*

In the upper left are the *Problems*, so called because they are high in food cost and low in weighted contribution margin. Often the items in this quadrant are children's menu items and desserts. Children's menu items may run 100 percent food cost in some restaurants where kids eat free with adults. As part of a marketing strategy to attract families, these items must be viewed differently than ordinary menu items.

It is important to point out that decisions on how to deal with *Problems* are not made solely on quantitative data. If that were the case, the computer could replace management when it comes to adding and deleting items from the menu. Many non-quantifiable factors must be included in menu planning and pricing decisions. No simple quantitative rule of thumb is suggested here. Company policy, customer preferences, regional practices, competition, marketing policies, and company tradition are important factors that will override purely quantitative factors and keep certain items on the menu regardless of cost or contribution margin. Hopefully, management can make changes in price, portioning, and menu positioning that moves *Sleepers* into the *Primes* quadrant and moves *Standards* closer to the food cost cutoff line.

The menu items that fall closest to the intersecting lines are those easiest to improve or strengthen. Small changes in positioning on the menu to increase selection, adding and deleting accompaniments and portions to make an item either a better value to the customer or reducing the food cost and holding the price constant, or small incremental increases in price can improve item popularity and contribution margin.

The action taken on an individual menu item will also be influenced by how deeply it is positioned within a quadrant, its nearness to the intersecting lines, and whether it is above or below the PFC line or to the right of the AWCM line. Generally, one would seek to move items downward and to the right on the graph toward the *Primes* quadrant. Strategies for dealing with *Primes, Problems, Standards,* and *Sleepers* will be covered later in this chapter.

APPETIZERS

Upon examining the appetizers in Table 5.3 and Figure 5–5, one notes the concentration of items in the *Sleeper* quadrant. Items 2, 3, 6, and 7 appear the best menu items to improve. If the popularity of these items were improved, they could move into the *Prime* quadrant. Any internal promotion that would call attention to the items and increase their chance of selection would be in order. The dispersion of appetizers on the graph represents a very good mix of items relative to food costs. However, contribution margin can be improved. Most items are below the PFC line and to the left of the AWCM line.

SNACKS

In Table 5.4 and Figure 5–6, snack items 1, 3, 6, 8, 25, and 27 are the closest to the intersecting lines and therefore the best candidates for improvement. Closer examination of the items in the *Problems* quadrant reveals the worst items are children's portions. These items are purposely priced low and, because they represent such a small portion of the total items sold, have minimal impact on the overall food cost percentage.

ENTREES

Table 5.5 and Figure 5–7 shows the majority of entrée items in the *Standards* quadrant. If sales of entrées are increased through menu design and internal promotions, the Potential Food Cost of the total sales mix will increase since

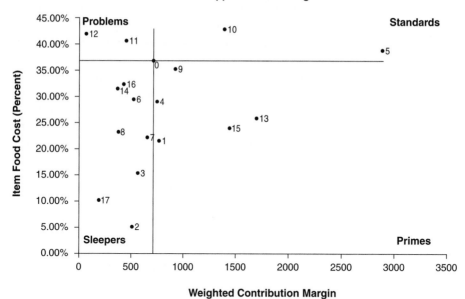

FIGURE 5–5
Appetizer Cost/Margin

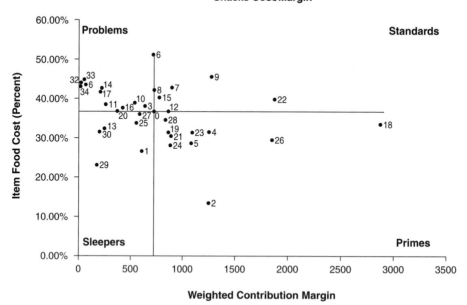

FIGURE 5–6
Snacks Cost/Margin

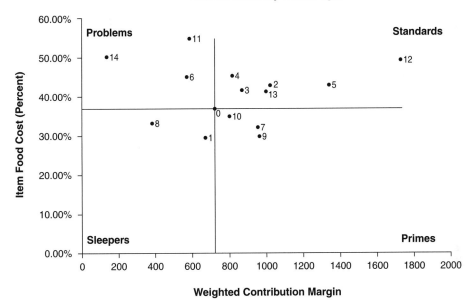

FIGURE 5–7
Entrees Cost/Margin

most of the items have a food cost higher than the 36.15 percent shown in Table 5.7. The plotted points of the entrees are fairly deep in the Standards quadrant, indicating that movement downward and closer to the Primes quadrant would require several changes involving price, portion size and accompaniments to minimize negative reactions from customers.

DESSERTS

The desserts shown in Table 5.6 and Figure 5–8 are skewed severely to the left. Most items are borderline *Problems* and may be moved into the *Sleepers* quadrant if costs can be reduced or prices raised. These items might appear at first to have a negative effect on overall figures, but because they account for such an insignificant number of items sold, their impact on food cost and gross profit is negligible.

The desserts present another example of why it is important to use a "desserts only" average for food cost percentage and average weighted contribution instead of the averages for the entire sales mix. If only desserts are averaged according to the formulas shown for cutoff points for food cost and average contribution margin, the food cost cutoff is 46.48 percent (compared to the 36.15 percent for the entire menu sales mix) and the weighted contribu-

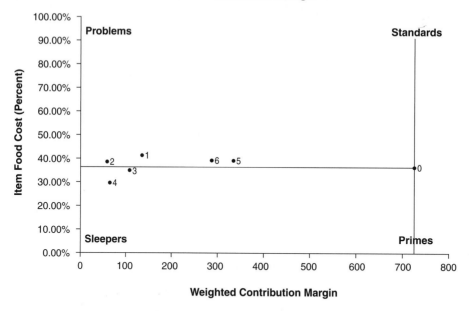

FIGURE 5–8
Dessert Cost/Margin

tion margin cutoff is $145.86 (compared to $724.24) (see Table 5.6). This would put dessert items 5 and 6 into the dessert *Primes* category, whereas they show up as *Problems* when compared to the overall sales mix. This is due to the fact that they have a lower markup, higher food cost percentage, and account for only 4.16 percent of all items sold. A very low percentage of customers order desserts compared to snacks and appetizers.

The data in Table 5.8 reveal that appetizers and snacks have a "lowering" effect on the PFC as both have average food cost percentages below 36.15 percent, the PFC for the entire menu sales mix. The highest volume items are in the appetizer category where the average number sold exceeds the menu average by 72 (257.60 minus 185.68). This is occurring at the expense of the entrées, which account for less than 18 percent of the total items sold. The data show that customers apparently order an appetizer or side order and do not consider entrees. This was partially due to the design of the menu, a multi-paged booklet where the entrees were located on the last two pages.

Snacks and appetizers made up 78 percent of the total items sold. These two categories have the greatest impact on overall cost, contribution margin, and sales revenue and deserve management's closest attention. They account for 68 percent of the food cost dollar, 75 percent of the contribution margin, and 72.5 percent of the sales revenue. (See Table 5.8.)

Table 5.8 Cost/Margin Average Menu Category Averages & Totals

Menu Category	Potential Food Cost	Average No. Sold	Average Item C.M.	Average Weighted C.M.	% of Items Sold	% of Food Cost	% of Cont. Margin	% of Sales Dollars
Appetizers	31.14%	257.60	$2.26	$832.55	32.76%	21.68%	27.14%	25.17%
Snacks	35.35%	178.11	$2.90	$737.81	45.30%	46.46%	48.11%	47.51%
Entrées	41.76%	169.85	$3.50	$848.88	17.79%	28.86%	22.79%	24.99%
Desserts	46.48%	79.40	$1.29	$145.92	4.16%	3.01%	1.96%	2.34%
Miscellaneous					0.00%	0.00%	0.00%	0.00%
Totals	36.15%	185.68	$2.73	$724.23	100.00%	100.00%	100.00%	100.00%

Cost/Margin Analysis should be conducted on a quarterly basis to reveal trends in popularity, costs, and contribution margin. An operator can quickly and easily see which items on the graph are the best candidates for improvement. If the graphs are printed on clear transparencies instead of paper, the movement of cutoff lines and menu item placement can be readily compared from one period to the next. If changes are made that lower the food cost line and move the average weighted contribution margin line to the right, the changes made are having positive effects on the sales mix.

Cost/Margin Analysis allows one to objectively view the effects of the menu design, pricing, and food cost changes through the plotting of the cutoff lines and menu items on a graph. Marketing and cost control efforts can be targeted to the menu categories and items where the greatest need exists. When changes are made, cost/margin analysis will indicate whether improvements to the sales mix have taken place.

The Cost/Margin Analysis is applicable to fast-food operations. There is a separate column in the spreadsheet titled "Supplemental Cost," which can be used to include packaging materials like beverage cups and styrofoam containers. This can also be used to add a "direct labor cost value" for items requiring direct labor. In the case of alcoholic beverages, it can be used for the mix and garnish costs of the drink. The data can also be used by multi-unit operations to compare units.

The Seven P's of Menu Design

The marketing mix consists of the four P's of promotion, place, price, and product. We can apply a similar marketing mix of seven P's to examine the role of the menu in marketing items to the customers.

Through menu design, we can influence the sales mix of menu items by altering certain aspects within the following areas:

Purchase price: The purchase price of the ingredients can relate to the "quality" of the item. Higher quality costs more than lesser quality. You could "shop" for the best price of ingredients to lower your food cost without sacrificing quality.

Portioning: The portion size and the accompaniments that are included are treated in the same manner to project "value" to the customer. Larger portions and more accompaniments translate to increased value for the customer.

Positioning: Positioning has to do with the placement or prominence given to an item on the menu. Primacy and recency principles and gaze motion can be used to increase the likelihood of selection.

Promotion: Anything done to increase attention to certain items will increase its chance of selection; e.g., table tents, suggestive selling, menu emphasis with graphics or bold typeface. When new items are added and old ones deleted, the number of portions sold of the items deleted will shift to other items. How much they affect the overall sales mix will depend on the promotion or attention given to the changes.

Product presentation: Doing something unique to the product and transforming it from a "commodity" to a "specialty" item allows you to create a monopoly of sorts, and with that designation comes a group of distinct advantages over the competition. The effective use of flatware and garnitures will certainly enhance the visual presentation and increase the value perception of the customer. We do not eat as much with our sense of taste as we do with our eyes. This also refers to the dining room amenities like tablecloths, candles, and fresh flowers.

Price (Menu): The price you charge can certainly influence selection. Pricing can also refer to whether the menu item is priced à la carte or table d'hôte. Further emphasis can be drawn to the item by price promotions such as discounting or by adding or deleting accompaniments or by giving larger portions. However, discounting or low price leaders are not the recommended way to build an image of quality and elegance that some restaurants seek to achieve.

Place: By altering the "place" aspects of marketing strategy, (i.e., home delivery, carryout service, picnic lunches, catering services) further competitive distinctiveness can be created. These factors are used in any strategy to improve the position of items in your sales mix to enhance whatever it is you are trying to accomplish, whether it be lowering food cost, or increasing popularity, the contribution margin, or the average check.

S trategies for Primes, Standards, Sleepers, and Problems

Once the Cost/Margin menu analysis has classified the menu items into one of the four categories, a strategy for improving or optimizing their overall impact on the menu sales mix can be put into action. The characteristics of the menu items will point you in the direction of what specific strategy would be best.

Primes: Remember, *Primes* are popular items that are low in food cost and high in weighted contribution margin. You want to sell the heck out of these items. Therefore you should utilize menu design psychology to make these items **STAND OUT** on the menu. Use techniques such as bold and oversized lettering, placing the menu item in its own outlined box, featuring it on a chalkboard or lit menu board, suggestive selling by servers, and so on.

Maintaining high visibility is recommended for *Primes.* It is very important to keep quality high and portions adequate because these menu items are likely house specialties or signature items that are specifically sought by customers. Because they are popular, you might test for price elasticity and increase the price if you felt it was low relative to competing items on the menu and if an item was one of your moderate to lowest priced items in its respective menu category. Monitor quality and presentation standards to insure high standards on these items.

Standards: These are also popular items that have high food costs and high weighted contribution margins. You can test for price elasticity by raising the price to lower the food cost percentage. If the item were a signature item on your menu, this option is one you might consider. The proximity to the food cost line on the graph will tell you exactly how much you have to raise the price to move it on or below the food cost line. If it is only a matter of $.25 to $.95, it might be worth a try. If raising the price were not an option, if the portion were large, you could lower the food cost by reducing the portion without the customer noticing the change.

If you could do neither, you might move it to a less noticeable position on the menu to lower its selection odds. At the same time you may want to emphasize another item in its place that is lower in food cost and higher in contribution margin. Food cost can also be lowered by reducing accompaniments or perhaps finding a purveyor who has a lower price on some of the key ingredients. You may be able to develop a similar item that is combined with a low-cost ingredient (e.g., pasta or rice) and promote that item. Also, promote sleepers to soften the high cost aspects of the popular standards.

Sleepers: Since these items are slow-selling, low food cost items, they also have a low weighted contribution margin. Therefore, anything you do to increase the likelihood that these items are selected by the guest is recommended. Prominently display them on the menu; feature them on menu boards; use table tents and suggestive selling by the servers. Since they are very low in food cost, you can lower the price via discounts or early bird specials to stimulate sales. Also, increase portions or accompaniments to create a better value at a low price to stimulate sales. Rename the item and promote it as a signature item.

Problems: These items are high in food cost and low in contribution margin. You can raise the price or lower the product cost. If you cannot do either, hide it on the menu. Develop and promote substitute items.

Combine this item with inexpensive ingredients to lower portion cost. If sales do not pick up, take it off the menu.*

ey Concepts

- The menu is the starting point for all restaurant planning and design.
- The menu is not just a list of what you have to sell, but rather a cost control, merchandising, and communication tool.
- Cost/Margin Analysis is a practical tool for analyzing the menu sales mix to find the items that contribute most to your sales, cost, and profit objectives.
- The items you want to promote are those that are popular, bring in a high weighted gross profit, and are low in food cost.

ey Terms

Menu sales mix	Gaze motion	Weighted sales
Extensive menus	Cost/Margin Analysis	Primes
Limited menus	Weighted contribution	Problems
Static menu	margin	Standards
Cycle menu	Individual contribu-	Sleepers
Combination menus	tion margin	Seven "P's" of menu
Menu psychology	Weighted food cost	design

iscussion Questions

1. Explain why the time and effort placed on designing a menu should be as much as that given to major financial and capital asset decisions.
2. What is the purpose for conducting the menu sales mix analysis? *Your answer should touch upon the information it provides management and how it aids in decision making and developing strategies for optimizing the menu sales mix.*

Authors' Note: For additional of Cost/Margin Analysis see "Prime Numbers: Finding Your Menu's Strengths," Cornell Quarterly, Nov. 1985, Vol 26, No. 3, pp. 71–77 and "Cost/Margin Analysis: A Third Approach to Menu Pricing and Design," International Journal of Hospitality Management, 1983, Vol 2, No. 3, pp. 127–134.

3. Define and explain the theory of *Primacy and Recency* and how it is applied to menu design.

4. Explain why and how a *Cost/Margin Analysis* improves upon the Miller Matrix and Menu Engineering menu sales analysis.

5. What four (4) criteria are used to analyze the menu sales mix? *Hint: Think of the three methods of menu sales analysis and the criteria plotted on the graphs.*

Problem 1 Menu Sales Mix Analysis

Using the Cost/Margin disk that came with your text, enter the data from the table below to complete this problem. *Use the* Appetizers *tab for Sales Mix "A" and the* Snacks *tab for Sales Mix "B". Do not change the names of the tabs or the macros will malfunction.* When you print your graphs, use the "individual" option, not the "summary" option. Using the data found on the spreadsheets and graphs, answer the following questions. *Use the accompanying Excel Template given for this problem to indicate your answers.*

1. Which Menu Items have the "best" food cost percentages?

	Item	Food Cost %
1st	_____	_____
2nd	_____	_____
3rd	_____	_____

2. Which menu items have the "worst" food cost percentages?

	Item	Food Cost %
1st	_____	_____
2nd	_____	_____
3rd	_____	_____

3. Which items have the "best" *individual* contribution margin/gross profit?

	Item	Indiv. CM/GP
1st	_____	_____
2nd	_____	_____
3rd	_____	_____

4. Which items return the "best" *total or weighted* contribution margin?

	Sales Mix A Menu Item	Sales Mix A Wgtd CM$	Sales Mix B Menu Item	Sales Mix B Wgtd CM $
1st	_____	_____	_____	_____
2nd	_____	_____	_____	_____
3rd	_____	_____	_____	_____

5. Which Sales Mix, A or B, returns the best weighted/potential food cost percentage? Show the amounts for both.

6. Which Sales Mix, A or B, returns the best weighted contribution margin/gross profit? Indicate the actual amount.

7. Using the Cost/Margin diskette that came with the text, enter the data for this problem and **print the graphs for both sales mixes** using all three of the menu analysis methods, i.e., the Miller Matrix, Menu Engineering, and Cost Margin Analysis. *You will have a total of six graphs.* Using the following table, summarize all the menu items that fall into each category. *Note: A menu item may appear more than once in the same category because of the common elements within the three methodologies.* **Using the problem template, indicate the distribution of menu items in each of the four quadrants for all three menu sales analysis methodologies.**

8. This is the most critical question in this assignment and is worth 30% of the grade. Crunching the numbers with this special software is only valuable if you can interpret the numbers. The tables, graphs and spreadsheets contain the quantitative information you need to support your conclusions. Considering all the information you have at your disposal, write a report that indicates which one of the two sales mixes is financially superior, and why. You must back up your answer with **quantifiable data**. Follow the logic in the explanation of "the fallacy of gross profit" at the end of Chapter 3, Food Cost Control. A template has been provided for your use in compiling the appropriate "quantifiable data."

   You must include your spreadsheets, tables, and graphs with your report. The sales mix data for this problem is shown in the table below.

Data for Problem 1

Item No.	Menu Item	Menu Price	Food Cost $	No. Sold A	No. Sold B
			Cost/Margin Sales Analysis Problem		
1	Quesadilla	$ 6.99	$ 1.63	222	200
2	Crab Cakes	$ 6.99	$ 3.89	158	188
3	Fried Shrimp	$ 10.99	$ 2.65	241	123
4	Chicken Tenders	$ 8.99	$ 2.43	508	365
5	Half Rack Ribs	$ 11.99	$ 4.41	365	508
6	Ribeye Steak	$ 14.99	$ 5.72	151	223
7	Shrimp Pasta	$ 13.99	$ 6.20	123	241
8	Creole Salmon	$ 9.99	$ 2.27	188	158
9	Veggie Pasta	$ 9.99	$ 2.05	59	81
10	Petite Top Sirloin	$ 9.99	$ 2.67	223	151
	Totals			2,238	2,238

Problem 2
Exercise Comparing the Three Methods of Menu Sales Analysis

Given the following food menu sales data for the months of October and November, and using the Cost/Margin software program, develop the spreadsheets and graphs for the four menu categories of Appetizers, Entrées, Desserts, and Miscellaneous, and answer the following questions:

1. On which items do the three menu sales mix programs agree?
2. On which items do they not agree? When they do disagree, examine the characteristics of the menu item as to food cost percentage, individual contribution margin, number sold, and weighted contribution margin to find the reason for their disagreement.
3. What is the Potential Food Cost of the entire sales mix for each month? Which month has the best financial results? Back up your answer with quantifiable data. Refer back to Chapter 3 and *the fallacy of gross profit* explanation.

Problem 2 Menu Sales Data

Menu Item	Oct Sales	Nov Sales	Menu Price	Food Cost
Appetizers				
Calamari	120	65	$ 8.00	$ 0.98
Caesar Salad	251	137	$ 6.00	$ 1.28
Frog Legs	33	0	$ 7.00	$ 2.08
Tiger Shrimp	68	57	$ 9.00	$ 2.46
Panzanella Salad	105	0	$ 6.00	$ 1.98
Spring Rolls	120	0	$ 9.00	$ 1.37
Insalata	126	49	$ 9.00	$ 2.19
Scallops	69	49	$ 9.00	$ 1.98
Endive Salad	0	56	$ 6.00	$ 0.65
Mesclun Salad	0	117	$ 7.00	$ 1.06
Crab Cakes	0	42	$10.00	$ 3.00
Vol Au Vent	0	53	$ 9.00	$ 1.81
Entrees				
Catfish	0	39	$13.00	$ 2.20
Kids Pasta	2	7	$ 5.00	$ 0.85

(continued)

Menu Item	Oct Sales	Nov Sales	Menu Price	Food Cost
Tandoori Salmon	0	49	$19.00	$ 2.47
Quail	0	29	$ 22.00	$ 5.71
Pork Chop	0	20	$ 22.00	$ 6.25
Veal Chop	127	64	$ 19.00	$ 4.77
Angry Trout	0	34	$ 21.00	$ 2.90
Romagoli	0	50	$ 19.00	$ 4.79
NY Strip	158	121	$ 24.00	$ 7.00
Lasagna	55	34	$ 16.00	$ 2.22
Crab Cakes	150	66	$ 24.00	$ 7.49
Short Ribs	0	58	$ 15.00	$ 2.67
Meatloaf	0	66	$ 14.00	$ 2.50
Special Char	47	0	$ 24.00	$ 3.50
Salmon	58	0	$ 22.00	$ 3.25
Duck	83	0	$ 23.00	$ 4.94
Tuna	85	0	$ 25.00	$ 6.61
Pasta	78	0	$ 20.00	$ 4.79
Lamb	121	0	$ 18.00	$ 3.50
Special Sable	137	0	$ 24.00	$ 5.50
Special Chop	106	0	$ 24.00	$ 6.38
Special Rock Fish	136	0	$ 22.00	$ 3.41
Special Tuna	11	0	$ 25.00	$ 7.10
Desserts				
Ice Cream	27	0	$ 7.00	$ 0.75
Vanilla Brulee	118	64	$ 6.00	$ 0.64
Special Clefouti	11	0	$ 7.00	$ 0.36
Godiva Cake	199	117	$ 7.00	$ 0.91
Special Tart	35	0	$ 6.00	$ 0.97
Bread Pudding	76	66	$ 6.00	$ 1.12
Special Cake	58	0	$ 6.00	$ 1.10
Lemon Cake	25	0	$ 6.00	$ 1.10
Cheese Cake 1	9	0	$ 6.00	$ 1.26
Apple Pie	7	0	$ 6.00	$ 1.32
White Chocolate	4	0	$ 6.00	$ 1.16
Cheese Cake 2	0	36	$ 6.00	$ 0.90
Panna Cotta	0	46	$ 5.00	$ 0.74

(*continued*)

Menu Item	Oct Sales	Nov Sales	Menu Price	Food Cost
Miscellaneous				
Corned Beef Hash	12	56	$ 7.00	$ 0.81
Eggs Benedict	45	66	$ 10.00	$ 1.22
She Crab Soup	34	45	$ 5.00	$ 1.20
Bacon	15	1	$ 1.50	$ 0.20
Chicken Salad	8	28	$ 7.00	$ 1.28
Dog Catcher	15	34	$ 7.00	$ 1.05
Add One Egg	15	2	$ 1.25	$ 0.11
TD Burger	20	51	$ 8.00	$ 2.37
Crab Cake Sandwich	26	59	$ 9.00	$ 2.24
Meatloaf	19	0	$ 8.00	$ 1.05
Catfish	6	0	$ 7.00	$ 1.20
Pancakes	27	0	$ 7.00	$ 0.72
Burrito	15	0	$ 6.00	$ 1.23
Grits	5	0	$ 1.25	$ 0.10
Tortilla Espagnole	5	0	$ 5.00	$ 1.25
Crab Quesadilla	32	0	$ 7.00	$ 1.56

6

Menu Pricing Methodology and Theory

■   ■   ■   ■   ■   ■   ■   ■   ■   ■

FUNDAMENTAL PRINCIPLES OF MENU PRICING

1. Although calculating the raw food cost of any given menu item is an objective and logical process, setting the price is subjective and enigmatic.

2. Pricing requires a combination of factors that involve both financial and competitive elements.

3. There is no single pricing method that can be used effectively on every menu.

4. The customer will ultimately determine the price you can charge.

5. You must be able to make a profit selling at the price the customer is willing to pay.

6. You cannot mark up every item to return the same gross profit percentage.

7. Cost is not the only consideration in pricing any given menu item.

8. Every restaurant will be placed into a price category by its customers.

9. Your average check is more than just the calculation of total sales divided by the total number of customers.

10. Prices are either *market driven* or *demand driven*.

Regardless of the methodology used to mark up food and beverages, prices charged by commercial food services must not only cover costs but return a profit as well. Pricing is an important function that directly influences customer counts and sales revenues. The optimum price must not only include some contribution to profit but also be deemed fair and reasonable by the public. One cannot remain in business very long if costs are not covered. However, costs are not the sole consideration in determining menu prices, but costs must be known in order to measure profit contribution on each sale. Some costs can be directly assigned to specific menu items while others must be subjectively allocated across the entire menu. At most, cost serves as a reference point to begin developing a pricing strategy.

Many operators experience increasing competition for their customers and have to constantly deal with rising operating costs, labor shortages, and legislation impacting their business. Such factors will definitely impact their profits. Therefore, the pricing strategy they use is a major factor in developing an overall plan to deal with such obstacles.

Most businesspeople seek logical and objective criteria on which to base their pricing strategy. This is the main reason we start with determining the cost of a product or service. The costing process is objective and absolute. There is a tendency to rationalize price as a means of returning an amount that will reflect a fair profit for the risk incurred and the time, effort, and materials consumed.

Of all the business decisions a restaurateur has to make, one that causes much anxiety is pricing the menu. Whenever pricing decisions require raising prices, the operator mentally prepares for some adverse customer response. The usual feedback comes in the form of spoken comments and the dreaded dropping customer counts. Consequently, the task of menu pricing is beset with misgivings and uncertainty. Prices that are too high will drive customers away, and prices that are too low will sacrifice profit. The main reason for this anxiety may well be the highly subjective methodology used to price menus in the first place. Anxiety results when trying to determine whether the approach used for pricing is the best or the right one for the respective menu items, existing market conditions, and operational concept.

Prices partially influence which menu items will sell and therefore impact the overall profitability of the sales mix. In fact, hospitality marketing experts will tell us that prices have a more direct and immediate impact on shifts in demand, profits, and customer reactions than any other hospitality marketing variable. While pricing is just one element in the marketing mix, it definitely influences guests' expectations of food quality and service, décor, image, and their level of satisfaction with the total dining experience. The menu sales mix will, in turn, influence everything from equipment utilization to marketing efforts. Menu items will differ widely in cost, popularity, and profitability. In addition, the amount of labor required will differ from item to item. Thus, pricing is not a simple matter of markup over cost but an intricate combination of factors that involve both financial and competitive elements.

Menu pricing philosophies are as diverse as political and theological beliefs and sometimes just as controversial. Initially, it was the popular belief that only raw food costs should be marked up to obtain a targeted food cost percentage. More often than not, the targeted food cost percentage was arbitrarily determined by simply copying a successful competitor or trying to match some industry average. We have subsequently improved upon the method of determining a targeted food cost percentage and can analytically determine a realistic food cost standard based on each operation's financial and budgetary idiosyncrasies. However, a unit's financial limitations or profit demands may not be realistic or compatible with the existing economic or market conditions. If prices are too high relative to what the competition is charging, quality is too low, or portions are so small as to negate the price-value relationship, sales and profit objectives may still not be realized.

M arket and Demand Driven Pricing

What it basically comes down to is that prices can be either *market driven* or *demand driven*, and depending on the uniqueness or monopolistic aspects of the menu item and operational concept, the approach to pricing will differ significantly. **Market driven pricing** must be responsive to competitors' prices. Menu items that are relatively common (commodities in an economic goods sense) and found on most menus (e.g., hamburgers, barbecue ribs, Prime rib) and in markets where there are several restaurants where customers can get these items, must be priced competitively. The markup is usually moderate on the pricing continuum. This perspective on pricing is also used when introducing new menu items before any substantial demand has been established. Therefore, *market driven* prices tend to be on the moderate to low side. When you are involved in pricing a menu, you will find it useful to assess your customers' price sensitivity before increasing prices.

In contrast is **demand driven pricing** where the customers openly ask for an item and demand exceeds the ability of restaurants in the market able to supply that item. The item becomes more of a "specialty good" in the economic sense, and a "monopoly" of sorts exists for the short term. Thus, pricing on an item that is demand driven can be more toward the higher end of the pricing continuum than on a market driven item. This is the case until demand starts to wane or competitors add the item to their menus. When this occurs, prices will stabilize and become more market driven.

Cost Markup

While costing out an entrée and accompaniments is a relatively objective and logical process, establishing a selling price is more of an art. Whatever the pricing methodology, no *single* method can be used to mark up *every* item on any given restaurant menu. You must employ a combination of methodologies and theories. Therefore, when properly carried out, prices will reflect food cost percentages, individual and/or weighted contribution margins, price points, and desired check averages, as well as factors driven by intuition, competition, and demand.

If pricing were a purely quantitative exercise, a computer program that would incorporate operating costs, profit objectives, and raw food costs could be used to set menu prices. However, such an approach lacks important "qualitative" factors that enter into the pricing decision. It has been said of most retail products and services that the buyer determines the price, not the seller. Therefore, the seller must be able to offer a product or service and make a profit selling it at the price the customer is willing to pay. Value judgments are hard to encode into a cost-markup pricing program.

Customer Price-Point Pricing

Consider the pricing wars that have transpired in the fast food segment such as Wendy's $.99 menu that was copied by McDonald's and Burger King. Wendy's initially dropped the price of the "Single" to $.99 and added french fries, chili, and a Frosty. McDonald's brought out their "Big Deluxe" for $.99 along with accompaniments like fries and drinks for the same price. Burger King also had its version of what has come to be called "value pricing." Basically, all three took the approach of dropping the prices on items already on the menu to meet a price point they felt the customer was looking to spend. In the process they experienced reduced profit margins on each item. It was a disguised form of discounting.

The traditional approach to pricing has always been to develop a product and then determine what the price should be based on our standard food cost. Taco Bell, on the other hand, was more successful with its value pricing of menu items because it did not simply reduce the cost on its existing items or start with a product and then arrive at the selling price. Rather, they first studied their customers' pricing perceptions and then developed menu items for the price range their customers were willing to spend. If the price customers were willing to pay would not return a profit, the menu item was rejected.

The pricing method used by Taco Bell was to first determine the price the customer is willing to pay and then develop menu items that will achieve profit and cost objectives selling for that price. Taco Bell was able to sell $.39 tacos and maintain a food cost percentage in the mid thirties. Taco Bell even considered that the customer reaction to a price that was so cheap might raise concerns about the quality. Subsequently, there was a pricing minimum they did not want to go below.

You are probably asking if this approach to pricing applies to full service restaurants. The answer is a resounding, YES IT DOES! Even the fine dining, white tablecloth restaurants have found themselves in a situation that required this approach to pricing. Since the World Trade Center tragedy on September 11, 2001, the hospitality industry in general has been facing difficult economic times. All segments of the food service industry have seen significant declines in customer traffic. Heretofore, fine dining had not resorted to discounting like the other segments of the industry. However, this is no longer the case.

In Atlanta, Georgia and other metropolitan areas like Chicago and New York, many fine dining restaurants have resorted to offering "early bird specials" for patrons who arrive at their restaurants prior to 6:00 PM. Several restaurants advertise "$10 Steaks," "$10 Fish," and "$1 Sushi." Initially, most simply cut their prices on one or two entrees and accepted the lower margin because they were able to fill their dining rooms that were otherwise empty between 5:00–6:00 PM. "Earlybird Specials" are a regular feature in many restaurants even today and is offered seven days per week.

However, not all fine dining operations took this approach. They used the Taco Bell approach of first developing a price point and then developing menu items that they could offer at that price that would not require them to lower their profit margin. They abandoned their original pricing strategy of gross profit return to a menu with lower prices and lower individual gross profits. This resulted in increased customer counts and a higher overall total gross profit return.

Subsequently, several operators took the approach of developing a special early bird menu of 4–6 choices priced at $10. Thus, like Taco Bell did with their $.39 taco, so these operations do with their special menus. In addition, the sale of a cocktail or a glass of wine improved the financial return of each transaction.

Determining the Price to Charge

A question often asked by restaurateurs is, "What price should I charge?" The response was, initially, "Charge the *highest* price you think the customer will pay." Finding that particular price point is not easy, and if you price at that point you can expect the customer to be more demanding and critical of the food and service. Getting the price right is one of the most fundamental and important management functions. In order to do this effectively, management must identify the level of customer price elasticity that will return the highest total gross profit.

A different perspective was offered by successful Ark Restaurants CEO Michael Weinstein during a past Multiple Unit Food Service Operators Conference, sponsored annually by Nation's Restaurant News. Rather than charging the highest price the customer will pay, his restaurants price at the lowest point at which they can still make a reasonable profit. His reasoning is that if you price at the high end, your operation must be on the "cutting edge" of excellence in food quality, preparation, service, and atmosphere. He achieves satisfaction from customers who praise the price-value offered on his menus. People almost always comment on the reasonableness of the prices, the large portion sizes, and the high quality of the ingredients. Therefore, the two perspectives on how much to charge are: Charge as much as you can or charge as little as you can. Keep in mind that the success of any pricing methodology is influenced by many factors including, among others, location, competition, clientele, and restaurant concept. What works on the Upper West Side of New York may flop in Atlanta, Georgia.

More often than not, prices are predominantly influenced by competition and/or customer demand. Whenever demand is greater than supply, pricing methodologies that favor higher gross profits and higher check averages can be effective in maximizing revenue. On the other hand, if customer counts are flat and strong competition exists for the products and services, such pricing could be disastrous.

The restaurant's menu prices must be in line with the price category in which the majority of its customers place the operation. If prices exceed that range, customers will not purchase many of those items. If your prices are too low, you run the danger of lowering your overall image and will find the check average falling.

The market ultimately determines the price one can charge. If you charge too much, your customers will go somewhere else. However, it is important to interject a warning at this point. Lower prices do not automatically translate into "value" and "bargain" in the minds of the customers. Having the lowest prices in your market may not bring customers or profit. Too often operators engage in price wars through discount promotions and find that profits fall and their image in the marketplace is lowered.

Once initial prices are determined, adjustments up and down will be made after examining the price spread between the lowest and the highest priced items. Every restaurant will be categorized by customers according to the prices it charges. Customers will place a restaurant into one of three categories: low-priced, moderate-priced, and high-priced. Specific numerical check averages are not given because customers, depending upon their incomes, will apply their own dollar ranges when rating restaurants in each category.

Some operators may temper markups on other factors besides food cost percentages. The desired check average, or price point, can strongly impact pricing philosophy, and it should be determined before the menu is initially priced. If you can forecast the number of customers you will serve at each meal period, a properly designed menu will help to influence your sales revenues by making it less likely for a customer to spend less than the predetermined amount needed to achieve your desired check average. This is a different definition of average check. Traditionally, it is calculated by dividing food and/or beverage sales by the number of covers.

For example, assume that sales were $2,000 and you served 125 covers. The average check is therefore $16 ($2,000/125). However, if you were seeking a $20 average check, you are $4 short of your objective. If a $20 check average is the goal or price point you want to achieve, this should be reflected in the prices charged. The majority of entrees (60 to 75 percent) should be priced within a range of $17.95 to $21.95 and predominantly positioned on the menu.

If the price range is as described and the check average is still below $20, the menu design may be encouraging customers to purchase lower-priced entrees. Menu design can influence customer selection. (See Chapter 5 on "Psychology of Menu Design.") Forcing a price point or check average will not be effective either. Price-value relationships must always be considered. Do not try to force up prices on common items offered by most competitors (e.g., steaks and Prime rib). Utilize house specialties and unique signature foods as your price point leaders. Because these items are unique to your operation, you enjoy the pricing advantages of having a monopoly—at least for the short run. This allows you to price closer to the high end of your price range.

As stated previously, menu prices must be in line with the price category in which the majority of its customers place the operation. If prices of some items exceed that range, customers will not purchase many of those items. If prices are too low, there is a danger of lowering the overall image and the check average may drop.

Pricing to Achieve a Specific Food Cost Percentage

Exclusive reliance on a menu pricing philosophy that seeks to achieve an unrealistically determined food cost percentage can create problems. Assume that the food cost goal is the oft-quoted 40 percent. If *all* items are marked up 2½ times their cost, one could theoretically achieve a 40 percent cost (allowances for employee meals and unavoidable waste factored in) and still not realize sales or profit objectives. Clearly, food cost percentage cannot be the sole consideration in establishing the selling price. All items cannot be marked up the same amount. Pricing or markup is rarely exclusively cost driven. If it were, many items would be greatly underpriced relative to what the public is willing to pay, while others would be overpriced. In the case of the former, a simple cup of beef bouillon with a food cost of less than 2 cents per ounce would have a total cost of 10 cents for a 5-ounce portion. A 40 percent food cost would be achieved if it were sold for 25 cents. It could sell for $3.95 in a white tablecloth restaurant and not be considered overpriced by patrons.

In the same restaurant, pricing a 1½-pound live lobster that costs $8.95 per pound would require a menu price of $33.50, without including the costs of accompaniments. Most patrons would consider this price excessive. In addition, marking up every item to achieve a single food cost percentage ignores price-value aspects of competitive pricing and does not allow for the fact that costs are not equally distributed among all items on the menu. Some items are purchased in convenience form and require little or no effort to prepare. An 8-ounce carton of milk, bottled or canned soft drinks, beer and wine, and coffee are examples. Such items do not require as high a markup as others requiring preparation and processing.

Customer Perceptions of the Restaurant and the Pricing Decision

In addition to placing the restaurant into a price category, customers will evaluate a restaurant as a place to "eat out" or as a place to "dine out." If a restaurant is considered an eat-out operation during the week (a substitute for cooking at home), customers will be more price-conscious, because "mental accounting" has them allocating grocery budgeted funds to eating out. If a restaurant is considered a dine-out operation, the visit is regarded more as a social and entertainment occasion rather than merely a trip to satiate one's hunger. The "mental accounting" in this situation takes funds from an entertainment budget, which is more liberal than a grocery budget.

Rarely will a restaurant be rated as both an eat out and dine out category by the same patron. Frequency of visits to an eat-out operation will be greater than to the dine-out operation, but amounts spent will be considerably less than in the latter. Regular weekday customers may go elsewhere for special celebrations like anniversaries or birthdays. Weekend clientele may differ greatly from weeknight customers. For example, local residents may be the bulk of the traffic during the week, while weekends may bring visitors, tourists, or people traveling from outside the restaurant's normal market area. Such patrons categorize the operation as a dine-out or special occasion restaurant. "Diners" will travel farther than those patrons "eating out" and are willing to spend more.

Four "Costless" Approaches to Pricing

One cannot arrive at a selling price without considering some highly subjective factors that have "refined" the interpretation of traditional economic theory on consumer buying behavior. Psychologists are teaming up with marketing analysts and economists to provide some new perspectives on pricing. The most common methods employed are logical in the accounting sense of the word. The methods offered here are largely subjective and, for the most part, ignore cost considerations. These "costless" approaches to pricing are (1) competitive pricing, (2) intuitive pricing, (3) psychological pricing, and (4) trial-and-error pricing (Schmidgall, 1990, pp. 282–85). Regardless of what they are called, these approaches reflect two of the three critical factors in pricing: demand and competition; the third is cost.

COMPETITIVE PRICING

The **competitive pricing** approach is very simple. The operator collects menus from competitors and then meets or beats their prices. This method is highly ineffective because it assumes that the customer makes the purchase decision based on price alone. It fails to take into account the many other factors that influence choice and preference such as product quality, ambience, service, and even location.

INTUITIVE PRICING

Intuitive pricing is practiced by operators who do not want to take the time to gather menu prices from competitors. They rely instead on what they can remember from past experiences and set prices based on what they feel the guests are willing to pay. This method relies on evaluating the competition and the demand for one's particular products or services.

PSYCHOLOGICAL ASPECTS OF PRICING

In another pricing approach, **psychological pricing**, a number of interesting theories enter into the pricing decision and a few are offered here. Buyer "price consciousness" influences the way prices are perceived and the importance of price in the buyer's choice of products or services (Monroe and Kirshnan, 1984). Researchers have suggested that "price consciousness" is inversely correlated with social class, implying that price is more a factor to low-income customers frequenting lower-priced restaurants (Gabor and Granger, 1961).

When a buyer lacks specific qualitative information about a menu item and is unable to judge quality prior to purchase, higher prices are associated with higher quality. Price perceptions are sometimes based on the "last price paid," or reference price (Monroe and Petroshius, 1973). The reference price may be the price charged by a competitor, and if it was lower, value perceptions are lowered.

The order in which buyers are exposed to alternative prices affects their perceptions. Buyers exposed initially to high prices will perceive subsequent lower prices as bargains. However, dropping prices to meet a competitor's is not always effective (Della Bitta and Monroe, 1973). Low price does not always result in a dominant market position because people refrain from purchasing a product not only when the price is perceived as too high but also when it is perceived to be too low. When prices for two competing products are perceived to be similar, the price is unlikely to be a factor when a buyer chooses between similar products or services (Monroe and Petroshius, 1973).

Current evidence would suggest that it is the buyer's perception of the total relative value of the product or service that provides the willingness to pay a particular price for a given offering. The total relative value in the restaurant sense consists of such elements as atmosphere, convenience, quality, service, and location. The relative value is enhanced by either *value analysis* or *value engineering*. Value analysis concentrates on increasing perceived value through improving performance (service) relative to customer needs. Value engineering concentrates on increasing value by decreasing costs while maintaining performance standards (Monroe, 1986). The element of customer perception is an important determinant of buyer behavior. Buyers use such cues as product quality, corporate image, and name recognition, along with price, to differentiate among alternatives and to form impressions of product and service quality (Monroe and Kirshnan, 1984).

The driving force in psychological approaches to pricing addresses the important aspect of customer perceptions that will influence the purchase decision (Pavesic, 1989, pp. 43–49). Whether the customer will pay the price or balk is the question. Should one start off low and increase the price or start off on the high side and then discount? Answers to such questions depend upon one's market position, the demand for the product or service, and the stage in the market life cycle of the operation and/or product.

Another psychological theory on pricing looks at the impact of "mental accounting" (Thaler, 1985). This theory suggests that consumers mentally code purchases into categories (e.g., food, housing, entertainment) and that each category is controlled to some degree by a budget constraint. Consequently, the amount spent on a meal away from home will vary depending on whether the expenditure is debited to the food or to the entertainment expense.

In a football stadium, the price for a hot dog and Coke is higher than the price for the same at the neighborhood sandwich shop. However, there are no other choices so the customers are forced to pay the price. This is analogous to the customer eating out while on vacation versus eating dinner on a weeknight in a neighborhood restaurant. Spending is more liberal in recreational or entertainment situations.

Because restaurant expenditures can be assigned to the budget categories of either food, entertainment, or recreation, the objective is to get the expenditure classified into a higher budget category or to combine two categories together. The mental budget category may change depending upon the occasion and day of the week. Such considerations may prompt promotions such as early bird specials and discount coupons to entice weeknight diners using their food budget to eat out. Such strategy may not be necessary on weekends, when dining out is done primarily for entertainment or social purposes because spending constraints are more relaxed.

In any purchase decision there are elements of "pleasure" and "pain" to be derived from the transaction (Kahneman and Tversky, 1979). The pleasure comes from the enjoyment of, or benefits derived from, the purchase, and the pain comes from having to part with one's hard-earned cash. The pain—pleasure aspect of parting with one's money suggests two pricing perspectives: à la carte, and modified table d'hôte or combination pricing. In price-sensitive markets, operators in the low-price units usually price each menu component separately (à la carte) to keep prices down and leave it up to the customer to decide whether to purchase extra items. Up-selling strategy is employed by servers and order takers to increase check averages. The combination pricing, or table d'hôte, charges a higher price but includes accompaniments that otherwise must be purchased separately. The combination price is lower than the sum of the accompaniments purchased à la carte. These concepts are covered in greater detail later in the chapter.

In addition to these pricing perspectives, the practice of using certain combinations of numbers to stimulate sales has been studied (Kreul, 1982). The most popular terminal digits used for prices on restaurant menus are 5, 9, and 0. This "fine-tuning" of prices affects only the terminal digits and has little cost implication. Its greatest impact is on customer perception of the value when contemplating the purchase of two or more competing items. This has been referred to as "odd-cents" pricing. The assumption is that customers will perceive a price of $9.95 as a better buy than $10.00. The use of odd-cents pricing also makes price increases less noticeable to the customer; for example, $9.50 to $9.75.

TRIAL-AND-ERROR PRICING

The last subjective method of menu pricing is simply **trial and error pricing**. This is another "non-cost" approach that claims to be responsive to customer perceptions of prices and is based on customer reactions and comments to pricing decisions. This can be employed on individual menu items to bring them closer to the price the customer is willing to pay. This "wait-and-see" perspective is not practical, especially when it comes to increasing prices.

The price differential between similar or competing items on the menu is another reason for adjusting prices upward or downward after initial pricing is completed. For example, consider the competitive similarity between baked chicken and roast duck. The cost of chicken will be much lower than the cost of duck, even if a larger portion of chicken is served. Duck can command a much higher price than chicken but has a higher food cost. If a menu offers both, the price differential between the two could be a determining factor in the customer selection process. By the same token, in the case of two similar veal dishes, with one requiring an inordinate amount of labor and ingredients and the other quickly and easily prepared, the former should be priced higher because of the preparation methods and ingredients. If the price spread is too close, the number sold of the more costly veal selection may increase. In both previous examples, two entrees had a lower food cost and lower price while the others had a higher food cost and higher price. The price spread can influence selection and therefore impact on check averages, food cost percentage, and gross profit.

Perhaps you have noticed on some restaurant menus that the price of a trip to the salad bar is within a dollar or two of the lowest priced entree that includes the salad bar. This is done partially to achieve a minimum expenditure from each guest and to encourage purchase of combination dinners rather than à la carte portions.

In addition, a steak house selling its steak trimmings as chopped sirloin at $7.95 may appear to be offering a bargain to price-conscious patrons when steaks range upward to $24.95. One must be cognizant of the desired check average and control the number of entrees priced above and below the average check target. The spread, or difference, between the highest and lowest priced entrees should be around 2-1/2 times the lowest priced entree. Therefore, if the lowest priced entree is $7.95, the highest should be around $19.95.

This is not a strict rule that forbids any entrée from being priced above $19.95; however, if the menu has more than three or four items higher than this amount, adjustments should be made. Similarly, if there are more than three or four items at the extreme low end of the menu price range, one may find that the overall check average will be lowered if such items account for greater than 20 percent of items sold. The adjustments needed in order to bring pricing in line would mandate raising the prices at the low end, not lowering prices at the high end.

Operators also set menu price points to cover food costs and achieve a certain profit margin. This method is tempered according to what the competition is doing. Today, operators must study customer demographics and market trends, and must give more thought to the wants and needs of their customers. In maturing and saturated markets, strategically set price points are critical to building and holding market share.

The challenge is to offer high value and low menu prices. This philosophy has spawned the introduction of lower-priced and lower-cost food items on many menus. Menus are showing upgraded à la carte offerings and increased variety. When prices are lowered, check averages decline, but the hope is that traffic will increase and build unit volumes. Portions on high-cost items are being reduced or combined with inexpensive accompaniments because patrons are balking at paying higher prices and seem less inclined to eat so much food at one sitting. The strategy with à la carte pricing is to build check averages through add-on sales of lower-cost side dishes and desserts. However, price-value perception does not evolve solely from low price; it is a feeling that the customers have about receiving their money's worth when they pay their check. It is a combination of price, quality, portion size, ambience, service, and psychological aspects.

ndirect Cost Factors in Menu Pricing

Up to this point the discussion has been primarily on pricing methodologies that have traditionally employed quantitative factors to mark up food cost, beverage cost, or food and labor costs. These costs can be allocated to specific menu items. There are, however, a number of indirect costs that can influence the price charged because they provide "added value" to the customer or are affected by supply/demand factors. These **indirect cost factors** are (1) market standing, (2) service commitment, (3) ambience, (4) customer profile, (5) location, (6) amenities, (7) product presentation, (8) desired check average, and (9) price elasticity (Pavesic, 1988).

MARKET STANDING

Market standing relates to the operation's position in a particular market segment; that is, whether it is a "leader" or a "follower." Is it considered the "number one" operation in its concept category or one that is just marginally competitive? Usually, the first one into the marketplace has an advantage over others that follow. Eventually, "copycat" operations go head-to-head in the same market. The one that was there first can usually be more aggressive in its pricing strategy than the "clones;" however, competition will eventually moderate aggressive pricing strategy. This holds true for both fast-food operations and the higher check average, table-service restaurants. The number one operation in a particular food service segment usually finds that the competition tries to outdo it. To do so, copycats must go at least one step further than the leader in menu selection, service, ambience, and value in order to gain ground. The leader can never become complacent and let standards decline or market share may begin to erode.

SERVICE COMMITMENT

The service element can be just as important as the actual food being served in the customer's decision on which restaurant to patronize. This is especially true when the differences in product quality, quantity, and price are seen as negligible by the customer. In addition, the costs of providing table service versus self-service must be reflected in pricing structure. When the customer performs many of the duties of service personnel, prices must be lowered to compensate for the inconveniences. But even self-service restaurants have opportunities to provide service that will distinguish them from their competition. The "invisible product"—the service component—is becoming an important measure of competitive distinctiveness.

Truly personalized service, driven by the needs of the customer, becomes an intangible that is recognized as an added value by the customer and can be reflected in the prices charged. Increased competition leads to increased demand for services, and service can become the basis for improving one's market position. (See Appendix A, *The Economic Value of Customer Service*).

AMBIENCE

The atmosphere and decor of a restaurant can add much to the enjoyment of a meal. It can turn the experience of eating out into a pleasant social occasion. People want quality food products regardless of whether they pay a little or a lot. However, the perception of value is certainly enhanced for the customer eating in a beautifully decorated, carpeted, appointed, and lighted dining room. Some operators spare no expense in trying to create atmosphere in their restaurants. The atmosphere can be informal or formal, casual or elegant. The more luxurious the atmosphere, the higher prices are likely to be. The customer does not usually object to paying a little more to dine in such surroundings.

CUSTOMER PROFILE

Although the type of clientele that regularly frequents a restaurant is influenced to a great degree by all of the factors listed, the pricing structure can dictate the status or economic class of clientele it will attract. The higher the average check or price range, the more selective and limited your customer base will be. Whether you are attempting to attract professional businessmen and women on their lunch hour, teenagers, baby boomer adults, or families with small children, the target customer will dictate to a great degree the prices you can charge.

LOCATION

Where the restaurant is located significantly influences the prices the customer will be willing to pay and whether the operator should price at "what the market will bear" or at relatively competitive levels. Usually, restaurants with lower check averages and prices must be located in areas of dense population and high traffic. They require many transactions to achieve sales goals. On the other hand, white tablecloth restaurants serving French and continental fare will need fewer covers per meal period and make up for it with high average checks.

Location also refers to geographic area of the country (i.e., Northeast, South, Midwest) and even to certain parts of a city. These conditions may predispose a restaurant operator to a menu pricing structure; for example, Lower Manhattan versus the Upper West Side of New York City, Chicago's South Side versus the Rush Street area, a small rural town versus a large metropolitan city, and a residential neighborhood versus a commercial district. If a location is accessible to tourists more than to local residents, higher prices are more likely than if only local customers are sought.

AMENITIES

Amenities cover a number of factors that can raise the value-added perceptions of the customer. Most definitely, with all other things being equal between two competing restaurants, one with live entertainment could have a competitive edge over one without it, in terms of customer perceptions of value. Other examples may be free valet parking, complimentary hors d'oeuvres in the lounge, taking reservations, fresh flowers on the table, and house charge accounts. Such extras must eventually be reflected in prices charged.

PRODUCT PRESENTATION

This marketing concept proclaims, "Sell the sizzle, not the steak." The product presentation is very important in the patron's value perception. It is often said that "we eat with our eyes." If it looks good the guests are likely to enjoy it. The same concept works for alcoholic beverages. Restaurants spend considerable time and money selecting appropriate china and glassware to "display" food and drink. They do many things to make the product stand out and be noticed by the customer ordering it. Some even turn the presentation into a production that causes other diners in the restaurant to take notice.

The presentation can be enhanced by visual or audio accents. The hot sizzle platter (audio) used by some steak houses can get the patron's attention when the waiter places the steak in front of the guest. A seafood assortment served on a fish-shaped platter is not common and will elicit favorable comments from customers. One restaurant serving "London broil for two" created attention by serving from a cart that was rolled through the dining room. When it reached the table, the maitre d' would hone the carving knife before slicing the London broil. The slices were placed on a super-heated steak liner that sizzled and steamed when a ladle of au jus was added. Since this was the most expensive dinner on the menu, its presentation was deserved (visual).

This type of presentation costs very little in relation to the additional price that can be charged. Another example pertains to alcoholic beverage service. If you have ever been to Pat O'Brien's in the French Quarter of New Orleans or at a luau at the Polynesian Village at Disney World, you probably ordered or saw many unique drinks being served in hollowed out pineapples, melons, and coconuts as well as glasses and mugs of unique shapes and sizes. They were colorfully garnished with fruit, flowers, and bamboo parasols. You probably paid in excess of $8.00 for what amounted to less than $.50 worth of liquor and fruit juice. Nobody complained about the prices because the presentation was unique and not available anywhere but in New Orleans or at Disney World.

DESIRED CHECK AVERAGE

One cannot rely on what is referred to as the "secondary sales effect" to reach a desired check average if entrees are priced too low (secondary sales effect: sell appetizers, side dishes, and desserts at à la carte prices to build check averages). The reason for this is that although every customer will buy one entrée, less than 50 percent will likely order an appetizer, side dish, or dessert. The addition of such add-ons cannot be relied upon to upgrade a $6.95 entree to achieve a $10 average check. Pricing structure should be designed to make it difficult for a customer to spend less than a specified amount.

PRICE ELASTICITY

Although related to the aspect of market standing, price elasticity for a product or service is a key element in the pricing decisions. Whenever demand is high (if the restaurant has waiting lines every night), the approach to pricing can be more aggressive than if the operation were one of four similar operations all within a mile of one another. In the latter situation, supply is greater than demand. In such a market, sales volume may be very sensitive to a change in price. (See the discussion on discount pricing later in this chapter.)

However, certain items on the menu can be priced higher because of their uniqueness. Signature items or house specialties can be priced at the higher end of your price range because they are only available at your operation. You create a "monopolistic" pricing situation where you can charge the "highest price the customer is willing to pay." This type of aggressive pricing cannot be employed on highly competitive or common items like prime rib or sirloin steak. It will be limited to unique appetizers, entrées, and desserts prepared from scratch with the owner's, manager's, or chef's "secret" recipe.

À LA CARTE AND TABLE D'HÔTE PRICING

Two approaches to pricing menu items are used in concert with one another. They are à la carte, where each course is priced separately, and table d'hôte or combination pricing, where several courses or accompaniments are included at one price. The price of the items purchased à la carte should always be higher than the combination price for the same entree accompaniments.

Combination pricing is a modified table d'hôte that includes everything from appetizer to dessert and beverage at one price. The more accompaniments or courses, the higher the price that must be charged. It is a pricing strategy that "packages" menu items to make it easier for the customer to order. Most club breakfasts are typical examples of combination pricing. A club breakfast that includes two eggs, bacon, toast, juice, hash browns, and coffee may be offered at $4.95 whereas the same items ordered à la carte may come to $5.25.

Combination pricing also helps to increase the check average. Even fast-food operations that have exclusively priced items on an à la carte basis are promoting "value meals" which combine a hamburger, french fries, and soft drink at a reduced price. À la carte pricing allows the customers to select accompaniments with greater freedom and control the amount they spend.

The classical table d'hôte pricing, appetizer to dessert at one price, is being modified to include fewer courses in order to keep prices down and give customers greater choice. Most patrons do not want a seven-course meal. Most menus will be a mix of à la carte and combination pricing where appetizers, side dishes, and desserts are priced à la carte and the entree, bread, and vegetable or salad are included at one price.

When pricing combinations that provide choices among two or more accompaniments—for example, baked, french fried, or mashed potatoes; French, thousand island, or blue cheese salad dressing—it is much better to price the combination slightly higher and not make additional charges for sour cream or blue cheese dressing. Many times the customer is not informed

Table 6.1   Menu Listings for Pricing

Old Way		Better Way	
Spaghetti with Meatballs	$3.50	Spaghetti Marinara	$3.50
Spaghetti with Sausage	$3.95		
Spaghetti with Mushrooms	$3.75	Spaghetti with meatballs, sausage, mushrooms, or meat sauce	$3.95
Spaghetti with Meat Sauce	$3.75		
Spaghetti Marinara	$3.50		
Small Pizza with cheese	$6.95	Small Pizza with cheese	$6.95
Pepperoni	$7.50	One Topping	$7.50
Sausage	$7.75	Two Toppings	$7.75
Peppers and Onions	$7.25		
Anchovies	$7.80		

of the extra charge and is annoyed when the check arrives. In addition, the server may fail to charge for these extras.

The practice of offering several choices at one price is even more practical when pricing such items as pizza toppings and sauces for spaghetti or lasagna. Instead of having five prices differing by less than $.50 for meatballs, sausage, mushrooms, ground beef, and clam sauce, have one premium price for the choice of any one of them.

Most pizza restaurants list prices according to the number of toppings and allow the customer to select any combination from the full offering. There is rarely a need for price differentiation to be less than $.25 to $.50 between certain combinations of accompaniments. This is especially true when servers must price each item manually and memorize prices (see Table 6.1).

The total food cost range may vary 1 to 7 percent, depending on the topping at the single price, but the sales mix will result in a food cost reflecting a weighted average of all items. The item with the highest cost will likely set the upper limit on the price to charge, but if that particular item is ordered only 2 to 3 percent of the time and the lowest cost item is the most popular, the average single price charged can be lower than the upper limit item would be on an à la carte basis.

Changing Menu Prices

When cost of ingredients or other expenses increase, the operator must adjust menu prices upward. However, a price increase can often result in an immediate drop in the demand for an item and generally, as the average check moves up, the number of meals served begins to level off and sometimes begins to decline. The operator cannot always pass on cost increases to the customer in the form of higher prices. This is especially true in fast-food and moderate-priced food-service operations. The higher average check white tablecloth restaurants seem to show less sensitivity to price increases because their clientele are in higher income brackets.

Changes in restaurant prices should always be done with merchandising skill and finesse. The less attention called to price increases the better, and the less chance of adverse customer responses. The following suggestions are offered as ways to disguise the fact that prices have been raised (Pavesic, 1988).

1. Use increments of .25, .50, .75, and .95 or .29, .59, .79 and .99 for the digits to the right of the decimal point. An item raised in $.25 increments from $4.25 to $4.50 is less likely to stand out and be noticed by the customers.

2. Never raise prices when you change the design of the menu. Raise prices on the last reprint of the old menu. Patrons will be more price conscious with a new menu because they expect prices to increase and will therefore be more sensitive to changes.

3. Never cross out old prices and write over them with a pen. However, this would be effective if prices were lowered, as a bargain is implied when a higher price is crossed out.

4. Hold off as long as possible on price increases that change the dollars digit (e.g., $9.95 to $10.25), as these changes are most likely to be noticed.

5. If a price increase cannot be avoided, consider increasing portions or accompaniments to create a "new" and "improved" item and give it a new name. In this way, one provides "added value" that becomes a trade-off for the price increase.

6. Reposition items that have been noticeably increased to less visible parts of the menu and emphasize lower priced substitutes in their place.

7. Consider reducing portions or accompaniments in lieu of raising prices. This may be an appropriate strategy in highly competitive markets that are price sensitive. Many operators have dropped either the vegetable or salad accompaniments in lieu of raising prices.

8. Never raise prices across the board. It is better to raise only a few items with each reprinting of the menu. It is also better to increase popular items by a small amount than to try to recover costs by sizable increases in marginally popular items.

9. Items with volatile and unpredictable costs should be listed as "market priced" so prices can be verbally quoted. Remember that prices

of à la carte accompaniments must be adjusted to remain in line with combination prices. The à la carte prices should always be higher than the same items priced together.

10. Do not align prices in a continuous order and never list menu items in price sequence. Doing either makes price dominate and biases the purchase decision. The most common mistake used in menu format is aligning prices in a straight line down the right side of a column or page (see Figure 6–1). The price range can be quickly determined and price comparisons easily made. Descriptive menu copy that has been written to "sell" the customer on each respective item may be overlooked. The price becomes the major determinant in the purchase decision. To overcome such shortcomings, do not align prices. Instead, place the price immediately after the last word in the menu description. The price will not be placed in any set location and the focus is transferred to the "sell" copy (see Figure 6–2).

Although the concept of primacy and recency says to list the higher-priced and higher-profit items first or last in a list to improve the likelihood of their being ordered, it is not recommended to list them in rank price order. Customers may never read past a certain price point and usually the lower-priced entrees will dominate, dropping the check average. When prices are

---

SPECIALTIES

Veal Francese   20.95
A Trotters tradition with lemon-butter sauce

Veal and Mushrooms   19.95
Tender milk-fed veal sauteed in fresh cream with mushrooms and herbs and served with fettuccine

Sauteed Medallions of Veal   19.95
With tomato and basil cream sauce

Calves Liver   13.95
Thinly cut and sauteed with bacon and raspberry-vinegar sauce

Long Island Duckling   15.95
Roasted and grilled with thin pancakes; served with a black currant sauce

Rack of Spring Lamb   20.95
Roasted with an herb breading and served with a rich brown sauce

---

FIGURE 6–1
Traditional Alignment of Prices

POISSONS ET CRUSTACÉS

NORWEGIAN SALMON STEAK BARBECUED ORIENTAL STYLE
With Sesame Seeds, Ginger, and Garlic 17.75

DOVER SOLE FILLETS POACHED IN SAUVIGNON BLANC
With Shrimp, Mussels, and Mushrooms 20.00

GULF SNAPPER FILLET
In Romaine Lettuce with Beaujolais Sauce and Mediterranean Eggplant 18.00

DOVER SOLE FILLETS SAUTEED GOLDEN BROWN
"Noisette Butter" and Lemon 20.00

SWORDFISH PICCATA
With Linguini, Spinach, and Tomato Concasse 17.75

SEA SCALLOPS WITH LEEK SAUCE
In Phylio Crust 18.00

FIGURE 6–2
Recommended Placement of Prices

listed in a mixed (random) order, there is a greater likelihood that the customer will read through the entire list of selections before making a decision. Some operators of formal dining establishments, particularly private clubs and hotel dining rooms, will omit the price completely on all but the host or hostess menu, and where price is shown it is written out in words rather than arabic numerals (e.g. twenty-one dollars rather than $21.00). These practices are only appropriate in high average check operations, and arabic numerals will be used in the majority of restaurants.

Discount Pricing

In an attempt to increase volume, many operators have employed some form of **discount pricing** strategy. Discounts are being renewed so often that regular menu prices have almost become meaningless. The increasing use of discount promotions would seem to endorse its effectiveness, but many operators remain unconvinced that discounting is cost-effective. Many fear that repeated use of discounting erodes pricing policy, detracts from one's image, and attracts fickle bargain hunters by "buying" their loyalty.

There are two considerations with discounting: its appropriateness or effectiveness as a strategy for increasing traffic, attracting new clientele, and introducing new products; and the consequences discounting has on overall financial results. Profit margins are lowered with discounting and sales may be too low to cover costs.

The use of discounting assumes that demand is elastic or price sensitive. The philosophy of discounting states that reduced prices will increase demand. Failure to realize sufficient increases in sales volume to offset the lower margins of each discounted transaction can have detrimental effects on financial outcomes.

The increased redemption rates necessary for high value discounts (e.g. two-for-one) may not be realized. The higher the discount and the greater the percentage of discounted transactions, the more sales volume must rise to achieve the same return realized prior to the discount (Pavesic, 1985, pp. 67–73).

Sales volume must improve if the costs of discounting are to be recovered. The break-even point is increased, because discounting increases the food cost percentage. This variable cost increase can be offset only by a decrease in the percentage of fixed costs, which in turn can occur only if sales volume increases.

The operator needs to examine the impact of any given discount on profit margins and check averages. Each discount has a "trigger point" of increased volume that must be reached to offset the reduced margins of each discounted sale. A simple calculation, using a variation of the traditional break-even formula, can be used to estimate the approximate increase in sales required to reach the "trigger point." The operator first needs to estimate an increase in sales and set a discount rate that is appropriate to existing competitive conditions, historical sales trends, and realistic redemption rates. Before discounting can be successful in a financial sense, overall sales must increase so that the percentage of fixed costs declines more than variable cost percentage increases.

The chances of realizing an increase in overall profit from a discount promotion is greatly improved if the business is already operating at or above break-even. Because the gross margin per sale is reduced by discounting, an operation that is below break-even will take longer (more sales) to reach break-even. For example, assume that "buy-one-get-a-second-at-half-price" is contemplated. Start with an estimate of the number of discounted entrees you expect to serve. If you assume that 10 percent of the entrees served will be discounted, the equivalent of a 5 percent reduction in sales revenue will result.

10% of entrees @ 50% discount

90% of entrees @ 100% (no discount)

0.10 (.50) + 0.90 (1.00) = 0.95 or 95%

100% − 95% = 5% reduction

Table 6.2 shows the break-even point without the discount. Theoretically, the 5 percent reduction in sales would cause the food cost to increase by 2 percent. Instead of $1,000 in sales, only $950 would be received, and if the same number of dinners are served, the total food cost would still be $380. The new food cost percentage would therefore be 40 percent, not 38 percent ($380/$950).

Table 6.3 shows how break-even is affected by the discount. Assume that although customer traffic may increase slightly, total sales do not increase. If all other costs remain constant, a loss of 2 percent will be incurred. Realistically, promotion costs would likely increase expenses and result in a greater loss than 2 percent.

Total variable costs have increased from 54 to 56 percent. Because sales did not increase, the percentage of fixed costs remained the same. However, you can estimate the approximate increase in sales necessary to be no worse off than before the discount. Table 6.4 presents the figures in statement format. The calculation for the "trigger point" is simply,

$$\frac{1}{1 - \text{Var Cost\% w/discount}} \times \text{Change in Variable Cost\%}$$

The variable costs before and after the discount are 54 and 56 percent, respectively. Substituting into the equation:

Table 6.2   Break-Even Without Discount

	Amount	Percent
Sales	$1,000*	100
Less Variable Costs:		
Food Cost	(380)	(38)
Operating Expenses	(160)	(16)
	(540)	(54)
Contribution Margin	$460	46
Less Fixed Costs		
Labor Cost	(280)	(28)
Occupational Expenses	(180)	(18)
	(460)	(46)
Net Profit (Loss)	$0	0

*Break-Even Sales = $460/0.46 = $1,000

Formula: $\dfrac{\text{Fixed Cost \$}}{\text{Contribution Margin (100\% − Variable Cost 54\%)}}$

$$\frac{1}{1 - .56}(.56 - .54) = \frac{1}{.44}(.02) = 2.273(.02) = .04546 \text{ or } 4.546\%$$

$$0.04546 \, (\$1,000) = \$45.46 \text{ increase in sales to } \$1,045.46$$

Therefore, the 2 percent increase in variable costs can be offset if sales increase by 4.546 percent, because fixed cost percentage will be reduced from 46 to 44 percent. The sales increase can be expressed in customer counts by simply dividing sales by the average check.

Table 6.3   Loss After Discount Without Sales Increase

	Amount	Percent
Sales	$1,000	100
Less Variable Costs:		
Food Cost	(400)	(40)
Operating Expenses	(160)	(16)
	(560)	(56)
Contribution Margin	$440	44
Less Fixed Costs		
Labor Cost	(280)	(28)
Occupational Expenses	(180)	(18)
	(460)	(46)
Net Profit (Loss)	$(20)	(2)

Table 6.4   Break-Even with Discount

	Amount	Percent
Sales	$1,045	100
Less Variable Costs:		
Food Cost	(418)	(40)
Operating Expenses	(167)	(16)
	(585)	(56)
Contribution Margin	$460	44
Less Fixed Costs		
Labor Cost	(280)	(27)
Occupational Expenses	(180)	(17)
Total	(460)	(44)
Net Profit (Loss)	$0	0

The check average before the discount was $10 ($1,000/100 covers). If 10 percent of the entrees were discounted by 50 percent, the new check average would be approximately $9.50 ($950/100 covers). Therefore, an additional 10 covers must be served in order to break even when the discount is running ($1,045/$9.50 = 110 covers).

The operation would need to serve more than 110 covers before any incremental profit would be realized. If the promotion increased customer traffic and sales improved by 20 percent, the financial results would resemble that shown in Table 6.5, assuming that only 10 percent of the entrees were discounted.

Although the contribution margin remains at 44 percent, a sales increase of 20 percent reduces the percentage of fixed costs by 5.7 percent, to 38.3 percent. It is important to understand that the greater the value of the discount and the higher the percentage of discounted transactions, the greater the resulting increase in the variable food cost percentage and the higher the break-even point will go.

In the example given, only 10 percent of the meals were discounted and food cost increased by 2 percent. If 15 percent of the meals were discounted, the food cost would increase to 41 percent.

$$15\% @ 50\% \text{ discount}$$

$$85\% @ 100\% \text{ (no discount)}$$

$$0.15 (.50) + .85 (1.00) = 0.925 \text{ or } 92.5\%$$

This is theoretically equivalent to a reduction in sales of 7.5 percent. Sales would therefore be $925 with a food cost of $380 or 41 percent. Food cost will

Table 6.5 Profit After Discount with 20 Percent Increase in Sales

	Amount	Percent
Sales	$1,200	100.0
Less Variable Costs:		
Food Cost	(480)	(40.0)
Operating Expenses	(192)	(16.0)
	(672)	(56)
Contribution Margin	$528	44.0
Less Fixed Costs		
Labor Cost	(280)	(23.3)
Occupational Expenses	(180)	(15.0)
TOTAL	(460)	(38.3)
Net Profit (Loss)	$68	5.7

continue to increase as the percentage of discounted meals rises. Having a dining room full of customers redeeming coupons could be financially disastrous. There needs to be a substantial number of customers paying full price along with the bargain seekers to "soften" the effects of the discount.

Further, if a "buy one, get one free" discount were employed, the consequences would be as follows: Assuming that 20 percent of the meals are discounted and 100 covers are served, food cost would increase from the original 38 percent to 47.5 percent. This would require that sales increase by 26 percent just to break even. This requires an additional $260 in sales and 58 more covers to reach the "trigger point."

$$20\% \text{ @ Free} = 0$$

$$80\% \text{ @ } 100\% = 8.0$$

$$100\% - 80\% = 20\% \text{ reduction in sales}$$

$$\$1000 - \$200 = \$800/100 \text{ covers} = \$8.00 \text{ average check}$$

$$\text{Food Cost } \% = \$380/\$800 = 47.5\%$$

$$\frac{1}{(1 - .635)}(63.5 - 54\%) = \frac{1}{.365}(9.5\%) = 2.74(0.095) = 0.26 \text{ or } 26\%$$

$$\$1,260/\$8.00 = 158 \text{ covers}$$

Using this information, the operator can examine actual cover counts to see if the promotion is drawing enough additional business. If the promotion does not draw more than 58 additional covers, it should be adjusted or discontinued because the operation will be in worse financial condition than it was before the discount.

The trigger point is not an absolute number and will vary up or down depending on the percentage of discounted meals served and the sales mix of accompanying items sold. Studies have revealed that too large or too small a discount does not pay off relative to additional sales, customer counts, and profits. Over-discounting can cause profits to be reduced, even with increased traffic and sales. The amount of the discount is important to optimizing sales increases and profit return. Small price reductions do not stimulate traffic, and over-discounting does not bring in significantly more traffic than slightly smaller discounts would have captured ("Restaurant Technology," 1984).

It is therefore logical to conclude that every promotion offering some discount has a "relevant" range such that the optimum increase in sales allows the operator to offset the increased costs and improve on the return that would have been realized had the discount promotion not been used. Using the simple calculation, one can estimate the increases in traffic needed to make the discount pay off in the financial sense. If the increases are unrealistic given competitive and historical redemption rates, the discount can be altered to improve the likelihood of financial success.

Discounting prices is therefore a somewhat risky pricing strategy. Additional sales cannot be guaranteed, especially in markets experiencing flat or declining customer counts. The additional cost incurred in offering a discount raises the break-even point. Therefore, the amount of the discount must be adjusted to achieve financial benefits that can be seen in the form of bottom line profit return.

Pricing in Private Clubs

Pricing menu items in private clubs is largely influenced by the markup limits mandated by the club's board of directors. Prices charged by clubs may be somewhat lower than prices for comparable items offered by commercial restaurants, and food cost percentages in clubs may sometimes exceed 50 percent. Clubs are more likely to price to return high gross profits rather than to achieve low food costs.

In those clubs that desire just to break even on their food and beverage operations, price markup will cover only raw food cost and labor. Some may include an additional 3 to 5 percent markup as a "safety factor" to cover cost overrides. To avoid having to assess members if costs are not covered, clubs charge members monthly food and beverage minimums to cover fixed overhead expenses. Therefore, the budget and policies of each club's board of directors will determine the markup on food and beverage items.

Pricing in Nonprofit Operations

Many industrial or institutional food services set prices on the basis of a minimum markup to cover costs. The rationale is that there is an average cost incurred in serving every patron and if this average cost is recovered on every sale, break-even is assured. The allocation of cost is based on dividing total costs by the number of customers. However, if customer counts are less than projected, costs will not be covered unless prices are increased. This pricing method is used in state- and federally-subsidized convalescent homes, where residents are charged a daily rate for meals regardless of their individual dietary requirements. In commercial operations, a minimum cover charge would be required. Nonprofit operations do not utilize cost percentages for control and pricing the way commercial operations use them. Most often, institutional food services operate on budgeted cash allowances per meal, per person, per bed, or per day. For example, a nursing home may have a yearly allowance of $2,400 per person to feed and care for the patient. This allowance may be allocated as follows: food, 50 percent; labor, 30 percent; supplies and overhead, 20 percent. This breaks down to $6.58 per day, with a food portion of $3.28 for meals and snacks.

Determining prices in nonprofit or subsidized operations primarily involves recovering costs or staying within a budgeted amount per day, per person, or per meal. This approach is taken by public schools and state-run institutions such as prisons and nursing homes, and in some cases by employee food services operated by business and industry.

Cost markup varies because the cost may be covered, all or in part, by federal or state funds or by company subsidy. The patrons pay only a portion of the cost, as with school lunch programs and employee cafeterias. Generally, pricing in nonprofit operations involves selling at cost and there is no need to include margin for profit in the price. At most, they are required to stay within a budget and perhaps add a small allowance above cost as a safety factor to make up for fluctuations in costs and volume. Covering costs becomes critical to keeping within budgets. Accurate cost information must be assembled and updated to be sure that costs remain in line. Monitoring of standardized purchase specifications, recipes, and portions are critical elements in nonprofit operations.

In some institutions, a cost allowance is established based on specific quantities of foods from different food groups allocated per day or per meal in order to provide a balanced diet. The cost allowance per person is determined after combining the items from each food group making up the entire meal. Our armed forces operate on a system referred to as a "ration allowance." In many state tax-supported institutions, such as hospitals and prisons, ration systems are used.

Ration allowances are determined by standards developed by the United States Department of Agriculture based on current prices of commodities. There are three levels for these allowances—low, moderate, and liberal—based on the quantities needed by elementary school children, elderly patients, or military personnel. When a ration system is used, only the cost of food is used to establish allowances per person. Other costs must be kept separate (e.g., labor, overhead).

E mployee Meals

Policy regarding employee meal allowances is determined by each operation. There is no requirement to provide free meals to employees in the wage and hour law. Employers may charge employees full price, discount meals, or give them away without charge. The wage and hour laws do allow operators who provide free meals to take a credit against the minimum wage in an amount equal to the reasonable cost of the food and beverage provided.

Employee meals are often considered a fringe benefit, and the cost is included as a payroll related expense. Employee meals must be monitored because the food used can account for over 2 percent of the cost of food consumed. Employees are often limited as to what they can eat for free, and additional charges are made if they choose to order from the regular menu. Regardless, some type of employee meal policy needs to be made, for it is generally expected that meals will be part of the overall compensation.

Pricing Catering

Since caterers often provide more than just the food and beverage, price is determined more by the perceived value for the management of an entire event and is not a simple markup of food cost. In fact, pricing one's services too low may result in lost sales.

Cost is merely a minimum that helps you determine whether you can afford to sell the function for the value the client assigns to it. Never forget that catering is a personal service; too often one reduces the services to a list of groceries. You must understand your clients' needs. Ask them to describe the party they have in mind; that is, buffet or sit-down dinner, self-service or servers, silver chafing dishes or ceramic bowls. Once you get an idea of their budget, you can offer a price range. Their reaction to your price range will be an indication of their interest.

Your objective is to get past negotiating over price. Once they feel that you are going to provide an affair that will satisfy their guests, price will not be as much a factor. In pricing catering, determine what value the clients place on your services and give them their money's worth. The minimum price can be assumed to be 100 percent markup, or double your total costs. But remember, this is a minimum price. Sell the party for what it is worth to the customer—what the market will bear. Other caterers may sell it cheaper, but they may not provide a better catered event. If the customers are satisfied, they will feel that any price was worth it (Mossman, 1987).

Current food service wisdom says that caterers must offer strong price-value to capture consumers. In past years, caterers set menu price points to cover food costs and achieve a certain profit margin. This decision was tempered according to what the competition was doing. Today, caterers must study customer demographics and market trends, and must give more thought to the wants and needs of their clients. In maturing and saturated markets, strategically set price points are critical to building and holding market shares.

For every caterer who prices the menu by marking up cost, there is one who says prices are market driven. Realistically, it is a combination of the two, but more and more market pressures and not cost pressures are driving menu prices. To achieve the right mix of prices, caterers must be willing to adjust prices up and down as needed.

The Texas Restaurant Association (TRA) Pricing Method

Most menu pricing methodologies covered in books and articles on the subject are cost driven or are intuitive, subjective, and arbitrary. Pricing must be carried out with the ultimate objective of planning for a profit, and costs must be covered; that is a must. The question is, however, how much over cost should one charge? Charging too much drives down demand and sales while charging too little sacrifices marginal income.

The first step in pricing out a menu is to get a firm grasp of the cost structure. In the early 1960s, a group of restaurateurs in Texas developed a method that remains an efficient way to assess cost structure implications prior to pricing decisions. No two restaurants are exactly alike in all costs, even if they are chain affiliated. Therefore, if the food cost objectives of two operations were set at the same percentage, and even if this food cost were achieved, there is still no guarantee that bottom line profit and return on investment would be the same.

The reason for this is that every restaurant operation has distinctly different and unique costs, investment, and financial idiosyncrasies that will cause cost standards and profit goals to vary. This is the reason why copying the budget of another operator will not achieve the same results. In addition, due to different menu sales mixes, food cost objectives cannot be the same. Yet multiple unit operators continue to apply a single food cost standard to all units under their supervision.

The Texas Restaurant Association (TRA) method answers the question, "What does the food cost need to be in order to achieve the desired profit?" The TRA methodology works equally well with proforma financial information of proposed properties and with existing operations.

The **TRA pricing methodology** follows the identical procedures explained in Chapter 3 on the discussion of *maximum allowable food cost*. Start with a realistic estimate of costs and revenues if working with a proforma. Actual costs should be expressed in dollar values rather than percentages. Do not heavily rely on industry averages; instead, call insurance agents, utility departments, and the telephone company, and get cost figures based on actual billings in the market of the proposed building and property. Labor costs can be determined by preparing a manpower schedule based on staffing requirements and the going wage rates. Most operating costs have a large "fixed" portion and are therefore better expressed in dollars than in percentages. Be liberal when estimating expenses; you are better off overstating costs. After all costs have been estimated, impute a minimum profit expectation. Be reasonable; don't set it unrealistically high, as it will impact the food cost figure. Food cost is the only expense that is not estimated. It is calculated after other costs and profit have been projected.

The next step is estimating sales revenues for a comparable accounting period that relates to the cost projections. Be conservative in the sales forecasts; in fact, show three different sales levels—the best or highest volume expected, the worst, and a realistic level somewhere between the high and the low. However, for purposes of the proforma, use the lowest sales projections to determine the food cost percentage.

Sales are projected based on estimating check averages and customer counts by meal periods and days of the week. If there are three meal periods per day using different menus, project sales of each separately. Once sales are projected, convert expenses to percentages of sales, add the profit percentage based on the minimum sales projections, and subtract this total from 100 percent. The difference is the food cost percentage objective used in pricing decisions. To achieve the profit objective, food and operating cost percentages must stay within the expense projections. Compare these figures to industry averages to see if they are in line. In reality, actual revenues should be higher and expenses lower than the projections, not the other way around.

As an example, assume that the following figures have been derived from an existing operation. Start with an unbiased accounting period, one that is neither too high nor too low in sales. A six-month or year-to-date average can be used. Separate costs into two categories: labor, and all other operating expenses including controllable and fixed expenses but *excluding* food cost. Profit must also be expressed and is a critical element in determining the food cost goal. All expenses must be expressed as dollars initially and then converted to percentages of the sales for the same accounting period. Assume that the following totals were calculated for the accounting period used:

Sales Revenue	$30,000	
Labor Cost	$ 6,900	23%
Overhead	$ 7,500	25%
Profit	$ 3,000	10%
Total Cost & Profit (w/o food cost)	$17,400	58%

Food Cost % = 100% − 58% = 42%

This tells us that we must achieve a food cost objective of 42 percent or less to realize a 10 percent profit. Because these expenses are unique to this particular operation, the food cost goal is equally unique and demonstrates why this exercise must be performed on an individual unit basis. The computed food cost percentage becomes the basis for pricing the menu. Every item cannot be marked up the same amount. The TRA uses subjective markups based on such factors as menu category (i.e., appetizers, entrees, and desserts), the popularity of the item, its perishability, and preparation requirements. This is where objectivity ends and the "art" enters into the menu pricing decision.

The TRA menu pricing methodology is demonstrated in the following example. Assume that we are concerned with two menu items, one a half of broiled chicken and the other an 8-ounce top sirloin steak. The food costs, including salad, potato, and bread, are $1.75 for the chicken and $4.50 for the steak. The TRA arrives at the initial price by dividing raw food cost by a desired food cost percentage. We previously calculated the TRA desired food cost percentage to be 42 percent (100% − 58%); therefore, the starting point for pricing the chicken would be $4.16 ($1.75 divided by .42) and $10.71 for the steak ($4.50 divided by .42). Remember, these are just starting points for the menu price, as the pricing decision cannot be exclusively cost driven.

Pricing to achieve a 42 percent food cost should return a profit of 10 percent. If you can charge more and achieve a lower food cost percentage, profit will increase. If the chicken is plain broiled or barbecued, a minimum price must be charged. However, if it is "honey basted" or "mesquite broiled," it may get a premium price. You may further adjust the price upward to close the spread between the highest and lowest priced entrees. The competitive position in the marketplace may allow you to charge the highest the customer is willing to pay, or it may require a price below the competition. The price must be tempered with subjective, competitive, and economic considerations.

The steak, initially priced at $10.71, may not be acceptable in the marketplace. If the operation is not noted for its steaks and has them on the menu to accommodate a small percentage of the customers, it should not price them at the high end of the market. In such a case, market position and competition may require lowering the price to $8.95. This would increase the food cost to over 50 percent, eight points higher than our 42 percent target. However, we may not be competitive at $10.71 and need to set the price on something other than the food cost percentage; for example, the gross profit or contribution margin. It represents the difference between the menu price and the raw food cost. In this case it is $4.45 for the steak ($8.95 − $4.50) and $2.75 for the chicken ($4.50 − $1.75). Although the food cost is higher on the steak, it brings in $1.70 more in gross profit. We are reminded that we bank dollars, not percentages, and are likely to sell more steaks at $8.95 than at $10.71.

The TRA methodology recognizes that the menu price is determined primarily by the market. However, a higher markup is taken when the risk of a loss or spoilage increases. Regardless of this logic, the customer will determine the correct price. The pricing methodology cannot force a food cost percentage or gross profit by charging a price that the customer does not deem fair and acceptable. You may employ low markups on high-cost items to stimulate sales, and although the food cost percentage may be higher, as with the steak, hopefully the gross profit will make up for it. Fast-selling items can have only moderate markups, as the volume allows for sizable gross profit return. High markups can be taken on specialty items that are unique to the operation, as there is little competition and one enjoys a monopolistic position.

In summary, the procedures for using the TRA menu pricing methodology are as follows.

1. Select an unbiased accounting period and divide expenses into the following categories:

   Labor and related expenses

   Overhead (which will include controllable as well as fixed expenses, but without food cost)

   Profit (minimum profit expectations)

2. Express all costs and profit as dollar values (e.g., labor $6,900, overhead $7,500, profit $3,000, sales $30,000).

3. Convert dollar values to percentages by dividing by sales (e.g., labor 23%, overhead 25%, profit 10%, total 58%).

4. Total the percentages to arrive at total operating costs and profit without food costs. Subtract from 100% to determine the TRA food cost percentage (100% − 58% = 42%).

5. Divide the raw food cost of each menu item by the TRA food cost percentage to arrive at the initial price (e.g., chicken: $1.75/0.42 = $4.16; steak: $4.50/0.42 = $10.71).

6. Adjust the price upward or downward depending on such factors as perishability, popularity, uniqueness, and demand.

The most important aspect of the TRA methodology is that it forces the operators to study their true operating costs. The figures used in the calculation must be realistic, accurate, and reflect the operation's unique financial and competitive position. Covering costs is a basic tenet of any business; however, in addition to the raw food cost, prices must reflect the risks of doing business and the nature of the product itself. For example, more must be charged if the product is delicate or highly perishable and the risk of loss or spoilage is great.

The old saying, "Volume hides a multitude of ills," refers to spoilage, waste, and operating inefficiencies and their effects on bottom line profits. The higher the total sales volume, the lower the markup has to be because such "ills" are absorbed in the marginal profits realized. The other side of the coin is that low volume requires higher markups because the bottom line cannot absorb much loss. Each item in the menu must be assessed and priced according to uniqueness, popularity, and whether you want to price at the high or low end of the market. No simple quantitative formula can be used in menu pricing. A proper and effective pricing policy results from management's understanding of costs, sales, volume, profit, competition, and customer demand.

Prime Cost Pricing Methodology

Another major cost-driven menu pricing philosophy states that the cost of preparation labor must be added to the raw food cost of all menu items made from scratch. In some instances the cost of direct preparation labor can exceed the cost of the ingredients. St. Louis restaurateur Harry Pope is credited with introducing this pricing theory. He noted that certain items on his menu had considerable labor involved in their preparation. The conventional method of marking up only raw food cost often omitted a significant part of the cost incurred in making an item ready for service to the customer.

The theory of including direct labor with raw food cost is referred to as the *prime food cost pricing methodology*. Direct labor is precisely defined as that labor incurred as a result of making an item from scratch on the premises. Direct labor is labor specifically involved in the "preparation" of menu items (e.g., butchering meats, vegetable cutting, and in-house baking). The operation must pay the meat cutter, salad maker, and baker because the restaurant manufactures its own products in-house. If the operation were to purchase precut steaks, premade salads and dressing, and baked goods from a commercial bakery, it would not employ or schedule labor to prepare such items from scratch (see Figure 6–3).

However, the price of convenience foods (items that are purchased partially processed) will cost the operator more per pound or unit of purchase, because the price paid reflects both raw food and labor for processing. Therefore, both cost aspects of items prepared on premises should be considered when determining markups. Examples of items that incur more labor costs than food costs are homemade soups, pastries, decorative garnishes, canapes, and hors d'oeuvres. Main entrees requiring cleaning, peeling, cutting, breading, partial cooking, or other time-consuming processes add a labor element that needs to be reflected in the total cost of the item.

PRIME COST = RAW FOOD COST + DIRECT LABOR

Direct Labor: Any labor incurred as a result of making an item from scratch on premises

Direct Labor	Indirect Labor
Pre-preparation	Bus Staff
Meat Cutting	Dishwashers
Baking	Wait Staff
Vegetable/Salad Preparation	Hostess
	Cashiers
	Line Servers

FIGURE 6–3
Prime cost.

Prime cost methodology, when used, raises the markup on items with high food costs and little direct labor and lowers the markup on items that have low food costs and considerable direct labor. Convenience foods, with built-in labor costs, will not be marked up as high as they would with the more conventional Texas Restaurant Association method because the cost of the labor is already reflected in the higher purchase price.

In order to assign labor costs to the specific menu items causing the labor to be incurred in the first place, you must first divide your menu items into two categories, those items needing direct preparation labor and those that have little or no direct labor. Labor that cannot be directly charged to specific menu items is designated "indirect" labor cost and is allocated evenly across all menu items, just like overhead expenses. Wait staff, line servers, and cooks used to "finish cook" items are not direct labor. Remember, direct labor is essentially initial production labor or preprep labor.

The cost of this direct labor can be determined by having employees note the amount of time they are involved in direct preparation activities each day. Not all of a kitchen worker's time will be classified as direct labor. For example, the head cook may cut steaks only 20 percent of the time; the rest of the time he or she may be working on the serving line plating food or finishing cooking entrees. Only the time used to cut the steaks is considered in prime food cost.

By noting the amount of time an employee spends in the preparation of a recipe, the labor cost per unit produced can be determined. Include the time it takes to assemble ingredients, utensils, and equipment. This is referred to as the "get-ready" stage. Washing, peeling, cutting, trimming, weighing, mixing, breading, and preliminary cooking such as parboiling and blanching must be considered direct labor. Do not forget to include the cleanup process that concludes the task. Once the time has been determined, the labor cost can be quickly calculated by multiplying the hours by the hourly wage. This labor cost is then divided by the number of pies, salads, or steaks produced to determine the labor cost per unit. When this is added to the raw food cost, prime food cost will be determined.

If a restaurant elects not to recognize the direct labor aspect in menu pricing, then the cost of steak cutting, baking, or salad preparation will be charged to menu items that do not benefit from the labor. Spaghetti, baked chicken, Prime rib, and other items with little or no direct labor must carry an unfair burden of recovering the expense of the meat cutter. Prime cost allocates the direct labor incurred to the item that caused it to be incurred in the first place.

Those that argue against prime cost may assume that direct labor will be covered by spreading the cost throughout the entire menu sales mix. However, smart operators quickly realize that they are not assured of selling one spaghetti for every steak sold. They recognize the benefit of a method that equitably costs out and prices each item to obtain the necessary return.

Pricing the steak with the prime cost method requires the inclusion of the direct labor element with the raw food cost. The operating budget is the same as that given in the TRA example. The first step is to calculate the portion of the total labor expense that is direct labor.

Assume that the total labor hours worked per week are 100, and of that 25 hours are required to trim and cut steaks. Assume that the total payroll is $500 and the average hourly wage is $5 per hour ($500/100 hours). The direct labor cost would then be $125 ($5 × 25 hours). If 500 steaks were produced during this time period, the direct labor cost per steak would be $.25 ($125/500 steaks). If the steaks were purchased precut, we would not have to schedule the meat cutter for the 25 hours. (The TRA pricing methodology considers only raw food cost and makes no distinction between direct and indirect labor).

The prime cost of the steak is $4.50 + $.25, or $4.75. The chicken is not priced with the prime food cost methodology because it does not require any direct labor to prepare and serve. The amount of direct labor, $125, represents one fourth of the total labor, or 25 percent ($125/500). Since a portion of the total labor cost is added to the raw food cost, do not use the formula, Raw Food Cost divided by Desired Food Cost Percentage, to arrive at a starting point for pricing.

If one divides the prime cost by the TRA calculated food cost, the markup double-charges for the direct labor. If one fourth of total labor is direct labor, represented by the $.25 per steak, the total labor cost percentage needs to be reduced to reflect this fact. The remaining three fourths, or 75 percent of the total labor, is indirect labor that is allocated across all menu items. The direct labor will be added only to steaks cut on the premises. Figure 6–4 shows all the costs in a pie chart format.

The total labor percentage must be reduced by the direct labor portion of one fourth of 25 percent, or 6.25 percent. Therefore, the indirect labor por-

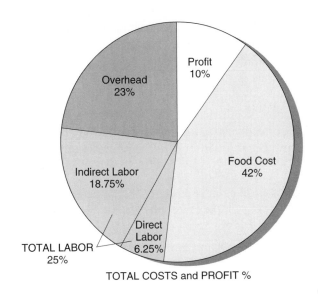

TOTAL COSTS and PROFIT %

FIGURE 6–4
Prime Food Cost

tion is 18.75 percent (25% − 6.25%). The prime food cost percentage can be determined by adding the indirect labor percentage to overhead and profit and subtracting this total from 100 percent (18.75% + 23% + 10% = 51.75%). The prime food cost percentage is therefore 48.25 percent (100% − 51.75%).

The prime cost price, $9.84, is calculated by dividing prime food cost by the prime food cost percentage ($4.75/48.25% = $9.84). When you examine the difference between the TRA and prime cost methodology in pricing the steak, the prime cost method needs to generate only $2.07 in sales for every dollar of prime cost ($1.00/48.25%), compared to $2.38 for every dollar of raw food cost with the TRA or conventional markup theory ($1.00/ 42%).

In summary, the steps in determining the prime cost markup are:

1. Determine the percentage of total labor that is direct labor. ($125/500 = 25%)

2. Multiply the total labor percentage by the percentage of direct labor. (0.25 × 0.25 = 6.25%)

3. Subtract the percentage of direct labor from total labor to determine indirect labor. (25% − 6.25% = 18.75%)

4. Add the indirect labor to overhead and profit and subtract the sum from 100 percent to get the prime food cost percent. (18.75% + 23% + 10% = 51.75%; 100% − 51.75% = 48.25%)

5. Divide the prime food cost by the prime food cost percentage to arrive at a starting point for price evaluation of the item. ($4.75/48.25% = $9.84)

6. Adjust the price upward or downward depending on competitive and economic factors. Since the chicken does not require direct labor, it is priced using the TRA or conventional markup with appropriate adjustments up or down based on product uniqueness and the relevant indirect cost factors that may apply.

B y-The-Ounce Pricing for Salad and Food Bars

A new pricing strategy is being tried in operations offering self-service salad and food bars. Restaurants are experimenting with *by-the-ounce* **pricing** as an alternative to the traditional per-person price for all you can eat. One of the ideas they are testing is whether pricing by the ounce will increase the marketing value of all-you-can-eat promotions to nutrition- and diet-conscious patrons. In addition, all-you-can-eat operations that do not permit carryouts or doggy bags for leftovers can do so with pricing by the ounce. With the increasing demand for takeout service, by-the-ounce pricing would allow operations to offer the same price value to both carryout and dine-in customers. Restaurants can basically charge customers for only what they take.

Arriving at a by-the-ounce price is complex because items offered range from inexpensive croutons and bean sprouts to the more costly chicken and salmon salad. A random check of operations pricing by the ounce revealed prices ranging from $.15 to $.28 per ounce. The per-person prices for all you can eat ranged from a low of $1.99 for a basic salad bar to double digits for elaborate buffets with meat and seafood entrees. How does one arrive at a price that is acceptable to the customer's price-value perceptions and the operator's profit and food cost goals?

The most widespread method used today for pricing all-you-can-eat food bars is the set per-person price. Operations offering smorgasbords, buffets, and the traditional Sunday brunch typically charge one price for all you can eat. Other operations serve family-style at the table for a set price per-person. In each case, the portion size and food cost varies with each man, woman, and child that partakes. These two key cost factors make it difficult to arrive at a single price point that is acceptable to all customers because of the individual differences in *perceptions* of what constitutes *value.* Unlike the controlled plating of food served from a kitchen, there is no such thing as a *standardized portion* with salad bars. The variance in individual portions complicates the task of determining a single food cost that will serve as the basis for a single price for all adult customers.

The National Restaurant Association's study on price-value relationships at restaurants reported that value is not absolute and cannot be determined without considering price and cost. Consumers determine the value of a restaurant meal based on the combination of goods and services they receive for the price paid. Customers see themselves as more *quality* and *value* conscious as opposed to *price* conscious (February 1992, p. 30).

Pricing by-the-ounce provides the operator with an opportunity to establish what is perhaps the most *equitable* menu pricing methodology for all customers regardless of sex, age, or income level. The operator seeks to set a price that will cover costs and return the desired profit margin. Arriving at a set price per-person requires an estimate of the average food cost per customer. The question is, how does one determine the average cost of food per customer when on any given day the mix of customers may range from senior citizens to growing adolescents? When a single price is used, it must reflect the wide range of portion sizes that are consumed by the total mix of customers.

The set-price-per-person pricing decision begins by determining the food cost for all the items needed to set up the bar plus the backup inventory used to replenish the bar during the meal period. Assume that $794 represents the beginning inventory of food and $258 represents the food remaining at the end of the meal period. The cost of food consumed is the difference between the opening inventory and the ending inventory, which in this case is $536. If the number of customers going through the buffet that day was 223, the average cost per customer served can be determined by dividing the number of customers into the cost of food consumed ($536/223). In this case, $2.40 is the average food cost per customer. This procedure is repeated for each meal period for two to three weeks. The average food cost per customer will vary slightly from day to day because the mix of customers, the meal period, and day of the week all impact business. A weighted average can be calculated to approximate a **standard portion cost** for a set price per person. Although this is a satisfactory way to estimate average food cost prior to setting the price, certain customers, especially women, dieters, and older patrons, are likely to question the price-value.

With per-person pricing, the light eaters subsidize the heavy eaters because they pay just as much as the customer who goes back for seconds and thirds. Nutrition-conscious customers are not as motivated to purchase by all-you-can-eat promotions. In fact, all you can eat may be viewed negatively by those who want only salads and vegetables and feel that they should pay less than those eating meats and desserts. Operators that use multiple price categories for children, adults, and seniors are often challenged by the customer, and in all likelihood, charges are not consistently applied by the servers who must classify the customer into a price category.

Pricing by-the-ounce addresses two other difficulties sometimes associated with per-person pricing of all-you-can-eat food and salad bars. They are

(1) the customer who shares food with another member of his or her party who did not order and (2) the issue of taking home leftovers in doggy bags. Carry-out meals could also be sold by the ounce, thereby allowing customers to pay only for what they take and so creating additional marketing opportunities.

The process of arriving at a price per ounce is not difficult. However, there are items whose weight and density are at different ends of the weight continuum. For example, three ounces of bean sprouts will fill a medium salad bowl while three ounces of potato salad would amount to only three or four tablespoons. Items usually measured in *liquid* ounces must now be measured by *avoirdupois* ounces. It cannot be assumed that two liquid ounces will weigh two avoirdupois ounces. When pricing by-the-ounce, all items must be weighed. Divide the weight, expressed in ounces, into the total recipe cost to arrive at the cost per ounce for each item on the salad or food bar. Calculations will reveal costs ranging from $0.02 to $0.30 per ounce. Table 6.6 shows the cost per ounce of common salad bar items.

A cost markup based on highest cost item will result in grossly overpricing the salad bar. When pricing by the ounce, consider the customer's perspective on the quality, quantity, and value. Keep in mind the price range the market will permit. For example, students and faculty patronizing a college cafeteria have expectations of lower prices there than at a nearby commercial cafeteria serving identical food. There are definite price points for each concept, menu, and service delivery system that must be considered before setting the price.

Setting a price per ounce that will achieve a specific average check is important. First estimate the weight of an average portion in ounces and divide the number of ounces into the desired average food check. If the average check target is $3.95 and the average portion size is 16 ounces, a price of $.25 per ounce is needed in order to achieve the desired average check. However, *forcing* a price to achieve a desired average check without providing value to the customer would be a mistake.

Costs of *premium* salad bar items are shown in Table 6.7. The cost per ounce of *premium* items like pasta salads with tuna or shrimp, chicken salad, and ham salad can reach $.40 per ounce, especially if pre-made products are used. Technically, a customer could fill the plate with high-cost items such as anchovies and smoked salmon and exceed the average portion cost target. One should not be overly concerned when this happens because it will generally average out over the month. The rounded straight average for all items found on *typical* salad bars is approximately $.07 per ounce. With a price to the customer of $.25 per ounce, the food cost is a respectable 28 percent.

A bar with both cold salads and hot entrees will be perceived as a better value than one with only cold items. A national supermarket chain with in-store food bars prices both by per-person and by-the-ounce. Its dine-in-store all-you-can-eat price is $5.29 per person, and the take-home price is $3.99 per pound or $.25 per ounce. Hot selections include fried chicken and pot roast

Table 6.6   Cost Per Ounce for Standard Salad Bar Items

Item	Price per Ounce
Canned Pickled Beets	$.03
3 Bean Salad	$.05
Shredded Carrots	$.03
Yellow Onions	$.03
Green Peppers	$.06
Garbanzo Beans	$.02
Sliced Cucumbers	$.02
Iceberg Lettuce	$.04
Broccoli	$.04
Yellow Squash	$.03
Croutons	$.06
Imitation Bacon Bits	$.05
Mixed Citrus Fruit Sections	$.07
Pineapple Chunks	$.05
Peach Halves	$.04
Cottage Cheese	$.05
Kidney Beans	$.02
Ranch Dressing	$.05
Italian Dressing	$.05
French Dressing	$.05
Bleu Cheese Dressing	$.08
Thousand Island	$.05

and desserts like banana pudding and cherry cobbler. The food bars found in many budget steak houses offer similar low-cost hot food items, that is, meat loaf, fish sticks, and spaghetti and meatballs. The cost of most items will still be under $.25 per ounce.

Premium cold items like pasta, chicken, and tuna salad provide value and command higher prices. Even the quality of the salad dressing can impact price-value perceptions of the customer. Does the blue cheese dressing contain chunks of real blue cheese? Specialty items like anchovy fillets, stuffed manzanilla olives, and pickled corn are premium items too.

Cost markup of salad bars and buffets is typically lower than plated items in full-service operations. The overall food cost percentage with a food bar or buffet will usually run four to six percentage points higher than with table service. This translates to a better value on the plate. The added costs are recovered from the lower labor cost associated with self-service. In high-

Table 6.7 Cost Per Ounce for Premium Salad Bar Items

Item	Price per Ounce
Fresh Mushrooms	$.15
Sliced Tomatoes	$.15
Shredded Cheddar	$.13
Parmesan Cheese	$.19
Real Bacon Bits	$.19
Chicken Salad	$.25
Tortellini Salad	$.26
Provolone Cheese	$.24
Broccoli Salad	$.22
Hot Chicken Wings	$.25
Ham Salad	$.22
Sliced Pepperoni	$.30
Potato Salad	$.07
Cole Slaw	$.04
Jello w/fruit	$.08

volume operations, once the sales exceed the break-even, every percentage point that fixed costs are lowered goes directly to bottom line profit.

Eleven food service operations in a large southeastern city offering all-you-can-eat salad or food bars were surveyed to ascertain offerings and prices. Only one commercial operation priced its salad bar by the ounce; it charged $0.25 per ounce. Four of the restaurants offered only cold items with prices that ranged from $2.50 to $5.45 per person. The higher price was indicative of more extensive offerings, the higher quality of their selections, and intangibles such as location, ambiance, and service. Six operations offered hot entrees along with salad items with prices ranging from $3.99 to $6.49 per person. Carryout was permitted in all but one of the operations, and the price was the same as the dine-in price.

Pricing by-the-ounce does have some weaknesses that need to be considered before switching over. For example, the *daily* average check may fluctuate and run lower than with a set price per-person. However, this does not necessarily mean lower overall revenue if daily customer counts increase to offset lower check averages. In addition, digital portion scales must be purchased, and the logistics of having to weigh each plate before the customer is seated may be disruptive to the service delivery system already in place. Many customers like to return to the bar for seconds, and pricing by the ounce precludes return trips, which could lower the value perceptions of the customer who expects to return for seconds.

Pricing of all-you-can-eat salad and food bars in commercial food services by a per-person charge is the most widely used pricing strategy largely for reasons of marketing, logistics, and customer price-value perceptions. Institutional food service operations and retail grocery stores may find that pricing their food and salad bars by the ounce is an acceptable alternative pricing strategy. Hotels and private clubs offering elaborate buffets containing boiled shrimp, Prime rib, and other premium items may find a per-ounce pricing structure impractical. Changing over from a per-person price would likely lower the price-value perceptions of regular customers. For the present time, commercial operations featuring food and salad bars are likely to remain with the per-person price for all-you-can-eat and leave the institutional food services to experiment with pricing by-the-ounce.

Determining the Average Cost Per Ounce

1. Make a list of all items offered.

2. Determine the recipe cost for each item. Calculating the cost per servable pound/ounce on items with shrinkage or waste in preparation (e.g., beef roasts and fresh fish) or items that increase in volume and weight (e.g., rice and pasta) are more difficult to compute than on products that basically combine ingredients that neither shrink nor expand. Carefully weigh raw products and ingredients before and after cooking or preparation. Keep in mind that your total food cost is the same before and after cooking or preparation. However, depending on the yield, the cost per servable pound will likely increase considerably. Assume you start with 25 pounds of raw headless shrimp (as-purchased price of $124.75, or $4.99/lb) that weigh only 13 pounds when peeled, deveined, and cooked. Exclusive of the cost of added spices and other ingredients, the cost of the shrimp is now $9.60/lb ($124.75/13). In addition, direct labor costs are added to items requiring extensive amounts of preparation labor, increasing the cost per servable pound/ounce even more.

3. Record the weight of each batch of product prepared.

4. Divide the weight of the item into the raw food cost of the item.

5. List the cost per pound of each item and then convert to the cost per ounce.

6. Rank order the items by cost per ounce from most to least.

7. Estimate the popularity of each item and the quantities you will likely consume each day. These key items will shape your price per ounce.

8. Compute a weighted average price per pound of the entire list of ingredients. Method: pounds consumed per meal × the cost per pound

(do this for each item on the salad and food bar). Divide the total weight into the total food cost. This is your weighted average cost per pound. Estimates are adjusted after an actual sales analysis can be taken and estimates of consumption are replaced with actual figures. Daily inventories and monitoring of high-cost items should be done. The determination of the quantities consumed of each item on the food bar will allow you to recalculate the weighted cost of the food consumed. This will impact your overall food cost and the price you must charge to recover cost and return a fair profit.

9. Determine your desired average food check for the meal period. This is an imputed amount based on realistic customer counts and minimum sales needed to cover costs and produce a profit.

10. Estimate the "average" portion size of an "average" customer.

11. Divide the weight of the average portion into your desired check average. This is what you need to charge *(price)* per ounce in order to achieve your desired average check based on the average portion. You want to compare this figure to the *cost* per ounce calculated in step 8.

12. Subjectively adjust your price per ounce. You are the only person who can effectively do this; there is no magic formula for marking up your food cost and establishing a menu price. As stated before, the two ends of the pricing continuum are (a) charging the highest price the market will bear and (b) charging the lowest price that will still produce a profit.

Regardless of the menu pricing philosophy, in the long run it is the customer who ultimately determines what price is acceptable. Therefore, only after knowing the acceptable price does cost come into play. The operator must be able to make a profit selling at the price the market says he or she must charge. What is the proper price? From the customers' point of view, it is the one that makes them buy. From the seller's perspective, the successful price is one that moves the product and produces a profit. If a menu item is common or ordinary and offered by many competitors, the price will likely be at the low end. However, if the item is special or unique and not easily duplicated by the competition, it can be priced at the high end. It behooves management to have several "specialty" items on the menu to create some competitive distinctiveness. Competitive distinctiveness can be enhanced by other factors such as location, atmosphere, service, entertainment, and unique product presentation (Pavesic, 1994).

When students were asked to price three non-descript menu items identified only by the letters A, B, & C along with raw food cost amounts for each one, the following questions were generated as they felt the answers were relevant before they could attempt to price each item.

1. What kind of menu item is it, e.g., appetizer, entree, dessert, side dish, etc.?
2. What is the direct labor involved in its preparation? Does it require special skilled preparation or simple heating and plating?
3. What is the portion size?
4. Is it a seasonal item of limited availability?
5. What are competitor's charging for the same thing?
6. It is a commodity or a specialty item on the menu?
7. What is the desired food cost percentage?
8. Is it a demand or market driven menu item?
9. What kind of restaurant is serving it, e.g., fast food, fast casual, limited service, full service?
10. What meal period are we pricing it for, e.g., breakfast, lunch, or dinner?
11. Where is the location of the restaurant, e.g., center city, suburban, office building, shopping center, etc.?
12. What are the accompaniments served with it?
13. Who is our target market or clientele, local residents or tourists, business people, shoppers, etc.?
14. What is the perishability of the product and its cost, e.g., live lobster, fresh seafood?
15. What is the service delivery method in the restaurant, e.g., table service, self-service, drive-thru?
16. What is the desired check average?
17. What are the prices of the other menu categories and the spread among items in each category?
18. What are the prices of complimentary and competing items on the menu?
19. What is the ambiance of the restaurant?
20. What is the plate presentation for the menu item
21. Is there live entertainment or music?

These are the subjective aspects that will impact the price you should charge for the menu item. Customers come in with reference prices that they expect to pay for certain items and will not blink an eye at paying $1.50 for a glass of iced tea with a cost of less than $0.05 with sugar and lemon and complain loudly if they feel that the price you are charging for fried chicken tenders or a hamburger is perceived as too high. Each menu item will be marked up individually and produce a range of food costs from single digits to the high forties. But remember, it is the sales mix of all the menu items that produces the food cost that shows up on your monthly income statement.*

Key Concepts

- Pricing cannot be reduced to a simple mark up of cost.
- You cannot mark up every menu item to achieve the same food cost.
- There are many indirect cost factors that must be considered in the pricing decision.
- There are ways to make price increases less noticeable to your customers.
- In order for discounting to work correctly, you need to increase sales and bring in more customers.
- Prices will be either "market driven" or "demand driven".
- There are several "psychological aspects" of menu pricing that are used to "adjust" prices.
- Pricing all-you-can-eat buffets can be done by-the-person and by-the-ounce.

Key Terms

Market driven pricing	Trial and error pricing	Prime food cost pricing methodology
Demand driven pricing	Indirect cost factors	
Competitive pricing	Discount pricing	By-the-ounce pricing
Intuitive pricing	TRA pricing methodology	
Psychological pricing		

Discussion Questions

1. If an operator marked up every item on the menu the same amount in order to achieve a desired food cost percentage that would achieve the profit objective, it would not be an effective pricing strategy. Give three reasons why it would not be effective.

*For an in-depth discussion of pricing, see Menu Pricing and Strategy, 4th ed., by J. Miller and D. Pavesic (Van Nostrand Reinhold Publishers, 1996).

2. Explain the difference between "eat out" and "dine out" restaurants and how it impacts customer spending and restaurant pricing strategy.
3. List five (5) ways to disguise menu price increases so they are less noticeable to customers.
4. Give three (3) indirect cost factors that can influence the markup or price of menu items and explain how they can influence the price direction on the price continuum.

Problems

Problem 1

a. A seafood dinner with all accompaniments, e.g. salad, bread and potato, has a food cost of $5.85 and is priced at $13.95. What is the food cost percentage?
b. If the cost of the ingredients increased by $.15 (fifteen cents), what would the new menu price need to be to maintain the same food cost percentage calculated above?

Problem 2
TRA & Prime Cost Pricing

Use the Excel template found on your diskette for this problem.

Given:		
	Food Sales	$40,000
	Labor Cost	$10,400
	Overhead	$8,800
	Profit	$6,000

1/5 of total labor is direct labor

Assume the meat cutter spends one hour per day cutting steaks and earns $30/hr. The total number of steaks cut in an hour are 120.

Entree costs:

Spaghetti and Meatballs Food Cost is $2.25

Top Sirloin Butt Steak is $4.70

Cost of accompaniments $1.25 (same for both entrees)

Compute the following and show and label all calculations;

1. Total Raw Food Cost for both Entrees
2. TRA food cost percentage

3. TRA suggested starting menu price
4. Portion of Total Labor that is Direct Labor
5. Indirect Labor Percentage for Prime Food Cost Calculation
6. Prime Food Cost percentage
7. Prime Food Cost suggested starting menu price

Problem 3
Discount Pricing

Each discount promotion has a "trigger point" or the amount of increased sales that must be realized just to offset the reduced margin of each discounted sale. A simple modification of the traditional break-even formula (fixed costs/contribution margin), can be used to approximate the increase in sales required to reach the "trigger point." Use the templates provided on your diskette.

- In this example, you are contemplating running a "buy-one-get-one-free" dinner entree promotion on Monday-Thursday nights.

- You estimate that 25 percent of the customers will redeem this coupon and eat free.

- Assume the check average without any discount is $15 and the Monday-Thursday customer counts average 125 per night.

- Assume that Food Cost is 38 percent and that Operating Expenses are $300 when sales are $1875 or below and will run 17% of sales over $1875. (*Operating expenses will increase as customer counts increase and are not purely variable expenses.*)

- Assume that Labor is $525 with sales of $1875 or less and will increase by $100 if sales exceed $1875. Assume that Occupational Expense remains constant at $337.

1. Using the methodology shown in the chapter, calculate the percentage and dollar amount of the sales reduction due to the discount redemption rate given. Also show the increase in the food cost percentage due to the discounted meals and the change in the average check.
2. Show the amount of loss that could result with the promotion redemption rate of 25% and when sales remain at $1875 per day.
3. Determine the trigger point in both sales and customer counts for this proposed promotion.
4. Prepare an income statement with the trigger point sales showing the net profit/loss that results.
5. After calculating the figures, comment on whether the trigger point is achievable and whether you would recommend proceeding with the pro-

motion. You can speculate on what additional items you might sell, their prices, and the percentage of customers who might purchase these items to help increase your average check.

Problem 4

Using the Excel template provided on your diskette, solve the following problem. Assume your restaurant is doing $1,000 per day with an average check of $10 and your current variable and fixed costs are as follows:

Sales	$1,000	100%
Less Variable Costs		
Food Cost	$350	35%
Variable Operating Exp	$160	16%
Total Variable Costs	$510	51%
Contribution Margin	$490	49%
Fixed Costs	$440	44%
Net Profit	$50	5%

You are considering running a discount promotion to increase business of buy-one-dinner and get the second at half price. You estimate that 15% of the entrees served will be discounted. Assume that Variable Operating Costs remain at $160 even with the reduced sales level.

1. What is the equivalent reduction in sales with the discount and redemption rate of 15%.
2. What would the check average be if 100 covers were served?
3. What is the new food cost percentage if 15% of the meals were sold at the discount?
4. What is the total sales needed (trigger point) to be no worse off than before the discount for the promotion?
5. How many additional customers must be served to reach the trigger sales point?

R eferences

"Computer Applications in Marketing." *Nation's Restaurant News,* July 1984.

"Coupon Promotions." *Independent Restaurants,* February 1985, pp. 68–71.

Degen, James M. "How Price Promotions Affect Profits." *Restaurant Business,* April 1, 1983, pp. 169–170.

Della Bitta, A. J., and Kent B. Monroe. "The Influence of Adaptation Levels on Subjective Price Perceptions." In *Advances in Consumer Research,* Vol. 1., eds. Scott Ward and Peter Wright. Ann Arbor, MI: Association for Consumer Research, 1973, pp. 353–369.

Ferguson, Dennis H. "Hidden Agendas in Consumer Purchase Decisions." *Cornell Quarterly,* 28, no. 1 (May 1987), 31–39.

Gabor, André, and Clive Granger. "On the Price Consciousness of Consumers." *Applied Statistics,* 10 (November 1961): 170–188.

Jeffrey, Don. "The Battle for the Spotlight." *Nation's Restaurant News,* 17, no. 17 (March 28, 1983), 31, 33–34.

Kahneman, Daniel, and Amos Tversky. "Prospect Theory: An Analysis of Decision under Risk." *Econometrica,* March 1979, pp. 263–291.

Keister, Douglas C. *Food and Beverage Control.* Englewood Cliffs, NJ: Prentice Hall, 1977.

Kotschevar, Lendal H. *Management by Menu.* Wm. C. Brown Publishers, National Institute for the Foodservice Industry, 1987.

Kreul, Lee M. "Magic Numbers: Psychological Aspects of Menu Pricing." *Cornell Quarterly,* August 1982, pp. 70–75.

Levinson, Charles. *Food and Beverage Operation: Cost Control and Systems Management.* Englewood Cliffs, NJ: Prentice Hall, 1976.

Miller, Jack and David Pavesic. *Menu Pricing and Strategy,* 4th ed. New York: Van Nostrand Reinhold Co., 1996.

Monroe, Kent B. "Techniques for Pricing New Products and Services." Virginia Polytechnic Institute, 1986.

Monroe, Kent B., and Kirshnan. "The Effect of Price on Subjective Product Evaluations" in *Perceived Quality,* eds. Jacob Jacoby and Jerry C. Olson. pp. 209–231 Lexington Books, 1984.

Monroe Kent B., and Susan M. Petroshius. "Buyer's Perceptions of Price: An Update of the Evidence." *Journal of Marketing Research,* 10 (February 1973): 70–80. Published by American Marketing Association.

Mossman, John. "How to Set Prices." *Restaurant Management,* June 1987, pp. 76, 85.

Pavesic, David V., "Indirect Cost Factors in Menu Pricing," *FIU Review,* Vol. 6, No. 2, Fall 1988, pp. 13–22.

Pavesic, David V. "Psychological Aspects of Menu Pricing," *International Journal of Hospitality Management,* Vol. 8, No. 2, 1989, pp. 43–49.

Pavesic, David V. "Taking the Anxiety Out of Menu Price Increases," *Restaurant Management,* February 1988, pp. 56–57.

Pavesic, David V. "The Myth of Discount Promotions," *International Journal of Hospitality Management,* Vol. 4, No. 2, 1985, pp. 67–73.

Pavesic, David V. "By-The-Ounce Pricing for Salad Bars," *Journal of College and University Foodservice*, Vol. 1(4), 1994, pp. 3–11.

"Price-value relationships at restaurants," National Restaurant Association Research and Information Service Department, Feb. 1992, p. 30.

"Restaurant Technology, Computer Applications in Marketing." *Nation's Restaurant News*, July 2, 1984, Sec. 2, p. 33.

Schmidgall, Raymond S., *Hospitality Industry Managerial Accounting*, 2nd ed., East Lansing, MI: Educational Institute of the American Hotel and Motel Association, 1990.

Thaler, Richard. "Mental Accounting and Consumer Choice." *Marketing Service*, Summer 1985, pp. 199–214.

7

Purchasing

FOOD PURCHASING AND ORDERING

Fundamental Principles of Cost Control

1. Develop your own purchase specifications.
2. *Purchasing* is an administrative function.
3. *Ordering* is a management function.
4. Know the prerequisites and objectives of the purchasing function and the channels of distribution.
5. Purchasing techniques improve your buying efficiency.
6. Consolidate your buying power.
7. Use the bid process to benefit your purchasing program.
8. Develop a *partnership* with each of your purveyors.
9. Don't make overly restrictive demands on your suppliers.
10. Price is not the only or even the primary factor in selecting your suppliers.

The purchasing and ordering functions have a significant impact on food costs and are two of the most important activities in any cost control program. An operator who monitors what is purchased and sold can closely monitor the pulse of the business. Purchasing cannot be performed casually or delegated to rank-and-file employees or purveyor representatives. The ordering function can be delegated but purchasing policy is always the domain of the owner or general manager.

Ordering takes place *after* purchasing policy has been set. Using purchase specifications as a guide, competitive bids can be obtained from potential suppliers. Once bids have been returned and purveyors selected, the process of ordering the appropriate quantities can be delegated.

Parameters of Effective Ordering

Managers of corporate or franchise restaurants are not given "purchasing" authority. They do have authority to *order* necessary quantities of the specified merchandise from approved purveyors. Therefore, **ordering** determines the *quantities* that will be purchased and kept in inventory. Ordering can be delegated; purchasing authority is not. A purchasing agent for a hotel chain makes both ordering and purchasing decisions as do some corporate chefs and club chefs.

Efficient ordering brings together the right items, in the right quantity, in the right place, at the right price, at the right time. Once menus have been written offering items that will result in optimum customer satisfaction and will return the desired food cost percentage and gross profit, a purchasing program designed to assure profit margins can be developed.

To order efficiently and effectively, the buyer will need the following information:

1. Product descriptions and specifications
2. Unit size per case or individual package
3. Unit price
4. Purveyors who carry items
5. How much to order and keep on hand

Any efficient purchasing program must also incorporate the following:

1. Standard purchase specifications based on,
2. Standardized recipes that result in,

3. Standardized yields that, with portion control that allow for,

4. Accurate costs based on portions actually served

Standards assure consistency in each area, and if standards change, costs must be recalculated. Once you have determined the specific varieties, grades, and brands, you must adhere to these specifications. Although a bid process is usually undertaken to determine possible suppliers, rarely is the decision on which purveyor to use is based on price considerations alone. Other factors that enter the decision process will be covered in detail later in this chapter. The exceptions are state and municipal governments that are bound by statute to go with the lowest bidder. As those who have to follow such regulations have told me, there are disadvantages to this, and low initial price does not always translate to low cost over the long run. Given the choice, another vendor might be selected even if the price were a little higher. The missing element in making a buying decision on the basis of price alone is *service after the sale.*

One thing that both chains and independents strive for with their menus is consistency in taste, appearance, and cost. If different brands of product are purchased without regard for standardized recipes, in consistency in cost and quality will result. As any kitchen manager, chef, or cook knows, mayonnaise quality is not the same with all brands. The same holds true for salad dressings and most other foods. Consider the color, taste, and consistency of the brands of French dressing available on the market today. An order placed with three different purveyors for French dressing will produce three different-tasting products ranging from sweet to a definite vinegar tartness. In addition, the color may range from a deep orange color to a pale orange or yellow.

There is an old saying in the pizza business: "You don't have to make the best pizza sauce, just be consistent." After a while, your customers will become accustomed to your sauce. If it changes in taste and texture on subsequent visits, customers will complain. They do not want to be surprised when they get their pizza and find it different from the last time they ate in the restaurant.

Ordering for a restaurant operation is complicated by the fact that a restaurant is essentially a manufacturing operation producing a large number of highly perishable products. Some restaurants serving breakfast, lunch, and dinner have three different menus to order for, each containing dozens of different items.

In order to effectively carry out the ordering function and control costs, the operator must be able to do four things: accurately predict how much will be needed, maintain purchase specifications, follow standardized recipes, and enforce portioning standards. Only when these four things are under control can the person doing the ordering determine the optimum quantities to keep on hand.

It is important to understand that written standards are not a guarantee that they will be effective. There can be compliance in the absence of written standards. It is not what is *written* that makes it formal, but what is actually *practiced.* Standards are followed to the extent that management demands. It is management and employees who make standards work, not the mere fact that they are codified in some policy manual. There must be continual follow-up and appraisal because employees will deviate from prescribed standards only as far as management allows.

If the ordering function is not done properly and shortages occur, food cost will fluctuate and standardized recipes may be altered. Ingredients may be left out of a recipe or substitutions made that not only affect the taste but the cost as well. Quantities can be accurately predicted if standards of purchasing, preparation and portioning are followed.

The Buyer's Credentials

Purchasing is an administrative function requiring technical knowledge about the products being purchased and the market dynamics that affect prices and supply. To fill the position of purchasing agent, the buyer should be experienced in food production procedures. The buyer must understand the workings of a kitchen and be familiar with equipment and the skill levels of employees in the kitchen. It is also critically important to be familiar with market trends and sources of supply and to keep up with new products coming on the market. The buyer needs to know how the primary markets impact prices paid in local markets and how quickly the prices in local markets will change relative to the major market indicators.

The purchasing agent should be able to judge if a fair price is being quoted by a distributor based on current market reports. Foodstuffs and supplies ordered must be matched to the purchase specifications for each outlet. For example, the specifications for a fast-food versus a full-service restaurant will find that more prepared or convenience products are used in the former. Also impacted will be the grade, variety, size, or count of food items ordered. The lack of space, equipment, and skilled employees may require pre-portioned or processed ingredients be purchased.

If ordering is to meet the needs of the system it serves, the buyer must be familiar with the use to be made of each food item as this will impact the various types, grades, and forms in which they will be purchased. The buyer must also know the grading criteria, labeling terminology, and the standards of quality used in grading.

Buyers need to follow market conditions closely as supply and price follow predictable seasonal variations. The United States Department of Agriculture (USDA) provides free reports indicating the percentage of total crop that is marketed during each of the twelve months of the year. The greater the probability of price and supply changes, the greater the need to follow the market closely, especially on items purchased in significant quantities. Some of the USDA reports are available for seafood, fruits and vegetables, and beef, pork, veal, and lamb.

A very few buyers may physically go to the market to select their own merchandise. Exclusive restaurants sometimes purchase directly from farmers, fishermen, and growers who sell organically raised products. They are willing to pay a premium for these products as are their customers.

Types of Buying

Different types of buying are employed in the food-service industry. *Open* or **informal buying** is where the contact between the buyer and seller is made through a sales representative in face-to-face meetings or over the phone. Negotiations are largely oral, and conditions of purchase and product specifications are given orally. This is not unlike a unit manager calling a produce supplier checking supply and prices of items needed.

Formal buying means that the terms are put in writing and procedures for payment of invoices and terms are stated as conditions for quoting prices and service commitments. This is what corporate administrators will arrange for multi-unit purchasing programs. However, individual operators also enter into formal buying agreements with suppliers.

Sales Representatives

The traditional purveyor representative will usually make weekly stops at the company's top accounts to get the order directly from the manager or purchasing agent. Some may also collect payment for last week's delivery. Occasionally, they will bring in new product samples; they are sales representatives first and foremost. The role of the sales rep cannot be overstated as companies realize that anyone can sell a particular product and that the determination of who gets the order is not simply based on the purveyor with the lowest price. If the price advantage is neutralized, the customer will make the purchasing decision on other services and benefits received from dealing with a particular purveyor and their sales rep.

The most important aspect of purveyor selection is perhaps customer service. It is here where the purveyor representative has to be much more than an *order taker*. Representatives not only must be knowledgeable about product lines but also must have an understanding of the needs and problems of the operator and be able to offer suggestions. The major food-service distributors are offering a package of what is being called "value-added services," or buyer benefits. These include such things as recipes for products, point-of-sale information, training sessions for kitchen and service personnel, special reports detailing the use levels of all items purchased, and special presentations on new products.

Professional sales representatives will not take up a lot of an operator's or manager's valuable time and interrupt his or her daily routine just to get an order. However, they want to sell to you every week and would very much like you to expand what you purchase from them. They gain your confidence by offering solutions to your food related problems.

Some of the old-time sales reps will take as long as you let them to get an order. They will stand around chatting with the kitchen personnel and dining room staff and keep them from being productive. These types give sales reps a bad reputation; but they will stay only as long as management allows them to stay. Many managers will only see sales reps with appointments or at a set time each week.

With certain items like dairy products, fountain syrups, coffee, crackers, and bread, the delivery person and the sales rep are one and the same. Orders are prepared at the time of delivery after counting what is currently on hand. A par level of stock is usually kept with the approval of the operator. In cases of product sold on guaranteed sales, day-old bread and outdated dairy products are replaced for credit unless they were specifically ordered by the operator. This kind of conditional sale is a self-regulating inventory process. There is little benefit in overstocking when the product has to be returned for credit and returns are subtracted from the commission of the sales representative.

However, we recall one restaurant where the bread delivery person had his product stocked in the freezer of the restaurant. The manager did not realize that he was paying for this unused inventory when it should have been credited to his account. In addition, we have observed occasions where nonperishable items were overstocked by ambitious commissioned sales reps. Paper suppliers and dish detergent sales reps should always be required to obtain management approval on all reorders. If you are not careful, you will be tying up your cash in excess inventory.

Some managers prefer to give their order over the phone to eliminate the time spent dealing with sales representatives. This is the practice with most chain restaurant operations. It is unnecessary for the sales representative to make personal visits because the prices and products supplied have been agreed upon by corporate executives and payment is not made from the individual unit. The manager has no authority to change product specifications and cannot authorize purchase of items not preapproved by corporate. The weekly visits to restaurants still occur within the independently owned and operated units that account for roughly 60 percent of the 595,000 commercial food-service units. Most commercial restaurants purchase from distributors and orders are placed over the phone, given to sales representatives, or submitted in writing. The amount of formality varies, but there is negotiation and agreement over the terms of sale that specify quantities, prices, deliveries, payment of invoices, and notification of price increases.

Purchasing Channels

The path that food products take to ultimately end up in the storerooms of the food service operation is quite complex. As products move from the grower or producer to the end user, costs increase with each successive transfer. The route begins with the producer and grower, who in turn sell their products to a processor. Often, an intermediary, called a *concentrator*, is necessary to gather the output of many small producers and growers into transportable quantities. Examples of concentrators are grain elevators, receiving plants, and cooperative marketing organizations. They primarily aid the small farmers in getting their goods to the larger markets.

A **broker** represents a packer or processor who in turn sells the processed products, canned tomato products for example, to distributors and wholesalers who may put their private label on the can. They in turn will sell direct to the end users, the restaurants, and food-service outlets. It is estimated that approximately 60 percent of the price of the product goes to cover the cost of marketing and transporting the product to the end user. Only 40 percent goes to the farmer.

There are also primary and secondary markets. Prices quoted on primary markets influence the pricing on all other markets. The Chicago Livestock Market is a primary market that affects the prices charged in Kansas City and New York. Boston is a primary seafood market, and the prices charged there drive the prices in other cities from Atlanta to Dallas. Buyers learn to watch the activity on the primary markets to forecast what will happen to the price and supply in secondary and local markets. The larger chain operators like McDonald's and Red Lobster purchase in such large quantities that they can bypass the primary markets and buy directly from the producer, grower, or trawler. This allows the chains to save on middleman handling costs.

The Buyer-Seller Relationship

The operator-supplier interaction is a mutually beneficial relationship. Each party is dependent on the other for its existence; neither can prosper without the other. In nature, this type of relationship is referred to as *symbiosis* and means "consorting together of two dissimilar organisms in a mutually advantageous partnership."

Although some vendors have vertically integrated into the food-service business (e.g., Pepsico, General Mills, and Pillsbury are three that come to mind), the majority of vendor-operator relationships are best described as symbiotic where either one can end the relationship at any time.

It seems to work best when both sides view each other in a mutually advantageous partnership. But often, one of the parties, usually the restaurant operator, will approach the negotiation table and present a one-sided unilateral position of demands and conditions the vendor must abide by to get the restaurant's business. The larger the account, the greater the stipulations and the greater the likelihood of the supplier yielding to the buyer's terms. We are not referring to product specifications here, but to the conditions of the agreement, prices, delivery terms, and payment policy.

We are not going to take sides as we have bargained from both sides of the table. Obviously, in such negotiations both parties are attempting to protect their respective interests. But sometimes the attitude of the negotiators is heavily one-sided due to the belief of some operators that you have to be tough on purveyors or they will take advantage of you. Conversely, the attitude of some purveyors is that they cannot let the operator get the upper hand because he or she will take advantage of them.

The food-service operator who is inflexible as to delivery times, days, and payment terms is just as unrealistic as the purveyor who sets the terms for ordering and delivery, returns, and credits without consideration for the needs of the client. This operator seems to be saying, "If you want my business, this is what you must do for me, regardless of how it increases your distribution cost and disrupts your operating procedures." The other side of the coin has the autocratic vendor saying, "If you want to buy from me, this is what you have to do before I will consider serving your account."

The negotiation process can be made more equitable for both parties if each understands the other's situation. We believe that these extreme attitudes have become the exception rather than the rule, thanks to allied memberships of national and local restaurant associations and the International Food Service Executives Association (IFSEA), where operators and vendors can meet in a nonthreatening social and professional setting.

A number of things will determine the vendors you choose to deal with. And from the vendor side, purveyors also analyze the operators to see if it is feasible to do business with them.

ow Purveyors Analyze Food-Service Accounts

First, the account is probably analyzed by the distributor for your total purchases over a 12-month period. The percentage of increase or decrease will be noted. If it has decreased, the vendor will seek to learn the reason why—for example, ordering from another supplier, change in specifications to a brand not carried—and try to increase your business.

Once these data have been gathered, the restaurant accounts are put into one of three categories.

A Accounts: Profitable accounts in sales volume, order size, gross profit, required service level, and payment history. These are their best customers and they do not want to lose them to a competitor.

B Accounts: These do not meet the minimum A levels but are still profitable.

C Accounts: These are marginal customers whose order size, profitability, bill paying, or service levels cause second thought as to maintaining these accounts. In the scheduling of the sales reps' time, more time needs to be devoted to service A accounts and to improve B accounts. Marginal C accounts are time-consuming.

A distributor's sales manager is likely to tell sales reps that if they are calling on a large number of C accounts, they may be costing themselves and the company money. Unless these accounts show potential in terms of sales volume growth and profitability, their time can be better spent with A and B category customers.

How Purveyors Can Improve Buyer Relations

1. Be consistent with order taking, deliveries, and product quality; charge a fair price.

2. Look out for the interests of the operators. Keep them in mind when certain products they need are going into short supply or where prices are likely to increase, inform clients of market conditions, protect them from shortages, and/or allow them to benefit from lower prices due to surpluses or special discounts from processors.

3. Maintain an adequate stock level of products they need, and in case of emergencies when stocks are low on certain items, make sure they have the first right of refusal to purchase additional quantities before selling stock to new accounts.

4. Give adequate notice of price increases and invoice them at prices quoted at the time the order was taken. Be responsive to their specific needs, and give them the benefit of your superior knowledge about market supply and demand.

The buyer and seller who are aware of each other's interests can work together for their mutual benefit. Although they are "dissimilar organisms," they need each other to prosper and succeed. I love this quotation by the great statesman, John Ruskin: "There is always someone who is willing to make a product a little worse and sell it a little cheaper. Those who consider price only are this man's lawful prey."

Things Operators Can Do To Improve Vendor Relations

Don't be a fickle buyer who is "penny-wise and dollar-foolish." Look at the cost of your overall food order and not the prices of specific items. Value is determined by more than just low price. Consider the extra services the purveyor provides; for example, merchandising and marketing assistance, cooperative advertising, order summary reports, handling of credits and returns, special deliveries, and credit policies. The more business you do with a purveyor, the more important your account becomes and the greater the likelihood the vendor will work closely to satisfy your special needs.

Examine your purveyor relationships and determine where you are likely classified as an A account. You should be receiving special consideration in terms of prices, payment terms, and deliveries. Also, understand that you need to be at least a B account with the majority of your suppliers.

Don't make overly restrictive demands on delivery times or demand special deliveries on items *you overlooked* after the regular delivery has been made. Remember, they probably route their trucks to keep delivery costs down so they can charge more competitive prices. A mutually agreed-upon delivery schedule should be negotiated.

Pay your account on time, adhering to agreed-upon terms. The more frequently you pay, the lower prices you should be able to negotiate. The longer you take to pay or the longer the credit period, the higher prices they must charge. There are not too many other businesses who can get merchandise delivered today and not have to pay for it until next week.

Purveyors have the same demands on their cash flow as restaurant operators. Many have to pay their suppliers quickly, and if they are on a 14-day billing period with their suppliers, they cannot give you the lowest price if you take 45 days to pay your invoices. It costs both parties money to extend credit terms.

Don't spread out your orders too thinly between more than two purveyors of similar items. Work to make your account an A or B rating; you will get better prices and service. You want to limit your purveyors so each gets a reasonable slice of your business. They will tell you that the more you buy from them, the more they can save you on your overall food purchases. The fewer vendors you have to deal with, the more time you can give to your operations, employee training, and customer relations. When a vendor meets your standards on a consistent basis and charges you a fair price, it deserves your business and loyalty. Switching purveyors over a few cents per pound when they have been reliable and service minded in the past is unwarranted. A good purveyor will treat the operators' interests as though they were as important as those of his or her own company, for, in fact, they are. Support the vendors who work with you. Be mindful that they are in business to make a profit for their time and expertise. It will all come back to you when product shortages occur or when you need some extra time to pay your bills.

Here is a list of questions that you might ask when you are interviewing suppliers for your operation:

1. Are you willing to stock private label (for chain concepts), or are you willing to add to your line the special brands we specify?
2. Can or will you enter into long-term contracts that will guarantee price and product supply?
3. Will the quality/brands/labels of your products remain consistent?
4. Will you agree to 30- to 60-day notification for price and product changes?
5. What is your policy on returns and credits?
6. What is your policy on deliveries:

   Frequency: number of days and which days?

   Emergency deliveries: extra charges?

   Will you agree to our delivery schedule requirements?

7. Who are your sales representatives in our area that we can call if there is a problem with our account? Or will we be considered a "corporate account" with the regional sales manager as our contact? Will orders be called in or will a sales rep call on the unit manager?

8. Will the delivery drivers put away the delivery or just unload the truck?

9. What are your payment terms?

10. What is your policy on notification of out-of-stock items?

11. Can you provide references of satisfied clients? (Check on their reliability and reputation.)

12. What value-added services can you provide? (For example, point-of-sale pieces, nutritional analysis, product development, recipes, reports of product use levels, and market information about price and supply.)

13. May I visit your distribution center to check on cleanliness and organization of your warehouse?

Sometimes operators and managers try to take advantage of purveyors. One of the authors recalls a young assistant manager he inherited when he accepted a position of food-service director at a small private college and how the assistant held suppliers in contempt. He would ask them for tickets to football games and Disney World because he felt they could not refuse if they wanted to get our business. On one occasion, a case of frozen product was accidentally put into the walk-in refrigerator and not the freezer and spoiled. He called the supplier and demanded that the company pick it up and give us full credit for the product.

When the sales representative came in with the replacement case, I had a talk with him and told him that it was not the vendor's fault and what actually happened. He had already assessed my assistant and knew it was not his company's fault because it was the only incident reported in his district. If it had been the vendor's fault, others who used the product would have reported the same thing. You are not going to put one over on your supplier for very long. Either the vendor will stop doing business with you or recover the extra costs in the prices you are charged.

The operator has obligations to the purveyor just as the purveyor has obligations to the operator. Developing an honest working relationship of mutual respect will pay off during times of product shortages and questions over billing and spoiled merchandise. Changing purveyors over small price differentials can work against the operator in the long run. There is a fine line between using competitive bidding to one's advantage and being known as a fickle buyer who can be swayed by price alone. Orders must be coordinated with purveyors' delivery schedules and restaurant production requirements. The ingredients need to be delivered in advance of the day they are required for preparation, or a disruption of production will occur should the needed ingredients not be in stock. Efficient ordering has the product in stock when it is needed.

While price is certainly a factor in the selection of approved purveyors, other factors can override a few cents per pound or per case. Very few purveyors will allow an independent operator or chain to "cherry pick" its bids. That term describes purchasing only the items with the lowest prices from a purveyor, leaving the supplier little margin of profit. Keep in mind that, like a restaurant menu, the list of items carried by a supplier are not subject to the same identical markup.

Just as the restaurant operator monitors the sales mix of menu items, noting the food cost and gross profit return, so do vendors. They like to use the example that many supermarkets are using to demonstrate to the public that when you look at a typical shopping cart full of groceries, the total cost of the basket is lower than the competition's. If you examine the individual prices of the goods in the basket, you will find that certain items are higher than at a competitor, but the total market basket price for identical brands, grades, and sizes is less.

Factors That Influence Purveyor Selection

When sending out bids to potential suppliers, here are some other considerations you will need to obtain clarification.

THE EXTENT OF BRANDS, GRADES, VARIETIES, AND SIZES CARRIED

If a standardized recipe calls for a specific brand name product and that brand is carried by only one purveyor, the operator has little choice in purveyors and price. Usually, in such cases, one brand is deemed superior to all others and is considered critical for quality control purposes. If sizable quantities are purchased, the operator has leverage to get another supplier to start handling the item. If the supplier agrees to carry a particular brand because you request it, that is a value-added service that you must take into account.

A purveyor cannot carry every brand and variety of canned good or frozen shrimp. Some purveyors offer low prices but are limited in the number of brands and sizes they carry. Having to purchase items in smaller or larger units than is practical for standardized recipe batches can become a disadvantage in quality and cost control. The greater the varieties and lines carried, the greater will be the prices charged. The same holds true for certain unit sizes of items, e.g., pints, quarts, gallons, or 5 gallon buckets. If you want to purchase items in sizes that are best for your standardized recipes instead of bulk packs, that is another factor that may override having to pay a little more. Purveyors do not want to carry items that do not sell well or that they cannot turn over quickly in their inventories. For the same reasons that restaurants try to limit their menu offerings, purveyors try to limit their inventory of brands, varieties, and sizes.

MINIMUM ORDER QUANTITIES FOR DELIVERY

The cost of making a stop at a restaurant to drop off one case or twenty cases is the same. When the driver's salary, truck lease, maintenance, gas and oil, insurance, and tolls are totaled and divided by the number of deliveries made over a year, the fixed overhead cost for a delivery of 30 cases of product is over $90. That cost needs to be spread over each item ordered. If the order quantity and items ordered (remember the low bid items) do not leave sufficient margin to cover fixed overhead, the vendor may not deliver or may tack on a minimum delivery charge. Therefore, the profit on a small delivery can be very little so the supplier must charge more per case or unit for small deliveries. If you regularly divide up a 30-case order between three different purveyors, the delivery cost per case would be $90/10 = $9.00. But if the order for all 30 cases were placed with a single vendor, the delivery cost per case would be reduced to $90/30 = $3.00, or a total saving of $180.00, which we assume would be reflected in lower prices.

Of course, there will always be purveyors who suspend the minimum order quantity to regular customers when circumstances dictate; that is just good business sense. However, if the customers regularly order below the minimum, the policy will be invoked. There are always competitors who want your business and will not impose minimum order quantities, but if they do not have the brands, sizes, and varieties you request, it becomes a moot point. In addition, expect to pay more per case or per pound when you are regularly ordering less than the minimum orders. You cannot negotiate the lowest price when you are ordering at minimum levels.

CREDIT POLICIES

It is not the price but the payment terms that are important. If you are paying COD (cash on delivery) for your food and supplies, you should be negotiating the lowest possible prices with your purveyor regardless of the fact that you are an independent operator. It is when you are extended credit that the price will go up. However, purchasing on credit is critically important to an independent operator trying to manage working capital.

Purveyors have the same cash flow pressures as the independent restaurant operator and corporate chain. They cannot give the buyer any better terms than they are being charged by their brokers or master distributors. If they must pay their invoices within 30 days, they cannot extend you credit for 60 without having to charge you interest or raising their prices. Most purveyors give one week credit. That is really a fantastic advantage to the cash flow. Consider that what is delivered on Monday is processed and sold that week. We then take the sales to pay for last week's delivery. The longer you take to pay your bill, the higher will be the prices you will pay.

Most retailers must pay for merchandise before it is delivered. Auto and appliance dealers must arrange for loans for their floor inventory and pay off the loans as merchandise is sold. In the restaurant business, we get delivery and have a minimum of one week to pay for the merchandise. If a purveyor will extend credit, it is a tremendous consideration to do business with the supplier and again overrides a slightly higher price than if we paid COD. There are times during the month and year when those workers' compensation premiums and other expenses that cannot be put off must be paid. The credit extended by purveyors is a very low-interest loan, and many restaurant operators, independents and chains alike, have used purveyor credit as a way to finance expansion and get low-interest loans. Bill-paying flexibility is what credit affords the restaurant operator. Purchase on credit allows the operator to spread out the payment of accounts. Having to pay a few cents more per pound to get additional time to pay is more than worth it during periods when cash flow is strained to a dangerously low point.

What is important is the cash-to-cash cycle. Supplies purchased on COD must be sold to *replenish* the cash that was paid out. If this cycle takes too long because excessive amounts were purchased or business was less than anticipated, the cash position of the operation will be strained. This was the case during the 1996 Summer Olympics in Atlanta. Both purveyors and restaurants increased inventories in anticipation of record sales to the tourists and Olympic officials. What occurred was just the opposite. Business activity was lower than would have been the case without the Olympics. Regular customers stayed away, and the out-of-town business did not make up for the loss of local trade. Restaurants expecting to turn over inventories more quickly were burdened with excessive purchases and invoices to pay. Without the anticipated sales, their cash flow was severely strained. Perishable products spoiled and could not be used. Purveyors could not take back much of what went unused because they too increased their inventories and had to pay their suppliers from cash reserves. This is why the credit policies of purveyors is an important factor in the selection of one purveyor over another.

FREQUENCY OF DELIVERIES

Like minimum order quantities, how often a purveyor will deliver is a very important consideration. Purveyors are experiencing the same cost constraints as any business in the economy today. Many are cutting back on the number of trucks used for delivery and that means reducing the number of deliveries per week.

Daily deliveries may become a thing of the past except for some very high-volume operators with good payment histories. Traditionally, bread, produce, and dairy suppliers delivered daily. Those that continue to do so will need to charge more for such services.

The purveyor-operator relationship cannot be a one-sided unilateral arrangement. There must be give-and-take on both sides. For example, the routing of the purveyor's delivery trucks may require that the delivery be made between 11:30 A.M. and 1:30 P.M., traditionally a time when restaurants, open for lunch, will not accept deliveries. The delivery routes are programmed to have the trucks traveling the shortest distances when empty. One of the author's restaurants in Orlando was only a quarter mile from one supplier's warehouse, but because they were not able to accept delivery before 8:00 A.M. on Thursdays, we became the last delivery on that truck, which sometimes did not get there until 7:30 P.M. After two of these night deliveries, he changed his schedule to be at the restaurant by 8:00 A.M.

SALES REPRESENTATIVE SERVICES

A "professional" purveyor sales representative is more than a simple salesperson or order taker. The sales rep who can provide the independent operator with new product information, market supply and demand reports, and suggestions on product usage can provide tangible services to the independent operator. These types of services are not requested or needed by the large chain and franchise accounts because franchisees and managers do not have the authority to change purchase specifications or menu items. Subsequently, the number of full-service sales reps is shrinking every year.

Chain and franchise operations are usually on national accounts, and orders are either called in or transmitted electronically so there is no need for a sales rep except when problems arise. Many independent operators rely heavily on their sales rep, and it is not uncommon for the sales rep to spend upward of thirty minutes to an hour talking with management when taking an order. They get the order and collect the check for last week's delivery. Many sales reps go into the storage areas and write the order for the operator. They maximize their commission this way and reduce the likelihood that they will have to make a personal delivery because of something the operator forgot to order. This scenario occurs in operations where the owner is unorganized and not in control of his purchasing.

One independent operator related how he gets the "best" prices for the items he needs. He said he quit mailing out individual closed bids to his suppliers because every Monday morning all the sales reps he used would come into his restaurant to get an order. He handed each of them a list of what he needed for the week and allowed them to meet together in one of his empty banquet rooms to fill out the bid sheets. When they emerged, the bid sheets were filled out and he seriously thought he had stumbled on the most effective way to assure he was getting the best prices in a competitive bidding process.

After he had finished his remarks and we sat down in his office with a cup of coffee, we explained that what was likely happening was that the sales reps were "taking turns" being low bidder, and they were likely inflating their prices and made the "low" bid look good by comparison.

Sales representatives are your voice with the purveyor. They can help you extend your credit when you are experiencing cash flow stress and protect you if certain products you need are in short supply. When they suggest that you purchase a few extra cases because the price is likely to increase next time or that they are running low on inventory and are not sure when the next truckload will be arriving, you are protected. This is the kind of service you expect from a sales representative who has your business interests first and foremost in mind. He or she wants to continue doing business with you, and in many cases a special bond develops with your sales representative.

EQUIPMENT SUPPLIED OR MAINTAINED

Some purveyors are able to help an operator defer purchase of certain pieces of equipment by offering to provide what is needed if the operator agrees to purchase certain items from them. Most often provided are coffee makers, soft drink dispensers, ice cream cabinets, milk dispensers, and instant tea and hot chocolate dispensers. If an operator has the needed equipment, it is serviced free by the supplier. The cost of providing the equipment or the maintenance is added to the cost of the product. In the case of the coffee equipment, a few cents per pound is added to the cost of the coffee. Some will lease their equipment like ice makers at a greatly reduced price if the customer purchases their soft drink mix. Again, these benefits may outweigh the additional costs for the coffee, milk, ice cream, and soft drink syrup.

RELIABILITY AND REPUTATION

Regardless of how low prices are, the integrity of the suppliers outweighs most of the factors mentioned. If they do not deliver what they promise, it is no bargain at half the going price. Purveyors will sometimes get into bidding wars when one of their top accounts switches to the competition. The losing purveyor immediately sets out to "get even" by getting clients of the rival to switch to his or her company. We recall being in the middle of a linen rental company war when the rival linen company cut the prices it was charging for napkins, aprons, and swipe towels in half. It was a deal we could not refuse, and the rival knew our current supplier would not outbid it because they could not do it without incurring a loss. Of course after a month when emotions subsided, the new linen company representative came to see us, begging to allow his company to increase the price. We had gotten a six-month term on the prices and technically the company had to honor it. We negotiated a higher price that was still less than we had been paying previously. If we had not allowed the supplier to raise the price, we are sure the product and service it would have provided would have had us terminating the agreement. Eventually, prices returned to normal after a few more months.

Purveyors who want your business often come in and quote very low prices on products they want us to buy from them. This is referred to in the industry as "lowballing." They offer a one-time or short-term price to get you to try their product and then raise the price after you order it on a regular basis. Loyalty to your supplier is important, and if you get a reputation as a price-fickle buyer, you will get exactly what you pay for. When there is a question about a price charged or a credit for returned or spoiled merchandise, a quick and equitable settling of discrepancies makes any additional cost small in terms of the satisfaction that one is being treated fairly and professionally.

ow Many Purveyors?

When it comes to selecting purveyors to supply the needed items, one must decide on the actual number of companies that will be used. An operator can use as few or as many suppliers as is practical for the volume of product purchased. One option is to use what is called a "total supplier." This is as close to one-stop shopping as an independent operator can come, short of owning and operating its own commissary or distribution center. US Foods and SYSCO are two such companies that can supply everything from kitchen equipment and china to precut steaks and dry goods.

The alternative is to use several small specialty suppliers for specific items like seafood, red meats, poultry, and produce. Certain food items of a specialized type that are purchased in minimal quantities are usually purchased from a single supplier (e.g., coffee and tea, dairy products, and bread). If more than one supplier were used for such items, order amounts would not meet minimum order quantities required for delivery. In addition, the total value of your account would diminish to prospective suppliers.

The minimum order and frequency of delivery policies of suppliers will determine the number of purveyors that the product use levels of the restaurant can support. If a restaurant becomes an unprofitable account due to small orders, slow paying, and returns and credits, purveyors will not want to service the account because the "slice of the business pie" is too small to bother with, compared to other accounts who deserve their attention and service commitment.

A dvantages of a Total Supplier

When deciding between the total supplier and specialty supplier route, consider the following points. The **total supplier** is the way to go if you have multiple units and can combine their buying power to be able to negotiate the best prices and service. There are fewer deliveries and fewer invoices to process when you use a total supplier. However, the deliveries and invoices are much larger than would be the case with several specialty suppliers. Consequently, some bill-paying flexibility is lost. But perhaps the greatest drawback comes from putting "all your eggs in one basket." With a total supplier you do not have an alternative source of supply to go to in the event of shortages or stock-outs of critical items. Also, you do not have the market information available from multiple suppliers, and no competitive bidding is present to be sure you are getting the best prices. However, there are a number of market reports on supply and price for meat, produce, eggs, and seafood that can keep you informed of market conditions.

Because total suppliers carry a broad line of products, they are forced to cut back on the number of brands, grades, and varieties of canned, fresh, and frozen products. Thus, product specifications may need to reflect allowable substitutions.

Total suppliers claim to offer the lowest overall "food bill." They say, "The more you spend with us, the more we can save you." The only way you can be sure this is true is to obtain prices from rival companies. It is recommended that you have alternative sources of supply for your most critical items so you are not left in a lurch when your supplier is out of stock on an item.

Multi-unit operators like the total supplier concept because it helps control costs and quality. If everyone buys from the same company and pays a corporate negotiated price, managers do not have to spend time on the phone getting price quotations every Monday morning. Standard purchase specifications can be upheld more easily because the supplier is instructed to deliver specified brands and grades.

Because every unit is purchasing the same items at the same price, food cost comparisons between like units can be made (allowing for differences in the menu sales mix). Better service to individual locations is another benefit of the total supplier. Smaller, low-volume units can demand the same service as the high-volume units because they have combined their influence. Unit management is not required to spend time seeking out the best prices. They can use the extra time to train employees, do community service, and interact with customers.

In multi-unit operations total suppliers reduce the likelihood of fraud between the buyer and seller. Only approved purveyors are authorized to sell to restaurants and managers do not have purchasing authority. This is an important aspect in corporately owned units and independent operations with absentee ownership. In order to control cost and assure product consistency, purchasing from total suppliers makes for a more centralized control over ordering.

Quality, service, and price were mentioned by more than half of all operators when asked for the criteria they use when selecting a purveyor. The biggest complaints voiced were sales reps with insufficient product knowledge, lack of responsiveness to problems, and late deliveries. An average of eleven purveyors were used regularly by the operators in the survey. Those that use full-line distributors (75.8%) used an average of four different sources. Those that use specialty suppliers (43.4%) use an average of seven different sources ("An Operator's Guide for Foodservice Distribution," advertising supplement, *Nation's Restaurant News*, August 1982).

L ocal Speciality Suppliers

Local **specialty suppliers** still rule food-service distribution. Forced to reckon with the broad-line giants, distributors everywhere have become increasingly sophisticated, deploying computer technology and expanding the range of services they offer.

During the past two decades, the rise of national food service chains has spawned the need for larger distributors that can provide state, regional, and even national distribution. To combat such development, independent distributors have organized to offset the marketing and distribution clout of the giants. Three of the largest and better known are Comsource, Code, and NIFDA.

The giant distributors have expanded their territories through the acquisition of local independent distributors. Between 1982 and 1987, the aforementioned firms collectively acquired 89 independent distribution companies. Payoffs to the operators of restaurants dealing with these distributors comes in the form of better value-added services because cost efficiencies allow them to charge lower prices. Operators will still need to deal with the local specialty distributors who are in a position to provide better service to local accounts than the big suppliers. The broad-line suppliers have minimum order quantities and do not seek out the smaller lower-volume independent operations; they typically go after the chain accounts and large hotels and country clubs. This leaves a sizable unserved market for the specialty suppliers.

The value-added services provided by the largest distributors are: one-stop shopping; reduced time spent on ordering and receiving; fewer deliveries and invoices; menu planning services; merchandising assistance; quality control; inventory control; and direct ordering through computers.

In the meantime, chains continue to vertically integrate and operate their own distribution companies. Denny's, Wyatt Cafeterias, Hardee's, and Yum Brands are some that have tried this route. They claim that they are saving 1 to 2 percent of total food cost. Even remote units get excellent service that would otherwise be unavailable from regular purveyors. Some are even into food processing such as cutting steaks, and making hamburger patties, sauces, dressings, and pastry dough.

Other companies have abandoned their distribution systems in favor of broad-line suppliers—for example, Collins (Sizzler) and Morrison's (Morco)—conceding that instead of yielding great self-sufficiency, it may have dulled their ability to focus on operations and expansion.

A dvantages of Using Local Specialty Suppliers

Many of the disadvantages of a total supplier are the advantages of using multiple specialty suppliers. Since you are dealing with more than one supplier, you have smaller bills and therefore more bill-paying flexibility. You have alternative sources of supply in the event a critical item is out of stock. You have multiple sources for market information and always will have the element of competitive bidding to keep prices in check. In addition, specialty suppliers will carry a greater line of brands, grades, and sizes, which broad-line distributors may not provide.

As for disadvantages, there are more invoices to process and deliveries to check. If you are a multi-unit operation, it is more difficult to monitor cost and quality consistency between units. Management will spend more time with ordering and receiving than with total suppliers. There is also some increased exposure to fraud when you are dealing with more purveyors. Competitive bidding can result in lower prices and better services than can be obtained with total suppliers.

Independent operators will likely prefer the multiple specialty purveyors to the total supplier primarily because of the minimum delivery requirements. Whichever option is preferred is indicative of one's buying philosophy. Motives can be either rational or emotional. The predominant motivators should be quality of products, service, dependability, and price.

Determining the Quantity to Order

How much should you order? This question has important implications on preparation, cash flow, theft, spoilage, and space. Let us relate a story that answers this question. Upon graduation from the master's program in Hotel, Restaurant, and Institutional Management at Michigan State, one of the authors interviewed for a position as head of a junior college hotel and restaurant management program in Kansas City, Missouri. The dean of the college brought him to interview the president of the college. After giving him some background on his last job as president of a small, private women's college that included room and board in its tuition, he related they fed 500 women three meals a day for a total cost of $5.00 per student.

His question was, "How much food inventory should such an operation carry?" I started to do some calculations in my head, multiplying 5×500 and assumed a 40 percent food cost as a standard when it came to me that the answer was not a specific dollar amount. I responded with, "*As little as possible.*" It was an answer he liked, and he told me that the foodservice director had submitted an invoice for $30,000 from a single purveyor that put quite a strain on the cash flow of the small private school. However, there can be some very legitimate reasons for such a large order, although such a large order should not have been made without his approval.

The amount to keep on hand must be qualified by a number of factors that influence the quantities ordered at any one time. Perhaps of greatest influence is the frequency of deliveries by the purveyor. In this case, the school was in a rural area where the purveyor required the purchase an entire semi trailer full of product to make the delivery. The order quantity was driven by the purveyor's delivery policy, not the use level of the school cafeteria.

The accurate estimation of order quantities is frequently a problem for many operators. This is easily remedied. An inventory system is presented in Chapter 10 that will allow any manager to interpret what to buy, how much to buy, the price, and which purveyor to use on his or her first day in the unit. It is all possible because proper written records are kept. There will not be run-outs or overstocked items for fear of running out. The quantities kept on hand will convert cash into perishable foodstuffs.

Overstocking of food and supplies seems to encourage lax standards, resulting in increased waste and theft. The amounts kept in inventory are inversely related to the frequency of deliveries from suppliers. In a city like Atlanta, Georgia, inventories can be kept relatively small as many purveyors will deliver five days a week and even on weekends. Conversely, if you are located in Opp, Alabama, you may be able to get only one delivery per week on some items. Included here are nine conditions that will influence order quantities and inventory levels. Using the inventory forms shown in this chapter, this information can be quickly and easily assembled.

FREQUENCY OF DELIVERIES

The first condition for determining whether one or two cases should be purchased is how often deliveries can be made to the restaurant. The more frequent the deliveries, the less that needs to be ordered and kept on hand between deliveries. Typically, grocery items like flour, sugar, canned goods, and items not requiring refrigeration are ordered and delivered once a week in most metropolitan markets. Perishable items like produce and fresh fish need to be delivered more frequently unless they are going to be frozen.

Any restaurant located in an area where less than weekly deliveries are made will need to carry a greater supply of nonperishable items. The frequency of delivery may be related to how close the supplier or actual source of the product is to the operation. Restaurants located in Gulf or coastal cities where fishing fleets dock will be able to get fresh fish more readily than a restaurant in Kansas City, Missouri. The quantities ordered and kept on hand are also affected by the distance the product must be shipped. A Kansas City restaurant may order 500 pounds of lobster tails shipped from a distributor in Tampa, Florida where a Tampa restaurant could order only 50 pounds.

USE LEVELS BETWEEN DELIVERIES

The amount of inventory consumed between deliveries is the next condition that influences order quantities. Since business volume fluctuates from week to week and month to month, so will purchase quantities and inventory levels. When the busy season ends, staff must be reduced and purchases cut back. Typically, in a chain of family restaurants every September sales volumes dropped because the family business dropped significantly as parents outfitted their children for the coming school year.

We monitored labor costs and purchased more closely in September because many units continued to staff and purchase according to sales levels of the previous month. Subsequently, they ended up with excessive inventories and invoices to be paid in September where business volume dropped almost 50 percent over the previous month. Restrictions were placed on managers purchasing multiple cases of expensive food items.

The calculation of the amount of product used between deliveries and the minimum amount needed to get to the next delivery will be covered in Chapter 8. Now inexpensive items are not as much a concern. An extra case of catsup or mayonnaise is hardly noticeable; but an extra case of breaded shrimp is what you should seek to avoid.

PRODUCT PERISHABILITY

This is a self-limiting factor that is obvious. Lettuce, for example, cannot be held more than a few days without deterioration. Fresh poultry will spoil if not used in three or four days. Fresh shrimp and fish begin to lose quality after a few days even under ideal refrigeration conditions.

STORAGE SPACE AND TEMPERATURE

Restaurants with limited storage space have much higher inventory turnover levels than restaurants with large storage areas. Therefore, the conclusion seems to be that storage space should be designed with frequency of deliveries in mind. When visiting the Buckhead Diner in Atlanta, Georgia, it was noted that every square inch of the building was being used and that the storage area was far less than what would be expected for an operation doing approximately $5 million a year. The Diner is able to function because of daily delivery of foodstuffs by its purveyors.

If you have a large storage area, there may be a tendency to "fill it up." If this occurs, more dollars are converted into food inventory and cash flow can become strained. If food inventory is not turned over at least three times a month in dollar value, you need to reduce your inventory levels. A simple calculation of use levels between deliveries will identify overstocked items.

In addition to the square feet of overall storage space, the amount of refrigeration and freezer space will influence quantities you can keep on hand. If you have only a small reach-in freezer, quantities kept in inventory will be limited to the capacity of the freezer unit. Again, inventories need to be tied to frequency of deliveries and use levels between deliveries, not storage area available. It is much easier to control cash in a bank account than food in your restaurant.

MARKET CONDITIONS

There will be times when heavier than normal inventories will be needed. Such conditions may arise if there is a likelihood of short supplies or significant price increases. This was the case with tomato products several years ago. If there is a shortage in supply, price will likely increase and product will be harder to find. If you have advance notice and can stock up, you will carry much more than your normal weekly inventory.

QUANTITY DISCOUNTS

We recommend resisting the temptation to purchase more than you will use in a given month just to save a few dollars in quantity discounts. What the supplier is doing is reducing his inventory and replacing it with cash. You, on the other hand, are depleting your cash position and increasing your inventory of perishable foodstuffs. However, there are times when it works to the operator's advantage to purchase enough to qualify for discounts. The operator must have the capital resources to take advantage of discounted quantity purchases. Remember, money tied up in perishable inventory can put a strain on cash flow.

CASH POSITION

Your cash position will dictate whether you can take advantage of quantity discounts or purchase extra quantities when market conditions call for it. If you do not have the excess capital and the discounts are predicated on quick payment, you may have to continue to purchase on the "spot" market, and pay higher prices.

CREDIT TERMS

When a purveyor offers you favorable credit terms for quantity or bulk purchases, you may wish to take advantage and purchase more than necessary. However, your cash position and the credit terms will keep your purchases at manageable levels.

PROXIMITY TO SUPPLY/SUPPLIER

There is a relationship between the quantities purchased and the proximity to supplier or supply. The farther away you are, the more you will likely have to purchase or keep on hand. The distance from the supplier impacts the frequency of deliveries, and the less frequent the deliveries, the greater will be the amounts ordered and kept on hand.

Competitive Bidding

Buying competitively requires having a clear understanding of what prices different purveyors can offer. Even the single operation independent operator can exert some purchasing clout on purveyors seeking their business. You need to obtain comparative bid prices from a minimum of two different purveyors of similar product lines to see the range of prices and products available.

However, this is not saying that price is the only or even the most important factor in the bid process. This formal type of buying is a way to survey potential suppliers when one first enters a new market. This is not a process that one does more than two or three times a year. Competitive bidding can be a waste of time unless you utilize the bid process to its fullest advantage. When service and other factors in the purchase decision are equal, you will then turn to the lowest bidder for its products. However, in reality, service can override price considerations more often than not.

Buyers who say they purchase only the highest quality ingredients need to qualify their statement with the words, "as determined by the intended use." Depending on how an item is incorporated into a recipe, varying levels of quality can be acceptable without lowering the overall quality of the end product. An example would be common Pascal celery used for soup stocks, gravies, and mirepoix. It does not need to be of the size, color, and texture required for decorative relish platters. A can of sliced peaches graded choice because of lack of uniformity in size may be perfectly acceptable for a Jello salad.

Although one would expect that price and quality are always directly related, this is not the case. High prices do not automatically equate to high quality just as low prices do not always mean poor quality. Perhaps the best example of this is fresh produce. When the price of certain produce is high, quality is usually the poorest. The best quality comes when prices are low and supply plentiful because it is in season. It seems that when lettuce is $24.00 a case, it is small and light. When it is $12.00, the heads are heavy and dense.

The prices change due to supply and demand. Fresh products like produce, chicken, fish, and red meats are more likely to fluctuate in price than processed foods. However, there have been times when prices of canned or processed foods have been unstable even after the season's crops have been processed and canned. Several years ago, all products containing tomatoes increased dramatically as California tomato farmers plowed under a season's crop because they could not get enough money for them. This produced a shortage on the market and significantly increased the price.

There are times when you are happy to get any product, whatever the price or brand. A buyer must know what constitutes quality and be able to recognize it to make effective price comparisons when bids are obtained. Having more than one supplier increases your bargaining power.

There are two approaches to commercial food buying: the needs of the operation and the availability of products on the market. The buyer may have to begin with what is available in the local market area. This may mean that adjustments must be made on the menu and preparation methods. Very often, the products purchased are a compromise between need and availability. For example, if you need a prepared meatball for your sandwich shop and there is only one brand being carried by your suppliers, even though you are not completely satisfied with that product, you will buy it until something better can be obtained. This kind of purchase decision must be kept to a minimum or your quality standards will be compromised.

When you have more than two sources of supply for a particular food item and you have multiple units using the same items, it makes more sense to pool your purchasing power and negotiate for all locations instead of having each manager hunt for the best price *he or she* can get. In the case of a midwestern family restaurant chain, each manager was left to purchase for his restaurant individually. It was discovered that each manager had his own favorite purveyor and substituted its brands instead of what the president of the company thought they were using. The prices paid were not the same; in fact, different restaurants purchasing the same items from the same purveyors were being charged different prices.

On items in which brand names were specified—for example, Heinz catsup, Cattleman's bbq sauce, Comet Cleanser, Trio hash browns, Coca Cola fountain syrup, and similar items—price was the determining factor for which purveyor was given the order. There were exclusive suppliers of other "custom" items (e.g., dinner rolls, steaks and ground beef, and dairy products). Here, the corporate office negotiated with the supplier or meat fabricator and required all units to purchase only from these approved sources.

The bid process on grocery items was the first step in enforcing a company purchase policy on *all* items. Even repair and maintenance services were bid out with the condition that the successful plumbing or heating and air conditioning repair company would be given all the company's business. However, even much smaller chains and large-volume single-unit operations can obtain better prices by the bidding process. The smaller operations will not receive the same prices as the larger accounts, but they can move toward being in the top 5 percent of operations their size in getting optimum pricing from their suppliers, especially on high-volume items. A small Italian restaurant may purchase large quantities of canned tomato products. Even a small pizza parlor can be a significant user of mozzarella cheese and therefore be able to negotiate a very good price from its supplier. The quantities it uses may allow the supplier to purchase quantities that qualify for a lower price bracket because of quantity discounts from its cheese supplier.

Being too large of an account by having too many units distributed across a larger part of the state or region may reduce the number of potential suppliers who can handle *all* your units. This is what motivated some larger chains to develop their own distribution companies or commissaries. When they had the processors deliver truckloads of product to their warehouses for their trucks to deliver, they saved on the cost of delivery and eliminated a middleman markup. Smaller chains that do not want to get into the distribution business contract with certain regional distributors to stock and deliver their custom-packed products to their stores.

Some chains are so large and purchase such large quantities of certain items, they seek to deal directly with the source of the item they need. In some cases they will vertically integrate and own cattle farms and fishing fleets. Red Lobster requires many thousands of pounds of shrimp to supply its restaurants across the country. The company has contracted directly with trawlers on the ocean to supply a certain number of tons of shrimp and get a guaranteed price. Bonds are taken out to insure that if Red Lobster must go to the spot market to get shrimp because of weather or because an oil spill reduced the catch, driving up price, it will be indemnified for the difference in price.

Sometimes, smaller operations will try to hedge against price increases, especially if supply is limited and demand is holding constant. One such example in the past involved all tomato products from catsup and barbecue sauce to tomato paste and puree. When suppliers of one of the authors told him that there was about to be a severe shortage in all canned tomato products he used in his restaurant and that prices were going to increase, he had to make a unique purchase decision. He needed to have assurance of a steady supply of canned tomatoes to keep his restaurant operating profitably. He was able to purchase 400 cases (what amounted to a six month supply) at the current market price but would be required to take delivery of all 400 cases and pay the invoice within 30 days. Fortunately, we had the cash in the bank to cover the cost so the purchase of a six month supply of tomatoes was made. The market price of all canned tomatoes products doubled over the next three months and it was the right decision.

The following year, the supplier stated that he was not sure that he could hold the price for six months and wanted to know if the restaurant wanted another 400 cases. After checking with other suppliers who stated that price might fluctuate some but not more than $1.00 a case, if at all and inquiring about future supply, with the reply that there was a significant increase in processed inventories and supply was more than adequate, only the amount needed from week to week was purchased. Prices and supply remained stable that entire year.

The formal bid process also puts into place other standards and procedures that removes the purchasing authority of the unit managers and replaced it with ordering responsibility. Sales reps were told that price increases had to be submitted to the corporate office a minimum of one week prior to going into effect. Telling a unit manager was not considered notification to the corporation. Subsequently, if invoice prices did not match those in the bid, they took a credit on the invoices. Once the vendors saw we meant business, they notified us as requested. This gave us time to shop around for substitutes, for a better price, or to instruct our units to increase their orders before the price increase. Information about prices, purveyors, and specifications now came from the corporate office in the form of official memos, which in turn became part of the unit manager's purchase notebook for future reference.

STANDARD PURCHASE SPECIFICATIONS

One of the first "purchasing" decisions that an owner-operator has to make are the specifications for the products the restaurant will use. **Purchase specifications** are precise statements of quality and other factors required in a commodity to suit production needs. Specifications should be brief but complete enough to assure proper identification of the item. If properly used, purchase specifications will provide suitable buying standards for the food buyers and purveyors.

Specifications allow for purveyor price bids to be compared from item to item. Specifications also give uniformity and consistency to purchasing and receiving that will help maintain consistency in cost and quality. Specifications usually include the following:

1. Trade name or common name of the product (e.g., sliced apples)
2. Quantity in a case, pound, carton (e.g., 6/#10 cans)
3. Trade or federal grade (e.g., USDA Choice)
4. Size of the container (e.g., No. 10 cans)
5. Geographic origin (e.g., Michigan Bing Cherries)
6. Variety (e.g., York Imperial Apples)
7. Style (e.g., solid pack pie apples)
8. Count (size) when applicable (e.g., spiced apple rings 30 count per No. 10 can)
9. Condition upon receipt (e.g., fresh, frozen)
10. Unit size on which price is quoted (e.g., case, 6/#10 cans)
11. Other specific factors such as specific gravity, drained weight, packing medium, degree of ripeness, length of age.

The inclusion of brand names in specifications reduces the amount of written detail in a specification. However, numerous private label products offer quality products at sizable savings over the branded products. The buyer may then decide on a lesser brand after testing of samples.

When you find a particular brand that meets your specifications, add it to your purchase specifications. There are the well-known national manufacturer brands like Hunts, Heinz, Delmonte, and Kraft, but there are also distributor group brands like Code, Nifda, Nugget, Pocahontas, and Plee-Zing that are comparable in quality and lower in cost than national brands.

Formal bids will contain the buyer's name and address, closing dates for returned bids, delivery address, payment terms, delivery frequency and location, number of invoice copies required, terms of price change notice, minimum order quantities, and policy on stock-outs and substitutions. Figure 7–1 shows a sample of a letter accompanying the bid sheet sent to purveyors.

In these times of increasing costs of both materials and operating expenditures, all of us are even more conscious of our cash outlays. We have received notices of price increases and minimum order quantities for delivery from many of our purveyors who are just as concerned with rising costs as we are.

We, too, have found it necessary to consolidate our buying to counter these cost increases. We have four full-line restaurants and one drive-in requiring the food and supply items listed on the enclosed commodity list. The corporate office, from which all bills are paid, will be directing each unit as to where specific commodities are to be purchased. In effect, all five of our units will then buy specific items only from approved purveyors.

We are already purchasing many of the listed items from you, but prices have been only quoted to each unit individually. We in the corporate office have not been directly involved in the ordering process. We have noticed from our invoices that prices many times vary from unit to unit from the same purveyor on identical products.

We request that you review our product list and quote your prices with the following conditions:

1. In most cases there must be individual unit deliveries (of your minimum amounts). Our locations are: 8031 Metcalf (restaurant and commissary), 6500 N. Oak Trafficway, 9500 Nall, 11121 Holmes, and 2514 Johnson Drive.
2. Certain items, storage space allowing, may be purchased in larger lots and delivered to the commissary.
3. Items listed bearing a double asterisk (**) cannot be substituted.
4. When a brand is specified without asterisks, bid on identical or better quality brands.
5. State can counts and size of net can contents on applicable items, for example, fruits, when quoting house brands or private labels.
6. When a grade is specified, it is the *minimum* grade acceptable for our need. Bid on equal or better grades.
7. State length of time quoted prices will be honored. After stated time, *we will call* to reestablish prices and make necessary changes.
8. If price changes should occur prior to the stated quotation period expiration, *we will require you to notify this office a minimum of seven days prior to the price increase.* Without advance notice, we reserve the right to pay previously quoted prices.

Please return the bid sheet with your terms before February 1. Thank you for your cooperation. Should you have any questions, please direct them to me at 312-555-0000.

FIGURE 7–1
Bid letter.

A sample of the **bid sheet** is shown in Figure 7–2.

When the bids were returned, a memo, shown in Figure 7–3, was sent to restaurant general managers along with the price list and approved purveyors.

Each unit manager had in his or her possession a list of the approved purveyors and the quoted prices for the specified items. They used this list to compare to the prices on their invoices. Part of the obligation of restaurants was to use the approved purveyors and not purchase from any others. The purveyors entered into the agreement based on the condition that they would

NAME OF PURVEYOR			
Sales Manager	**Telephone**		
Item	**Grade or Brand**	**Size/Count/Weight**	**Price**
Salt Pellets		100 lbs	
Gelatin		case/1.5# boxes	
Toothpicks (round)		case	
Kitchen Cleanser		case/14 oz	
Worcestershire	Lea & Perrins	case/5 oz	
Heinz 57		case/5.5 oz	
Red Beans	Choice	6/10	
Butter Flavored Oil	Koala Gold/Low Melt	35# 5 gal	
Long Spaghetti		20#	
Assorted Cereals (indiv)	Kelloggs	50 or 100/case	
RG Black Pepper		6#	
Hot Chocolate Mix	Jubilee/Nestlé	case	
Quick Oats	Quaker	42 oz case	
Powdered Sugar	4x	case 1# boxes	
Vinegar	White	4/gal	
	Cider	4/gal	
Paprika		1#	
Granulated Sugar	Cane	100#	
	Beet	100#	
Pancake Syrup		4/gal	
Tartar Sauce	Fancy	4/gal	
Cocktail Sauce	Fancy	6/10 case	
Sliced Dill Pickles	Extra standard	4/gal	
	Choice	4/gal	
Mustard	Heinz	case 6 oz	
	French's	case 6 oz	

FIGURE 7–2
Bid sheet for Regan's Restaurants.

Enclosed is a copy of the letter sent from our office to the following purveyors: Isis, Lady Baltimore, John J. Meier, Pisciotta, Sun-ra, and Better Foods. Bids were not received back from Sun-ra and Better Foods.

Because we cannot adjust our prices as frequently as our purveyors increase theirs, we are forced to ride out inflation by methods under our direct control. Our last menu price increase has not been able to keep up with our recent cost increases. This is the reason we have consolidated our five-unit buying power. You will no longer be responsible for "shopping the market" for the best prices.

We cannot just consider price if quality is lowered. We will not resort to lowering our quality standards in the face of rising prices. The enclosed bid sheets show the lowest prices *on specified grades and brands*. We believe we can keep cost increases to a minimum if we all purchase the lowest priced items from the purveyors indicated.

We know that you cannot search the market for the best prices as easily as we can do with a formal bid system. In addition, purveyors are required to notify the corporate office of impending prices increases. Telling you when you call in your order *is not considered notice* of price increases. Remind them that they must call the office if prices are going to be changed from those quoted on the bid sheet. Check your invoices for correct prices and circle any that are higher than your official price list.

FIGURE 7–3
Bid instructions memo.

be the exclusive suppliers of all units. When price increases were called into the corporate office, memos were immediately sent to each unit either approving the price increase or instructing the unit to switch to another brand or purveyor.

This is one way to deal with price increases over the short term or until menu prices can be raised. Once purchase specifications are written, and the bid issued and accepted, the control over perishable inventory begins. The delivery of orders must be checked and stored for eventually use. In Chapter 8, the critical inventory process will be covered.

ey Concepts

- Purchasing is an administrative decision made by owners and top management and is not delegated to unit management in chain operations.
- Ordering is determining the quantity to purchase and following purchase specifications.

- Both operator and purveyor need to be reasonable in their requests from the other party.
- Establish purchase specifications for your key ingredients
- Do not be penny-wise and dollar-foolish when it comes to selecting your suppliers.
- Think of your major suppliers as business colleagues, not adversaries.

ey Terms

Purchasing	Purchase specifications	Broker
Ordering	Bid sheets	Distributor
Total supplier	Informal buying	
Specialty supplier	Formal buying	

iscussion Questions

1. Assume you operate a small regional chain of identical restaurants. Give three (3) advantages of using a Total Supplier over multiple Specialty Purveyors.
2. List six (6) factors that will influence quantities ordered and kept in inventory.
3. Distinguish between the terms "purchasing" and "ordering."
4. Take the perspective of either (a) an independent operator or (b) a multiple unit chain administrator (state which perspective) and give four (4) reasons for using either (c) a total supplier or (d) multiple specialty purveyors for your purchasing needs. Choose either (a) or (b) and either (c) or (d).

Problem 1 (next page)

Daily Food Sales to Food Purchases Record

Date	Sales	Sales Week to Date	Sales Month do Date	Daily Purchases	Purchases Week to Date	Purchases Month do Date	Daily Purchases to Sales %	Week To Date %	Month To Date %
Mon 12–29	$1,701	$1,701	$1,701	$1,258	$1,258	$1,258	73.96%	73.96%	73.96%
Tu 12–30	$1,904	$3,605	$3,605	$2,378	$3,636	$3,636	124.89%	100.86%	100.86%
Wed 12–31	$2,160	$5,765	$5,765	$462	$4,098	$4,098	21.39%	71.08%	71.08%
Th 1–1	$2,160	$7,925	$7,925	$903	$5,001	$5,001	41.81%	63.10%	63.10%
Fri 1–2	$4,496	$12,421	$12,421	$2,365	$7,366	$7,366	52.60%	59.30%	59.30%
Sat 1–3	$3,713	$16,134	$16,134	$1,414	$8,780	$8,780	38.08%	54.42%	54.42%
Sun 1–4	$4,163	$20,297	$20,297						
Weekly Total	$20,297			$8,780				43.26%	43.26%
Mon 1–5	$1,998								
Tu 1–6	$1,836								
Wed 1–7	$2,052								
Th 1–8	$2,255								
Fri 1–9	$4,958								
Sat 1–10	$5,439								
Sun 1–11	$4,588								
Weekly Total	$23,126								
Mon 1–12	$1,850								
Tu 1–13	$1,728								
Wed 1–14	$2,376								
Th 1–15	$2,255								
Fri-1–16	$3,108								
Sat 1–17	$5,439								
Sun 1–18	$4,348			-					
Weekly Total	$21,104								

Instructions: Assume you are the owner of the Buckhead Grill in Grand Rapids, Michigan and you are seeking to minimize your purchases to keep your inventory turnover between 3 and four times per month. After looking at month end inventories for the past six months, you believe that by the third week of the month purchases for food should be no more than 45% of your month to date sales. In order to test this standard, you have prepared a form that tracks daily, weekly, and monthly sales and purchases. The dollar amount in the purchase column represents the total of the delivery invoices for that particular day of the week. You have completed the first week of the month but need to fill out the form through the third week of the month to see if your goal of 45% percent is realistic.

- Using the Excel template diskette for Chapter 7, Problem 1, complete the Daily Food Sales to Food Purchases Record.

- Is the standard of keeping purchases to 45% of monthly sales a feasible one?

- Why are the week-to-date percentages higher than the weekly Total Purchases to Sales percentage?

- What happens to the month-to-date percentage of food purchases to food sales after the first week on the month? Does it increase or decrease? Why?

- What are some possible reasons for purchases to vary from week to week?

- What information does this record provide management regarding purchasing, inventory and food costs?

Problem 2-Inventory Review

Ending Inventory May 31	$6,200
Total Delivery Invoices for April	$9,700
Employee Meals	$860
Food Sales for April	$31,775

Compute the following:

1. Total Food Available for Sale in April
2. Cost of Food Consumed in April
3. Cost of Food Sold in April
4. Cost of Food Consumed Percent
5. Cost of Food Sold Percent
6. Inventory turnover in times per month
7. Average number of days of inventory on hand
8. Comment on the amount of inventory kept on hand and assume that this restaurant is in a large metropolitan city, like Chicago or Kansas City.

8

Inventory and Storeroom Management; Receiving; and Accounts Payable

■   ■   ■   ■   ■   ■   ■   ■   □   □

FUNDAMENTAL PRINCIPLES OF COST CONTROL

1. Have a written record of your all purchase requirements.
2. Take inventory prior to placing your orders.
3. Take a physical inventory at least once a month.
4. Separate non-food items when you are totaling inventory figures.
5. Organize your inventory records to expedite taking inventory and improve its accuracy.
6. Take inventory on the same day of the week to establish use levels between deliveries.
7. Inspect each delivery before signing the invoice.
8. Pay from invoices, not from statements.
9. Quantity discounts on slow moving items is not an effective use of your capital.
10. Audit delivery invoices for prices and extensions before paying.

The Inventory Process

You cannot carry out effective ordering unless you count and control your inventory. Fiscal counts of items in stock should be made before an order is placed with a purveyor. Some computer software programs used by chains are able to determine order quantities directly from sales reports by deducting from inventory the items required for its preparation. However, without such a system, one must inventory what is on hand before ordering. This may mean daily counts on items like produce or weekly counts on canned goods and paper supplies.

We understand that in many restaurants the taking of the month-end inventory is a tedious and dreaded activity. When that is the case, it is because management must remain until the early morning hours counting items. This important activity should not be any more unpleasant than reconciling the sales for the day. Considering that knowledge of what is on hand must be determined before the quantity to order can be determined, inventory is something that must be performed as frequently as one places orders for food items.

If you are buying an existing business and the current owner does not take monthly inventories, the food cost figures shown on the financial statement are not accurate. Ask to see the balance sheets as well. Look for inventory figures in the *current assets* section, and if nothing is shown, you know that the business is simply reporting purchases, not cost of food consumed or sold. If there is only one inventory figure, you will need to ask if it contains the total of food, beverage, and supplies, and get individual category amounts. Do not place much reliability on reported operational results that lack inventory figures. They cannot even be called "cost estimates" because they are based on incomplete information. In such cases, an inventory should be taken and a true cost of food consumed determined.

There must be documented inventory records listing all goods purchased. The owner or manager who claims to have it all in his or her head and shuns documentation leaves the operation open to serious problems. In the event of illness, vacations, dismissal, or transfer, other management personnel can use the permanent records and continue to order in an efficient manner.

Food cost control requires that regular and accurate inventories of food, beverage, and supplies be kept. Taking inventory prior to placing an order provides management with the "pulse" of the restaurant activity. When you combine the inventory and purchasing information with sales and customer counts, you develop an important perspective on the business activity. As owner-operators of our own restaurants, we did the majority of the ordering. We knew our restaurants so well that we could detect breakage, recipes that were not followed correctly, and errors in deliveries because we knew how much we had on hand, how much we ordered, and how much we sold of the key ingredients. A manager or operator must have intimate knowledge of food production, sales, customer counts, and purchase quantities to be able to detect variances early.

Without taking time to count what you have on hand prior to placing an order, one of two problems will likely occur. First, you may run out of something before the next delivery and be forced to substitute and disappoint customers who cannot obtain their first choice; or you will have more than is necessary, tying up capital in perishable food products, taking up valuable storage space, and increasing the likelihood of spoilage and theft.

In order for the monthly income statement to accurately reflect the cost of food consumed and sold, you must take a complete food inventory at the end of the month. This **fiscal inventory** means counting and extending the prices on all food, beverage, and supply items. There is no substitute or shortcut for taking a fiscal count of all food, beverage, and supply items if you expect your cost ratios and percentages to reflect what is actually taking place in the operation. Without a fiscal inventory and the proper posting of purchase invoices for the month, it is impossible to compute an accurate cost of food consumed or sold. Every operation needs to take inventory at least once a month for accounting purposes. However, the number of operations that do not take monthly inventories is alarmingly high, and some of these operations are doing over $3 million dollars per year in sales. Not only do they not take monthly inventories; they do not prepare monthly income statements and balance sheets. A consultant colleague told of a client with five hotels and sales in excess of $24 million that prepared only annual financial statements. The income statement should not be viewed as only an IRS report. Chapter 12 covers the income statement and how it can become a management tool for cost analysis.

The Inventory System

The inventory system described in this chapter is a basic manual system (vis-à-vis a computer system) that can quickly and inexpensively be started in any operation. The computer programs for inventory were developed from this manual system. The inventory forms are available from most office supply stores (see Figure 8–1). With this system in place, a record of purveyors, product specifications, prices, and usage levels can be interpreted by any management employee. This is especially important in the restaurant industry because of management turnover from year to year.

The following information is found in an **inventory book**:

	STOCK NO.	DESCRIPTION	AVERAGE MONTHLY CONSUMP-TION	DATE		DATE		DATE		DATE		DATE		DATE		
				ON HAND	ORDERED	ON HAND	ORDERED	ON HAND	ORDERED	ON HAND	ORDERED	ON HAND	ORDERED	ON HAND	ORDERED	
1																1
2																2
3																3
4																4
5																5
6																6
7																7
8																8
9																9
10																10
11																11
12																12
13																13
14																14
15																15
16																16
17																17
18																18
19																19
20																20
21																21
22																22
23																23
24																24
25																25
26																26
27																27
28																28
29																29
30																30
31																31
32																32
33																33
34																34
35																35
36																36
37																37
38																38

NATIONAL · MADE IN U.S.A. · 15-006 · "COUNT OF STOCK" INVENTORY

FIGURE 8–1
National form no. 15-006, "Count of Stock" inventory.

1. Provides a record of what is needed
2. Provides a record of product specifications
3. Provides a record of the purveyors
4. Provides a record of prices and unit of purchase
5. Provides a record of product use levels
6. Makes it easy to interpret for efficient ordering
7. Increases the accuracy of inventory
8. Makes the inventory process easier and faster
9. Makes it easier to detect variance in inventory levels

Monthly fiscal inventories of bulk foods in the walk-ins and storeroom can be taken on the same form. The current prices are indicated for ease of extension of inventory values at the end of the month. In addition, a separate page/section should be available for *food in process,* which should also be inventoried. Food in process is all the foods on the serving line or salad bar, sugar, salt, pepper, and condiments in the dining room and food in line refrigerators. Inventory should also include food prepared for service but not yet used, such as prepped vegetables and meats, pasta, and rice. If these items are not counted, your food cost will be overstated (because you will show a lower inventory value and therefore a higher cost of food consumed).

The column "Stock No." can be used to indicate the purveyor from which the item is ordered. If there is an alternative or secondary supplier, it should also be indicated. Buyers know that the purveyor listed first is the primary supplier. The "Description" column is used for detailed product specifications. This is necessary to be sure the proper items are ordered and received. Examples of entries are shown in Figure 8–2.

The column "Average Monthly Consumption" is used to indicate the price and unit of purchase. The price should be written in pencil so it can be easily changed when price increases occur. The "Date," "On Hand," and "Ordered" columns are used as they are shown. Before an order can be given, an inventory must be taken. The date the count is taken is indicated and the amount on hand is recorded. The amount needed to meet forecasted business volume (including a small safety factor), is reflected in the *ordered* column. The *use levels between deliveries* will become apparent after several weeks of taking inventory. For example, in Figure 8–2, if there was one case (six no. 10 cans) of green beans on 12-1 and only two cans on 12-8, the use level is four cans. Therefore, another case must be ordered to have enough to get through to 12-15. Since cases are not broken by vendors, there will be a built-in safety margin of four cans.

Every item that is purchased, from perishables to paper supplies and china, can be listed on this form. It allows inventories to be taken as often as

Purveyors*	Item Description	$/Unit	Date 12-1		Date 12-8		Date 12-15		Date
			OH	Ord.	OH	Ord.	OH	Ord.	
US Foods PF&G	Cut Gr Beans, 4 sieve, BL, Ex Stand	$9.86 6/10	0	1 cs	2	1 cs	3	1 cs	
US Foods PF&G	Gabonzo Beans Fancy	$11.50 6/10	0	1 cs	2	1 cs	3	1 cs	
Sysco US Foods	Tomato Sauce Hunts	$17.50 6/10	0	4 cs	1+3	3 cs	2	4 cs	
Manco Bari	Crushed Tomatoes Fancy	$14.60 6/10	0	3 cs	2+2	2 cs	3 cs	1 cs	

*Primary and alternative suppliers

FIGURE 8–2
Inventory book page format.

ordering requires. The information provided allows management to set par stock quantities if it so chooses. The inventory can be reduced to as small as conditions will allow without fear of running short in the middle of the week. Slow moving expensive items can be given special reorder points to limit the dollars tied up in inventory.

The value of this inventory record is extensive. It provides a record of what is purchased, the product specifications, the primary and alternative purveyors, the price, and the unit in which the item is purchased. In addition, and equally important, it indicates the use levels between deliveries. It is easily interpreted by other management personnel, increases the accuracy in taking inventory, and expedites the counting process. Regular inventory taking also helps detect shortages and overages. It allows for comparisons to be made from month to month and between units in a multi-unit operation.

Taking Inventory

The process of taking inventory can be accomplished quickly and efficiently by following some very basic practices. First, organize the pages of the inventory book to correspond to specific products and/or storage areas. For example, the items kept in the freezer should be put on one page to keep from having to turn pages or move back and forth between storage locations. Group like items (e.g., seafood, vegetables) on consecutive lines on the page. Like items should also be stored together so counts can be quickly taken. If items are stored on shelves in the order they are listed on the inventory record, the counting can proceed more quickly and with less chance of omitting an item.

The month-end inventory can be taken right on this form. Since the current prices are indicated, there is no time lost checking old invoices that have been paid and filed away. Remember to indicate food in process on a separate page. In some operations, backup stocks of prepared foods can account for a significant dollar amount of food cost.

Inventory should be taken on the same day(s) each week. Making up orders on a specific day, regardless of when the delivery is made, will determine the proper amounts that should be kept on hand between deliveries. Items ordered once a week (e.g., canned goods and supplies) can be counted all at once, even when several purveyors are used and their order days are different. In this way, the operator is organized to give orders on certain days and receive deliveries on others.

Don't forget to also include all the spices and condiments that are on the shelves by the cooks' station. This can be a sizable amount so it must be inventoried. Since food in process stays relatively constant over time, a weighted average value can be applied to the inventory after six months. The only thing that will impact the value of food in process is the day of the week that the last day of the month falls on. Another variance will occur when business volume reaches its maximum due to seasonal or special event reasons.

The food cost percentage should reflect only the cost of food consumed or sold. Supplies (nonfood items like plastic wrap, plastic gloves, paper towels, pan liners, carryout containers, paper napkins, cocktail napkins, etc.) need to be inventoried separately from food. Some fast-food operators count paper food containers against food cost because every food item served must be either wrapped or in a cardboard or put into a Styrofoam clamshell. If supplies are counted as food inventory, your cost of food consumed will be understated (because you will show an inflated food inventory, thus lowering your cost of food consumed).

The Month-End Inventory Process

The end-of-the-month inventory process is absolutely essential for accurate food cost calculation and the preparation of the income statement. A set procedure needs to be established and followed month after month. Since the inventory book contains all the items that are to be counted, copies of the pages can be used for accounting purposes. As the prices paid are part of the information contained in the inventory book, all units need only provide the actual counts of items on hand.

Invoices for the month are tallied to arrive at total purchases. If an inventory book is not being used, separate sheets will need to be prepared for ease of comparing figures from unit to unit and from month to month. Separate sheets should be provided for produce, meat, frozen foods, groceries, fountain, paper items, dairy products, fish and seafood, and miscellaneous. Inventory sheets should already contain the names of the common items purchased but space should be left for specific brands, grades, and units of purchase and price to be added. You may even leave a space for the name of the purveyor the product was purchased from. This is especially important if you do not have a centralized purchasing system and unit managers can purchase a variety of brands from different purveyors. Prices shown should be those on the most current invoices.

An example of an inventory entry might contain the following under the description column; *Long Spaghetti, Lee, Isis, 20 lb box @ $8.50.* The extension would include the quantity on hand and the value of the inventory, for example, *35 lb @ $14.88.* The value of the inventory can be computed based on either **LIFO (last-in, first-out)** or **FIFO (first-in, first-out)**. Under LIFO, inventory is valued on the basis of the cost of the first items placed in stock. The last items purchased, usually at higher prices, are assumed to be the first sold. By using LIFO, inflation is removed from your inventory value. This eliminates phantom profits, reduces taxable income and income tax, and increases cash flow.

Accountants will tell you that LIFO is a tax planning tool. LIFO does its job best when you are having a good year. In general, the more LIFO inventory you have on hand at year-end, the lower your profit will be. No other day in your year counts; only the last day of the year. Tax laws will allow you to use FIFO to value your inventory for balance sheet purposes, where you want to increase your assets, and LIFO for income statement and tax purposes. Check with your accountant before valuing your inventory to see which is best for your tax bracket and purposes.

Organization of the Inventory Book

The order and sequence of the inventory book allows one to see the quantity and dollar value of various food classifications. The *Uniform System of Accounts for Restaurants* (USAFR) identifies 20 such categories but typical classifications might include: Meats, Dairy, Poultry, Fruits and Vegetables, Fish and Seafood, and Canned Goods. You may further define certain classifications such as Meat by having separate sections for beef, pork, veal, lamb; and

Poultry by chicken, turkey, duck, and so forth. The more detailed the breakdown of your inventory, the easier it is to locate the exact cause of problems. You may find it useful to calculate the percentage of your total food cost dollar or inventory value for each of the separate food categories. You will probably find that over 50 percent of your inventory value is tied up in fresh meats and seafood. This knowledge will help you set controls and procedures to monitor more closely those food items that have the biggest impact on your overall food cost. The more expensive the food item, the more control management must be placed over that item.

For example, if the monthly food purchases amounted to $16,800 and the total amount of fresh meat purchased totaled $9,875, approximately 59 percent of your food dollar was spent on meat. When this is tracked over several months, management can see a trend or discover variances that will signal where costs may be out of line.

By comparing monthly inventory totals by food categories to the total value of food inventory, another view of food cost is provided. This kind of detailed analysis is very easy to accomplish at basically no cost. In general, the percentage of the food dollar that is spent on various food categories will show that only 12 to 15 percent is tied up in canned and dry goods. It is somewhat ironic to see the dry goods storeroom locked up tight while the walk-in refrigerators and freezers remain open. The cost of a case of cut green beans disappearing from the storeroom is practically nil while just a few pounds of shrimp or beef tenderloin disappearing could easily exceed a cost of $25. The control needs to be placed where the loss is likely to be the greatest.

In the cost control process *total control* is the objective. It is impossible to monitor every item equally and management should never let the employees know that they are practicing cost control in a "selective" manner. If management cannot monitor all costs they must prioritize their attention; in other words, shrimp and steaks are closely watched while green beans are for the most part ignored. The largest or the most frequently occurring costs are those that are most closely monitored.

Many chain operations monitor weekly purchases by having each of their operations summarize their delivery invoices when they are turned in for payment. The purpose of the sheet is to uniformly summarize all food, supplies, laundry, and repair invoices received during the week. This allows the corporate office to have a "snapshot" of what occurred in each of its operations. Each unit is required to turn in all invoices, deposit slips, time cards, and other internal paperwork to the corporate office for processing. The Weekly Invoice Summary Report, shown in Figure 8–3, summarizes all invoices received that week on a single page.

The form is broken down into sections that separate food, nonfood supplies, pay-outs for food and supplies, miscellaneous and commissary, returns and credits. There is a spot for weekly sales so percentages can be calculated

Week of: 2-4

	Food Purveyors					Supplies/Nonfood			
Date	Invoice	Vendor	Amount	Date	Invoice	Vendor	Linen	R & M	Supplies
2-4	1090013	Sunshine	127.94	2-5		St. John		128.50	
2-3	09763	A Reich	124.20	2/1 - 2/7		Faultless	450.00		
2-5	12960	Presto	40.50	2-3	7900	KC Air filters			25.00
2-6	94122	Pisciotta	160.80						
2-7	40716	Overland	480.30						
2-5	40762	"	123.75						
2-3	06761	JJ Meier	180.60						
2-6	20063	Kelly	53.76						
2-3	5621	Henkle	149.50						
2/1 - 2/7	–	Manor	488.30						
2-5	067112	Lady Balt	553.60						
2/1 -2/7	–	Foremost	236.70						
Totals			2719.95				450.00	128.50	25.00

	Pay-outs			Miscellaneous and Commissary		
Date	Description		Amount	Date	Description	Amount
2-4	Red Beans		10.89	2-2	Commissary	318.00
2-6	Band aids		2.50	2-5	"	393.73
				2-7	"	229.48
				2-3	Eli Witt	88.50
Total			13.39	Total		1029.71

	Returns and Credits					Summary			
Date	Invoice	Vendor	Item	Amount		Sales	Cost	Percent	
2-5		Commis.	16 Filets	(21.70)	Food	8742.85	3652.85	41.78 %	
					Linen		450.00	5.1 %	
					Supplies		25.00	.285 %	
					Miscell.		88.50	1.0 %	

FIGURE 8–3
Weeky invoice summary report.

for food purchases, laundry, and supplies. This form is useful in keeping managers mindful of their purchases relative to their sales.

For purveyors who deliver three or more times per week the *total* of the invoices for the week is posted. For purveyors having one or two deliveries per week, their invoices are posted separately but consecutively. The total of food invoices is placed at the bottom right of the form.

Under the section titled "Supplies/Nonfood," all laundry, repairs, and nonfood supplies are recorded. Managers are instructed to adjust food invoices if supplies are delivered by broad-line suppliers or they will overstate their food cost. In the "Pay-outs" section they list all food and supplies purchased with petty cash. Limits are placed on the total amount of any single pay-out, with approval required from the corporate office if a pay-out exceeds the maximum allowed. In the section on "Miscellaneous and Commissary," invoices from the commissary are listed. Miscellaneous includes deliveries of cigarettes, cigars, candy, and gum. In the section "Returns and Credits," credits due for returned goods or merchandise billed for but shorted on deliveries are indicated.

Order Quantities

Once product specifications have been determined and the purveyors have been selected, the next step is to establish **order quantities** and inventory levels. A number of factors will influence the quantities purchased and kept on hand (see Chapter 9). Generally, the amounts purchased and kept in stock should be as small as conditions will allow. It is impossible to set a dollar amount or a quantity that will apply to every operation or even to a single operation over the entire year. If one were to base inventory levels on the busiest week of the year, it might mean tying up space and dollars over the other 51 weeks.

Writing the Order

Now that the quantities needed have been determined, an order can be prepared. Because the inventory book is not organized by purveyors, it is not easy to use when giving your orders to the sales rep or calling them in over the phone. You do not order every item you stock each time an order is made. In addition, a record of what was ordered from each purveyor is needed to check deliveries against purveyor invoices.

This is the purpose of the purchase order shown in Figure 8–4. It is basically a retrofitted bid sheet where the purveyors and their prices were recorded and the purveyor getting the order was circled. The names of the purveyors are written in at the top of each column. To the left are three columns containing the item purchased, the unit, and the amount. It is filled out by going down the inventory book pages, with an entry being made for each item that needs to be ordered.

The circle placed in the cell opposite an item description and in a purveyor's column indicates that the order will be placed with that supplier. The checkmark (4) placed inside the circle means that the order has been placed. An X in the circle means one of two things: Either the purveyor was out-of-stock, or the minimum order was not met so the order was given to the secondary vendor.

When the sales rep comes in or calls, all the operator has to do is check the order sheet and read down the column for the company for the order. There is no need for the salesperson even to come to the operation as the order can be placed over the telephone. If the owner or manager is not available when the sales rep calls, the assistant manager or lead cook can read off the order. Deliveries can also be double-checked against this purchase order when the person doing the receiving is different from the one who placed the order.

The Week Of: 12-1			Purveyors						
Item Description	Unit	Quan.	US Foods	CFS	SYSCO	PYA	Kraft	Wilson	
Cut Green Beans	6/10	1 cs	⊗	⊘					
Garbonzo Beans	6/10	1 cs	O						
Tomato Sauce	6/10	4 cs		⊘					
Crushed Tomatoes	6/10	3 cs		⊘					
Provolone	15#	6 ea					O		
Tomato Puree	6/10	2 cs		⊘					
Chopped Clams	12/52 oz	1 cs	O						

FIGURE 8–4
Purchase order sheet.

Receiving

Now that the ordering function has been completed, the next step is to assure the proper items are received at the restaurant. Receiving is the *quality assurance* part of the buying function. A well thought-out receiving system can catch errors, verify vendor billing, and often signal supplier problems before they become crippling to the operation. A receiving system does not have to be elaborate and overdocumented; the most important element is responsibility.

Although it seems that the examples dwell on food items, the same care must be given to checking deliveries of such products as linens, chemicals and detergents, paper supplies, small wares, printed menus, and placemats. Since these items are all "consumed" in the operation of a foodservice establishment, they should be as rigidly accounted for as the larger volumes of food and beverages that are delivered to the operation.

The time to detect errors in orders is when they arrive. In the vast majority of restaurants, the delivery is checked against the invoice that the driver hands the person checking the order. Let it be clear, the invoice is not necessarily an accurate record of what has been *ordered*; it is a record of what has been *delivered*. The invoice may be accurate most of the time, but unless the person checking in deliveries was the one who called in the order, mistakes will likely go undetected at the time of delivery. Consequently, the order form becomes a backup record to refer to when discrepancies arise about the quantity and quality of delivered items.

With the new electronic ordering systems, where numbers are entered over a telephone line or computer terminal, a simple transposition of a number on an order can change olive oil into graham cracker crumbs. This kind of error is more likely to happen with electronic order taking than with manual systems so it is even more important to have something to compare to the delivery invoice at the time of delivery.

What about price extensions? Well, that is another item that must be checked, but it is usually caught before the payment is made. Credit memos, discussed later, will address this occurrence. However, should a pricing error be discovered at the time of delivery, it needs to be noted on the invoice. Circling the error and writing in the correct price will alert the accounts payable clerk prior to writing a check.

There may be times when an item ordered is left off the delivery invoice. This is impossible to detect unless the person receiving can check the invoice against the purchase order. In other instances the invoice will list an ordered item as "back-ordered." The receiving person must notify the manager so the latter can contact another purveyor to get the needed product. If this is discovered when the order is being given, the sales rep will notify the manager and get authorization for a substitute item.

Many regional and local distributors will never back order an item and always ship a substitute brand. They leave it up to the operator to accept or return the item; it cannot be accepted if it would compromise quality or cost standards. This should be worked out with your purveyor beforehand. Chains cannot accept substitutes whereas independent operators can. This is a frequent occurrence with country clubs, hospitals, and contract feeders.

Products sold by the pound must be weighed for correct weight. Items like fresh whole or cut fryers packed in ice need to be checked for total weight and for the average size of the chickens supplied. If the total weight is correct, but the purveyor shipped 2.5-pound fryers when the specifications called for 2-pound fryers, the delivery must be returned. Precut steaks must be similarly weighed. A quality scale is an essential piece of receiving equipment. A digital scale with 150-pound capacity is recommended as it should handle the vast majority of quantities delivered by weight. Digital portion scales with a 5-pound capacity would also be helpful.

Not every single item needs to be weighed during each delivery. Random weighing will expose problems. However, if you become predictable as to whether or not you will check weights, you become vulnerable to **fraud**. If you do not have scales to weigh product sold by weight, you are also vulnerable. Each randomly weighed item should be compared to the weight shown on the box, label, or invoice. If the item is in a cardboard box, the tare weight of the box should be deducted. The scale weight should be written down on the invoice beside the figure supplied by the purveyor, even if the two weights are the same. By accepting this marked invoice, the driver agrees to the weights recorded.

The vast majority of purveyors will be accurate and fair and will not risk your business for a few dollars. However, the delivery personnel are most aware of your receiving vulnerability. Sometimes a driver will purposely leave something on the truck to see if you catch if it's missing. Don't compromise your receiving security because the driver is running behind on his route and is in a hurry.

The person receiving the deliveries must also check the condition of the product when it is received. For example, if frozen product is partially thawed, it should be refused. The ripeness of fresh vegetables must also be verified. Freshness is extremely critical when checking fresh fish. Sometimes it is difficult to tell the variety of the fish that is delivered if it is already cut into fillets. The product identification of what can be sold as "snapper," for instance, does not mean you are getting "red" snapper.

Once discrepancies are discovered, the responsibility for rectifying the mistakes must be clear. A note left for the relief shift manager that an important item was not delivered may not be enough. The note should more properly notify the manager that the missing item has been ordered from another purveyor and when to expect delivery. The sooner an error is discovered, the sooner the remedy can be administered. Remember, the objective of ordering is to have the right product and quantity in the right place at the time it is needed. Sometimes price is secondary to these objectives.

The problems encountered with purveyors on deliveries, back orders, and shortages will impact the amount of business given that purveyor. If problems occur frequently, it is likely that the operator will look for a new supplier or substantially reduce the amount of business done with that particular supplier.

When items are returned or not accepted, the procedure is to fill out a *credit memorandum*, attach it to the invoice, or check when payment is made. Either the delivery driver or the operator can issue the credit. When it comes from the operator, it is a *request for credit memo*. It is a simple form containing the following information: name of purveyor, name of restaurant, amount of credit requested/taken, the reason for the credit, and the date and number of the delivery invoice (see Figure 8–5). Two copies are made: one for the restaurant records and one for the purveyor.

The delivery invoices are often signed by a dishwasher or cook. Some purveyors have delivery policies that state once the invoice is signed, shortages are the responsibility of the operator. Consequently, each and every item on the invoice must be verified by the person signing the invoice. One of the authors remembers how this was indelibly imprinted in his mind from his teenage years when he went to his stepfather's restaurant. A delivery came in and he was told to check it in. The driver said he was behind on his route and was double-parked. He signed the invoice without checking it against the items. When he handed the invoice to his stepfather he asked him if he had checked the delivery

---

Request for Credit Memo
Regan's Restaurants, Inc.

Restaurant Location:

Purveyor		Date	
Invoice Number		Please Credit Our Account For:	
Unit/Quantity	Description	Credit Amount	

Reason for Credit: Wrong Mdse. _____ Shorted Order _____ Wrong Price _____

Requested By: _____ Spoiled/Damaged _____

Prepared in duplicate: One copy to Purveyor; One copy attached to original invoice.

FIGURE 8–5
Request of credit memo.

for accuracy and he told him what had happened. Well, he learned that the delivery driver should not dictate that receiving procedures be compromised. His stepfather said, "Next time he makes a delivery and says that, you tell him to put everything back on the truck and come back later so you can properly check it."

Deliveries should be arranged to arrive at least one day before supplies will be needed, especially prior to heavy preparation days. Nothing is more disruptive than being unable to complete preparation for lack of a key ingredient; production schedules are disrupted and substitutions that impact quality and cost occur.

Purveyors will make their deliveries on set days of the week and generally at the same time of the day, give or take an hour or so. Some establishments make a hard and fast rule that deliveries will not be accepted between the hours of 11 A.M. and 2:00 P.M. if they are open for lunch. Most purveyors honor this request and route their trucks to locations without this limitation.

S torage

Few restaurants can afford the luxury of a full-time storeroom attendant, even those doing $2 million to $3 million in sales. It is impractical because the bulk of food cost is most likely in the walk-in refrigerators and freezers, not the dry storeroom. In addition, these areas are not in a central location where a single door provides access to all.

One key to taking a quick and accurate inventory is to have a set place in the storeroom, freezer, walk-in, and the like for each item purchased. Many times an item thought to be out-of-stock has been stored in the wrong bin or shelf where no one thought to look for it. If the storage area is not organized, moving from one area to another, flipping pages, and skipping lines will increase the time it takes to complete the inventory and raises the possibility of mistakes being made.

To simplify the inventory-taking process, the following practices will make a difference:

1. Group items on shelves to listings on pages.
2. Organize pages by storage location or major food classifications.
3. Have a set storage space for every item.
4. Do not store similar goods in more than one place.
5. Keep storage areas neat and orderly.

Too often, the storeroom in a restaurant is a hodgepodge of supplies and foodstuffs and a convenient place for old or broken equipment, chairs, and utensils. The condition and layout of the storage facilities can actually hinder the efficiency of the inventory and cost control function. The size and type of storage area needs to fit the menu, your standardized recipes, and the frequency of deliveries. Unused storage space is a waste of valuable building space, and excessive inventory is a waste of financial resources. You can tell a lot about the owner or manager of a restaurant by the condition of the storeroom and walk-ins. By looking on the shelves you can ascertain whether those in charge have purchase specifications, are diligently following standardized recipes, and if their food costs are stable or fluctuating. If you see more than one brand of mustard, mayonnaise, or Italian salad dressing on the shelf, it indicates stock is not being rotated so that the oldest is used first; the operation's food costs will probably fluctuate because those ordering are likely buying from different purveyors with different prices; they have no purchase specifications or are not following them; and there will likely be inconsistency in the taste of products using those ingredients.

Control over inventory and storage areas can take place without full- or part-time storeroom personnel. Control is greatly enhanced when inventory is taken on a regular basis and storage areas are kept clean and organized. An operator relying exclusively on what he or she can see with the naked eye, hear with his or her ears, or remember in his or her head to control costs will be far less aware of what is taking place than the operator who supplements this intuitive information with written records. Written records reveal what cannot be seen, heard, or remembered.

Limit access to storage areas to authorized personnel only. Storage areas should be off-limits to certain employee job categories such that their presence in those areas would be questioned. The only employees allowed to remove food from storage areas are the kitchen preparation staff or a member of management. The only personnel allowed in the liquor storeroom would be the bar manager or head bartender. When a dishwasher or waiter is in either of these areas without direct supervision of a member of management, one would immediately question the person's reason for being there.

The best way to increase control is to limit access to restricted locations by locking storage areas. The use of bin cards or requisitions are not practical except for liquor and certain meats and seafood. By being able to detect shortages, even though you cannot determine individual responsibility, you will slow down your losses. Being aware of a problem is the first step in finding a solution. It may take a while, but the person or persons responsible will be discovered through the process of elimination and investigative activity.

Limiting access to only certain employees narrows down the number of individuals who could be the cause of any discrepancies. The following ideas also help:

1. Have all employees enter and depart through one door that is monitored by management.
2. Check all packages and backpacks.

3. Do not leave the back door unlocked. Keep it locked, and when trash is emptied, have a member of management stand next to the door and check the garbage and linen that go out.

4. Keep expensive inventory under lock and key.

Walk-ins should be locked when all preparation has been completed. Items should be given date stamps and rotated to the front whenever fresh inventory arrives. When storing items, you may find keeping items in their original packages provides greater control and counting efficiency. Multiple case purchases of canned goods need only have a weekly supply on the shelves. Floor pallets are better suited than shelves for cases of products.

Recipes are likely to call for case quantities of ingredients, and it is more efficient to remove a single case than try to handle six loose number 10 cans. If your par stock never exceeds two cases, always remove items from their shipping containers before placing them on the shelf. The boxes are breeding and hiding places for roaches and other vermin.

In most restaurants' operations, the storage area cannot be secured and requires management to control inventory on a selective basis. One places the greatest control on items that will result in the greatest loss. Therefore, more control is placed over 10 pounds of steaks or shrimp than 100 pounds of flour. Expensive items like saffron, truffles, caviar, and other items in small containers are usually kept in locked cabinets or cages. Remove items in set lots, (e.g., lots of three, six, nine). Keep perpetual inventory records of expensive items that are likely targets of theft.

The biggest deterrent to theft is letting the word get out to the employees that management is aware something is missing. Also, make it clear that those caught stealing will be prosecuted to the full extent of the law. The more quickly shortages can be detected, the less likely they are to occur. Management is naive to think that employees will inform them of dishonest employees freely. The only time they may is when the dishonesty reflects back upon them personally. They are doing it in either case for *their own* protection, not for the operators' sake.

Don't think it is just the hourly employees and the delivery people who are the perpetrators of all the fraud and dishonesty. The biggest losses probably occur between the sale reps and managers or the employees entrusted to handle cash and pay bills. Kickbacks to managers, which are actually discounts and credits that should be given to the company, are ways that the manager and the purveyor steal from the operator. This is why chain operations have national accounts set up with virtually all suppliers and have very strict guidelines if one of their unit managers wants to purchase from a purveyor not on the approved list.

Offers of tickets to basketball, baseball, and football games, junkets to topless bars, and even dates have been arranged by purveyors for clients. If you are purchasing from these companies because of such considerations, you are compromising your professional credibility.

Don't ever risk compromising your professional integrity that you have worked long and hard to get. That is why many companies do not allow managers or employees to accept gifts or favors from purveyors. We are seeing governmental agencies drafting codes of ethics regulating such activities in political fund-raising and lobbying activities. There will always be someone willing to test you in this regard.

A ccounts Payable Procedures

Once the deliveries have been received, invoices checked for correct pricing extensions, and returns and allowances deducted, the invoices are sent in for payment. Each month, the purveyor will mail a statement of account listing all the invoices and amounts due. One very important rule to remember is, *pay from invoices, not the statement.* The invoices you have in your possession should be current and reflect all returns and allowances. Sometimes it takes weeks for credits issued by your purveyor to show up on statements. One sales representative instructed an operator who was due a credit to go ahead and pay the full amount and a credit memo would be forthcoming. He paid the full amount, including the amount of the credit he was due. Since he was owed money, he had to remember to watch for the forthcoming credit on the next statement to be sure he got it. The more he thought about what he had done, the more determined he was not to let it happen again.

He, in essence, had overpaid his account so the purveyor had his money. It was money he needed more than the purveyor did. He had to keep checking to see if the credit was applied to his account. In addition, he realized that this procedure was a huge inconvenience that was done to accommodate the purveyor's bookkeeping procedures. From that time on, he paid from the signed invoices, less any credits he had coming. He was in control of his invoices and credits. As an owner-operator, it makes your job a lot less stressful when you pay only what you owe.

Another reason to pay from invoices and not statements is the accounting cycle for restaurants and for purveyors are not the same. Purveyors may close their books one week before the last day of the month to get their statements out by the first. Most restaurants, on the other hand, will use the full month for their accounting period. This means that invoices from two different months are shown on a single statement. This makes monthly income statements inaccurate in terms of food cost. If you deal with as few as 15 different purveyors, there could be different statement dates for every one of them. Consider that some operations have twice that number of suppliers they regularly deal with every month. Such variances in billing periods complicates your bill-paying routine. Being able to determine accurate **accounts payable** information would be difficult and time-consuming to assemble.

If you are a multi-unit operation and pay bills from a corporate office, never have the statements mailed to the unit; have the statements mailed to the corporate office. The statements can be compared to the invoices turned in by the units. Remember, since most operators pay from invoices, there have been instances where unit managers have withheld invoices for payment to make their purchases look lower than they actually are to get bonuses or bring their monthly food cost into line.

One absentee restaurant owner who was having problems with cash flow went to his minority partner, who was manager of the restaurant, and told him he needed to bring the food cost in line. The next month he saw a sizable turnaround and thought that they were now on the road to profitability. He liquidated some personal assets to pay the restaurant bills and even changed the menu in an effort to turn business around. The finances reached a point where he had to manage the restaurant himself and when he went through the manager's desk he found statements and invoices totaling more than $25,000 that were never turned in for payment. The same ploy was used by a manager of a very successful restaurant chain. By withholding invoices, his food cost was such that he was paid several thousand dollars in bonuses that he did not earn or deserve. So the moral is, have the statements mailed to the corporate office, not the individual unit.

Set up two checking accounts; one general account into which your sales are deposited and from which you write the checks to pay the bills. The second checking account is for payroll. Special checks are used there also. Transfer funds from the general checking account to the payroll account only as needed to cover checks written.

Many managers of chain operations doing $2 million to $5 million annually will never experience the cash flow pressures that an independent operator deals with every day. That is why bill-paying flexibility is such an important element in selecting purveyors. While it is true that chains experience similar cash flow problems from time to time, the independent operator deals with it every day of the year.

Invoices received at the time of delivery should be filed alphabetically by company. Invoices are collected on a weekly or monthly basis for payment. Prices charged should be checked along with price extensions, especially on handwritten invoices. Stapling the adding machine tape to the bundle of invoices being paid is recommended. This speeds up the check writing step.

Earlier in this chapter I said that the time to catch errors in deliveries and on invoices was at the time of delivery. The truth is that often errors are found long after the driver has left, sometimes even days later. You open a case to find a broken bottle of mayonnaise; a price extension error is discovered when you are getting ready to pay your bills. In both cases, the credits from these errors will lower your outstanding balance. What do you do?

If you write your check for an amount less than what is showing on the statement, the purveyor's accounts receivable clerk will call to ask why you did not pay your account in full. One thing you can do is attach a *request for credit memo* to your check with an explanation of the credit taken. It is recommended that you order checks that have a space on them for you to list the invoice dates, numbers, and amounts right on the check (see Figure 8–6). The check is your proof of payment, and the check lists the specific invoices you paid and the amount of each.

You can expect a call from one of your purveyors telling you that its record keeping does not show payment of an invoice from six months ago. Since you pay from invoices, the only way you would not have paid it would be because you misfiled or lost the invoice. Given the invoice number and month in which it was delivered, you go back to your paid invoice file for that particular company. You find the invoices for each week stapled together with the adding machine tape. On each bundle of paid invoices you have listed the number of the check used to pay those invoices. You retrieve your canceled check to verify that it cleared. If the number of the missing invoice is on the check, you have proof that it has been paid and the error is likely due to a posting error of the purveyor.

The canceled check is proof of payment and this system, which is simple and inexpensive to install, will be used many times to verify payment of invoices and taxes. On another occasion, I was unable to locate the invoice the purveyor said remained outstanding so I asked the company to mail me a copy. When it arrived I noted that the signature on the invoice was not one of

Date	Invoice	Amount
Total		

Angelo's Restaurants, Inc.
6233 S. Orange Blossom Tr.
Orlando, FL   32810
Tele: 912-555-6223

Check 100

_____ 19 ____

Pay to the order of _____

_____ Dollars

Memo _____

⑈000019⑈ ⑆001113326⑆⑈ 1336⑈00132⑈ 9⑈

FIGURE 8–6
Check design for bill paying

my employees. The invoice was for a dock pickup, not a unit delivery. Since we had not had any previous billing problems with this purveyor, the supplier removed the invoice from our account when it was realized that either some unauthorized person used our name to get a dock pickup or the person writing the invoice put down the wrong account name.

Another time this system was used to prove that an invoice had been paid was when a notice of delinquent beverage license fees was received from the Bureau of Alcohol and Firearms. This was far more important than missing an invoice to a purveyor. Knowing that the license fee had been paid four months before it was actually due, the canceled check was located and a photocopy mailed to the bureau and they corrected their records.

If all your bills are paid by check, your ledger and journal records can all be done with a computer software program. All you have to do is provide your accountant with your check register, list of deposits, payroll records, and invoices for the month. Inventory figures and pay-outs complete the accounting information needed to completely prepare your monthly income statement, balance sheet, as well as your sales tax, payroll tax, and income tax withholding.

Records management is an extremely important aspect of running a restaurant. If you are not organized, mistakes go undetected and you can be taken advantage of by customers, employees, and purveyors. While many of the errors are unintentional, if undetected, they can cost you hard earned dollars that should be going into your bank account and not out the front or back door. This is not a difficult process to organize. You can start by purchasing one of those accordion files from any office supply store. Sort your invoices alphabetically and summarize them each week and group them into monthly periods. If a question arises about a missing invoice or payment, you can quickly go to your files and find it.

ey Concepts

- You cannot carry out effective ordering unless you count and control your inventory.
- You must take an inventory at least monthly for accounting purposes to accurately calculate your cost of food consumed and sold.
- Organize you inventory book into food categories and storage location.
- Order levels are affected by frequency of delivery, perishability of the product, and use levels between deliveries.
- An invoice is not an accurate record of what was ordered.
- Pay by invoice totals, not statement totals.

- Deduct credits owed from your payments and enclose a Request for Credit Memo.
- Pay by check and write the number of the check on your invoice. Write the invoice number being paid on your check.

Key Terms

Fiscal inventory	Accounts payable
Inventory book	Order quantities

Discussion Questions

1. Discuss how often inventory is actually taken. A physical/fiscal inventory must be taken once a month for accounting purposes, but how often is it taken during the month?
2. Why must you take a month end physical/fiscal inventory and not use "food purchases" as your cost of food consumed?
3. What are the benefits to you as a manager of having an inventory book or record?
4. Why is it recommended that you pay from invoices, not statements?

Problem: 1 Determining Order Quantities

Assume that you get once a week deliveries from your grocery supplier. The following data is taken from your inventory book. The use level between deliveries is determined by adding the amount on hand to the amount ordered for the previous week and then subtracting the amount on hand for the current week. For example, with tomato sauce, the amount on hand on 2-16 was 3 cases. Six cases were ordered. That means a total of 9 cases were available and with two cases in inventory on 2-23, it tells us that seven cases were used. That would mean that we would need to order a minimum of 5 cases to get us to the next delivery. However, this would not leave any back up should we use more than seven cases. Therefore, we need to add a sixth case as a safety factor.

With this in mind, using the Excel template on your diskette, complete the inventory spreadsheet by filling in the order quantities for selecting items on 3-1 and compute the price extensions for the amounts on hand on 3-8.

Description	Pack/Count	Price	Date 2-16 On Hand	Date 2-16 Ordered	Date 2-23 On Hand	Date 2-23 Ordered	Date 3-1 On Hand	Date 3-1 Ordered	Date 3-8 On Hand	Price Extension
Tomato Sauce	6-No. 10 cans	$ 16.95	3 cs	6 cs	2 cs	6 cs	1 1/3 cs		1 1/2 cs	
Tomato Puree	6-No. 10 cans	$ 17.15	2 cs	2 cs	1 cs	2 cs	1 cs	1 cs	4 cans	
Crushed Tomatoes	6-No. 10 cans	$ 23.65	2 cs	2 cs	1 cs	2 cs	1 cs	1 cs	4 cans	
Mayonnaise, Whole Egg	30# pail	$ 30.80	15#	30#	15#	1 pail	15#		12#	
Olive Oil, Extra Virgin	3-1 gal	$ 59.50	1 gal	3-1 gal	2 gal	3 gal	2 gal		1 1/2 gal	
Chopped Clams	12/51 oz cans	$ 93.75	8 cans	0	6	0	4 cans	0	2 cans	
Kidney Beans	6-No. 10 cans	$ 17.30	3 cans	1 cs	4 cans	1 cs	5 cans		5 cans	
Garbonza Beans	6-No. 10 cans	$ 17.60	3 cans	1 cs	4 cans	1 cs	5 cans		5 cans	
Green Beans	6-No. 10 cans	$ 22.90	3 cans	1 cs	4 cans	1 cs	5 cans		5 cans	
Wax Beans	6-No. 10 cans	$ 17.60	3 cans	1 cs	4 cans	1 cs	5 cans		5 cans	
Brown Sugar	24-1#	$ 15.50	12#	0	8#	0	3#		5 cans	
Corn Starch	24-1#	$ 17.05	22	0	21	0	20	0	19	
Dry Oregano	5 oz	$ 7.72	15 oz	0	10 oz	0	5 oz	2	7 oz	
Dry Basil	22 oz	$ 24.77	44 oz	0	11 oz	1	11 oz	1	16 oz	
Garlic Powder	19 oz	$ 7.03	29 oz	0	10 oz	1	16 oz	0	5 oz	

Item	Pack	Price							
Pepper, Black, Table Grind	1#	$ 11.15	6#	1	2#	4	3#	1	1#
Clam Base	6-1#/cs	$ 46.05	4#	0	2#	1 cs	6#	0	4#
Lobster Base	6-1#/cs	$ 78.23	5#	0	4#	0	3#	0	2#
Chicken Base	3-4# tubs/cs	$ 88.65	10#	0	5#	1 cs	16#	0	8#
Beef Base	4-5# tubs/cs	$ 145.70	15#	0	10#	0	5#	1 cs	19#
All Purpose Flour	50#	$ 11.20	45#	0	20#	50#	35#	50#	45#
Bread Crumbs, Plain	12-24 oz/cs	$ 34.75	11	0	2	1 cs	11 pkgs	0	10 pkgs
Japanese Bread-crumbs (Panko)	25#	$ 30.70	12#	0	4#	25#	21#	0	19#
Oreo Cookie Crumbs	25#	$ 79.65	18#	0	15#	0	12#	0	10#
Polenta, Stone Ground	25#	$ 14.55	20#	0	17#	0	15#	0	12#
Aborio Rice, Imported	10 #	$ 38.10	9#	0	6#	0	3#	10#	9#
Basmati Rice	10 #	$ 29.65	2#	10#	6#	10#	12#	0	8#
Linguini	20#	$ 19.00	5#	40#	10#	40#	15#		10#
Penne Rigati	20#	$ 21.60	7#	20#	6#	20#	4#		8#
Ziti	20#	$ 18.40	4#	20#	12#	20#	25#		12#
Spaghettini	20 #	$ 19.00	40#	80#	20#	100#	45#		25#
Total									

Description	Pack/Count	Price	Date 2-16 On Hand	Date 2-16 Ordered	Date 2-23 On Hand	Date 2-23 Ordered	Date 3-1 On Hand	Date 3-1 Ordered	Date 3-8 On Hand	Price Extension
Butter, Unsalted	30 lbs/cs	$ 72.60	15#	60#	25#	2 cs	1 1/2 cs		20#	
Fry Max Liquid Shortening	35# jugs	$ 41.80	2 jugs	5 jugs	3	2 jugs	1 jug		2 jugs	
Blue Cheese Crumbles	4–5# bags/cs	$ 73.55	10#	0	5#	1 cs	15#	0	0	
Whole Eggs, large	15 doz/cs	$ 20.45	6 doz	2 cs	12 dz	2 cs	1 1/2 cs		1 cs	
Mozzarella Cheese, Part Skim	5# blocks	$ 8.25	35#	20#	15#	45#	35#	0	5#	
Lettuce, Iceberg	24 heads/cs	$ 20.35	2 cs	6 cs	2 cs	5 cs	2 cs	6 cs	1 cs	
Romaine	24 heads/cs	$ 16.60	1/2 cs	1 cs	1/2 cs	1 cs	0		1/2 cs	
Endive	24 heads/cs	$ 15.80	1/2 cs	1 cs	1/2 cs	1 cs	0		1/2 cs	
Portabello Mushrooms	5# box	$ 20.45	3 boxes	0	1 box	2 boxes	2.5#	3 boxes	5#	
Spanish Onions	50 #	$ 9.60	60#	2 bags	40#	3 bags	1 bag	3 bags	75#	
Red Bell Peppers	5# bag	$ 10.85	4 bags	4 bags	2 bags	5 bags	3 bags	2 bags	1 bag	
Russet Bakers 50# 100 count	50 lbs/cs	$ 12.50	2 cs	2 cs	25#	4 cs	100#	3 cs	1 cs	
Tomatoes, Roma	25# flat	$ 25.10	2 flats	2 flats	12.5#	4 flats	1 flat		3/4 flat	
Tomatoes 5×6 60 count	20 lb lugs	$ 25.70	2 lugs	3 lugs	15#	3 lugs	1 lug	2 lugs	1 1/2 lugs	
Lemons, 115 count	box 40#	$ 23.15	1/2 box	1 box	1/2 box	1 box	1/2 box	1 box	1/4 box	
Limes 200 count	box 40#	$ 19.25	3/4 box	0	1/4 box	1 box	3/4 box	1 box	3/4 box	

Item	Pack	Price							
Ground Beef, 80–20	4–5# bags/cs	$ 32.15	40#	40#	30#	1 cs	20#	1 cs	10#
Striploin Choice 180A 13 lb average	pound	$ 63.83	4 each	4 each	3 each	3 each	2 each	1 cs	1 each
Prime Rib 109 23# average Choice	pound	$ 5.51	6 each	12 each	4 each	7 each	4 each	4 each	3 each
Sirloin Butt #184 Choice	3 ea / 13# ea	$ 122.46	6 each	2 each	1 each	7 each	4 each	4 each	2 each
Baby Back Ribs (NAM) 422	50# case	$ 154.50	2 cs	2 cs	1 cs	3 cs	1/2 cs	4 cs	2 cs
Chicken Breast Boneless/Skinless 5 oz	24/case	$ 23.15	36 ea	2 cases	1 case	3 cs	1 cs	3 cs	2 cs
Whole Broiler-Fryers 2.75 # WOG	38.5#/14 ea	$ 40.42	3 cs	1 cs	1 case	3 cs	1 cs	3 cs	1 1/2 cs
Shrimp, Tiger 16/20 raw	6–4# boxes/cs	$ 281.95	3 boxes	6 boxes	3 boxes	1 cs	4 boxes		5 boxes
Salmon Fillets, Coho, IQF 8 oz	10 lbs/cs	$ 72.65	8 lbs	0	5 lbs	0	2 lbs	1 cs	9#
Trout, Boned, 8 oz	6–5# boxes/cs	$ 132.30	4 boxes	0	2 boxes	1 cs	5 boxes	0	3 boxes
Crabmeant, Snowcrab	6–5# boxes	$ 498.35	5 boxes	0	4.5 boxes	0	4 boxes	0	3.5 boxes
Bay Scallops, 80–120 count	2–5# boxes/cs	$ 68.75	15#	0	5 lbs	10#	8#	0	6#
Total									

Problem 2

Transcribe the following invoices from The Seafood Shanty restaurant to the Weekly Invoice Summary Report shown below in their proper category. An Excel template has been provided for your use.

Date	Vendor	Invoice No.	Amount	Description
2-16	Bari Imports	12356	$356	Groceries
2-16	Lady Baltimore	2367	$256	Groceries
2-16	Eli Witt	2232	$145	Cigars & Mints
2-16	Atlanta Fixture	2345	$235	Kitchen Supplies
2-16	Red's Market	45789	$457	Produce
2-16	SYSCO	34567	$895	Beef and Poultry
2-17	Lombardi Fish	567890	$765	Seafood
2-17	TG Lee Dairy	2345	$79	Milk and Cream
2-17	Faultless Linen	11134	$259	Napkins and Tablecloths
2-18	Coca Cola	98765	$125	Fountain Syrup
2-19	B & B Bakery	501	$135	Bread and Rolls
2-19	A & A Printers	2209	$1,500	New Menus
2-20	Manco Foods	6665	$350	Olives and Cheese
2-20	St. John Paper	4445	$345	Carry-out Containers
2-21	Stella Doro	8885	$45	Breadsticks

In addition to the above invoices, the following transactions took place and need to be included on the Weekly Invoice Summary.

- Cool Ray Heating and Air was called to repair a broken thermostat on 2-18. The repair bill was for $245, invoice number 543.
- Roto-Rooter was called on 2-20 to unclog a floor drain. The invoice left was for $75, number 2334
- Band aids were purchased with petty cash on 2-17 for $7.50.
- The chef sent a busser to the local grocery store for more arugula on 2-20. Petty cash was used in the amount of $4.50.
- The weekly window washing service was paid out of the register on 2-21 in the amount of $20.
- The squid delivered by Lombardi Fish was returned with the driver and a credit memo was requested for the amount of $45 (which will be deducted from invoice number 567890 when paid). This was recorded on 2-17.

Sales for the week were $15,360. Total the amounts for Food, Linen, Supplies, Repairs & Maintenance and Miscellaneous and compute their respective percent of weekly sales.

Weekly Invoice Summary Report   The Seafood Shanty

Problem 2
Week of: 2-16

| | | FOOD PURVEYORS | | | | SUPPLIES/NON-FOOD | | | | | |
Date	Invoice No.	Vendor	Amount	Date	Invoice	Vendor	Linen	Repairs	Supplies
Totals									

PAID-OUTS

Date	Description	Amount
Total		

MISCELLANEOUS

Date	Description	Vendor	Invoice	Amount
Total				

Returns and Credits

Date	Invoice	Vendor	Item	Amount

SUMMARY

	Sales	Cost	Percent
Food	$ 15,360.00		
Linen			
Supplies			
Repairs & Main.			
Miscellaneous			

Problem 3-Analysis of Inventory

This simple, but relevant exercise is a valuable tool to owners and managers to help where the majority of their food inventory dollars are being spent. Below are the totals for the end of the month for the Cattleman's Steak House in Houston, TX. Find the percentage that each food category is to the total inventory. Review the figures and tell how you would use this information to improve your cost control procedures. What areas do you think you need to pay the closest attention to? Use the Excel template provided on your diskette.

Analysis of Inventory

Category	$	% of Composition
Meat	$2,568.00	
Seafood	$1,468.00	
Dairy	$ 425.00	
Produce	$ 620.00	
Bakery	$ 190.00	
Grocery	$1,255.00	
Total	$6,526.00	

9

Beverage Cost Controls

FUNDAMENTAL PRINCIPLES OF BEVERAGE COST CONTROL

1. Many of the principles of food cost control apply to beverage cost control.

2. Beverage cost percentage will always be higher in a restaurant than a lounge or night club.

3. Wine and beer have higher beverage cost (lower mark-up) than mixed drinks.

4. The sale of beer, wine, and spirits need to be rung up on separate keys.

5. You do not necessarily need an expensive liquor dispensing system to control liquor costs.

6. There is no need to "shop around" for the best deals when purchasing branded alcoholic beverages.

7. Establish a par stock level for all bottles kept behind the bar.

8. Standardize glassware for all drinks.

9. Record all beverage transactions like you do food orders.

10. Price and markup is not based solely on beverage cost.

Factors Impacting Beverage Cost

If you were asked what is an average bar cost or liquor cost percentage, how would you respond? We should first remember that in the foodservice industry we classify all alcoholic beverages as a **beverage** sale". This does not include coffee, tea, soda, or orange juice at breakfast. The reasons for this are varied. They include compliance with many local, state or federal laws on the recording of these sales for sales tax valuation to Generally Accepted Accounting Practices **(GAAP)** and the *Uniform System of Accounts for Restaurants* **(USAR)**. The GAAP rules are a set of standards that are used to insure conformity in the way we all keep our records and the USAR has become the common accounting language for the industry.

Why is the beverage cost percentage more likely to be higher in a restaurant than in a lounge with live entertainment not serving food? Or, why the difference between a family style restaurant, fine dining, or a sports bar? How does the sales mix of beer, wine, and spirits affect the overall beverage cost percentage?

The answer to the first question is that there is not a straightforward direct answer. The response would have to be, "It all depends." First determine what type of operation the questioner has in mind. A lounge with live entertainment will have a higher drink price structure because it will sell more mixed drinks than beer and wine. The fine dining operation will sell more high-end spirits, cordials, wine, and less beer. The sports bar will most likely sell more beer and wine to their clientele. These conditions will result in different costs of beverages sold depending on the demand of the customers who patronize the establishments.

Markup of Alcoholic Beverages

Beer and wine, the beverages commonly consumed with food, have a lower **markup** than mixed drinks. Beer and wine are typically marked up two or three times their cost, resulting in 33 to 50 percent cost to price. Think about it; if domestic beer costs $14.50 for a case of twenty-four 12-ounce bottles, the cost per bottle is $.60. To return a 33 percent cost, it would be priced at $1.82. Knowing this, what is the customers' perceived price-value when it is priced at $2.50 or $2.95? That is a 20–24 percent cost to price.

Case Price	Portion Cost (bottle)	Desired Cost %	Suggested Selling Price
$14.50	*$14.50/24 count = .60*	*33%*	*$.60/.33 = $1.82*

Now that you have the suggested price you can test the results of additional price points on your cost.

$$\$.60/\$2.50 = 24\% \text{ Beverage Cost}$$

$$\$.60/\$2.95 = 20\% \text{ Beverage Cost}$$

This is another example that demonstrates that pricing decisions on food or beverage are not simply a cost markup exercise. The subjective (your immediate micro-market) and indirect cost factors (location, labor, and distribution) that must be taken into account will sometimes allow an operator to charge far more (or less) than originally considered. A bottle of Corona beer or a Margarita sold at a restaurant on the water in Key West Florida will be priced much higher than if they were being sold in a neighborhood Mexican restaurant in the suburbs of Tampa. The pricing decision must take regional demand for particular brands of beer and spirits into account. If customers request specific brands of beer or spirits, higher prices can be charged because of the demand. In fact, all of the indirect cost factors previously mentioned in the chapter on pricing food items apply to pricing of alcoholic beverages. Today we see a resurgence in the promotion of specialty martinis made with premium vodkas and infused with flavors like cranberry, orange, and citron. Demand driven pricing is more toward the high end of the pricing continuum. Even some beers can be priced this way. However, most restaurants with bars will have what we call "house" brands of spirits and beers that are priced at the low end of the pricing continuum to appeal to the price-conscious customer.

The markup on liquor, beer, and wine in restaurants is still lower than the markup in operations where liquor makes up the majority of sales such as entertainment night clubs where live entertainment and/or state-of-the-art sound systems play recorded music. The prices reflect the uniqueness of the operation and the overhead costs of equipment, entertainers, and liability insurance. If the restaurant or lounge becomes a leader in the market, more aggressive pricing strategies can be used. This creates a situation where you will choose a pricing strategy where you will either charge the highest price the customer is willing to pay or the lowest price at which you can make your profit.

A bottle of domestic white wine that costs $6 a bottle would have to be priced at $24 to return a 25 percent beverage cost and may not sell because of the price. If it is a popular wine sold in grocery or liquor stores, the customers will know the retail price and refuse to pay more than $4 to $5 more than retail. The public will generally pay more to be served but not an extravagant amount. Remember that the general public is much more informed about the wine selections being offered. Many wine distributors will have several labels that are not sold through normal retail outlets. Restaurants will want to have several of these labels on their wine list.

Both grocery retail chains as well as the commercial distributors of wine are looking for new ways to sell more products to the public. Even the producers of wine have found ways to sell more by increasing the advertising on several media outlets like radio, television, and print. By doing this the producers create the "pull-through" demand for the product whether it is the grocery store market or the foodservice industry. Restaurant operators should be mindful that there is virtually no labor involved in selling wine to your dining room customers. Therefore, it can be marked up only 50 percent. A $6 cost would mean an $11.95 price. This produces a gross profit of $5.95 for just uncorking the wine and pouring it. The lower price stimulates sales and increases the number of bottles sold, therefore increasing profits on an item that has almost no labor. It really is like finding new incremental profits at very little cost to the operation. Another thing to keep in mind when pricing bottle wine is your average entree price. You need to have several bottles of wine priced between 1 ½ and 2 times your average entree price for price-conscious customers.

Example

Cost	Price	Cost % (Cost/Price)	Gross Profit (Price-Cost)
$6.00	$24.00	25%	$18.00

This is often more than the customer is willing to pay, they feel taken advantage of and your wine stays on your storage shelf.

Cost	Price	Cost %	Gross Profit
$6.00	$11.95	50%	$ 5.95

This is more realistic for the customer; they feel they received value for the money spent.

Average Entree Price	Lower Price Range of Bottle Wines
$12.95	$19.25–$24.95

Contrast this to the prices of mixed drinks with a portion of 1.5 ounces. A quart of premium vodka, with a cost to the operation of $17.50, should yield twenty-one 1.5-ounce shots. This is the **bottle portion yield**. That leaves a slight allowance of 1/3 ounce for spillage and over-pouring. That makes the cost approximately $.84 each. If we poured 1-3/4 ounce we would get a yield of approximately 18 drinks at $.97. A martini using the particular brand of vodka, depending on the type of operation and its location, could be priced anywhere from $1.95 up. If a 1.5-ounce shot is used and priced at $2.95, the beverage cost percentage would be just over 28 percent. At $4.95 for a 1.75-ounce pour, the cost is just over 19.5 percent. What, then is the proper price to charge? From the customer' perspective, it is the price they are willing to pay. From the restaurant's perspective, it is the price that moves the product and produces a profit. It is not just the cost of the ingredients that drives the price, it is also the ambiance, location, product presentation, and service that are reflected in your price.

Example

Bottle Cost	Portions Yield	Portion Cost	Price	Cost%
$17.50	1.5 oz 21	$.84	$2.95	28%

This strategy focuses on the beverage cost %.

Bottle Cost	Portions Yield	Portion Cost	Price	Cost%
$17.50	1.75 oz 18	$.97	$4.95	19.5%

This strategy focuses on the portion size and cost %.

Typically, **mixed drinks** produce beverage cost percentages in the low to high teens. The double and triple liquor drinks are in the low to mid twenties. Most patrons of all ages are curbing the quantity of what they drink when they go out. When people order a drink, they are more likely to request a premium brand and have only one or two drinks. The market demand is one of quality and variety to replace the previous levels of higher consumption. We are seeing an emergence of wine and beer bars that carry hundreds of varieties. The premium vodkas and tequilas have replaced the single malt scotches and premium bourbons as the most demanded spirits today. You can see that the ratio of beer, wine, and liquor sold can impact the overall liquor cost when you examine the beverage sales mix analysis.

Monitoring Beverage Cost

In order to monitor your liquor costs accurately, you need to separately record the sales of each type of alcoholic beverage within the liquor, beer or wine category. A single "beverage" key on the cash register is not sufficient. To report "total" beverage sales is not enough for proper analysis. Separate keys for liquor, beer, and wine should be used. Obtaining a representative sales mix of liquor sold has traditionally been much more difficult to accomplish than it has with food sold.

When the back bar inventory of bourbon, scotch, rum, gin, vodka, tequila, beer, and wine contains dozens of brands of each type, the pricing structure recognizes only **"selling tiers"** of drinks and not specific brands. For example, the price structure at a typical bar or restaurant lounge would show three pricing tiers (levels) for mixed drinks: well brands, call brands, and premium brands. A house brand of vodka might be Popov (the least expensive); a **call brand** Smirnoff 80 proof (slightly more expensive and better quality); and a **premium call brand** Stolichnaya (even more expensive and of the highest quality).

Example

Spirit Type	Well Brand	Call Brand	Premium Brand
Scotch	Inverhouse	Dewars, Chivas Regal	Johnny Walker Black
Bourbon	Mattingley & Moore	Jim Beam	Jack Daniels
Whiskey (Rye)	Haller's	Seagram's 7	Crown Royal
Rum	Castillo	Bacardi Silver	Bacardi 151
Gin	Bowman's	Beefeater	Tanqueray
Vodka	Popov	Smirnoff 80	Stolichnaya
Price	$3.25	$4.50	$5.75

Further, mixed drinks like Long Island Iced Tea, and Margaritas that already have multiple liquors in the recipe, may be upgraded by brand name addition such as Grand Marnier instead of house triple sec and with premium tequila like Jose Cuervo Gold. This will complicate your ability to get a true sales mix with manually written bar checks that typically do not fully describe the drink that was served. Usually, the order is verbally called in to the bartender by the customer and the price charged is the only indication of the "type of spirit" as shown in the example. Whether it was vodka, gin, or bourbon is sometimes difficult to tell from price. It should be noted that this is changing with the improvements in point-of-sale (POS) technology. The current systems in the market are capable of tracking exact recipes sold by almost any time period or individual server/bartender.

The same trade-off of pricing for specific brand identification may occur with beer and wine. When restaurants or bars inventory 40 or 50 different brands of bottled beer, they also may compromise with three pricing structures for domestic, imported, and microbrews/draught. Microbrewed beers are enjoying a demand-driven pricing period, as they are the trendy new choice of customers today.

Unless an electronic point-of-sale system is used, a detailed beverage sales mix (i.e., brands and type of drink) is extremely difficult and time-consuming to obtain. Several "touch screen" systems allow the server to quickly and completely identify the drink, brand, and even special preparation variances of the mixes and presentation.

iquor, Beer and Wine Ordering

The function of the purchasing agent or buyer of alcoholic beverages is simply to insure that an adequate supply of the required wines, beers, and spirits is available. There is no need to "shop around" for the best deal as is done when purchasing food and supplies because:

1. Specific brands are sold by specific dealers only; they each have an exclusive right to distribute all of the brands that they carry.
2. Wholesaling of alcoholic beverages is state regulated and controlled.
3. Retail Prices are published in monthly journals and there is little change from month to month.
4. Only quantity discounts are available.
5. Purchase is done by brand name.

Factors that determine the number of brands to be stocked are:

1. Customer preferences in the area of the country.
2. Class of clientele and operation; that is, country clubs will carry more brands than a chain restaurant.

3. What is used as the **"well brand"** or "house brands." Well and house brands are poured when a customer requests a drink like gin and tonic or bourbon and seven and does not specify a particular "call" brand. For example: well bourbon—Cabin Stills; call bourbon—Jim Beam; premium call bourbon—Jack Daniels Black.

4. Drink price structure: cheaper prices, fewer brands. This strategy is not used in hotels and restaurants.

5. Volume of the operation: the greater the volume, the greater variety that can be stocked. Convention hotels like the Hyatt Regency in Chicago carry over 1,100 different bottles of spirits and wines.

Purchasing

We should note that different states have laws that regulate who are authorized to wholesale to foodservice operations and who can sell alcoholic beverages to the public. The license state is one who allows independent liquor, beer, and wine distributors to wholesale the brands that they are authorized to sell to foodservice operators as well as liquor and convenience stores. A state controlled system is one that the state is the wholesaler and liquor store for liquor, beer, and wine. While this may vary by state, in other words a control state may allow convenience stores to sell beer and wine as well as a grocery store they cannot sell liquor.

In a state controlled system the liquor prices are set and there are virtually no discounting or allowances associated with volume discounts. Furthermore operators are prohibited from purchasing these items from out of state. What can be an important cost implication aside from the steadfast pricing is that if you need to have the items delivered you may hire a bonded delivery service to pick up the inventory you purchase and deliver it to your location as your temporary legal agent. There is usually a fee associated with this service.

Accounting principles state that these fees must be added to our cost of goods sold on the income statement. This is a cost that should be forecasted during the budget time and will most likely have an impact on a manager's purchasing decisions. An example of how this may effect an operation is in the beverage inventory turnover calculation. If you wish to save money on the delivery service you will have to weigh this cost against the increased inventory par levels you will need to carry. This means that if your beverage inventory ratio decreases you have more money tied up in inventory on the shelf instead of in your bank account where it could be earning interest for you.

COST OF BEVERAGES SOLD CALCULATIONS

We follow the identical format shown for calculating the cost of food sold for determining the cost of beverage sold that will be shown on the monthly income statement.

- $+$ Beginning Inventory
- $+$ Purchases
- $-$ Bar to Food Transfers
- $+$ Food to Bar Transfers
- $-$ Beverages (alcoholic) ordered by management for consumption or guest relations
- $-$ Promotions/Coupons for free or reduced drinks
- $-$ Ending Inventory
- $=$ Cost of Beverages in Dollars ($)

Example

1.	Beginning Inventory	$+$ $ 8,500
2.	Purchases this month	$+$ $15,350
3.	Bar to Food Transfers	$-$ $ 670
4.	Food to Bar Transfers	$+$ $ 3,200
5.	Management Signing	$-$ $ 1,300
6.	Promotions	$-$ $ 710
7.	Ending Inventory	$-$ $ 7,985
8.	Cost of Beverages Consumed	$=$ $16,385

Note that without the tracking and adjustments of numbers 3, 4, 5, and 6 you would have the cost of beverage sold of $15,865. This would understate your beverage cost and make your cost ratio's look worse than they should.

Beginning Inventory is the amount of product you began the accounting period with. We usually evaluate this on a monthly basis. You count your inventory and complete the extensions of the cost and count to arrive at a dollar value at the end of the month, usually the last day, by midnight or close of business. By the virtue of your efforts you now can use this number twice! It also becomes the value of the inventory you begin the next month with, hence your beginning inventory for the upcoming month, which began just after midnight or at the end of business on the last day.

Purchases for the month are the total of all invoices and receipts during the month for liquor, beer, and wine that you purchased. You can separate these by category or put them all into one, it depends on the level of analysis you want to perform each month. We recommend separating out the three so as to also be able to use this information for further profitability analysis later.

Bar to Food Transfers are items that originally were purchased for the bar and the invoice total was added to the monthly purchases. From time to time the chef will require liquor, beer, or wine for one or more of the recipes. This may include Marsala wine for a sauce, or Grand Marnier for marinating fruit on a dessert menu or a favorite beer for making a nice beer batter for a fish fry. All of these items were taken from the bar and used in a recipe to make a food item, which was sold to the customers and rung up by the service staff as a food sale. Therefore, the food department (in accounting terms) should pay for the ingredient (liquor, beer, wine). This is accomplished by recording the entire product that is taken to the kitchen for preparation and sale.

Food to Bar Transfers includes items that are ordered and paid for by the food department and then taken to the bar for use in serving beverages. Items that are included in this category are: fruit for garnishing drinks, juices for mixing, kosher salt or sugar for the preparation of drink rims for margarita's or a cosmopolitan. Just as in the case of the chef obtaining wine or liquor, the ingredients taken from the chef's cooler and storeroom are used to sell drinks where the money from the sale is credited entirely to the beverage department. Therefore, they should pay for all of the ingredients that they use to make the sale. This includes all free food served during happy hours.

Management Signing is a privilege given to many managers. Whether they are to consume the drink themselves while off duty or are purchasing it for some guest relation's reason it is made and served without collecting any payment. Keep in mind, ingredients left your inventory and no money came in. That will cause the cost to increase. The accurate place for these expenses is in the advertising and promotion (A & P) or the administrative and general (A & G) expense accounts. *It should be noted that giving away free drinks, a common practice in restaurants, is technically against the law. As it was explained by an alcohol agent, "Since our agency collects taxes on each alcoholic beverage sold, when drinks are given away, no tax is collected, and this is a violation."*

Promotions include any couponing or complimentary drinks to guests. This may be in the form of a two-for-one special, free glass of wine with dinner, or drink coupons used in the lodging industry. Here, the same situation applies as in management signing privileges. Inventory left the bar without any money changing hands. This is charged off to the advertising and promotion (A & P) account.

Ending Inventory is the final count as mentioned in the beginning inventory explanation provided earlier.

Cost of Beverages Consumed is the dollar amount of all inventories that was used during the month, including items in the food department and marketing department. This number is reflected on the income statement under cost of goods sold and is one of the three prime cost areas that must be monitored by operators in order to be profitable.

Cost/Margin Sales Mix Analysis

The same sales mix analysis that is used to determine the impact each food item has on resulting sales, costs, and profits, can be applied to your beverage sales mix. The gross profit on each dollar sale of alcoholic beverages is about 30–40 percent higher than food. The bar is also were many dollars of profit are lost due to fraud and poor controls. How do you know if your monthly liquor cost is good or bad? In order to answer that question you need to know what your potential liquor cost should be given your sales mix, your drink sizes, and your actual liquor costs.

In this chapter, you will see that we have simply adapted the **Cost/Margin Analysis program** to accommodate alcoholic beverages. You need the same basic data to do you beverage sales analysis; drink name, selling price, number sold, and drink cost. The key to consistency is accurate pouring and recording of every drink prepared into your POS system.

Beverage sales are categorized as Spirits, Beer, Glass Wine, Liqueurs, and Bottle Wine. *We have put "glass wines" under the tab designated as "wine" and the "bottled wine" in the tab designated as "miscellaneous" in the software program.*

Tables 9.1 to 9.5 show the breakdown of sales, costs, and profits for all five beverage categories. This analysis tracked 150 different alcoholic beverages. The total beverage sales was $21,431 and the total beverage cost was $6,180. This produces a weighted overall beverage cost of 28.84 percent. This is the percentage that is compared to your *Actual Beverage Cost Percentage* shown on your monthly income statement. *(Refer to the Summary Spreadsheet in the software program for these figures).*

Note the different cut-off points for number sold, item contribution margin, weighted contribution margin, and beverage cost. These cut-off points are summarized in Table 9.6. You can see in the **%** *of Items Sold* column the differences in numbers sold of each category of alcoholic beverages. Immediately, one notices that Bottled Wine accounts for just under 3% of the beverages sold. This coupled with the wide range of potential beverage costs,

Table 9.1   Spirits Cost/Margin Spreadsheet

Item No.	Item Name	No. Sold	Menu Price	Item Bev Cost	Supp. Cost	Total Cost	Item Cont Margin	Wgtd Bev Cost	Wgtd Cont Margin	Wgtd Sales	Item Bev Cost %
0	Midpoint	52.88					$2.58		$193.45		26.21%
1	Crystal Pal Vodka	333	$2.17	$0.30		$0.30	$1.87	$99.90	$622.71	$722.61	13.82%
2	Absolut	94	$4.25	$1.20		$1.20	$3.05	$112.80	$286.70	$399.50	28.24%
3	Smirnoff	10	$3.75	$1.20		$1.20	$2.55	$12.00	$25.50	$37.50	32.00%
4	Stoli	60	$4.75	$1.20		$1.20	$3.55	$72.00	$213.00	$285.00	25.26%
5	Ketel One	42	$5.25	$1.53		$1.53	$3.72	$64.26	$156.24	$220.50	29.14%
6	Skyy	14	$4.75	$0.90		$0.90	$3.85	$12.60	$53.90	$66.50	18.95%
7	Ron Liave Rum	118	$2.58	$0.60		$0.60	$1.98	$70.80	$233.64	$304.44	23.26%
8	Bacardi light	49	$4.25	$0.75		$0.75	$3.50	$36.75	$171.50	$208.25	17.65%
9	Capt. Morgan	55	$3.75	$0.75		$0.75	$3.00	$41.25	$165.00	$206.25	20.00%
10	Meyers	23	$4.25	$1.20		$1.20	$3.05	$27.60	$70.15	$97.75	28.24%
11	Crystal Pal Gin	138	$2.58	$0.54		$0.54	$2.04	$74.52	$281.52	$356.04	20.93%
12	Beefeaters	44	$4.25	$1.03		$1.03	$3.22	$45.32	$141.68	$187.00	24.24%
13	Bombay	42	$4.75	$1.26		$1.26	$3.49	$52.92	$146.58	$199.50	26.53%
14	Tanqueray	29	$4.25	$1.26		$1.26	$2.99	$36.54	$86.71	$123.25	29.65%
15	Canadian Mist	114	$2.58	$1.06		$1.06	$1.52	$120.84	$173.28	$294.12	41.09%
16	Canadian Club	42	$4.75	$1.25		$1.25	$3.50	$52.50	$147.00	$199.50	26.32%
17	Crown Royal	81	$4.75	$1.35		$1.35	$3.40	$109.35	$275.40	$384.75	28.42%
18	Seagrams VO	62	$2.58	$1.06		$1.06	$1.52	$65.72	$94.24	$159.96	41.09%
19	Clan Mac Scotch	124	$4.25	$0.80		$0.80	$3.45	$99.20	$427.80	$527.00	18.82%
20	Chivas	14	$4.25	$1.60		$1.60	$2.65	$22.40	$37.10	$59.50	37.65%
21	Dewars	62	$4.25	$1.25		$1.25	$3.00	$77.50	$186.00	$263.50	29.41%
22	Johnny Walker	29	$4.25	$1.40		$1.40	$2.85	$40.60	$82.65	$123.25	32.94%
23	Early Times	246	$2.92	$0.70		$0.70	$2.22	$172.20	$546.12	$718.32	23.97%
24	Jim Beam	142	$4.25	$1.00		$1.00	$3.25	$142.00	$461.50	$603.50	23.53%
25	Jack Daniel's Green	28	$3.75	$1.23		$1.23	$2.52	$34.44	$70.56	$105.00	32.80%
26	Jack Daniel Blk	12	$4.75	$1.62		$1.62	$3.13	$19.44	$37.56	$57.00	34.11%
27	Wild Turkey	16	$4.75	$1.75		$1.75	$3.00	$28.00	$48.00	$76.00	36.84%
28	Maker's Mark	36	$4.25	$1.62		$1.62	$2.63	$58.32	$94.68	$153.00	38.12%
29	Cuervo Gold	119	$4.75	$1.40		$1.40	$3.35	$166.60	$398.65	$565.25	29.47%
30	Sauza Tree	26	$4.75	$1.75		$1.75	$3.00	$45.50	$78.00	$123.50	36.84%
31	Montezuma	138	$2.17	$0.84		$0.84	$1.33	$115.92	$183.54	$299.46	38.71%
	Total	2,342						$2,130	$5,997	$8,127	

Total Sales %	Total Bev Cost %	Items Sold %	Wgtd Cont Margin %	Popularity	Bev Cost	Indv. Cont Margin	Wgted Cont Margin	Miller Matrix	Cost Margin	Menu Engineering
8.89%	4.69%	14.22%	10.38%	Popular	Low	Low	High	Winner	Prime	Plowhorses
4.92%	5.30%	4.01%	4.78%	Popular	High	High	High	HVHCMARG	Standards	Stars
0.46%	0.56%	0.43%	0.43%	Not Popular	High	Low	Low	Loser	Problems	Dogs
3.51%	3.38%	2.56%	3.55%	Popular	Low	High	High	Winner	Prime	Stars
2.71%	3.02%	1.79%	2.61%	Not Popular	High	High	Low	Loser	Problems	Puzzles
0.82%	0.59%	0.60%	0.90%	Not Popular	Low	High	Low	LVLCMARG	Sleepers	Puzzles
3.75%	3.32%	5.04%	3.90%	Popular	Low	Low	High	Winner	Prime	Plowhorses
2.56%	1.73%	2.09%	2.86%	Not Popular	Low	High	Low	LVLCMARG	Sleepers	Puzzles
2.54%	1.94%	2.35%	2.75%	Popular	Low	High	Low	Winner	Sleepers	Stars
1.20%	1.30%	0.98%	1.17%	Not Popular	High	High	Low	Loser	Problems	Puzzles
4.38%	3.50%	5.89%	4.69%	Popular	Low	Low	High	Winner	Prime	Plowhorses
2.30%	2.13%	1.88%	2.36%	Not Popular	Low	High	Low	LVLCMARG	Sleepers	Puzzles
2.45%	2.48%	1.79%	2.44%	Not Popular	High	High	Low	Loser	Problems	Puzzles
1.52%	1.72%	1.24%	1.45%	Not Popular	High	High	Low	Loser	Problems	Puzzles
3.62%	5.67%	4.87%	2.89%	Popular	High	Low	Low	HVHCMARG	Problems	Plowhorses
2.45%	2.47%	1.79%	2.45%	Not Popular	High	High	Low	Loser	Problems	Puzzles
4.73%	5.13%	3.46%	4.59%	Popular	High	High	High	HVHCMARG	Standards	Stars
1.97%	3.09%	2.65%	1.57%	Popular	High	Low	Low	HVHCMARG	Problems	Plowhorses
6.48%	4.66%	5.29%	7.13%	Popular	Low	High	High	Winner	Prime	Stars
0.73%	1.05%	0.60%	0.62%	Not Popular	High	High	Low	Loser	Problems	Puzzles
3.24%	3.64%	2.65%	3.10%	Popular	High	High	Low	HVHCMARG	Problems	Stars
1.52%	1.91%	1.24%	1.38%	Not Popular	High	High	Low	Loser	Problems	Puzzles
8.84%	8.09%	10.50%	9.11%	Popular	Low	Low	High	Winner	Prime	Plowhorses
7.43%	6.67%	6.06%	7.70%	Popular	Low	High	High	Winner	Prime	Stars
1.29%	1.62%	1.20%	1.18%	Not Popular	High	Low	Low	Loser	Problems	Dogs
0.70%	0.91%	0.51%	0.63%	Not Popular	High	High	Low	Loser	Problems	Puzzles
0.94%	1.31%	0.68%	0.80%	Not Popular	High	High	Low	Loser	Problems	Puzzles
1.88%	2.74%	1.54%	1.58%	Not Popular	High	High	Low	Loser	Problems	Puzzles
6.96%	7.82%	5.08%	6.65%	Popular	High	High	High	HVHCMARG	Standards	Stars
1.52%	2.14%	1.11%	1.30%	Not Popular	High	High	Low	Loser	Problems	Puzzles
3.68%	5.44%	5.89%	3.06%	Popular	High	Low	Low	HVHCMARG	Problems	Plowhorses

Table 9.2 Beers Cost/Margin Spreadsheet

Item No.	Item Name	No. Sold	Menu Price	Item Bev Cost	Supp. Cost	Total Cost	Item Cont Margin	Wgtd Bev Cost	Wgtd Cont Margin	Wgtd Sales	Item Bev Cost %
0	Midpoint	33.46					$2.67		$127.60		20.31%
1	Bud	40	$2.95	$0.62		$0.62	$2.33	$24.80	$93.20	$118.00	21.02%
2	Legend Porter	67	$3.50	$0.53		$0.53	$2.97	$35.51	$198.99	$234.50	15.14%
3	Miller Lite	165	$2.95	$0.62		$0.62	$2.33	$102.30	$384.45	$486.75	21.02%
4	Corona	38	$3.75	$0.95		$0.95	$2.80	$36.10	$106.40	$142.50	25.33%
5	Heineken	64	$3.75	$0.90		$0.90	$2.85	$57.60	$182.40	$240.00	24.00%
6	Mobjack Pale	64	$3.75	$0.57		$0.57	$3.18	$36.48	$203.52	$240.00	15.20%
7	Bass Ale	0	$3.50	$1.09		$1.09	$2.41	$0.00	$0.00	$0.00	31.14%
8	Amstel Lite	13	$3.75	$0.91		$0.91	$2.84	$11.83	$36.92	$48.75	24.27%
9	Kaliber	28	$3.75	$0.93		$0.93	$2.82	$26.04	$78.96	$105.00	24.80%
10	Trick Dog	81	$3.25	$0.57		$0.57	$2.68	$46.17	$217.08	$263.25	17.54%
11	Legend	20	$3.50	$0.53		$0.53	$2.97	$10.60	$59.40	$70.00	15.14%
12	Wild Goose	0	$3.95	$0.51		$0.51	$3.44	$0.00	$0.00	$0.00	12.91%
13	Tucher Heffe	26	$3.95	$0.97		$0.97	$2.98	$25.22	$77.48	$102.70	24.56%
14	Bud Light	88	$2.95	$0.62		$0.62	$2.33	$54.56	$205.04	$259.60	21.02%
15	Flying Dog	23	$3.95	$0.90		$0.90	$3.05	$20.70	$70.15	$90.85	22.78%
	Total	**717**						**$488**	**$1,914**	**$2,402**	

ranging from a low of 20.31 (Beers) to a high of 36.28% (Bottle Wine) results in a 28.84% beverage cost for the entire sales mix (total potential beverage cost percentage). *Keep in mind that this percentage is not an average of the five categories but rather the quotient of the total weighted beverage cost divided by the total weighted beverage sales or $6,180/$21,431.*

You can lower your overall beverage cost percentage by promoting more beer sales. If you increased your bottle wine sales, your overall beverage cost percentage would increase. In this example, the prices for vodka are the reason for the high cost percentage. Typically, spirits costs will be in the mid to high teens. Either prices need to be increased or the portion reduced to bring costs down. Also, Canadian Mist and Seagrams's VO are showing costs of 41%, which is much too high. In reviewing the Item Beverage Cost % column, several other items are running costs in the mid thirties. These items need to have prices increased or portions reduced. However, you must consider the amount of dollars you actually put into the bank when you sell bottle wine. While the cost is high, the gross profit dollars are also high and you bank more than on the sale of a bottle of beer.

Total Sales %	Total Bev Cost %	Items Sold %	Wgtd Cont Margin %	Popularity	Bev Cost	Indv. Cont Margin	Wgted Cont Margin	Miller Matrix	Cost Margin	Menu Engineering
4.91%	5.08%	5.58%	4.87%	Popular	High	Low	Low	HVHCMARG	Problems	Plowhorses
9.76%	7.28%	9.34%	10.40%	Popular	Low	High	High	Winner	Prime	Stars
20.27%	20.97%	23.01%	20.09%	Popular	High	Low	High	HVHCMARG	Standards	Plowhorses
5.93%	7.40%	5.30%	5.56%	Popular	High	High	Low	HVHCMARG	Problems	Stars
9.99%	11.81%	8.93%	9.53%	Popular	High	High	High	HVHCMARG	Standards	Stars
9.99%	7.48%	8.93%	10.63%	Popular	Low	High	High	Winner	Prime	Stars
0.00%	0.00%	0.00%	0.00%	Not Popular	High	Low	Low	Loser	Problems	Dogs
2.03%	2.42%	1.81%	1.93%	Not Popular	High	High	Low	Loser	Problems	Puzzles
4.37%	5.34%	3.91%	4.13%	Not Popular	High	High	Low	Loser	Problems	Puzzles
10.96%	9.46%	11.30%	11.34%	Popular	Low	High	High	Winner	Prime	Stars
2.91%	2.17%	2.79%	3.10%	Not Popular	Low	High	Low	LVLCMARG	Sleepers	Puzzles
0.00%	0.00%	0.00%	0.00%	Not Popular	Low	High	Low	LVLCMARG	Sleepers	Puzzles
4.28%	5.17%	3.63%	4.05%	Not Popular	High	High	Low	Loser	Problems	Puzzles
10.81%	11.18%	12.27%	10.71%	Popular	High	Low	High	HVHCMARG	Standards	Plowhorses
3.78%	4.24%	3.21%	3.67%	Not Popular	High	High	Low	Loser	Problems	Puzzles

Additional insight into which items need to be promoted or adjusted in price or portions can be seen when the spreadsheet data is put into graph format. Figures 9–1 to 9–5 show the five beverage categories in graph format.

S pirits

Upon examining the Spirits in Figure 9–1 you can quickly see the concentration of items in the Problems quadrant. The farther the plot is from the intersection of the lines, the higher the beverage cost percentage. There are too few items in the Primes quadrant to offset the high number in the Problems quadrant. Items 20, 27, 18 and 26 (Chivas, Wild Turkey, Seagram's VO, and Jack Daniels Black) are well known brands that support higher prices. Fortunately, most of the house brands are Primes, e.g., Crystal Pal Vodka and Gin, Ron Llave Rum, Clan Mac Scotch, and Early Times.

Table 9.3　Glass Wine Cost/Margin Spreadsheet

Item No.	Item Name	No. Sold	Menu Price	Item Bev Cost	Supp. Cost	Total Cost	Item Cont Margin	Wgtd Bev Cost	Wgtd Cont Margin	Wgtd Sales	Item Bev Cost %
0	Midpoint	22.98					$3.70		$121.33		31.49%
1	Don Conde' Brut	59	$4.95	$0.58		$0.58	$4.37	$34.22	$257.83	$292.05	11.72%
2	Alamos Chard	216	$4.95	$1.33		$1.33	$3.62	$287.28	$781.92	$1,069.20	26.87%
3	Borgo Pinot Grigio	63	$5.25	$1.50		$1.50	$3.75	$94.50	$236.25	$330.75	28.57%
4	Guy Saget Vouvray	37	$5.75	$1.50		$1.50	$4.25	$55.50	$157.25	$212.75	26.09%
5	Ingleside Viognier	3	$7.50	$4.00		$4.00	$3.50	$12.00	$10.50	$22.50	53.33%
6	Joe Ballard Sauv Blanc	18	$5.50	$1.65		$1.65	$3.85	$29.70	$69.30	$99.00	30.00%
7	Latour Macon Chard	22	$5.25	$1.65		$1.65	$3.60	$36.30	$79.20	$115.50	31.43%
8	Barboursville Phileo	0	$5.25	$1.04		$1.04	$4.21	$0.00	$0.00	$0.00	19.81%
9	Boillot Bourgogne Pinot	28	$7.25	$2.33		$2.33	$4.92	$65.24	$137.76	$203.00	32.14%
10	Cline Cotes d'Oakley	30	$5.25	$1.50		$1.50	$3.75	$45.00	$112.50	$157.50	28.57%
11	Blushing Dog	22	$4.95	$1.40		$1.40	$3.55	$30.80	$78.10	$108.90	28.28%
12	Feudi Merlot	90	$4.95	$1.75		$1.75	$3.20	$157.50	$288.00	$445.50	35.35%
13	Alamos Cabernet	88	$4.95	$1.65		$1.65	$3.30	$145.20	$290.40	$435.60	33.33%
14	Jaboulet Parallele	4	$5.25	$1.84		$1.84	$3.41	$7.36	$13.64	$21.00	35.05%
15	Domaine Artois Dry Rose	0	$5.25	$1.33		$1.33	$3.92	$0.00	$0.00	$0.00	25.33%
16	Fife Merlot	21	$10.00	$5.06		$5.06	$4.94	$106.26	$103.74	$210.00	50.60%
17	Chateau La Paws	2	$6.00	$2.25		$2.25	$3.75	$4.50	$7.50	$12.00	37.50%
18	Dry Creek Cabernet	4	$12.00	$6.00		$6.00	$6.00	$24.00	$24.00	$48.00	50.00%
19	Seghezio Zinfandel	34	$6.25	$3.04		$3.04	$3.21	$103.36	$109.14	$212.50	48.64%
20	Oakencroft Merlot	23	$5.50	$2.42		$2.42	$3.08	$55.66	$70.84	$126.50	44.00%
21	P/M Chard	23	$5.25	$1.75		$1.75	$3.50	$40.25	$80.50	$120.75	33.33%
22	Ch. Maltroye Bourgogne	0	$7.25	$2.75		$2.75	$4.50	$0.00	$0.00	$0.00	37.93%
23	Churchill 10 Year Port	0	$6.00	$2.20		$2.20	$3.80	$0.00	$0.00	$0.00	36.67%
24	Graham's 20 Year Port	1	$7.00	$3.50		$3.50	$3.50	$3.50	$3.50	$7.00	50.00%
	Total	788						$1,338	$2,912	$4,250	

Total Sales %	Total Bev Cost %	Items Sold %	Wgtd Cont Margin %	Popularity	Bev Cost	Indv. Cont Margin	Wgted Cont Margin	Miller Matrix	Cost Margin	Menu Engineering
6.87%	2.56%	7.49%	8.85%	Popular	Low	High	High	Winner	Prime	Stars
25.16%	21.47%	27.41%	26.85%	Popular	Low	Low	High	Winner	Prime	Plowhorses
7.78%	7.06%	7.99%	8.11%	Popular	Low	High	High	Winner	Prime	Stars
5.01%	4.15%	4.70%	5.40%	Popular	Low	High	High	Winner	Prime	Stars
0.53%	0.90%	0.38%	0.36%	Not Popular	High	Low	Low	Loser	Problems	Dogs
2.33%	2.22%	2.28%	2.38%	Not Popular	Low	High	Low	LVLCMARG	Sleepers	Puzzles
2.72%	2.71%	2.79%	2.72%	Not Popular	Low	Low	Low	LVLCMARG	Sleepers	Dogs
0.00%	0.00%	0.00%	0.00%	Not Popular	Low	High	Low	LVLCMARG	Sleepers	Puzzles
4.78%	4.88%	3.55%	4.73%	Popular	High	High	High	HVHCMARG	Standards	Stars
3.71%	3.36%	3.81%	3.86%	Popular	Low	High	Low	Winner	Sleepers	Stars
2.56%	2.30%	2.79%	2.68%	Not Popular	Low	Low	Low	LVLCMARG	Sleepers	Dogs
10.48%	11.77%	11.42%	9.89%	Popular	High	Low	High	HVHCMARG	Standards	Plowhorses
10.25%	10.85%	11.17%	9.97%	Popular	High	Low	High	HVHCMARG	Standards	Plowhorses
0.49%	0.55%	0.51%	0.47%	Not Popular	High	Low	Low	Loser	Problems	Dogs
0.00%	0.00%	0.00%	0.00%	Not Popular	Low	High	Low	LVLCMARG	Sleepers	Puzzles
4.94%	7.94%	2.66%	3.56%	Not Popular	High	High	Low	Loser	Problems	Puzzles
0.28%	0.34%	0.25%	0.26%	Not Popular	High	High	Low	Loser	Problems	Puzzles
1.13%	1.79%	0.51%	0.82%	Not Popular	High	High	Low	Loser	Problems	Puzzles
5.00%	7.72%	4.31%	3.75%	Popular	High	Low	Low	HVHCMARG	Problems	Plowhorses
2.98%	4.16%	2.92%	2.43%	Popular	High	Low	Low	HVHCMARG	Problems	Plowhorses
2.84%	3.01%	2.92%	2.76%	Popular	High	Low	Low	HVHCMARG	Problems	Plowhorses
0.00%	0.00%	0.00%	0.00%	Not Popular	High	High	Low	Loser	Problems	Puzzles
0.00%	0.00%	0.00%	0.00%	Not Popular	High	High	Low	Loser	Problems	Puzzles
0.16%	0.26%	0.13%	0.12%	Not Popular	High	Low	Low	Loser	Problems	Dogs

Table 9.4 Liqueurs Cost/Margin Spreadsheet

Item No.	Item Name	No. Sold	Menu Price	Item Bev Cost	Supp. Cost	Total Cost	Item Cont Margin	Wgtd Bev Cost	Wgtd Cont Margin	Wgtd Sales	Item Bev Cost %
0	Midpoint	20.14					$1.21		$34.89		24.57%
1	Amaretto Di Saronno	21	$4.25	$0.95		$0.95	$3.30	$19.95	$69.30	$89	22.35%
2	B & B	7	$5.25	$1.88		$1.88	$3.37	$13.16	$23.59	$37	35.81%
3	Bailey's	36	$4.25	$0.90		$0.90	$3.35	$32.40	$120.60	$153	21.18%
4	Chambord	5	$4.25	$0.74		$0.74	$3.51	$3.70	$17.55	$21	17.41%
5	Cointreau	10	$5.25	$1.29		$1.29	$3.96	$12.90	$39.60	$53	24.57%
6	Courvoisier	5	$5.25	$1.20		$1.20	$4.05	$6.00	$20.25	$26	22.86%
7	Drambuie	13	$5.15	$1.35		$1.35	$3.80	$17.55	$49.40	$67	26.21%
8	Frangelico	26	$4.25	$0.73		$0.73	$3.52	$18.98	$91.52	$111	17.18%
9	Galliano	5	$4.25	$1.05		$1.05	$3.20	$5.25	$16.00	$21	24.71%
10	Goldschlager	5	$4.25	$0.90		$0.90	$3.35	$4.50	$16.75	$21	21.18%
11	Grand Marnier	16	$5.25	$1.46		$1.46	$3.79	$23.36	$60.64	$84	27.81%
12	Irish Mist	26	$5.25	$0.88		$0.88	$4.37	$22.88	$113.62	$137	16.76%
13	Yukon Jack	3	$4.25	$0.65		$0.65	$3.60	$1.95	$10.80	$13	15.29%
14	Kahlua	73	$2.13	$0.84		$0.84	$1.29	$61.32	$94.17	$155	39.44%
15	Midori	8	$4.25	$0.72		$0.72	$3.53	$5.76	$28.24	$34	16.94%
16	Sambuca	3	$4.75	$1.02		$1.02	$3.73	$3.06	$11.19	$14	21.47%
17	Southern Comfort	16	$4.25	$0.64		$0.64	$3.61	$10.24	$57.76	$68	15.06%
18	Annisette	22	$0.50	$0.20		$0.20	$0.30	$4.40	$6.60	$11	40.00%
19	Banana Liqueur	9	$0.50	$0.20		$0.20	$0.30	$1.80	$2.70	$5	40.00%
20	Apricot Brandy	4	$0.50	$0.20		$0.20	$0.30	$0.80	$1.20	$2	40.00%
21	Blackberry Brandy	22	$0.50	$0.20		$0.20	$0.30	$4.40	$6.60	$11	40.00%
22	Cherry Brandy	4	$0.50	$0.20		$0.20	$0.30	$0.80	$1.20	$2	40.00%
23	White Cacao	13	$0.50	$0.19		$0.19	$0.31	$2.47	$4.03	$7	38.00%
24	Crème de Almond	4	$0.50	$0.20		$0.20	$0.30	$0.80	$1.20	$2	40.00%
25	Green Crème de Menthe	31	$0.50	$0.20		$0.20	$0.30	$6.20	$9.30	$16	40.00%
26	White Crème de Menthe	40	$0.50	$0.20		$0.20	$0.30	$8.00	$12.00	$20	40.00%
27	Razmataz Raspberry	31	$3.25	$0.35		$0.35	$2.90	$10.85	$89.90	$101	10.77%
28	Peach Schnapps	26	$3.25	$0.35		$0.35	$2.90	$9.10	$75.40	$85	10.77%
29	Peppermint Schnapps	8	$3.25	$0.35		$0.35	$2.90	$2.80	$23.20	$26	10.77%
30	Peach Brandy	53	$0.50	$0.17		$0.17	$0.33	$9.01	$17.49	$27	34.00%
31	Strawberry Liqueur	13	$0.50	$0.20		$0.20	$0.30	$2.60	$3.90	$7	40.00%
32	Triple Sec	141	$0.30	$0.17		$0.17	$0.13	$23.97	$18.33	$42	56.67%
33	Vermouth Dry	136	$0.50	$0.14		$0.14	$0.36	$19.04	$48.96	$68	28.00%
34	Vermouth Sweet	110	$0.50	$0.14		$0.14	$0.36	$15.40	$39.60	$55	28.00%
35	Amaretto	62	$0.50	$0.20		$0.20	$0.30	$12.40	$18.60	$31	40.00%
	Total	1,007						$398	$1,221	$1,619	

Total Sales %	Total Bev Cost %	Items Sold %	Wgtd Cont Margin %	Popularity	Bev Cost	Indv. Cont Margin	Wgted Cont Margin	Miller Matrix	Cost Margin	Menu Engineering
5.51%	5.02%	2.09%	5.67%	Popular	Low	High	High	Winner	Prime	Stars
2.27%	3.31%	0.70%	1.93%	Not Popular	High	High	Low	Loser	Problems	Puzzles
9.45%	8.14%	3.57%	9.88%	Popular	Low	High	High	Winner	Prime	Stars
1.31%	0.93%	0.50%	1.44%	Not Popular	Low	High	Low	LVLCMARG	Sleepers	Puzzles
3.24%	3.24%	0.99%	3.24%	Not Popular	Low	High	High	LVLCMARG	Prime	Puzzles
1.62%	1.51%	0.50%	1.66%	Not Popular	Low	High	Low	LVLCMARG	Sleepers	Puzzles
4.14%	4.41%	1.29%	4.05%	Not Popular	High	High	High	Loser	Standards	Puzzles
6.83%	4.77%	2.58%	7.49%	Popular	Low	High	High	Winner	Prime	Stars
1.31%	1.32%	0.50%	1.31%	Not Popular	High	High	Low	Loser	Problems	Puzzles
1.31%	1.13%	0.50%	1.37%	Not Popular	Low	High	Low	LVLCMARG	Sleepers	Puzzles
5.19%	5.87%	1.59%	4.97%	Not Popular	High	High	High	Loser	Standards	Puzzles
8.43%	5.75%	2.58%	9.30%	Popular	Low	High	High	Winner	Prime	Stars
0.79%	0.49%	0.30%	0.88%	Not Popular	Low	High	Low	LVLCMARG	Sleepers	Puzzles
9.60%	15.41%	7.25%	7.71%	Popular	High	High	High	HVHCMARG	Standards	Stars
2.10%	1.45%	0.79%	2.31%	Not Popular	Low	High	Low	LVLCMARG	Sleepers	Puzzles
0.88%	0.77%	0.30%	0.92%	Not Popular	Low	High	Low	LVLCMARG	Sleepers	Puzzles
4.20%	2.57%	1.59%	4.73%	Not Popular	Low	High	High	LVLCMARG	Prime	Puzzles
0.68%	1.11%	2.18%	0.54%	Popular	High	Low	Low	HVHCMARG	Problems	Plowhorses
0.28%	0.45%	0.89%	0.22%	Not Popular	High	Low	Low	Loser	Problems	Dogs
0.12%	0.20%	0.40%	0.10%	Not Popular	High	Low	Low	Loser	Problems	Dogs
0.68%	1.11%	2.18%	0.54%	Popular	High	Low	Low	HVHCMARG	Problems	Plowhorses
0.12%	0.20%	0.40%	0.10%	Not Popular	High	Low	Low	Loser	Problems	Dogs
0.40%	0.62%	1.29%	0.33%	Not Popular	High	Low	Low	Loser	Problems	Dogs
0.12%	0.20%	0.40%	0.10%	Not Popular	High	Low	Low	Loser	Problems	Dogs
0.96%	1.56%	3.08%	0.76%	Popular	High	Low	Low	HVHCMARG	Problems	Plowhorses
1.24%	2.01%	3.97%	0.98%	Popular	High	Low	Low	HVHCMARG	Problems	Plowhorses
6.22%	2.73%	3.08%	7.36%	Popular	Low	High	High	Winner	Prime	Stars
5.22%	2.29%	2.58%	6.17%	Popular	Low	High	High	Winner	Prime	Stars
1.61%	0.70%	0.79%	1.90%	Not Popular	Low	High	Low	LVLCMARG	Sleepers	Puzzles
1.64%	2.26%	5.26%	1.43%	Popular	High	Low	Low	HVHCMARG	Problems	Plowhorses
0.40%	0.65%	1.29%	0.32%	Not Popular	High	Low	Low	Loser	Problems	Dogs
2.61%	6.03%	14.00%	1.50%	Popular	High	Low	Low	HVHCMARG	Problems	Plowhorses
4.20%	4.79%	13.51%	4.01%	Popular	High	Low	High	HVHCMARG	Standards	Plowhorses
3.40%	3.87%	10.92%	3.24%	Popular	High	Low	High	HVHCMARG	Standards	Plowhorses
1.91%	3.12%	6.16%	1.52%	Popular	High	Low	Low	HVHCMARG	Problems	Plowhorses

Table 9.5 Bottle Wine Cost/Margin Spreadsheet

Item No.	Item Name	No. Sold	Menu Price	Item Bev Cost	Supp. Cost	Total Cost	Item Cont Margin	Wgtd Bev Cost	Wgtd Cont Margin	Wgtd Sales	Item Bev Cost %
0	Midpoint	2.27					$21.97		$71.27		36.28%
1	Don Conde Brut	1	$20.00	$4.66		$4.66	$15.34	$4.66	$15.34	$20.00	23.30%
2	J & Jacques Berat Brut	0	$60.00	$15.00		$15.00	$45.00	$0.00	$0.00	$0.00	25.00%
3	Mumm's Cuvee Napa	3	$40.00	$16.42		$16.42	$23.58	$49.26	$70.74	$120.00	41.05%
4	Billecart Brut Rose	1	$125.00	$46.66		$46.66	$78.34	$46.66	$78.34	$125.00	37.33%
5	Alamos Chardonay	0	$24.00	$5.99		$5.99	$18.01	$0.00	$0.00	$0.00	24.96%
6	Rapidan River Riesling	2	$20.00	$7.33		$7.33	$12.67	$14.66	$25.34	$40.00	36.65%
7	Borgo Pinot Grigio	6	$18.00	$5.99		$5.99	$12.01	$35.94	$72.06	$108.00	33.28%
8	Guy Saget Vouvray	8	$25.00	$5.99		$5.99	$19.01	$47.92	$152.08	$200.00	23.96%
9	Civrac Lagrange Graves	0	$23.00	$5.00		$5.00	$18.00	$0.00	$0.00	$0.00	21.74%
10	Joe Ballard Sauv Blanc	0	$18.00	$6.59		$6.59	$11.41	$0.00	$0.00	$0.00	36.61%
11	Mills Reef Sauv Blanc	7	$28.00	$10.66		$10.66	$17.34	$74.62	$121.38	$196.00	38.07%
12	Fess Parker Chard	10	$33.00	$9.99		$9.99	$23.01	$99.90	$230.10	$330.00	30.27%
13	Sonoma Cutrer Chard	4	$50.00	$19.99		$19.99	$30.01	$79.96	$120.04	$200.00	38.98%
14	Genot Boulanger Montrac	7	$68.00	$25.99		$25.99	$42.01	$181.93	$294.07	$476.00	38.22%
15	Latour Macon Chard	1	$20.00	$6.59		$6.59	$13.41	$6.59	$13.41	$20.00	32.95%
16	Prince Michel Chard	5	$21.00	$6.99		$6.99	$14.01	$34.95	$70.05	$105.00	33.29%
17	Catene Chard	3	$38.00	$11.99		$11.99	$26.01	$35.97	$78.03	$114.00	31.55%
18	Ingle Viog	0	$38.00	$15.97		$15.97	$22.03	$0.00	$0.00	$0.00	42.03%
19	Cline Cotes d'Oakley	11	$22.00	$5.99		$5.99	$16.01	$65.89	$176.11	$242.00	27.23%
20	Blushing Dog	2	$18.00	$6.79		$6.79	$11.21	$13.58	$22.42	$36.00	37.72%
21	Ingle Brut	2	$32.00	$18.54		$18.54	$13.46	$37.08	$26.92	$64.00	57.94%
22	Clicquot La Grande Dame	0	$225.00	$100.00		$100.00	$125.00	$0.00	$0.00	$0.00	44.44%
23	Jaboulet 45	1	$21.00	$7.33		$7.33	$13.67	$7.33	$13.87	$21.00	34.90%
24	Thomas Mitchell Marsanne	4	$28.00	$6.66		$6.66	$21.34	$26.64	$85.36	$112.00	23.79%
25	Alessandria Barolo	5	$39.00	$16.66		$16.66	$22.34	$83.30	$111.70	$195.00	42.72%
26	Domaine Artois Dry Rose	0	$22.00	$5.32		$5.32	$16.68	$0.00	$0.00	$0.00	24.18%
27	Syrah-Syrah	6	$30.00	$7.99		$7.99	$22.01	$47.94	$132.06	$180.00	26.63%
28	De Cheil Pinot Noir	5	$30.00	$11.99		$11.99	$18.01	$59.95	$90.05	$150.00	39.97%

Total Sales %	Total Bev Cost %	Items Sold %	Wgtd Cont Margin %	Popularity	Bev Cost	Indv. Cont Margin	Wgted Cont Margin	Miller Matrix	Cost Margin	Menu Engineering
0.40%	0.26%	0.68%	0.48%	Not Popular	Low	Low	Low	LVLCMARG	Sleepers	Dogs
0.00%	0.00%	0.00%	0.00%	Not Popular	Low	High	Low	LVLCMARG	Sleepers	Puzzles
2.38%	2.70%	2.05%	2.21%	Popular	High	High	Low	HVHCMARG	Problems	Stars
2.48%	2.56%	0.68%	2.44%	Not Popular	High	High	High	Loser	Standards	Puzzles
0.00%	0.00%	0.00%	0.00%	Not Popular	Low	Low	Low	LVLCMARG	Sleepers	Dogs
0.79%	0.80%	1.37%	0.79%	Not Popular	High	Low	Low	Loser	Problems	Dogs
2.15%	1.97%	4.11%	2.25%	Popular	Low	Low	High	Winner	Prime	Plowhorses
3.97%	2.62%	5.48%	4.74%	Popular	Low	Low	High	Winner	Prime	Plowhorses
0.00%	0.00%	0.00%	0.00%	Not Popular	Low	Low	Low	LVLCMARG	Sleepers	Dogs
0.00%	0.00%	0.00%	0.00%	Not Popular	High	Low	Low	Loser	Problems	Dogs
3.89%	4.09%	4.79%	3.78%	Popular	High	Low	High	HVHCMARG	Standards	Plowhorses
6.56%	5.47%	6.85%	7.17%	Popular	Low	High	High	Winner	Prime	Stars
3.97%	4.38%	2.74%	3.74%	Popular	High	High	High	HVHCMARG	Standards	Stars
9.46%	9.96%	4.79%	9.17%	Popular	High	High	High	HVHCMARG	Standards	Stars
0.40%	0.36%	0.68%	0.42%	Not Popular	Low	Low	Low	LVLCMARG	Sleepers	Dogs
2.09%	1.91%	3.42%	2.18%	Popular	Low	Low	Low	Winner	Sleepers	Plowhorses
2.27%	1.97%	2.05%	2.43%	Popular	Low	High	High	Winner	Prime	Stars
0.00%	0.00%	0.00%	0.00%	Not Popular	High	High	Low	Loser	Problems	Puzzles
4.81%	3.61%	7.53%	5.49%	Popular	Low	Low	High	Winner	Prime	Plowhorses
0.72%	0.74%	1.37%	0.70%	Not Popular	High	Low	Low	Loser	Problems	Dogs
1.27%	2.03%	1.37%	0.84%	Not Popular	High	Low	Low	Loser	Problems	Dogs
0.00%	0.00%	0.00%	0.00%	Not Popular	High	High	Low	Loser	Problems	Puzzles
0.42%	0.40%	0.68%	0.43%	Not Popular	Low	Low	Low	LVLCMARG	Sleepers	Dogs
2.23%	1.46%	2.74%	2.66%	Popular	Low	Low	High	Winner	Prime	Plowhorses
3.87%	4.56%	3.42%	3.48%	Popular	High	High	High	HVHCMARG	Standards	Stars
0.00%	0.00%	0.00%	0.00%	Not Popular	Low	Low	Low	LVLCMARG	Sleepers	Dogs
3.58%	2.63%	4.11%	4.12%	Popular	Low	High	High	Winner	Prime	Stars
2.98%	3.28%	3.42%	2.81%	Popular	High	Low	High	HVHCMARG	Standards	Plowhorses

(continued)

Table 9.5 *Continued*

Item No.	Item Name	No. Sold	Menu Price	Item Bev Cost	Supp. Cost	Total Cost	Item Cont Margin	Wgtd Bev Cost	Wgtd Cont Margin	Wgtd Sales	Item Bev Cost %
29	Clos Daviaud St. Emillon	1	$38.00	$9.99		$9.99	$28.01	$9.99	$28.01	$38.00	26.29%
30	Barboursbille Barbera	1	$26.00	$10.39		$10.39	$15.61	$10.39	$15.61	$26.00	39.96%
31	Thomas Mitchell Shiraz	2	$28.00	$6.66		$6.66	$21.34	$13.32	$42.68	$56.00	23.79%
32	Fife Merlot	6	$48.00	$20.25		$20.25	$27.75	$121.50	$166.50	$288.00	42.19%
33	La Magia Rosso	1	$31.00	$10.99		$10.99	$20.01	$10.99	$20.01	$31.00	35.45%
34	Chateau Montrose	1	$90.00	$47.99		$47.99	$42.01	$47.99	$42.01	$90.00	53.32%
35	Cape Mentelle Shiraz	5	$35.00	$13.99		$13.99	$21.01	$69.95	$105.05	$175.00	39.97%
36	J Lohr Cabernet	2	$48.00	$19.17		$19.17	$28.83	$38.34	$57.66	$96.00	39.94%
37	Aresti Merlot	6	$28.00	$5.99		$5.99	$22.01	$35.94	$132.06	$168.00	21.39%
38	Chateau La Paws	0	$25.00	$8.99		$8.99	$16.01	$0.00	$0.00	$0.00	35.96%
39	Dry Creek Cabernet	3	$49.00	$23.99		$23.99	$25.01	$71.97	$75.03	$147.00	48.96%
40	Seghezio Zinfandel	7	$29.00	$11.25		$11.25	$17.75	$78.75	$124.25	$203.00	38.79%
41	Panther Creek Pinot Noir	1	$55.00	$34.99		$34.99	$20.01	$34.99	$20.01	$55.00	63.62%
42	David Bruce Pinot Noir	4	$69.00	$28.66		$28.66	$40.34	$114.64	$161.36	$276.00	41.54%
43	Oakencroft Merlot	2	$25.00	$9.67		$9.67	$15.33	$19.34	$30.66	$50.00	38.68%
44	Catena Cabernet	0	$36.00	$13.99		$13.99	$22.01	$0.00	$0.00	$0.00	38.86%
45	Boilot Bourgogne Pinot	10	$28.00	$9.32		$9.32	$18.68	$93.20	$186.80	$280.00	33.29%
	Total	**146**						**$1,826**	**$3,207**	**$5,033**	

Table 9.6 Beverages Sales Mix Category Totals

Menu Category	Potential Beverage Cost	Average No. Sold	Average Item C.M.	Average Weighted C.M.	% of Items Sold	% of Beverage Cost	% of Cont. Margin	% of Sales Dollars
Spirits	26.21%	52.88	$2.56	$193.45	46.84%	34.46%	39.32%	37.92%
Beer	20.31%	33.46	$2.67	$127.60	14.34%	7.90%	12.55%	11.21%
Glass Wine	31.49%	22.98	$3.70	$121.33	15.76%	21.65%	19.09%	19.83%
Liqueurs	24.57%	20.14	$1.21	$34.89	20.14%	6.44%	8.01%	7.55%
Botttle Wine	36.28%	2.27	$21.97	$71.27	2.92%	29.55%	21.03%	23.49%
Totals	28.84%	23.33	$3.05	$101.67	100.00%	100.00%	100.00%	100.00%

Total Sales %	Total Bev Cost %	Items Sold %	Wgtd Cont Margin %	Popularity	Bev Cost	Indv. Cont Margin	Wgted Cont Margin	Miller Matrix	Cost Margin	Menu Engineering
0.76%	0.55%	0.68%	0.87%	Not Popular	Low	High	Low	LVLCMARG	Sleepers	Puzzles
0.52%	0.57%	0.68%	0.49%	Not Popular	High	Low	Low	Loser	Problems	Dogs
1.11%	0.73%	1.37%	1.33%	Not Popular	Low	Low	Low	LVLCMARG	Sleepers	Dogs
5.72%	6.65%	4.11%	5.19%	Popular	High	High	High	HVHCMARG	Standards	Stars
0.62%	0.60%	0.68%	0.62%	Not Popular	Low	Low	Low	LVLCMARG	Sleepers	Dogs
1.79%	2.63%	0.68%	1.31%	Not Popular	High	High	Low	Loser	Problems	Puzzles
3.48%	3.83%	3.42%	3.28%	Popular	High	Low	High	HVHCMARG	Standards	Plowhorses
1.91%	2.10%	1.37%	1.80%	Not Popular	High	High	Low	Loser	Problems	Puzzles
3.34%	1.97%	4.11%	4.12%	Popular	Low	High	High	Winner	Prime	Stars
0.00%	0.00%	0.00%	0.00%	Not Popular	Low	Low	Low	LVLCMARG	Sleepers	Dogs
2.92%	3.94%	2.05%	2.34%	Popular	High	High	High	HVHCMARG	Standards	Stars
4.03%	4.31%	4.79%	3.87%	Popular	High	Low	High	HVHCMARG	Standards	Plowhorses
1.09%	1.92%	0.68%	0.62%	Not Popular	High	Low	Low	Loser	Problems	Dogs
5.48%	6.28%	2.74%	5.03%	Popular	High	High	High	HVHCMARG	Standards	Stars
0.99%	1.06%	1.37%	0.96%	Not Popular	High	Low	Low	Loser	Problems	Dogs
0.00%	0.00%	0.00%	0.00%	Not Popular	High	High	Low	Loser	Problems	Puzzles
5.56%	5.10%	6.85%	5.82%	Popular	Low	Low	High	Winner	Prime	Plowhorses

B eer

Looking at Figure 9–2, you will note that the highest concentration of plots is in the Problems quadrant. Bass Ale (7) is not popular and carries a 31% cost. Although none were sold during the period, it is likely to be discontinued. If inventory remains to be sold, prices should be raised to lower the cost percentage. Kaliber and Tucher Heff are also high cost items that should be re-priced. Bud Light and Miller Lite have the best potential for becoming Primes given their proximity to the cut-off line. A price increase to $3.25 (assuming that this is still a competitive price point in the market) should be attempted.

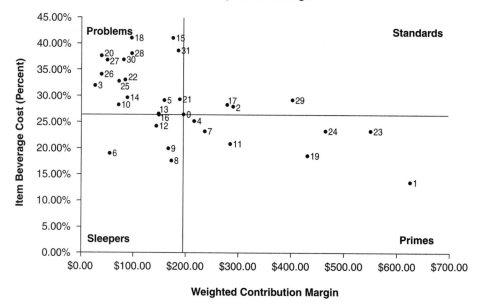

FIGURE 9–1
Spirits Cost/Margin Graph

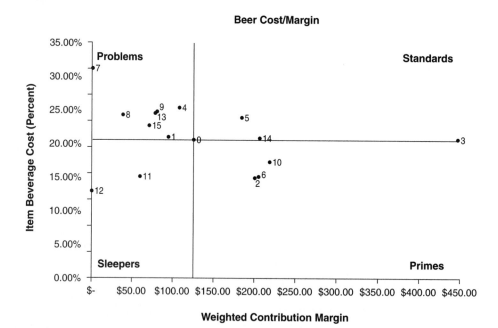

FIGURE 9–2
Beer Cost/Margin Graph

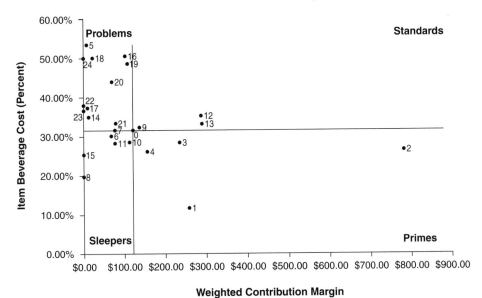

Glass Wine Cost/Margin

FIGURE 9–3
Glass Wine Cost/Margin Graph

G lass Wine

Figure 9–3 again tells us that there is a disproportionate number of items in the Problems quadrant. However, there are a number of good candidates for the Primes quadrant, e.g., Boillot Pinot, Cline Coates d'Oakley, and Alamos Cabernet (9, 10, and 13). Because they are so close to the beverage cost line, a price increase of $.25 would put them in the Primes quadrant.

L iqueurs

When you examine the graph of the Liqueurs in Figure 9–4, you will notice the high concentration of items at the 40% point in the Problems quadrant. These are items 18-26 which are not sold separately but rather are ingredients for other mixed drinks. Because the restaurant chooses to assign them a cost price value of $.50, the cost percentages are somewhat overstated. One finds that the majority of items in the Problems quadrant are ingredients rather

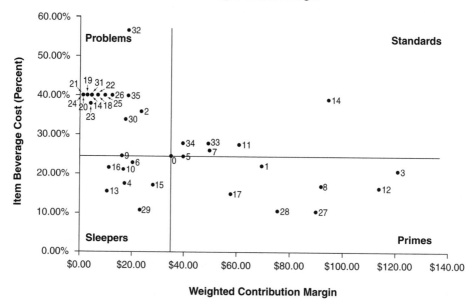

FIGURE 9–4
Liqueurs Cost/Margin Graph

than drinks. With that knowledge, you can turn your attention to the other items closest to the intersecting lines and explore strategies for moving them down and or to the right by adjusting prices, portions, and promotions.

Bottle Wine

Considering the small number of bottles of wine sold compared to drinks (this is not unusual), it is quite amazing to see that bottle wines, which account for only 2.92% of all beverages sold, bring in 23.49% of beverage sales! However, it would appear that the wine inventory could be pared down to fewer labels and still contribute to the overall beverage gross profit. Here you see a significant number of wines in the Primes quadrant, indicating they are the wines that should be promoted and given top billing on the wine list. The items that are just above the cut-off line in the Standards quadrant are the candidates for moving into the Primes quadrant by increasing their prices $1.50–$2.00.

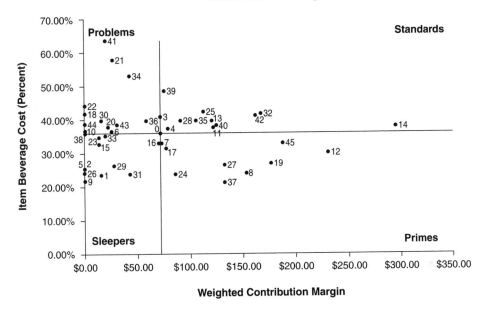

Bottle Wine Cost/Margin

FIGURE 9–5
Bottle Wine Cost/Margin Graph

The graphing of the spreadsheet data is a useful tool for interpreting the sales mix and identifying the best candidates for pricing or portioning changes. This type of analysis should be conducted at least four times per year. Cost/Margin analysis allows you to objectively analyze the effects of your beverage menus and wine lists and the effects of your pricing changes and promotions.

Inventory

Liquor, beer, and wine need to be inventoried just like food. In fact, greater security is given to alcoholic beverages because of the cost and abuses that can take place if they are not watched closely. Liquor inventory is kept under lock and key in separate storerooms from the food such as in locked cages, or cabinets in storerooms and walk-ins. Only authorized individuals have access to such areas, and requisitions must be filled out to record any withdrawals.

It is also recommended that you establish par stock levels for all remote and service bars and replenish stock from stamped empty bottles. Bottle stamping is used to prevent bartenders from bringing in their own bottle and selling it. If they do, even with close inventory controls, shortages are not detectible because there are none. When a bottle is brought in from the outside and is not part of the operation's inventory it is called a phantom bottle. The receipts from the bar register are kept by the guilty employee for each sale made with this phantom liquor. This results in a drop in sales levels of $50 to $100 a night.

Inventories must be audited to verify that the liquor is actually in the storeroom. If phantom inventory is reported and/or a purchase invoice is not turned in, the cost of liquor consumed will be understated and show a lower beverage cost than actually exists. This is why monthly statements from vendors should be mailed to the corporate office and not the individual unit. Bills are paid from invoices, not statements. However, statements let the comptroller know that all invoices have been submitted for payment.

Deliveries need to be checked for completeness and accuracy. Again, too often, the driver's delivery invoice is used to check the delivery. It is recommended that a purchase order be available to verify the invoice for correct brands, units, quantities, and prices. Some companies that are allowed by state statue may provide a separate invoice for bottles awarded at no cost as an incentive for volume purchases. By having a second party compare the perpetual inventory to the invoices with the statement as a guide, an audit can be performed monthly along with inventories.

PERPETUAL INVENTORY

The most common method for controlling and recording beverage inventories is the **perpetual inventory system**. This method takes a constant count, recording all merchandise ordered and requisitioned so that a running count is kept for every brand in inventory. A master record (Figure 9–6) is main-

---

BIN NUMBER 34   BRAND: CHIVAS REGAL   UNIT: QUARTS
DISTRIBUTOR: AMERICAN BEVERAGE

Date	Quantity on Hand	Quantity Delivered	Total	Quantity Issued	Balance in Stock	Issued To:	Issued By:
7-22-98	18	12	30	6	24	RRF	DVP
7-23-98	24	na	na	4	20	DDR	DVP
7-24-98	20	na	na	2	18	RRF	DVP

FIGURE 9–6
Perpetual Inventory Control Record

BIN NO. 34	BRAND: CHIVAS REGAL		UNIT: QUARTS	
DISTRIBUTOR: AMERICAN BEVERAGE				

Date	Amount on Hand		Amount Delivered		Amount Issued		Balance in Stock
7-22-98	18	+	12	−	6	=	24
7-23-98	24		na		4		20
7-24-98	20		na		2		18

FIGURE 9–7
Bin Card

tained by the accounting department that records all deliveries and subtracts all requisitions. There would be a similar record kept by management in the liquor storeroom. A separate bin card (Figure 9–7), may be used in place of a record book but a book is recommended over the bin cards. Duplicates of liquor requisitions (Figure 9–8) are made, one going to the accounting department and one kept by management to update their inventory book.

At the end of the month, a complete fiscal inventory is taken and compared to the perpetual inventory amounts. The two should be the same. If

DATE: *7-22-98*	BAR STATION: *MAIN BAR*	REQUESTED BY: *RRF*	

Quantity	Brand	Unit Size	Empties Returned
6	*Chivas Regal*	*Quarts*	6
3	*Dewars*	*Quarts*	3
1	*Glenlivet 12 yr*	*Fifth*	1
3	*Jim Beam*	*Quarts*	2
2	*Skyy Vodka*	*Quarts*	3
1	*Cuervo 1800*	*Quarts*	1
1	*Amaretto Di Saronno*	*Quarts*	1

Filled By: *DVP*

FIGURE 9–8
Liquor, Wine, and Beer Requisition

not, the discrepancy needs to be investigated. No merchandise should be taken from the liquor storeroom without recording it on the requisition form containing the proper authorization signature. The information contained on the requisition is the brand, size, number of bottles, date, name of person filling out the requisition, and the authorized signature. If the *par stock–empty bottle requisition system* is used, an empty one must be returned to the storage cabinet in exchange for every full bottle issued. The empty bottle is then left on the shelf in the storeroom until a new one is received and takes its place. By using this system the total number of bottles (in all bars and storage) always stays the same.

Controlling Sales of Beverages

Controls for determining dispensing costs, recording sales, and accounting for beverage consumed is accomplished by use of three different systems.

1. Automated: systems that dispense and count

2. Ounce or drink controls

3. Par stock or bottle control

AUTOMATED DISPENSING SYSTEMS

Automated dispensing systems are being installed in many of the chain operations. The better-known ABC Computerbar and the Berg system are just a few of dozens of systems on the market. They range from mechanical dispensers attached to individual bottles to magnetic pourers that can be activated when the cash register records the sale. These systems dispense the exact amount every time, allow for more consistent drinks, reduce spillage, cannot give free drinks, and allow no over- or under-pouring. With some systems the bartender never touches the bottles. Liquor cannot be dispensed without being recorded in the system.

The suppliers of these systems will tell you that you will need to dispense at least 80 percent of all alcohol through the system to receive the optimum benefits. Since each magnetic pourer or dispensing head is not cheap, it requires that you reduce the number of brands offered. More than likely, a premium well program would be used. Cordials and liqueurs both have high sugar content and will clog up the sensitive moving parts that control the amount dispensed. Such items may be left off the system or require frequent maintenance of pouring heads to keep them flowing.

Dispensing systems that measure and count portions are available for draft beer and draft wines. Their use allows servers to dispense their own orders and not require a bartender. This is highly useful in restaurants without full liquor licenses. The systems have portion meters that count each glass, pitcher, or carafe served. At the end of the shift, the readings are taken and the number of servings at the different sizes can be quickly tallied and compared to point-of-sale records.

Bottled beer and wine can be controlled by a perpetual inventory system that counts what is on hand at the beginning and end of the meal period and compares the difference to the sales records or guest checks. One server is given the responsibility of taking inventory and replenishing the par stock of beer and wine. Management should spot check and sign off on the count when the server has completed the restocking. This provides the operator with virtually 100 percent control.

Advantages of dispensing systems

1. Systems provide measured pouring, which eliminates problems of under- and over-pouring.
2. Drinks are more consistent.
3. Systems can utilize 1.75-liter bottles, which reduce the cost per ounce of the liquor. In this instance, the bartender does not handle any bottles behind the bar.
4. Liquor is counted every time it is dispensed and, therefore, can be tracked.
5. They provide sales mix information for use in sales analysis.
6. They speed up the service in high-volume bars and increase productivity.
7. No requisitions need to be used since the liquor is dispensed from the secure liquor storeroom.

OUNCE OR DRINK CONTROLS

Prior to the development of automatic dispensing systems, the most common method for determining the sales mix of liquor sold was through counting the drinks sold. This was extremely difficult because of the manual recording of beverages and the multi-tiered price structure to identify the house, call, and premium call brands used in the drinks. It was further complicated by the fact that there were numerous ways the liquor could be sold and combined with other wines and spirits that significantly impacted the price and cost percentages. Note the information contained on the beverage check produced with a point-of-sale system shown in Figure 9–9 and the additional printouts it produces providing management with detailed information for beverage cost analysis in Figures 9–10 and 9–11. In the absence of a point-of-

THE ABC GUEST CHECK
AND PAPER RECEIPT

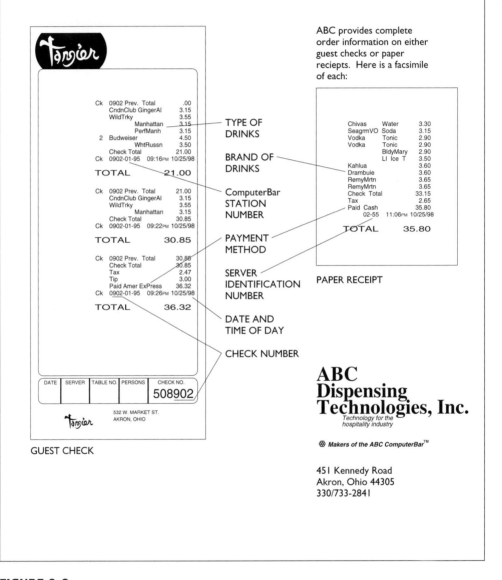

ABC provides complete order information on either guest checks or paper receipts. Here is a facsimile of each:

GUEST CHECK

PAPER RECEIPT

**ABC
Dispensing
Technologies, Inc.**
Technology for the hospitality industry

⊛ *Makers of the ABC ComputerBar™*

451 Kennedy Road
Akron, Ohio 44305
330/733-2841

FIGURE 9–9
ABC Computebar Management Report (Courtesy of ABC Dispensing Technologies, Akron, Ohio 44305).

ABC COMPUTERBAR MANAGEMENT REPORT

X-Read Ringoff #02	- 01:33 p.m.	06/08/92	
Accumulators Cleared	- 01:00 a.m.	06/07/92	

REPORT #1 – SALES BY MAJOR CATEGORY

Sales by Major Category	STATION 1 SALES	STATION 2 SALES	TOTAL SALES
Liquor	334.10	668.20	1002.30
Draft Beer	48.85	97.70	146.55
Bottled Beer	60.30	120.60	180.90
Wine	.00	.00	.00
Soft Drinks	32.30	64.60	96.90
Misc A	.00	.00	.00
Misc B	.00	.00	.00
Misc C	.00	.00	.00
PLU	.00	.00	.00
Non-Taxable Food	.00	.00	.00
Taxable Food	82.00	164.00	246.00
Special	.00	.00	.00
Beverages	475.55	951.10	1426.65
Non-Taxable Food	.00	.00	.00
Taxable Food	82.00	164.00	246.00
Special #1	.00	.00	.00
Special #2	.00	.00	.00
Price Mode 1	562.55	1125.10	1687.65
Mode 2	.00	.00	.00
Mode 3	.00	.00	.00
Tax Rate #1	.00	.00	.00
Rate #2	.00	.00	.00
Rate #3	.00	.00	.00
G.S.T. Rate #4	.00	.00	.00
Extracted Rate #5	.00	.00	.00
Reported Tips	5.00	10.00	15.00
Void Total	4.50	.00	4.50
Void Count	02	00	02
Transactions	36	72	108
Non-Clearing Sale	585.80	1171.60	1757.40
Gross Sales	562.55	1125.10	1687.65
Net Sales	557.55	1115.10	1672.65

MONITORS UP TO FOUR SEPARATE STATIONS

ABC Version JOT4B3   ✹ *ABC ComputerBar*™

FIGURE 9–10
ABC Computerbar Management Report
(Courtesy of ABC Dispensing Technologies, Akron, Ohio 44305).

ABC COMPUTERBAR MANAGEMENT REPORT

REPORT #3 – SALES BY SERVER

Reported Server	Total Tip-ES	Sales	Cash	Visa	MC	Amex	Dine	Voids
			[All Sales Include Tax and Tips]					
02	7.38	92.40	73.35	19.05	.00	.00	.00	.00
04	16.62	208.05	129.15	78.90	.00	.00	.00	.00
05	16.65	105.00	20.70	84.30	.00	.00	.00	.00
08	1.92	24.30	24.30	.00	.00	.00	.00	.00
09	2.16	27.00	27.00	.00	.00	.00	.00	.00
22	98.46	1230.90	916.35	223.80	10.50	80.25	.00	4.50
Totals	135.01	1687.65	1190.85	406.05	10.50	80.25	.00	4.50

REPORT #4 – SALES BY SETTLEMENT METHOD

Settlement Methods	STATION 01 SALES	STATION 02 SALES	TOTAL SALES
Cash	396.95	793.90	1190.85
VISA	135.35	270.70	406.15
MasterCard	3.50	7.00	10.50
AmericanExpr	26.75	53.50	80.25
Discover	.00	.00	.00
Total Settlements	562.55	1125.10	1687.65

ABC Version JOT4B3

⬡ *ABC ComputerBar*™

FIGURE 9–11
ABC Computerbar Management Report
(Courtesy of ABL Dispensing Technologies, Akron, Ohio 44305).

sale system, the drink control system can be used for a period of time to determine the drink sales mix so a potential, standard, and actual beverage cost percentage can be estimated.

The ounce or drink control requires the following actions:

1. Standardize glassware and recipes
2. Record each drink sold for sales analysis
3. Determine the cost of beverage consumed
4. Compare actual use levels to "potential" consumption based on the sales mix
5. Compare actual beverage cost percent to the "potential" beverage cost percent

PAR STOCK–EMPTY BOTTLE CONTROL

Par stock or **empty bottle control** is the third method of control used for alcoholic beverages. The steps are:

1. Determine the maximum consumption/usage for each type of liquor and add a small safety factor; state in terms of number of bottles to keep behind the bar. This becomes the "par stock" that is maintained.
2. All empty bottles are turned in for full ones; no full bottles are issued without an empty turned in.
3. A standard sales value per bottle is determined based on the types of drinks made from each liquor.
4. A sales value is determined from consumption and compared to actual sales for variances. If more was consumed than sold, investigate.

STANDARDIZED DRINK RECIPES, GLASSWARE, AND ICE

Like food, all drinks must be prepared according to standards. If dispensers are not used, measures like jiggers or "Posi-Pourers" are used. When first learning to mix drinks, measures should be used. You should not learn by "eye" or "count." A drink recipe is much the same as one for a menu item. It lists ingredients, portions, and method of preparation.

Ingredients	Portion	Cost
Cost of Liquor	1 1/2 ounces @ $8 qt	$.375
Cost of Mix	4 oz @ $.025 oz	.10
Cost of Garnish		$.02
Total		$.495

Prices charged are influenced by the same factors used in pricing menu items. Divide the beverage cost by the desired beverage cost percentage and adjust up or down according to indirect cost factors. The effects of a Happy Hour Special with two-for-one would double each of the above percentages.

Happy Hour Two-for-One Special

Ingredients	Portion	Cost
Cost of Liquor	1 1/2 ounces @ $8 qt	$.375
Cost of Mix	4 oz @ $.025 oz	.10
Cost of Garnish		$.02
Total		$.495

Double for Happy Hour would cost $.99

Cost	Price	Beverage Cost %
$.50	$1.95	25.6%
$.50	$2.50	20.0%
$.50	$2.95	16.9%

DRINK CATEGORIES

Operations that do not have elaborate point-of-sale units to record beverage sales usually classify their drinks into one of the following categories with a separate price for each category.

Highballs: vodka tonic, scotch and soda, 7 & 7

Cocktails: martini, manhattan

Collins/sours: whiskey sour, tom collins

Frozen drinks: frozen daiquiri, margarita

Double liquor drinks: harvey wallbanger, tequila sunrise, rusty nail, godfather

Cream drinks: grasshopper, pink squirrel

Cordials and liqueurs: Amaretto, Grand Marnier

Specialty drinks: Zombie, Long Island Iced Tea

In addition, prices are increased in each category when the customer requests a call or premium call brand be used (e.g., Stoli vodka and tonic; Tanqueray martini).

Glassware must be standardized (see Figure 9–12) and so must the size and quantity of ice used. Larger cubes are harder, melt slowly, and are best for making cocktails. However, they do not displace much liquid when used for on-the-rocks drinks where "mini-cubes" are recommended. When making cocktails, always start with fresh ice.

All transactions need to be entered into the system. If you do not possess a point-of-sale system, each order needs to be written on a check similar to a food order so you can go back and determine the sales mix of alcoholic beverages. No drinks should be issued without a written requisition also known as a "guest check". In some bars and lounges, servers carry their own banks and pay for every drink they serve. Such a system guarantees that the house is paid first.

B everage Frauds

Only a few of the most common beverage frauds perpetrated on restaurant and lounge owners are discussed here. Whenever the bartender has access to the cash drawer, such frauds can occur. If bartenders do not handle cash, as with service bars and banquet bars, or the operation utilizes liquor-dispensing systems that measure each drink dispensed or the bartender never touches the actual bottles, the likelihood of fraud diminishes. When the servers carry their own banks, occasionally collusion between a server and a bartender can occur. But this happens less frequently than when the employee can act alone. This list is by no means exhaustive and is offered only to show the most common kinds of fraud and how they can be detected and prevented.

SHORT POURING

Realistically, not every transaction can be monitored. Short pouring is where the drink is under-portioned and the amount "stockpiled" until, after four or

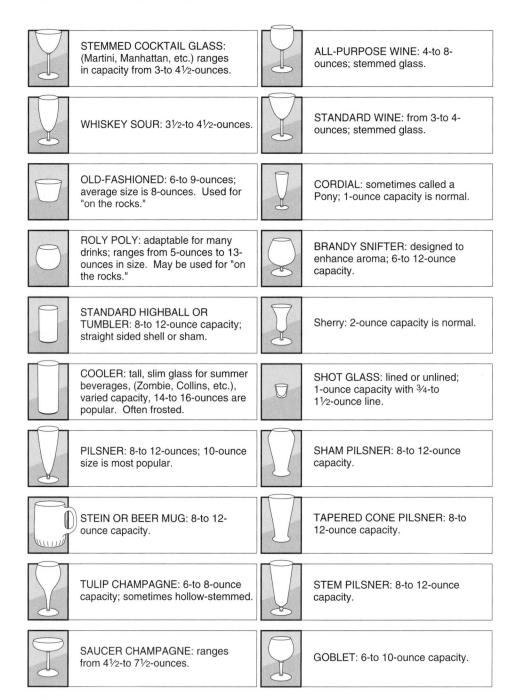

FIGURE 9–12
Common Sizes and Shapes of Liquor Glasses

five drinks, a full drink can be made and sold without showing a deduction from inventory. This can be done even with automatic dispensing systems.

1. Watch for bartenders keeping a glass under the bar with liquor in it. This is not a frequent occurrence since it takes so much time and can be easily observed.
2. Require bartenders to use a jigger to measure all drinks.

Customers especially vulnerable to short-pour fraud are those requesting doubles. Happy hour is another time when free-pouring bartenders can make a lot of money with short pouring because of the two-for-one or doubles-for-one price structure.

SUBSTITUTING HOUSE BRANDS FOR CALL BRANDS

Because there is a price differential between house brands and call brands, a bartender can substitute a house brand and charge for a call brand. This is a difficult one to control. Many restaurants have limited the number of brands of liquor served and are using a call brand as their house brand. For example, they may use Jack Daniels Green as their well bourbon. They will subsequently reduce the number of premium call brands on the back bar.

Only a few customers will be able to detect that their Black Jack and Coke has been substituted with Old Library. The substitution will not likely be made when bourbon and water or soda is ordered. If you suspect that this is being done, a secret shopper may be able to detect it.

DILUTION OF LIQUOR

This occurs typically at inventory time to cover up missing liquor. The white spirits like your gins and vodkas are the most vulnerable to be diluted with water. However, if this is taking place you will likely be receiving a lot of complaints about weak drinks. Look for more than one bottle of a particular brand open behind the bar. The diluted bottle can be used in drinks like Screwdrivers, Bloody Marys, and Long Island Iced Tea because the mix overpowers the taste of the white liquor.

BRINGING IN OWN BOTTLE

Bartenders can easily bring in their own bottle of stock liquor and pour from their own bottle and never record the usage or sale. With 30 shots per bottle at $2.95 per drink, a bartender can steal close to $90 a shift, and the inventory will never show that the sales ever took place. There are several things an operator can do to prevent this occurrence or increase the likelihood that it will be detected.

1. Use an indelible stamp on all bottles leaving the liquor storeroom. A black ultraviolet light reveals the stamp on authorized bottles. Periodically check the bottles at the bar. Also, the tax stamp on liquor sold by the wholesale distributor or state liquor store is a different color than the stamp of bottles sold in retail outlets. Look for the different stamp color.

2. Keep a par stock number of each type of liquor behind the bar. If you notice that there is an extra bottle of bourbon, get out the black light and look for the bottle stamp.

3. Inspect all empty bottles before breaking and discarding. If you use the empty bottles to determine the issues from the storeroom to replenish the stock, you have another check point for foreign bottles.

4. Do not let employees bring backpacks or large handbags behind the bar. Have employees enter and leave through one entrance and check all packages large enough to hide a bottle.

5. If you have an automatic dispensing system, the bartenders may never touch the bottle so it eliminates free pouring completely. However, it is an expensive mechanical cost control system.

GIVING AWAY FREE DRINKS

This is a ploy for bartenders to increase their tips or simply pocket the money from the customer without ringing the transaction. It is usually used with over-pouring as a strong drink is considered better than a weak one. This is used when the restaurant has a lounge with stools and customers come in just to drink and socialize.

Require a cash register receipt to be printed for each drink and placed down with the drink when served. Require a tab be run with the check placed in front of the customer or in a rack with slots corresponding to seats at the bar. If the problem is excessive, some have initiated a procedure that is prominently posted, "Your drink is free if we fail to give you a receipt." Some even use a tape with randomly printed "stars" that qualify the patron for a free drink. The object is to get the transaction recorded and entered into the system.

The sale of nonalcoholic beverages including virgin Bloody Marys, Piña Coladas, and soft drinks from the bar are virtually untraceable, even with a point-of-sale system, unless the sale is entered into the register. The policy that a check or receipt must be printed on each sale is still the only way to control this fraud, but management must routinely check for compliance. In some instances, these virgin drinks and mocktails could be charged as alcohol drinks and rung in as nonalcoholic.

Money can be taken directly from the cash register and be undetectable until the drawer is reconciled at the end of the night. If more than one bartender is working out of a cash drawer, one could steal knowing that they will all have to make it up. But if $60 is taken and each bartender has to ante up $20, the guilty one still comes out $40 ahead. Limit access to cash drawers to one bartender so each is responsible for his or her own cash.

There are only three places where bartenders can keep their "extra earnings": in the register, in their pockets, or in their tip jars. Putting money into their pockets would be risky and likely questioned by management. If a tip jar is used, "extra" money will be placed into it immediately. Without the tip jar, the only other place the money could be is in the register.

Extra funds placed in the tip jar are usually divided among all the bartenders working. Consequently, the bartender who took the extra will likely retrieve it before it is divided, a difficult task to go undetected by the other bartenders. If the cash drawer is the location of the extra earnings, and management, not the bartender counts the drawer at the end of the night; the money will have to be removed from the register before the closing reading. If management suspects that this might be occurring, a random change of the drawer in the middle of the shift will result in cash over in the drawer.

COLLUSION BETWEEN SERVER AND BARTENDER

Again, the greatest likelihood of this type of fraud occurs because management cannot obtain an accurate sales mix of drinks served. If your operation does not have a point-of-sale system, you are vulnerable. With a point-of-sale system, you reduce the likelihood of fraud because your records will reveal that you have a problem.

The most important element of control is getting the transaction recorded and entered into the system *before* the drink is made and served. You can still have control without a point-of-sale system, and restaurant and lounges have used these controls for many years. Steak & Ale restaurants had a very effective system that still works well today in operations with written guest and bar checks. They issued servers separate checks for food and liquor. They did not allow the server to *verbally* transmit the beverage order to the bartender. This simple rule required them to write the order on the beverage check. The bar check was placed in a check rack at the service bar. A system of abbreviations and descriptions was used to identify what was ordered.

The bartender filled the order and placed a grease pencil line under the last drink prepared to indicate it was completed. He did not accept cash but could not make a drink without that check being submitted. The server attached the beverage check to the food check when presenting the bill to the guest for payment.

This system, however, can be beaten as explained by a former student who worked in a hotel lounge. It requires the bartender to be lax about marking the ticket with the grease pencil. This allows the server to "resubmit" the same check when a second round of the same drinks are ordered. Since the server also collects the money, she can collect for all the drinks served but show that only one round is written on the check. She splits her earnings with the bartender at the end of the night. This student related that cocktail waitresses were stealing up to $100 per shift in a very busy downtown commercial hotel lounge. No system is foolproof. You need to check for compliance and make it very clear that noncompliance will result in dismissal and prosecution.

INVENTORY FRAUD

Inventory fraud occurs with beverage as well as food. In operations where month-end inventories are taken to compute cost of food or beverage consumed and sold, verification of inventory is a critically important element of this calculation. In chain-owned corporate restaurants, the corporate or district supervisor or vice president will likely make only a few physical visits to the locations each year unless there are problems with food, labor, or beverage cost.

Each manager is given certain cost standards that they are expected to meet to earn bonuses, raises, and promotions. Some managers have learned how to "manipulate" the numbers to get the results that corporate management expects. One way they always achieve their food and beverage cost percentages is by falsifying their inventory amounts. By overstating their liquor inventories, they will *reduce* the cost of beverage consumed. Thus when that amount is divided by the beverage sales, the smaller cost of beverage consumed produces a lower beverage cost percentage.

Whenever a manager is transferred from one store to another, or when a new bar manager takes over a different store, you must verify the inventory amounts. This is especially important if the previous manager had been at that location for an extended period of time. Since the general manager approves all the reports sent to corporate, he or she will have the opportunity to "adjust" the figures to make costs come out.

We have been told of auditors discovering as much as $15,000 in missing liquor inventory when a new manager took control. Corporate management and ownership must physically certify inventory and petty cash at least once a year to detect this kind of fraud.

In all these cases, the use of *secret shopper* services can help find fraud if you expect it. You instruct the company to send in shoppers to observe bartenders, servers, and management and specifically tell them what you want them to look for.

Serving Alcohol Responsibly

Any restaurant that serves alcoholic beverages must do so responsibly. We must be careful in how we promote and serve alcoholic beverages. The authority to regulate the sale of alcoholic beverages is given to the individual states by the United States Constitution. Each state can decide the age limit for someone to sell or consume, the days that it can be sold, who can sell it (vendors), and what products can be sold by different retailers. Individual states issue licenses to retail alcoholic beverages in the foodservice industry. Within each state there is a regulatory agency that applies and enforces the law through their individual policies. These vary according to state.

The most noteworthy change in the accountability of selling alcoholic beverages is what is referred to as "**Dram Shop Acts/Laws**". Dram shop legislation is written by the individual state legislature and varies according to state. The focus is on the responsibility to the victims and their families of a tragedy as a result of the actions taken by an intoxicated person. In general, not only is the person responsible for causing the tragedy, car accident or a fight, held liable but so is the establishment and the individual who served the intoxicated person. This focus on assigning accountability to the seller is a shift from previous legislation (common law) that exclusively held the person consuming the alcohol responsible.

There are several ways that an operation can limit their exposure to liquor liability. The first and most important is to have policies that are supported and enforced by the owner/operator. These may include employee-training programs. We advocate programs that have been tested for reliability and validity such as ones offered by the National Restaurant Association Educational Foundation or the Educational Institute of the American Hotel and Lodging Association. Both of these programs include an examination and certification upon successful completion of the course. Within both of these programs you will find various methods for prevention and recognition, and suggestions on how to deal with different situations when they occur.

The second is to obtain liquor liability insurance. This is an expense that should be planned for and included in your fixed overhead expenses. By purchasing this insurance you shift the exposure (at some negotiated level of coverage) to the insurance company. The cost of this insurance is based on food and beverage sales volume, the variety of beverage products you serve (liquor, beer, wine), your operating hours (noon to 2 AM versus noon to 9 PM), whether or not you also serve food, the location (geographic population density), and your experience rating (whether you have had any previous incidents).

Lastly, an operation should have continuous and ongoing training in responsible alcohol service. Any server or bartender must be given this training. It is not just something you casually cover in the pre-meal meetings. The attention you give this subject will impact your ability to obtain liability insurance and the premium you will pay. In the event a patron who was served in your establishment is involved in an incident that is alcohol-related, how your employees treated this patron may have a bearing on your legal position should action be taken through dram shop law.

Here are some suggestions for daily reviews; checking ID of patrons who appear to be underage, offering alternative non-alcoholic beverages, development and featuring of specialty non-alcoholic beverages, providing a coffee cart with natural flavorings with dessert. You should also document the items covered in your management log book. Do not let impaired customers drive when they leave the restaurant. Get their keys and call them a cab. Tell them that you will notify the police if they attempt to drive. This will be helpful to you in a reasonable person defense should you ever have an incident involving one of your patrons in a tragedy with a victim.

In actuality, they should never have been allowed to become inebriated in your restaurant. Your servers and bartenders need to know the signs of intoxication. Individuals may have been drinking before they arrive at your restaurant so even counting the number of drinks served cannot be enough. Mood, body type, and mental state all impact the ability to absorb and tolerate alcohol. Remember, it takes the liver one hour to absorb one ounce of alcohol. So, if a patron has more than two ounces of alcohol in an hour, the liver cannot absorb it and it goes into their blood. This is when it affects the ability to think clearly and maintain the motor skills needed for driving. We recommend the Responsible Alcohol Awareness certification offered through the National Restaurant Association as a program you should follow.

Finally, we should mention the fact that society has decided to control the problem by encouraging legislators to enact laws that hold factors in the environment, and the agent responsible for service, accountable. For a very long time, common law only held the host responsible for their actions. Well, if the host is obviously and visibly intoxicated, they are not capable of making rational decisions. That is why interest groups have successfully lobbied lawmakers to use different strategies to address this problem through public policy. Even local law enforcement agencies have increased the frequency of sobriety checkpoints in municipalities to control the public environment.

ey Concepts

- Principles of food cost control can be applied to beverage cost control.
- Beverage cost will always be higher in a foodservice operation than a bar.
- Wine and beer have higher beverage cost (lower mark-up) than mixed drinks.
- Recording of the sales of liquor, beer, and wine needs to be done separately.
- You do not have to purchase an expensive liquor dispensing system to control liquor costs.
- Pricing of beverage items is established and controlled by exclusive distributors of these products and you cannot shop among purveyors for the best price.
- Inventory levels for all bottles kept behind the bar need to be standardized using pars.
- Standardized glassware for all drinks are a part of your "system" and need to be established well in advance of costing/pricing decisions.
- Record all beverage transactions like you do food orders.
- Prices and markup percentages are not based solely on beverage cost.

ey Terms

USAR	Selling Tier	Food to Bar Transfer
GAAP	Well Brand	Cost/Margin Analysis
Beverage	Call Brand	Par Stock
Markup	Premium Call Brand	Perpetual Inventory
Bottle Portion Yield	Management Signing	Empty Bottle Control
Mixed Drink	Bar to Food Transfer	Dram Shop Acts/Laws

iscussion Questions

1. Explain what is considered a "beverage" in cost control and how it is different from what is classified as a beverage in service training.
2. What part of a restaurant's revenue center is more profitable, food or beverage? Can you explain why?

3. What are the "other" factors that affect the pricing strategy of beverage items?

4. What are the reasons that full bottle wine pricing strategy has changed in recent years?

Problem 1

Assume you are the bar manager for the Chicago Steak House and are looking into the impact that each category of alcoholic beverages has on your overall beverage cost percentage. Using the Excel template to calculate your numbers, complete the following spreadsheet and determine which of the two sales mixes, A or B, is the most profitable. Explain why you picked the one you did, citing quantitative data to support your conclusion.

Chapter 9, Problem 1			
	Sales Mix A		
Beverage Sales Mix		**$**	**%**
	Liquor	$12,562	
	Beer	$ 4,720	
	Wine	$ 2,431	
	Total	$ 19,713	
Beverage COGS Mix			
	Liquor	$ 1,532	
	Beer	$ 1,564	
	Wine	$ 925	
	Total	$ 4,021	
Gross Profit Margin "A"			
	Liquor		
	Beer		
	Wine		
	Total		

Sales Mix B		$	%
Beverage Sales Mix			
	Liquor	$ 8,952	
	Beer	$ 5,819	
	Wine	$ 4,942	
	Total	$ 19,713	
Beverage COGS Mix			
	Liquor	$ 1,092	
	Beer	$ 1,926	
	Wine	$ 1,882	
	Total	$ 4,900	
Gross Profit Margin "B"			
	Liquor		
	Beer		
	Wine		
	Total		

Problem 2

Using the Excel template on your disk, complete the following spreadsheets showing activity for the months of April, May and June at Bob Russell's Sports Bar in Decatur, GA. Analyze the three month figures and point out any significant differences between them. What are the reasons for the differences?

April Sales		**$ 33,562**
	add or subtract	
Beginning Inventory		$ 12,564
Purchases		$ 9,264
Total Available for Sale	*equals*	
Ending Inventory		$ 10,924
Cost of Beverage Consumed	*equals*	
Bar to Food Transfers		$ 863
Food to Bar Transfers		$ 1,100
Manager Signing Privileges		$ 659
Complimentary Promotions		$ 4,250
Cost of Beverage Sold	*equals*	
Beverage Cost Percentage for April		
B.C. % without any adjustments		
May Sales		**$ 18,925**
	add or subtract	
Beginning Inventory		$ 10,924
Purchases		$ 8,795
Total Available for Sale	*equals*	
Ending Inventory		$ 9,632
Cost of Beverages Consumed	*equals*	
Bar to Food Transfers	subtract	$ 965
Food to Bar Transfers	Add	$ 963
Manager Signing Privileges	subtract	$ 1,256
Complimentary Promotions	subtract	$ 4,825
Cost of Beverages Sold	*equals*	

Beverage Cost Percentage for May		
B.C. % without any adjustments		
June Sales		**$ 33,579.00**
Beginning Inventory		$ 9,632
Purchases		$ 11,563
Total Available for Sale	*equals*	
Ending Inventory		$ 9,561
Cost of Beverages Consumed	**equals**	
Bar to Food Transfers		$ 1,568
Food to Bar Transfers		$ 1,432
Manager Signing Privileges		$ 1,899
Complimentary Promotions	subtract	$ 3,825
Cost of Beverages Sold	*equals*	
Beverage Cost Percentage for June		
B.C. % without any adjustments		

Problem 3 Cost/Margin Analysis:

Use the following data for this problem.

Item No.	Menu Item	Menu Price	Bev Cost $	No. Sold A	No. Sold B
	Wines by the Glass		**Cost/Margin Sales Analysis Problem**		
1	Kendall-Jackson Chardonnay	$ 8.95	$ 4.32	222	200
2	Penfold's Shiraz	$ 6.50	$ 2.95	158	188
3	Sutter Home Pinot Noir	$ 5.95	$ 2.10	241	123
4	Kendall-Jackson Sauvignon Blanc	$ 8.00	$ 3.25	508	365
5	Jacob's Creek Shiraz Cabernet	$ 6.50	$ 2.45	365	508
6	Louis Jardot Beaujolais-Village	$ 5.95	$ 2.75	151	223
7	St. Michelle Chardonnay	$10.00	$ 4.85	123	241
8	Coppla Cabernet Sauvignon	$ 9.95	$ 3.65	188	158
9	Cakebread Cellars Chardonnay	$11.00	$ 4.95	59	81
10	Sterling Vineyards Merlot	$ 8.00	$ 3.90	223	151
	Totals			2238	2238

Using the Cost/Margin disk that came with your text, enter the data from the table below to complete this problem. *Open up the cost margin program for beverage and use the "Wine" tab, located at the bottom of the page for Sales Mix "A" and the "Beer" tab next to the wine tab for Sales Mix "B". Do not change the names of the tabs or the macros will malfunction.* When you print your graphs, use the "individual" option, not the "summary" option. Using the data found on the spreadsheets and graphs, answer the following questions.

1. Which Wine by the Glass Menu Items have the "best" beverage cost percentages?

                Item   Bev Cost %

    1st   ____   ____

    2nd ____   ____

    3rd   ____   ____

2. Which Wine by the Glass Menu Items have the "worst" beverage cost percentages?

	Item	Bev Cost %
1st	____	____
2nd	____	____
3rd	____	____

3. Which wines have the "best" *individual* contribution margin/gross profit?

	Item	Indiv. CM/GP
1st	____	____
2nd	____	____
3rd	____	____

4. Which wines return the "best" *total or weighted* contribution margin?

	Sales Mix A Menu Item	Sales Mix A Wgtd CM $	Sales Mix B Menu Item	Sales Mix B Wgtd CM $
1st	____	____	____	____
2nd	____	____	____	____
3rd	____	____	____	____

5. Which Sales Mix, A or B, returns the best weighted/potential beverage cost percentage? Show the amounts for both.

6. Which sales mix, A or B, returns the best weighted contribution margin/gross profit? Indicate the actual amount.

7. Using the Cost/Margin diskette that came with the text, enter the data for this problem and print the graphs for both sales mixes using the Miller Matrix, Menu Engineering, and Cost Margin Analysis. *You will have a total of six graphs.* Using the following table, summarize all the menu items that fall into each category. *Note: A beverage item may appear more than once in the same category because of the common elements within the three methodologies.*

	Sales Mix A	Sales Mix B	Total A	Total B
Primes				
Stars				
Winners				
Standards				
Plowhorses				
HCHV Marginals				
Sleepers				
Puzzles				
LCLV Marginals				
Problems				
Dogs				
Losers				
Totals				

Based on the graph data, which sales mix would you say is better? _____

Considering all the information you have at your disposal, including graphs and spreadsheets, potential beverage cost percentage and individual and weighted contribution margin, indicate which sales mix is financially superior and why. You must back up your answer with *quantifiable data.* Follow the logic in the explanation of "the fallacy of gross profit" at the end of Chapter 3, Food Cost Control and apply the same principle to your beverage analysis.

Problem 4

1. The owners of the Trick Dog Café want you to compare the beer and wine sales for two months, March and September, and tell them why their beverage costs at the end of each month were different. Utilizing the Cost/Margin Beverage Sales Analysis diskette provided with your text, enter the data below in separate categories and run a summary of the results of each. Print out the graphs using Cost/Margin and Menu Engineering. Compare the results.

   ■ What items are Primes and Stars? What items are Problems and Dogs? Comment on the similarity or differences in the items identified. On which items do the three menu sales mix programs agree?

- When they do disagree, examine the characteristics of the item as to beverage cost percentage, individual contribution margin, number sold, and weighted contribution margin to see the reason for their disagreement.
- What is the Potential Beverage Cost of the entire sales mix for each month? Which month has the best financial results and why?

Item No.	Item Name	No. Sold March	No. Sold Sept.	Menu Price	Item Beverage Cost
0	Beer				
1	Bud	59	80	$2.95	$0.62
2	Coors Lite		2	$2.95	$0.62
3	Miller Lite	143	157	$2.95	$0.62
4	Corona	94	107	$3.75	$0.95
5	Heineken	50	58	$3.75	$0.90
6	Mobjack Pale	68	89	$3.75	$0.57
7	Bass Ale		36	$3.50	$1.09
8	Amstel Lite	27	28	$3.75	$0.91
9	Kaliber	47	31	$3.75	$0.93
10	Trick Dog	136	102	$3.25	$0.57
11	Legend	26	31	$3.50	$0.53
12	Wild Goose	20	55	$3.95	$0.51
13	Tucher Heffe		33	$3.95	$0.97
14	Bud Light	122	115	$2.95	$0.62
15	Flying Dog	5	17	$3.95	$0.90
16	Flying Dog Draft	55	0	$2.95	$.62
	Total				

Item No.	Item Name	No. Sold March	No. Sold Sept.	Menu Price	Item Beverage Cost
0	**Wine By-the-Glass**				
1	Don Conde Brut	47	58	$4.95	$0.58
2	Alamos Chard	155	256	$4.95	$1.33
3	Borgo Pinot Grigio	109	74	$5.25	$1.50
4	Guy Saget Vouvray	32	17	$5.75	$1.50
5	Ingleside Viognier	0	6	$7.50	$4.00
6	Joe Ballard Sauv Blanc	20	34	$5.50	$1.65
7	Latour Macon Chard	21	45	$5.25	$1.65
8	Barboursville Phileo	1	6	$5.25	$1.04
9	Boillot Bourgogne Pinot	47	0	$7.25	$2.33
10	Cline Cotes d'Oakley	34	23	$5.25	$1.50
11	Blushing Dog	15	30	$4.95	$1.40
12	Feudi Merlot	107	79	$4.95	$1.75
13	Alamos Cabernet	74	69	$4.95	$1.65
14	Jaboulet Parallele	0	3	$5.25	$1.84
15	Domaine Artois Dry Rose	0	1	$5.25	$1.33
16	Fife Merlot	6	22	$10.00	$5.06
17	Chateau La Paws	1	6	$6.00	$2.25
18	Dry Creek Cabernet	0	19	$12.00	$6.00
19	Seghezio Zinfandel	31	30	$6.25	$3.04
20	Oakencroft Merlot	23	0	$5.50	$2.42
21	Ingleside Cabernet	0	0	$5.50	$2.54
22	Ch. Maltroye Bourgogne	0	0	$7.25	$2.75
23	Churchill 10 Year Port	0	3	$6.00	$2.20
24	Graham's 20 Year Port	0	0	$7.00	$3.50

(continued)

Item No.	Item Name	No. Sold March	No. Sold Sept.	Menu Price	Item Beverage Cost
25	P/M Chardonnay	35	0	$5.25	$1.75
26	Dry Creek Reserve	10	0	$12.50	$6.00
27	Aresti Merlot	15	0	$7.25	$1.34
28	Fess Parker Chardonnay	74	0	$8.50	$2.22
29	Ubet Shiraz	35	0	$5.50	$1.78
	Total				

Item No.	Item Name	No. Sold March	No. Sold Sept.	Menu Price	Item Beverage Cost
0	**Bottle Wines**				
1	Don Conde Brut	2	0	$20.00	$4.66
2	J & Jacques Berat Brut	7	4	$60.00	$15.00
3	Mumm's Cuvee Napa	7	4	$40.00	$16.42
4	Billecart Brut Rose	0	0	$125.00	$46.66
5	Alamos Chardonay	0	0	$24.00	$5.99
6	Rapidan River Riesling	0	0	$20.00	$7.33
7	Borgo Pinot Grigio	25	13	$18.00	$5.99
8	Guy Saget Vouvray	1	0	$25.00	$5.99
9	Civrac Lagrange Graves	5	3	$23.00	$5.00
10	Joe Ballard Sauv Blanc	5	3	$18.00	$6.59
11	Mills Reef Sauv Blanc	1	18	$28.00	$10.66
12	Fess Parker Chard	12	9	$33.00	$9.99
13	Sonoma Cutrer Chard	5	5	$50.00	$19.99
14	Genot Boulanger Montrac	1	4	$68.00	$25.99
15	Latour Macon Chard	1	1	$20.00	$6.59

(continued)

Item No.	Item Name	No. Sold March	No. Sold Sept.	Menu Price	Item Beverage Cost
16	Prince Michel Chard	2	16	$21.00	$6.99
17	Catena Chard	4	9	$38.00	$11.99
18	ZD Chard	0	3	$82.00	$35.99
19	Cline Cotes d'Oakley	4	0	$22.00	$5.99
20	Blushing Dog	1	3	$18.00	$6.79
21	Ingle Brut	0	0	$32.00	$18.54
22	Clicquot La Grande Dame	0	0	$225.00	$100.00
23	Jaboulet 45	1	1	$21.00	$7.33
24	Thomas Mitchell Marsanne	0	6	$28.00	$6.66
25	Alessandria Barolo	4	5	$39.00	$16.66
26	Domaine Artois Dry Rose	0	0	$22.00	$5.32
27	Syrah-Syrah	2	1	$30.00	$7.99
28	De Cheil Pinot Noir	4	2	$30.00	$11.99
29	Clos Daviaud St. Emilion	2	2	$38.00	$9.99
30	Barboursbille Barbera	0	0	$26.00	$10.39
31	Thomas Mitchell Shiraz	9	2	$28.00	$6.66
32	Fife Merlot	0	0	$48.00	$20.25
33	La Magia Rosso	1	2	$31.00	$10.99
34	Chateau Montrose	0	1	$90.00	$47.99
35	Cape Mentelle Shiraz	0	2	$35.00	$13.99
36	J Lohr Cabernet	2	1	$48.00	$19.17
37	Aresti Merlot	4	4	$28.00	$5.99
38	Chateau La Paws	0	3	$25.00	$8.99
39	Dry Creek Cabernet	3	11	$49.00	$23.99

(*continued*)

Item No.	Item Name	No. Sold March	No. Sold Sept.	Menu Price	Item Beverage Cost
40	Seghezio Zinfandel	4	8	$29.00	$11.25
41	Panther Creek Pinot Noir	2	1	$55.00	$34.99
42	David Bruce Pinot Noir	2	4	$69.00	$28.66
43	Oakencroft Merlot	4	6	$25.00	$9.67
44	Catena Cabernet	0	0	$36.00	$13.99
45	Chateau Maltroye Bourg	0	0	$28.00	$10.99
46	Boillot Bourgogne Pinot Noir	7	0	$28.00	$9.99
47	Ubet Shiraz	7	0	$22.00	$7.99
48	House Chardonnay	5	0	$22.00	$5.32
49	House Merlot	2	0	$22.00	$5.66
50	House Cabernet	2	0	$22.00	$6.59
	Total				

From the results, why is there a sizable difference in the potential cost of beverage sold between the two periods? What happened within the sales mix? Which menu category had the biggest change? What would be some of the reasons for this kind of change in the sales mix of beer and wine? Cite the information from the spreadsheets and graphs to support your conclusions.

Problem 5

Given the following spreadsheet with the three tiers of categories of alcoholic beverages sold in your restaurant, calculate the portion costs, cost percentage, contribution margin dollars, and contribution margin percentage. Use the Excel spreadsheet on your diskette to calculate your numbers.

Tier Level	Category	Item	Bottle Cost	Portion Yield	Portion Cost	Selling Price	Cost %	Cont Marg $	Cont Marg %
I	Scotch	Inverhouse	$8.17	21		$3.25			
II	Scotch	Dewar's White Label	$21.68	13		$4.50			
III	Scotch	Johnny Walker Black	$28.39	17		$5.75			
I	Whiskey	Haller's	$7.42	21		$3.25			
II	Whiskey	Seagram's 7	$13.18	13		$4.50			
III	Whiskey	Crown Royal	$21.98	17		$5.75			
I	Bourbon	Mattingley & Moore	$6.25	21		$3.25			
II	Bourbon	Jim Beam	$12.39	13		$4.50			
III	Bourbon	Jack Daniels	$15.40	17		$5.75			

	Category	Brand				
I	Rum	Castillo	$8.27	21		$3.25
II	Rum	Bacardi Silver	$14.62	13		$4.50
III	Rum	Bacardi 151	$17.63	17		$5.75
I	Vodka	Popov	$5.26	21		$3.25
II	Vodka	Smirnoff 80	$10.85	13		$4.50
III	Vodka	Stoyli	$18.38	17		$5.75
I	Gin	Bowman's	$5.67	21		$3.25
II	Gin	Beefeater	$18.02	13		$4.50
III	Gin	Tanqueray	$18.27	17		$5.75
I	Tequilla	Montezuma	$6.72	21		$3.25
II	Tequilla	Jose Cuervo Gold	$15.26	13		$4.50
III	Tequilla	Jose Cuervo 1800	$22.63	17		$5.75

10
Labor Productivity Analysis

■   ■   ■   ■   ■   ■   ■   ■   □   □

1. You need more than the traditional labor cost percentage to accurately measure worker productivity and scheduling efficiency.

2. You do not control labor cost by paying low wages.

3. If you want to increase worker productivity, you need to invest in your employees.

4. Labor cost must be pre-controlled.

5. Scheduling is the key to effective labor cost control.

6. Turnover will happen, however it can be controlled.

7. Management is the key to improved employee productivity.

8. Paying higher wages to a lazy employee will not improve their productivity.

9. Labor cost can only be reduced so far.

10. Not all employees are equal. Don't schedule them like they are.

When restaurant executives are asked to indicate the most strategic issues facing the industry in the immediate future, in almost all surveys labor costs and turnover will very likely be mentioned. Increasing costs cannot continue to be passed on in the form of higher prices without impacting customer counts and market share.

Top management must recognize the need to improve on operating efficiencies or run the risk of being displaced by more efficient operators. The challenge is to improve efficiencies and increase worker productivity so fewer can do more. The initial steps are to establish standards for employee productivity and control labor costs.

You cannot control labor costs until you realize that you are not hiring people but rather purchasing a potential to do work. The only conceivable reason for hiring or scheduling an additional employee is that certain work needs to be done and that person will be able to do the required job.

In the United States, employee benefits are approaching 50 percent of an employee's "real wage cost." The federal and state government have supported efforts to pass legislation requiring operators to offer medical insurance and paid maternity leave, on top of unemployment insurance, workers' compensation insurance, and Social Security. When voluntary vacation pay, sick leave, bereavement, life insurance, and disability benefits are added to administrative payroll costs, this percentage will continue to increase.

An employee's "real wage" is far greater than his or her total net pay, whether computed on a hourly rate or as straight salary. You can estimate that an employee's total remuneration, deferred or otherwise, is at least double his or her earnings before taxes. Added benefits and fringes are becoming a necessity to attract and retain qualified employees. Therefore, *total labor cost* is defined as *any cost incurred as a result of employing a worker*. A list of labor-related expenses are shown in Figure 10–1.

Hourly wage, weekly salary, holiday pay, bonus pay, sick leave, vacation, bereavement leave, meals, uniforms, shift and holiday differential, insurance (all), retirement plans, severance pay, training costs, recruiting costs, employee development programs, educational expense reimbursement, travel expenses, moving allowances and expenses, loans, Social Security, discounts on meals, recreational or social activities, and sponsorships

---

FIGURE 10–1
Costs of Employing a Worker

Labor Supply and Demand

Labor costs have always been a significant concern of both independent and chain restaurant operators. The supply of potential employees who are willing to work at low starting wages is diminishing every year. The industry is not attracting enough young people as a long-term career choice. Employment in food service continues to be an entry level for unskilled, uneducated individuals of all ages. The industry continues to report that there are an insufficient number of "qualified" applicants. This may be due in part to the low entry-level pay and low quality of life associated with the foodservice industry. To make matters worse, we do not do an adequate job in selecting applicants for jobs. After running an ad in the newspaper and hardly getting a call, we rationalize that we are not going to get a qualified applicant so we hire the "best of the lot" from those who did apply.

When demand exceeds the supply of qualified applicants, management often resorts to adopting a rationale of selecting the "best applicants" even when they do not meet their original minimal qualifications for the position. When we are operating shorthanded and need some relief, we are forced to lower our standards to fill the open position. However, in the long run, we create a self-fulfilling prophecy of high labor turnover and poor productivity. Then we exacerbate our labor woes by not adequately training the unskilled employees. We complain that employees today have poor work habits and a bad attitude about working in foodservice operations. Maybe we expect them to come already trained and motivated. Another fatal error we make is failing to provide adequate supervision while on the job.

Basic management principles tell us that unskilled workers need more direct supervision than skilled workers. Without adequate training or supervision, is it any wonder that we get poor productivity, bad service, waste, and inefficiency in our operations? When management and workers are unhappy, the result is high turnover and low retention rates. It is a self-fulfilling prophecy without an end in sight. When demand for labor exceeds supply, we begin to treat good employees with more respect and appreciation. We want to keep them and not surprisingly, wage rates go up. We begin to understand that a manager or cook needs to have "quality time" away from the stress and pressures of the business. We develop more of a human relations attitude toward our employees.

However, when business is down and labor in excess supply, we abandon the human relations approach and return to the "bottom line mentality." We stop increasing wages, eliminate the higher paid hourly and salaried workers, and work the remaining employees six and seven days a week without adequate time off. The quality of life issues are thrown out the window.

We continue to expect employees to "adapt" to a "workaholic" environment and lifestyle.

Quality of Life Issues

Today, men and women do not feel it is right to have to make a choice between their family and professional career; they want both. When 25-year-old college graduates who had a full social life are suddenly given a schedule that takes their social life away from them, it is not surprising that they leave the industry for other careers after just four or five years. Research has shown that there is no correlation between work ethic or previous experience and industry burnout. Even the employee with a workaholic mentality eventually gets burned out, albeit a little later than some of the others (Pavesic and Brymer, 1990 and Brymer and Pavesic, 1990).

We seem to be saying to employees that they have to "adapt to the industry environment" rather than changing the conditions in the industry that are contributing to the attrition rate affecting many good people. The industry environment is "killing off" many potential employees. There are still some around who can deal with the long hours, low pay, and high stress. However, as the industry grows, there are fewer of those kinds of employees in existence. The industry needs to address this before its too late. It is not the intention of this chapter to get into the factors that create turnover and lower worker productivity. This is a subject for our colleagues in the human resources area. Yet we note other reasons for high labor costs and low productivity including poor layout and design of operation, lack of labor-saving equipment, poor scheduling, and no regular detailed system to collect and analyze payroll data.

Labor Cost Standards

A continuing dialogue exists between top management and operations management concerning labor cost standards with top management inclined to give priority to low labor cost percentages and to monitoring the ratio of payroll to sales. Unit managers tend to rationalize higher labor cost percentages on a qualitative as well as quantitative basis. They reason that the level of service provided to the customer is equally important to income and profits.

During periods when labor cost percentages are low and service is at its best, both top and unit management are in harmony on labor cost. However, when labor costs are high and service has not been improved in proportion to the additional costs incurred, top management will demand a reduction in labor cost.

Both levels of management need to have a common benchmark to analyze labor productivity effectively. The traditional measure of labor cost—the ratio of payroll to total sales revenue—is a poor measure of labor productivity. The *Uniform System of Accounts for Restaurants* (USAR) groups management salaries with hourly payroll when reporting industry labor cost figures. While this is an acceptable accounting practice, it is better to separate management and hourly payroll for cost and productivity analysis.

Salaries for management are really "fixed" labor costs, and in multi-unit chain operations, starting salaries are negotiated by corporate administrators, not unit managers. Salaries of managers should be included in administrative overhead on the income statement. The payroll shown in examples in this chapter reflects only hourly employees hired, trained, and scheduled by unit management.

As stated earlier, labor cost can be defined as any cost incurred as a result of employing a worker, but labor cost analysis focuses primarily on hourly wages and employment taxes when examining labor cost. According to the latest figures in the Restaurant Industry Operations Report for 2002, p. 48, the average labor cost percentage, excluding benefits, for full-service restaurants with average check per person <$25 ranged from a low of 25.0 percent to a high of 34.5 percent.

If you were asked to give a "good" labor cost percent goal, it would be difficult to quote a single percentage applicable to all types of operations. As a rule of thumb, labor costs, including employee benefits and payroll taxes will run in the low to mid thirties. In many operations, the labor cost percentage exceeds the food cost percentage. However, there is no *average labor cost* standard that can be cited that would be representative for every foodservice operation. That is why we believe that you must look at the *combined* food and labor cost percentage, referred to as *prime* cost. Table 10.1 shows some possible cost ratios for different types of restaurant operations. Note how the labor cost percentage varies.

Generally speaking, each operation's financial idiosyncrasies make its food, beverage, labor, and prime cost unique, so it is impractical to arrive at a useful and valid industry average. Since labor cost is calculated based on *total* sales revenue, those operations serving liquor will run a lower payroll ratio than operations without liquor. This is because the gross profit return on every dollar of beverage revenue is much higher than that on each dollar of food revenue. Here we can say with a high degree of confidence that regardless of the type of food service operation, keeping your prime costs in the mid-sixties, e.g. 64–67 percent, should result in sufficient gross profit to cover fixed and overhead expenses and produce a profit.

Table 10.1   Prime Cost Examples

	Local Steak House	Fast Food	Hotel Dining	Units Earning Profits	Units Incurring Losses
Food Cost %	49	41	34***	41	41
Beverage Cost %	25	0	18	28	29
Total Cost %*	42	41	28.5	37	39
Payroll Cost %	24	19**	34****	31	37
Prime Cost %	66	60	62.5	68	76

*% of total food and beverage sales

**Automation, training, labor-saving equipment keep it low

***Higher overhead of downtown locations requires lower food cost

****Union wages

Deficiencies of the Traditional Labor Cost Ratio

The traditional labor cost ratio calls management's attention to higher payroll percentages, but it has some definite deficiencies. First, it is an *aggregate* labor cost ratio and therefore too generalized to interpret. Typically, we report the entire weekly or monthly payroll as a single figure. Since the figure is compiled from employees in all job categories (i.e., wait staff, cooks, bartenders, busboys, dishwashers, etc.), it is impossible to tell from the percentage which employee or employee group, and which day or meal period may have caused the variance.

Second, percentages calculated for weekly or monthly periods are historical, after-the-fact figures. The information comes too late to do anything about it. To be effectively controlled, variations in labor cost must be monitored at least weekly and preferably daily. In some cases, hour-by-hour labor scheduling is conducted.

Third, since labor cost has a large "fixed cost" element as well as a variable element, it is subject to showing percentage increases or decreases that vary inversely with sales levels. When business is good, the ratio of payroll to sales is low. Exactly the opposite occurs when sales are low. This decline or increase in the percentage of sales is in no way an indication that labor productivity is higher or lower; it is partially due to the fixed cost component of labor cost. As sales increase, the payroll percentage will usually decrease without any direct managerial action.

In addition, the ratio can be further distorted by menu price increases and wage rate increases. This too is caused by the fact that labor cost has both fixed and variable cost components. The fixed cost portion is not just salaries, but the cost of scheduling the employees needed at the slowest time, day, or meal period of the week. The minimum staff needed to start a meal period, whether there are customers being served or not, is the lowest payroll can be if the restaurant opens for business. Fixed cost labor is the bare bones or skeleton crew. Even when sales revenues fall to their lowest levels, a minimum staff must still be scheduled. During these periods, further reduction in labor hours is not feasible. Cost can only be reduced so far and then only increases in sales can lower the labor cost percentage. If management is required to act as host, cook, and bartender to cut payroll costs, the restaurant will likely be close to closing its doors. Eventually, you have to increase your sales.

The variable portion of labor cost are those employees added to the schedule as business volume warrants. Few restaurants bring in the entire crew at the same time. They arrive on staggered schedules corresponding to the customers in the restaurant. On busy nights, more servers and bus help are scheduled to handle the increased volume of business. It is the overscheduling of variable cost labor that puts payroll figures over standard costs.

Labor cost does not increase proportionally with sales increases; therefore, changes in sales levels will cause the traditional labor cost ratio to fluctuate. Table 10.2 shows three different sales levels of a restaurant and the resulting impact on labor cost. In this case, it is assumed that minimum or fixed labor is adequate to handle the volume of business. Only certain employee classifications are increased when customer counts increase. Eventually, no additional employees can be added to a particular shift regardless of business level because they become counterproductive; for example, putting three bartenders on two stations, adding additional servers, and reducing the station size.

While, in Table 10.2, the productivity of the employees definitely improved from period I to III as the same number of employees had to handle 40 more customers, it is no reflection of poor productivity in period I. The operation could not reduce labor, and the only thing that improved the labor cost ratio was the increase in sales.

To prove that reliance on the traditional ratio of labor cost to sales can result in some incorrect conclusions about labor productivity and scheduling efficiency, consider the following figures in Table 10.3 from two identical

Table 10.2   Impact of Sales on Labor Cost Ratio

	I	II	III
Customer Count	80	100	120
Sales @ $10 Average Check	$800	$1,000	$1,200
Fixed Labor	$200	$200	$200
Labor Cost %	25%	20%	16.6%

Table 10.3   Labor Cost Analysis

	Unit A	Unit B
Sales	$28,636	$32,593
Payroll	$8,856	$8,856
Payroll %	30.9%	27.2%
Labor Hours	2,360	2,360
Cost per Labor Hour	$3.75	$3.75
Sales per Labor Hour	$12.13	$13.81
Average Check	$5.50	$7.30
Covers	5,206	4,465
Covers/Labor Hour	2.2	1.9
Labor Cost/Cover	$1.70	$1.98

restaurants in different locations. In addition to the traditional labor cost percentage, four other ratios are offered to assess productivity more discriminately.

From the information in Table 10-3, which unit is using labor more productively? The majority of us would look at the traditional labor cost ratio and feel very confident that Unit B, with the lower labor cost percentage, would be the one. It has a higher sales level and a higher average check than Unit A. The sales are greater for Unit B, but sales alone do not indicate better employee productivity. What if you discovered that Unit B was located in a tourist area of the city and Unit A in a residential area? Do you think the spending habits of the restaurant clientele would be affected by location?

The payroll is identical for both locations since they are the same size with identical layouts. The next figure is *labor hours* worked and that, too, is identical for both locations. Thus the average *cost per labor hour* is also the same at both locations. The only differences to this point are the sales and labor cost percentages.

While *sales per labor hour* and *average check* are higher at Unit B, neither are indicators that labor is being utilized more productively. Tourists are more likely to purchase appetizers, wine, and desserts than local residents. It is a classic example of the spending habits of clientele "dining out" and "eating out" discussed in Chapter 6. Most would still feel comfortable with their decision that Unit B is doing a better job with labor cost.

The number of covers (customers or meals) served is higher at Unit A, which seems somewhat contradictory to the previous information. Ask yourself, "What criteria does management use when making up employee schedules and determining how many employees are needed?" Most will respond with *the number of customers we expect to serve.* Thus customer count must be included in any labor productivity analysis.

The number of *covers per labor hour* was greater at Unit A, and the *labor cost per cover* was also lower. Although Unit A had a higher labor cost percentage, it is getting more productivity out of its employees than Unit B. In fact, if Unit B had been as productive as Unit A, its payroll should have been only $7,590.50 ($1.70 × 4,465), which would have meant a labor cost ratio of 23.3 percent instead of the 27.2 percent.

Using such nonproductive indicators as the traditional labor cost ratio, sales per labor hour, and average check to assess labor productivity, we would end up criticizing the manager of Unit A and praising the manager of Unit B. Criteria such as covers per labor hour and labor cost per cover are needed to get the complete picture of payroll management and productivity. This same information is used to establish employee schedules and hold payroll costs in check.

Much of the necessary data needed for this analysis is already collected and reported elsewhere in the cost control system. It is part of the daily sales reports and weekly payroll reports. All that needs to be done is to put this information into a format conducive for analysis.

Management must have an accurate index of **labor productivity**. Simply stated, productivity is the relationship between output of goods or services and the input of manpower, money, or materials. When output grows faster than input, goods and services are being produced more efficiently and at a lower per unit cost, thereby generating a rise in productivity.

No single measure can be used to evaluate labor productivity efficiently; therefore, management must employ multiple measures collectively. The five additional measures that need to be included with the traditional labor cost ratio are:

1. Total labor hours
2. Sales per labor hour
3. Covers per labor hour
4. Labor cost per labor hour
5. Labor cost per cover

TOTAL LABOR HOURS

Each time payroll is processed, total labor hours worked is tallied. When there is a variance in the total hours actually worked compared to those scheduled, management must investigate to discover the reason for the overage. If labor hours are further broken down by job categories (e.g., busboys, cooks, dishwashers, etc.), the employee category causing the overage can be discovered. See Table 10.4.

Table 10.4 Total Labor Hours by Job Categories

Job Category	Labor Hours	% Labor Hours	Payroll $	% Payroll	LC/LH	Sales/LH	Covers/LH	LC/Cover
Servers	850	36	1912.50	22	$2.25	$33.69	6	$.37
Busboys	500	21	1875.00	21	$3.75	$57.27	10	$.36
Dishwashers	85	4	318.75	3.5	$3.75	$336.89	61	$.06
Hostesses	80	3	383.50	4.3	$4.79	$357.95	65	$.07
Cashiers	40	2	190.00	2	$4.75	$715.90	130	$.04
Cooks	605	26	3176.25	36	$5.25	$47.33	9	$.61
Bartenders	200	8	1000.00	11.2	$5.00	$143.18	26	$.19
Totals	2360	100	8856.00	100	$3.75 (avg)	$12.13 (avg)	2.2 (avg)	$1.70

LC/LH = Labor Cost per Labor Hour
Sales/LH = Sales per Labor Hour
Covers/LH = Covers per Labor Hour
LC/Cover = Labor Cost per Cover

SALES PER LABOR HOUR

This index is only marginally better than the aggregate labor cost percentage and has some weaknesses that must be carefully noted. It is calculated by dividing sales by the total labor hours worked. Many fast-food operators have used this figure to schedule labor hours. For example, if the standard were sales of $25 per labor hour, one employee is scheduled based on the hourly sales divided by $25. Thus if sales of $125 per hour were forecasted, up to five labor hours could be scheduled during that hour.

If the operation's sales per labor hour met or exceeded the standard, the manager is thought to be scheduling his labor productively. This conclusion has proven to be inadequate for several reasons. First, with menu price increases, this index will appear to improve without scheduling changes. Second, many fastfood operations with drive-through windows found that labor hours scheduled according to a sales per labor hour standard were sometimes inadequate to provide the level of service needed to satisfy customers. The drive-through window resulted in a significant increase in the number of transactions (the fastfood equivalent of customer counts and average check). In addition, fastfood operations soon discovered that breakfast required more transactions to achieve the sales per labor hour standard because of a lower average transaction amount than lunch and dinner.

In some operations, sales per labor hour are decreasing even with rising prices. This may indicate poor worker productivity, but it can at least be partially explained by the fact that many operations are opening earlier and staying open longer in an attempt to maximize the use of their physical facilities. In 24-hour operations, a skeleton crew must be on hand during the early morning hours when business is so slow that even the minimum number of employees cannot be kept productive. It can also be attributed in part to the high percentage of part-time workers who are inexperienced. Until these workers are trained and gain experience, their productivity is generally lower than more seasoned workers.

COVERS PER LABOR HOUR

Because of the inefficiencies of the sales per labor hour index, operators switched to what is perhaps the most "inflation-proof" indicator of productivity, *covers per labor hour.* Here the customer count or meals served is divided by the total number of labor hours worked. The covers per labor hour is also calculated for each job category.

Covers or customer counts are not distorted the way sales are affected by price increases. Although operations typically experience declines in customer counts after price increases, covers per labor hour remains the most effective indicator of employee productivity from month to month.

LABOR COST PER LABOR HOUR

This index is calculated by dividing total payroll by total labor hours. One can readily see the wage differential between employee job classifications when labor cost per labor hour is calculated for each job category. This information can assist management in establishing wage ranges for the various job categories. In both food-only operations and operations serving both food and beverage, service employees (e.g., servers, hostess, cashier, bus help, etc.) account for the greatest percentage of total payroll. In food-only operations, preparation labor is next in percentage of total payroll while in food and beverage operations, the management and administrative employee category is the second greatest percentage of total payroll.

An aggregate **labor cost percentage** of 27.5 percent does not indicate how much each employee category contributes to the total percentage. By calculating the percentage of total payroll for each employee category, areas where payroll costs are concentrated can be isolated to show where the greatest savings can be obtained.

LABOR COST PER COVER

This index is calculated by dividing payroll by the number of covers served during the period the payroll covers. Analysis of this index by job category will reveal the employee group with the highest and lowest cost per cover. This index is affected by the wages paid and will show distinct differences because of the usual wage differentials between bus help, cooks, hostesses, bartenders, etc. and the number of employees scheduled for the meal period. For example, there will be more servers than cooks and more busboys than bartenders scheduled on any given day.

Productivity Standards

Before productivity standards can be established, relevant data must be assembled and analyzed. The following steps are necessary to establish the information base required to develop productivity standards for any given restaurant.

The determination of realistic productivity standards, those that are attainable, involves careful planning. In order to accomplish this, standards must be developed from and be representative of actual on-the-job conditions. A standard of productivity must be general enough to compensate for different employees and the actual circumstances of the task and work environment. It also must be specific enough to be used repeatedly without capriciousness on the part of the evaluator.

Before attempting to develop any standard of employee performance, an operator must first have a clear and detailed image of the restaurant. This includes an understanding of the quality standards for food and beverage offered, the level of service, and the nature of the clientele. Only then can productivity standards be set realistically and practically.

Realistic minimum activity levels must be established for each job classification. An efficient measurement must be made of both *the amount of work that must be accomplished within a time frame* and *the qualitative level of performance required.* These activity levels are then used as the standard of performance for scheduling employees in each job category.

Once the products and service to be offered have been determined and what jobs will exist as a result, it becomes possible to determine the regular assignment of work. The first jobs filled are the *fixed labor* positions that must be staffed regardless of sales volume.

Do not expect overall industry standards or those of a competitor to work for your operation. Develop standards that reflect the uniqueness of your operation. No sound automatic rules of thumb can apply to any given restaurant and be accurate. Review labor hours worked by job categories. Break the payroll information down by days and meal periods. Observe employees at work and judge their productive effort throughout their shift.

You will quickly identify the employees and shifts with the best and poorest productive efforts. Use the most productive employees as the minimum standard for that job category. Keep in mind that employees cannot be expected to perform at 100 percent efficiency all shift long; they are not machines. Many do feel, however, that productivity can be immensely improved if the work effort expended averages 75 percent over the workday. An average of 90 percent for a shift would be close to optimum productivity. Ask questions like: What makes an efficient dishwasher? What is it that makes Tom a more productive dishwasher than Bill? How many covers can be served before it is necessary to schedule a second dishwasher? What you are doing is conducting a form of *work analysis* utilized by industrial engineers in designing assembly lines and workstations. Your observations help ascertain whether quality as well as quantity standards are being met in the performance of the job at various levels of business activity. The information gathered will serve as a basis for job descriptions as well as setting staffing guidelines. It may also reveal inefficiencies and the opportunity for improving operations with labor-saving equipment, a more efficient layout of the equipment, and changes in the ingredients to eliminate certain steps completely.

SETTING UP A REPORTING AND EVALUATION SYSTEM

The measurement criteria used to analyze labor productivity must be held constant over time. If the criteria change, interpretation against historical records is clouded. For example, customers or covers must be counted by the meal period. It must be perfectly clear as to who is to be counted as *one cover*. Do you count small children? Do you count adults ordering only coffee? How do you count children in high chairs or boosters seats? These management decisions can be different from one operation to another. The important thing is to do it one way consistently.

A restaurant that had been operating for about seven years kept track of customer counts through counting the number in the party listed on the guest check. Then for some reason, it stopped including customers who ordered only coffee. The restaurant had a counter where these coffee drinkers would regularly come on a daily basis. Although it is management's prerogative as to how to "count customers," the problem with this change in policy made comparisons to past records impossible. If the customer count was down, it was usually explained with the coffee customers. However, there was no way to tell what was really happening. Average check increased and covers per labor hour decreased by simply eliminating the coffee-only customers. The variances that were showing up were at least partially influenced by the changing of the criteria, not employee productivity.

A stable database is necessary if one expects to pre-control labor cost. Pre-control implies advance planning versus after-the-fact corrective action. You wish to maximize profits first as opposed to reducing the losses after the damage has occurred. Scheduling too much labor is an expense that can never be recovered. The comparison of data from past periods to current figures is very important in pre-controlling labor cost. The essence of pre-controlling costs is knowing where you are going as opposed to using the information to discover where you've been.

The point-of-sale computer systems being used today make gathering of productivity information easy, accurate, and timely. In fact, several systems have employees using the system like a time clock to time in and out. The programs can calculate all the productivity indicators automatically and print them out at any time.

The information is collected, summarized, and printed out in a comparative analysis against previous periods and budget standards, showing positive or negative variances. Breaking the payroll data down by job categories will show management where scheduling needs to be adjusted. The faster management is made aware of negative variances and trends, the faster they can take preventive measures to keep them from reoccurring.

PREPARING FORECASTS FROM THE INFORMATION

Data must be gathered regularly, treated as critically as opening and closing readings of the cash register, and assembled at least every pay period. Many operations, especially when labor costs are excessive, accumulate data daily and even by meal periods to keep on top of the problem.

A minimum test period of four to five weeks is recommended before forecasting labor hour requirements can be reasonably representative. As time goes by and the historical database increases, the easier it is to predict customer counts. Any external factors that may influence the volume of business should be noted. The initial test period should include periods of both high and low volume. You need to arrive at the standards you will require for both a minimum and maximum staff schedule. Over a period of time a pattern will evolve revealing trends that enable an operator to forecast quantities to purchase and prepare as well as set labor hour schedules.

Forecasts must be constantly adjusted when actual data are gathered. The comparison of actual data to forecasts is the critical step in locating trouble areas. It does not necessarily tell you what is happening or why; that must be ascertained by closely examining the conditions. But the first step in correcting a problem is being able to detect that something is out of the ordinary.

These three steps have been referred to as a "systems" approach to labor cost. The system is that it combines customer count predictions with labor hour scheduling. By combining these two criteria, productivity standards can be established allowing management to prepare daily and weekly schedules that will optimize the use of labor while providing the quality and quantity of service expected by the customers.

S cheduling Techniques

Labor cost control involves proper hiring, training, and supervision. The assumption is made that these are being done to the optimum, and therefore your biggest concern is to schedule your employees so they will be on the job when you need them and off the clock when they are not needed. The key to controlling labor cost is not having a low average hourly wage but by proper scheduling of productive employees.

A restaurant's business is characterized by periods of idleness followed by periods of intense rushing. This "hurried" activity should be avoided as it causes mistakes and service flaws. When operating shorthanded, your labor problems take on a different nature than when you are overstaffed. If your valued employees are the ones who must "cover" for the slackers, eventually they will become discouraged, burn out, and quit.

Everything must be done to facilitate the flow of materials and manpower to minimize the hectic "lost it" or "in-the-weeds" pace where qualitative standards are disregarded in an effort to get caught up.

Customers notice disorganization and poor service, which will eventually cause them to not return to your establishment. Schedules become complicated and restrictive when you try to factor in all employee requests when making them out. You have to arrange for adequate coverage with the employees available for that day and time period.

Like a baseball manager or basketball coach, you want to start your best athletes when you have an important game. Such is the case when a restaurant manager makes up the schedule. He or she wants to place the best servers, cooks, bartenders, and dishwashers strategically to optimize productivity and customer service. Scheduling is complicated by the fact that it must reflect the variations in business volume that occur daily and within meal periods. The goal is to accomplish the necessary qualitative and quantitative productivity standards with a minimum number of labor hours.

If the forecasted customer count for the period is 350, the number of employees scheduled will be determined by such factors as the length of the meal period, the number of tables and seats in the dining room, the number of tables assigned per station, the maximum number that can be served at one time, and table turnover rates.

The staffing requirements for each and every job category will reflect the forecasted customer count. An example scenario might be as follows: using waiters, the meal period is six hours long, the dining room has 40 tables and 160 seats, and an average of 130 seats are occupied. Each waiter will be assigned a 5 to 6 table station and will serve 40 to 50 covers over the course of the shift. Seven *experienced* waiters will likely need to be scheduled. If one of the seven is a trainee, service may not be up to standard. Subsequently, even with seven waiters scheduled, management may consider they are still "understaffed" to handle the business effectively. An additional trainee may be added to the schedule, thus raising the labor cost without appreciably increasing the level of service.

Scheduling is not just a mathematical numbers game. When scheduling employees, the manager must put the *right* employee in the right time slot. This implies that in order to schedule effectively, a manager must know the strengths and weaknesses of each employee. Most operators and managers can recall a day when they struggled through a meal period with a weak cook, dishwasher, or bartender. They were not "shorthanded" in terms of the number of employees but were "understaffed" because standards of service and preparation could not be sustained without considerable assistance. The skills and capabilities of each employee must be examined when making up schedules for maximum productivity. The most productive and efficient employees need to be scheduled on the busiest days while trainees are broken in on slower volume days.

In addition to customer counts and employee capabilities, physical conditions of the facility itself pose additional considerations that need to be factored into the scheduling of employees. Two factors that can affect scheduling of servers, for example, are the number of tables in the dining room and the distance of stations to the kitchen and/or bar. Regardless of the total covers served during a meal period, a restaurant can serve only what the table turnover will allow. The physical limitations caused by the number of tables, seats, and the length of time it takes to be seated, order, be served, eat, pay, clear the table, and set it for the next party will all influence scheduling.

Other factors influence scheduling, such as the duties and responsibilities of the employee. Using the service staff as an example, do they serve both food and beverage? Do the customers serve themselves at a salad bar? Are there busboys to bring water, clear, and set tables? The same holds true for dishwashers, busboys, and cooks. The more they are required to do, the fewer customers they will be able to handle. This is why it is impractical to use scheduling guidelines from another operation for your business.

Table 10.5 is a chart of labor hour guidelines based on forecasted covers for three meal periods by job categories. Note that the number of covers per labor hour (C/LH) is different for each job category and that the number of scheduled labor hours does not increase incrementally with customer counts. The labor hours scheduled for 0 to 50 covers represents the minimum or fixed labor hours. Labor hours added as customer counts increase are the variable employee labor hours. Each meal period has different guidelines reflecting the varied demands brought on by the menu, preparation, and service requirements. Management must first prepare a forecast of expected covers and required (standard) labor hours. The actual labor hours worked and covers served must be compared to the forecast. In so doing, management can determine the meal periods and employee job categories that are performing up to standard. Variance from the standards must be examined closely to detect causes unrelated to scheduling and employee productivity; for example, equipment breakdowns, poor forecasting, training new employees. Also, the covers per labor hour actually served may show an increase, which may have been brought about by absenteeism and working shorthanded. Although labor cost will be lower and productivity higher when we work understaffed, quality standards may have been adversely affected. If allowed to continue, sales may decline due to customer dissatisfaction with service quality.

Scheduling would be fixed if customers arrived at a steady pace all day long. Some restaurants enjoy this kind of steady traffic (e.g., Houston's and the Cheesecake Factory), but most find their business volume fluctuating between very slow and frantically busy. The length of an employee's shift depends on the operating hours of the restaurant. Ideally, the operation sets its hours according to customer patterns. This is not always the case in restaurants located in hotels and motels. It may be their policy to provide both dining-room and room service during very slow periods.

The times of day customers enter your operation needs to be monitored if you expect to schedule effectively. This kind of information can be obtained in a number of ways. One way would be for the server or hostess to note the

Table 10.5   Covers Per Labor Hour Chart

Forecasted Covers	Cooks: LH and C/LH	Dishwashers: LH and C/LH	Busboys: LH and C/LH	Servers: LH and C/LH	Total LH and C/LH
Breakfast 7–11 A.M.					
0–50	4.5 and 11.0	4.0 and 12.5	4.5 and 11.0	4.5 and 11.0	17.5 and 2.8*
51–100	4.5 and 22.0	4.0 and 25.0	4.5 and 22.0	8.0 and 12.5	21.0 and 4.7
101–150	5.5 and 27.0	4.0 and 37.5	4.5 and 33.3	10.0 and 15.0	24.0 and 6.25
Lunch 11 A.M.–4 P.M.					
0–50	5.0 and 10.0	5.0 and 10.0	5.0 and 10.0	8.0 and 6.25	23.0 and 2.1*
51–100	8.0 and 12.5	5.0 and 20.0	5.0 and 20.0	8.0 and 12.5	26.0 and 3.8
101–150	10.0 and 15.0	7.0 and 21.4	7.0 and 21.0	10.0 and 15.0	34.0 and 6.7
151–300	10.0 and 30.0	7.0 and 42.8	10.0 and 30.0	15.0 and 20.0	42.0 and 7.7
301–400	13.0 and 30.7	9.0 and 44.4	12.0 and 33.0	20.0 and 20.0	54.0 and 7.4
Dinner 4–10 P.M.					
0–50	6.5 and 7.6	6.5 and 7.6	6.5 and 7.6	13.0 and 3.8	32.5 and 1.5*
51–100	10.0 and 10.0	6.5 and 15.2	6.5 and 15.2	19.0 and 5.2	42.0 and 2.3
101–200	13.0 and 15.4	9.5 and 21.0	13.0 and 15.4	24.0 and 8.3	59.5 and 3.4
201–300	15.0 and 20.0	9.5 and 31.5	16.0 and 18.8	29.0 and 10.3	69.5 and 4.3
301–400	15.0 and 26.6	11.5 and 34.7	19.0 and 21.0	33.0 and 12.1	78.5 and 5.0

LH = Labor Hours

C/LH = Covers per Labor Hour

*Fixed Labor Hours (Minimum Labor)

time each party is seated. The point-of-sale programs in use in most restaurants note the time an order is entered into the system. Another way would be to note the time an order is placed in the kitchen by the server. The ticket is usually timed in and out to check the ticket times. If the timer is set at the correct time, it can be used to gauge the customer count in the dining room.

The information about customer counts can be plotted on a chart by hours of operation (see Figure 10–2). Cover per labor hour guidelines can be used to develop the optimum schedule shown in Figure 10–3. (Adapted from Dittmer and Griffin, 1976.)

The schedule shown is for the service staff and made with the following standards: maximum number of covers that can be properly served by each service employee is 25 covers per hour; company policy requires a minimum of two (2) service personnel be scheduled at all times; the company pays employees for a minimum of four hours each time they report to work; no employee can work more than eight hours per shift; and a 30-minute break is given to all employees working over 4.5 hours. By computing the number of labor hours for each hour of operation, the exact time of day labor productivity can be improved may be determined.

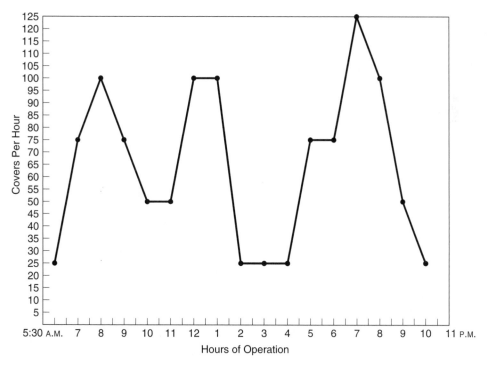

FIGURE 10–2
Customer Counts by Hours of Operation

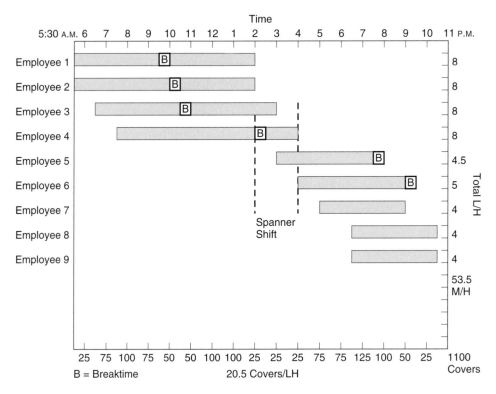

FIGURE 10–3
Spanner Shift Schedule

STAGGERED ARRIVALS AND DEPARTURES

The arrival and departure of the employees should correspond to the volume of customers expected so maximum labor hours are scheduled during peak periods and minimum labor hours during slack times. This is referred to as *staggered arrival and departure scheduling.* The number of employees gradually increases to its maximum during the peak volume periods and is gradually reduced as the restaurant approaches closing time.

SPANNER SHIFTS

When an operation is open for two or more consecutive meal periods, employees should arrive and leave without inconvenience to customers and allow departing employees to complete their side work and time out at scheduled times. Many times employees remain on the clock past their scheduled departure time because they are still cleaning up, doing side work, or waiting for a table they are serving to pay up and leave.

Staying past scheduled departure time can be minimized through another scheduling technique called **spanner shifts**. Note the overlapping schedules in Figure 10–3. For example, if the lunch shift ends at 4:00 P.M., there will be an employee scheduled to come in from 30 minutes to one hour earlier, depending on the duties that need to be completed and the table turnover rate. The departing server(s) will cease to take new parties after the spanner shift employee arrives. They will be able to complete side work and be through with all customers by 4:00 P.M. This helps reduce the amount of overtime employees work.

ON-CALL SCHEDULING

When forecasts of customer counts are not accurate, scheduled labor hours must be adjusted down or up as necessary for productivity standards. For those unpredictable periods of time, management can utilize *on-call scheduling* and *send home early* scheduling. What is meant by *on-call* is that employees remain at home where they wait for a call to come in to work. If the call does not come in by a certain time, they know they are not needed. This is preferred to driving in and then having to be sent home. It was the waiters in one of the author's restaurants who came up with this system when it seemed that we were overstaffed more often than understaffed. Tipped employees do not want to work when there is little business.

In order to be fair to all employees, different individuals are placed on-call each shift. This is strictly a short-term solution to uncertain business volumes. If you never call in the employee on-call, then there is no need to use it. If you are regularly calling the waiting employee, he or she should be placed on the regular schedule.

There are those who use *on-call* as an emergency backup to cover for employees who call in sick or simply do not show up. This is not the purpose of on-call and its use for this is actually counterproductive and shows disregard for formal scheduling. It should be the responsibility of an employee scheduled to fill a shift or get someone to cover if he or she needs the shift off or if anything short of an emergency occurs. Employees who are absent without cause will not be on the schedule for long.

On-call is also a way to increase the hours of newly hired employees who have not been given a full schedule. It is a good probationary period scheduling technique to test the dedication of new employees before giving them a permanent shift. Of course, local wage practices, union, and corporate policy will determine whether this technique is used and its effectiveness. Remember, these techniques are used for scheduling "variable cost" employees. If neither of these methods can be employed to help scheduling efficiency, then marketing and advertising will need to be used to increase customer traffic with early bird specials, happy hours, and so forth.

SEND HOME EARLY

As for *send home early*, no restriction under the Federal Wage and Hour Law says that if you discover you have too many employees scheduled that you have to keep them on the clock and pay them. Union contracts, corporate policy, and local wage practices may require minimum "show-up" pay to be provided, especially in the case of banquet servers at hotels. In the case that weather conditions deteriorate (e.g., blizzard, tornado, or hurricane watches), keeping most of your anticipated business away, your tipped employees will volunteer to leave.

Also, if you have overscheduled and are having to send someone home every night, you will need to find a way to fairly determine who goes home. If it is the same employee every shift, that employee will find that his or her paycheck is greatly reduced. When it comes to hourly employees, keeping them on the clock will increase your payroll costs if they are variable cost employees on the schedule when they are not needed. Drawing straws from a broom or asking for volunteers are two fair ways to select the employee to leave early.

In addition to the spanner shift, staggered arrival and departure, the on call, and send home early scheduling techniques, four more are worth mentioning. These scheduling techniques may be known by other names and you may already be using them and never thought of them as scheduling techniques.

PART-TIME SCHEDULING

Another way to keep payroll to the minimum in times of uncertain business activity is the use of **part-time schedules**. Part-time in the scheduling sense does not mean "fewer than 40 hours a week"; that is a Department of Labor term that does not apply here. What we mean by part-time employees are those former employees in good standing who are no longer on the permanent schedule. If you have college students working for you, you know what I mean. They may have to drop off the permanent schedule for a semester because they are taking a difficult load of classes or have other school-related obligations. They go on a list to call in an emergency to fill a shift where an employee wants off or is sick or injured. Part-time employees' names and telephone numbers are posted for full-time employees to call if no one on the permanent schedule wants the extra work. We have found that part-time employees will either come back to work after six months or will take their name off the call list. It is a source of trained employees you can call on with short notice.

SPLIT SHIFTS

Split shifts are another scheduling technique with limited application but excellent results if you can find people to work them. Split shift entails scheduling employees to work a short shift, usually a peak period, and then clocking out. It works especially well on residential college campuses. Students can work a few hours in the dining hall between classes and during peak meal periods when you need more employees to handle the rush. Contrast this to having to schedule employees for a full eight-hour shift because they cannot be sent home.

ON BREAK SCHEDULES

When you cannot send people home, put them *on break.* When you give an employee a 30-minute break and provide a meal, you can deduct the 30 minutes off his or her time card and take a credit for the reasonable cost of the meal provided against the minimum wage. Here is an example that shows the savings that can result from break and meal deductions being taken.

Assume that the average hourly wage is $6.00. Your policy is to give all employees who work more than 4.5 hours a meal and a 30-minute break. Further assume that the reasonable cost of the food provided is $2.00. That converts to approximately $.25 an hour based on an 8-hour shift. That amount can be credited against the hourly wage, whereby you will not pay $6.00/ hour but $5.75/hour. In addition, the 30 minutes of break time is not paid, resulting in an additional savings of $3.00 per shift over 4.5 hours. Assuming a 40-hour/5-day workweek, the savings in payroll costs from providing meals is $10.00 ($.25 × 40 hr) and $15.00 in breaks ($3.00 × 5 days). That totals to $25.00 a week and $108.33 per month. When you add up the savings over a 12-month period for several employees, the average cost reduction is $1,300 per employee!

SHORT-RUN USE OF OVERTIME

Although *overtime* is forbidden in many companies, it can be used to reduce labor costs *in the short run.* With temporary emergencies that occur due to injury, illness, vacations, and termination for cause, overtime paid another experienced employee can be less expensive than the hiring and training of a temporary employee. However, overtime becomes counterproductive when allowed to go on for too long. Not only are labor costs increased, you run the risk of burning out an employee who has not had a day off in several weeks.

The Consequences of the Productivity Push

The effects of understaffing are immediately detectable. However, overstaffing is more difficult to detect unless your staffing standards are in place. If you assign two employees one hour to do a job that one could have finished in the same time, they will divide the work between them and take one hour to finish it. This is referred to as Parkinson's Law—work expands to the time allowed.

Once employees have been used to dividing up work because you have been overstaffed, they are not receptive to increasing their output when the labor hours have been cut back and the output or time in which they have to accomplish the work remains the same. Some employees develop what can be called an "overstaffing bias." They have adjusted their productivity to a lower standard and have difficulty stepping up their efforts, especially for their "old" boss. When management changes, they are more responsive to changes of this nature.

Even when the upgraded output level is only 70 to 80 percent of the individual's capability, the employee may still complain. Once employees have adjusted their work habits to slow down in service or production, they are rarely receptive to speeding up unless closely supervised and have sanctions placed on performance. They develop poor work techniques and habits that prevent them from becoming productive on their own.

In addition, unneeded personnel on the schedule creates idle time that contributes to inefficiencies in productivity. The staff is inclined to become too relaxed when business is slow; this is not the case when it is busy. It also seems that more complaints about service and food occur during slow periods than in the heat of a rush. Most of the complaints could have been eliminated if the employees kept on their toes.

Physical and mental fatigue develop as does an attitude of "no need to hurry." Extra steps and motions become habitual; like employees who go to the dishroom for stock and bring out only what they need instead of the tray of cups or rack of silverware. We find that they procrastinate doing their side work and the housekeeping standards slip. Morale drops, too, because management is always on their case and tips are low.

When changes are constantly being made, as often occurs in a developing company, many times it is the employees with the longest tenure who have difficulty taking on increased job responsibilities. Contrast this attitude to that of the newer hires who accept whatever job responsibilities you give them without question.

One of the authors recalls an incident in his restaurant when he decided to change the cleanup assignments at closing by having the waiters vacuum the dining room at the end of the day. Heretofore, it was the busboys that vacuumed. He was approached by my two most senior waiters who voiced their displeasure with the new work assignments. They even complained to the new waiters about this change. They wanted to have a meeting after closing to discuss the matter. The owner took them aside and told them that this was necessary for our company to reduce costs and that he expected their support for this new side duty. The newer waiters had no problem with the duty, it was only the most senior employees.

There was no waiters meeting and the two senior waiters supported the new changes. The story got around to all the employees through the grapevine and later that same month when the duties of the cooks were expanded to sweeping and mopping the food line, there was not one comment about the addition of the new duties from the senior cooks. Because it is a natural occurrence that senior employees exert some informal influence over the newer employees, care must be taken to be sure their reluctant attitudes are not passed on to new hires. The old adage "A few bad apples can spoil the barrel" is very true with employee attitudes.

You are always better off to begin somewhat understaffed than over-staffed. Employees rarely complain when you give them additional help (unless they are tipped employees and it takes money out of their pockets). They are less receptive when they are asked to do what more than one person in the past was asked to do. In the late 1980s and early 1990s, the hotel industry went through a major downsizing. Many positions were eliminated and combined. One hotel food and beverage manager told me he was now doing the work that just three months earlier was assigned to six other people. He was getting it all done too, an indication of earlier overstaffing.

Many times, an increase in wage or salary provides an incentive to take on the added duties enthusiastically. It is not that you have added a burden to employees' job responsibilities that they cannot do; it is just that over-staffing was recognized and eliminated. Sometimes the only way to get employees to increase their productivity is by replacing the employee or manager of a particular department or unit. If these employees transfer their bad attitude to new hires, the problem will continue. Controlling labor cost is the biggest challenge you will face as a restaurant manager. You will leave for another company more often for reasons related to the way you were treated as an individual than for monetary reasons. Managers are terminated more for their inability to deal with employees than for their inability to control food cost or beverage cost.

Understaffing can cause problems with efficiency and morale as well. Good hardworking employees can become burned out because they are frequently asked to fill in when short-handed or during busy periods. They are usually the most loyal and productive employees on the schedule. If their efforts are not recognized by management, they will soon lose incentive to remain more productive.

Wages and Productivity

Would you agree that if you pay employees a premium wage they will be more productive than if they were paid just the minimum wage? Or to put another way, you have a worker who is not performing to your level of qualitative and quantitative standards. You tell him that you are increasing his wages by 25 percent. Can you be assured that his productivity will improve? If it were true, higher wages would guarantee higher productivity, and the National Restaurant Association would not be against raising the minimum wage. The truth is that it just doesn't work that way.

It is said that over one third of all employees leave a job voluntarily for better pay. However, this is relative to the working conditions and their job satisfaction. You may believe more money cannot be a motivator for increasing productivity. While it is true that high wages and high productivity do not always go hand-in-hand, money can be used as an effective reward for outstanding performance and loyalty. When it accompanies outstanding performance, it can be an effective productivity motivator. When it comes to raises and bonuses, if they are doled out on seniority and not performance, they are not effective motivators. In fact, they become sources of dissatisfaction and negative reinforcement. If everyone receives the same bonus, it devalues the bonus in the minds of the employees who have gone the extra mile and put out extra effort. You need to rank order your employees and pay and reward them accordingly. The fact that employees come to work on time and do their job is not sufficient grounds for raises and promotions. Think about that. That's what they are hired to do. It is like customers praising your restaurant because you serve hot food and have a clean operation. These are minimum expectations that all restaurants are expected to meet, and you should not reward employees for doing what is expected. Those who go beyond the normal scope of their duties are the exceptional ones who should be duly compensated and rewarded.

You cannot turn an unproductive employee around by simply paying him or her more money. Consider the employee who approaches management and says, "If you pay me $1.00 more per hour, I will work twice as hard for you." When you think about it, we are all somewhat underpaid for our jobs. If everyone who felt that way lowered his or her productivity to a level commensurate with his or her pay, there would be a drastic reduction in the output of goods and services. The American way is to first prove your worth to your employer and then be rewarded monetarily. Make your boss feel guilty about not paying you enough by identifying with ownership interests. Management will realize that they have a valuable asset that they want to keep. If they do not treat you any differently, leave and go to work for someone who will appreciate your work ethic.

It is not unusual to find low productivity and inefficiency in establishments paying below average wages to their employees and management personnel. It is likely that businesses that pay below the market average will not attract the more productive workers. Such places attract marginally productive employees who cannot qualify for the higher paying positions at the better restaurants or who were let go because they did not perform well enough to earn their pay. If you consider yourself an exceptional manager or chef, would you work for someone who paid you wages far below what you are currently making? The same holds true when you are hiring servers, bartenders, cooks, and dishwashers. If you want to attract the best employees, you better pay premium wages because you will not attract them without it. Therefore, the places that pay above the going wage rate in the area will likely get the more productive applicants.

We need to include a word about employee benefits. The competition to attract, hire, and retain the top candidates in the food service labor pool has made employee compensation packages an important negotiation tool in the hiring process. Benefits like health insurance, paid vacations, tuition reimbursements, profit sharing, and retirement programs, typically only offered to members of management, are now being used to attract and retain hourly employees as well. You will need to offer competitive benefit packages to attract and retain your productive employees. Eligibility of employees and the percentage of the premiums paid by the restaurant increases the longer the worker remains in your employ. This incentive appears to be effective in lengthening the term of employment of both management and hourly employees. If the average restaurant could increase the average term of employment to just six months, it would reduce turnover by 50 percent and increase profits by a like amount.

Supervision and Productivity

The importance of management supervision in labor cost control and productivity cannot be overstated. Much of the attitude, ability, and professionalism of a manager is reflected in the type of employees attracted to a restaurant and the staff a manager eventually hires, trains, and retains.

The manager remains the key element in improving labor productivity. It is imperative that management inform the employees right from the start what is expected of them in terms of attitude and performance. They must explain the "why" behind the procedures to keep employees from taking shortcuts that compromise quality for the sake of quantity. A conscious effort must be made to implement standards and monitor performance. Employees need objective measurements to guide them while management acts as the scorekeeper.

If management allows the standards to slip or accepts less than the established standards, it will become more difficult to set standards in the future. Remember, employees will deviate from standards only as far as management allows. Follow-up and constant appraisal are necessary to permanently implant standards in the minds of the employees.

Like a coach, the chef and manager helps sets the team spirit. As management goes, so goes the restaurant. Systematic evaluation of an employee's job performance is essential to measure progress in developing job skills, to identify substandard performance and correct it, and to provide a basis for recognition, promotion, and merit wage increases.

To illustrate how payroll data can be organized into a format conducive to in-depth analysis, the following payroll worksheets are offered (see Tables 10.6 and 10.7).

Organizing weekly payroll data into a format that will allow the operator to see exactly how payroll costs are allocated to individual job categories as well as the aggregate figures, will greatly improve labor cost data analysis. The comparison of current figures with past periods will show where variances are occurring. The *total* payroll figure by itself does not provide enough detail that in depth analysis demands. Staffing and scheduling guidelines can be developed from monitoring the sales and covers per labor hour. By closely monitoring the labor cost per cover, the job categories where overscheduling has occurred can be quickly detected.

The information that is recorded over a period of weeks and months will provide management with information to set and assess productivity and cost standards. The criterion used to determine the number of labor hours needed to be scheduled will be the forecasted customer counts by separate meal periods. Separate standards will be set for each respective job category. To illustrate, assume the server schedule for the evening meal is being prepared. The projected number of covers will be indicated for each day of the week as shown in Table 10.8.

After the customer counts have been estimated, divide them by the standard covers per labor hour to determine the optimum number of labor hours

Table 10.6 Weekly Payroll Analysis Worksheet
Food Sales: $12,000 Customer Count: 1,600

	Servers	Bus Help	Dishers	Cooks	Host/ Cash	Totals
Payroll	$455.10	$338.10	$196.00	$882.00	$168.00	$2039.20
Labor Hours	222	98	56	168	42	586
% of LH	37.9%	16.7%	9.5%	28.7%	7.2%	100.00%
Labor Cost %	3.8%	2.8%	1.6%	7.4%	1.4%	17.0%
% of Payroll	22.3%	16.6%	9.6%	43.3%	8.2%	100.0%
Cost/LH	$2.05	$3.45	$3.50	$5.25	$4.00	$3.48
Sales/LH	$54.05	$122.45	$214.29	$71.43	$285.71	$20.48
Covers/LH	7.2	16.3	28.6	9.5	38.1	2.7
Labor Cost/Cover	$.284	$.211	$.1225	$.551	$.105	$1.275

Table 10.7　Weekly Payroll Analysis Worksheet
Beverage Sales: $4500　Customer Count: 850

	Bartenders	Servers	Totals
Payroll	$280.00	$245.00	$525.00
Labor Hours	56	98	154
% of Labor Hours	36.4%	63.6%	100.0%
Labor Cost %	6.2%	5.4%	11.6%
% of Payroll	53.3%	46.7%	100.0%
Labor Cost/Labor Hour	$5.00	$2.50	$3.41
Sales/Labor Hour	$80.36	$45.92	$29.22
Covers/Labor Hour	15.2	8.7	5.5
Labor Cost/Cover	$.33	$.29	$.62

that should be scheduled. This is converted to the number of actual servers that needs to be scheduled. The most efficient form of scheduling would examine customer counts by the hour and schedule accordingly.

Comparison of actual labor hours and customer counts to forecasted numbers must be done to fine-tune scheduling. A comparison of actual to forecasted labor hours in shown on the Weekly Payroll Summary, Table 10.9.

The format of the schedule provides management with a breakdown of labor hours by job categories so variances can be readily seen. If totals are monitored daily, management can send employees home early or adjust schedules to meet the weekly labor hour standards. However, it would be impractical and impossible to have every day and shift exactly within standard. Consequently, it is the weekly average that management will look at as the overall indication of how well labor scheduling is being conducted. A day or shift where standards were not met will be canceled out when fore-

Table 10.8　Schedule Worksheet
Job Category: Servers　Meal Period: Dinner (5–11 P.M.)

Day of Week	Projected Customer Count	Covers/Labor Hour Standard	Total Labor Hours to Schedule
Saturday	300	7.2	41.7
Sunday	280	7.2	38.9
Monday	180	7.2	25
Tuesday	150	7.2	20.8
Wednesday	160	7.2	22.2
Thursday	170	7.2	23.6
Friday	320	7.2	44.4

Table 10.9 Weekly Payroll Summary
Dinner Labor Hours Schedule: Standard Versus Actual

	Servers *Standard/ Actual	Busboys Standard/ Actual	Dishwashers Standard/ Actual	Cooks Standard/ Actual	Hostess-Cashier Standard/ Actual	Daily Total Standard/ Actual
Saturday	42/47	18.5/19.5	10.5/11.5	32/30	6**/6	109/114
Variance	+5	+1	+1	-2	0	+5
Sunday	40/37	17.5/18.0	10.0/11.0	29.5/27	6/5.5	103/98.5
Variance	-3	+.5	+1	-2.5	-.5	-4.5
Monday	25/27	11/10.5	6.5*/6.5	19/20	6/6.5	67.5/70.5
Variance	+2	-.5	0	+1	+.5	+3
Tuesday	21**/21	9.5/9.5	6.5/6.5	16/20	6/6	59/63
Variance	0	0	0	+4	0	+4
Wednesday	22.5/20	10/10	6.5/6.5	17/19	6/6	62/61.5
Variance	-2.5	0	0	+2	0	-.5
Thursday	24/24	10.5/11	6.5/7	18/18	6/6	65/66
Variance	0	+.5	+.5	0	0	+1
Friday	44.5/43	20/21	11.5/12.5	34/32	6/6.5	116/115
Variance	-1.5	+1	+1	-2	+.5	-1
Totals	219/219	97/99.5	58/61.5	165.5/166	42/42.5	581.5/588.5
Variance	0	+2.5	+3.5	+.5	+.5	+7.0

*Standard LH based on forecasted customer counts divided by standard covers per labor hour as shown on Weekly Payroll Analysis Worksheet, Tables 10.6 and 10.7.

**Minimum LH; equivalent of Fixed Labor Cost.

casted customer counts exceeded expectations and actual productivity exceeded the standard.

The actual labor hours worked were +7 and thus exceeded the standard number of labor hours for the period. The cause of the variance can be seen in the bus help and dishwasher job categories. This small variance would be considered within a tolerable range and not be seen as a problem. Justification of the extra labor hours may be explained by reasons not related to scheduling.

The type of specific conclusions that can be drawn from review of payroll-related data containing multiple measures cannot be made from review of payroll ratios and sales per labor hour figures. The key to controlling labor is scheduling and the use of covers per labor hour as the standard for determining labor requirements. Accurate forecasting of customer counts is also critical to effective labor cost analysis. The cost information must be compiled and reviewed at least on a weekly basis so schedules can reflect actual business activity.

The U.S. Congress approved an increase in the minimum wage to $5.15. The following is a list of things to do that will help reduce the impact of rising wage rates.

1. Employees should be cross-trained to do more than one job. This allows them to fill in during slow periods and keeps you from having to schedule additional workers. When employees distinguish themselves by being able to perform several jobs, they need to be appropriately compensated.

2. Use time clocks and time cards. Set up procedures for breaks and meal allowances. Have time-in and time-out rules; for example, manager's OK needed if more than 12 minutes early or late timing in or out.

3. Eliminate the need for a worker whenever feasible. Try to get the work done with the least number of people. Invest in labor saving equipment or purchase in a form that eliminates the need for the worker. Increase your inventory of glassware and china so you lower the turnover of flatware and china. It may allow you to reduce the dishwashing crew.

4. Go to self-service where feasible.

5. Hire and train skilled employees. Two lesser skilled and lower paid employees are far more expensive than one skilled, well-compensated employee.

6. Place emphasis on marketing and ways to increase overall sales. Remember, labor has a significant fixed cost component and increasing sales will lower labor cost percentage. The old adage is still true, "Volume hides a multitude of sins."

7. You could always raise your prices as a last resort.

8. Cut back on overhead by closing during unprofitable times of the day.

9. Schedule more closely using the techniques given in this chapter.

10. Look into rearranging your layout if it would improve productivity without increasing labor cost.

 ## Key Points

- You need more than the traditional labor cost percentage to assess labor productivity.
- Scheduling is the key to controlling labor cost.
- Labor must be pre-controlled.
- You must have a reporting and evaluating systems for labor cost analysis.
- Wages and supervision impact labor productivity.

 ## Key Terms

Labor productivity	Spanner shifts	Split shifts
Labor cost percentage	On-call scheduling	
Staggered arrival and departure scheduling	Part-time schedules	

Discussion Questions

1. What are the three deficiencies or limitations of the traditional labor cost percentage shown on all income statements?

2. Explain when and how staggered schedules and spanner shifts are used to keep labor costs within standards.

3. Scheduling can never be reduced to a simple numbers game of scheduling a certain number of employees based only on customer counts. What other considerations must management use in order to schedule and keep qualitative as well as quantitative standards. List 3 things.

4. Can the going wage rate paid by a restaurant affect the qualitative and quantitative level of the applicants it hires? Explain.

Problem 1

Given the following:

	Unit 1	Unit 2
Sales	$35,600	$38,900
Labor Cost	$ 8,188	$ 8,947
Covers	6,300	6,500
Labor Hours	1,638	1,720

Using the Excel template provided, compute and show all calculations for:

1. Average Check
2. Labor Cost Percentage
3. Sales per labor hour
4. Labor cost per labor hour
5. Covers per labor hour
6. Labor cost per cover
7. Which unit is using labor more productively? How do you know?

Problem 2

David A. is the owner and general manager of the new Insignia Restaurant in the trendy Buckhead area of Atlanta. He and his executive chef, Pete P. are concerned that their labor cost is out of line with the volume of business and customers they are serving. David feels that the staff needs to be trimmed. In order to objectively examine their scheduling and payroll decisions, the office manager has provided them with the following payroll data. The sales and customer counts for a typical week are $22,500 and 840.

Job Category	Labor Hours	Payroll
Servers	280	$ 653
Bussers	84	$ 675
Dishwashers	75	$ 563
Hostesses	60	$ 555
Cashiers	60	$ 555
Cooks	175	$2,349
Bartenders	56	$ 504
Totals	790	$5,854

From this data and the sales and customer count figures and using the Excel template on your diskette, which follows the format shown in Table 10-4, indicate the job categories with the *best* and *worst* productivity.

1. Which two job categories account for over 57% of the total labor hours scheduled?
2. Which job category accounts for over 40% of the total payroll expense?
3. What is the average labor cost per labor hour for the entire payroll?
4. Which job category has the lowest sales per labor hour? Why?
5. Which job category has the highest number of covers served for every hour scheduled?
6. Which job category has the lowest labor cost per cover?
7. What is the average labor cost per cover served in the restaurant?
8. What is the weekly payroll percent to sales?
9. Which job category would result in the greatest savings in payroll and increase in productivity if you were to cut hours by just 28 hours per week?

B ibliography

Brymer, Robert A. and David V. Pavesic. "Personality Characteristics and Profiles of Hospitality Management Graduates," *Hospitality Research Journal,* Vol. 14, No. 1, 1990, pp. 77–86.

Dittmer, Paul R. and Gerald G. Griffin. *Principles of Food, Beverage, and Labor Cost Controls,* Boston: Cahners Books, Inc., 1976.

Pavesic, David V., "Myth of Labor Cost Percentages," *Cornell Quarterly,* Vol. 24, No. 3, Nov. 1983, pp. 26–38.

Pavesic, David V. and Robert A. Brymer. "Why Young Managers are Quitting," *Cornell Quarterly,* Vol. 30, No. 4, Feb. 1990, pp. 90–96.

National Restaurant Association, Deloitte & Touche, "2002 Restaurant Industry Operations Report," Washington, D.C. p. 48.

Restaurant Industry Operations Report 1996, National Restaurant Association, Deloitte & Touche Ltd., pp. 68–69.

11

Internal Controls

THE FUNDAMENTAL PRINCIPLES OF COST CONTROL

1. Separate the authority and responsibility for cash deposits and the writing of checks.

2. Each transaction needs to be recorded in order to be tracked and audited.

3. Identify the authority and responsibilities of all members of your team.

4. Internal cost control systems serve as checks and balances in the absence of management or owners.

5. The basis for all control is the comparison of current results to standards or budgets.

6. The basic control procedure is an independent verification at control points during and after the completion of a task.

7. There are telltale signs of possible theft that management can observe.

8. Pay everything by check so you have a record of the payment.

9. Internal reports will contain both objective quantitative data and subjective qualitative information.

10. Prevention is the key to internal control.

Restaurant owners and security experts estimate that about five cents of every dollar spent in U.S. restaurants is lost to theft. To discourage theft, management establishes clear controls and must be sure they are, in fact, followed and practiced. The most fundamental aspects of **internal control** are the separation of duties and the recording of each transaction. Most of us are guided by a high degree of personal integrity and moral standards that keep us honest. The total humiliation of being accused, let alone being arrested, is also a huge deterrent to honest people.

The procedural checks and balances discussed in this chapter and the perseverance of management toward avoiding fraud will strongly limit the opportunity to steal and increase the likelihood of being detected.

However, one's personal circumstances can reach such a desperate point that previously honest and law-abiding employees are driven to steal, often as a result of severe debt or catastrophic financial loss. Tax-free money becomes very tempting to an individual experiencing such stress.

Internal controls are a critical component to any cost control program. They identify the authority and responsibilities of all members of the organization at each and every level. They also define the ways by which cost objectives will be achieved. Many operations install a management information system for data accumulation, preparation, analyzing, and reporting.

M anagement Information Systems (MIS)

Management information systems (MIS) help establish clear and proper rules for consistent and prompt reporting. MIS sets up efficient paperwork flow and data collection that reduces errors and omissions so as not to compromise their interpretation and decision making. The accumulation and preparation of reports must be done economically to keep duplication and over-reporting to a minimum.

An MIS seeks to prevent fraudulent conversions at all levels. Although no system will prevent all fraud because the cost could far exceed the losses from it, a soundly designed system that is followed and maintained will reveal areas of loss if fraudulent conversions do occur. A system will not identify specifically what caused the loss or variance from standard, but it will alert management that investigation is warranted. For example, when the sales records show fewer items were sold than were used, the food cost will certainly be affected. However, at this stage one cannot determine whether the kitchen or dining room is the cause and who in particular is at fault. The system alerted management to a potential problem and now they must investigate.

The Association of Independent Certified Public Accountants (AICPA) defines internal controls as follows: *Internal control comprises the plan of organi-*

zation . . . adopted to safeguard the assets of a business, check the accuracy and relia-bility of its accounting data, promote operational efficiency, and encourage adherence to prescribed managerial policies.

The definition goes beyond simple checks and balances in paperwork flow, using cash registers, prenumbered guest checks, time cards, and inventory records. It includes such techniques and control devices as:

1. Budgets
2. Standards of performance
3. Personnel policies
4. Statistical analysis
5. Physical safeguards
6. Sales and production planning and forecasting
7. Continuous follow-up and appraisal of compliance and accuracy of reports and activities.

A well-designed system of control is so important to the efficient conduct of the business that it is incumbent upon management to continually review and evaluate their control system. From time to time, controls might break down from the lack of supervision and continuous review. This may happen when an employee fails to perform a particular procedure one time and, because no one challenged the lack of procedure, the employee continues to omit the procedure periodically; for example, putting guest checks in numerical order and matching kitchen copies with hard copies to detect walkouts and missing checks.

The key to internal control is *entering the transaction into the system.* That may be accomplished electronically as with a computer driven sales system or when a handwritten, serially numbered guest check is given to the cook or bartender to fill an order. If food or beverage can be obtained by servers or customers without being entered into the system, the system is flawed and control can be compromised.

The basis for all control is comparison. Menu sales mix analysis is useful only when the totals can be compared against the amounts on hand, issued, and remaining in inventory. The figures are compared to either a preestablished or concurrently established standard or goal.

Most activities performed in a restaurant are cyclical and begin with preparation, proceed to action, and then the cycle starts over again. By inserting a comparison stage in the cycle, you create a control sub-system that becomes the basis for your system of internal control. The sub-systems interlock and feed into a reporting cycle since the final stage in a control system is a written report of the results. It is used to assess the persons responsible for the reported activity as well as the activity itself.

In addition to establishing a control point against which results can be compared, five other general cost control concepts are integral to control systems. They are:

1. Documentation: A description of the task, activity, or transaction including a physical record of the result. Written procedures and report forms are essential.

2. Supervision and review by someone familiar with performance standards.

3. Segregation of duties so no one person is responsible for or involved in all parts of the task cycle.

4. Timeliness: All tasks must be performed within the appropriate time. Comparisons must be made at established control points and reports made available at scheduled times in order to solve problems that are detected.

5. The cost–benefit relationship of procedures used and benefits derived must exceed the cost of implementing the controls.

The basic control procedure is an independent verification at control points during and after the completion of a task. Although normally done visually or manually, verification is now being accomplished through written reports and the use of electronic devices and generated reports. The verification, however accomplished, is for the purpose of determining one or more of the following:

1. Proper authority to perform the task

2. Quantity available must be verified

3. Quality must meet preset standards

4. Performance results must be in accordance with proper guidelines

Techniques used include observation, inspection, and physical counts. The cycles of control must be examined from the perspectives of control objectives, control sub-systems, control points, and special procedures and techniques. The aspects of control include operational control, accounting control, and administrative control.

D aily Sales Report

A MIS is a network for the generation and communication of pertinent and timely quantitative and qualitative information to all levels of management to be used for planning, directing, and controlling the operations of an organization. Internal managerial accounting records are necessary for the control of day-to-day operational activity.

The primary record is perhaps the **daily sales report**. If a restaurant has more than one cash register, it will require reports for each register. A sample of a restaurant's daily report is shown in Figure 11–1. The information contained in a sales report can include any of the following information:

1. Register readings, beginning and ending
2. Sales breakdowns, by meal periods, types of sale (e.g., food, beverage, merchandise, cigars, candy, etc.)
3. Type of payment (i.e., cash, charge, check, employee discount, or complimentary)
4. Over-rings, under-rings, voids, paid-outs
5. Comments on activity, weather, special parties, events affecting business
6. Sales tax
7. Amount of deposit
8. Name of person preparing report
9. Customer counts

Guest Check Register

Forms that monitor guest checks, if check books are issued to servers, are an important control when the guest check is used to requisition food and beverage from the kitchen and bar. A **guest check register** should record the beginning numbers of all check books. See Figure 11–2. Checks should not be left out in the open but kept under lock and key with unused checks turned in at the end of the shift and the ending number written on the check register. Servers should write their name on all their checks when issued a new book to discourage others from using their checks when they are not working.

Checks should be sorted by server and put in numerical order to check for missing checks. If a soft duplicate copy (dupe) is used to requisition food from the kitchen, kitchen copies should be collated with the customer copy to detect missing checks or omitted food items. Checks should be audited for register verification of payment and the amounts verified. Price extensions and additions should also be audited.

If food and beverage can be obtained without submitting a guest check (i.e., oral orders), the system has a flaw. Once an item is written on a check or

DATE / /

RESTAURANT DAILY REPORT

DAY OF WEEK _____ WEATHER _____

NAME _____

ADD BEGINNING REGISTER CASH _____

ADD CREDIT CARDS NOT DEPOSITED TO DATE _____

ADD NSF CHECKS ON HAND _____

(MEMO ONLY) SALES		(MEMO ONLY) NON TAX SALES OR CONTROL INFO.	SALES CATEGORIES	CLOSING READINGS		LESS: OVERRINGS & UNDERRINGS	TOTALS
FORWARD	MONTH-TO-DATE						
			FOOD				
			LIQUOR				
			BEER				
			WINE				
			PROMOTIONAL SALES				
			VENDING				
		Ⓑ	TOTALS Ⓕ			ADD TOTAL SALES → Ⓐ	

COMMENTS _____

ADD SALES TAX COLLECTED: USE ONLY FOR THE AMOUNT OF SALES TAX NOT ALREADY INCLUDED IN Ⓐ ABOVE:

1. AMOUNT COLLECTED PER SEPARATE REGISTER KEY
   — OR —
2. TAXABLE SALES: (POSSIBLY JUST TAXABLE FOOD) TIMES ____ %

(SEE A/R PAGE) ADD COLLECTIONS ON CHARGE SALES

← (EXPLANATION) ADD OTHER INCOME OR RECEIPTS

EQUALS TOTAL TO ACCOUNT FOR Ⓒ

PAID OUT OF REGISTER CASH					
PAYEE AND DESCRIPTION	FOOD	LIQUOR	BEER	WINE	PROMO SALES
TOTALS					

ADD TOTAL PAID OUTS →

PERPETUAL REGISTER READING RECONCILIATION	
PERPETUAL READING TODAY	
LESS: PERPETUAL READING YESTERDAY	
= AUDIT TOTAL	
LESS: TODAY'S READINGS (Ⓕ ABOVE)	
= DIFFERENCE TO ACCOUNT FOR	

(MEMO ONLY) DISCOUNT	DEPOSITS	
	CASH	
	MASTERCHARGE	
	VISA	

ADD TOTAL DEPOSITS →

SEE A/R PAGE FOR CREDIT CARD RECEIVABLE CONTROL SECTIONS	OTHER CREDIT CARDS	
	AMERICAN EXPRESS	

CONTROL & ANALYSIS SECTION				
TICKET CONTROL	TOTAL	LOCATION	LOCATION	LOCATION
CLOSING TICKET # +				
OPENING TICKET # −				
TICKETS ISSUED =				
TICKETS VOIDED −				
TICKETS USED = Ⓖ				
CUSTOMER ANALYSIS				
AVG. CHECK Ⓐ ÷ Ⓖ				
CUSTOMER COUNT				
AVG. PER CUSTOMER				

ADD TOTAL CREDIT SLIPS SUBMITTED FOR COLLECTION →

(SEE A/R PAGE) ADD CHARGE SALES

ADD OWNER CASH WITHDRAWALS

ADD ENDING REGISTER CASH

ADD CREDIT CARDS NOT DEPOSITED TO DATE

ADD NSF CHECKS ON HAND

EQUALS TOTAL ACCOUNTED FOR Ⓓ

CASH OVER/(SHORT) TODAY Ⓓ MINUS Ⓒ

CASH OVER/(SHORT) MONTH TO DATE

© 1979 Edwin K. Williams & Co.

FIGURE 11-1
Daily sales report. Permission granted by Edwin K. Williams & Company, Waco, TX 76707.

Date: *7-22-98*		Shift: *Lunch*		Prepared By: *DVP*			
Checks Issued		Server Initials	No.	Checks Returned		Server Initials	No.
Beginning Number	Ending Number			Beginning Number	Ending Number		
001	*025*	*RRF*	*25*	*016*	*025*	*RRF*	*15*
026	*050*	*DDR*	*25*	*036*	*050*	*DDR*	*10*
051	*075*	*PRC*	*25*	*069*	*075*	*PRC*	*18*

Missing or Voided Check Record			
Check Number	Server	Comments	Mgt. Authorization
065-067	*PRC*	*Checks voided due to beverage spill. New checks prepared. Voids attached.*	*DVP*

FIGURE 11–2
Guest Check Register

entered electronically, it can be tracked. That is why so many operations have eliminated oral transmission of food and beverage orders. All cross-outs of food and beverage items should be initialed by management. If they cannot present it orally, it must be written. Checks that have been filled should be marked or perforated to keep them from being resubmitted. If checks are monitored, controls will be effective.

The data assembled on the reports may be pertinent enough to be presented in raw data form for decision-making purposes. More often data are included with other information for comparative and ancillary purposes. For example, the sales mix information taken from guest orders or checks is useful to the kitchen manager to forecast preparation quantities. This same information is used by the buyer to determine what and how much to purchase.

All they need is summary information of what was recorded on the guest checks, not the checks themselves.

The actual guest check is passed from server to guest to cashier. Sometimes the server also acts as the cashier and keeps a personal bank. If a separate cashier is used, the guest check is collected when paid for future auditing. The sales data needed by the kitchen and buyer may be extracted electronically with a point-of-sale system. In the absence of such technology, the sales mix information will be collected manually. The checks are also audited for errors in addition, price extensions, and verification stamps that checks have been paid. Most cash registers will print PAID on the check and the amount tendered. A detailed sales report of the daily sales for food and beverage is also garnered from the guest check. Sales reports are prepared and management uses this information to compare to forecasts, standards, and budgets. It also provides information helpful to management in scheduling workers and forecasting business activity. Finally, the information on sales is compiled and entered into sales journals for financial reports where further decisions will be made after interpreting the information.

B asic Principles for Cash Control

No matter which method of cash collection is used by an operator, basic **cash control** principles apply.

1. With all systems, any handwritten check should be added up with an adding machine. The tape should be stapled to the check so the customer can see that the bill has been added correctly. This also speeds up the auditing of prices and extensions.

2. The guest check should be rung into a cash register that cancels the check by printing a paid total on the check so it cannot be resubmitted for payment. In coffee shop operations where the same check is used to requisition food from the kitchen and given to the guest at the end of the meal, some marking or perforation should be done when the order is filled to prevent the check from being reused on another table. In the case of alcoholic beverages, the simple grease pencil line drawn under the order indicates it has been filled.

3. Require that the guest check be submitted *before* food or beverage will be prepared. Do not under any circumstances fill requests from oral orders. Remember, it must be written on the guest check or entered electronically for it to be tracked by the cost control system.

4. All checks should be rung up individually and the cash drawer should be closed after each check is rung up. The checks should be

audited to see that the verified amount paid is the same as the written total on the check. A newly hired cashier under-rang checks totaling $1,200, which we did not discover until after she had left town. The system was there but management failed to check for compliance.

5. Use a pre-check or dual system of ordering. Checks not only are to be written out but also rung into a pre-check register under the food or beverage key. The check must be verified by the register stamp or receipt before an order is filled. At the end of the night, the totals from the pre-check register are compared to those at the cashier station.

6. Require management initials on all altered checks, especially once the food order has been issued from the kitchen.

7. Limit the access to the cash register to as few individuals as possible. Verify the contents of the drawer whenever there is a shift change. Conduct random drawer changes in the middle of a meal period to check for under-rings.

8. Do not allow the register to be "Z'ed out." Remove the ability to set the register reading back to zero. Make sure register tapes are included with the drawer contents at the end of the shift. The ending reading should be verified by the tape.

9. Guest checks should be custom printed and serially numbered. Issue checks to specific servers and have them turn in unused checks at the end of the shift. Keep unused guest checks in a secure location. Sort used guest checks by number order and compare ending number of unused book to verify that all checks have been accounted for.

10. Have management initial any checks that are over-rung or under-rung and attach an over/under-ring slip. See Figure 11–3. Do not make up over-rings by under-ringing checks. If a check is under-rung, put it in sideways and ring the shorted amount.

11. Develop a uniform set of menu abbreviations for handwritten guest checks, and develop a format that divides the check into sections for food and beverage.

12. Have management approve all voided checks and do not discard voided checks no matter how soiled or torn they may be.

13. Do not deviate from your procedures for cash and check control.

14. Print notices on the checks, menu, and at the cashier's station that inform the customer as to how and whom to pay.

15. If you have a cashier, do not allow servers to collect cash. Direct customer traffic in such a manner that those who pass the cashier's stand without paying can be detected.

```
                    Regan's Restaurants, Inc.

Unit Location:

            Over-Ring/Under-Ring Voucher

  Over-Ring Key No.:            Amount $:

  Under-Ring Key No.:           Amount $:

  Transaction No.:          Check Number:

  Comments:




  Authorization:


         GUEST CHECK MUST ACCOMPANY THIS VOUCHER
```

FIGURE 11–3
Over-ring/Under-ring Voucher

16. Use a duplicate check or pre-check system for main dish items and all food items issued from the kitchen. Inventory pies and other desserts so you can check the sales records against the usage at the end of a meal period.

17. Inventory all bottled beers and wines before and after each meal period and compare to guest checks.

18. Audit checks regularly for correct prices, price extensions, and addition.

19. Use secret shopper services to see that correct procedures are being followed.

20. When coupon promotions are used, require that coupons be stapled to the guest check prior to payment at the cashier to reduce coupon fraud by the cashier or server.

21. If management makes bank deposits, set strict procedures on how often deposits are made. This is especially important for out-of-town locations. Have deposit slips turned in weekly or even better, obtain electronic verification of deposit amounts from bank. This is a particularly vulnerable area where large losses can occur. Management

```
                        Regan's Restaurants, Inc.

    Unit Location:

              CASH PAID-OUT VOUCHER

      Date:                          Amount $:

      Paid To:

      Justification:


      Expense Category:

      Paid Out By:

      Received By:


          RECEIPT MUST ACCOMPANY THIS VOUCHER
```

FIGURE 11–4
Cash Paid-out Voucher

typically prepares and completes sales and deposit reports. If they also count or prepare the daily deposit, ownership must be especially vigilant in monitoring these activities.

22. **Cash paid-out vouchers** and correction vouchers (Figure 11–4) should be reviewed and approved. Authority to approve these vouchers should not be given to persons involved in the cash or check register duties.

Sometimes management can directly contribute to putting employees in a position that the temptation to steal and go undetected is too much. Ironically, the techniques used by employees to steal are not sophisticated or complicated. A large percentage of the theft goes undetected simply because management does not consistently follow up on the very procedures they have in place. Recalling a situation faced at a restaurant where they were just not happy with the amount of profit given the volume of business the restaurant was doing; we suspected that food cost was too high and concentrated our efforts in the back of the house on waste, portioning, and purchase price. We inventoried items that were not rung into the register to tally against the guest checks. Nothing missing could be detected.

It was not until a friend and regular customer, who stopped in for breakfast before his weekly golf game, related that his waitress never gave him a check and made change from her apron. When confronted, the waitress admitted to taking an average of $12 a day for the previous 6 years. We estimate that she took over $30,000. This was made possible because the manager wanted to save money and did not schedule a cashier one until 8:00 A.M. when the restaurant opened at 6:00 A.M.

Telltale Signs of Possible Theft

A number of "danger signs" can point toward the possibility of theft. Sometimes the thief is the person you least expect. It may be a loyal, long-term employee, a close friend, or even a relative.

1. Are you at a loss to explain why your restaurant is not making the profit it should, given the volume of business you are doing?

2. Is any employee or manager overextended to creditors?

3. Has any employee incurred extensive personal or family medical bills without a way to pay them?

4. Has any employee displayed spending habits that surprise you given his or her pay rate (e.g., new car, furniture, clothes, recreational equipment)?

5. Does any employee appear to have a drug or drinking problem and a habit of "partying"?

6. Is any employee openly showing dissatisfaction with his or her rate of pay?

7. Is any employee unusually friendly with one of your supplier's sales or delivery personnel, or your regular customers?

8. Have you been receiving more than the normal number of calls from creditors to verify employment of one employee in particular? Have collection agency personnel or creditors called your company because of one of your employees?

9. Is any employee openly lobbying you to give him or her more responsibility in one or more of the following tasks: receiving cash, recording to accounts, preparing bank deposits, auditing guest checks, or checking deliveries?

10. Is there any employee who constantly asks for advances on his or her pay? (Source: Thomas L. LaJeunesse, "Is Your Company Safe

from Embezzlement?" *The Bottomline*, August–September, 1987, pp. 7–7, 11).

Point-of-Sale Systems for Control

One effective way to reduce and control the loss of cash receipts is through tight inventory control and **point-of-sale systems**. If servers are unable to obtain food or beverage without a hard-copy check or entering the sale electronically, you have eliminated 99 percent of the opportunity for theft. Once a check has been written or entered into the system, an audit trail is established.

Several great products are available to the industry to speed up data accumulation, sorting, and report preparation. Total systems require extensive training of the entire staff as well as management. At first, employees will be intimidated by the new hardware and software. It may take longer for the older employees to feel comfortable and accept the registers and dispensers than the younger ones.

Once installed, operators report a significant reduction in pilferage and theft. Food cost and liquor cost savings often pay for the system in a very short time. This is referred to as the "Big Brother Syndrome." Employees are uncertain of the system's capabilities and are therefore inclined to watch their step. Some operators will report that long-time employees will quit or retire.

One restaurant manager who asked our advice about which system to purchase, related the true story of two long-time employees who left soon after he purchased a system. One was his head bartender and the other his cashier. His head bartender never took a vacation, and the cashier always came out exactly to the penny when she reconciled her register drawer. We surmise that both were stealing heavily from the business.

With a press of a key, a manager can discover which items sell the best at different times of the day. The manager can then order more efficiently and keep inventory to a minimum, eliminating overstocking and running out. The option on the point-of-sale system is referred to as "menu explosion." It has the ability to subtract out of inventory all the ingredients used in the preparation of the item sold. Example: When a cheese enchilada is sold, the prescribed amounts of cheese, lettuce, tomato, spices, and corn enchilada are used. You compare the amount the standardized recipe says you should use to the actual amount left in inventory at the end of the month. What in essence the system does is compare cost of food sold to cost of food consumed. If there is a significant variance in one or more of the ingredients, it "flags" that item on the printout. While it does not tell what was causing the over-usage of a particular ingredient, it alerts the operator to a potential problem area for management to investigate. In this case the variance could be caused by the service person not putting the item on the check, a cook's over-portioning, the ticket not being rung, and so on.

The data such a system provides can be used to track server productivity, initiate promotions and contests for servers, and keep the servers with their customers and not in the kitchen. These systems can also give you sales on a monthly, weekly, daily, meal, or hourly basis. Peak periods can be discovered to assist in scheduling workers more efficiently.

The majority of what is stolen in restaurants comes out of the bar. In a tightly run operation, cash is more likely to be taken by management-level employees than by hourly workers. They know the system better, have a much greater access to cash and inventory, and have considerable autonomy. Hourly employees are more likely to take things. If there is any food or beverage near an open back door, you increase the opportunity for theft.

One of the deterrents management uses to slow down thieves is simply making them aware that they suspect someone to be stealing and letting them know that they are investigating to determine who the person or persons are. In addition, the announcement that management will prosecute to the full extent of the law is also a significant deterrent to petty theft. The habitual thief or person who has a drug problem will not be as motivated not to steal, but it will slow them down for a while.

The internal control process is built from all the rules, regulations, policies, and procedures in place for ordering, receiving, storage, preparation, portioning, and the like. Every activity occurring within the restaurant is linked to your internal controls.

The transmission of information for such controls includes visual inspections or observations. However, it also means checking to see that schedules are manned properly and taking the necessary action when they are not (e.g., calling in another employee and disciplining the absentee). Information flows horizontally and vertically in the organization as well as through the formal and informal communication channels.

P ay By Check, Not Cash

In the restaurant industry, the central collection point for data is the accounting department or, in the case of an independent operation, the accounts payable function. A systematic record-keeping system must be established to record daily sales and organize invoices for payment. To establish **accounts payable control**, it is recommended that all your bills be paid by check and that you open two checking accounts for the business. One is your *general account* into which you deposit your daily sales and from which you write checks to pay your bills. The second checking account is used exclusively for *payroll*. You move funds from your general account to the payroll account as payrolls are processed. Basically, the payroll account "zeros out" each pay period when employees cash their checks.

By using checks to pay 99.9 percent of your bills, only small cash paid-outs are allowed. The check register, along with your invoices, inventory, and deposit slips, is all your accountant needs to prepare your financial statements for the month.

Management Reports

As the level of management for which the reports are intended moves higher, the nature of the information contained in the reports changes. At the departmental or unit manager level, the information is rather detailed and frequently is expressed in such terms as cover per labor hour or labor cost per cover served. These reports provide information that allows the department heads to immediately isolate deficiencies in the operation under their direct control.

At higher levels of management, the information tends to become broader and more summarial in nature. At the level of chief executive, the information is presented in the form of financial statements, operating statistics, departmental performance, budgets, or special reports. Since upper management is responsible for the performance of the total operation, it must be able to take the appropriate action, preventive or corrective, in the event of unsatisfactory performance.

An efficient method of keeping management informed, but not buried in data, is through what is referred to as *exception reporting.* Here management can be kept informed about the current deficiencies and favorable information that exceeds standards. Standards are set that provide for an acceptable range of performance. Only data that deviates to an unacceptable level from the standard are flagged for upper management's attention.

The frequency of **management reports** should be closely related to management's ability to influence or control items included within particular reports. Food and beverage reports must be frequently prepared, but schedules showing insurance and or depreciation schedules are not readily controllable and thus compiled less frequently.

Some reports will contain only objective quantitative information while others may have more subjective qualitative information, as with secret shopper reports on quality of food and service. Examples of both types of reports are given throughout this book and include both financial and statistical information. Financial information requires reporting of absolute dollar values as with the monthly financial statements. Statistical information includes percentages, ratios, and averages; other statistics include units of activity, number sold, customer counts, and productivity indices.

The period of time a report covers is related to the length of the reported activity covered. For example, dining room sales could be reported over the time period of the whole day, meal period, or hour while the report is transmitted to management every day.

The length of time between the end of the reporting period and the delivery of the report must be kept to a minimum. It is related to the time it takes to prepare the report and deliver it. Daily reports, for example, are prepared early the following day to maintain their value for prompt corrective action. The problem with the traditional accounting reports was the time lapse between their preparation and delivery to appropriate management. The fifteenth of the following month is not timely enough. With electronic data processing, reports can be compiled in one third the time it previously took to prepare monthly financial statements.

Internal control covers a broad field and involves far more than cash and check control. Prevention is the key to internal control as it is impossible to completely eliminate fraud when an employee, customer, or purveyor is motivated to steal. Such internal controls are needed most in operations with absentee ownership. Actual visual observation is not sufficient to insure adequate control. Written reports and adherence to standards are critical to minimizing the occurrence of internal theft.

ey Points

- You must be able to identify and describe the various elements of internal control.
- Know the purpose of management information systems.
- Daily departmental reports like the sales report and guest check register are key to internal control of cash receipts.
- Point-of-Sale systems (POS) can make the internal control function more efficient.

ey Terms

Internal controls
Management information systems (MIS)
Daily sales report

Guest check register
Cash control
Point-of-sale systems

Accounts payable control
Management reports

Discussion Questions

1. List and describe the various elements of internal control in a restaurant.
2. What is the purpose of Management Information Systems (MIS)?
3. What is the difference between a POS and a cash register?
4. What are the signs you can look for that may indicate internal theft or fraud may be taking place in your restaurant?

Problem 1

Restaurant Book Daily Exercise
Use the Daily Sales Report shown in Figure 11–1.

1. You are ready to close your cash register. It's is Friday night, 4/23/XX. The weather was rainy and cold all day. *Record these facts.*
2. Yesterday's cash drawer closing readings (today's opening readings) are:
   a. Ending cash $300
   b. Credit cards not deposited $ 75
   c. NSF Checks (to be redeposited) $25

   Instructions: Record these amounts.
3. Zee out the register (you are the owner). The bottom of the tape shows the following readings:

ZZZZZ	**$1,510.00 Food**
ZZZZZ	**$200.00 Beer**
ZZZZZ	**$200.00 Wine**
ZZZZZ	**$100.00 Gifts/Sundries**
ZZZZZ	**$100.00 Sales Tax**

   Instructions: Record the register closing readings.
4. There is an over-ring voucher in the register showing a Food over-ring of $10.

   Instruction: Record this wrong ringup. Note: all wrong ringups are subsequently rung up correctly.
5. Total out the Sales to Line A.
6. Yesterday's Month-to-Date Sales were as follows:
   1. Food $21,500
   2. Beer $ 2,800
   3. Wine $2,800
   4. Gifts/Sundries $ 900

   Instruction: Fill in the above figures and complete the MTD Sales Section.

7. For analysis purposes, a tabulation of revenue from the Dinner Special (Prime rib) is being kept.

   Instruction: Record $420 in the place provided.

8. The cash drawer contains a $200 check from Bob Jones as payment on his "House charge account." *Instruction: record this payment.*

9. The bank returned a twice deposited check of Joe Smith for $100. Your recourse is to hold the check and contact Joe Smith for collection. *Instruction: Record as an item introduced into the cash drawer which should be accounted for.*

10. You added $200 cash into the drawer during the day. *Instruction: Record this addition.*

11. *Instruction: Determine the "TOTAL TO ACCOUNT FOR"*

12. The cash drawer contains two paid out slips. 1. Acme Meats $50 2. Ajax Repair Co. $50 *Instruction: Record, total, and extend the paid outs section.*

13. Checks and cash total to $1,400. $300 is put back in the drawer for tomorrow's open and the rest is deposited. *Instruction: Record this transaction.*

14. Credit card slips total to $1,300 as follows: Mastercard $500; VISA $400; AMX $200, Diner's $100; Carte Blanche $100. All will be deposited **except the Carte Blanche.** *Instruction: Record this transaction.*

15. Bob Jones charged his dinner on his HOUSE ACCOUNT for $98. *Instruction: Record this transaction.*

    INSTRUCTION: CLOSE OUT THE DAILY REPORT <u>NOTE</u>: *Through yesterday 4/22/XX you had a $6 cash overage.*

16. Yesterday's perpetual register count was $202,000. Today's is $204,030. A "perpetual reading" is a *"nonresetable"* total that accumulates all the sales rung into the register. *Instruction: Determine the "Difference to Account For."*

17. You serve only dinner on Saturday.

Facts: Closing Check	$7,204
Opening Check	$7,000
# of Voided Checks	4
Customer Count	200

    Instruction: Determine the Average Check and Average Per Customer.

    Notes:

    1. If the restaurant has a second cash register (bar), use the column to the right of the "Closing Readings" for that register's closing. Remember that for proper control PAID OUTS should only be allowed from one register.

2. The "MEMO ONLY" Sales column could be used for many purposes, i.e., lunch totals, Non-taxable /Sales, Specific Product Sales, etc. . .
3. The Control & Analysis Section may be used to analyze check and customer sales by meal, Dining Room or Bar, or Server.

Note: You will not on the Excel template for this problem that several of the items have been inserted for you. This is to assist you in interpreting the instructions.

12

Financial Analysis

■   ■   ■   ■   ■   ■   ■   ■   ■   ■

THE FUNDAMENTAL PRINCIPLES OF COST CONTROLS

1. Most restaurant operators plan not to fail; however, many who fail do not have a financial plan.

2. In order to make a profit, you have to plan for a profit.

3. Financial management stresses the interpretation of financial data.

4. Financial accounting is primarily intended to provide external user groups with financial data.

5. Managerial accounting is exclusively intended to provide internal users with financial data on operations.

6. Your income statement must be a cost control tool and not just another IRS form.

7. Non-financial data must be incorporated into your accounting reports.

8. Costs are not purely fixed or purely variable.

9. Break-Even and Closing Point analyses are important financial management tools.

10. Follow *Uniform System of Accounts for Restaurants* for all your financial accounting reports.

When you hear and read about successful restaurants, whether independent, franchise, or chain operated, you must realize that their success didn't happen all by good luck and timing but as a result of some very careful and detailed planning. In order to make a profit, one must plan for a profit. All aspects of an operation must be designed to achieve the profit plan. Richard Melman, chairman of Lettuce Entertain You Enterprises, perhaps the most successful restaurant concept developer, addressed the attendees at a past National Restaurant Show in Chicago. His company has launched over 30 different restaurant concepts, most of which have been great successes. His words to the audience were that 85 percent of a concept's success is determined before a restaurant opens its doors to the public. This speaks directly to the importance of due diligence in all areas of site selection, menu, equipment selection, layout, staffing, and the like. The unsuccessful entrepreneur did not plan to fail; he likely *failed to plan.*

Many food service operations offering well-prepared and served food, in attractive surroundings, in good locations, and having adequate customer counts still go out of business. The reason that many businesses fail is the inability of the owner-manager to manage the financial aspects of the business. Now while it is true that volume will make up for minor flaws in your managerial style, poor cost control management will eventually be fatal.

While operators cannot avoid many of the consequences brought about by factors affecting the economy as a whole, those who are prepared in advance can often "weather the storm" while the less prepared close their doors. The critical function of financial management goes hand in hand with cost control. Financial management has three perspectives for assessing the profitability of an enterprise. First, in the beginning and growth stages of the business, decisions surrounding long-term assets and capital expenditures for physical facilities and equipment must be made. The decisions management makes today are a future commitment and long-term financial obligation that must be well planned. The way these assets are financed is the second perspective from which management must assess its financial commitments. The ratio of borrowed funds to owner's investment should not put a strain on the cash flow. Ideally, it should provide an adequate rate of return to the investors while not taxing the operation's ability to retire the debt. Third, current assets and operating capital must be monitored on a day-to-day basis to detect variances from operating standards and serve as the basis for management planning and control in both the short- and long-term decision-making process.

Financial management stresses the *interpretation* rather than the preparation of financial statements and internal reports. Preparation of the forms is an accounting function, but to interpret the data one must have an understanding of what each figure or ratio represents. This requires an insight into the relationships between revenues and expenditures.

Financial Semantics

Let us distinguish the sometimes subtle differences in meaning of several terms used in the area of financial management. There are many kinds of financial records, and their preparation depends upon who ultimately has to interpret them. **Financial accounting** is primarily intended to provide *external user groups* with information concerning the current status of the firm and the results of its operations. It is historical in nature and must be reported precisely and without bias. Reports for the Internal Revenue and Securities and Exchange Commission demand this kind of reporting. Accounting information is the basis for cost standards, budgets, and departmental controls. The information provided by the accounting function is essentially financial in nature and is used by management to compare actual to projected results, direct daily operations, and assist in controlling costs.

Distinctively different is the concept of **managerial accounting**. Where financial accounting provides information concerning the financial status of the firm and the results of its operations, managerial accounting attempts to provide *internal users* with data and information that will serve as a basis for day-to-day operational decision making. Because its use is internal, report preparation is more specific and emphasizes departmental operations; uses nonfinancial data like customer counts, menu sales mix, and labor hours; draws from other disciplines (e.g., marketing, human resources, and production); and supplements financial accounting information.

Cost accounting is a concept that utilizes techniques designed to standardize and systematize the accumulation and analysis of cost data for use in financial management decisions. This is a two-step process. First, management must set the control standards that will be compared to the actual costs incurred. Second, through the use of a cost accounting system, the actual unit costs must be accumulated. Variances between standard and actual costs identify areas for management emphasis either to maximize returns or minimize losses. Knowledge of current and past cost trends allows management to better forecast the future. Pricing policy is also dependent upon cost accounting analysis. With *managerial accounting,* internal reports break down revenues and expenses by department, day, and meal period to make them easier to interpret and to locate the areas that need attention. The aggregate figures on the standard income statement do not allow management to pinpoint the causes of variances. Each revenue producing department must be analyzed separately and then comparisons made between the actual expenses incurred and the revenues produced.

This is why financial statements must be designed as *management tools.* They should *not* be just IRS forms for income tax purposes. The most important financial statement from an operational perspective is the Statement of

Income and Retained Earnings, also known as the Statement of Profit and Loss, which summarizes the historical results of operations for a previous period, usually one month. Management needs the information it contains much more frequently than once a month; daily and weekly reports must be prepared to see emerging trends.

The monitoring of current assets—food and beverage inventory in particular—and operating capital is accomplished through the interpretation of the daily and weekly operating reports prepared for internal control purposes. *Working capital,* defined as the excess of current assets over current liabilities, is the liquid cash the business has to work with. **Working capital turnover** is a measure of short-term cash position. Because the majority of transactions are for cash rather than extended credit terms, a restaurant per se does not need as much working capital as a retail operation. Lending institutions and creditors sometimes use working capital to assess the financial position of the borrower. Adequate working capital gives the business protection against financial stress and is a strong indicator of being able to meet current debt.

A restaurant has a considerably smaller percentage of its total assets in current assets as compared to retail or industrial firms. This is due to the small inventories of perishable commodities that are turned over frequently and the fact that restaurants deal primarily in cash transactions. Credit card charges are debited daily to bank accounts and are treated as cash.

Effective internal reports contain departmental data that can be directly measured and controlled by unit management. Prompt remedial action can be taken when unacceptable variances are detected. Major costs or recurring costs are monitored closely. An effective internal reporting systems organizes operations by revenue centers and assigns cost and income to each. The monitoring of cash receipts and accounts payable is a daily function of management. Cash flow management is perhaps the most critical task for the owner/manager. Funds must be allocated to pay the outstanding bills in a timely manner.

The Uniform System of Accounts for Restaurants (USAR)

The National Restaurant Association has endorsed a uniform accounting system in response to restaurant operators' demand for authentic data on operating results and guidance on their financial problems. With a uniform format for reporting financial data, industry-wide analysis and comparison will be possible. In addition, the USAR provides a turn-key accounting system and it is a system developed by some of the foodservice industry's top financial analysts. It is recommended that you own a copy of the 7th edition of the *Uniform System of Accounts for Restaurants* in your personal library so you will have it for a reference for both you and your accountant. The USAR gives restaurant operators a common language to use in their accounting statements, making it easier to discuss and compare food and labor cost figures with other operators at association meetings.

Management Tools for Financial Analysis

The typical financial statements used by all businesses are the Balance Sheet, Income Statement, and Statement of Cash Flow. The balance sheet reflects the financial position of the foodservice operation and records the assets, liabilities, and owners equity as of a given date. While creditors and investors will find the information on the balance sheet of interest, management's primary financial statement is the income statement. For that reason, the format of the income statement needs to contain far more detail than that required for tax reporting purposes.

Balance Sheet Analysis

While the information contained on the balance sheet does not relate directly to the efficient operation of the foodservice entity, creditors and investors will use the balance sheet to assess the ability of the business to pay its current and future obligations. The format of a restaurant balance sheet is basically the same as any other business.

The fixed assets represent the largest amount of investment, e.g., land, building, furniture, equipment, and leasehold improvements. Because virtually all of the transactions are for cash or cash equivalents, very little working capital is required to operate a restaurant. Suppliers generally do not require payment upon delivery of goods; the restaurant operator actually sells the goods to get the money to make payment to the supplier the following week. This is unlike the retail sector (e.g., appliances, electronics, and automobiles) where dealers are required to take out bank loans to purchase their goods before they are sold to the public.

BALANCE SHEET FORMATS FOR ANALYSIS

There are two primary ways the balance sheet can be arranged for financial analysis: 1. **Comparative Statements** or Horizontal Analysis and 2. **Common-size Statements** or Vertical Analysis. The comparative format compares two balance sheets, the one for the current year and one from the previous year. Month to month comparison of balance sheets will not show significant differences except in the current assets, current liabilities and retained earnings in owners' equity. Table 12.1 shows a balance sheet in both comparative and common-size "report" format. Comparative or horizontal analysis shows both the absolute or dollar variance and the relative or percentage variance between statements. The absolute difference between the current period and the past period value for each asset, liability, and owners' equity line item is converted to a percentage by dividing the change in value by the amount for the previous period. For example, General Bank balance went from a positive $2,878.82 to a negative $6,030.28 or a difference of ($8,909.10). When divided by $2,878.82 the percentage difference is over 300 percent. *The reason this occurred was due to writing checks on the last day of the month using sales from the first few days of the new month to cover them. Subsequently, the General Bank account would be "overdrawn" on the last day of the month.*

The common-size statements, or vertical analysis, reduces each asset line item to a percentage of total assets. Therefore, total assets equal 100% and likewise, total liabilities and owners' equity equals 100%. When you total the percentages of the individual assets, they will equal 100%. In the example shown in Table 12.1, the amount of cash in the General Bank account was a minus 8.39% in 1998 compared to the equivalent of 3.55% of total assets the previous year. Such variances are investigated to determine the cause. In this case it was due to overdrawing the checking account at the end of the month. In both **comparative balance sheets** and **common-size balance sheets**, all changes from one period to the next are easily detected. Management then investigates any significant changes to determine the cause.

R atios

In addition to the comparative and common-size balance sheets, management will also utilize a number of balance sheet ratios to analyze and measure the amount of debt versus equity and the liquidity of the operation. Ratio analysis is a tool to assess whether the financial condition has remained unchanged, improved, or declined from one fiscal period to another. It is important to understand that computing a **ratio** is not financial analysis but simply a way to express numerical relationships between two numbers. The interpretation of whether a ratio is acceptable or not depends on which side of the negotiation table you are sitting. Creditors and investors have different perspectives and standards than owners and managers when it comes to interpreting balance sheet ratios.

Table 12.1 Comparative Balance Sheet

| | | | | Common-Size Balance Sheet | | |
| | | | | Assets | | |
Assets	2004	2003	$ Variance	% Variance	2004	2003
Current Assets						
Petty Cash	$ 946	$ 946	$ 0 -	0.00%	1.32%	1.17%
General Bank	$ (6,030)	$ 2,879	$ (8,909)	-309.47%	-8.39%	3.55%
Payroll Bank	$ 1,185	$ 1,230	$ (44)	-3.59%	1.65%	1.52%
Barnett-BAC Bank	$ 15	$ 2,503	$ (2,489)	-99.41%	0.02%	3.09%
Sun Bank	$ 5,105	$ 1,295	$ 3,811	294.31%	7.10%	1.60%
Savings	$ 5,562	$ 5,291	$ 271	5.13%	7.74%	6.52%
Sun Bank Central Park	$ 10,260	$ 5,605	$ 4,655	83.05%	14.28%	6.91%
Accts Rec AMX	$ 3,466	$ 3,317	$ 148	4.47%	4.82%	4.09%
Accts Rec Diners Club	$ 708	$ -	$ 708	100.00%	0.98%	0.00%
Supplies Inventory	$ 2,075	$ 1,733	$ 342	19.71%	2.89%	2.14%
Food Inventory	$ 7,992	$ 5,499	$ 2,494	45.35%	11.12%	6.78%
Beverage Inventory	$ 1,742	$ 1,458	$ 284	19.49%	2.42%	1.80%
Prepaid Insurance	$ 3,439	$ 2,295	$ 1,145	49.90%	4.79%	2.83%
Prepaid Rent	$ 1,700	$ 1,700	$ 0 -	0.00%	2.37%	2.10%
Prepaid Equip Rental	$ 1,150	$ 1,150	$ 0 -	0.00%	1.60%	1.42%

(continued)

Table 12.1   Comparative Balance Sheet (Continued)

| | | | | | Common-Size Balance Sheet | |
| | | | | | **Assets** | | |
Assets	2004	2003	$ Variance	% Variance	2004	2003
Total Current Assets	$ 39,316	$ 36,900	$ 2,416	6.55%	54.71%	45.49%
Fixed Assets						
Auto and Trucks	$ 3,800	$ 3,800	0 -		5.29%	4.68%
Leasehold Improvements	$ 37,778	$ 35,793	$ 1,985	5.54%	52.57%	44.13%
Furn/Fixt/Equip	$ 9,843	$ 9,336	$ 507	5.43%	13.70%	11.51%
Machinery-Equip	$ 47,575	$ 44,570	$ 3,005	6.74%	66.20%	54.95%
Less Depreciation	$ (68,795)	$ (51,635)	$ (17,160)	33.23%	−95.72%	−63.66%
Net Fixed Assets	$ 30,202	$ 41,865	$ (11,664)	−27.86%	42.02%	51.61%
Other Assets						
Deposits	$ 2,350	$ 2,350	0 -	0.00%	3.27%	2.90%
Total Assets	$71,868	$ 81,115	$ (9,248)	−11.40%	100.00%	100.00%
Current Liabilities						
Accounts Payable	$ (17,434)	$ (8,771)	$ 8,663	−98.76%	24.26%	10.81%
Social Security Fund	$ (14,484)	$ (3,772)	$ 10,712	−283.95%	20.15%	4.65%
Withholding Tax	$ 5,288	$ (3,846)	$ (9,134)	237.48%	−7.36%	4.74%
Federal Depository	$ 6,141	$ 5,737	$ (404)	−7.04%	−8.55%	−7.07%

Sales Tax Fund	$ (2,941)	$ (2,517)	$ 424	−16.83%	4.09%	3.10%
Total Current Liabilities	$ (23,430)	$ (13,169)	$ 10,260	−16.83%	32.60%	16.24%
Long Term Liabilities						
N/P Atlantic Bank	$ (2,001)	$ (10,002)	$ (8,002)	80.00%	2.78%	12.33%
N/P INS-SOBT	$ (407)	$ (1,017)	$ (610)	60.01%	0.57%	1.25%
N/P 3M Music System	$ (1,023)	$ (1,047)	$ (23)	2.24%	1.42%	1.29%
N/P Atlantic Auto	$ -	$ (146)	$ (146)	100.00%	0.00%	0.18%
N/P Insurance	$ (700)	$ (342)	$ 358	−104.84%	0.97%	0.42%
N/P Sun Bank CPK	$ (25,250)	$ (31,000)	$ (5,750)	18.55%	35.13%	38.22%
N/P Sun CPK	$ (2,500)	$ -	$ 2,500	100.00%	3.48%	0.00%
Accr Prop Taxes	$ (2,982)	$ (2,600)	$ 382	−14.68%	4.15%	3.21%
Total Long Term Liabilities	$ (34,862)	$ (46,153)	$ (11,291)	24.46%	48.51%	56.91%
Total Liabilities	$ (58,292)	$ (59,323)	$ (1,031)	1.74%	81.11%	73.14%
Owner's Equity			0 -			
Capital Stock Issued	$ (20,500)	$ (20,500)	0 -	0.00%	28.52%	25.28%
Retained Earnings	$ (1,293)	$ (433)	$ 860	−198.78%	1.80%	0.53%
Net Profit or Loss	$ 8,217	$ (850)	$ (9,067)	1066.77%	−11.43%	1.05%
Total Equity	$ (13,576)	$ (21,783)	$ (8,207)	37.68%	18.89%	26.86%
Total Liabilities & OE	$ (71,868)	$ (81,105)	$ (9,238)	11.39%	100.00%	100.00%

There are three standards used to evaluate ratios for the current accounting period. They can be compared to ratios from a previous period, e.g., last month, last year; they can be compared to forecasted expectations or budgets; and they can be compared to other units, if a chain operation, or to industry averages for similar types of foodservices. Comparison to industry averages is the least reliable of the standards one can use. You are better off comparing to past periods budgeted figures.

The evaluation of the ratio will also depend on which standards are used by internal or external reviewers. For example, a current ratio of 1.5:1 may be unacceptable to a lender who wants to see a ratio of $2 in current assets for every $1 of current liabilities. On the other hand, an owner may find that 1.5:1 is too high and that a .5:1 reflects a better use of the liquid cash generated by the operation. A current ratio of .5:1 is what two of the top fast food hamburger chains show on their annual report to stockholders. The textbook interpretation that a current ratio of less than 2:1 means that the operation is not able to meet current liabilities out of operating revenue does not necessarily apply to restaurant operations where the cash-to-cash cycle is much shorter than what occurs in normal retail stores who have to pre-pay for their merchandise. Of course, the assumption is that the ratio standards were objectively and realistically determined by management. If the standards were unrealistic to begin with, comparisons to actual ratios will cause your analysis to be flawed.

Regardless of these shortcomings, ratios are of significant value in helping managers assess the effectiveness of their operational decisions, the performance of units, departments, shifts, and individuals. Financial ratios allow absentee owners and managers to monitor the efficiency of their operations without having to be there during all operating hours. When ratios are used with other financial and operating reports, owners and managers now have more detailed information than is typically found on standard financial statements.

Balance sheet ratios are separated into the following classes:

1. Liquidity Ratios
2. Solvency Ratios
3. Activity Ratios
4. Profitability Ratios.

LIQUIDITY RATIOS

Liquidity ratios are used to assess the ability of the food service operation to meet its current liabilities without having to convert assets to cash. The formula for the *current ratio* is current assets divided by current liabilities.

Using the figures from Table 12.1, the current ratio for Angelo's Restaurant can be calculated as follows:

2003

$$\frac{\$36,900}{\$28,323} = 1.30{:}1 \text{ or } \$1.30 \text{ in current assets for every } \$1 \text{ of current liabilities, leaving a "cushion" of } \$.30$$

2004

$$\frac{\$39,366}{\$33,042} = 1.19{:}1 \text{ or } \$1.19 \text{ in current assets for every } \$1 \text{ in current liabilities.}$$

The current ratio for 2004 was lower than in 2003 indicating that there were fewer dollars of current assets to pay for the current liabilities. However, it is still greater than a .5:1 ratio which is considered acceptable by industry standards. Again, if you were a lender, you might find cause for some concern if you required a minimum current ratio higher than 1.19:1. After reviewing the current assets for both periods, one sees that the reason for the decline was the negative value in the General Bank account at the end of the last accounting period. If this occurred every month, management and creditors would both be questioning the ratio.

Another important liquidity measure is Working Capital. The formula for working capital is current assets minus current liabilities.

$$2003 \text{ WC} = \$36,900 - \$13,169 = \$23,731$$
$$2004 \text{ WC} = \$39,316 - \$23,430 = \$15,886$$

In this example, there is positive working capital for both years, although the amount of working capital has declined by $7,845. Management will want to watch to see if working capital continues to erode. The primary cause would be declining sales and loss of market share. However, many food service operations have negative working capital and are still solvent operations that pay their bills on time. Negative working capital typically is found in newly opened businesses where they have not had time to build cash reserves from operations. Again, one must look at more than just one ratio when seeking to assess the financial condition of a foodservice enterprise.

SOLVENCY RATIOS

Solvency ratios measure the degree of debt financing by a food service enterprise and are used as indicators of the operation's ability to meet its long-term debt obligations. Solvency ratios are used primarily by external users like lenders and creditors. Generally speaking, if a restaurant operation has assets valued at more than its liabilities it is considered solvent. The formula for computing the solvency ratio is simply Total Assets divided by Total Liabilities.

$$2003 \ \frac{\$81,115}{\$59,323} = 1.36{:}1 \text{ or that there are \$1.36 in assets for every \$1}$$

of liability.

$$2004 \ \frac{\$71,868}{\$58,292} = 1.23{:}1 \text{ or that there were \$1.23 in assets for every \$1}$$

of liability. This shows a decline over the previous year.

The difference is only $.13 but it represents a 9.55% decrease over 2003. Again, much of it can be attributed to the deficit in the General Bank account balance.

Another solvency ratio used by external financial analysts is the Debt-Equity Ratio. It compares the establishment's debt to its net worth or owners' equity. It is an indication of the restaurant's ability to meet its long-tem debt obligations.

The formula is Total Liabilities divided by Total Owners' Equity. Using the figures from Table 12.1, we calculate the following:

$$2003 \ \frac{\$59,323}{\$21,783} = 2.72{:}1 \text{ or \$2.72 in debt for every \$1 of owners' equity.}$$

$$2004 \ \frac{\$58,292}{\$13,576} = 4.29{:}1 \text{ or \$4.29 in debt for every \$1 of owners' equity.}$$

Management and creditors would likely be concerned over this dramatic decline. The increase in the ratio of $1.57 is a 58% increase over the previous year. There are indications that financial stress is occurring and if it continues, it will most certainly have negative repercussions on the operation's credit-worthiness with lenders and suppliers. It would appear the profitability of the operation is eroding. If revenues are also declining, marketing efforts will need to be intensified to regain market share.

ACTIVITY RATIOS

Activity ratios measure internal management's use of the firm's financial resources. Ratios such as inventory turnover, average guest check, seat turn over, prime cost, and food, beverage and labor cost ratios are included in this category.

PROFITABILITY RATIOS

Profitability ratios are used to examine the results of all areas of management responsibility. The primary ratio is of course, net profit. On the income statement, we would look at gross profit dollars and percentage as an indication of management's effectiveness in utilizing the business's assets.

There are many more ratios that are utilized by management and financial analysts in assessing the financial condition of a business. While it is beyond the scope of this text to cover them all in detail, the reader is advised to ask an accountant or financial advisor about which ones are most relevant for their purposes.

Turning the Common Income Statement into a Cost Control Tool

The standard income statement format shown in Figure 12–1 can be improved even further to be a useful tool to management in financial analysis. It is the recommended system format for restaurants according to the seventh edition of the *Uniform System of Accounts for Restaurants,* published by the National Restaurant Association.

The major weakness of this format is that it provides only *summary* information that totals income and expense during a particular period of time. In order for management to be on top of day-to-day operations, the financial data must be supplemented with *managerial accounting* information, much of which is non-financial data. Examples of non-financial data that aid in turning the common income statement into a managerial accounting tool are shown in Table 12.2.

The income statement needs to include information that will provide specific facts about the operation that add detail, to the financial information it reports. Most financial statements are prepared only once a month. The supporting information is compiled weekly and even daily.

The daily and weekly internal operating reports emphasize departmental breakdowns of both financial and non-financial statistics; for example, customer counts, labor hours, and menu sales mix. This information is needed to pinpoint variances and check compliance to cost standards. The traditional income statement merely *summarizes* accounting data where departmental reports emphasize specific detailed operating statistics.

The assumption is made that in the absence of departmental reports, the income statement will be the primary tool for assessing operational efficiency. This makes it imperative that financial data is presented in a manner that provides management with a clear picture of revenues and costs.

NAME OF RESTAURANT PERIOD COVERED BY STATEMENT		
	$ Amounts	**% Percent**
Sales		
Food		
Beverages		
Total Sales		
Cost of Sales		
Food		
Beverage		
Total Cost of Sales		
Gross Profit		
Food		
Beverage		
Total Gross Profit		
Other Income		
Total Income		
Operating Expenses		
Salaries and Wages		
Employee Benefits		
Direct Operating Expenses		
Music and Entertainment		
Marketing		
Energy and Utility Services		
Administrative and General Expenses		
Repairs and Maintenance		
Total Operating Expenses		
Income before Occupancy Costs, Interest, Depreciation, Corporate Overhead, and Income Taxes		
Rent		
Property Taxes		
Property Insurance		
Total Occupancy Costs		
Income before Interest, Depreciation, Corporate Overhead, and Income Taxes		
Interest		
Depreciation		
Corporate Overhead Charges		
Income before Income Taxes		
Income Taxes		
Net Income		
Retained Earnings, Beginning of Period		
Less Dividends		
Retained Earnings, End of Period		

FIGURE 12–1
Statement of Income and Retained Earnings
Source: Uniform System of Accounts for Restaurants, 7th Ed. National Restaurant Association, 1996.

Table 12.2   Monthly Income Statement\Internal Management Tool Format

	$ Amount	% of Sales	Cost per Cover
Sales			
Food	34,499	70.5	$6.63
Beer/Wine	5,919	12.1	$1.14
Liquor	8,107	16.6	$1.56
Vending	23	.0	$.0
Promotional Sales	368	.8	$.07
Cash Over/Under	35	.1	$.0
Total Sales	**48,951**	**100.0**	**$9.41**
Direct Departmental Expenses			
Cost of Food Consumed	14,696	42.6	$2.83
Less Employee Meals	(690)	(2.0)	($.13)
Cost of Food Sold	14,006	40.6	$2.69
Beer/Wine	1,378	23.3	$.26
Liquor	1,443	17.8	$.28
Cost of Beverage Sold	2,821	21.1	$.54
Promotional Items	294	79.9	$.06
Food Wages	7,850	22.7	$1.51
Beverage Wages	1,000	7.1	$.19
Total Wages	8,850	18.2	$1.70
Employee Meals	690	2.0	$.13
Payroll Taxes/Insurance	760	1.5	$.14
Total Departmental Expenses	**27,421**	**56.0**	**$5.27**
Gross Margin	**21,530**	**44.0**	**$4.14**
Operating Expenses			
Laundry and Uniforms	950	1.9	$.18
Bar Supplies	250	.5	$.05
Kitchen Supplies	275	.6	$.05
Cleaning Supplies	459	.9	$.09
Utilities	1,350	2.8	$.26
Telephone	50	.1	$.01
Repairs and Maintenance	250	.5	$.05
Equipment Leases	475	.9	$.09
Printing and Menus	168	.3	$.03
Credit Card Expense	125	.25	$.02
Advertising	900	1.8	$.17
Total Operating Expenses	**5,252**	**10.7**	**$1.00**

(continued)

Table 12.2 *Continued*

	$ Amount	% of Sales	Cost per Cover
Profit before Admin. and Gen. Expense	**16,278**	**33.3**	**$3.13**
Administrative and General Expenses			
Management Salaries	4,000	8.3	$.77
Management Benefits and Taxes	810	1.7	$.16
Office Expense	525	1.0	$.10
Travel and Entertainment	195	.4	$.03
Automobile	275	.6	$.05
Accounting and Legal Fees	325	.7	$.06
Licenses and Fees	25	0	$.0
Total	**6,155**	**12.6**	**$1.18**
Profit before Occupational Expenses	**10,123**	**20.7**	**$1.95**
Occupational Expense			
Rent	2,500	5.1	$.48
Interest	400	.8	$.08
Property Taxes	325	.7	$.06
Insurance	475	.9	$.09
Total	3,700	7.5	$.71
Profit before Depreciation	6,423	13.2	$1.24
Depreciation	200	.4	$.04
Pretax Profit	6,223	12.8	$1.20

Nonfinancial Data	
Food Labor Hours	2,160
Beverage Labor Hours	200
Total Labor Hours	2,360
Wage per Food LH	$3.63
Wage per Beverage LH	$5.00
Average Wage per LH	$3.75
Sales per Food LH	$15.97
Sales per Beverage LH	$70.13
Average Sales per LH	$20.56
Customer Count	5,200
Average Sales per Cover	$9.33
Labor Cost per Cover	$1.70
Covers per LH	2.2

The general organization of the income statement shown in Table 12.2 indicates a *detailed* breakdown of sales and expenses. The IRS does not require this kind of detail. Management, on the other hand, needs to have separate sales figures for food, beverage, and banquets broken down separately. This detail is missing from most monthly income statements; your accountant should provide you with the information you want, not just what a computer is programmed to prepare for some generic accounting software program.

Expenses should be similarly separated to correspond to the same sales breakdowns. The section of the statement, **Direct Departmental Expenses,** groups all expenses that can be directly attributed to the revenues they produce. *Operating Expenses* are those costs that can be at least partially controlled by management and follow in the format. Expenses such as laundry and uniforms, utilities, and supplies are examples.

They are followed by *Administrative and General Expenses,* commonly grouped under the category with fixed and non-controllable expenses. They are typically not a responsibility of the operational management team in an absentee owner operation. Included here are management salaries, fringe benefits, licenses, and fees.

Another category of expenses are identified as *Occupational Expenses,* also referred to as fixed expenses, that include rent, interest, property taxes, and depreciation. Note that regardless of the classification, every revenue and expense is expressed as a dollar value, a percentage of *total* sales, and as a cost per cover.

Ratios and percentages are not effective in localizing trouble spots or measuring performance of individual departments unless they can be calculated by figures taken exclusively from their respective departments. For example, the *total* cost of beverage sold is 21.1 percent, but there is a 5.5 percent differential between beer/wine and liquor cost that would not have been readily noticed were they not broken down and reported separately.

Operators like to compare their percentages with industry averages published in trade journals as a reference point for their cost standards. The fact that a difference is found or that they have identical numbers does not necessarily mean that cost optimization has or has not been achieved. The reasons that can be causing the differences or similarities can be due to prices, costs, and menu sales mix.

One of the likely reasons for differences in payroll, food cost, or beverage cost percentages comes from the way revenues and expenses are separated. For example, if beer, wine, and spirits are all grouped into the categories "beverage sales" and "beverage costs," the percentages that result will be significantly different from another operator who separates the three. Restaurants typically sell more beer and wine than mixed drinks, thereby driving up the overall beverage cost percentage. See Chapter 9 for more beverage cost information.

Unless identical records are kept, it is not likely that two independent operators can use each other's cost standards interchangeably. The same caution holds true for food and labor cost comparisons. If salaried personnel are included with hourly workers, the percentage will be greater than if they were separated. The message here is simply to be aware when comparing operational data with industry averages or other operations.

When the standard accounting information is combined with certain non-financial data on the income statement, it becomes much more valuable as a management tool. Most of the non-financial data is already assembled on daily cash reports and payroll records so it is easy and inexpensive to incorporate it into your income statement format.

Daily sales reports will give you sales by meal periods and corresponding customer counts. Labor hours are tallied for every hourly paid employee and are recorded every time a payroll is processed. By simply separating time cards by job categories—that is, busboys, cooks, servers, and so on—labor hour distribution among employees can be seen.

Sales can then be shown on a per labor hour basis and supplement the traditional labor cost percentage used by all operators. Evaluating the number of customers served for every labor hour worked will indicate the true productivity of the employee. Calculation of average wage per labor hour worked and customer served can indicate far more specific causes of payroll problems than can an aggregate ratio of total labor to total sales. Refer to Chapter 10 for detailed report formats.

While food, beverage, and labor costs get the majority of management's attention, and rightly so, what remains cannot be ignored. With the nickels and dimes that are made or lost on each dollar of sales, even the smallest expense must be kept in line. By calculating the *cost per cover* for all the controllable expenses over a period of time, comparisons to past periods can reveal much in the search for causes of profit declines.

In the example statement provided, Table 12.2, total wages were $8,850, or 18.2 percent of total sales. But further breakdown indicates that food related payroll of $7,850, was 22.7 percent of *food* sales and that beverage payroll of $1,000 was 7.1 percent of *beverage* sales. This is an example of why it is important to separate revenues and costs by department. Food related payroll makes up 88.7 percent of the total payroll, indicating that improvements made there are likely to be reflected in a lower overall payroll percentage.

Payroll records show that 2,360 labor hours were worked (2,160 in food and 200 in beverage). The average cost per labor hour was $3.75 ($8,850/ 2,360). By separating food and beverage labor, the cost per labor hour proves to be $3.63 in the food area ($7,850/2,160) and $5.00 in the beverage area ($1,000/200). This information can be broken down further by individual job categories so the average cost per labor hour can be shown for servers, cooks, busboys, cocktail waitresses, bartenders, and so forth.

Sales per labor hour can be similarly calculated and compared. The average sales per labor hour worked was $20.56 ($48,525/2,360). When broken down by food and beverage, it is $15.97 ($34,499/2,160) and $70.13 ($14,026/200), respectively. The figures can be broken down further by meal periods to see the times of day when sales per labor hour are highest.

Although this type of information can increase the management value of the income statement and help establish standards for forecasting and costs, it is subject to distortion and therefore inaccurate interpretation. Inflation and wage and menu price increases will require some type of adjustment over time to keep comparison of present figures to past figures relevant. The inclusion of customer counts is very important because it is perhaps the one true inflation-proof figure.

During the statement period, 5,200 covers were served. This information was obtained from guest checks and server counts. Utilizing this with the previous revenues and cost breakdowns, the value of the income statement as a management tool increases.

The labor cost per cover served is $1.70 ($8,850/5,200), and the average number of covers served per labor hour was 2.2 (5,200/2,360). The initial calculation of this type of information becomes more useful over time as comparisons of one period to another are made. You can begin to see trends that are developing and the highs and lows in sales and costs.

Every item on the income statement can be expressed as a cost per cover served. The data can be presented to show current period, year to date, and the previous year's results (not shown). Computer software makes such detailed financial statement reporting easy and inexpensive to produce. The majority of management's time no longer is spent on the preparation of the cost control documents, but in the interpretation of the data.

The Statement of Cash Flows

The third and last statement of financial analysis is the **Statement of Cash Flows** (SCF). It is a necessary addition because the balance sheet and income statement do not provide all of the financial information about a restaurant's operation. The income statement and balance sheet do not provide information on how cash generated from operations was used during the period to create the financial position shown on the balance sheet (see Table 12.1). The preferred format for the SCF is the Indirect Method. It starts with net income which is then adjusted for non-cash items included on the income statement, e.g. depreciation and amortization. Table 12.3 shows a cash flow statement prepared by the indirect method.

Table 12.3   Statement of Cash Flow

Name of Restaurant or Company

Period Covered by Statement (Indirect Method)

	Current Period	Previous Period	Change
Cash Flows From Operating Activities			
Net Income *(From Income Statement)*	na	na	$ 3,112
Adjustments to Reconcile Net Income to Net Cash Provided By Operating Activities			
Depreciation and Amortization	$ 200	na	$ 200
Changes in Assets and Liabilities			
Increase in Accounts Receivable	$ 4,174	$ 3,317	$ (857)
Increase in Inventories	$ 11,809	$ 8,690	$ (3,119)
Increase in Prepaid Expenses	$ 6,289	$ 5,145	$ (1,144)
Increase in Accounts Payable	$ 17,434	$ 8,771	$ 8,663
Increase in Accured Expenses	$ 2,982	$ 2,600	$ 382
Decrease in Interest	$ 400	$ 600	$ (200)
Increase in Taxes Payable *(All)*	$ 8,977	$ 6,998	$ 1,979
Total Adjustments			$ 5,704
Net Cash Provided by Operating Activities			$ 8,816
Cash Flows from Investing Activities			
Proceeds from Sale of Equipment	$ 2,500	$ -	$ 2,500
Cash Payments for Leasehold Improvements	$ 10,000	$ -	$ (10,000)
Down Payment on Equipment Purchases	$ 1,200	$ -	$ (1,200)
Net Cash Used in Investing Activities			$ (8,700)
Cash Flows from Financing Activities			
Net Borrowings under Line-of-Credit	$ 18,852.00	$ 10,000.00	$ 8,852
Decrease in Notes Payable	$ 31,881	$ 43,554	$ (11,673)
Net Cash Provided by Financing Activities			$ (2,821)
Net Increase/Decrease in Cash and Cash Equiv.			$ (2,705)
Cash and Cash Equivalents: Beginning of Period			$ 19,748
Cash and Cash Equivalents: End of Period			$ 17,043
Supplemental Disclosures of cash flow information			
Cash Paid During Period for:			
Interest (net of amount capitalized)	$ 400		
Income Taxes	$ 3,112		
Cash Inflow (+) when Assets Decrease & Liabilities Increase			
Cash Outflow (–) when Assets Increase & Liabilities Decrease			

The SCF reports cash receipts and cash payments in three categories or activities: operating, investing, and financing. The major purpose of the SCF is to provide relevant information about the cash receipts and disbursements. The information contained on the SCF will assist investors, creditors, and managers to:

- Assess the restaurant's ability to generate positive future cash flows
- Assess the restaurant's ability to meet its financial obligations
- Assess the major sources of cash and how much relates to the restaurant's operations
- Assess the effect investing and financing during the accounting period.

The major users of the SCF are management, investors and creditors.

As a rule of thumb, there will be a cash outflow when assets *increase* or when liabilities *decrease*. For example, Inventories increased from $8,690 to $11,809 on successive balance sheets and there was a cash *outflow* of $3,119. Inventories of food, beverage, and supplies are *current assets* that have increased from the previous balance sheet. Therefore, this results in a cash outflow to pay for the additional inventory. Cash outflows from operating activities include cash payments for food, beverage, supplies, and other operating expenses not resulting from transactions defined as investing or financing activities.

Cash inflows from operating activities are the cash received from transactions involving the production, delivery, and sale of goods and services and all other cash receipts, but not from transactions defined as investing or financing activities. Cash inflows occur when assets decrease or liabilities increase. You will note that Accounts Payable increased from $8,771 to $17,434. This results in a cash inflow of $8,663 for the accounting period.

A way of distinguishing between cash inflow and outflow transactions is to remember the following:

	Assets	Liabilities
Cash Inflow (+) when	Decrease	Increase
Cash Outflow	Increase	Decrease

Investing activities relate primarily to cash flows from the acquisition and disposition of non-current assets, particularly investments, property, and equipment. Financing activities relate to cash flows resulting from the issuance or retirement of debt and the issuance and re-purchase of capital stock. On the cash flows statement we see that as the combined result of selling some equipment, paying cash for leasehold improvements, and putting a down payment on new equipment, the net result of investing activities during the period was a cash outflow of $8700. Cash inflow from investing activity of $2,500 occurred with the sale of the old equipment, a fixed asset.

Financing activities include increases in owner's equity and/or payments to owners for their investment. **Cash inflows** from financing activities occur when owners increase their capital investment in the business (put more of their own money into the business) or from proceeds from mortgages, notes, and other borrowings from outside lenders. **Cash outflows** occur when loans are paid to these creditors and long term debt is retired.

During the accounting period shown on the Statement of Cash Flows, we see on the monthly income statement that the restaurant took in $48,951 in total sales that resulted in a Pretax Profit of $6,223. The Statement of Cash Flows tells us that the amount of cash and cash equivalents decreased by $2,705 dollars during the accounting period. When you calculate the difference in all the cash related asset accounts on the consecutive balance sheets, you will see that the total decreased by $2,705 from the previous period. The Statement of Cash Flow tells us how our cash was used.

BREAK-EVEN ANALYSIS FOR RESTAURANT OPERATIONS

A helpful technique that provides additional information in making financial and operation decisions is **break-even point analysis** (BEP). Break-even is a cost accounting tool commonly defined as the volume point at which an operation becomes profitable. You need to understand the general effects of what is referred to as the **volume-cost-profit ratio**. When a change occurs in either sales volume or cost, the profit will be affected. Therefore, there is no single or absolute BEP for a restaurant. It is constantly changing and may actually be several hundred dollars more or less than the theoretical calculated BEP. The reason for this is that costs are *not perfectly fixed or variable.* Many expenses on the income statement possess, at different levels of volume, both fixed and **variable cost** components. *Semi-fixed* is used on those fixed costs with some variable cost tendencies, and **semi-variable cost** is used to describe variable costs with some fixed cost properties. If purely fixed and variable costs were shown on a graph, like those in Figures 12–2 and 12–3, they would make the break-even analysis much more precise. Some expenses behave like those shown in Figure 12–4, with both fixed and variable properties at different sales volumes.

All restaurants have fixed costs, and these fixed costs continue to be incurred, even if a restaurant is closed. When it opens for business, it will incur additional variable costs. However, consider the fact that a **fixed cost** can be a **discretionary cost**, as with an advertising budget, or a *committed costs,* as with rent or principal loan payments.

Another term for *discretionary* is *managed,* in that fixed costs are *totally controlled* by management. They may be planned or budgeted, or they may be deleted if management sees that the restaurant is not deriving any additional business from the advertising. Expenses like depreciation and rent cannot be

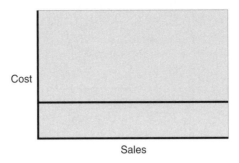

FIGURE 12–2
Fixed Cost Behavior

easily changed with just a management decision, as they require other parties to approve and negotiations must take place. While they are not *absolutely* fixed (committed), they are fixed for purposes of the accounting definition. Fixed cost behavior is not tied to or influenced by the level of business volume. In contrast, variable costs increase and decrease at a predictable percentage amount when volume increases or decreases. The two most exemplary variable costs are food and beverage cost. As long as the sales mix of food and beverage remains consistent to past sales mixes and prices, portioning, and recipe costs are held constant, the food and beverage percentage will be the same regardless of whether sales are $1,000 or $10,000.

However, some conditions cause these variable percentages to vary, and they have to do with the elements previously mentioned. If a discount promotion is run, it will change the sales mix, food costs, and sales volume. See Chapter 6 for coverage of discount pricing. Happy hours in the lounge or discount coupons in the paper will cause the cost of sales to increase.

Semi-fixed costs have characteristics of both fixed and variable costs. They are fixed to a point but after volume reaches a certain level, they will

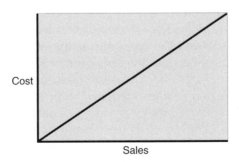

FIGURE 12–3
Variable Cost Behavior

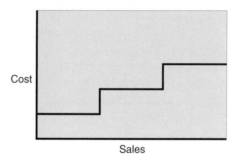

FIGURE 12–4
Semi-variable/fixed Cost Behavior

increase. Utilities are an example: When the volume of business increases, more gas and electricity will be needed for cooking, washing dishes, and cooling or heating the premises. These expenses may increase 4 to 5 percent in response to a 10 percent increase in volume.

Labor is another example of a semi-fixed expense. Labor cost is fixed at the "skeleton crew" level of staffing. Regardless of the slowness of business, management must schedule this minimum staff to open the doors. The skeleton crew can handle a pretty good number of customers, but after a certain number, additional employees must be scheduled in certain job categories to meet the quantitative and qualitative service standards. Typically, a restaurant will schedule additional service employees as the number of cooks, bartenders, and hostesses remains the same.

Since BEP analysis must assume that costs are purely fixed or variable, something must be done with these *semi*-costs so they fit into one of the two classifications of cost. What you can do is separate them into their fixed and variable components through statistical methods or by what we call an "educated estimate."

The terms *marginal income, contribution margin, profit-volume ratio,* **gross profit,** and *gross margin* have been used to describe basically the same thing; the amount that remains after variable costs have been deducted from sales. However, always check the meaning of the term used by an author when these terms are used because they may mean something other than what has been defined here. In this book, the preferred term is **contribution margin**. It is expressed as a percentage calculated with the formula: 100% − Variable Cost Percent. If total variable cost were 63.5 percent, the contribution margin would be 36.5 percent, which is the amount left to pay the remaining fixed-occupancy costs. Accounting and finance theory tell us that this represents the actual cost behavior and that every dollar brought in above the break-even point will produce added profit equal to the contribution margin ratio. The truth is that the ratio fluctuates because of the changes in costs or volume.

The traditional break-even formula seems so simple and easy to follow. It is the numbers and percentages you use in the formula that are difficult to compute accurately. The following assumptions are made for BEP in this chapter:

1. Food and beverage costs are 100% variable.

2. Hourly payroll is semi-fixed and management salaries and benefits are discretionary fixed costs.

3. Advertising and promotion are discretionary fixed costs because they can be increased, decreased, or totally eliminated by management.

4. Rent and occupancy expenses are committed fixed expenses. However, if you really want to split hairs, an expense like insurance has two elements, fixed for personal property coverage and variable for products and customer liability. Liability insurance premiums are sometimes determined by the sales volume much like workers' compensation insurance is computed as a percentage of your total payroll.

To take the BEP out of the realm of theory and put it to practical use, you must first recognize its limitations. The factors of cost and volume affect it in the following ways:

1. Changes in fixed costs will change the BEP but not the contribution margin percentage.

2. Variable cost changes will alter both the BEP and the contribution margin percentage.

3. Changes in menu prices will alter both the BEP and the contribution margin.

In order for BEP to work perfectly, the following must occur:

1. Prices should not change.

2. The sales mix should remain constant.

3. Variable costs should vary in direct proportion to sales.

4. Fixed costs should remain constant at all sales levels.

If all these conditions are met, the calculated BEP will remain the same for all levels of volume. This is rarely the case in the hospitality industry. Understand that a calculated BEP is *not* an absolute value calculated down to the exact dollar. It has value to management for use as a "what if . . ." in financial decision making.

Managers can consult the BEP as they consider alternatives to a variety of operational problems and conditions. Some applications for BEP analysis are:

1. determining the effects when sales rise or drop

2. determining the effects when variable costs rise

3. determining the effects when menu prices are increased/decreased

4. determining the effects of labor-saving devices or training

5. determining the effects from long-term capital expenditures

6. determining the sales levels needed to achieve a specific profit amount

7. determining the profit growth from expansion of the business

8. determining what increase in sales is necessary to offset a price reduction

9. deciding whether the restaurant should stay open or close for a given day/meal period?

Examples of BEP Analysis

Assume that management is considering putting additional seats in the restaurant's lounge and dining room. The plan calls for 10 additional seats in the bar and 30 more seats in the dining room. Further assume that the restaurant's sales volume has leveled off at $80,000 per month. The profit structure resembles that shown in Table 12.4.

The following monthly increases in fixed costs are anticipated from the expansion:

Utilities	$ 150
Rent	$ 250
Depreciation	$ 300
Administrative	$ 300
Total	$1,000

Table 12.4   Financial Summary for Cal-Mar Restaurant

	$ Amounts	% Percent
Sales	80,000	100
Cost of Sales (all variable costs)	30,400	38
Gross Margin	49,600	62
Operating and All Other Costs		
Variable Costs	20,800	26
Fixed Costs	17,600	22
Totals	38,400	48
Operating Profit before Taxes	11,200	14
Taxes	5,800	7.3
Net Profit	5,400	6.7

The new fixed costs are $17,600 + $1,000 = $18,600. The total variable costs are 38% + 26% = 64%. Therefore, the contribution margin is 100% − 64% = 36%. Substituting into the break-even formula, Fixed Cost $/Contribution Margin, or $18,600/0.36 = $51,667. The break-even without the expansion is $17,600/0.36 = $48,889. Therefore, it has increased $2,778 per month. That works out to about $650 a week in additional business, or $92 per day based on a seven-day week. This does not seem to be an unreasonable volume to achieve.

What sales level must be attained to make a $11,200 profit with the expansion? Using the same formula, we treat profit as a fixed expense and add it to the fixed cost in the numerator of the equation: ($18,600 + $11,200)/ 0.36 = $82,778. The previous sales level to achieve the same profit was $80,000 so an increase of only $2,778 per month is needed.

Since the expansion requires a cash investment, management expects an additional $1,000 in profit per month. The sales needed to achieve a $12,600 profit is $85,555 ([$18,600 + $12,200]/.36). Is an additional $5,555 per month a realistic amount given the competition and customer traffic in the restaurant's trading area? If volume has plateaued at $80,000 due to supply and demand, expansion may not increase customer counts. Perhaps money should be spent on marketing to increase business.

What is the profit before taxes at a sales level of $85,000 without expansion costs? The formula is Profit = Sales × Contribution Margin − Fixed Costs. In this case, $85,000 × .36 = $30,600 − $17,600 = $13,000.

What sales volume is needed to earn a $15,000 profit without the expansion? Again, profit is treated in the formula as if it were a fixed expense. So instead of fixed costs of $17,600, we have $32,600 in the numerator of the formula: $32,600/0.36 = $90,555.

What sales volume is needed to maintain the present profit if a discount promotion is run that, in effect, will decrease overall prices by 5 percent? Assume that $11,200 profit is acceptable. We already know that at regular prices sales of $80,000 are needed to earn $11,200 in profit. The formula is:

$$\frac{\text{DESIRED PROFIT} + \text{FIXED COST}}{1 - \left(\dfrac{\text{Present Variable Cost\%}}{100\% - 5\%}\right)}$$

$$\frac{\$11,200 + 17,600}{1 - \left(\dfrac{.64}{1.00 - .05}\right)}$$

$$\frac{\$28,000}{1 - \left(\dfrac{.64}{.95}\right)}$$

$$\frac{\$28,000}{1 - .6736} = \frac{\$28,000}{.3264} = \$88,235$$

The discount promotion would need to bring in an additional $8,235 to equal the profit the restaurant is earning without the discount. An increase in sales volume of over 10 percent is needed. That should be translated into the number of additional customers needed on the nights the discount is offered.

Food cost will increase as a result of the discount reducing the contribution margin and increasing the BEP. Remember, BEP assumes that costs remain constant or vary in the same proportion to sales. It is doubtful that this could be the case with a 10 percent increase in volume. Labor would most definitely have to increase. The actual BEP is probably much higher than this figure. It makes you wonder about the financial impact of discount promotions. See Chapter 6 for a full explanation of discount pricing.

What is the effect on profit if fixed and variable costs are changed? Assume that we lease $3,000 worth of new equipment that will enable us to reduce variable costs by 20 percent. A new contribution margin ratio needs to be computed. Present variable costs are 64% so a 20% reduction would be $0.20 \times 0.64 = 12.8\%$. $64\% - 12.8\% = 51.2\%$; $1.00 - 0.512 = .488$, the *new* contribution margin. Fixed costs will increase from $17,600 to $20,600 because of the equipment lease: $20,600/0.488 = $42,213$. The new BEP is lowered from $51,667 to $42,213. Go out and lease that equipment!

If sales were $85,000, how much profit would we earn with the leased equipment installed? The formula is Sales × Contribution Margin − Fixed Costs, or $85,000 \times 0.488 - \$20,600 = \$20,880$. This is almost $7,900 more than the profit we calculated earlier on this sales volume without the expansion in seats. *Remember, every time there is a change in fixed or variable costs, the break-even point must be recalculated.*

The Concept of Closing Point

Is a restaurant better off financially to close its doors earlier on certain days or cease to operate during a particular season of the year? Is it possible for an operation to make more money by closing one day a week or by operating one meal period instead of two? Should a restaurant expand its hours of operation to early in the morning? Whether you are trying to determine the most profitable hours or days of the week to open, the *closing point analysis* can help you make an informed decision.

Every operation has a break-even point and a closing point. Closing point is that point where sales revenues do not cover the costs of opening; for example, payroll, extra utilities, supplies, linens, and the like. If the operation remained closed, such "opening" expenses would not be incurred.

The closing point of any operation is based on the relationship of minimum opening costs to total sales. For example, as sales volume and customer counts drop, the cost-minded manager or owner will purchase and prepare less food, schedule fewer employees, and cut costs wherever possible. Yet, eventually he will reach a point where costs are fixed and cannot be further reduced if the business is to remain open and standards of food, beverage, and service are to be reasonably maintained.

In table-service operations, regardless of customer counts, when the doors are opened, food will be purchased and prepared and a minimum skeleton crew will need to be scheduled and paid. These minimum costs are fixed and the restaurant cannot open without incurring these opening costs. Consequently, sales revenue must be sufficient to recover these minimum opening costs. If sales fall below the closing point, not only will you have to pay the "sunk" fixed costs like rent, insurance, interest, and utilities, you will incur the additional expenses of opening. Simply stated, if it costs $100 to open the doors and you take in only $90, it will cost you $10 more than it would to remain closed in the first place.

To illustrate, if you decided to close your restaurant for any one day or perhaps at an earlier closing hour each day, you would save the expense of labor, food, and beverage, reduce your utility bill, not use up supplies, consume hot water, or turn on cooking equipment.

When you open the doors, you will incur these expenses and your sales must cover these operating costs. Of course, the alternative to closing is to try to increase sales volume and make it profitable to remain open. If your sales were $110 instead of $100, you would not only cover the costs of opening but an additional $10 of your sunk fixed costs. In that case, you are $10 better off by opening than staying closed.

Many operations have hours of the day and days of the week when they operate below their break-even point. But as long as they are above the closing point, they are better off remaining open than closing. To determine your operation's closing point, classify your costs into two categories: fixed and variable. Fixed costs are those that continue when you are closed. The remaining costs are not absolutely variable as the opening costs have a "programmed" fixed portion. For the sake of example and simplification, the only purely variable costs are food and beverage. These costs are expressed as percentages. Fixed costs are expressed in dollars.

The most logical expense of opening to express in dollar value would be your labor cost. Based on hourly wages and management salaries of those scheduled for the day, meal period, or hour, you can arrive at a definite dollar cost of labor for opening. Add any additional costs in dollars that you will incur by opening (e.g., laundry and linen, utilities, supplies, etc.). Compute a contribution margin by adding the food and beverage variable cost percentages, and subtract it from 100 percent. Divide the contribution margin into the fixed costs of opening to arrive at the closing point or sales level that will cover the costs of opening the doors to the public.

Assume the following costs of opening are:

> Labor $150
>
> Variable Costs 46%
>
> Contribution Margin $= 100\% - 46\% = 54\%$
>
> Closing Point $= \$150/0.54 = \$278$

Sales would need to exceed $278 to cover the costs of opening for the period of time the expenses represent.

Break-even and closing point analysis is best used for short-term periods like meal periods, days, and weeks. When break-even is calculated, try to express your costs from monthly or weekly figures. If you have annual figures and simply divide by 12 to get a monthly BEP and then by 4.3 to get a weekly figure, the figure you get is not exact to what BEP may be. BEP analysis is a helpful tool if costs used in its calculation are representative of the actual costs incurred. Most costs of operating a restaurant are not purely fixed or variable; they are a combination of each. This complicates the calculation of BEP and explains why it is just an estimated sales point and not an exact number.

I ntegrating Technology into Kitchen Management

Throughout your career as a culinary professional, you will find that your duties and responsibilities will not only include the knowledge of food and preparation skills, but also managing a foodservice kitchen. You will not only be responsible for food cost control and purchasing, you will also be in charge of hiring, training, and scheduling the kitchen staff. You may prepare delicious and creative menu items but if your food and labor costs are such that the operation does not make a profit, you reputation will suffer. In general, the foodservice industry and chefs more so than managers, lag behind others in using the Internet or World Wide Web, as a tool for collecting, sorting, and analyzing operational data.

Ten years ago, few chefs had computers in their offices. They kept track of purchases, food costs, employee schedules, and purveyor prices on paper records or in their heads. Today, not being able to use a computer or not having one in your office puts you in jeopardy of not being able to do your job properly. It has become an essential tool that one cannot be without in these days and times. Before the advent of computers, chefs and managers had to spend a large portion of their time assembling cost data and putting it in report format so it could be analyzed. Remember, the essence of cost control analysis is comparison of actual results to standards or to past periods. In terms of the time required to accomplish this important task, 80 percent of their time was spent in assembling and filling out the reports. That left only 20 percent of their time to analyze the data.

This was not surprising because many chefs had no time to spare from their busy production schedules to gather the necessary cost data and put it in a format they could analyze. If they did, they found that they were working 12–15 hours seven days a week. Computer technology has reversed this time allocation so chefs and managers spend less than 20 percent of their cost control analysis time assembling reports and now find that they have more time to analyze the data.

A computer is the hardware and without software, it really is of little assistance to a chef. Fortunately, there are many sources of software programs available to chefs including *ChefTec*, at ChefTec.com; *Escoffier Online* at escoffier.com; *MenuPro*, which also offers a labor scheduling program, an inventory, and recipe program at foodservice.com; RestaurantOperator.com at restaurantoperator.com; and *ChefDesk*, at chefdesk.com. These are only a few of the many software and web sites available. We suggest that you do a search on *Google* or *Yahoo* using the key words, "restaurant software."

Many suppliers to the foodservice industry now have on-line ordering where you place your weekly orders over the computer and avoid having to deal with a sales person. The software keeps track of your use levels of food stuffs you purchase so you can see how much you have been using between deliveries. This information allows you to optimize your purchase quantities so as not to run out or to over-buy and tie up your cash in perishable food commodities.

Computer software is now available that will monitor your inventory, check availability, and provide you with price and case quantities of the products. You can also produce spreadsheets showing prices of the vendors for like brands and grades of product. You can even create a matrix that shows cost comparisons based on product edible portion yield.

Technology is changing rapidly and new software and equipment is developed every year. We recommend that you attend the National Restaurant Association Show is Chicago to see the new technology that is displayed. This show is always held around the middle of May. Another show that we recommend you attend to learn about the latest foodservice technology is the Foodservice Technology Exposition. FS Tech, sponsored by Nation's Restaurant News since 1995, is held usually around the middle of November. These two shows will feature the very latest technology.

Your restaurant is already using computers to print guest checks that tell you which menu items have been ordered. Your restaurant more than likely has its own web site. You may be even doing web-based training for food sanitation and safety certification for your employees. You probably have at least one e-mail address and are already communicating with vendors, family, and using the Internet to search for new products, recipes, or menu ideas. The restaurant's POS system is tracking individual server sales and tallies the menu sales mix for each meal period. You are probably using this information to determine order quantities from your suppliers. You already know that the information you get from your restaurant's POS system is important and valuable to you in doing your job.

You need to leverage the power of your POS system in the kitchen with what is called *kitchen display system technology* (KDS). KDS has been used in the quick service sector for almost 25 years. Burger King and KFC have used KDS to smooth order flow and to get orders out fast and efficiently. The same technology has been improved and can be used in table service operations. KDS provides feedback on order preparation times and monitors the entire service transaction time for each guest table.

Here is how KDS works. The system records food and beverage orders and displays them on a screen at the expediting station and the work stations where the items are prepared. The times are monitored from start to finish and will alert management and service staff when preparation time parameters are being exceeded. Information is displayed graphically on a monitor. Management can tell at a glance the number of tables seated, the number of tables with orders placed, and the number of tables that have been served their entrees. With this knowledge, a manager can adjust staffing to meet serving needs and can tell when it is time to put in another tray of baked potatoes or notify the staff that they are approaching selling out of certain specials. These monitors are replacing the paper check.

Hand-held palm pilots are replacing paper checks and even touch screen terminals in the dining room. You may have seen them in action if you have attended a sporting event and sat in the box seats. They can even take payment from your credit card in the stands. Some industry prognosticators are saying that we are not far away from touch screen ordering and payment in fast food restaurants. We are already dealing with this kind of technology with ATMs at our bank and at the gas pump. In most quick service restaurants, customers verbalize their orders to an employee who in turn enters the information into a point of sale (POS) system. The order comes up on a screen in the preparation area and the order is prepared and assembled. With touch screen technology, ordering and payment with debit or credit cards would allow the customer to place their own orders without needing a minimum wage hourly employee to enter it. When an order is assembled and packaged, the customer returns to the counter and picks up their food.

The POS is also linked to your kitchen computer and your inventory management. In theory, every time an item is ordered at a POS terminal, it can be deleted from inventory in the amount of your standardized portion quantity. Counting cans and cartons at the end of the month is already being replaced by a hand-held bar-code reader. All you have to enter is the amount on hand and the program automatically calculates the inventory value using the most recent purchase price for each item. You compare the actual inventory figures to the theoretical figures based on standardized portions giving you a discrepancy report that can identify shortages due to theft, waste, or over-portioning.

Software sales analysis programs like the Cost/Margin Analysis program that accompanied this text are a valuable tool for analyzing your menu sales mix to ensure you are optimizing your menu's profit potential. It identifies which menu items return the highest gross profits and have the lowest costs so these items can be featured on your menu.

Many restaurants are printing their own menus in house with the use of several menu design software packages that are on the market. One we have used and find helpful is *Soft Cafe Menu Pro.* It has clip art, menu formats, and even a spell-check feature.

Management is likely using some kind of payroll program to schedule the dining room staff and track labor cost. You need to do it in the kitchen as well. In fact, the labor cost in the kitchen is likely a higher percentage of the restaurant's total labor cost than the tipped staff which is paid only $2.15 per hour. Have you noticed that time clocks are obsolete? The POS system has replaced it. Management can tally total labor cost as quickly as it totals food and beverage sales at the end of the meal period.

A chef is no longer just a culinarian. A chef needs to be a teacher, coach, accountant, negotiator, counselor, purchasing agent, and a manager. You need to embrace computer technology to make your job easier and make the restaurant run more efficiently.

In addition to internal operational data, many restaurants are tracking their frequent customers and giving them rewards for their loyalty. The computer software keeps track of every transaction and stores the data so it can be retrieved and analyzed by the operator. This is called "data warehousing." It is a process for assembling and managing data from various sources so you can answer business questions and make decisions that previously were not possible about customer behavior and trends.

Using the POS system along with credit card data or other transaction-driven programs like frequent diner and birthday clubs, can capture customer information that can be helpful in marketing to your guests. A credit card number can be used as the customer number eliminating the need for a separate loyalty card (which several companies are offering to restaurant operators). This number can be matched to a name and address for use in direct mail promotions. You can track the number of customer visits, average check, total dollars spent, and the date of the last visit. A large percentage of customers can be identified with full name and address; demographic, and geographic information.

Many restaurants with web pages have a link so customers can register on line for loyalty programs, print coupons, fill out comment cards regarding their food and service experience, order take-out, and make reservations from their homes or offices. *Xirius Concepts* offers such programs with their *Aloha QuickService* system.

What we have described here is just an overview of what is available. Your choices are so extensive that it is hard to know where to even start your search. One of the best starting points is to visit comparable operations and inquire as to what system they are using and if they are pleased with the reports and the service from the vendor. Be sure to ask about the reliability of the system, the track record of the company, its level of support, and any on-site maintenance options.

The benefits come from the fact that your restaurant will gain a competitive edge in marketing because you will have detailed knowledge about your customers that your competition does not have.

Key Points

- Most restaurant operators plan not to fail; however, many who fail do not have a financial plan.
- Financial management stresses the interpretation of financial data.
- Your income statement must be a cost control tool and not just another IRS form.
- Non-financial data must be incorporated into your accounting reports.
- Costs are not purely fixed or purely variable.
- Break-Even and Closing Point analysis are important financial management tools.
- Follow *Uniform System of Accounts for Restaurants* for all your financial accounting reports.
- A very significant portion of a restaurant's success is determined before it opens its doors to the public.
- Poor financial management can put a restaurant out of business even if has excellent food and service.
- Managerial accounting is far more specific and detailed than financial accounting.
- Internal management relies on managerial accounting reports; external constituencies such as creditors and investors, rely on financial accounting reports.
- Comparative and common-size balance sheet analysis are useful financial tools for owners and managers.

- Ratio analysis informs owners and managers about the effectiveness of their operational decisions.
- There is a difference between income and cash flow.

 ## Key Terms

Financial analysis
Financial management
Financial accounting
Managerial accounting
Cost accounting

Break-even point
    analysis
Closing point analysis
Volume-cost-profit ratio
Fixed cost

Variable cost
Semi-variable cost
Discretionary costs
Gross profit/
    contribution margin

 ## Discussion Questions

1. Distinguish the differences in the preparation and content of financial accounting and managerial accounting reports.
2. What is meant by making your income statement a management cost control tool and not just another Internal Revenue report?
3. What are the three major financial reports used by management? What information do they provide?
4. List the various ratios that management uses to analyze balance sheet numbers.

Problem 1

Instructions:

With the help of the Excel spreadsheet on your diskette, complete the income statement by filling in the percentage column and the totals for:

- Total Cost of Goods Consumed
- Total Gross Profit Margin
- Total Operating Expenses
- Income Before Occupation Cost, Interest, Depreciation, Corporate Overhead, and Income Taxes
- Total Occupancy Costs

- Income Before Interest, Depreciation, Overhead, and Income Taxes
- Total Interest, Depreciation, and Corporate Overhead
- Income Before Income Taxes
- Income Taxes
- Net Income after Taxes

Sales		$$	%
	Food Sales	$ 78,000	
	Beverage Sales	$ 30,000	
	Total Sales	**$ 108,000**	
Cost of Goods	Food Cost	$ 22,542	
	Beverage Cost	$ 4,530	
Cost of Goods Consumed	**Total COGC**		
Gross Profit Margin	Food Gross Profit	$ 55,458	
	Beverage Gross Profit	$ 25,470	
	Total Gross Profit Margin		
Direct Operating Expenses	Salaries and Wages	$ 39,250	
	Payroll Tax & Benefits	$ 6,280	
	Direct Operating Expenses	$ 1,650	
	Music and Entertainment	$ 210	
	Marketing	$ 1,435	
	Energy and Utility Services	$ 1,200	
	Administrative and General	$ 800	
	Repairs and Maintenance	$ 800	
	Total Operating Expenses		

(continued)

		$$	%
Income Before Occ Cost, Int, Depr, Corp OH, & Inc. Taxes			
	Rent	$ 5,260	4.87%
	Property Taxes	$ 890	0.82%
	Property Insurance	$ 560	0.52%
	Total Occupancy Costs		
Income Before Int, Depr, Overhead, & Inc. Taxes			
	Interest	$ 1,655	1.53%
	Depreciation	$ 2,865	2.65%
	Corporate Overhead Charges	$ 1,500	1.39%
Total Interest, Depreciation, Corporate Overhead	**Total**		
	Income Before Income Taxes		
	Income Taxes (at 32%)		
Net Income	**Net Income**		

Problem 2

The following income statement is prepared in the internal management tool format. Using the template provided on the accompanying diskette, complete the totals in the dollar column and then compute the percentages and cost per cover amounts. *Keep in mind that while most of the line items are divided by Total Sales to determine the percentage,* food and beverage cost-related expenses are divided by their respective sales amounts and not total sales. E.g., Cost of Food Consumed percentage is calculated by dividing Cost of Food Consumed by Food Sales. Also, complete the section utilizing non-accounting information utilizing customer counts and labor hours to make the income statement more of a management analysis tool and not just an accounting statement.

Sales	$	%	Cost/Cover
Total Food Sales	$137,500		
Beer	$ 12,500		
Wine	$ 15,000		
Liquor	$ 19,400		
Total Beverage Sales	$ 46,900		
Total Sales			
Direct Departmental Expenses			
Cost of Food Consumed	$ 44,000		
Less: Employee Meals	$ (3,438)		
Cost of Food Sold			
Beer Cost	$ 3,125		
Wine Cost	$ 6,000		
Liquor Cost	$ 2,910		
Cost of Beverages Sold			
Food Wages	$ 41,306		
Beverage Wages	$ 10,326		
Total Wages			
Employee Meals	$ 3,438		
Payroll Taxes/Insurance	$ 10,843		
Total Payroll Related Exp.			
Total Departmental Expenses			
Gross Margin			
Operating Expenses			
Laundry and Uniforms	$ 3,135		
Bar Supplies	$ 738		
Kitchen Supplies	$ 829		

(*continued*)

Operating expenses (*continued*)	$	%	Cost/Cover
Cleaning Supplies	$ 1,350		
Utilities	$ 4,232		
Repairs and Maintenance	$ 125		
Menu Printing	$ 850		
Credit Card Expense	$ 2,750		
Advertising and Promotion	$ 4,600		
Total Operating Expenses			
Profit Before A&G Expenses			
Administrative & General Expenses			
Management Salaries	$15,675		
Management Benefits and Taxes	$ 3,291		
Office Expense	$ 1,800		
Travel and Entertainment	$ 2,500		
Automobile	$ 2,900		
Accounting and Legal	$ 1,500		
Licenses and Fees	$ 500		
Total Admin. & General Exp.			
Profit Before Occupational Exp.			
Occupational Expenses			
Rent	$11,000		
Interest	$ 800		
Property Taxes	$ 750		
Insurance	$ 3,500		
Total Occupational Expense			
Profit Before Depreciation			
Depreciation	$ 550		
Pretax Profit			

Customer Count	12,293
Food Labor Hours	5,000
Beverage Labor Hours	1,120
Total Labor Hours	6,120
Food Wages per LH	
Bev. Wages per LH	
Avg. Wage per LH	
Food Sales Per Food LH	
Bev. Sales Per Bev. LH	
Avg. Sales per Total LH	
Avg. Check per Cover	
Total Labor Cost per Cover	
Covers Per LH	
Prime Cost $	
Prime Cost Percentage	

Problem 3

Given the following, calculate Break Even and Closing Point using the Excel template provided

Food Cost:	35%
Labor Cost:	$100/day minimum; $200/maximum
Rent:	$100/day
Utilities:	$75/day (Refrigeration $25; Lights and HVAC $50)
Cleaning	Supplies: $25/day
Maintenance:	$10/day
Variable Expenses:	5%

1. Determine Break Even for minimum and maximum labor cost.
2. Determine Closing Point.
3. Determine Sales to make $400 profit for minimum and maximum labor costs.
4. Determine Break Even with rental of equipment at $10 day that will reduce variable costs by 3% for minimum and maximum labor.
5. Determine what sales volume is necessary to maintain a $400 profit if a dining discount is given which will raise the food cost 2% for minimum and maximum labor cost.
6. What is the daily profit if sales are $1,500 per day at minimum and maximum labor with the above dining discount promotion?

Problem 4 Break Even Formula Applications Problem

Sample Income Statement Summary for Sidelines Grill Sports Bar Given:

Food Sales	$112,500
Beverage Sales	$37,000
Food Cost	32% of Food Sales
Beverage Cost	22% of Beverage Sales
Labor Cost	$30,000 of which 66.67% is fixed cost and 33.33% is variable cost
Other Variable Costs	$18,000
Fixed Costs	$48,750
Profit	$9,000

Compute:

The owners of the restaurant are looking into the benefits and costs of offering off-premise catering to tailgaters at local college and high school football games. The have done their preliminary cost estimates and have determined the following:

- Monthly fixed costs will increase as follows:

  Utilities $300; Rent $500; Depreciation Expense $600;

  Administrative and General expense $300.

- Catering sales is more profitable than regular menu prices and they estimate that total variable costs for the restaurant will be 1.5% lower each month.

- Fixed labor will increase by $1,500 a month but variable labor cost will remain the same.

- All other variable costs will remain the same percentage of sales.

Given these estimates, they want you to determine how these changes will affect their Break Even Point.

1. Break Even Point for existing sales and costs.
2. Compute their new Break Even Point and write an opinion on whether they should go ahead with their plans or they should not go forward as it is not financially feasible.
3. Compute the sales required for the restaurant to earn $12,000 in profit with the addition of the catering department.
4. Compute the sales volume they would need to maintain the current $9,000 profit with the catering changes if they ran an opening discount promotion that would decrease overall prices by 5 percent.

References

Pavesic, David V., "Financial Management for Hospitality Enterprises." In *Introduction to Hotel and Restaurant Management*, ed. Robert A. Brymer, 4th ed (Dabeque, Iowa Kendall-Hunt Publishers, 1979), pp. 212–216.

Appendix A
The Economic Value of Customer Service

FUNDAMENTAL PRINCIPLES OF COST CONTROL

1. Every restaurant's definition of *quality service* is unique because each one seeks to fulfill slightly different customer needs. *Bill Marvin*

2. Regardless of your service delivery system, *service quality* is always a combination of your service *procedures* and the *personality* of your service staff. *William B. Martin*

3. There is a cost you will incur to achieve *quality service. Daryl Wyckoff*

4. Service quality is more difficult to control than food or beverage costs. *Bill Marvin*

5. Develop a policy of service guarantees. *Tim Firnstahl*

6. Develop a *service first* mentality. *Frank Margarella*

7. Bend the customer service rules sometimes. *Karl Albrecht*

8. Be mindful of how damaging poorly rendered service can be to your business. *Charlie Trotter*

9. Service is "given." Hospitality is "felt." *Jim Sullivan*

10. Respect demanding customers: they can bring out the best in you and your staff. *Charlie Trotter*

Some of you reading the chapter are asking yourself, "What is an appendix on customer service doing in a book on restaurant cost controls?" It is here because of the economic impact it has on your business. It is common for chefs to open their own restaurants after working many years for someone else. However, many have found that culinary knowledge and skill and back-of-the-house operations knowledge does not automatically translate into a successful restaurant concept.

It is a wonder the level of service in all retail sectors has not been "kicked up a notch" given that so many college educated men and women have not been able to find work in the disciplines they studied in school and the multitude of other educated individuals that have lost their white collar jobs due to the downturn in the economy and stock markets. Whenever this occurs, many of these individuals will seek temporary positions in the service industries. The hotel and restaurant industry offers some of the most flexible and attractive positions while they hold out hope for better employment opportunities. The inference here is that these individuals are more likely to have a service-mentality that the normal employee pool for servers, sales representatives, and department store sales people.

When we started writing this appendix we collected over a dozen books with titles that told about dealing with complaints, managing customer service, how to deliver quality service, service guarantees, and handling difficult customers. We decided that if we were going to include an appendix on service, we would have to do something different. After all, we wrote a book on restaurant cost controls and other authors have devoted entire books to the subject. Therefore you will find that our approach to service is more of an overview that stresses its importance. We believe that if we can convince you of its importance you will then be motivated make whatever changes are necessary to improve the level of service in your restaurant.

In the well known service primer, *At America's Service,* (Karl Albrecht, Dow Jones-Irwin Publishers, 1988) the following tenets of service are the building blocks of a mindset that will motivate you to provide quality service in your restaurant.

1. Service has more economic impact than we thought.

2. Service is worse than we imagined.

3. You have to approach service from the perspective of the customer, not what management thinks it should be.

4. Service is a psychological and personal outcome and not a "physical" product.

5. The quality control of service is in the hands of the employees delivering the service.

6. It starts at the top. Top management and owners must be committed to quality service for it to permeate to the service delivery personnel.

7. You have to first sell your employees on service or they will never be able to sell it to your customers.

8. Systems and procedures are enemies of service. Employees must be "empowered" to rectify service breakdowns on the spot.

9. Service must become an "art form." The employees are obsessed and unrelenting in delivering quality service.

10. Quality service is defined by "outcomes," not "activities." The customer will decide whether you delivered on your promise.

While great food and sound fiscal management are two essentials for successful restaurant operation, the one other component that contributes enormously to getting repeat business is customer service. Depending on the perspective of the person evaluating a restaurant, the order and importance of components of success will be different. For example, if you were to ask a panel of professional dining critics what they would consider the number one factor in rating a restaurant, don't be surprised when they tell you it is the food. In fact, they can even overlook bad or indifferent service when the food is outstanding.

If you ask an operational consultant which is most important, you are likely to hear that restaurants with good food and service do not make it because of shoddy cost controls and financial management. While the opinions and recommendations of food critics and restaurant consultants must be heeded, they are not the most important people a restaurant operator has to please. That honor and distinction goes to people like you and me, in other words, the customers.

Research shows that during any given visit, one in four of your customers are dissatisfied enough to stop doing business with you for a significant period of time. Only one out of four dissatisfied customers will bother to tell you about it. The other three will not say anything, switch to a competitor, and mention their dissatisfaction to 8–10 of their friends and acquaintances.

"Good service" is difficult to define because service is described in "qualitative" terms. Quality means different things to different people. Some may rate elements relating to timing and speed while others look for more subtle nuances and technique. Speed is important when going through a drive-thru at a fast food restaurant. It is also important when you are checking out in a cafeteria line with hot food on your tray. Being served too fast may be a negative service quality in a table service restaurant where the patrons equate a leisurely pace with good service.

Providing "good service" is no longer enough to give you a competitive edge. Satisfaction is not enough anymore. It isn't powerful enough. It only means the customer got what they expected and simply meeting expectations is no longer enough to make you stand out in today's business climate. It only becomes a competitive edge if service is "exemplary." Exemplary service is delighting and astonishing your customers by totally *exceeding their expectations.* This has been called the "WOW" factor.

One study asked customers what single factor best defined quality service. The most frequent response was "personal attention." This was followed by responses mentioning *dependability, promptness, and employee competence.* Not only must we meet these expectations of our customers; we must do it consistently. In the widely read book, *At America's Service,* the authors suggested that those who are willing to serve as "champions" of service are obsessed with understanding and staying in tune with their customers' needs, attitudes, values, expectations, and perceptions.

Albrecht's definition of quality service taken from the book, *At America's Service* is:

> A level of service quality that, when compared to your competitors, is high enough in the eyes of your customers that it enables you to charge a higher price, gain a larger share of the market, and enjoy a higher profit margin than your competitors.

One of the reasons for this emphasis on quality service is that service has more economic impact than we thought and the level of service being provided is worse than we thought. Although "customer satisfaction" is usually part of an overall strategic plan, only a few forward thinking companies have made it their number one priority. Many companies have had honorable "intentions" for such strategy, but few have made it part of their corporate culture. When quality improvement turns to **total quality management** is when customer satisfaction is no longer a "program" but a "process" that becomes ingrained in the way they conduct all aspects of the business. "Programs" have beginnings, middles, and ends, whereas a "process" continues and becomes part of the culture of the company. TQM is a methodology that replaces the "old" ways and guides company activity year after year. TQM is a "journey" not a "destination."

In order for quality to become a "process" it must involve employees at all levels in the assessment and improvement of quality. You need to train your employees to deliver quality food and service. You need to empower employees to pursue quality improvements with a passion for excellence. You need to vigorously support and reward the employees who deliver the improvements that lead to satisfied customers. A total quality management process includes methods for accomplishing all these things.

A TQM process requires that you have a set of standards that are based upon the wants and expectations of your customers. The emphasis is on "prevention" and not "correction." The former is "proactive" the latter "reactive." In the early stages of a TQM process, reoccurring breakdowns in quality standards will be documented and corrective action taken to see that they do not reoccur in the future. The process also requires the need for quality teams or quality circles and empowering employees to guarantee customer satisfaction. This requires a major commitment on the part of ownership and management in order to be effective.

Most restaurants are "product" focused rather than "customer" focused. They set policy and procedure to be sure purchase specifications are followed, standardized recipes are used, proper portioning is done, and that the kitchen equipment is cleaned properly at closing. The result is mechanically correct service that may never respond to the customers' basic needs. We have been conditioned to focus on the wrong things and it is tough to change. We are too often focused on keeping costs down and meeting the inspection standards of our superiors. We are conditioned to evaluate everything from a cost perspective and that greatly limits our frame of reference when it comes to satisfying customers that complain about our not being able to substitute cottage cheese for a baked potato, or to request that we alter a recipe to accommodate their diet or taste. We even refuse to provide separate checks to large parties during busy periods because it is bothersome.

Service personnel need to be "aggressively friendly" and seek opportunities to help and they need to smile all the time they are doing it. Survey your guests after they have experienced the meal. Asking them for their opinion provides an outlet for them to voice their dissatisfaction which in itself greatly increases the likelihood they will give you another opportunity to make it right, even if you do nothing more than listen and apologize.

The common belief in the past has been that improvement in quality, whether product or service, will increase costs. It is true that quality does not come without real cost to the business. However, the cost of providing quality is far less costly than the cost of lost business due to customer complaints and dissatisfaction. Sometimes responding to guest complaints appears to conflict with some of your financial objectives. You start thinking that if you 'comp' the dinner your food cost will go up. In such a case, if you let the cost aspect control your decision, it would be to the detriment of repeat business from the customer. Whenever you feel the urge to put these kinds of interests before that of the customer, repeat the following to yourself: "This restaurant is run for the enjoyment and pleasure of our guests, not for the convenience of the staff and owners."

Traditionally, restaurants have relied on their food to provide them with their competitive edge in attracting and retaining customers. However, the difference between the signature steaks sold at an Outback, a Longhorn, and a Lonestar, for example, is difficult for the average customer to describe. While I am sure that the founders of those restaurants can explain how and why the way they do their steak is superior, I doubt that the customers see much of a difference. The point is that when food is considered at least equivalent in quality, and price and location are not a factors, service becomes the deciding criteria in restaurant selection.

Customer loyalty is fleeting and the frequency of visits may decline not because they are unhappy with the food or service, but because there are so many other dining choices. Take the popular Buckhead area in Atlanta, GA for example. It is home to many of the most popular, new, and trendy restaurants in the city. In fact, a few operators have multiple locations less than a mile from each other. In their entire business life many have seen steady increases in customer counts year after year until now.

Customer counts are now flat and in some cases declining. This typically is a sign that food quality or service is off and people are dining there less frequently because they are unhappy with either the food or service. This is not the case however. The reason for at least part of the decline in customer counts is the competition. There are twice the number of restaurants doing business as there was just six years ago. The clientele who dine in Buckhead are adventuresome diners who like to try new places. They are dining out just as frequently but they are spreading their food dollar among many more restaurants. This is referred to as the phenomenon of proportional market share. It means that whenever a new restaurant opens in a market area, it will take a portion of the business away from the existing restaurants.

Author and speaker Jim Sullivan believes that the word "service" has become so over-promised and under-delivered that its meaning and value have greatly diminished. If we focus on the procedural aspects of service we miss the true intent; that is to demonstrate a "feeling" of hospitality. A customer goes into a restaurant and is greeted by a host, escorted to a table and greeted again by a server. The order is taken, the food served and while the food was relatively well prepared, the entire service experience may come off as perfunctory and not convivial. Good service is described more by how we "feel" rather than how it was "given."

The main objective of service is to ensure complete customer satisfaction with all aspects of their dining experience. It is not difficult to provide pretty good food to the public. The challenge that faces the restaurant industry has always been to provide excellent service to accompany the food. Nearly all businesses proclaim that they want to provide "excellent customer service." Why is service in such a sad state in America today? It is not just in the food-service business where service has deteriorated, it is in retail, banking, insurance, telephone, airlines, and even government.

The National Restaurant Association reports that the number one concern of restaurant operators today is the inability to find and hire "qualified and motivated employees." That is quite interesting in that they are seeking those that are already trained and have a positive attitude about customer service. Those kinds of individuals would be just as hard to find even if unemployment levels were much higher than they are today. While there may be a small percentage of the unemployed work force that is "qualified and motivated," they are smart enough to get the maximum compensation for their services. Therefore, they are unlikely to seek employment anywhere they are not going to be compensated accordingly.

What it comes down to these days is that your service reputation can become your most effective weapon against losing market share to new restaurants. Marketing research into customers' decisions on whether to return to a particular restaurant a second time has revealed that service is the most important element in their decision. Poor service turns customers away faster than mediocre food.

Think of your service package in two parts. The first is providing quality food items, fairly priced, courteously and efficiently served in clean and attractive surroundings. This is what any restaurant is expected to provide. You do not get extra credit for having them; these are givens that are expected. It is what you do above and beyond these basics that adds value. It is what your restaurant does to support, complement, and add value to the expected practices. Examples are signature menu items; special meal deals; catering services; carryout and delivery services; special treatment of children or senior citizens. Such amenities and services provide "added value" to the purchase.

The reality is that no chain or independent will be able to sustain a product or price advantage over the competition over the long run. The reason is that competitors will copy your amenities and menu items and match or beat your prices. Serving good food and offering good service are essential and fundamental for success. It is the extras like calling customers by name, bringing them their usual cocktail, seating them at their favorite table, assigning them their favorite server, showing some special concession to them that first time customers do not get, thanking them personally and making them know their business is appreciated.

The difficulty in trying to state the elements of "exemplary service" is that each customer will assess it from a different perspective. Good or exemplary service is more easily recognized and described by what it does NOT provide than by what it provides. When expectations are not met, dissatisfaction occurs and because breakdowns occur even in the most service-minded restaurants, alternative strategies must be developed to handle these occasional breakdowns.

The manner in which your customer service breakdowns are resolved is a major component of your customer service policy. When do you begin the "moment of truth" of customer service? It starts when a customer telephones the restaurant to ask directions or make a reservation. It could be when they drive into the parking lot or when they walk in and are greeted by an employee. It continues when they are escorted to their table and greeted by their server. All are opportunities to demonstrate your service commitment. The customer's overall evaluation of your service commitment tends to be a composite of these many "moments of truth" that occur prior to and during the actual dining experience.

Restaurants have a natural advantage over other retail businesses in satisfying customers with their service. Consider that people go to restaurants expecting to have a good time and they usually arrive in a pleasant mood. Restaurants are places where very important life experiences and memories take place. Consider the number of birthdays, anniversaries, wedding receptions, job promotions, retirements, wedding proposals, and major business deals that take place in restaurants.

A higher state of mind predisposes people to enjoy themselves, and people will have a good time when they are in this mindset. They are more forgiving and generous. They spend more and the food tastes better. They are more open to recommendations on what to order. They tip better and they are more likely to tell their friends what a wonderful restaurant they visited.

As customers our expectations for the entire dining experience increase in direct proportion to the prices we are paying. When you go to a Waffle House and order one of their T-bone steaks at $7.95 and it comes with potato and salad, you probably will not complain if the steak was a little chewy. However, if you go to a prime steak restaurant like Ruth's Chris or Morton's, where you will pay $36 for a T-bone, you would complain if you had to remove gristle from the steak.

Will service continue to get worse before it gets better? Let's pose a question. How are "customer no-service" and alcohol and chemical dependence alike? Answer: You have to hit bottom before you realize that you have to change. The possible antidote for antisocial service will be discovered when desperate, insecure workers resort to politeness to keep their jobs. When will service hit the bottom? It could be shortly before the next major downsizing of white-collar jobs in the economy. As a result, at least in the short run, many college-educated and socially skilled individuals will be seeking work in the service sector while they wait for the economy to recover.

The reality is that there will be real estate and insurance agents who will never sell another property or policy again. There will be teachers, especially at the secondary and post-secondary levels, that will never teach in a conventional classroom again. What will they do? They will have to retool and go back to school or find employment in the service sector. Hotels and restaurants will go from famine to feast in terms of the quality of the workers they will find in the unemployment pool. With the influx of the displaced white-collar workers into the service industries, service will improve, albeit mostly by default.

Rudeness may have been good for some businesses (but it has quickly reached the point of diminishing returns). Restaurants and nightclubs have provided the best examples where customers were treated so rudely that they offered the staff bribes to ward off insult and to insure promptness. This is called "tipping." In some instances, the tip is given before they are seated and served to be assured of a "good table" and attentive waiter. Other industries have learned to sell ordinary service as a luxury item. Such marketing concepts as first-class travel, executive floors in hotels, and personal shoppers in stores are based on the idea that decent treatment and efficient service are not what the ordinary *customer* should expect.

The element of self-service has grown exponentially in the last decade for two reasons. It reduces labor cost and it reduces the likelihood of a bad service encounter with an employee. Think about it. Voice mail has eliminated talking to a rude receptionist or secretary and ATMs have eliminated having to deal with an indifferent teller. We now pump our own gas and pay by credit card at the pump so we do not have to deal with a human being during the entire transaction. We can now check out our own groceries at the supermarket or order them over the Internet and have them delivered to our homes. Self-service improves service by getting rid of it. Total self-service would have the etiquette advantages of eliminating opportunities to be rude and removing the incentive for issuing blame. More importantly, it could make customer service into a noble profession serving the unfortunate (who cannot help themselves).

One writer believes that the cause of bad service is the so-called service consultants. Consultants made people who had been reasonably content working in customer service turn disgruntled with their lot. In addition, the consultants annoyed customers who had been reasonably content with the level of service they had been receiving.

The first flaw in the consultant's recommendations on customer service was apparently the axiom that "the customer is *always* right." In addition, they stressed the idea that efforts should be made to please even unreasonable customers. The failure of this approach is that eventually the employee is reduced to a position where they are destined to *always be wrong*. This approach did not always bring out the best in the customers whom it is intended to attract.

The next well-meant axiom was the concept of "friendly service." The idea was to assure the customer that the service would not be "surly." The opposite of surly, in a business context, is not friendly but *cheeky*. What was really meant was *cheerfulness*. What often occurred was an employee unburdening their troubles on the customer and being completely honest about what was going on in the kitchen; too much information!

The third service axiom was *personal service* which meant to tailor the service to the requirements of the individual. However, when taken to the extreme, it was applied in situations in which altering the service for every customer was not possible. It has largely been practiced by reading the customers' first names from credit cards and reciting them back to them. Lately, with the help of those "smart cards" or "frequent user" cards, it has been a way to keep track of their purchases as a way of enticing the customer to purchase more. In other words, these "service techniques" have become a tool to get the customer to spend more, not provide them personal service.

When will service get better? It may take at least another decade. It will take us that long to realize that what the customer really wants is *fairness, efficiency and privacy.* The good news in that when the downsizing takes place, the employee pool will improve. However, there is some trepidation that we will be in a recession and dining out frequency will also decline. Such is the ebb and flow of the economy.

Restaurants will continue to be judged not by their service intentions, but by their actions. The best intentions in the world will not produce quality service or products. When the food quality of two competitors is viewed as equal, service can be the deciding factor on which restaurant to patronize. According to CREST (The NRA's Consumer Report on Eating Share Trends) more than 50 per cent of fast food customers and 60 percent of full service customers *always or regularly* consider service as their primary reason for choosing a restaurant. In fact, service is more important than price.

It has been mentioned that quality service does not come without increased costs. You have to train your employees and you have to pay those that really do their job well more than the going wage rate for their skills. Think about it. If you are an exceptional bartender, cook, or server, would you accept ordinary wages for your service? Of course not. You would work for the operator who recognized and rewarded your exceptional ability. Restaurant who pay well get a better pool of applicants applying for positions than those who pay on the low end of the going wage rate in the locality.

Restaurants that have been rated by their customers as having better than average food and service can charge and receive approximately 9 percent more for their products and services, grow twice as fast, and gain market share at a rate of 6 percent per year (compared to a 2 percent market share decline by those restaurant with below average service). There is approximately a 12 percent return on sales for those restaurants rated as being in the top half of service compared to only 1 percent for the rest.

Only 3 percent of your customers quit eating at your restaurant because they move away. Nine percent leave for competitive reasons and 14 percent due to product dissatisfaction. More than 65 percent of your customers will not do business with you again just because of the attitude or indifference toward them by one of your employees, not because they didn't like your location, menu, food preparation, or prices. There are too many alternatives for them to pick from and they are not going to give it to a business that treats them indifferently.

It is inevitable that even in operations with the best service intentions, breakdowns will occur and they will have to be resolved. The way you respond to breakdowns is a reflection of your true customer service commitment. In fact, the function of most "customer service" departments is to deal with customer complaints. Subsequently, dealing with dissatisfied customers and resolving their complaints is an important element of your customer service policy. For many years now we have fostered the belief that the customer is *always right*. Today, we are backing off from that because we have had it pointed out to us that if that is true, the employee is *always wrong*. We know that both of these statements are false; the customer is not always right and the employee is not always wrong. But the truth is that complaints are indications of the direction your customer service delivery needs to go. Therefore, you need to have a way for customers to voice their complaints and then pass those complaints on to top management.

One of the tenets of quality service is that a complaint must be corrected immediately if you are to negate negative feelings about your operation. Time does not heal service wounds; it just makes them worse. About one third of customers who did not voice their complaints will return to your restaurant a second time. Half of those who voiced their complaint before they left said they would return. What does this tell us? Even if a customer has a complaint about food or service you can get 17 percent more to return if you just provide them with a sounding board for their complaints. Over three-fourths of those who complained and had it resolved before they left said they would return to the restaurant.

You know it is very expensive to get a new customer in the first time. If a customer leaves with a bad first impression, you will not likely get them back. Even more disturbing is the fact that unhappy customers spread the word to twice as many of their friends and acquaintances as do happy satisfied customers. Think of how many times one of your acquaintances has gone on about a bad experience at a restaurant or department store. Didn't you respond with a story of your own? This negative word of mouth is devastating and that is why you need to resolve complaints before guests leave.

You must develop a responsive policy to deal with complaints immediately. Another of the service tenets is that you must empower your employees to deal directly with the customer to resolve complaints immediately. There is only one acceptable response to a complaint. This is a positive response that does not seek to assign blame or provide excuses. By handling the complaint immediately you will reduce the possibility that the complaint will escalate. If you keep a journal of the complaints, and you should, you will discover that the same two or three things are the cause of 75 percent of the complaints. You then take the necessary steps to stop them from reoccurring in the future.

Sometimes you need to look beyond the cost of the meal being 'comped' and look at the situation in terms of the future sales revenue a happy customer will bring to your restaurant. If a customer eats at your restaurant an average of just once a month and they bring in only one other person, he or she will have an economic impact equal to double your average check times twelve. This is a conservative estimate in that the people he or she may bring in may also return on their own with friends and family.

Some restaurants have experimented with service guarantees. Their guarantee does not just pertain to whether you like the food or not but with the whole experience of the restaurant's products and services. This extreme approach to service requires you to empower your employees with the complete responsibility and authority for making the guarantee effective. This provides management with a process for identifying aspects of system failure; the organizational problems that cause customer dissatisfaction.

Empowering the employees with the ability to make good on the promise of the guarantee eliminates any hassles for the customer. Houston's Restaurants recommends that managers carry at least fifty dollars on their person so he or she can handle a refund on the spot. It is also quite effective to have the manager personally paying for the inadequacies of his or her crew. Every dollar paid out to offset customer dissatisfaction is a signal that the company must change in some decisive way. The guarantee brings out a true, hard-dollars picture of company failures, and forces them to assume full responsibility for customer dissatisfaction.

Tim Firnstahl, the founder and CEO of Satisfaction Guarantee Eateries in Seattle, WA, was perhaps the first restaurateur to install an unconditional service guarantee program. He refers to it as the "hassle factor" allowance. His policy is simply, "Replace plus one." If a guest does not like her salad, not only will he not charge her for it, he will go one step beyond and buy her dessert or beverage, or whatever else it takes to make her happy. The guarantee has led to new training procedures, recipe and menu changes, restaurant redesign, equipment purchases, and whatever else it took to put things right and keep them that way. In the long run, the guarantee works only if it reduces system failure costs and increases customer satisfaction. Firnstahl cautions those of you who want to institute a service guarantee policy to be ready for costs to go up before they come down. As costs go up, complaints will start to go down and sales will go up. Costs will then start to go down (fewer breakdowns) and profits will begin to go up.

Service guarantees require an "attitude adjustment" for management and employees. The new attitude is that "the guest is never wrong." That is a different perspective of the view that the customer is always right. This policy means that a server or manager should never question a guest's judgment and perception. In other words, don't stand there and argue the technical difference between medium and medium rare; take the steak away and get it broiled the way the guest defines it.

Firnstahl offers this caveat; employee empowerment and responsibility are not enough. Employees must also be rewarded. Good thinking and positive action deserve money, praise, the limelight, advancement, and all the other encouragement a company can provide.

Here are some guidelines for handling customer complaints. Remember that anger is a potential response whenever a customer's needs are not being met. It is recommended that whenever you know that a service breakdown has occurred that you respond *before* the customer does. In other words, don't use the "do nothing and see if the customer says something" approach. Remember that only a small percentage of customers will even voice their complaints and a lack of complaints does not necessarily mean that you have been satisfying the majority of your customers. If you know you messed up, don't wait for the guest to mention it; respond immediately.

When approaching a guest introduce yourself by your first name and tell them that you are the manager. Eliminate the word "problem" in your vocabulary. If an employee has told you of the specific problem, go to the guest with a solution, *not with*, "I understand we had a problem with the food at your table." If the customer wants to vent, listen without interrupting them and respond with a solution, not an excuse.

Avoid becoming defensive and argumentative. Take responsibility for the mistake and don't offer excuses. Apologize and ensure that you will take the necessary action to see that it does not occur again. The customer must win all questionable calls, even when you know they are wrong. Remember the two rules of customer service.

1. The customer is never wrong.
2. If the customer is wrong, respond as if he was right.

Express empathy and understanding of their feelings. Let them know you are there to resolve the matter to their satisfaction. This normally calms the legitimate complainer and makes a solution easier. Determine exactly what the customer wants. Don't take their money! If you have difficulty with this rule, ask yourself, "Would you pay for a service/product that did not meet your expectations?" Supplemental responses to be used if you really want to be please customers who complain: "The answer is 'yes.' Now what is your request?" However, we do not recommend that approach until after you have offered a generous solution as a method of resolving the complaint.

Do not expect the guest to tell you what they want in return for their dissatisfaction. If you do ask that question, be prepared to provide whatever they ask for in return. When a manager approached the customer with, "What can I do to compensate you for this inconvenience?" in response to a request that the server return the barbecued chicken to be heated because it was only warm, he was offering to pick up the dinner, or buy a round of drinks, responses that were far more than would be expected for the complaint.

The customer left with a positive attitude about that restaurant. The moral of this anecdote is that you are far better off to err to the liberal side of compensating the guest than you are to not offer enough for the inconvenience.

Take action with the R + 1 rule. (Replace plus one). This strategy means going one step beyond what the customer sees as "adequate compensation" for the error or inconvenience. And follow up with the customer before they leave to be sure he or she feels adequately compensated. There may be instances that require a follow-up phone call or written letter of apology.

The following are examples of the most common service blunders.

1. Failing to acknowledge a customer when they approach you. How often have you waited for the hostess at the greeting stand to look up from her paperwork and officially greet you? This kind of body language says that the hostess sees her job as something other than greeting a guest in a friendly manner when they arrive. Typically, this kind of greeting will be followed by another service blunder in the initial verbal response. Your staff is making blunders if the first words out are any of the following commonly used greeting phrases;
   a. I'll be with you in just a minute.
   b. How many in your party?
   c. Smoking or non-smoking?
   d. There will be a 20-minute wait.
   e. Two this evening?

2. Not recognizing that the first person that comes in contact with the customer can set the mood for the rest of the dining experience. The first encounter with your restaurant personnel is often with the first person they see upon entering. It remains a mystery to me today why even the most expensive and full service restaurants entrust this important responsibility to an hourly employee who is titled a "hostess." Often there are two or three attractive young ladies handling the greeting and seating for the entire restaurant. In an independent restaurant, the owner or a member of management should be monitoring the greeting and seating of guests. In many chain operations, the manager is expediting the food out of the kitchen because they are obsessed with "ticket times." The only time they enter the dining room is when the window is clear of orders. This is when they make their obligatory walk-thru asking, "How was everything tonight folks?" The responses they get are, "fine," "good," "great," "no complaints." Customers treat that kind of comment the way we respond when a friend or acquaintance asks us, "How was your weekend?" Our response, "Great, and yours?" These are simply pleasantries that have little or no substance.

3. Assuming that employees know how to properly greet a customer before taking their order. Remember, if your servers see their job as taking orders and delivering food, they are not going to be providing the kind of service that earns points with your customers. It is expected that their orders will be taken and delivered correctly and in a timely manner. It is the little nuances that make the service encounter a pleasant one. Remember, good service is "felt" not "given."

4. Not knowing the answer to a customer's question may send another answer to the customer. Recently we attended an opening party for a grand new restaurant. The printed invitation indicated the time of our reservation and that a donation to a local charity would be taken at the door. After entering and donating, we approached the hostess stand where two attractive young ladies were positioned. I spoke first and gave my name and the time of our reservation. I then asked them how the dinner was to proceed, in particular if cocktails were extra or if everything was complimentary. They did not have an answer. They then handed us an envelope that we were told contained "our" menu and we were escorted to the table. I repeated the question to our server and his response was that he "thought" that cocktails were included but that they would be pouring wine with dinner. I must say that this vagueness in what we were going to be served that evening made us feel uncomfortable with a negative opinion about the training and instructions the employees were given. You expect that you are being taken care of by knowledgeable and well-trained employees and the higher the menu prices, the higher your expectations.

5. Not realizing that it is not just *what you say,* but *how you say it* that counts. What I am referring to is the tone of voice that is used when you are greeted or thanked for your patronage. I recall one New Year's Eve when my wife and I went out for an early dinner (7:00 PM). When we were close to finished, I could see the manager standing nearby with a bus tub in hand, eyeing our table. They had a waiting list and he was obviously anticipating where the next table would clear. Our waitress came over to remove our dinner plates and suggested dessert. When I commented that it appeared the manager wanted our table and that perhaps we should go, she put us at ease and told us to take our time. As we finished our dessert and were leaving, the manager said in a most insincere tone, that I am sure was not intended to be condescending, but he said it so fast that it would have better gone unsaid, *"Thankyouverymuchcomeandseeusagain."*

6. Speedy service can cut both ways in terms of customer satisfaction. Quality service (cannot be assessed) based on how quickly we

receive our order. In a fast food drive-thru this criteria is appropriate and slow times would be judged as poor service. However, being served too fast can lessen the value of the experience in full-service restaurants. While at our major shopping mall we decided to stop in at one of the anchor restaurants for dinner. While this did not happen to me, I did observe it at another table. The hostess led a party of four to their table, placed the menus down, and was already returning to the hostess stand at the entrance. The server assigned that station was right behind the party. While the guests were removing their coats and before they were seated, she was asking them if she could get them something from the bar and then started to recite the daily specials. I wonder if the guests felt rushed.

7. Assuming that each employee understands all that their job entails. The hostess in the previous scenario likely defined her job as "assigning guests to tables." Walking ten steps in front of the party, making them walk faster than normal just to catch up, dropping the menus, and quickly returning to the hostess stand leaves a lot to be desired and sends a negative customer service message to the guest. They should walk slowly just a step or two ahead of the guests, pull out the chairs, wait for them to seat themselves, and then hand them the menu. Then tell them the name of their server and that they will be right with them. On the way back to the hostess stand she is making mental notes of the empty tables and where the checks are down and tables will be clearing. She should also make eye contact with guests who are seeking to get an employee's attention. There is no rule that says you should not make eye contact with customers not seated at your station. Have you ever tried to get the attention of another server when you cannot see yours? They never look you in the eye and that drives guests crazy.

What do you do when a customer does not accept your complaint resolution as adequate compensation? Recently my family had lunch at a resort hotel in Central Florida. We had left the theme park crowds seeking refuge in the calm and serene atmosphere of one of the park's hotels. I noted some incongruities in service delivery immediately. The hostess who was taking names and quoting waiting times was literally yelling the names of the guests out when she was ready to seat them. I cannot overstate how loud she was yelling as she bellowed out, "Rose, party of five." However, we dismissed this as strange but turned our attention to the life-sized gingerbread house that was the focal point of the anteroom and waiting area.

When we were finally called, another hostess escorted us to our table in a most beautiful part of the dining room. She waited until we were seated before passing out the menus that were opened to the middle page. Our waiter greeted us in a timely manner and took our drink order and brought out some delicious sour dough bread and yeast rolls. He was very personable and engaged just about everyone in our party in some light-hearted conversation that put us all at ease and in a positive frame of mind. He returned to take our order and then we did not see him again for at least twenty minutes. We noted that parties that were seated when we arrived were leaving and their tables being cleared and set. Other parties that were seated after us were receiving their food while we sat with empty beverage glasses and no sign of our waiter.

Finally, at my wife's insistence, I got up from my seat and tracked down a hostess to check into our order and find our waiter. Within five minutes of that contact our order was being carried out of the kitchen and our waiter apologized profusely for the delay. According to our waiter, he had to "fight" for our order because another server had taken a hamburger that was part of our order and he had to find another. In other words, he held up the entire order because one item was missing. This was not the best way to handle that kind of error. Those things happen quite often in busy restaurants. Subsequently, the entire order remained under the heat lamps while he waited for another hamburger.

As one would expect, the fries had lost their crispness and were just warm. We asked for them to be replaced (which is what they should have done without our having to ask). By that time the entire mood of our table had gone from elation to disappointment. There was no sign of management until we were about halfway through our food. He apologized for the delay and told us he would speak to the kitchen to see that this does not happen again. I mentioned that not knowing what had happened to our food was the thing that upset us most. If the waiter had just come to our table to let us know that there was a mix-up we would have felt differently. I suspect that the real problem was the waiter and not the kitchen.

The manager listened to what I had to say and did not try to make excuses. I could see that they still had a line and were very likely understaffed. He offered to buy everyone a dessert as a gesture of compensation for our inconvenience. We declined the offer because we were full and had spent twice as much time as we intended for lunch. We then told him we were leaving for home and would not be able to return to the hotel again on this trip. He apologized again and excused himself from our table.

This is a case where the manager followed "suggested procedure" but was apparently not empowered to alter the response to fit the circumstances of the complaint. We did voice our complaint to management; management made an offer to compensate us with the dessert but for valid reasons we did accept the offer. Should a tourist be compensated differently than a local resident? Although this was not a "fatal" service experience, what is the downside to the hotel because of the way it was handled?

The demographics of our party consisted of a senior citizen, two middle-aged couples, a child and an adolescent. When they return to their respective hometowns and talk with their friends about their trip to this famous theme park and resort hotel, what do you think they are going to say about this experience? This is a case where the manager did not obtain closure that assured that the customer was leaving satisfied with the way their complaint was handled. Some key points in this scenario; the waiter apparently was not empowered to act to resolve the complaint. The manager was brought in late and offered only a perfunctory remedy that was not acceptable to the guests.

There were seven people in the party and if a dessert were ordered by all seven the value of the complimentary desserts would have been $26.25. Assuming that the food cost to the hotel was approximately 35 percent, the actual cost to the hotel would be only $9.19. If the manager would have thought about it in those terms, another form of compensation could have been offered. This hotel issues its own currency to use in its shops and theme park. Offering $15 in its own currency, redeemable only at its properties could have been another option. If this were a restaurant chain, a "be my guest" certificate would have been another way to provide compensation. Of course, they could have reduced the amount of the bill by a similar amount. They failed on all accounts to handle this service breakdown in a satisfactory manner. By the way, this happened over twelve years ago, and I am still using it as an example.

A list of books on customer service

Service America by Karl Albrecht and Ron Zemke, Dow Jones-Irwin, Homewood, IL, 1985.

At America's Service by Karl Albrecht, Dow Jones—Irwin Publishers, 1988.

The Service Edge by Ron Zemke with Dick Schaff, NAL Books, Canada, 1989.

The Spirit to Serve—Marriott's Way by J.W. Marriott, Jr., and Kathi Ann Brown, Harper Business Publishers, New York, 1997.

Delivering Quality Service by Valerie Zeithaml, A. Parasuraman & Leonard Berry, Collier MacMillan Publishers, London, 1990.

Managing Quality Customer Service by William B. Martin, Crisp Publications, Los Altos, CA, 1989.

Raving Fans by Ken Blanchard and Sheldon Bowles, William Morrow and Company, NY, 1993.

50 Proven Ways to Enhance Guest Service, Edited by William R. Marvin, Hospitality Masters Press, Gig Harbor, WA.

Quality Restaurant Service Guaranteed by Nancy Loman Scanlon, John Wiley Publishers, NY, 1998.

Contact-Customer Service in the Hospitality and Tourism Industry by Donald M. Davidoff, Prentice Hall Publishers, Englewood Cliffs, NJ, 1994.

Waiting on America by Mario Ponce, American Service Publications, Inc, Winter Park, FL, 1989.

Service That Sells! By Jim Sullivan and Phil Roberts, Pencom Press, Denver, CO, 1991.

Appendix B
Wage and Hour Laws

Introduction

The laws governing wages paid to workers in the U.S., officially called the Fair Labor Standards Act (FLSA) of 1938, volume 29 of the U.S. Code, sections 201-219, is one of the most important federal laws with which hotel and restaurant operators must comply. This appendix offers a brief explanation of the FLSA as of September 2003 and was adapted from their posted materials on their web sight, www.dol.gov.esa.

Important Note

The authors and the publisher wish to make it clear that they are not engaged in rendering legal, accounting, or other services and do not in any way claim that the interpretation of the content of this appendix is accurate and will hold up in a court of law. We, therefore, strongly suggest that you consult with an attorney or accountant on their interpretation of the laws as they may pertain to your circumstances. You should also be aware that federal law does not preempt state laws and the operator is obligated to comply with both federal and state laws.

Q uestions and Answers About the Minimum Wage

WHAT IS THE FEDERAL MINIMUM WAGE?

The federal minimum wage for covered nonexempt employees is currently *(09-2003)* $5.15 an hour. Many states also have minimum wage laws and the employee is entitled to the higher of the two minimum wages. If your state has a minimum wage of $5.65 per hour, employees in your state must be paid $5.65 per hour. However, if your state has an overtime threshold of 44 hours per week, employees must be paid overtime for all hours in excess of 40 hours, not 44. In other words, the federal law is more favorable to employees and will supersede the state's overtime threshold.

There are various minimum wage exemptions that apply under specific circumstances to workers with disabilities, full-time students, youth under age 20 in their first 90 consecutive calendar days of employment, tipped employees, and student-learners.

Young workers under the age of 20 can be paid a minimum wage of $4.25 per hour during their first 90 consecutive calendar days of employment as long as their work does not displace other workers. After 90 consecutive days of employment, or when the employee reaches 20 years of age, whichever comes first, the employee must receive a minimum wage of $5.15 per hour.

The Full-Time Student Program is for full-time students. An employer that hires students can obtain a certificate from the DOL which allows the student to be paid not less than 85 percent of the minimum wage. However, the certificate limits the number of hours the student may work to 8 hours per day and no more than 20 hours per week when school is in session and 40 hours per week when school is out. The employer must also comply with child labor laws. Once the students graduate or leave school for good, they must be paid $5.15 per hour. There are some limitations to the use of the full-time student program. For information on the limitations or to obtain a certificate, contact the Department of Labor Wage and Hour Western Region Office at 525 Griffin Square, Suite 800, Dallas, TX 75202, telephone: (972) 850-2601.

There is another program for high school students at least 16 years old who are enrolled in vocational education. If you hire these students, you can obtain a certificate from the DOL which will allow you to pay 75 percent of the minimum wage for as long as the student is enrolled in the vocational education program. Employers who seek this certificate should contact the DOL Wage and Hour Regional office with jurisdiction over their state. *Addresses and telephone numbers are available on the DOL web site* www.dol.gov.

WHAT IS THE MINIMUM WAGE FOR WORKERS WHO RECEIVE TIPS?

An employer of a tipped employee is only required to pay $2.13 an hour in direct wages if that amount, plus the tips received, equals at least the federal minimum wage, the employee retains all tips and the employee customarily and regularly receives more than $30 a month in tips. If an employee's tips plus the employer's direct wages of at least $2.13 an hour do not equal the federal hourly minimum wage, the employer must make up the difference.

HOW DOES THE DOL DETERMINE IF AN EMPLOYER IS REQUIRED TO PAY THE MINIMUM WAGE?

If your business does at least $500,000 in sales per year, you must pay the minimum wage. It also applies to businesses engaged in interstate commerce or in the production of goods for commerce.

There are two ways in which an employee can be covered by the law: "enterprise coverage" and "individual coverage." Generally, federal regulations define *enterprise* as "the same or similar activities performed by one or more persons, firms, or corporations for a common business purpose." For more detailed information on the definition of an enterprise, see volume 29 C.F.R., sections 770.200-779.269.

Even when there is no enterprise coverage, employees are protected by the FLSA if their work regularly involves them in commerce between states. This constitutes *interstate commerce.* In its own words, the law covers individual workers who are "engaged" in commerce or in the production of goods for commerce. The employer is required to pay the minimum wage even if the enterprise does not have annual gross sales of $500,000. If your restaurant has a commissary that delivers food and supplies over state lines, the employees who work in the commissary and drive the delivery trucks would have to be paid the minimum wage. This even includes employees in the corporate office whose duties involve processing credit card charges mailed or electronically transmitted across state lines for collections or your operators who take orders or reservations from individuals out-of-state.

The $500,000 threshold must be computed using annual gross dollar volume, using calendar-year accounting, and measuring gross dollar volume by quarters in January, April, July, and October, and by looking at sales during the preceding four quarters. An enterprise using fiscal-year accounting can also adopt the same method for determining annual gross volume.

New businesses, open fewer than twelve months, will need to rely on their proforma sales forecasts based on the sales history of other locations. In cases where forecasts cannot be done accurately, estimates of annual gross volume can be estimated using the gross receipts for the first quarter and extrapolating volume for the remaining three quarters. It is possible for a worker to be covered one workweek and not the next. Employees of enterprises with gross annual sales of less than $500,000 would not have to pay minimum wage for those workweeks during which the employees are *not* engaged in commerce or the production of goods for shipment out of state. There may also be circumstances where only a portion of your employees are covered.

W ages, Pay, and Benefits

WHEN ARE PAY RAISES REQUIRED?

Pay raises to amounts above the Federal minimum wage are NOT required by the FLSA. Pay raises are a matter of agreement between an employer and employee.

IS EXTRA PAY REQUIRED FOR WEEKEND OR NIGHT WORK?

While some employers *elect* to pay more for employees scheduled during weekends and nights as an incentive, it is strictly a matter for individual companies to decide. The FLSA does not require extra pay for weekend and night work.

HOW ARE VACATION PAY, SICK PAY, AND HOLIDAY PAY COMPUTED, AND WHEN ARE THEY DUE?

Again, benefits are strictly matters of agreement between an employer and its employees. None of these benefits is *required* by the FLSA.

WHAT ABOUT SEVERANCE PAY?

Again, there is no FLSA requirement for employers to pay severance pay. This is strictly a matter of elective company policy.

WHEN MUST BREAKS AND MEAL PERIODS BE GIVEN?

While it has become customary for many restaurants to provide meals for employees and give them time to eat it, it is NOT required under the laws of the FLSA. However, some states have passed laws requiring breaks or meal periods. Check with your respective state for such requirements.

ARE PERIODIC PERFORMANCE EVALUATIONS REQUIRED?

The FLSA does not require performance evaluations. However, most restaurant operators have them as they are necessary for determining wage increases and promotions. In addition, performance evaluations are relevant when an employee is terminated.

vertime and Work Hours

WHEN IS OVERTIME DUE?

For covered, nonexempt, employees, the FLSA requires overtime pay at a rate of not less than one an one-half times an employee's regular rate of pay after 40 hours of work in a workweek.

WHAT IS CONSIDERED A "WORKWEEK?"

An employee's workweek is a fixed and regularly recurring period of 168 hours—seven consecutive 24-hour periods. It need not coincide with the calendar week, but may begin on any day and at any hour of the day. Different workweeks may be established for different employees or groups of employees. Averaging of hours over two or more weeks is NOT permitted. Normally, overtime pay earned in a particular workweek must be paid on the regular pay day of the pay period in which the wages were earned.

HOW DOES SPECIAL PAY RATES FOR WEEKENDS, NIGHTS, AND HOLIDAYS AFFECT OVERTIME PAY?

The regular rate of pay cannot be less than the minimum wage. The regular rate includes all remuneration for employment except certain payments excluded by the Act itself. Payments which are not part of the regular rate include pay for expenses incurred on the employer's behalf, premium payments for overtime work, or the true premiums paid for work on Saturdays, Sundays, and holidays, discretionary bonuses, gifts and payments in the nature of gifts on special occasions, and payments for occasional periods when no work is performed due to vacation, holidays, or illness.

WHAT ABOUT AN EMPLOYEE WHO WORKS TWO DIFFERENT JOBS WITH TWO DIFFERENT PAY RATES?

If a server who is normally paid $2.13 per hour because they are a *tipped employee,* also works as a hostess on another shift or day and is paid $8.00 per hour, and does so in a single workweek, and works more than 40 hours, he or she shall have the overtime rate of pay determined by calculating the weighted average of such rates. That is, the earnings for all such rates are added together and this total is then divided by the total number of hours worked at both jobs. For example, if the employee worked 30 hours at $2.13 per hour and 15 hours at $8.00 per hour, the overtime pay rate for the five hours of overtime would be at $6.13 per hour. ([30 × $2.13 + 15 × $8]/ 45 hrs = $4.09; $4.09 × 1.5 = $6.13)

ARE THERE OVERTIME EXEMPTIONS FOR MANAGEMENT PERSONNEL?

Yes. Managers, supervisors, and assistant and associate managers are not subject to overtime pay. As a result, many restaurants attempt to classify employees into this category who really do not meet the requirements for exemption. If you spend a large portion of your time on the job performing tasks like ringing sales, working the food line, or filling in for absent non-management personnel, then you may not meet the requirements to be officially classified as a manager or supervisor and could be due overtime pay.

WHAT ARE THE REQUIREMENTS TO BE CONSIDERED EXEMPT FROM OVERTIME PAY?

Under volume 29 of the C.F.R., a series of requirements are spelled out in order for an employee to be a bona fide exempt executive. They are:

1. Paid a salary of at least $455 per week
2. Their primary duty is managing the enterprise
3. They regularly direct the work of two or more full-time employees
4. They have the authority to hire and fire
5. They regularly exercise discretionary powers
6. They spend less than 40 percent of their workweek duties on activities other than those mentioned above. *Note: There are situations where an employee can spend more than 40 percent of their time on non-managerial duties and still be considered an exempt employee if the employee is in "sole charge of an independent establishment" or if they own an interest of 20 percent of the business.*
7. If an employee is paid a salary not less than $250 per week, whose primary duties are the management of the enterprise and they direct two or more employees. These two requirements plus the increased salary qualify the employee as exempt under what has been referred to as the "short test."

8. There are no DOL regulations that allow an employer any exemption to overtime provisions for management trainees. If they do not meet the aforementioned requirements, they are NOT exempt from the overtime requirements of the FLSA.

HOW MANY HOURS PER DAY OR PER WEEK CAN AN EMPLOYEE WORK?

The FLSA does not limit the number of hours per day or per week that employees aged 16 years and older can be required to work.

HOW MANY HOURS IS FULL-TIME EMPLOYMENT? HOW MANY HOURS IS PART-TIME EMPLOYMENT?

The FLSA does not define full-time or part-time employment. This is a matter that will be determined by company policy and typically is tied to eligibility for company benefits or bonuses (which are also not required and are subject to what the employer *elects* to do). The designation of full-time or part-time employee does not change the application of the FLSA.

WHEN CAN AN EMPLOYEE'S SCHEDULED HOURS OF WORK BE CHANGED?

This is not an issue for the FLSA. The only exception is with child labor law provisions. Therefore, an employer may change an employee's work schedule with prior notice or by obtaining the employee's consent.

CAN CASH SHORTAGES AND BREAKAGE OF GLASSWARE OR CHINA BE DEDUCTED FROM AN EMPLOYEE'S PAY?

Deductions for cash shortages, walk-outs, under-charges, breakage, etc. can NOT be deducted from the wages of an employee being paid the minimum wage, currently at $5.15 per hour, nor can a minimum wage employee be required to pay for such losses. This is because their rate of pay for the time worked will be at less than the federal minimum wage rate.

For those employees who are paid rates above the minimum wage of $5.15 per hour, deductions for shortages, walk-outs, under-charges, breakage, etc can be made from the amount of earned wages in excess of the minimum wage rate of pay for the hours worked. For example, if an employee is paid $5.45 per hour and worked 30 hours, their gross pay would be $163.50. If this employee had cash shortages and breakage totaling $14 for the pay period, only $9.00 could be deducted on this pay check for to do otherwise would reduce total wages below the minimum wage rate of $5.15 or $154 for the hours worked. In addition, *tipped employees* may not be required to pay for such losses from their tips.

R ecordkeeping and Notices

ARE PAY STUBS REQUIRED?

The FLSA does require that employers keep accurate records of hours worked and wages paid to employees. However, pay stubs are NOT required by the FLSA. The majority of restaurants do provide them as a normal payroll record for the employee so they can check to see that their hours and pay rate are accurate.

WHAT NOTICES MUST BE GIVEN BEFORE AN EMPLOYEE IS TERMINATED OR LAID OFF?

The FLSA has no requirement for notice to an employee prior to termination or lay-off. Some states many have requirements for employee notification prior to termination or lay-off. Check the law in your state.

RECORDS TO BE KEPT BY EMPLOYERS

Every covered employer must keep certain records for each non-exempt worker. The Act requires no particular form for the records, but does require that the records include certain identifying information about the employee and data about the hours worked and the wages earned. The law requires this information be accurate. The following is a listing of the basic records that an employer must maintain:

1. Employee's full name and social security number
2. Address, including zip code
3. Birth date, if younger than 19
4. Sex and occupation
5. Time and day of the week when employee's workweek begins
6. Hours worked each day
7. Total hours worked each workweek
8. Basis on which employee's wages are paid (e.g., $6 an hour, $220 a week, piecework)

9. Regular hourly pay rate

10. Total daily or weekly straight-time earnings

11. Total overtime earning for the workweek

12. All additions to or deductions from the employee's wages

13. Total wages paid each pay period

14. Date of payment and the pay period covered by the payment

ours Worked Under the FLSA

DEFINITION OF "EMPLOY"

The definition of the term "employ" includes "to suffer or permit to work." The workweek ordinarily includes all the time during which an employee is necessarily required to be on the employer's premises, on duty, or at a prescribed work place. "Workday", in general, means the period between the time on any particular days when such employee commences his/her "principal activity" and that time on that day which he/she ceases such principal activity. The workday may therefore be longer than the employee's scheduled shift hours.

WAITING TIME

Whether waiting time is time worked under the Act depends upon the particular circumstances. Generally, the facts may show that the employee was engaged to wait (which is work time) or the facts may show that the employee was waiting to be engaged (which is not work time). For example, a server who is folding napkins while waiting to be assigned a table or a cook who arrives for work on time but cannot enter the restaurant because the manager is late, has been "engaged to wait." Similarly, an employee who is "off the clock" at the end of the shift who remains to finish an assigned task, re-clean a station, or compile written reports, this time is considered work time and must be paid. This basic rule applies to work performed away from the restaurant, if for example, the employee completes their written reports at home.

ON-CALL TIME

In an attempt to get around the requirements of waiting time, some operators have used the on-call system. They would tell an employee who was not put on the regular schedule, but wanted more shifts, that they would place them "on-call" for a shift. They were instructed that if they received a call by a certain time, they would be asked to come in to work. This was used during periods when business volume was unpredictable, and was an alternative to bringing an employee in and then sending them home early.

The FLSA says that an employee who is required to remain on call *at home*, or who is allowed to leave a message where she/he can be reached, is NOT working while on-call and therefore does not need to be paid. However, additional constraints on the employee's freedom could require compensation for this waiting time.

Employees who are asked to be on-call on the employer's premises are in fact "working" while on-call and must be paid. Thus, servers who are at the restaurant but told not to time in until they have a table, are in fact "waiting to be engaged" and must be paid.

BREAKS

Rest periods of short duration, usually 20 minutes or less, are common in the industry, are paid as working time. Unauthorized extensions of work breaks can be deducted assuming that the employer has expressly and unambiguously communicated to the employee that the authorized break may last only a specific length of time and that any extension of the break without management authorization is contrary to the break policy and deducted from time worked.

MEAL BREAKS

Bona fide meal periods (typically 30 minutes or more) generally are not be compensated as work time. In a restaurant environment, in order to deduct for meal breaks, the employee must be completely relieved from duty for the purpose of eating regular meals. The employee is not relieved if he/she is required to perform any duties, whether active or inactive, while eating. For example, a cashier who is collating guest checks while eating is technically not fully relieved. A server who does not want to miss getting a table of guests while on a meal break, is technically working. In this case, the employee, not the employer, has requested that they retain the meal benefit and voluntarily requests that they not be skipped in taking customers since they rely on tips for 75 percent of their wages. While the employee has, of their own volition, told management they wish to surrender their 30 minutes, regardless of the fact that they were not fully relieved, if payroll records were audited by the FLSA the fact that the employee was not "completely relieved" would most certainly come into question.

LECTURES, MEETINGS, AND TRAINING PROGRAMS

The FLSA considers time spent at these activities as time worked if one or more of the following conditions exist:

1. They are held during regular operating hours;
2. Attendance is mandatory; and
3. It is job-related.

Attendance at these activities need NOT be counted as working time if four criteria are met. They are:

1. It is outside normal hours;
2. It is *voluntary*;
3. It is not job-related; and
4. No other work is concurrently performed.

Thus time spent by employees attending the National Restaurant Show or an association seminar on sanitation and safety would not be considered as time worked. However, mandatory attendance would change this interpretation.

CLOTHES-CHANGING AND PRE-SHIFT AND CLOSING ACTIVITIES

If uniforms are issued and required attire for the work, and the employer requires that it be done on the premises, changing in and out of uniform is considered as time worked. Getting dressed at home, even if a uniform is required, is NOT regarded as working time. However, the washing time of a uniform may be considered working time.

MEDICAL ATTENTION

Because cuts and burns are common injuries in a restaurant, should an employee be injured on the job and require medical attention, the time spent by the employee on premises or in a hospital emergency room on normal working hours and on days when the employee is working, are considered working time and must be paid to the employee.

Tipped Employees Under the FLSA

CHARACTERISTICS

Tipped employees are those who customarily and regularly receive more that $30 a month in tips. Tips actually received by tipped employees may be counted as wages for the purposes of the FLSA, but the employer must pay not less than $2.13 and hour in direct wages.

REQUIREMENTS

If an employer elects to use the tip credit provision, the employer must:

- Inform each tipped employee in writing about the tip credit allowance (including the amount credited) before the tip credit is utilized.
- Be able to show that the employee receives at least the minimum wage when direct wages and the tip credit allowance are combined.
- Allow the tipped employee to retain all tips, whether or not the employer elects to take a tips credit for tips received, except to the extent the employee participates in a valid tip pooling arrangement.

If an employee's tips combined with the employer's direct wages of at least $2.13 an hour do not equal the minimum wage of $5.15 an hour, the employer must make up the difference.

Retention of Tips: The law forbids any arrangement between the employer and the tipped employee whereby any part of the tip received becomes the property of the employer. A tip is the sole property of the tipped employee. Where the employer does not strictly observe the tip credit provisions of the Act, no tip credit may be claimed and the employees are entitled to receive the full cash minimum wage, in addition to retaining tips they may/should have received.

Service Charges: A compulsory charge for service, for example, 15 percent of the bill, is NOT a tip. Such charges are part of the employer's gross receipts. Where service charges are imposed and the employee receives no tips, the employer must pay the entire minimum wage and overtime required by the Act.

Tip Pooling: The requirement that an employee must retain all tips does not preclude tip splitting or pooling arrangements among employees who customarily and regularly receive tips, such as waiters, waitresses, bellhops, counter personnel (who serve customers), busboys/girls, and service bartenders. Tipped employees may NOT be required to share their tips with employees who have not customarily and regularly participated in tip pooling arrangements, such as dishwashers, cooks, chefs, and janitors. Only those tips that are in excess of tips used for the tips credit may be taken for a pool. Tipped employees cannot be required to contribute a greater percentage of their tips than is customary and reasonable.

Credit Cards: Where tips are charged on a credit card and the employer must pay the credit card company a percentage on each sale, then the employer may pay the employee the tip, less that percentage. This charge on the tip may not reduce the employer's wage below the minimum wage. The amount due the employee must be paid no later than the regular pay day and may not be held while the employer is awaiting reimbursement from the credit card company.

TIP REPORTING

What you need to know if you employ tipped workers

- All tips are taxable and employees must be told to report 100 percent of their tips. *There exists a "myth" that tipped employees need only report a percentage, between 8 and 12 percent, of their cash tips and 100 percent of their charge tips. This is not a good idea. If a restaurant is audited, the DOL will audit charge sales, (which are a much larger percentage of sales than cash sales) to determine the tip percentage of sales. If 68 percent of the restaurant's sales are credit cards, they will use the percentage of tips to estimate what tips were on the 32 percent cash sales.*

- You are required to gather employees' tip reports, report the amount to the IRS, and withhold payroll and income taxes.

- The IRS requires any employee who receives more than $20 per month in tips to report those tips at least once a month and no later than the 10th of the month for the previous month's tips. The IRS Publication 1244, Employee's Daily Record of Tips and Report to Employer, contains a form employees can use and it can be downloaded from the IRS Web site.

- You must report employee tips to the IRS and withhold taxes on the amount of the tips.
  The taxes include the employer's share of FICA and the income tax and other payroll taxes on direct wages and reported tips. This information must be reported at the end of the year on the employee's W-2 form as "wages" along with cash wages.

- If tipping is customary in your establishment, you serve food and drink for on-premise consumption, and you employ more than ten employees on a typical day, you must file IRS Form 8027, *Employer's Annual*

Information Return of Tip Income and Allocated Tips, with the IRS each February. With the information on this form, the IRS examines your annual gross sales, your charge card sales, charge card tips, and reported tips. If the total tips reported by employees do not add up to 12 percent of your restaurant sales, the IRS will be able to estimate how much they under-reported and the restaurant may be required to pay FICA taxes on the shortage.

■ The Zero Paycheck
Since tipped employees are typically paid only $2.13 per hour and earn the majority of their wages through tips, more often than not, the employee's direct wages are not enough to cover the income and payroll taxes on the total of direct wages plus tips. Subsequently, a $0 paycheck results. When this occurs, inform employees that they need to give the extra money to apply toward these taxes so at income tax time they do not owe a large amount of unpaid income tax and FICA.

■ Tip Rate Determination Agreement (TRDA)
As a way of avoiding tips audits by the IRS, many restaurant operators will voluntarily participate in a tip compliance agreement with the IRS. The three types of tip agreements available for the food and beverage industry are:
1. Tip Rate Determination Agreement (TRDA)

Requirements
   ■ The IRS and the restaurant must establish a tips rate for its various occupations
   ■ At least 75 percent of the employees sign a Tipped Employee Participation Agreement with the employer and report at or above the determined rate. *If employees do not report at or above the determined rate, the employer is obligated to give the IRS the names of those employees.*
2. Tip Reporting Alternative Commitment (TRAC) With TRAC, the restaurant is not required to establish tips rates and employees do not need to sign an agreement. Instead, the restaurant must do the following:
   ■ Educate and re-educate all employees and new hires every quarter on their statutory requirement to report all tips to their employer.
   ■ A minimum of once a month, give all tipped employees a written statement of their cash and charge tips, and tell them the process for correcting inaccurate reporting.
   The IRS maintains that they will not audit the employer while the TRAC agreement is in effect, but they can audit any individual employee that is under-reporting their tip wages.
3. Employer-designed Tip Reporting Alternative Commitment (EmTRAC)
   The main difference between the two is that with the EmTRAC the

employer has more latitude designing its educational program and tip reporting procedures.

Restaurants wanting to enter into a TRDA or TRAC arrangement need to send a letter to the IRS Chief, Examination/Compliance Division, Attention: Tip Coordinator.

SUMMARY OF EMPLOYER AND EMPLOYEE RESPONSIBILITIES FOR TIPPED CREDIT

- Educate employees regularly on their statutory requirement to report 100 percent of their tips
- Allocate tips when needed and show allocations on employee's W-2 forms
- Fulfill tip allocation responsibilities
- Collect and pay taxes on tips reported by employees
- Keep records to support the data on your returns
- Keep daily records of all tips
- Report all tips in writing to employer by the 10th of the month
- Include all tips on your income tax return

Employee Meal Credits

The FLSA allows any employer who customarily offers meals to employees while working to reduce their hourly wage by an amount equal to the *reasonable food cost and supplies used in the preparation* of the meal (not the menu price, but the raw food cost). For example, if the reasonable food cost of a furnished meal amounts to $2.00, the employer can reduce the hourly wage paid the employee by $.25 per hour for an eight hour shift. In addition, if the employee is given a 30 minute break and is fully relieved of duties, this is not considered "work time" and 30 minutes can be deducted from their time card to reduce the time from 8 hours to 7.5 hours.

DO EMPLOYEES HAVE TO AGREE TO PARTICIPATE IN THE MEAL PLAN BEFORE AN EMPLOYER CAN DEDUCT MEAL CREDIT?

Since a court case in 1983, employers are allowed to take credit on the cash components of the minimum wage for meals regularly provided even if the employees are not given the option to take cash instead. *Some state laws permit employees to take a meal credit only if the meal is consumed by the employee. New*

York state currently allows a meal credit of $1.65 for tipped employees and $1.75 for nontipped employees.

HOW DO MEAL CREDITS IMPACT FEDERAL TAXES?

Meal credits are NOT subject to federal income tax withholding, FICA, or FUTA taxes. Employees do not have to pay federal taxes on meals as they are considered a non-taxable fringe benefit if the meals are furnished on the premises of the employer and the meals are furnished for the convenience of the employer.

DISCOUNTS ON EMPLOYEE MEALS

Some employers choose to discount menu prices for employees who eat while working. The value of the discount can be credited against the employee's wages just as long as the discount does not exceed the gross profit the employer receives on the meal and the discount is taken on the prices regularly charged to customers.

OTHER MEAL CREDITS

In establishments where an employee dining room or cafeteria is maintained, the value of the meals can be deducted from employees' gross income if certain requirements are met. (Refer to volume 26 of the C.F.R., section 1.132.7)

Sources of Wage and Hour Information

U.S. Department of Labor

Employment Standards

Administration Wage and Hour Division

www.dol.gov/esa

National Restaurant Association

The Legal Problem Solver for Restaurant Operators, 2001 is an excellent reference that all restaurateurs should have in their files.

www.restaurant.org/legal/tips/employertips.cfm

PAYCHEX

www.paychex.com/restaurant/managing/tipreporting/html

Appendix C
Glossary of Cost Control, Finance, and Culinary Terms

Actual Food Cost (AFC)   The second of the 4 faces of food cost based on the food cost percentage that the restaurant is actually running. It is the one typically reported on the monthly income statement and is calculated by dividing cost of food sold by food sales. If employee meals are not deducted, the percentage will be cost of food consumed and will be a higher percentage than cost of food sold.

As-Purchased (AP) weight   Referring to the weight (or count) of a product upon delivery to the restaurant and prior to processing or cooking. Includes bones, fat, and unusable trim.

Average Check   Calculated by dividing total revenue by number of customers. Also is the minimum amount that a guest needs to spend for the restaurant to realize its daily sales objectives based on the number of customers it serves. In the latter, the menu is priced to realize the minimum check average needed to achieve daily sales objectives given normal customer counts.

Back-of-the-house   Also called "heart of the house" and is the back area of the front office, kitchen, housekeeping, and engineering. These are the working areas of the hotel or restaurant where the vast majority of the employees are located.

Beating   A mixing method in which foods are vigorously agitated to incorporate air to increase volume or to develop gluten.

Bid Sheet   Used to get price quotes from suppliers on food and supplies.

Bottle Portion Yield   The number of measured portions of a specific quantity, e.g., 1.5 ozs. that one gets from a 750 liters or litre bottle.

Break-Even Point   That point where sales and expenses are equal and neither a loss or profit is incurred.

Break-Even Analysis   A valuable financial management tool for analyzing income and expenses and the impact of financial decisions.

Broker   The middleman between the producer-packer and the distributor.

Burnoff   Restrictions on refinancing (penalties for prepayment) burnoff over time. It is not so much risk related, as it guarantees a given return to the lender or buyer of securities for a given period of time.

By-the-ounce-pricing   In food bars and buffets, an alternative to one price for all you can eat is pricing by the ounce where the customer weighs their plate of food and pays anywhere from $.25 to $.40 per ounce or $4–$7.20 per pound. Thus individuals pay for only what they take, as much or as little as they want.

Call Brand   A premium brand of liquor usually specified by the customer when ordering a drink.

Cash Control   The system put in place to safeguard the cash receipts of the business. This includes devices, e.g., POS systems, cash registers, and safes; procedures and rules regarding handling of cash receipts, credit sales, and personal checks; to instructions on taking sales readings and making deposits to a bank or drop box safe.

Cash Inflows   Cash received by a hospitality organization during an accounting period; occurs when liabilities increase and assets decrease.

Cash Management   The management of a hospitality operation's cash balances (currency and demand deposits), cash flow (cash receipts and disbursements), and short-term investment securities to earn as much as possible within limits of liquidity requirements.

Cash Outflows   Cash disbursed by a hospitality organization during an accounting period; occurs when a liability decreases and an asset increases.

Cash Paid-Out Voucher   A form used to record money taken out of the cash register to pay for goods or services needed by the restaurant. Typically, management will set a maximum limit on amounts that can be removed for paid-outs. The voucher will contain the following information: unit; location; date, paid to; amount; justification (reason); expense category, e.g., food, beverage, labor, repairs; signature of person issuing the paid-out; signature of individual receiving the cash; and a receipt or invoice supporting the amount.

Closing Point   That level of sales at which the costs of opening are not even covered, thereby causing the owner to spend more than if the business remained closed.

Closing Point Analysis   A valuable financial management tool for analyzing the costs of opening during specific hours of the day or days of the week. Used to determine the sales needed to cover the costs of opening the restaurant for business.

Combination Menu   A menu format that incorporates both static and changing (cycle) menu items and à la carte and table d'hôte pricing techniques to provide variety to a customer base that frequents the operation more than twice per week. A steakhouse with a static menu may incorporate a cycle menu for their daily luncheon specials.

Common-size balance sheets   Statements shown in vertical analysis and where dollar figures are converted to percentages of total assets and total liabilities and owners' equity to facilitate comparison and note changes from period to period.

Comparative balance sheets   Balance sheets from two or more successive periods used in horizontal analysis were the difference between the current and past period is expressed in both relative (%) and absolute ($) format for in-depth comparison and analysis.

Competitive Bids   The process of putting your product specifications out for bid among the preferred suppliers in your market area in an effort to get competition for your business and get better prices, payment and delivery terms. Interested vendors will return your bid sheet with their prices and you can then select which products to purchase from each purveyor.

Competitive Pricing   Pricing that considers the prices charged for similar or identical menu items in restaurants competing for the same market or customer and either matches or beats their prices. This pricing is ineffective because the assumption is that the customer makes their purchase decision on price alone. It fails to take into account many other factors that influence choice and preference, e.g., product quality, ambiance, service, and even location. Consider the cost of a quarter pound hamburger with lettuce and tomato. Compare the prices at Wendy's, Burger King and McDonald's. There is a price threshold on a quarter pound hamburger that not even the big three will exceed.

Competitive-based pricing method   A pricing method that bases the menu price on the relative cost charged by similar restaurants for a comparable menu item rather than on the direct food and labor costs.

Contribution Margin   The amount that remains after direct costs have been subtracted from revenue to cover labor, overhead and profit. This is also referred to as Gross Profit.

Control/Controlling   The process of regulating, checking, and verifying compliance to standards through the use of authority, devices, systems, rules, and procedures.

Convenience Food   Any food product item that has been partially or completely prepared or processed by the manufacturer thus eliminating some processing step at the restaurant. Products can be raw and portioned to completely cooked and ready to eat. The AP price will be more than for raw and unprocessed foods because trim, cooking shrinkage, and preparation labor have been performed. However, convenience foods eliminate the need for the operator to have labor or equipment needed for the pre-preparation of the ingredients and therefore eliminate those costs.

Cooking from scratch   The preparation of recipes from raw ingredients and referred to as "homemade."

Cost Accounting   A concept that utilizes techniques designed to standardize and systematize the accumulation and analysis of revenue and expense for use in financial management decisions.

Cost Approach   A method of appraising property based on the depreciated reproduction or replacement cost (new) of improvements, plus the market value of the site.

Cost Control   The process of accumulation and interpretation of information on the day-to-day business activities. It requires the filling out of departmental reports, inventory records, recipe costing, and the computing of ratios and percentages of revenues and expenses. Provides management with the necessary information for determining the efficiency of the operation and operational decisions.

Cost Control Cycle   The cost control cycle consists of 15 function areas and all functions must be monitored because the cost control system is only as strong as its weakest link. The areas are: purchasing, receiving, storage, issuing, pre-preparation, portioning, preparation for service, transfer of food from kitchen to dining room, order taking and guest check control, cash receipts, bank deposits, accounts payable, menu planning and design, menu sales mix analysis, and inventory process.

Cost Control Strategy   The strategy must produce relevant information, reported in a timely manner, that is easily assembled and organized, is easy to interpret and the cost savings is greater than the cost of implementing the strategy. It is not an end in itself but rather just one component in the overall business plan that includes marketing, customer relations, employee relations, service commitment, and competitive distinctiveness.

Cost Per Servable Pound   A mathematical constant that is used to convert the AP price per pound to the cost per servable pound. It assumes that standard purchase specifications, standardized recipes, and portioning are adhered to such that estimated yields and actual yields are the same or close to the same. It is calculated by dividing the cost per servable pound by the original AP price per pound.

Cost Management   An awareness of the various types of cost and the effect that the relevant costs have on individual business decisions.

Cost of Food Consumed   All food that is sold, eaten, wasted, stolen, discarded, or used up and for which no revenue was received. Employee meals, discounted or complimentary meals, theft, and waste cause the food cost percentage to rise. Cost of food consumed is always a larger number than cost of food sold. It is calculated by adding beginning inventory plus purchases and then subtracting ending inventory.

Cost of Food Sold   Cost of food consumed less employee meals and other food consumed but not sold, e.g., known waste, food transfers to bar, complimentary meals, etc. Will always be a lower percentage than cost of food consumed. Also the total cost of food items sold during a given period.

Cost per portion   The cost of one serving calculated by dividing the cost of the batch one recipe produces by the number of portions it makes.

Cost per Servable Pound   In calculating standard portion costs, you divide the as purchased price per pound by the percentage of servable yield. It can also be found by dividing the total AP price by the weight of the servable yield.

Cost Reduction   The action taken by management to bring costs within accepted standards or budgets. For example, the control action taken when portion sizes are too large or too small would be to require the use of a portioning tool or scale to measure each portion before serving.

Cost Standards   A measure that establishes a value for comparison of actual results to the established standard. Standards are the "yardsticks" with which management measures quantitative and qualitative results to assess the level of performance of individuals, departments and units. Actual results are compared to standards to see if they exceed or fall below accepted levels.

Cost-Volume-Profit Analysis   An analysis of fixed and variable costs in relation to sales. Is used as a tool in decision making and is also referred to as Break-Even Analysis.

Cost/Margin Analysis   A menu sales mix analysis methodology that looks at food cost percentage, popularity, and weighted contribution margin of menu items. Menu items that have a low food cost percentage, return a high weighted contribution margin, and are relatively popular are then placed in primary sales areas on the menu to increase the likelihood of their selection by the guest. This method is considered unbiased to either food cost percentage or contribution margin. Can be used in competitive markets where price elasticity exists.

Creative Financing   Any financing arrangement other than a traditional mortgage from a third party lending institution. Examples of creative financing devices are: Balloon Payment Loans: the balloon mortgage called for payments of $500 per month for five years, followed by a balloon payment of $50,000. The "balloon" is the final payment on the loan and is typically greater than the preceding installment payments and pays the loan in full. For example, if the debt requires interest-only payments annually for five years, at the end of which time the principle balance a balloon payment is due.

Credit Memorandum   A slip that is attached to a vendor invoice or statement describing why the amount paid is less than the invoice amount. The reason for the credit is indicated, e.g., wrong brand, grade, or size; breakage or spoilage; incorrect price extension or quoted unit price.

Cycle Menu   A menu format used in institutional and school foodservice where the daily menu selections repeat over a period of time, usually 10–21 days. This format allows management to forecast quantities more accurately while offering a changing menu to a somewhat captive customer base.

Daily Sales Report   A report prepared at the end of each shift and/or business day detailing all the sales activities and transactions affecting cash accounts. Sales is shown by category, e.g., food, beverage, miscellaneous, etc., by meal period, and by cash receipts, charge sales, and personal and travelers checks. Also, any paid-outs, over-rings and under-rings, and voided guest checks are also recorded. It will also contain customer counts and commentary on unusual or unique conditions that may have contributed to the level of business activity, e.g., weather, special events going on in the city, and special advertising promotions. This information is useful to management in forecasting sales. This information is sent to the accounting department and recorded in sales journals and accounting records.

Demand Driven Pricing Pricing applied if customers openly seek out the item and demand is greater than supply. These menu items are "specialty goods" (in the economic sense) and enjoy a special status, as least in the short run. The first restaurants offering these items have a "monopoly" of sorts. Thus pricing items that are demand driven can be at the high end of the pricing continuum. As more competition adds these menu items to their menus, prices will stabilize and become market driven.

Differential Costs Costs that differ between two alternatives.

Dilution Fraud The bartender will cover up his free drinks by adding water to the white liquors so upon looking at the amount in the bottle you cannot tell there has been a theft.

Direct Departmental Expenses Expenses that can be directly attributed to the revenues they produce. For the most part, they are expenses directly involved in the service to the customer. This includes operating expenses that can as least be partially controlled by unit management. Included are: food and beverage cost, labor, linens, supplies, menus, replacement of silverware, china, and glassware.

Direct Labor Those costs that can be directly assigned to a particular menu item as is the case with a butcher who cuts steaks or a baker who makes fantastic breads and desserts. There labor is charged like an ingredient when calculating the Prime Food Cost of items requiring direct labor.

Discount Pricing The reduction in regular menu price that is undertaken to increase the number of transaction. When you consider the use of premiums as purchase incentives, e.g., McDonald's and Beanie Babies, Burger King and Lion King toys, these are basically other forms of discounting.

Discretionary Cost or Expense An expense that management can choose to incur or eliminate at a given point in time; e.g., replacement of carpeting in the lobby, resurfacing of the swimming pool.

Discretionary Fixed Cost   A contractual obligation that an owner or manager commits to for a prescribed period of time; e.g., an advertising contract with a local radio station to run 20–60 advertisements a week for a period of three months at a agreed upon rate. The cost is fixed for three months and was made at the discretion of the owner. Also called, managed fixed cost.

Distributor   The supplier to the restaurant. They purchase from producer-packers and distribute to restaurants.

Dram Shop Acts/Laws   Laws that hold the business serving alcoholic beverages liable for damages if a customer becomes inebriated and injures or kills someone after leaving the establishment.

Edible Portion (EP) Weight   The weight (or count) of a product after it has been trimmed, cooked, and portioned. It is almost always less than the AP weight. This is also referred to as "as served" and "plate cost." No further losses will occur due to trimming or shrinkage in cooking.

Empty Bottle Control   Empty bottles are turned in for full bottles at the end of each shift.

Entree   The main dish of an American meal, usually meat, poultry, fish or shellfish and accompanied by a green vegetable and a starch. In French service, the first course served before the fish and meat courses.

Extensive Menus   Menus that have a large number of menu offerings and require an extensive number of ingredients, preparation methods and ingredient combinations. A menu can be limited in terms of number of selections but extensive in the variety of preparation methods as is typically the case in specialty restaurants like Chili's and Applebee's.

Eye Magnet   A menu design technique used to draw the reader's attention to a particular section or item on the menu through the use of a graphic design, illustration, color screen or bold type font. This is reserved for items that are Primes, Stars, or Winners.

Financial Accounting   Primarily intended to provide external user groups and contains information concerning the current status of the firm and the results of its operations. It is historical in nature and must be reported precisely and without bias. Reports for the IRS and SEC demand this kind of reporting.

Financial Analysis   Understanding the "story behind the numbers." Calculating ratios and percentages is done in advance of any analysis. One must understand "the how and why" behind the financial figures. Compares figures from different periods of operation. Will reveal causes and identify positive and negative variances from desired outcomes. The interpretation of reports is the analysis management uses to compare actual outcomes with budgets and standards.

Financial Management Like Financial Accounting, Financial Management focuses upon internal financial statements, budgeting, and internal control. It stresses the interpretation rather than the preparation of schedules and reports. Its objective is to design financial statements to be management tools and not just IRS forms for income tax purposes.

First-In, First-Out Method (FIFO) An inventory valuation methodology that is based on the assumption that the units in stock are used in the order of purchase, such that the remaining units at the end of the month are the most recently purchased. The values can then be determined from the prices on the most recent invoices. In times of inflation and rising prices, FIFO results in a slightly lower cost of food consumed or sold.

Fiscal Inventory See Physical Inventory.

Fixed Cost or Expense A cost that does not change in the short run with changes in the volume of business.

Fixed Labor (Payroll) That portion of payroll that represents the minimum skeleton crew necessary to open for business at the slowest times or on the slowest days. Since it cannot be lowered, it is considered a fixed cost.

Food Cost Percentage A ratio that shows food cost as a percentage of food sales; calculated by dividing cost of food consumed/sold by food sales.

Food Transfers to Bar This reflects food used by the bar, e.g., fruits, juices, olives, food items served during happy hours, etc. The amount is deducted from the kitchen food cost and charged to the bar cost.

Formal Buying Terms and conditions are put in writing and procedures for payment of invoices and terms are stated as conditions for quoting prices and special service commitments. A buyer agrees to give the purveyor all their business for certain items and in return the supplier agrees to offer special prices and value added services in return for this loyalty. A supplier may agree to carry a certain brand or grade of product for the exclusive use of one major chain client. The supplier may agree to a special billing procedure with discounts and rebates. Formal buying can also be used by independent owner-operators.

Front-of-the-House This is an very old term used to describe the part of the restaurant or hotel that the guests and customers see, e.g., the dining room, lobby, and front desk.

Gaze Motion   The eye movement that naturally occurs when scanning a printed menu.

Gross Margin   See Contribution Margin or Gross Profit.

Guest Check Register   Used in operations using duplicate checks; a record of the beginning and ending numbers of the serially numbered custom-printed guest checks assigned to each server.

High/Low Price Differential   The price spread between the lowest and highest priced entree should not exceed 2.5 times the lowest priced entree. This will help achieve a minimum check average and not make the highest priced items seem over-priced in relation to the rest of the menu.

Income Approach   A method of appraising real estate like hotels and restaurants based on the property's anticipated future income. The formula for determining *Market Value* by the income approach is *Expected Annual Income* divided by *Capitalization Rate*. For example, a restaurant is expected to produce a net operating income of $100,000 annually after paying management salaries. Recent sales data (of similar properties that have sold in the area) indicate that the capitalization rate of 10%. By the income approach, the business is said to have a market value of $1,000,000. That means that you would recover your investment in ten years. This approach does not apply when the business is closed. One must then base it on anticipated income.

Indirect Cost Factors   A series of factors other than raw food cost and direct labor that can be reflected in the prices of menu items because they provide "added value" to the customer and are impacted by supply and demand. Such factors are: market standing, service commitment, ambiance, location, customer profile, product presentation, desired check average, and price elasticity.

Individual Contribution Margin (aka Individual Gross Profit)   The amount that remains after the raw food cost is subtracted from the menu price. This is what remains after food cost is deducted to cover labor, overhead and profit.

Informal Buying   Also called "Open Buying." The contact between the buyer and seller is made through a sales representative face-to-face, over the phone, or by Internet. Negotiation of price and terms for payment are by oral agreement or prices charged vary only according to quantity discounts or payment frequency that are agreed upon. This is not unlike an owner or manager calling a supplier to check on supply and prices of needed items prior to placing an order.

Internal Controls A system of procedures and forms established to safeguard the assets of a business and help monitor individuals, departments, and units. It includes accounting practices and security procedures for employees and guests. Seeks to prevent fraudulent conversions and disclose loss in the event they do occur by establishing a system of checks and balances and separation of duties. The Association of Independent Certified Public Accountants defines it as a" . . . a plan of organization . . . adopted to safeguard the assets of a business, check the accuracy and reliability of its accounting data, promote operational efficiency and encourage adherence to prescribed managerial policies."

Intuitive Pricing This pricing relies on memory as to prices previously paid or charged by other restaurants and sets the menu price on what they think the customer is willing to pay. This method relies on evaluating the competition and the demand for one's products and services.

Inventory Book/Record A written or electronic record of all food, beverage, and supplies used in the sale and service of food and beverage. It will contain the names of the primary and secondary suppliers, a product description, the unit of purchase and the current price, the amount currently on hand, and the use levels between deliveries. This record allows anyone who understands the content to know what to order, how much to order, the name of the primary supplier, and the correct order quantity. (See pp. 222–223 of *Fundamental Principles of Restaurant Cost Control*.)

Inventory Turnover A ratio showing how quickly inventory is moving from storage to productive use. Looks at the average inventory compared to the cost of goods consumed. Calculated by dividing cost of goods consumed by average inventory. The turnover should be relatively quick and the average inventory very small relative to the frequency of deliveries. The more frequent you can get deliveries, the smaller the average inventory and the higher the turnover.

Labor Cost Percentage (Traditional) Calculated by dividing total hourly payroll by total sales. Management salaries are usually not included in this percentage. Some operations will include employee benefits (including employee meals) as total payroll expense. This has become the largest single recurring operating expense in the restaurant and hotel industry, usually running more the 30 percent of sales.

Labor Productivity The output of the scheduled employees measured in terms of covers per labor hour, labor cost per cover, and labor cost per labor hour.

Last-in, first-out method (LIFO)   A inventory valuation method that assigns to remaining units the earliest prices paid for units. In a period of inflation and rising prices, LIFO results in a slightly higher cost of food consumed or sold.

Leftover   Any menu item that is prepared today but not sold. Further, it cannot be sold the next day in its original form at full price. Typically, it must be combined with other ingredients and sold as an extended dish. For example, leftover baked potatoes may be sold as hash browns or used in potato salad. Leftover Prime rib can be sliced thin and sold as a hot roast beef sandwich. However, the item made with the leftovers is priced much lower than the price that would have been received if it had sold as it was originally intended. Subsequently, this will raise the food cost percentage rather than lower it.

Limited Menus   Menu with a small number of menu offerings and needing only a moderate amount of ingredients. Typically, only one preparation method is used on each ingredient as is the case in most quick service restaurants, e.g., hamburgers and fried chicken. A menu can be extensive in terms of the number of menu selections but limited in terms of variety of preparation methods. Coffee shop restaurants like IHOP and Denny's have such menus.

Managed Fixed Cost   See Discretionary Fixed Cost.

Management Information Systems (MIS)   An efficient way to accumulate data needed by owners and managers. Establishes rules and procedures for consistent and timely reports, efficient flow of information to management on an as needed basis, data collection, and organization.

Management Reports   Departmental reports showing sales activity, labor hours, inventory, menu sales mix, and other financial and nonfinancial information broken down by meal periods, hours, and day of the week. These managerial accounting reports are in far greater detail than is required for income tax purposes. These reports provide information that allows the department heads to immediately isolate deficiencies in the operation under their direct control. These reports will contain qualitative as well as quantitative information.

Managerial Accounting   Primarily intended for internal user groups and contains information that will serve as a basis for day-to-day operational decision making. Because its use is internal, report preparation is more operationally specific and contains details such as menu sales mix, customer counts, average check and total labor hours. In addition, it will draw from other disciplines, e.g., marketing, human resources, and food production to supplement financial accounting reports.

Mark-up   An approach to pricing a hotel room, menu item or service that determines retail prices by adding a certain percentage to the cost of goods sold. The mark-up is designed to cover all non-product costs (overhead like labor, utilities, supplies, interest, taxes, etc.) as well as a desired profit. Ingredient mark-up is based on the entree and surrounding dish costs. However, price is NOT simply a mark-up over cost. See Demand driven and Market driven prices.

Markup   The difference between the cost of an item and its selling price.

Market Driven Pricing   Pricing is applied to items that are relatively "common" commodities (in the economic sense) and are found on most menus, e.g., hamburgers, ribs, prime rib, grilled chicken breast. Also used in markets where there are several restaurants that offer these items making prices very competitive. This is sometimes the pricing perspective applied when introducing new menu items before any substantial demand has been established. Market driven prices tend to be moderate to low on the pricing continuum.

Maximum Allowable Food Cost (MFC)   The first of the 4 faces of food cost. It is the highest the food cost can be and still allow the operation to realize its profit goal. It is the high-water mark for food cost. It is computed using the actual operating costs of the operation, either actual or projected. It will be different for every operation because of the financial idiosyncrasies of each operation. (See pp. 21–22 of *Fundamental Principles of Restaurant Cost Controls.*)

Menu Engineering   A menu sales analysis methodology that looks at individual gross profit and popularity (number sold). Biased toward items that are popular and return a high individual gross profit. Subsequently, this results in a higher food cost because items with high individual gross profits are typically the highest food cost items on the menu, e.g., steaks, seafood, veal. It is used by country club and resort restaurants and in markets where demand is greater than supply or where price inelasticity exists.

Menu Psychology   All the techniques used in menu design and production to make the menu a more effective cost control, merchandising, and communication tool. The methodology borrows techniques used in retail merchandising displays to call attention to the menu items the operation wants to sell more than some other menu items. It typically will feature the menu items that are low in food cost, high in gross profit, are easy to prepare, and are popular. Subsequently, the forecasting of menu sales can be made more accurate, thus improving the accuracy of order quantities and preparation quantities to eliminate the likelihood of unplanned leftovers.

Menu Sales Mix   A record showing the number sold of each menu item. Can be expressed as a whole number or percentage of total menu items sold. It is usually broken down by menu category, e.g., entrees, appetizers, salads, desserts.

Mise en Place   French term meaning "everything in its place." The gathering of all your ingredients, utensils, and pans prior to beginning the preparation of a recipe. It also includes all the preparations and organization that must be made before actual production can begin.

Mix   A culinary term meaning to combine ingredients in such a way that they are evenly disbursed throughout the mixture.

Mixed Drink   Any cocktail, or highball that combinations of spirits, wines, or liqueurs and optional non-alcoholic mixer, e.g., cola, water, fruit juice, tonic water, soda water, etc.

On-Call Scheduling   Used temporarily when business volume is unpredictable and when scheduled labor hours must be adjusted downward for productivity standards. Typically, one or more variable cost employees will be asked to remain at home up until a specified time and wait for a telephone call to come to work. If they are not called by a specified time, they know they will not be needed. This eliminates having employees fight traffic traveling to work only to be told to go home early because there is not enough business. This system was developed at the request of tipped servers who did not make much money on slow nights. If you are regularly calling in the on-call person you should discontinue the on-call and have them come in at the regular time. If you are never calling in the person on-call, discontinue the on-call scheduling.

Par Stock (Level of Inventory)   A system of determining the amount that needs to be kept on hand relative to usage and delivery frequency. It may also be the point at which an order is placed for additional product.

Par Stock-Empty Bottle Requisition System   A set number of bottles of every variety and type of liquor is determined based on maximum use level. Full bottles are requisitioned from the liquor storeroom only when an empty bottle is returned. A sales value of the liquor consumed is estimated from the empties and compared to the amount of sales reported.

Part-time Schedules   This does not mean "less than 40 hours per week," the traditional Labor Department definition of a part-time worker. In the hospitality industry, a person can work five or even six days and not work forty hours. What it means here is that when you are trying to hold down your labor cost you may call upon former employees in good standing who are no longer on the permanent schedule. College students, for example, may have a particularly heavy course load one semester and ask to have their hours cut back or even be taken off the regular schedule. However, they may be interested in filling in when someone needs time off, is injured, or is too sick to work. The names and telephone numbers of these part-time employees is posted so they can be contacted by employees or management to fill in when needed. You have a trained employee to step in during an emergency.

Percentage of Servable Weight   The actual amount of yield that results after preparation, cooking, and portioning losses have been deducted. This amount is divided by the original as purchased weight to obtain the percentage of servable weight.

Perpetual Inventory   A control where an ongoing record is maintained each time a delivery is made or part of the stock is removed from inventory. A card or electronic entry records each addition or subtraction from inventory such that an on-hand balance is constantly updated. The amount on the record and the amount actually in inventory should be the same.

Physical Inventory   Also called Fiscal Inventory. At least once a month, the amount of food and beverage currently in inventory is counted and price-extended for purposes of month-end bookkeeping and to determine cost of food and beverage sold.

Physical or Fiscal Inventory   The actual counting, recording, and pricing of food, beverage and supplies inventory. This needs to be done for every accounting period to determine the true cost of goods.

Point of Sale System (POS)   A computerized system for recording sales transactions and tracking food and beverage item by item. Called "point of sale" because the terminals are located in the dining room. Information is transferred electronically to the kitchen printers and the back office for record keeping.

Portion Cost Multiplier   A mathematical factor that allows you to convert the as purchased price into the cost per portion by multiplying the PCM by the as purchased price per pound. It is calculated by dividing the cost factor per servable pound by the number of portions per pound.

Portion Divider   A mathematical factor that tells you the quantity you need to purchase given the shrinkage and carving waste you will incur. It is calculated by dividing the percentage of servable weight by the number of portions per pound. You then divide the number of portion needed by the portion divider to get the gross amount you need to purchase. The same result can be obtained by dividing the percentage of servable weight into the total of the portion size times the number of portions needed.

Potential Food Cost (PFC)   This is the third of the 4 faces of food cost and is also know as theoretical food cost percentage but the least subjective of the 4 faces of food cost. It is the lowest your food cost can be and it assumes that all food consumed is sold and that there is no waste, theft, or over-portioning. It is based on the standard portion costs of each menu item multiplied by the number sold. This is done for the entire menu sales mix. This number is then divided by the total sales revenue for the menu sales mix (which is the sum of all menu item's revenue calculated by multiplying the number sold of each menu item times its menu price).

Pre-cut produce   This is produce (fruits and vegetables) that have been cut to order eliminating the need for processing at the restaurant. Examples are: cole slaw, shredded lettuce, sliced tomatoes, cut melon, etc. They are ready to serve without further processing. The cost per pound is higher than bulk because the cost of the labor to clean and cut the produce has been included. The restaurant saves the labor cost when it purchases pre-cut produce.

Pre-preparation   AKA "rough" preparation. The function of preliminary processing of food to make them ready for the final cooking to order prior to serving to the guest. Examples are: vegetable cleaning and chopping, meat cutting, and processing of ingredients for recipes. Also see Scratch Preparation

Premium Call Brand   Also Ultra Premium Call Brands that specify the very best and most expensive brands of scotch, tequila, vodka, etc.

Present Value of One   The value today of an amount to be received in the future, based on a compound interest rate. Example: At a 12% interest rate, the receipt of $1 one year from now has a present value of $.89286 (slightly more than 89 cents). One dollar to be received in 2 years has a present value of $.79719 (under 80 cents). Refer to your text for the formula.

Prime Cost   In addition to raw food cost plus direct labor, Prime Cost is the combined cost of food, beverage and labor. Together they are the three largest and most important costs incurred by a hospitality enterprise. It is generally felt that these three major costs cannot exceed 65% of total sales if the operation is to cover other direct departmental expenses, occupation costs, and leave anything left over for profit.

Prime Food Cost Pricing Methodology   Developed by Harry Pope of Pope's Cafeterias. Incorporates the cost of direct labor along with raw food cost. Items requiring extensive direct preparation because they are made from scratch must reflect the cost of the direct labor. Examples of direct labor would be the butcher to cuts steaks, the baker, the garde manger for the salad bar. The Prime Food Cost Percentage will be higher than the raw food cost percentage computed in the TRA methodology thus the markup will be lower.

Primes Menu items that are low in food cost, high in weighted gross profit and are relatively popular. (See Cost/Margin Analysis)

Problems Menu items that are high in food cost and return a low weighted gross profit. (See Cost/Margin Analysis)

Profitability Ratios A group of ratios which reflect the results of all areas of management's responsibilities.

Psychological Pricing This covers a number of interesting theories that are used to "adjust" menu prices because buyer "price consciousness" influences the way prices are perceived and the importance of price in the buyer's choice of restaurants and menu prices. Examples of psychological pricing are: reference pricing, mental accounting, pain and pleasure, price differential and odd cents pricing. (See pp. 123-126 in *Fundamental Principles of Restaurant Cost Control* for descriptions of each of these aspects).

Purchasing Purchasing involves setting policy as to which purveyors, brands, grades, and varieties of foodstuffs and supplies will be ordered. Prices, credit terms, delivery schedules, discounts, and return allowances are all part of the "purchasing function" that is negotiated between the distributor and the independent owner or the corporate officer. It is an administrative decision that authorizes the product specifications, vendor, price to be paid, payment terms, and delivery schedule. Purchasing policy is made at a corporate level for chain franchises. The independent owner-operators and corporate executives (not unit general managers) have the authority to make "purchasing decisions." Unit managers "order" specified grades and brands of food and supplies.

Purchase Specifications A detailed description of the attributes sought in a food product. It will include the grade, size, pack, weight, condition upon receipt, and other qualitative and quantitative descriptors.

Ratios The mathematical relationship between two relevant numbers. A relevant ratio must have some redeeming value to management in terms of assessing financial performance, or a measure of liquidity, solvency, profitability, or activity.

Request for Credit Memo When a mistake is discovered on a vendor's invoice due to a price extension or missing item, or returned merchandise, one copy of credit memorandum can be attached to the vendor's copy of the delivery invoice explaining the reason for the credit. A second copy is attached to the restaurant's copy of the invoice. The form contains the name and address of the restaurant, the name of the purveyor, the invoice number, date, amount of credit, a description of the returned or shorted merchandise, the reason for the credit request and the individual requesting the credit.

Rough Prep   The preliminary processing of ingredients to the point at which they can be finished for addition to a recipe. For example, peeling onions is rough prep. Taking the peeled onions and dicing prior to adding to a recipe if final prep.

Salamander   A type of over-counter broiler used to brown foods or glazing the tops of certain cheese dishes.

Sauté   To cook quickly at rather high heat in a small amount of fat.

Scratch Preparation   Menu items that are processed from raw to servable menu portion on the premises. This is the opposite of convenience foods which are purchased with all of the pre-preparation and preparation completed.

Seat Turnover   A ratio indicating the number of times that a given seat in a dining room area is occupied during a meal period; calculated by dividing the number of guests by the number of available seats.

Semi-variable or Semi-fixed Cost or Expense   A characteristic of most expenses as they are rarely purely fixed or variable. Costs need to be separated into their fixed and variable components. The fixed portion is expressed in dollars and the variable portion as a percentage. A fixed cost with some variable properties would be classified as semi-fixed and a variable cost with some fixed cost properties would be a semi-variable cost. Do not confuse fixed and variable costs with uncontrollable and controllable costs as they are not necessarily the same.

Seven P's of Menu Design   Purchase price, portioning, positioning, promotion, product presentation, price, and place.

Short Pouring   A fraud where the bartender will serve less than the prescribed portion and when they short the equivalent of a normal drink portion they can sell it and keep the money. The inventory will not reveal that there was a shortage in liquor.

Sleeper   A menu item that has a low food cost and a low weighted gross profit. (See Cost/Margin Analysis)

Solvency Ratios   Measure the ability of the business to meet its debts as they become due. The extent to which the enterprise has been financed by debt and is able to meet its long-term obligations. E.g., solvency ratio, debt equity ratio, operating cash flows to total liabilities.

Spanner Shifts   A scheduling technique used by operations open for two or three consecutive meals periods without closing that allows shift changes to occur without interruption to customer service and employees staying on the clock longer than their scheduled time. An arriving employee is scheduled to arrive at a time that "spans" the end of one shift and the beginning of the next shift. The departing employee is relieved of duties so they can close out their existing customers and complete their side work.

Specialty Supplier   A supplier that carries a rather narrow product line but with many grades, varieties, sizes, and packs of those products. An example of a specialty supplier would be a fresh seafood supplier or an ethnic import specialty supplier, e.g., Chinese or Italian groceries. Examples of specialty suppliers would be Inland Seafood, Buckhead Beef, and Atlanta's Finest Produce.

Split Shifts   This works very well on residential college campuses where students have a long break between classes and can come in and work during the peak volume periods and then leave. Contrast this to having to schedule employees a full shift because they cannot be sent home.

Staggered Arrivals and Departure Scheduling   A schedule that has employees arriving to correspond with the number of customers in the restaurant. The times of arrival and departure of the employees corresponds to the volume of customers expected so the maximum labor hours are scheduled during peak periods and minimum labor hours during slack times. The number of employees brought in gradually increases to its maximum during the peak volume periods.

Standards   Menu items that have a high food cost percentage but bring in a high weighted gross profit. (See Cost/Margin Analysis.)

Standard Food Cost (SFC)   The fourth and final food cost is simply the Potential Food Cost to which is added management allowances for unavoidable waste, employee meals, quality control waste, and complimentary meals and discounts. It becomes the benchmark to which the AFC is compared at the end of the accounting period. This is why it is critical to ascertain whether AFC is cost of food consumed or sold. This is the most subjective of the 4 faces of food cost because the management allowance is largely subjective.

Standard Portion Cost   The cost of preparing and serving one portion of food or one drink following the recipe and portioning standards.

Standard Portion Size   The prescribed weight, number of ounces, or count of a each food and beverage item. This is typically controlled by measuring portions with scales, scoops or serving container.

Standard Yield   What results when standard purchase specifications, recipes, and portions are followed. It is the amount of usable product available for portioning after all processing and cooking have been completed. The yield percentage is calculated by dividing the as-purchased weight by the actual yield. It should result in actual yield being the same as the standard yield.

Standardized Recipe   A specific recipe that has been customized to your operation's ingredient specifications, equipment, and menu presentation such that it produces a consistent product in taste, yield, and cost each time it is prepared.

Standards   A benchmark used to compare with actual performance or results.

Statement of Cash Flows   Explains the change in cash for the accounting period by showing the effects on cash of a business's operating, investing, and financing activities for an accounting period.

Static Menu   A menu format used in most table service and quick service operations where the selection of menu offerings remains the same from day to day. This allows for greater speed of preparation, cost and quality consistency, and easier forecasting of purchase and preparation quantities.

Stew   A moist heat cooking method that simmers food in a moderate amount of liquid that is usually served with the food item. Also a dish cooked by stewing uses less tender cuts of meat that have been cut into small bite-size pieces and seared before being cooking in the seasoned liquid containing vegetables.

Systems Approach   A management technique that enables a business to break the management of their operation down into subsystems or smaller, more manageable pieces.

Table d'hôte menu   A menu that includes multiple courses at one set price. This is the opposite of a la carte pricing.

Four Faces of Food Cost   The four different perspectives that food cost must be reviewed. They are: maximum allowable, actual, potential and standard. See individual glossary terms for full explanation.

Total Supplier   These are very large broad line suppliers that carry a very extensive inventory of all types of food products. However, because they carry such a broad line of products, they typically cut back on the number of brands, grades, sizes, and varieties of canned, fresh, and frozen products as compared to what might be carried by a "specialty supplier." Companies like Sysco and US Foods carry virtually all products needed by a foodservice operation including kitchen equipment, utensils, and fresh produce. They are beginning to acquire small specialty suppliers to further expand the depth of their product lines. For example, Sysco recently purchased Buckhead Beef, a meat specialty supplier with a very extensive product line and Atlanta's Finest Produce.

TRA Pricing Method Texas Restaurant Association came up with a method of arriving at a desired or target food cost percentage based on the financial idiosyncrasies of the operation. It then added certain markup suggestions based on popularity, cost, risk of spoiling, and menu category. (See pp. 142–146 of *Fundament Principles of Restaurant Cost Control*).

Traditional Labor Cost Ratio Total Payroll divided by Total Sales. Sometimes includes employee benefits and payroll related taxes. Payroll if for hourly employees and not management. The latter is an administrative and general expense.

Trial and Error Pricing This is another non-cost approach that claims to be responsive to customer perceptions of prices and is based on customer reactions and comments on prices. Once priced, the operator monitors sales and listens to customer comments and then adjusts prices upward or downward.

Triple Net Lease A lease agreement where the lessee is responsible for all three of the executory costs including property taxes, insurance and maintenance.

USAR—Uniform System of Accounts for Restaurants The established standard accounting language for the industry that makes it possible to compare ratios and percentages across the restaurant industry and to assure that numbers reported have been calculated according to set guidelines established for the restaurant industry. Includes detailed information about expense categories and classifications, formats of statements, and the content and uses of financial statements.

Usable Trim These are salable by-products that result when certain food ingredients are processed in-house that can be utilized in other menu items to recover all or part of their cost. For example, when cutting steaks there will be trim in the form of stew meat, ground beef trimming, steak sandwiches, and the like. These items can be incorporated into menu items that will recover the cost of the trim, thus the name, usable trim. The value of the usable trim based on their market price if purchased separately is deducted from the total AP price of the primal cut when determining the cost per servable pound.

Variable Cost/Expense   An expense that increases proportionally with sales but remains at a constant percentage of sales. The two purely variable costs on the income statement are food and beverage cost, all the others are mixed costs.

Weighted Contribution Margin aka Weighted Gross Profit   The sum total of the entire menu sales mix (number sold times the individual gross profit).

Well Brand   Also referred to as house pour and is used in generic drinks where brand of liquor is not specified.

Working Capital Turnover   Assuming a positive working capital, it is a liquidity ratio that compares working capital to revenue (Revenue divided by Average Working Capital). A turnover of greater than 17 times may be cause for concern should there be a slowdown in business. However, a turnover of 35 times may not be cause for concern in a restaurant operation that has transferred its cash into higher interest earning accounts.

Yield factors (food related)   These include the cost factor per servable pound, portion cost multiplier and portion divider. They are mathematical constants that reflect the standard yields that result if standardized purchase specifications, standardized recipes and standardized portioning is followed.

Yield tests (food related)   The process of measuring and weighing the yields that result when recipes are followed. For the yields to be realistic, the tests should be conducted under conditions similar to those in the restaurant.

Index

Q

R

S

storage, 20, 92–93, 304–7; *see also* inventory
    limiting access to, 305–6
    space and temperature, 276
    theft of, 306
substitution fraud, 359
summary report, weekly invoice, 298
supervision and productivity, 407–12
supply/supplier, proximity to, 277
symmetry, menu design, 168
systems approach, 3, 6
    to managing costs, 11–15

T

table d'hôte pricing, 161, 193, 217–18
Taco Bell, 205
technology, kitchen management and,
    464–68
temperature, storage, 276
Texas Restaurant Association (TRA) pric-
    ing methodology, 230–34
TGI Fridays, 157
theft, 306, 426
    deterrent, 306
    of storage, 306
    telltale signs of, 426
theoretical food cost. *see* potential food
    cost (PFC)
total food available for sale (TFAS), 86
total supplier, advantages of a, 271–72
traditional labor cost ratio, 42
transfer (food leaves kitchen for dining
    room), 22–23
transformation stage, 14
trial-and-error pricing, 211–13
turnover, 46–48
    inventory, 47–48
    seat, 46–47

U

understaffing, 403, 405
Uniform System of Accounts for Restau-
    rants, 36, 53, 78, 296, 322, 438–39

U.S. Department of Agriculture (USDA),
    228, 257
usable trim, 104

V

value-added services, 273
value analysis, 210
value engineering, 210
value meals, 161
variable costs, 146, 456
varieties, purveyor selection factor, 265–66
vendor relations, improving, 262–65
visual elements of menu psychology,
    166–68
volume-cost-profit ratio, 456

W

Wage and Hour Law, 80
wages and productivity, 405–7
waste, 104
weekly invoice summary report, 298
weekly payroll
    analysis, 408–9
    summary, 410
weighted contribution margin, 170
weighted food cost, 84
Weinstein, Michael, 206
well brand liquor, 328
Wendy's, 151, 204
wine cost/margin analysis, 336–37,
    340–42, 346–47
work analysis, 393
working capital turnover, 438
writing the order, 299–300
Wyatt Cafeterias, 273

Y

yield, 108, 120, 122, 130
    bulk produce, 130